*Paucis natus est, qui populum aetatis
suae cogitat.* Seneca [*Epist.* 79, 17]

("Whoever in his thinking takes note of his
own age will influence only a few." [Tr.])

THE WORLD AS WILL AND REPRESENTATION

by

ARTHUR SCHOPENHAUER

Translated from the German
by
E. F. J. Payne

In two volumes:
VOLUME II

Dover Publications, Inc.

New York

Published in Canada by General Publishing Company, Ltd., 30 Lesmill Road, Don Mills, Toronto, Ontario.

This Dover edition, first published in 1966, is a republication, with minor corrections, of the work originally published by The Falcon's Wing Press, Indian Hills, Colorado, in 1958. This edition is unabridged with the exception that the General Editor's Preface to the original edition has been omitted.
This edition is published by special arrangement with The Falcon's Wing Press.

Standard Book Number: 486-21762-0

Library of Congress Catalog Card Number: 66-29058

Manufactured in the United States of America
Dover Publications, Inc.
180 Varick Street
New York, N. Y. 10014

Contents, Volume II

"Warum willst du dich von uns Allen
Und unsrer Meinung entfernen?"—
Ich schreibe nicht euch zu gefallen,
Ihr sollt was lernen.

Goethe
Zahme Xenien, I, 2.

("Why wilt thou withdraw from us all
And from our way of thinking?"—
I do not write for your pleasure,
You shall learn something. [Tr.])

THE WORLD AS WILL AND
REPRESENTATION

VOLUME II

To the First Book

First Half

The Doctrine of the Representation of Perception
(Through § 1-7 of Volume I)

CHAPTER I

On the Fundamental View of Idealism

In endless space countless luminous spheres, round each of which some dozen smaller illuminated ones revolve, hot at the core and covered over with a hard cold crust; on this crust a mouldy film has produced living and knowing beings: this is empirical truth, the real, the world. Yet for a being who thinks, it is a precarious position to stand on one of those numberless spheres freely floating in boundless space, without knowing whence or whither, and to be only one of innumerable similar beings that throng, press, and toil, restlessly and rapidly arising and passing away in beginningless and endless time. Here there is nothing permanent but matter alone, and the recurrence of the same varied organic forms by means of certain ways and channels that inevitably exist as they do. All that empirical science can teach is only the more precise nature and rule of these events. But at last the philosophy of modern times, especially through Berkeley and Kant, has called to mind that all this in the first instance is only *phenomenon of the brain,* and is encumbered by so many great and different *subjective* conditions that its supposed absolute reality vanishes, and leaves room for an entirely different world-order that lies at the root of that phenomenon, in other words, is related to it as is the thing-in-itself to the mere appearance.

"The world is my representation" is, like the axioms of Euclid, a proposition which everyone must recognize as true as soon as he understands it, although it is not a proposition that everyone understands as soon as he hears it. To have brought this proposition to consciousness and to have connected it with the problem of the relation of the ideal to the real, in other words, of the world in the head to the world outside the head, constitutes, together with the problem of moral freedom, the distinctive characteristic of the philosophy of the moderns. For only after men had tried their hand for thousands of years at merely *objective* philosophizing did they discover that, among the many things that make the world so puzzling and precarious, the first and foremost is that, however immeasurable and massive it may be, its existence hangs nevertheless on a single thread; and this thread is the actual consciousness in which it exists. This condition, with which the existence of the world is irrevocably encumbered, marks it with the stamp of *ideality,* in spite of all *empirical* reality, and consequently with the stamp of the mere *phenomenon.* Thus the world must be recognized, from one aspect at least, as akin to a dream, indeed as capable of being put in the same class with a dream. For the same brain-function that conjures up during sleep a perfectly objective, perceptible, and indeed palpable world must have just as large a share in the presentation of the objective world of wakefulness. Though different as regards their matter, the two worlds are nevertheless obviously moulded from one form. This form is the intellect, the brain-function. Descartes was probably the first to attain the degree of reflection demanded by that fundamental truth; consequently, he made that truth the starting-point of his philosophy, although provisionally only in the form of sceptical doubt. By his taking *cogito ergo sum*[1] as the only thing certain, and provisionally regarding the existence of the world as problematical, the essential and only correct starting-point, and at the same time the true point of support, of all philosophy was really found. This point, indeed, is essentially and of necessity *the subjective, our own consciousness.* For this alone is and remains that which is immediate; everything else, be it what it may, is first mediated and conditioned by consciousness, and therefore dependent on it. It is thus rightly considered that the philosophy of the moderns starts from Descartes as its father. Not long afterwards, Berkeley went farther along this path, and arrived at *idealism* proper; in other words, at the knowledge that what is extended in space, and hence the objective, material world in general, exists as such simply and solely in our *representation,* and that it is false and indeed absurd to attribute to it, *as such,* an existence outside all representation and independent of the knowing subject, and so to assume a matter positively and absolutely existing in itself. But this very correct and deep insight really constitutes the whole of Berkeley's philosophy; in it he had exhausted himself.

Accordingly, true philosophy must at all costs be *idealistic;* indeed, it must be so merely to be honest. For nothing is more certain than that no one ever came out of himself in order to identify himself immediately with things different from him; but everything of which he has certain, sure, and hence immediate knowledge, lies within his consciousness. Beyond this consciousness, therefore, there can be no *immediate* certainty; but the first principles of a science must have

---

[1] "I think, therefore I am." [Tr.]

such a certainty. It is quite appropriate to the empirical standpoint of all the other sciences to assume the objective world as positively and actually existing; it is not appropriate to the standpoint of philosophy, which has to go back to what is primary and original. *Consciousness* alone is immediately given, hence the basis of philosophy is limited to the facts of consciousness; in other words, philosophy is essentially *idealistic*. Realism, which commends itself to the crude understanding by appearing to be founded on fact, starts precisely from an arbitrary assumption, and is in consequence an empty castle in the air, since it skips or denies the first fact of all, namely that all that we know lies within consciousness. For that the *objective existence* of things is conditioned by a representer of them, and that consequently the objective world exists only *as representation,* is no hypothesis, still less a peremptory pronouncement, or even a paradox put forward for the sake of debate or argument. On the contrary, it is the surest and simplest truth, and a knowledge of it is rendered more difficult only by the fact that it is indeed too simple, and that not everyone has sufficient power of reflection to go back to the first elements of his consciousness of things. There can never be an existence that is objective absolutely and in itself; such an existence, indeed, is positively inconceivable. For the objective, as such, always and essentially has its existence in the consciousness of a subject; it is therefore the representation of this subject, and consequently is conditioned by the subject, and moreover by the subject's forms of representation, which belong to the subject and not to the object.

That the *objective world would exist* even if there existed no knowing being at all, naturally seems at the first onset to be sure and certain, because it can be thought in the abstract, without the contradiction that it carries within itself coming to light. But if we try to *realize* this abstract thought, in other words, to reduce it to representations of perception, from which alone (like everything abstract) it can have content and truth; and if accordingly we attempt to *imagine an objective world without a knowing subject,* then we become aware that what we are imagining at that moment is in truth the opposite of what we intended, namely nothing but just the process in the intellect of a knowing being who perceives an objective world, that is to say, precisely that which we had sought to exclude. For this perceptible and real world is obviously a phenomenon of the brain; and so in the assumption that the world as such might exist independently of all brains there lies a contradiction.

The principal objection to the inevitable and essential *ideality of every object,* the objection which arises distinctly or indistinctly in everyone, is certainly as follows: Even my own person is object for another, and is therefore that other's representation, and yet I know certainly that I should exist even without that other representing me in his mind. But all other objects also stand in the same relation to his intellect as *I* stand; consequently, they too would exist without his representing them in his mind. The answer to this is as follows: That other being, whose object I am now considering my person to be, is not absolutely *the subject,* but is in the first instance a knowing individual. Therefore, if he too did *not* exist, in fact, even if there existed in general no other knowing being except myself, this would still by no means be the elimination of the *subject* in whose representation alone all objects exist. For I myself am in fact that *subject,* just as is every knowing being. Consequently, in the case here assumed, my person would certainly still exist, but again as representation, namely in my own knowledge. For even by myself it is always known only indirectly, never directly, since all existence as representation is an indirect existence. Thus as *object,* in other words as extended, filling space, and acting, I know my body only in the perception of my brain. This perception is brought about through the senses, and on their data the perceiving understanding carries out its function of passing from the effect to the cause. In this way, by the eye seeing the body, or the hands touching it, the understanding constructs the spatial figure that presents itself in space as my body. In no way, however, are there given to me directly, in some general feeling of the body or in inner self-consciousness, any extension, shape, and activity that would coincide with my inner being itself, and that inner being accordingly requires no other being in whose knowledge it would manifest itself, in order so to exist. On the contrary, that general feeling, just like self-consciousness, exists directly only in relation to the *will,* namely as comfortable or uncomfortable, and as active in the acts of will, which exhibit themselves for external perception as actions of the body. It follows from this that the existence of my person or of my body *as an extended and acting thing* always presupposes a *knowing being* different from it, since it is essentially an existence in the apprehension, in the representation, and hence an existence *for another being.* In fact, it is a phenomenon of the brain, no matter whether the brain in which it exhibits itself belongs to my own person or to another's. In the first case, one's own person is then split up into the knowing and the known, into object and subject, and here, as everywhere, these two face each other inseparable and irreconcilable. Therefore, if my own person, in order to exist as such, always requires a knower, this will apply at any rate just as much to all other objects; and to vindicate for these an existence independent of knowledge and of the subject of knowledge was the aim of the above objection.

However, it is evident that the existence conditioned through a knowing being is simply and solely existence *in space,* and hence that of a thing extended and acting. This alone is always a known thing, and consequently an existence *for another being.* At the same time, everything that exists in this way may still have *an existence for itself,* for which it requires no subject. This existence by itself, however, cannot be extension and activity (together space-occupation), but is necessarily another kind of being, namely that of a *thing-in-itself,* which, purely as such, can never be *object.* This, therefore, is the answer to the principal objection stated above, and accordingly this objection does not overthrow the fundamental truth that the objectively present and existing world can exist only in the representation, and so only for a subject.

It is also to be noted here that even Kant, at any rate so long as he remained consistent, cannot have thought of any *objects* among his things-in-themselves. For this follows already from the fact that he proved space as well as time to be a mere form of our intuition or perception, which in consequence does not belong to the things-in-themselves. What is not in space or in time cannot be *object;* therefore the being or existence of *things-in-themselves* can no longer be *objective,* but only of quite a different kind, namely a metaphysical being or existence. Consequently, there is already to be found in that Kantian principle also the proposition that the *objective* world exists only as *representation.*

In spite of all that may be said, nothing is so persistently and constantly misunderstood as *idealism,* since it is interpreted as meaning that the *empirical* reality of the external world is denied. On this rests the constant return of the appeal to common sense, which appears in many different turns and guises, for example, as *"fundamental conviction"* in the Scottish school, or as Jacobi's *faith or belief* in the reality of the external world. The external world by no means gives itself, as Jacobi explains, merely on credit; nor is it accepted by us on faith and trust. It gives itself as what it is, and performs directly what it promises. It must be remembered that Jacobi set up such a credit system of the world, and was lucky enough to impose it on a few professors of philosophy, who for thirty years went on philosophizing about it extensively and at their ease; and that it was this same Jacobi who once denounced Lessing as a Spinozist, and later Schelling as an atheist, and received from the latter the well-known and well-merited reprimand. In accordance with such zeal, by reducing the external world to a matter of faith, he wanted merely to open a little door for faith in general, and to prepare the credit for that which was afterwards actually to be offered on credit; just as if, to introduce paper money, we tried to appeal to the fact that the value of the ringing coin depended merely on the stamp the State put on it. In his philosopheme on the reality of the external world assumed on faith, Jacobi is precisely the "transcendental realist playing the part of the empirical idealist," whom Kant censured in the *Critique of Pure Reason,* first edition, p. 369.

True idealism, on the other hand, is not the empirical, but the transcendental. It leaves the *empirical* reality of the world untouched, but adheres to the fact that all *object,* and hence the empirically real in general, is conditioned by the *subject* in a twofold manner. In the first place it is conditioned *materially,* or as *object* in general, since an objective existence is conceivable only in face of a subject and as the representation of this subject. In the second place, it is conditioned *formally,* since the *mode and manner* of the object's existence, in other words, of its being represented (space, time, causality), proceed from the subject, and are predisposed in the subject. Therefore immediately connected with simple or *Berkeleian* idealism, which concerns the *object in general,* is *Kantian* idealism, which concerns the specially given *mode and manner* of objective existence. This proves that the whole of the material world with its bodies in space, extended and, by means of time, having causal relations with one another, and everything attached to this—all this is not something existing *independently* of our mind, but something that has its fundamental presuppositions in our brain-functions, *by means of* which and *in* which alone is *such* an objective order of things possible. For time, space, and causality, on which all those real and objective events rest, are themselves nothing more than functions of the brain; so that, therefore, this unchangeable *order* of things, affording the criterion and the clue to their empirical *reality,* itself comes first from the brain, and has its credentials from that alone. Kant has discussed this thoroughly and in detail; though he does not mention the brain, but says "the faculty of knowledge." He has even attempted to prove that that objective order in time, space, causality, matter, and so on, on which all the events of the real world ultimately rest, cannot even be *conceived,* when closely considered, as a self-existing order, i.e., an order of things-in-themselves, or as something absolutely objective and positively existing; for if we attempt to think it out to the end, it leads to contradictions. To demonstrate this was the purpose of the antinomies; in the appendix to my work,[2] how-

---

[2] "Criticism of the Kantian Philosophy" at the end of volume 1. [Tr.]

ever, I have demonstrated the failure of the attempt. On the other hand, the Kantian teaching, even without the antinomies, leads to the insight that things and their whole mode and manner of existence are inseparably associated with our consciousness of them. Therefore he who has clearly grasped this soon reaches the conviction that the assumption that things exist as such, even outside and independently of our consciousness, is really absurd. Thus are we so deeply immersed in time, space, causality, and in the whole regular course of experience resting on these; we (and in fact even the animals) are so completely at home, and know how to find our way in experience from the very beginning. This would not be possible if our intellect were one thing and things another; but it can be explained only from the fact that the two constitute a whole; that the intellect itself creates that order, and exists only for things, but that things also exist only for it.

But even apart from the deep insight and discernment revealed only by the Kantian philosophy, the inadmissible character of the assumption of absolute *realism,* clung to so obstinately, can indeed be directly demonstrated, or at any rate felt, by the mere elucidation of its meaning through considerations such as the following. According to realism, the world is supposed to exist, as we know it, independently of this knowledge. Now let us once remove from it all knowing beings, and thus leave behind only inorganic and vegetable nature. Rock, tree, and brook are there, and the blue sky; sun, moon, and stars illuminate this world, as before, only of course to no purpose, since there exists no eye to see such things. But then let us subsequently put into the world a knowing being. That world then presents itself *once more* in his brain, and repeats itself inside that brain exactly as it was previously outside it. Thus to the *first* world a *second* has been added, which, although completely separated from the first, resembles it to a nicety. Now the *subjective* world of this perception is constituted in *subjective,* known space exactly as the *objective* world is in *objective,* infinite space. But the subjective world still has an advantage over the objective, namely the knowledge that that external space is infinite; in fact, it can state beforehand most minutely and accurately the full conformity to law of all the relations in that space which are possible and not yet actual, and it does not need to examine them first. It can state just as much about the course of time, as also about the relation of cause and effect which governs the changes in outer space. I think that, on closer consideration, all this proves absurd enough, and thus leads to the conviction that that absolutely *objective* world outside the head, independent of it and *prior* to all knowledge, which we at first imagined we had conceived, was really no other than the second world already known *subjectively,* the world of the representation, and that it is this alone which we are actually capable of conceiving. Accordingly the assumption is automatically forced on us that the world, as we know it, exists only for our knowledge, and consequently in the *representation* alone, and not once again outside that representation.* In keeping with this assumption, then, the thing-in-itself, in other words, that which exists independently of our knowledge and of all knowledge, is to be regarded as something quite different from the *representation* and all its attributes, and hence from objectivity in general. What this is, will afterwards be the theme of our second book.

On the other hand, the controversy about the reality of the external world, considered in § 5 of our first volume, rests on the assumption, just criticized, of an objective and a subjective world both in *space,* and on the impossibility, arising in the case of this presupposition, of a transition, a bridge, between the two. On this controversy I have to make the following remarks.

Subjective and objective do not form a continuum. That of which we are immediately conscious is bounded by the skin, or rather by the extreme ends of the nerves proceeding from the cerebral system. Beyond this lies a world of which we have no other knowledge than that gained through pictures in our mind. Now the question is whether and to what extent a world existing independently of us corresponds to these pictures. The relation between the two could be brought about only by means of the law of causality, for this law alone leads from something given to something quite different from it. This law itself, however, has first of all to substantiate its validity. Now it must be either of *objective* or of *subjective* origin; but in either case it lies on one bank or the other, and therefore cannot serve as a bridge. If, as Locke and Hume assumed, it is *a posteriori,* and hence drawn from experience, it is of *objective* origin; it then

---

* Here I specially recommend the passage in Lichtenberg's *Vermischte Schriften* (Göttingen, 1801, Vol. II, page 12 *seq.*): "Euler says in his letters on various subjects of natural science (Vol. II, p. 228), that it would thunder and lighten just as well, even if there existed no human being whom the lightning could strike. It is a very common expression, but I must confess that it has never been easy for me to grasp it completely. It always seems to me as if the concept of *being* were something borrowed from our thinking, and that if there are no longer any sentient and thinking creatures, then also there *is* nothing any more."

* [Footnotes so marked represent additions made by Schopenhauer in his interleaved copy of the third edition between its appearance in 1859 and his death in 1860. Tr.]

itself belongs to the external world in question, and therefore cannot vouch for the reality of that world. For then, according to Locke's method, the law of causality would be demonstrated from experience, and the reality of experience from the law of causality. If, on the other hand, it is given *a priori,* as Kant more correctly taught, then it is of *subjective* origin; and so it is clear that with it we always remain in the *subjective.* For the only thing actually given *empirically* in the case of perception is the occurrence of a sensation in the organ of sense. The assumption that this sensation, even only in general, must have a *cause* rests on a law that is rooted in the form of our knowledge, in other words, in the functions of our brain. The origin of this law is therefore just as subjective as is that sensation itself. The *cause* of the given sensation, assumed as a result of this law, immediately manifests itself in perception as *object,* having space and time as the form of its appearance. But again, even *these* forms themselves are of entirely subjective origin, for they are the mode and manner of our faculty of perception. That transition from the sensation to its cause, which, as I have repeatedly shown, lies at the foundation of all sense-perception, is certainly sufficient for indicating to us the empirical presence in space and time of an empirical object, and is therefore fully satisfactory for practical life. But it is by no means sufficient for giving us information about the existence and real inner nature of the phenomena that arise for us in such a way, or rather of their intelligible substratum. Therefore, the fact that, on the occasion of certain sensations occurring in my organs of sense, there arises in my head a *perception* of things extended in space, permanent in time, and causally operative, by no means justifies me in assuming that such things also exist in themselves, in other words, that they exist with such properties absolutely belonging to them, independently of my head and outside it. This is the correct conclusion of the *Kantian* philosophy. It is connected with an earlier result of Locke which is just as correct, and very much easier to understand. Thus, although, as is allowed by Locke's teaching, external things are positively assumed to be the causes of the sensations, there cannot be any *resemblance* at all between the *sensation,* in which the *effect* consists, and the objective *nature* or *quality* of the *cause* that gives rise to this sensation. For the sensation, as organic function, is above all determined by the very artificial and complicated nature of our sense-organs; thus it is merely stimulated by the external cause, but is then perfected entirely in accordance with its own laws, and hence is wholly subjective. Locke's philosophy was the criticism of the functions of sense; but Kant has furnished the criticism of the functions of the brain. But to all this we still have to add the result of Berkeley, which has been revised by me, namely that every *object,* whatever its origin, is, *as object,* already conditioned by the subject, and thus is essentially only the subject's *representation.* The aim of realism is just the object without subject; but it is impossible even to conceive such an object clearly.

From the whole of this discussion it follows with certainty and distinctness that it is absolutely impossible to arrive at a comprehension of the *inner nature* of things on the path of mere *knowledge* and *representation,* since this knowledge always comes to things *from without,* and must therefore remain eternally *outside* them. This purpose could be attained only by our finding *ourselves* in the inside of things, so that this inside would be known to us directly. My second book considers to what extent this is actually the case. However, so long as we stop, as in this first book we do, at objective comprehension, and hence at *knowledge,* the world is and remains for us a mere *representation,* since no path is here possible which leads beyond this.

But in addition to this, adherence to the *idealistic* point of view is a necessary counterpoise to the *materialistic.* Thus the controversy over the real and the ideal can also be regarded as one concerning the existence of *matter.* For it is ultimately the reality or ideality of matter which is the point in question. Is matter as such present merely in our representation, or is it also independent thereof? In the latter case, it would be the thing-in-itself; and he who assumes a matter existing in itself must also consistently be a materialist, in other words, must make matter the principle of explanation of all things. On the other hand, he who denies it to be a thing-in-itself is *eo ipso* an idealist. Among the moderns only Locke has asserted positively and straightforwardly the reality of matter; therefore his teaching, through the instrumentality of Condillac, led to the sensualism and materialism of the French. Berkeley alone has denied matter positively and without modifications. Therefore the complete antithesis is that of idealism and materialism, represented in its extremes by Berkeley and the French materialists (Holbach). Fichte is not to be mentioned here; he deserves no place among real philosophers, those elect of mankind who with deep earnestness seek not their own affairs, but the *truth.* They must therefore not be confused with those who under this pretext have only their personal advancement in view. Fichte is the father of *sham philosophy,* of the *underhand* method that by ambiguity in the use of words, incomprehensible talk, and sophisms, tries to deceive, to impress by an air of importance, and thus to befool those eager to learn. After this method had been applied by Schelling, it reached its height, as is well known, in Hegel, with whom it ripened into real charlatanism. But whoever in all seriousness even mentions that Fichte along with Kant shows that he has no notion of what Kant is. On the other hand, materialism also has its justification. It is just as true that the knower is a product of matter as that matter is a mere representation of the knower; but it is also just as one-sided. For materialism is the philosophy of the subject who forgets to take account of himself. Therefore, against the assertion that I am a mere modification of matter, it must also be asserted that all matter exists merely in my representation, and this assertion is no less right. An as yet obscure knowledge of these relations appears to have evoked the Platonic saying ὕλη ἀληθινὸν ψεῦδος (*materia mendacium verax*).[3]

Realism, as I have said, necessarily leads to *materialism.* For while empirical perception gives us things-in-themselves, as they exist independently of our knowledge, experience also gives us the *order* of things-in-themselves, in other words, the true and only world-order. But this way leads to the assumption that there is only *one* thing-in-itself, namely matter, of which everything else is a modification; for the course of nature is the absolute and only world-order. To avoid these consequences, *spiritualism* was set up along with *realism,* so long as the latter was in undisputed authority; thus the assumption was made of a second substance, outside and along with matter, namely an *immaterial substance.* This dualism and *spiritualism,* devoid equally of experience, proofs, and comprehensibility, was denied by Spinoza, and shown to be false by Kant, who ventured to do this because at the same time he established *idealism* in its rights. For with *realism, materialism,* as the counterpoise to which *spiritualism* had been devised, falls to the ground of its own accord, since matter and the course of nature then become mere *phenomenon,* conditioned by the intellect; for the phenomenon has its existence only in the *representation* of the intellect. Accordingly, *spiritualism* is the specious and false safeguard against *materialism;* but the real and true safeguard is *idealism.* By making the objective world dependent *on us,* idealism gives the necessary counterpoise to the dependence *on* the objective world in which *we* are placed by the course of nature. The world, from which I part at death, is, on the other hand, only my representation. The centre of gravity of existence falls back into the *subject.* What is proved is not, as in spiritualism, the knower's independence of matter, but the dependence of all

---

[3] "Matter is a lie, and yet true." [Tr.]

matter on the knower. Of course, this is not so easy to understand and so convenient to handle as is spiritualism with its two substances; but χαλεπὰ τὰ καλά.[4]

In opposition to the *subjective* starting-point, namely "the world is my representation," there certainly is at the moment with equal justification the *objective* starting-point, namely "the world is matter," or "matter alone positively exists" (as it alone is not liable to becoming and to passing away), or "all that exists is matter." This is the starting-point of Democritus, Leucippus, and Epicurus. More closely considered, however, starting from the *subject* retains a real advantage; it has the advantage of one perfectly justified step, for consciousness alone is what is *immediate*. We skip this, however, when we go straight to matter and make that our starting-point. On the other hand, it would be possible to construct the world from matter and its properties, if these were correctly, completely, and exhaustively known (and many of them we still lack). For everything that has come into existence has become actual through *causes,* that were able to operate and come together only in consequence of the *fundamental forces of matter.* But these must be capable of complete demonstration at least *objectively,* even if we shall never get to know them *subjectively.* But such an explanation and construction of the world would always have as its foundation not only the assumption of an existence-in-itself of matter (whereas in truth such existence is conditioned by the subject), but it would also have to let all the *original properties* in this matter remain in force, and yet be absolutely inexplicable, that is, be *qualitates occultae.* (See §§ 26, 27 of the first volume.) For matter is only the bearer of these forces, just as the law of causality is only the regulator of their phenomena. Consequently, such an explanation of the world would still be only relative and conditioned, really the work of a *physical science* that at every step longed for a *metaphysic.* On the other hand, even the subjective starting-point and axiom, "the world is my representation," has something inadequate about it, firstly inasmuch as it is one-sided, for the world is much more besides this (namely thing-in-itself, will); in fact, being representation is to a certain extent accidental to it; secondly also inasmuch as it expresses merely the object's being conditioned by the subject without at the same time stating that the subject as such is also conditioned by the object. For the proposition that "the subject would nevertheless be a knowing being, even if it had no object, in other words, no representation at all" is just as false as is the proposition of the crude understand-

---

[4] "What is noble is difficult." [Tr.]

ing to the effect that "the world, the object, would still exist, even if there were no subject." A consciousness without object is no consciousness at all. A thinking subject has *concepts* for its object; a sensuously perceiving subject has objects with the qualities corresponding to its organization. Now if we deprive the *subject* of all the particular determinations and forms of its knowing, all the properties in the *object* also disappear, and nothing but *matter without form and quality* is left. This matter can occur in experience as little as can the subject without the forms of its knowledge, yet it remains opposed to the bare subject as such, as its reflex, which can only disappear simultaneously with it. Although materialism imagines that it postulates nothing more than this matter—atoms for instance—yet it unconsciously adds not only the subject, but also space, time, and causality, which depend on special determinations of the subject.

The world as representation, the objective world, has thus, so to speak, two poles, namely the knowing subject plain and simple without the forms of its knowing, and crude matter without form and quality. Both are absolutely unknowable; the subject, because it is that which knows; matter, because without form and quality it cannot be perceived. Yet both are the fundamental conditions of all empirical perception. Thus the knowing subject, merely as such, which is likewise a presupposition of all experience, stands in opposition, as its clear counterpart, to crude, formless, quite dead (i.e., will-less) matter. This matter is not given in any experience, but is presupposed in every experience. This subject is not in time, for time is only the more direct form of all its representing. Matter, standing in opposition to the subject, is accordingly eternal, imperishable, endures through all time; but properly speaking it is not extended, since extension gives form, and hence it is not spatial. Everything else is involved in a constant arising and passing away, whereas these two constitute the static poles of the world as representation. We can therefore regard the permanence of matter as the reflex of the timelessness of the pure subject, that is simply taken to be the condition of every object. Both belong to the phenomenon, not to the thing-in-itself; but they are the framework of the phenomenon. Both are discovered only through abstraction; they are not given immediately, pure and by themselves.

The fundamental mistake of all systems is the failure to recognize this truth, namely that *the intellect and matter are correlatives,* in other words, the one exists only for the other; both stand and fall together; the one is only the other's reflex. They are in fact really one and the same thing, considered from two opposite points of view; and this one thing—here I am anticipating—is the phenomenon of the will or of the thing-in-itself. Consequently, both are second-ary, and therefore the origin of the world is not to be looked for in either of them. But in consequence of their failure to recognize this, all systems (with the possible exception of Spinoza's) have sought the origin of all things in one of those two. Thus some of them suppose an intellect, νοῦς, as positively the first thing and the δημιουργός; and accordingly they allow a *representation* in this of things and of the world to precede their real existence; consequently they distinguish the real world from the world as representation, which is false. Therefore, *matter* now appears as that by which the two are distinguished, namely as a thing-in-itself. Hence arises the difficulty of producing this matter, the ὕλη, so that, when added to the mere representation of the world, it may impart reality thereto. That original intellect must either find it already in existence; matter is then an absolutely first thing just as much as that intellect is, and we then get two absolutely first things, the δημιουργός and the ὕλη. Or the intellect produces matter out of nothing, an assumption that our understanding combats, for this understanding is capable of grasping only changes in matter, not an arising or passing away of that matter. At bottom, this rests on the very fact that matter is the essential correlative of the understanding. The systems opposed to these, which make the other of the two correlatives, namely mat-ter, the absolutely first thing, suppose a matter that exists without being represented by a subject; and, as is sufficiently clear from all that has been said above, this is a direct contradiction, for in the existence of matter we always think only of its being represented by a subject. But then there arises for them the difficulty of bringing to this matter, which alone is their absolutely first thing, the intellect that is ultimately to know it from experience. In § 7 of the first volume I have spoken of this weak side of materialism. With me, on the other hand, matter and intellect are inseparable correlatives, existing for each other, and therefore only relatively. Matter is the representation of the intellect; the intellect is that in the representa-tion of which alone matter exists. Both together constitute the *world as representation,* which is precisely Kant's *phenomenon,* and con-sequently something secondary. What is primary is that which ap-pears, namely the *thing-in-itself,* which we shall afterwards learn to recognize as the *will.* In itself this is neither the representer nor the represented, but is quite different from its mode of appearance.

As an impressive conclusion to this important and difficult dis-cussion, I will now personify those two abstractions, and introduce them into a dialogue, after the manner of *Prabodha Chandro Daya.*[5] We may also compare it with a similar dialogue between matter and form in Raymond Lull's *Duodecim Principia Philosophiae,* c. 1 and 2.

The Subject.

I am, and besides me there is nothing. For the world is my representation.

Matter.

Presumptuous folly! *I* am, and besides me there is nothing: For the world is my fleeting form. You are a mere result of a part of this form, and quite accidental.

The Subject.

What silly conceit! Neither you nor your form would exist without me; you are conditioned through me. Whoever thinks me away, and then believes he can still think of you, is involved in a gross delusion; for your existence outside my representation is a direct contradiction, a wooden-iron. *You are,* simply means you are represented by me. My representation is the locality of your existence; I am therefore its first condition.

Matter.

Fortunately the boldness of your assertion will soon be refuted in a real way, and not by mere words. A few more moments, and you—actually are no more; with all your boasting and bragging, you have sunk into nothing, floated past like a shadow, and suffered the fate of every one of my fleeting forms. But I, I remain intact and undiminished from millennium to millennium, throughout endless time, and behold unmoved the play of my changing forms.

The Subject.

This endless time, to live through which is your boast, is, like the endless space you fill, present merely in my representation; in fact, it is the mere form of my representation which I carry already prepared within me, and in which you manifest yourself. It receives you, and in this way do you first of all exist. But the annihilation with which you threaten me does not touch me, otherwise you also

---

[5] More correctly *Prabodha-candra-udaya,* "the rising of the moon of knowledge," an allegorical drama in six acts by Krishna Misra (about 1200 A.D.) in which philosophical concepts appear as persons. [Tr.]

would be annihilated. On the contrary, it concerns merely the individual which for a short time is my bearer, and which, like everything else, is my representation.

Matter.

Even if I grant you this, and go so far as to regard your existence, which is inseparably linked to that of these fleeting individuals, as something existing by itself, it nevertheless remains dependent on mine. For you are subject only in so far as you have an object; and that object is I. I am its kernel and content, that which is permanent in it, that which holds it together, without which it would be as incoherent and as wavering and unsubstantial as the dreams and fancies of your individuals, that have borrowed even their fictitious content from me.

The Subject.

You do well to refrain from disputing my existence on account of its being linked to individuals; for just as inseparably as I am tied to these, so are you tied to form, your sister, and you have never yet appeared without her. No eye has yet seen either you or me naked and isolated; for we are both only abstractions. At bottom it is *one* entity that perceives itself and is perceived by itself, but its being-in-itself cannot consist either in perceiving or in being perceived, as these are divided between us.

Both.

So we are inseparably connected as necessary parts of one whole, which includes us both and exists through us both. Only a misunderstanding can set up the two of us as enemies in opposition to each other, and lead to the false conclusion that the one contests the existence of the other, with which its own existence stands and falls.

* * *

This whole, including both, is the world as representation, or the phenomenon. After this is taken away, there remains only the purely metaphysical, the thing-in-itself, which in the second book we shall recognize as the will.

CHAPTER II

On the Doctrine of Knowledge of Perception or Knowledge of the Understanding

In spite of all *transcendental* ideality, the objective world retains *empirical* reality. It is true that the object is not the thing-in-itself; but as empirical object it is real. It is true that space is only in my head; but empirically my head is in space. The law of causality, of course, can never enable us to set aside idealism by forming a bridge between things-in-themselves and our knowledge of them, and thus assuring absolute reality to the world that manifests itself in consequence of the application of that law. But this by no means does away with the causal relation of objects to one another, and thus the relation that unquestionably occurs between every knower's own body and all other material objects. But the law of causality unites only phenomena; it does not, on the other hand, lead beyond them. With this law we are and remain in the world of objects, in other words, of phenomena, and thus really in the world of representations. Yet the whole of such a world of experience remains conditioned first by the knowledge of a subject in general as its necessary presupposition, and then by the special forms of our perception and apprehension; therefore it belongs necessarily to the mere *phenomenon,* and has no claim to pass for the world of things-in-themselves. Even the subject itself (in so far as it is merely knowing) belongs to the mere phenomenon, and constitutes the complementary half thereof.

Without the application of the law of causality, however, we could never arrive at the perception of an *objective* world, for, as I have explained, this perception is essentially a matter of the *intellect,* and not merely of the *senses.* The senses give us mere *sensation,* which is still far from being *perception.* The share of the sensation of the senses in perception was separated out by Locke under the name of *secondary qualities,* which he rightly denied to things-in-themselves. But Kant, carrying Locke's method farther, also separated out and denied to things-in-themselves what belongs to the *elaboration* of that material (the sensation of the senses) through the *brain*. The result was that included in this was all that Locke had left to things-in-themselves as *primary* qualities, namely extension, shape, solidity, and so on, and in this way the thing-in-itself becomes with Kant a wholly unknown quantity *x*. So with Locke the thing-in-itself is something indeed without colour, sound, smell, taste, neither warm nor cold, neither soft nor hard, neither smooth nor rough; yet it remains something that is extended, has form, is impenetrable, is at rest or in motion, and has measure and number. With Kant, on the other hand, the thing-in-itself has laid aside even all these last qualities also, because they are possible only through time, space, and causality. These latter, however, spring from our intellect (brain) just as do colours, tones, smells, and so on from the nerves of the sense-organs. With Kant the thing-in-itself has become spaceless, unextended, and incorporeal. Thus what the mere *senses* supply to perception, in which the objective world exists, is related to what is supplied to perception by the *brain-functions* (space, time, causality) as the mass of the sense-nerves is to the mass of the brain, after deduction of that part of the latter which is moreover applied to *thinking* proper, in other words, to making abstract representations, and which in animals is therefore lacking. For while the nerves of the sense-organs invest the appearing objects with colour, sound, taste, smell, temperature, and so on, the brain imparts to them extension, form, impenetrability, mobility, and so on, in short, all that can be represented in perception only by means of time, space, and causality. How small the share of the senses is in perception compared with that of the intellect is proved also by comparing the nerve-apparatus for receiving impressions with that for elaborating them. For the mass of the nerves of sensation of all the sense-organs is very small compared with the mass of the brain, even in the case of animals, whose brain, since they do not really think in the abstract, serves merely to produce perception, and yet where this is perfect, as in the case of mammals, has a considerable mass. This is so even after the deduction of the cerebellum, whose function is the regulated control of movement.

Thomas Reid's excellent book, *Inquiry into the Human Mind* (first edition 1764, sixth edition 1810), as a corroboration of the Kantian truths in the *negative* way, affords us a very thorough conviction of the inadequacy of the *senses* for producing the objective perception of things, and also of the non-empirical origin of the intuition of space and time. Reid refutes Locke's teaching that perception is a product of the *senses*. This he does by a thorough and acute demonstration that the collective sensations of the senses do not bear the least resemblance to the world known through perception, and in particular by showing that Locke's five primary qualities (extension, figure, solidity, movement, number) cannot possibly be supplied to us by any sensation of the senses. Accordingly, he abandons the question of the mode of origination and the source of perception as completely insoluble. Thus, although wholly unacquainted with Kant, he furnishes, so to speak, according to the *regula falsi,* a thorough proof of the intellectual nature of perception (which I was really the first to expound in consequence of the Kantian doctrine), and of the *a priori* source, discovered by Kant, of the constituent elements of perception, namely space, time, and causality, from which those primary qualities of Locke first arise, but by whose means they can easily be constructed. Thomas Reid's book is very instructive and well worth reading, ten times more so than all the philosophical stuff which has been written since Kant put together. Another indirect proof of the same doctrine, though on the path of error, is afforded by the French philosophers of sensualism. Since Condillac followed in the footsteps of Locke, these philosophers have laboured actually to show that the whole of our making of representations and our thinking go back to mere *sensations of the senses (penser c'est sentir)*,[1] which, after the manner of Locke, they call *idées simples.*[2] Through the coming together and comparison of these *idées,* the whole of the objective world is supposed to be constructed in our head. These gentlemen certainly have *des idées bien simples.*[3] It is amusing to see how, lacking the depth of the German philosopher and the honesty of the English, they turn that wretched material of the sensation of the senses this way and that, and try to make it important, in order to construct out of it the deeply significant phenomenon of the world of representation and of thought. But the man constructed by them would inevitably be, speaking anatomically, an *Anencephalus,* a *tête de crapaud,*[4] with sense-organs only and without brain. To quote, by way of example, only a couple of the better attempts of this kind from among innumerable others, I mention Condorcet at the beginning of his book, *Des progrès de l'esprit humain,* and Tourtual on vision in the second volume of the *Scriptores Ophthalmologici Minores,* published by Justus Radius (1828).

The feeling of inadequacy of a merely sensualistic explanation of perception shows itself likewise in an assertion made shortly before

---

[1] "To think is to be conscious." [Tr.]
[2] "Simple ideas." [Tr.]
[3] "Really simple ideas." [Tr.]
[4] "Toad's head." [Tr.]

the Kantian philosophy appeared. This is that we not only have *representations* of things stimulated by sensation of the senses, but that we directly perceive and apprehend *the things themselves,* although they lie outside us, which of course is inconceivable. And this was not meant in some idealistic sense, but was said from the ordinary realistic point of view. The celebrated Euler expresses this assertion well and to the point in his *Briefe an eine Deutsche Prinzessin,* vol. II, p. 68: "I therefore believe that the sensations (of the senses) still contain something more than the philosophers imagine. They are not merely empty perceptions of certain impressions made in the brain. They give to the soul not merely *Ideas* (*Ideen*) of things, but *actually place before it objects* that exist outside it, although how this really happens we cannot conceive." This opinion is explained from what follows. Although, as I have adequately demonstrated, perception is brought about by the application of the law of causality, of which we are *a priori* conscious, nevertheless in vision the act of the understanding, by means of which we pass from the effect to the cause, certainly does not enter into distinct consciousness. Therefore the sensation of the senses is not separated from the representation that is first formed by the understanding out of that sensation as raw material. Still less can there enter into consciousness a distinction, which generally does not take place, between object and representation, but we perceive quite directly the *things themselves,* and indeed as lying *outside us,* although it is certain that what is immediate can be only the *sensation;* and this is confined to the sphere beneath our skin. This can be explained from the fact that *outside us* is an exclusively *spatial* determination, but space itself is a form of our faculty of perception, in other words, a function of our brain. Therefore the *"outside us"* to which we refer objects on the occasion of the sensation of sight, itself resides inside our head, for there is its whole scene of action; much the same as in the theatre we see mountains, forest, and sea, yet everything remains within the house. From this we can understand that we perceive things with the determination *"outside,"* and yet quite *directly,* but that we do not have within us a representation of the things lying outside us which is different from them. For things are *in space* and consequently *outside us* only in so far as we *represent* them. Therefore these *things* that we perceive directly in such a manner and not some mere image or copy of them, are themselves also only *our representations,* and as such exist only in our head. Therefore we do not, as Euler says, directly perceive the things themselves lying outside us; on the contrary, the things perceived by us as lying outside us are only our representations, and consequently are something we immediately perceive or apprehend. Therefore the whole of the correct observation given above in Euler's words affords a fresh corroboration of Kant's *Transcendental Aesthetic,* and of my theory of perception based thereon, as well as of idealism generally. The directness and unconsciousness above mentioned, with which in perception we make the *transition from the sensation to its cause,* can be illustrated by an analogous occurrence when we make *abstract* representations or think. Thus when we read or listen, we receive mere words, but from these we pass over to the concepts denoted by them so immediately, that it is as if we received *the concepts immediately;* for we are in no way conscious of the transition to them. Therefore on occasion we do not know what was the language in which we yesterday read something which we remember. Nevertheless, that such a transition takes place every time becomes apparent when once it is omitted, in other words, when we are distracted or diverted, and read without thinking; then we become aware that we have taken in all the words indeed, but no concept. Only when we pass from abstract concepts to pictures of the imagination do we become aware of the transposition.

Moreover, with empirical apprehension, the unconsciousness with which the transition from the sensation to its cause is brought about really occurs only with perception in the narrowest sense, with *vision* or *sight.* On the other hand, with every other perception or apprehension of the senses the transition occurs with more or less clear consciousness; thus in the case of apprehension through the four coarser senses, the reality of the transition can be directly observed as a fact. In the dark we touch a thing on all sides for a long time, until from its different effects on our hands we are able to construct their cause as a definite shape. Further, if something feels smooth, we sometimes reflect as to whether we have fat or oil on our hands; and also when something feels cold, we wonder whether we have very warm hands. In the case of a sound, we sometimes doubt whether it was a merely inner affection of hearing or one that actually comes from outside; whether it sounded near and weak or far off and strong; from what direction it came; finally, whether it was the voice of a human being, of an animal, or the sound of an instrument. We therefore investigate the cause in the case of a given effect. With smell and taste, uncertainty as to the nature of the objective cause of the felt effect is of daily occurrence, so distinctly are they separated in this case. The fact that *in the case of seeing* the transition from the effect to the cause occurs quite unconsciously, and thus the illusion arises that this kind of perception is perfectly direct and consists only in the sensation of sense without the operation of the understanding—this fact is due partly to the great perfection of the organ, and partly to the exclusively rectilinear action of light. In virtue of this action, the impression itself leads to the place of the cause, and as the eye has the capacity of experiencing most delicately and at a glance all the nuances of light, shade, colour, and outline, as well as the data by which the understanding estimates distance, the operation of the understanding, in the case of impressions on this sense, takes place with a rapidity and certainty that no more allow it to enter consciousness than they allow spelling to do so in the case of reading. In this way, therefore, the illusion arises that the sensation itself gives us the objects directly. Nevertheless, it is precisely in vision that the operation of the *understanding,* which consists in knowing the cause from the effect, is most significant. By virtue of this operation, what is doubly felt with two eyes is singly perceived; by means of it, the impression arrives on the retina upside down, in consequence of the crossing of the rays in the pupil; and when its cause is pursued back in the same direction, the impression is corrected, or, as it is expressed, we see things upright, although their image in the eye is inverted and reversed. Finally, by virtue of that operation of the understanding, we estimate magnitude and distance in immediate perception from the five different data very clearly and beautifully described by Thomas Reid. I expounded all this, as well as the proofs which irrefutably establish the *intellectual nature of perception,* in 1816 in my essay *On Vision and Colours* (second edition 1854), and with important additions fifteen years later in the improved Latin version. This version appears with the title *Theoria Colorum physiologica eademque primaria* in the third volume of the *Scriptores Ophthalmologici Minores* published by Justus Radius in 1830. But all this has been most fully and thoroughly discussed in the second edition of my essay *On the Principle of Sufficient Reason,* § 21. Therefore on this important subject I refer to these works so as not to extend the present discussions still further.

On the other hand, an observation which comes within the province of the aesthetic may find place here. By virtue of the demonstrated intellectual nature of perception, the sight of beautiful objects, a beautiful view for example, is also a *phenomenon of the brain.* Therefore its purity and perfection depend not merely on the *object,* but also on the quality and constitution of the brain, that is on its form and size, the fineness of its texture, and the stimulation of its activity through the energy of the pulse of the brain-arteries. Accordingly, the picture of the same view appears in different heads, even when the eyes are equally keen, as differently as, say, the first and last impression from a much-used copperplate. To this is due the great difference in the capacity to enjoy the beauties of nature, and consequently to copy them, in other words, to produce the same phenomenon of the brain by means of an entirely different kind of cause, namely dabs of colour on a canvas.

Moreover, the apparent immediacy of perception, resting on its entirely intellectual nature, by virtue of which, as Euler says, we apprehend the things themselves as lying outside us, has an analogy in the way in which we feel the parts of our own body, especially when they experience pain, as is generally the case as soon as we feel them. Thus, just as we imagine we perceive things directly where they are, whereas in fact we do so in the brain, so do we also believe we feel the pain of a limb in the limb itself, whereas this pain also is felt in the brain to which it is guided by the nerve of the affected part. Therefore only the affections of those parts whose nerves go to the brain are felt, but not those whose nerves belong to the ganglionic system. It may happen, of course, that an unusually strong affection of these parts penetrates by roundabout ways as far as the brain. Usually, however, it makes itself known there only as a dull discomfort, and always without precise determination of its locality. Therefore we do not feel injuries to a limb whose nerve-trunk is severed or ligatured. Finally, a man who has lost a limb still sometimes feels pain in it, because the nerves going to the brain still exist. Thus, in the two phenomena here compared, what occurs in the brain is apprehended as outside the brain; in the case of perception, by means of the understanding extending its feelers into the external world; in the case of a sensation in the limbs, by means of the nerves.

CHAPTER III

On the Senses

To repeat what others have said is not the purpose of my works; here, therefore, I give only isolated remarks of my own concerning the senses.

The senses are merely the brain's outlets through which it receives material from outside (in the form of sensation); this material it elaborates into the representation of perception. Those sensations that are to serve mainly for the *objective* apprehension of the external world must not be in themselves either agreeable or disagreeable. This really means that they must leave the will entirely unaffected; otherwise the sensation *itself* would absorb our attention, and we should pause at the *effect,* instead of passing at once to the *cause,* as is intended. This is occasioned by the decided mastery that *the will,* for our consideration, everywhere has over the mere representation, and we turn to the latter only when the will is silent. Accordingly colours and sounds are in themselves, and so long as their impression does not go beyond the normal degree, neither painful nor agreeable sensations, but appear with that indifference that makes them suitable to be the material of purely objective perceptions or intuitions. This is the case in so far as it possibly could be in general in a body that is in itself through and through will; and it is precisely in this respect that it is worthy of admiration. Physiologically it rests on the fact that, in the organs of the nobler senses, sight and hearing, those nerves which have to receive the specific outward impression are in no way susceptible to any sensation of pain, but know no sensation other than that which is specifically peculiar to them and serves mere perception. Accordingly, the retina, and the optic nerve as well, are insensitive to every injury; and it is just the same with the auditory nerve. In both organs pain is felt only in their other parts, in the surroundings of the nerve of sense which is peculiar to them, never in that nerve itself. In the case of the eye, the pain is mainly in the *conjunctiva;* in the case of the ear, in the auditory meatus. Even with the brain it is just the same, since if it is cut into directly, from above, it has no sensation of

[26]

this. Thus only on account of this indifference, peculiar to them, with reference to the will do the eye's sensations become capable of supplying the understanding with such manifold and finely shaded data. From these the understanding constructs in our mind the marvellous objective world by the application of the law of causality and on the basis of the pure intuitions of space and time. It is precisely that want of effect on the *will* which enables colour-sensations, when their strength is enhanced by transparence, as in the case of the sunset glow, of coloured windows, and so on, to put us very easily into the state of purely objective, will-less perception. As I have shown in the third book, such perception forms a principal element of the aesthetic impression. It is just this indifference with regard to the *will* which makes sounds suitable for supplying the material to express the endless multiplicity and variety of the concepts of reason (*Vernunft*).

Since the *outer sense,* in other words receptivity for external impressions as pure data for the understanding, is divided into *five senses,* these conform to the four elements, in other words, to the four conditions or states of aggregation, together with that of imponderability. Thus the sense for the firm (earth) is touch, for the fluid (water) is taste, for the vaporous, i.e., the volatile (vapour, exhalation) is smell, for the permanently elastic (air) is hearing, for the imponderable (fire, light) is sight. The second imponderable, namely heat, is really an object not of the senses, but of general feeling; hence it always affects the *will* directly as pleasant or unpleasant. From this classification the relative dignity of the senses also follows. Sight has the highest rank, inasmuch as its sphere is the most far-reaching, and its receptivity and susceptibility the keenest. This is due to the fact that what stimulates it is an imponderable, in other words, something hardly corporeal, something quasi-spiritual. Hearing has the second place, corresponding to air. Touch, however, is a thorough, versatile, and well-informed sense. For whereas each of the other senses gives us only an entirely one-sided account of the object, such as its sound or its relation to light, touch, which is closely bound up with general feeling and muscular power, supplies the understanding with data regarding simultaneously the form, size, hardness, smoothness, texture, firmness, temperature, and weight of bodies; and it does all this with the least possibility of illusion and deception, to which all the other senses are far more liable. The two lowest senses, smell and taste, are not free from a direct stimulation of the *will;* thus they are always agreeably or disagreeably affected, and so are more subjective than objective.

Perceptions through *hearing* are exclusively in *time;* hence the whole nature of music consists in the measure of time, and on this depends not only the quality or pitch of tones by means of vibrations, but also their quantity or duration by means of the beat or time. The perceptions of *sight,* on the other hand, are primarily and predominantly in *space;* but secondarily, through their duration, they are in time also.

Sight is the sense of the *understanding* that perceives; hearing is the sense of the faculty of *reason* that thinks and comprehends. Visible signs only imperfectly take the place of words; therefore I doubt whether a deaf and dumb person, able to read but with no conception of the sound of the words, operates as readily in his thinking with the merely visible concept-signs as we do with the actual, i.e., audible words. If he cannot read, he is, as is well known, almost like an irrational animal; whereas the man born blind is from the beginning an entirely rational being.

Sight is an *active,* hearing a *passive* sense. Therefore, sounds affect our mind in a disturbing and hostile manner, the more so indeed, the more active and developed the mind. They can destroy all ideas, and instantly shatter the power of thought. On the other hand there is no analogous disturbance through the eye, no immediate effect of what is seen *as such* on the activity of thinking (for naturally it is not a question here of the influence of the perceived objects on the will), but the most varied multiplicity of things before our eyes admits of entirely unhindered and undisturbed thinking. Accordingly, the thinking mind lives in eternal peace with the eye, and at eternal war with the ear. This antagonism of the two senses is also confirmed by the fact that deaf-mutes, when cured by galvanism, become deadly pale with terror at the first sound they hear (Gilbert's *Annalen der Physik,* Vol. X, p. 382); on the other hand, blind persons operated on behold the first light with great joy, and only with reluctance do they allow the bandages to be put over their eyes again. However, all that has been mentioned can be explained from the fact that hearing takes place by virtue of a mechanical percussion on the auditory nerve which is at once transmitted to the brain; whereas vision is a real *action* of the retina, which is merely stimulated and brought about by light and its modifications, as I have shown in detail in my physiological theory of colours. On the other hand, the whole of this antagonism clashes with the coloured-ether drum-beating theory so shamelessly served up everywhere at the present time. This theory tries to degrade the eye's sensation of light to a mechanical percussion such as the sensation of hearing actually is; whereas nothing can be more heterogeneous than the placid, gentle effect of light and the alarm-drum of hearing. If we also associate with this the special circumstance that, although we hear with two ears, whose sensitiveness is often very different, we never hear a sound doubly, as we often see double with two eyes, we are led to the conjecture that the sensation of hearing does not originate in the labyrinth or in the cochlea, but only deep down in the brain where the two auditory nerves meet, through which the impression becomes single. But this is where the *pons Varolii* encloses the *medulla oblongata,* and thus at the absolutely lethal spot, by injury to which any animal is instantly killed, and from which the auditory nerve has only a short course to the labyrinth, the seat of the acoustic percussion. It is just because its source is here, in this dangerous place, from which all movement of limbs also arises, that we start at a sudden bang. This does not occur at all with a sudden illumination, e.g., a flash of lightning. On the other hand, the optic nerve proceeds much farther forward from its *thalami* (although perhaps its primary source lies behind these), and throughout its course it is covered by the anterior lobes of the brain, though always separated from them, until, having got right outside the brain, it is extended into the retina. On the retina the sensation arises first of all on the occasion of the light-stimulus, and there it actually has its seat, as is shown in my essay *On Vision and Colours.* From this origin of the auditory nerve is also explained the great disturbance that the power of thought suffers through sounds. Because of this disturbance, thinking minds, and people of great intellect generally, are without exception absolutely incapable of enduring any noise. For it disturbs the constant stream of their thoughts, interrupts and paralyses their thinking, just because the vibration of the auditory nerve is transmitted so deeply into the brain. The whole mass of the brain trembles and feels the vibrations and oscillations set up by the auditory nerve, because the brains of such persons are much more easily moved than are those of ordinary heads. On the same great agility and power of transmission of their brains depends precisely the fact that, with them, every thought so readily evokes all those that are analogous or related to it. In this way the similarities, analogies, and relations of things in general come so rapidly and readily into their minds, that the same occasion that millions of ordinary people had before them brings them to *the* thought, to *the* discovery. Other men are subsequently surprised at not having made the discovery, because they are certainly able to think afterwards, but not before. Thus the sun shone on all statues, but only the statue of Memnon emitted a sound. Accordingly Kant, Goethe, and Jean-Paul were highly sensitive to every noise, as their biographies testify.* In the last years of his life Goethe bought a dilapidated house close to his own, merely in order that he might not have to endure the noise made in repairing it. So it was in vain that he had followed the drum in his youth, in order to harden himself to noise. It is not a matter of habit. On the other hand, the truly stoical indifference of ordinary persons to noise is amazing; no noise disturbs them in their thinking, reading, writing, or other work, whereas the superior mind is rendered quite incapable by it. But that very thing which makes them so insensitive to noise of every kind also makes them insensitive to the beautiful in the plastic arts, and to profound thought and fine expression in the rhetorical arts, in short, to everything that does not touch their personal interest. The following remark of Lichtenberg can be applied to the paralysing effect that noise has on highly intellectual persons: "It is always a good sign when artists can be prevented by trifles from exercising their art. F. . . . stuck his fingers into sulphur when he wanted to play the piano. . . . Such things do not hinder the mediocre head; . . . it acts, so to speak, like a coarse sieve." (*Vermischte Schriften,* Vol. I, p. 398.) Actually, I have for a long time been of opinion that the quantity of noise anyone can comfortably endure is in inverse proportion to his mental powers, and may therefore be regarded as a rough estimate of them. Therefore, when I hear dogs barking unchecked for hours in the courtyard of a house, I know what to think of the mental powers of the inhabitants. The man who habitually slams doors instead of shutting them with the hand, or allows this to be done in his house, is not merely ill-mannered, but also coarse and narrow-minded. That *"sensible"* in English also means "intelligent," "judicious" (*verständig*), accordingly rests on an accurate and fine observation. We shall be quite civilized only when our ears are no longer outlawed, and it is no longer anyone's right to cut through the consciousness of every thinking being within a circuit of a thousand yards, by means of whistling, howling, bellowing, hammering, whip-cracking, letting dogs bark, and so on. The Sybarites banished all noisy trades from their city; the venerable sect of the Shakers in North America tolerate no unnecessary noise in their villages, and the same thing is reported of the Moravian brotherhood. A few more remarks on this subject are to be found in chapter 30 of the second volume of the *Parerga and Paralipomena.*

---

* Lichtenberg says in his "Information and Observations about himself" (*Vermischte Schriften,* Göttingen 1800, Vol. I, p. 43): "I am extraordinarily sensitive to all loud noises, but they entirely lose their disagreeable impression as soon as they are associated with a rational purpose."

The effect of music on the mind, so penetrating, so immediate, so unfailing, and also the after-effect that sometimes follows it, consisting in a specially sublime frame of mind, are explained by the *passive* nature of hearing just described. The vibrations of the tones following in combined, rational, numerical relations, set the brain-fibres themselves vibrating in a similar way. On the other hand, from the *active* nature of vision, the very opposite of hearing, we can understand why for the eye there can be nothing analogous to music, and why the colour-organ was a ludicrous error. Further, it is just by reason of the *active* nature of the sense of sight that it is exceedingly keen in the case of hunting animals, that is, beasts of prey, just as conversely the *passive* sense, hearing, is keenest in the case of hunted, fleeing, timid animals, so that it may give them timely warning of the pursuer hurrying or creeping towards them.

Just as in sight or vision we have recognized the sense of the understanding, and in hearing that of the faculty of reason, so smell might be called the sense of memory, because it recalls to our mind more directly than anything else the specific impression of an event or an environment, even from the most remote past.

CHAPTER IV

On Knowledge a Priori

From the fact that we can of ourselves state and define the laws of relations in space, without needing experience to do so, Plato inferred (*Meno* [81 D], p. 353, *Bip.*) that all learning is merely a recollecting. Kant, on the contrary, inferred that space is subjectively conditioned, and is merely a form of the faculty of knowledge. How far, in this respect, Kant stands above Plato!

Cogito, ergo sum[1] is an analytical judgement; Parmenides, in fact, held it to be an identical judgement: τὸ γὰρ αὐτὸ νοεῖν ἐστίν τε καὶ εἶναι (*nam intelligere et esse idem est,* Clement of Alexandria, *Stromata,* vi, 2, § 23).[2] As such, however, or even only as an analytical judgement, it cannot contain any particular truth, even if we wanted to go still more deeply, and deduce it as a conclusion from the major premiss *non-entis nulla sunt praedicata.*[3] But by this Descartes really wished to express the great truth that immediate certainty belongs only to self-consciousness, to the subjective. On the other hand, to the objective, and thus to everything else, as having been brought about by self-consciousness, belongs merely indirect certainty. Therefore, because this is at second hand, it is to be regarded as problematical. On this depends the value of this famous proposition. As its opposite we can set up, in the sense of the Kantian philosophy, *cogito, ergo est;* in other words, just as I think certain relations (the mathematical) in things, so must they always turn out exactly in every possible experience; this was an important, profound, and late *aperçu,* which appeared in the form of the problem of the *possibility of synthetic a priori judgements,* and actually opened up the way to deeper knowledge. This problem is the watchword of the Kantian philosophy, just as the former proposition is that of the Cartesian, and shows ἐξ οἴων εἰς οἶα.[4]

Kant very properly puts his investigations on time and space at

---

[1] "I think, therefore I am." [Tr.]
[2] "For thinking and being are the same thing." [Tr.]
[3] "That which is not, has no predicates." [Tr.]
[4] "From what to what." (From small to great.) [Tr.]

the head of all the others. These questions above all force themselves on the speculative mind: What is *time?* What is this entity consisting of mere movement without anything that moves? and, What is *space,* this omnipresent nothing out of which no thing can emerge without ceasing to be something?

That time and space belong to the *subject,* are the mode and manner in which the process of objective apperception is carried out in the brain, has already a sufficient proof in the absolute impossibility of thinking away time and space, whereas we very easily think away everything that appears in them. The hand can let go of everything, but not of itself. I wish here to illustrate the more detailed proofs of this truth given by Kant by a few examples and deductions, not for the refutation of silly objections, but for the use of those who in future will have to lecture on Kant's teachings.

"A right-angled equilateral triangle" contains no logical contradiction, for the predicates by no means eliminate the subject, nor are they inconsistent with each other. Only with the construction of their object in pure intuition or perception does their incompatibility in it appear. Now if on that account we wished to regard this as a contradiction, every physical impossibility discovered only after centuries would also be a contradiction, for example, the composition of a metal from its elements, or a mammal with more or less than seven cervical vertebrae,[5] or the coexistence of horns and upper incisors in the same animal. But only *logical* impossibility, not physical, is a contradiction; and mathematical just as little. Equilateral and right-angled do not contradict each other (they coexist in the square); nor does either of them contradict the triangle. Therefore the incompatibility of these concepts can never be known through mere *thinking,* but results only from perception. But this perception is such that no experience, no real object, is required for it; thus it is a merely mental perception. Here we may refer to the proposition of Giordano Bruno, to be found also in Aristotle: "An infinitely large body is necessarily immovable"; a proposition that cannot rest either on experience or on the principle of contradiction; for it speaks of things that cannot occur in any experience, and the concepts "infinitely large" and "movable" do not contradict each other, but only pure perception establishes that movement demands a space outside the body, yet its infinite size leaves no space over. Now if anyone wished to object to the first mathematical example, and to say that it was a question only of how complete the concept is which the person judging has of the triangle, and that

---

[5] That the three-toed sloth has nine is to be regarded as an error, yet Owen still states it, *Ostéologie comparée,* p. 405.

if it were quite complete, it would also contain the impossibility of a triangle being right-angled and yet equilateral, then the answer is as follows: Assume that his concept of the triangle is not so complete, then, without the addition of experience, he can, by the mere construction of the triangle in his imagination, extend his concept of it, and convince himself of the impossibility of that combination of concepts for all eternity. But this very process is a synthetic judgement *a priori,* in other words, a judgement by which we form and perfect our concepts without any experience, and yet with validity for all experience. For in general, whether a given judgement is analytic or synthetic can be determined in the particular case only according as the concept of the subject has in the mind of the person judging more or less completeness. The concept "cat" contains a hundred times more in Cuvier's mind than in his servant's; therefore the same judgements about it will be synthetic for the latter, merely analytic for the former. But if we take the concepts objectively, and then seek to decide whether a given judgement is analytic or synthetic, let us convert its predicate into its contradictory opposite, and assign this without copula to the subject. If this gives a *contradictio in adjecto,* the judgement was analytic; if otherwise it was synthetic.

That *arithmetic* rests on the pure intuition or perception of *time* is not so evident as that geometry is based on the intuition of space.[6] It can be demonstrated, however, as follows. All counting consists in the repeated setting down of unity; merely to know al-

---

[6] This, however, does not excuse a professor of philosophy who, sitting in Kant's chair, expresses himself thus: "That mathematics as such contains arithmetic and geometry is correct. Yet it is incorrect to conceive arithmetic as the science of time, in fact for no other reason than to give a pendant to geometry as the science of space." [The German is *"einen Pendanten,"* after which Schopenhauer added *"[sic]." "Pendant"* is neuter, and the professor of philosophy should have written *"ein Pendant."* Tr.] (Rosenkranz in the *Deutsches Museum,* 14 May, 1857, No. 20.) This is the fruit of Hegelism. If the mind is once thoroughly ruined by the senseless gibberish of this, serious Kantian philosophy no longer enters it. The audacity of talking at random about things one does not understand has been inherited from the master, and in the end one comes to condemn without ceremony the fundamental teachings of a great mind in a peremptory and decisive tone, just as though they were Hegelian tomfoolery. But we must not overlook the fact that little men are anxious to get out of the track of great thinkers. Therefore they would have done better not to attack Kant, but to content themselves with giving their public more detailed information about God, the soul, the freedom of the will founded on fact, and anything else in that line, and then indulge in a little private amusement in their obscure back-shop, the philosophical journal. There they can work without ceremony and do what they like, for no one looks at it.

ways how often we have already set down unity do we mark it each time with a different word; these are the numerals. Now repetition is possible only through succession; but succession, thus one thing after another, depends entirely on the intuition or perception of *time*. It is a concept that is intelligible only by means of this; and thus counting is possible only by means of time. This dependence of all counting on *time* is also betrayed by the fact that in all languages multiplication is expressed by *"time,"* and thus through a time-concept, *sexies, ἑξάκις, six fois, sechsmal,* six times. But simple counting is itself a multiplying by one, and for this reason in Pestalozzi's educational establishment the children have always to multiply thus: "Two times two are four times one." Aristotle also recognized the close relationship between number and time, and expounded it in chapter fourteen of the fourth book of the *Physics.* To him time is "the number of motion" (ὁ χρόνος ἀριθμός ἐστι κινήσεως). He very profoundly raises the question whether time could be if the soul were not, and answers it in the negative. If arithmetic did not have this pure intuition or perception of time as its foundation, it would not be a science *a priori,* and consequently its propositions would not be of infallible certainty.

Although *time,* like space is the subject's form of knowledge, it nevertheless presents itself, like space, as something that exists independently of the subject and wholly objectively. Against our will, or without our knowledge, it hastens or lingers. We ask what time it is; we investigate time as though it were something quite objective. And what is this objective thing? Not the progress of the stars, or of clocks, which merely serve to measure the course of time itself; but it is something different from all these, yet like these is something independent of our willing and knowing. It exists only in the heads of beings that know, but the uniformity of its course and its independence of the will give it the right and title to objectivity.

Time is primarily the form of the *inner* sense. Anticipating the following book, I remark that the sole object of the inner sense is the knower's own *will.* Time is therefore the form by means of which self-knowledge becomes possible to the individual will, which originally and in itself is without knowledge. Thus in time the essential nature of the will, in itself simple and identical, appears drawn out into a course of life. But precisely on account of that original simplicity and identity of what exhibits itself thus, its *character* always remains exactly the same. For this reason, the course of life itself retains throughout the same *fundamental tone;* in fact, its manifold events and scenes are at bottom like variations on one and the same theme.

The *a priori nature of the law of causality* has at times not been *seen* at all, at other times not rightly understood, by Englishmen and Frenchmen. Therefore some of them continue the earlier attempts at finding an *empirical* origin for it. Maine de Biran puts this origin in experience, and says that the act of will as cause is followed by the movement of the body as effect. But this fact itself is erroneous. We do not by any means recognize the real, immediate act of will as something different from the action of the body, and the two as connected by the bond of causality; both are one and indivisible. Between them there is no succession; they are simultaneous. They are one and the same thing perceived and apprehended in a twofold manner. Thus what makes itself known to *inner* apprehension or perception (self-consciousness) as real *act of will,* exhibits itself at once in *outer* perception, in which the body stands out *objectively,* as the *action* of the body. That physiologically the action of the nerve precedes that of the muscle is here of no importance, as it does not come into self-consciousness; and it is not a question here of the relation between muscle and nerve, but of that between act of will and action of body. Now this does not make itself known as a causal relation. If these two presented themselves to us as cause and effect, their connexion would not be so incomprehensible to us as it actually is; for what we understand from its cause we understand in so far as there is in general for us a comprehension of things. On the other hand, the movement of our limbs by virtue of mere acts of will is indeed a miracle of such common occurrence that we no longer notice it; but if we once turn our attention to it, we become vividly conscious of the incomprehensible nature of the matter, just because we have here before us something we do *not* understand as effect of its cause. Therefore this perception or apprehension could never lead us to the notion of causality, for that does not occur in it at all. Maine de Biran himself recognizes the complete simultaneity of the act of will and of the movement (*Nouvelles considérations des rapports du physique au moral,* pp. 377, 378). In England Thomas Reid (*On the First Principles of Contingent Truths,* Essay VI, c. 5) stated that the knowledge of the causal relation has its ground in the nature and constitution of our cognitive faculty itself. Quite recently Thomas Brown has taught much the same thing in his extremely tedious book *Inquiry into the Relation of Cause and Effect* (4th ed., 1835), namely that that knowledge springs from an innate, intuitive, and instinctive conviction; he is therefore essentially on the right path. However, the crass ignorance is unpardonable by which, in this book of 476 pages, 130 of which are devoted to the refutation of

Hume, no mention at all is made of Kant, who cleared up the matter seventy years ago. If Latin had remained the exclusive language of science and literature, such a thing would not have occurred. In spite of Brown's explanation, which is on the whole correct, a modification of the doctrine, advanced by Maine de Biran, of the empirical origin of the fundamental knowledge of the causal relation, has found favour in England, for it is not without some plausibility. It is that we abstract the law of causality from the empirically perceived or apprehended effect of our own body on other bodies. Hume had already refuted it. I, however, have demonstrated its inadmissibility in my work *On the Will in Nature* (p. 75 of the second edition) from the fact that, in order that we may objectively apprehend in spatial perception our own body as well as others, the knowledge of causality must already exist, since it is the condition of such perception. The only genuine and convincing proof that we are conscious of the law of causality *prior to all experience* is actually found in the very necessity of making a *transition* from the sensation of the senses, given only empirically, to its *cause,* in order that perception of the external world may come about. I have therefore substituted this proof for the *Kantian,* whose incorrectness I have shown. The most detailed and thorough exposition of the whole of this important subject, here only touched on, and thus of the *a priori* nature of the law of causality, and of the intellectual nature of empirical perception, is found in the second edition of my essay *On the Principle of Sufficient Reason,* § 21, to which I refer to avoid repeating here all that I have said in that work. I have there shown the immense difference between the mere sensation of the senses and the perception of an objective world, and have uncovered the wide gulf that lies between the two. The law of causality alone bridges this gulf; but for its application it presupposes the other two forms akin to it, space and time. By means of these three in union do we first arrive at the *objective* representation. Now essentially it is immaterial whether the *sensation,* starting from which we arrive at perception or apprehension, occurs through the resistance suffered by the exertion of our muscles, or through the impression of light on the retina, or of sound on the auditory nerve, etc. The *sensation* always remains a mere *datum* for the *understanding,* and the understanding alone is capable of grasping it as *effect* of a *cause* different from it. The understanding now perceives it as something external, that is to say, something put into the form of *space,* which is also inherent in the intellect prior to all experience, as something occupying and filling this space. Without this intellectual operation, for which the forms must lie ready within us, the perception of an *objective external world* could never arise from a mere *sensation* inside our skin. How can we even conceive that the mere feeling of being hindered in a desired movement, which, moreover, occurs also in cases of paralysis, would be sufficient for this? In addition to this there is still the fact that, in order for *me* to attempt to affect external things, *these* must necessarily have affected *me* previously as motives; but this presupposes the apprehension of the external world. According to the theory in question (as I have already remarked in the place mentioned above), a person born without arms and legs would necessarily be quite unable to arrive at the representation of causality, and consequently at the perception or apprehension of the external world. But that this is not so is proved by a fact communicated in Froriep's *Notizen* (1838, July, No. 133), namely the detailed account, accompanied by a portrait, of an Estonian girl, Eva Lauk, then fourteen years old, who was born entirely without arms and legs. The account ends with the following words: "According to her mother's statements, she developed mentally as rapidly as her brothers and sisters did; in particular, she attained just as soon as they to a correct judgement of the size and distance of visible objects, yet without being able to make use of her hands. Dorpat, 1 March 1838. Dr. A. Hueck."

Hume's doctrine that the concept of causality arises merely from the habit of seeing two states or conditions constantly follow each other finds a refutation based on *fact* in the oldest of all successions, that of day and night, which no one has ever yet regarded as cause and effect of each other. And this very succession also refutes Kant's false assertion that the *objective* reality of a succession would be known first of all by our apprehending the two succeeding things in the relation of cause and effect to each other. Indeed, the converse of this teaching of Kant is true; thus we know *empirically* only in their succession which of two connected states or conditions is *cause* and which *effect*. On the other hand, the absurd assertion of many professors of philosophy of our day that cause and effect are *simultaneous* can again be refuted by the fact that in cases where on account of its great rapidity the succession cannot be perceived at all, we nevertheless assume it with *a priori* certainty, and with it the lapse of a certain time. Thus, for example, we know that a certain time must elapse between the pressing of the trigger and the emission of the bullet, although we cannot perceive it. We know that this time must again be divided between several states appearing in a strictly definite succession, namely the pressure of the trigger, the striking of the spark, the ignition, the spreading of the fire, the explosion, and the departure of the bullet. No person has ever yet perceived this succession of states; but since we know which state *brings about* the other, we also know in precisely this way which state must *precede* the other in time, and consequently that during the course of the whole series a certain time elapses, although it is so short that it escapes our empirical apprehension. For no one will assert that the flying out of the bullet is actually simultaneous with the pressing of the trigger. Therefore not merely the law of causality, but also its relation to *time,* and the necessity of the *succession* of cause and effect, are known to us a priori. If we know which of two states is cause and which effect, we also know which state precedes the other in time. If, on the contrary, this is *not* known to us, but their causal relation in general is known, then we try to decide the succession empirically, and according to this determine which of the two states is cause and which effect. The falseness of the assertion that cause and effect are simultaneous appears moreover from the following consideration. An unbroken chain of causes and effects fills the whole of time. (For if this chain were interrupted, the world would stand still, or to set it in motion again an effect without a cause would have to appear.) Now if every effect were *simultaneous* with its cause, then every effect would be moved up into the time of its cause, and a chain of causes and effects with still the same number of links would fill no time at all, much less an infinite time, but the causes and effects would be all together in one moment. Therefore, on the assumption that cause and effect are simultaneous, the course of the world shrinks up into the business of a moment. This proof is analogous to the one that every sheet of paper must have a thickness, since otherwise a whole book would have no thickness. To state *when* the cause ceases and the effect begins is in almost all cases difficult, and often impossible. For the *changes* (in other words, the succession of states or conditions) are a continuum, like the time they fill; and therefore also like that time they are infinitely divisible. Their succession or sequence, however, is as necessarily determined and irreversible as is that of the moments of time itself, and each of them with reference to the one preceding it is called "effect," and with reference to the one succeeding it, "cause."

Every change in the material world can appear only in so far as another change has immediately preceded it; this is the true and entire content of the law of causality. But in philosophy no concept has been more wrongly used than that of *cause,* by the favourite trick or blunder of conceiving it too *widely,* of taking it too *generally,* through abstract thinking. Since scholasticism, really in fact since Plato and Aristotle, philosophy has been for the most part a *continued misuse of universal concepts,* such as, for example, substance, ground, cause, the good, perfection, necessity, possibility, and very many others. A tendency of minds to operate with such abstract and too widely comprehended concepts has shown itself at almost all times. Ultimately it may be due to a certain indolence of the intellect, which finds it too onerous to be always controlling thought through perception. Gradually such unduly wide concepts are then used like algebraical symbols, and cast about here and there like them. In this way philosophizing degenerates into a mere combining, a kind of lengthy reckoning, which (like all reckoning and calculating) employs and requires only the lower faculties. In fact, there ultimately results from this a mere *display of words,* the most monstrous example of which is afforded us by mind-destroying Hegelism, where it is carried to the extent of pure nonsense. But scholasticism also often degenerated into word-juggling. In fact, even the *Topi* of Aristotle—very abstract principles, conceived with complete generality, which could be applied to subjects of the most different kind, and be brought into the field everywhere for arguing either *pro* or *contra*—also have their origin in that wrong use of universal concepts. We find innumerable examples of the way in which the scholastics worked with such abstractions in their writings, particularly those of Thomas Aquinas. But philosophy, down to the time of Locke and Kant, really pursued the path prepared by the scholastics; these two men at last turned their attention to the origin of concepts. In fact, in his earlier years, we find Kant himself still on that path in his *Proof of the Existence of God* (p. 191 of the first volume of the Rosenkranz edition), where the concepts *substance, ground, reality,* are used in such a way as they could never have been if a return had been made to the *source* of those concepts and to their *true content* as determined by this source. For then matter only would have been found as the source and content of *substance,* and of *ground* (when it is a question of things of the real world) only cause, in other words, the previous change bringing about the later change, and so on. This, of course, would not have led here to the intended result. But everywhere, as here, there arose false principles from such concepts *too widely* comprehended, under which more could therefore be subsumed than their true content allowed; and from these false principles arose false systems. Even the whole of Spinoza's method of demonstration rests on such uninvestigated and too widely comprehended concepts. Here Locke's very great merit is to be found; in order to counteract all that dogmatic unreality, he insisted on an investigation of the *origin of concepts,* and thus led back to what is *perceptive* and to *experience.* Before him Bacon had worked in a similar sense, yet with reference to physics rather than metaphysics. Kant pursued the path prepared by Locke in a higher sense and much farther, as mentioned previously. The results of Locke and Kant were, however, annoying and inconvenient to the men of mere show who succeeded in diverting the public's attention from Kant to themselves. But in such a case they know quite well how to ignore the dead as well as the living. They therefore summarily forsook the only correct path found in the end by those wise men, and philosophized at random with all kinds of raked-up concepts, unconcerned as to their origin and true content, so that Hegel's pretended wisdom finally resulted in concepts which had no origin at all, but were rather themselves the origin and source of things. But Kant was wrong in neglecting empirical perception too much in favour of *pure* perception, and this I have discussed at length in my criticism of his philosophy. With me perception is throughout the source of all knowledge. Early recognizing the ensnaring and insidious nature of abstractions, I already in 1813, in my essay *On the Principle of Sufficient Reason,* pointed out the difference of the relations that are thought under *this* concept. It is true that universal concepts should be the material *in* which philosophy deposits and stores up its knowledge, but not the source *from* which it draws such knowledge; the *terminus ad quem,* not *a quo.* It is not, as Kant defines it, a science *from* concepts, but a science *in* concepts. Therefore the concept of *causality* which we are discussing here has always been comprehended far *too widely* by philosophers for the furtherance of their dogmatic ends; and in this way much came into it that is not to be found in it at all. Hence arose propositions such as: "All that *is,* has its cause"; "The effect cannot contain more than the cause, and so anything that was not also in this cause"; *"Causa est nobilior suo effectu,"*[7] and many others just as unwarranted. The following subtle sophistry of that humdrum prattler Proclus, in his *Institutio Theologica,* § 76, gives us a fuller and specially lucid example: Πᾶν τὸ ἀπὸ ἀκινήτου γιγνόμενον αἰτίας, ἀμετάβλητον ἔχει τὴν ὕπαρξιν· πᾶν δὲ τὸ ἀπὸ κινουμένης, μεταβλητήν. Εἰ γὰρ ἀκίνητόν ἐστι πάντῃ τὸ ποιοῦν, οὐ διὰ κινήσεως, ἀλλ᾽ αὐτῷ τῷ εἶναι παράγει τὸ δεύτερον ἀφ᾽ ἑαυτοῦ. (*Quidquid ab immobili causa manat, immutabilem habet essentiam [substantiam]. Quidquid vero a mobili causa manat, essentiam habet mutabilem. Si enim illud, quod aliquid facit, est prorsus immobile, non per motum, sed per*

---

[7] "The cause is nobler than its effect." [Tr.]

ipsum Esse producit ipsum secundum ex se ipso.)[8] Fine! But just show me an unmoved cause; it is simply impossible. But here, as in so many cases, abstraction has thought away all determinations down to the one we want to use, without regard to the fact that the latter cannot exist without the former. The only correct expression for the law of causality is this: *Every change has its cause in another change immediately preceding it.* If something *happens,* in other words, if a new state or condition appears, that is to say, if something *changes,* then something else must have *changed* just previously, and so on backwards into infinity; for a *first* cause is as impossible to conceive as is a beginning of time or a limit of space. The law of causality does not assert more than what is thus stated; hence its claims appear only in the case of *changes.* So long as nothing *changes,* there can be no question of a cause; for there is no *a priori* ground for inferring from the existence of things present, that is to say, of states of matter, their previous non-existence, and from this non-existence their coming into existence, hence a change. Therefore the mere *existence* of a thing does not entitle us to conclude that it has a cause. However, there can be grounds or reasons *a posteriori,* that is to say, reasons drawn from previous experience, for assuming that the present state has not existed *from all eternity,* but has *come into existence* only in consequence of another state, and thus through a *change,* whose cause is then to be sought, and also the cause of this cause. Here, then, we are involved in the *infinite regressus* to which the application of the law of causality always leads. It was said above: *"Things, that is to say, states of matter";* for *change* and *causality* refer only to *states or conditions.* It is these states which we understand by *form* in the wider sense; and the *forms* alone change; matter endures. Therefore only the *form* is amenable to the law of causality. But the *form* also constitutes *the thing,* that is to say, it establishes the *difference* of things, whereas matter must be conceived as homogeneous in all. The scholastics therefore said: *Forma dat esse rei.*[9] More accurately this proposition would run: *Forma dat rei essentiam, materia existentiam.*[10] Therefore the question as to the cause of a *thing* always concerns only its form, in other words, its condition or quality, not its matter; and even the condition or quality only in so far as we have grounds for assuming

---

[8] "All that arises out of an immovable cause has an immutable essence; but all that arises out of a movable cause has a mutable essence. For if the operating thing is in every sense unmoved, it will put forth the other thing out of itself not through a movement, but through its mere existence." [Tr.]

[9] "The form gives the thing being." [Tr.]

[10] "The form gives the thing essence, matter gives it existence." [Tr.]

that it has not existed *from all eternity,* but has come into existence through a change. The union of *form* with *matter,* or of *essentia* with *existentia,* gives the *concrete,* which is always an individual, hence *the thing.* It is the *forms,* whose union with *matter,* that is to say, whose appearance in matter, by means of a *change,* is subject to the law of *causality.* Therefore by *too wide* a comprehension of this concept in the abstract, crept in the misuse of extending causality to the thing absolutely, and thus to its entire essence and existence, and consequently to matter as well; and in the end it was considered justifiable to ask even about a cause of the world. This is the origin of the *cosmological proof.* This proof really starts from the fact that, without any justification, there is inferred from the existence of the world a non-existence preceding its existence. However, it has as its end the terrible inconsistency of doing away altogether with the law of causality itself, from which alone it derives all its conclusive force, since it stops at a *first* cause, and will go no farther. Therefore it ends, so to speak, with parricide, just as the bees kill the drones after they have done their work. All talk about the *Absolute,* however, can be referred to a shamefaced, and therefore disguised, cosmological proof; despite the *Critique of Pure Reason,* this has passed for philosophy in Germany for the last sixty years. Now what does the Absolute really mean? Something which is as it is, and of which we dare not ask further (on pain of punishment) whence and why it is. A precious rarity for professors of philosophy! But now, in the case of the honestly expressed cosmological proof through the assumption of a first cause, and consequently of a first beginning in a time absolutely without beginning, this beginning is moved up higher and higher by the question: Why not earlier? In fact, it is moved so high that we never reach down from it to the present, but must marvel that this present did not itself exist already millions of years ago. In general, therefore, the law of causality finds application to all things *in* the world, but not *to* the world itself, for this law is *immanent* to the world, not transcendent; *with the world* it is established, and *with the world* it is abolished. This depends ultimately on the fact that it belongs to the mere form of our understanding and, together with the objective world that is thus mere phenomenon, is conditioned by the understanding. Therefore the law of causality finds complete application, and admits of no exception, to all things *in* the world, in accordance with their form of course, to the variation of these forms, and hence to their changes. It holds good of the actions of man as it does of the impact of a stone, yet, as we have said, always only in reference to events, to *changes.* But if we abstract from its origin in the understanding, and try to comprehend it in a purely *objective* way, then fundamentally and ultimately it rests on the fact that every operative or causative thing acts by virtue of its original, and thus eternal, i.e. timeless, power. Therefore its present effect would necessarily have appeared infinitely earlier, and so prior to any conceivable time, if the temporal condition for this had not been lacking. This condition is the occasion, i.e., the cause, by virtue of which alone the effect appears only *now,* but now with necessity; the cause assigns it its place in time.

In consequence, however, of the above-mentioned *too wide* comprehension of the concept *cause* in abstract thinking, it has also been confounded with the concept *force.* Completely different from the cause, this force is nevertheless what imparts to every cause its causality, in other words, the possibility of acting. I have fully and thoroughly discussed this in the second book of volume one, also in my work *On the Will in Nature,* and finally in the second edition of the essay *On the Principle of Sufficient Reason,* § 20, p. 44. This confusion is found in its clumsiest form in Maine de Biran's book previously cited, and is dealt with in more detail at the place last mentioned. However, it is also usual apart from this, for example when one asks about the cause of any original force, say the force of gravity. Indeed Kant himself (*On the Only Possible Proof,* Vol. I, pp. 211 and 215 of the Rosenkranz edition) calls the forces of nature "effective causes," and says that "gravity is a cause." But it is impossible to have a clear understanding of his thought so long as force and cause in it are not distinctly recognized as completely different; the use of abstract concepts leads very easily to their confusion, if the consideration of their origin is set aside. Knowledge of causes and effects, resting on the form of the understanding and always *perceptive,* is abandoned, in order that one may stick to the abstraction *cause.* Merely in this way has the concept of causality so frequently been falsely comprehended, in spite of all its simplicity. Therefore even in Aristotle (*Metaphysics,* IV, 2) we find causes divided into four classes which are grasped in a fundamentally false and even crude way. Compare with this my division of causes, as set forth for the first time in my essay *On Vision and Colours,* Chap. I, briefly touched on in para. 6 of our first volume, and fully discussed in the essay *On the Freedom of the Will,* pp. 30-33 [2nd ed., pp. 29-32]. Two things in nature, namely matter and the forces of nature, remain untouched by the chain of causality which is endless in both directions. These two are the conditions of causality, whereas everything else is conditioned by it. For the one (matter) is that *in* which the states and their changes appear; the other (the forces of nature) that *by virtue of* which alone they are able to appear at all.

But we must bear in mind here that in the second book, and later and more thoroughly in the essay *On the Will in Nature,* the forces of nature are shown to be identical with the *will* in ourselves, but that matter appears as the mere *visibility of the will,* so that ultimately it too can be regarded in a certain sense as identical with the will.

On the other hand, what is explained in para. 4 of the first volume, and better still in the second edition of the essay *On the Principle of Sufficient Reason* at the end of para. 21, p. 77, is no less true and correct. This is to the effect that matter is objectively apprehended causality itself, since its entire nature consists in *action generally;* thus causality itself is the *effectiveness* (ἐνέργεια = actuality) of things generally, the abstraction, so to speak, of all their different kinds of acting. Accordingly, as the essence, *essentia,* of matter consists in *action generally,* and the actuality, *existentia,* of things in their materiality, which thus again is identical with action in general, it can be asserted of matter that in it *existentia* and *essentia* coincide and are one, for it has no other attributes than *existence itself* in general, and apart from any closer definition thereof. On the other hand, all *empirically given* matter, and thus all *material (Stoff)* (which our present-day ignorant materialists confuse with matter), has already entered the framework of the *forms,* and manifests itself only through their qualities and accidents, since in experience all acting is of a quite definite and special kind, and is never merely general. Therefore, pure matter is an object of *thought* alone, not of *perception;* and this led Plotinus (*Enneads,* II, Bk. 4, c. 8 and 9) and Giordano Bruno (*Della Causa,* dial. 4) to the paradoxical assertion that matter has no extension, for extension is inseparable from the form, and that it is therefore *incorporeal.* Yet Aristotle had already taught that it is not a body, although it is corporeal: σῶμα μὲν οὐκ ἂν εἴη, σωματικὴ δέ (Stobaeus, *Ecl.,* Bk. I, c. 12, § 5). Actually, under *pure matter* we think of mere *acting* in the abstract, quite apart from the nature of this acting, and thus of *pure causality* itself. As such, it is not *object* but *condition* of experience, just as are space and time. This is why, in the accompanying table of our pure fundamental knowledge *a priori, matter* has been able to take the place of *causality,* and, together with space and time, figures as the third thing which is purely formal, and therefore inherent in our intellect.

This table contains all the fundamental truths rooted in our *a priori* knowledge of perception, expressed as first principles independent of one another. But what is special, what constitutes the content of arithmetic and geometry, is not laid down here, or what results from the union and application of those formal kinds of knowledge. This is the subject of the *Metaphysical Rudiments of Natural Science* expounded by Kant, to which this table forms, to a certain extent, the propaedeutic and introduction, and with which it is therefore directly connected. In this table I have had in view first of all the very remarkable *parallelism* of our knowledge *a priori*, which forms the framework of all experience, especially also the fact that, as I explained in § 4 of volume one, matter (as also causality) is to be regarded as a combination, or if preferred, an amalgamation, of space with time. In harmony with this, we find that what geometry is for the pure perception or intuition of space, and arithmetic for that of time, Kant's phoronomy is for the pure perception or intuition of the two *in union*. For matter is primarily that which is *movable* in space. The mathematical point cannot even be conceived as movable, as Aristotle has explained (*Physics*, VI. 10). This philosopher himself has also furnished the first example of such a science, for in the fifth and sixth books of his *Physics* he determines *a priori* the laws of rest and motion.

Now we can, at our discretion, regard this table either as a collection of the eternal, basic laws of the world, and consequently as the basis of an ontology, or as a chapter from the physiology of the brain, according as we take up the realistic or the idealistic point of view, although the second is in the last instance right. We have, of course, already come to an understanding on this point in the first chapter; yet I still wish to illustrate it especially by an example. Aristotle's book *De Xenophane,* etc., begins with these weighty words of Xenophanes: ᾿Αΐδιον εἶναι φησιν, εἴ τί ἐστιν, εἴπερ μὴ ἐνδέχεται γενέσθαι μηδὲν ἐκ μηδενός (*Aeternum esse, inquit, quicquid est, siquidem fieri non potest, ut ex nihilo quippiam existat*).[11] Here, therefore, Xenophanes judges as to the origin of things according to its possibility, about which he can have no experience, not even an analogous experience; and he does not refer to any experience, but judges apodictically, and consequently *a priori*. How can he do this, if he looks from outside and as a stranger into a world that exists purely objectively, that is to say, independently of his knowledge? How can he, a transient and ephemeral being hurrying past, to whom is permitted only a fleeting glance into such a world, judge apodictically, beforehand, and without experience, about this world, about the possibility of its existence and origin? The solution of this riddle is that the man is concerned merely with his own representa-

---

[11] "He [not Xenophanes, but Melissus, of whom the passage narrates] asserts that if there is anything at all, it must be eternal, as it is impossible for anything to arise out of nothing." [Tr.]

tions, which as such are the work of his brain; therefore their conformity to law is merely the mode or manner in which the function of his brain alone can be carried out, in other words, the form of his representing. He therefore judges only about his own *brain-phenomenon,* and states what goes into its forms, time, space, and causality, and what does not. He is then perfectly at home, and speaks apodictically. Therefore *the following table of praedicabilia a priori* of time, space, and matter is to be taken in a similar sense.

Notes to the Annexed Table.

(1) To No. 4 of Matter.

The essential nature of matter consists in acting; it is action itself, in the abstract, and thus action in general, apart from all difference in the manner of acting; it is through and through causality. Precisely on this account, it itself, according to its existence, is not subject to the law of causality. Therefore it is without origin and everlasting, for otherwise the law of causality would be applied to itself. Now as causality is known to us *a priori,* the concept of matter, as the indestructible basis of all that exists, in that it is only the realization of a form of knowledge given to us *a priori,* can to this extent take its place among the different kinds of knowledge *a priori.* For as soon as we perceive something acting, it exhibits itself *eo ipso* as material; and conversely, something material necessarily exhibits itself as acting or effective; in fact, they are interchangeable concepts. Therefore the word "actual" is used as a synonym of "material," and also the Greek κατ' ἐνέργειαν, in contrast with κατὰ δύναμιν, shows the same origin, for ἐνέργεια signifies action in general; likewise *actu* in contrast with *potentiâ,* and also the English "actually" for *"wirklich."* What is called space-occupation or impenetrability, and is stated to be the essential attribute of body (i.e., of the material), is merely that *way of acting* which belongs to *all* bodies without exception, namely the mechanical. It is this universality alone, by virtue of which it belongs to the concept of a body, follows *a priori* from this concept, and so cannot be thought away without doing away with the concept itself—it is this, I say, that distinguishes it from other ways of acting, such as those of electricity, chemistry, light, or heat. Kant very rightly analysed this space-occupation or mechanical way of acting, into forces of repulsion and attraction, just as a given mechanical force is analysed into two others through the parallelogram of forces. At bottom, however, this is only the well thought-out analysis of the phenomenon into its constituent parts. The two forces in union exhibit the body within

Praedicabilia *A Priori*

Of Time

(1) There is only *one* time, and all different times are parts of it.

(2) Different times are not simultaneous but successive.

(3) Time cannot be thought away, yet everything can be thought away from it.

(4) Time has three divisions, past, present, and future, forming two directions with a neutral point of indifference.

(5) Time is infinitely divisible.

(6) Time is homogeneous and a *continuum,* in other words, no part of it is different from another, or is separated from it by anything that is not time.

Of Space

(1) There is only *one* space, and all different spaces are parts of it.

(2) Different spaces are not successive but simultaneous.

(3) Space cannot be thought away, yet everything can be thought away from it.

(4) Space has three dimensions, height, breadth, and length.

(5) Space is infinitely divisible.

(6) Space is homogeneous and a *continuum,* in other words, no part of it is different from another, or is separated from it by anything that is not space.

Of Matter

(1) There is only *one* matter, and all different materials are different states of it: as such it is called *substance.*

(2) Different matters (materials) are not so through substance but through accidents.

(3) The annihilation of matter cannot be conceived, yet the annihilation of all its forms and qualities can.

(4) Matter exists, i.e., acts in all the dimensions of space and throughout the whole length of time, and thus unites and thereby fills these two. In this consists the true nature of matter. It is therefore through and through causality.

(5) Matter is infinitely divisible.

(6) Matter is homogeneous and a *continuum,* in other words, it does not consist of originally heterogeneous (homoiomeries) or originally separated parts (atoms); it is therefore not composed of parts that would be separated essentially by something that was not matter.

(7) Time has no beginning or end, but all beginning and end are in time.

(8) By reason of time we count.

(9) Rhythm is alone in time.

(10) We know the laws of time *a priori*.

(11) Time is perceivable *a priori*, although only under the form of a line.

(12) Time has no permanence, but passes away as soon as it is there.

(13) Time is without rest.

(14) All that is in time has a duration.

(15) Time has no duration, but all duration is in time, and is the persistence of the permanent in contrast to its restless course.

(7) Space has no limits, but all limits are in space.

(8) By reason of space we measure.

(9) Symmetry is alone in space.

(10) We know the laws of space *a priori*.

(11) Space is immediately perceivable *a priori*.

(12) Space can never pass away, but always lasts.

(13) Space is immovable.

(14) All that is in space has a place.

(15) Space has no movement, but all movement is in space, and is the change of place of the movable in contrast to its unshakable rest.

(7) Matter has no origin or extinction, but all arising and passing away are in matter.

(8) By reason of matter we weigh.

(9) Equilibrium is alone in matter.

(10) We know the laws of the substance of accidents *a priori*.

(11) Matter is merely conceived *a priori*.

(12) The accidents change, the substance endures.

(13) Matter is indifferent to rest and motion, that is to say, originally it is not disposed either to the one or to the other.

(14) Everything material has an effectiveness.

(15) Matter is the persistent in time and the movable in space; by comparing what rests with what is moved we measure duration.

Of Time	Of Space	Of Matter
(16) All motion is possible only in time.	(16) All motion is possible only in space.	(16) All motion is possible only to matter.
(17) In equal spaces velocity is in inverse proportion to the time.	(17) In equal times velocity is in direct proportion to the space.	(17) With equal velocities the *magnitude of the motion* is in direct geometrical proportion to the matter (mass).
(18) Time is not measurable directly through itself, but only indirectly through motion, which is in space and time simultaneously; thus time is measured by the motion of the sun and of the clock.	(18) Space is measurable directly through itself, and indirectly through motion, which is in time and space simultaneously; thus, for example, an hour's walk, and the distance of the fixed stars expressed as so many light-years.	(18) Matter as such (mass) is measurable, i.e., determinable according to its quantity, only indirectly, thus only through the *magnitude of the motion*, which it receives and imparts by being repelled or attracted.
(19) Time is omnipresent; every part of time is everywhere, i.e., in the whole of space simultaneously.	(19) Space is eternal; every part of space exists always.	(19) Matter is absolute, in other words, it cannot come into being or pass away, hence its quantity cannot be either increased or diminished.
(20) In time by itself everything would be in succession.	(20) In space by itself everything would be simultaneous.	(20, 21) Matter unites the unstable flight of time with the rigid immobility of space. It is therefore the permanent substance of the changing accidents. This change is determined for every place at every time by causality, which in this very way combines time and space and constitutes the whole nature of matter.
(21) Time renders possible the change of accidents.	(21) Space renders possible the persistence of substance.	

(CONTINUED)

[50]

(22) For matter is permanent as well as impenetrable.

(23) Individuals are material.

(24) The atom is without reality.

(25) Matter in itself is without form and quality, and likewise inert, in other words, indifferent to rest or motion, hence without definition.

(26) Every change in matter can occur only by virtue of another change that preceded it. Therefore, a first change and hence also a first state or condition of matter are as unthinkable as is a beginning of time or a limit of space. (Principle of reason or ground of becoming.)

(27) Matter, as the movable in space, renders phoronomy possible.

(28) The simple element of phoronomy is the atom.

(22) No part of space contains the same matter with another part.

(23) Space is the *principium individuationis.*

(24) The point is without extension.

(25) Space in itself is empty and without definition.

(26) By the position of every limit in space compared with any other limit, its position compared with every possible limit is determined absolutely and exactly. (Principle of reason or ground of being in space.)

(27) Space renders geometry possible.

(28) The simple element of geometry is the point.

(22) Every part of time contains all parts of matter.

(23) Time is the *principium individuationis.*

(24) The Now is without duration.

(25) Time in itself is empty and without definition.

(26) Every moment is conditioned by the preceding moment, and exists only in so far as the preceding moment has ceased to be. (Principle of reason or ground of being in time.— See my essay *On the Principle of Sufficient Reason.*)

(27) Time renders arithmetic possible.

(28) The simple element of arithmetic is the unit.

its limits, in other words, in definite volume, whereas the one alone would diffuse the body into infinity, and the other alone would contract it into a point. In spite of this reciprocal balancing or neutralization, the body still acts on, and repels with the first force, other bodies that compete with it for space, and acts on, and attracts with the other force, all bodies generally in gravitation. Thus the two forces are not extinguished in their product, i.e., in the body, as are, for instance, two impulsive forces acting equally in opposite directions, or $+E$ and $-E$, or oxygen and hydrogen in water. That impenetrability and gravity really coincide exactly is established by their empirical inseparability, since the one never appears without the other, although we can separate them in thought.

But I must not omit to mention that Kant's doctrine here referred to, and constituting the fundamental idea of the second main portion of his *Metaphysical Rudiments of Natural Science,* namely of the dynamics, was expounded distinctly and in detail *before* Kant by Priestley in his excellent *Disquisitions on Matter and Spirit,* Sect. 1 and 2. This book appeared in 1777 (second edition 1782), whereas the *Metaphysical Rudiments* appeared in 1786. Unconscious reminiscences can perhaps be assumed in the case of subsidiary ideas, flashes of wit, comparisons, and so on, but not in the case of main and fundamental ideas. Therefore, are we to believe that Kant silently appropriated that very important idea of another man, and this from a book that was still new at the time? Or that this book was unknown to him, and the same idea arose in two minds within a short time? The explanation, given by Kant in the *Metaphysical Rudiments of Natural Science* (first edition p. 88, Rosenkranz edition p. 384), of the real difference between fluid and solid, is also to be found essentially in Caspar Friedrich Wolff's *Theorie von der Generation,* Berlin 1764, p. 132. But what are we to say when we find Kant's most important and brilliant doctrine, that of the ideality of space and of the merely phenomenal existence of the corporeal world, expressed already thirty years previously by Maupertuis? This is dealt with fully in Frauenstädt's letters on my philosophy, letter 14. Maupertuis expresses this paradoxical doctrine so decidedly, and yet without the addition of a proof, that it must be supposed that he also obtained it from somewhere else. It would be very desirable for the matter to be examined further, and as this calls for tedious and lengthy investigations, some German academy might well make the question the subject of a prize-essay. Just as Kant here stands to Priestley, and perhaps to Caspar Wolff also, and to Maupertuis or his predecessor, so does Laplace stand to Kant. The admirable and certainly correct theory of the origin of the planetary system, expounded in his *Exposition du système du monde,* Bk. V, c. 2, was in its main and fundamental ideas put forward by Kant some fifty years earlier, in 1755, in his *Natural History and Theory of the Heavens,* and more completely in 1763 in his *Only Possible Proof of the Existence of God,* chap. 7. Moreover, as he gives us to understand in the latter work that Lambert in his *Kosmologische Briefe,* 1761, silently borrowed that theory from him, but that at the same time these letters also appeared in French (*Lettres cosmologiques sur la constitution de l'univers*), we must assume that Laplace knew this theory of Kant's. He certainly expounds the matter more thoroughly, strikingly, fully, and yet more simply than Kant does, as is in keeping with his deeper astronomical knowledge. In the main, however, it is found clearly expressed in Kant, and, from the great importance of the matter, would alone be sufficient to immortalize his name. It must greatly distress us when we find minds of the first order suspected of dishonesty, a thing that is a disgrace even to those of the lowest rank. For we feel that theft is even less excusable in a rich man than in a poor one. But we dare not be silent about this, for here we are posterity and must be just, as we hope that one day posterity will be just to us. Therefore, as a third example, I will add to these cases that the fundamental ideas of Goethe's *Metamorphosis of Plants* were already expressed by Caspar Friedrich Wolff in 1764 in his *Theorie von der Generation,* pp. 148, 229, 243, etc. Indeed, is it otherwise with the *system of gravitation,* whose discovery on the continent of Europe is always ascribed to Newton? In England, on the other hand, the learned at any rate know quite well that the discovery belongs to Robert Hooke, who as early as the year 1666 in a *Communication to the Royal Society* expounded it quite clearly, yet only as a hypothesis and without proof. The principal passage of this communication is printed in Dugald Stewart's *Philosophy of the Human Mind,* Vol. II, p. 434, and is probably taken from R. Hooke's *Posthumous Works.* In the *Biographie Universelle,* article *Neuton* [Newton], we also find the details of the case, and how Newton got into difficulties over it. Hooke's priority is treated as an established fact in a short history of astronomy, *Quarterly Review,* August, 1828. More details on this subject are to be found in my *Parerga,* Vol. II, § 86. The story of the fall of the apple is a fairy-tale, as groundless as it is popular, and is without any authority.

(2) To No. 18 of Matter.

The magnitude of the motion (*quantitas motus* in Descartes) is the product of the mass into the velocity.

This law is the basis not only of the theory of impact in *mechanics,* but also of the theory of equilibrium in *statics.* From the force of impact manifested by two bodies with equal velocity, the relation of their masses to each other can be determined. Thus, of two hammers striking with equal velocity, the one of greater mass will drive the nail farther into the wall or the post deeper into the ground. For example, a hammer weighing six pounds with a velocity of six units will produce the same effect as a hammer of three pounds with a velocity of twelve units; for in both cases the *magnitude of the motion* is equal to thirty-six. Of two spheres rolling with the same velocity, the one of greater mass will push a third sphere at rest to a greater distance than can the one of smaller mass, since the mass of the first multiplied by the same velocity produces a greater *quantity of motion.* The gun has a greater range than the musket, since the same velocity communicated to a much greater mass produces a much greater *quantity of motion,* and this resists the retarding effect of gravity for a longer time. For the same reason, the same arm will throw a lead bullet farther than a stone bullet of the same size, or a large stone farther than a quite small one. Hence a discharge of canister-shot has not the same range as a cannon-ball.

The same law is the basis of the theory of the lever and the balance. For here also the smaller mass on the longer arm of the lever or beam of the balance has a greater velocity *in falling,* and, multiplied by this, can be equal to or even exceed in *magnitude of motion* the greater mass to be found at the shorter arm. In the state of *rest,* brought about by *equilibrium,* this velocity exists merely in intention or virtually, *potentiâ* not *actu;* yet its effect is as good as *actu,* which is very remarkable.

Now that these truths have been called to mind, the following explanation will be more easily understood.

The *quantity of a given matter* can be estimated in general only according to its *force,* and this force can be known only in its *manifestation.* Where matter is considered only as regards its quantity, not its quality, this manifestation can be only a *mechanical* one, in other words, can only consist in the *motion* imparted by it to other matter. For only in *motion* does the force of matter become, so to speak, alive; hence the expression *vis viva* for the force-manifestation of matter in motion. Accordingly, for the quantity of given matter the only measure is the *magnitude of its motion.* But if this is given, the quantity of matter still appears combined and amalgamated with its other factor, *velocity.* If, therefore, we want to know the quantity of matter (the mass), this other factor must be eliminated.

Now the *velocity* is known directly, for it is $\frac{S}{T}$; but the other factor, that remains after this is eliminated, can always be known only *relatively,* in comparison with other masses, and these themselves in turn can be known only by means of the *magnitude of their motion,* and so in their combination with velocity. We must therefore compare one *quantity of motion* with another, and then subtract the velocity from both, in order to see how much each of them owes to its mass. This is done by weighing the masses against each other; and here the *magnitude of motion* is compared which, in each of the two masses, produces the earth's attractive force that acts on both only in proportion to their *quantity*. Hence there are two kinds of weighing; either we impart *equal* velocity to the two masses to be compared, in order to see which of the two *communicates* motion to the other, and thus itself *has* a greater quantity of motion; and, as the velocity is the same on both sides, this quantity is to be ascribed to the other factor of the *magnitude of motion,* that is to the mass (hand-balance). Or we weigh by investigating how much *more velocity* the one mass must receive than the other has, in order to be equal to the latter in *magnitude of motion,* and to allow no more motion to be *communicated* to itself from the other. For then in proportion as its *velocity* must exceed that of the other, its mass, i.e., the quantity of its matter, is less than that of the other (steelyard). This estimation of masses by *weighing* rests on the favourable circumstance that the moving force, in itself, acts on both quite equally, and that each of the two is in a position to *communicate* directly to the other its surplus *magnitude of motion,* whereby it becomes visible.

What is essential in these theories was set forth long ago by Newton and Kant, but by the connexion and clearness of this discussion I believe I have made them more intelligible, and this brings within the reach of everyone the insight that I deemed to be necessary for the justification of proposition No. 18.

Second Half

The Doctrine of the Abstract Representation, or of Thinking

CHAPTER V[1]

On the Intellect Devoid of Reason

It must be possible to arrive at a complete knowledge of the consciousness of animals, in so far as we are able to construct such consciousness by merely taking away certain properties of our own. On the other hand, instinct is closely associated with animal consciousness, and in all animals this instinct is more developed than in man; in some animals it extends to mechanical instinct.

Animals have understanding without the faculty of reason, and consequently they have knowledge of *perception,* but no abstract knowledge. They apprehend correctly, and also grasp the immediate causal connexion, the higher animals even through several links of its chain; but properly speaking they do not *think.* For they lack *concepts,* in other words abstract representations. The first consequence of this is the want of a real memory, which applies even to the most intelligent animals; and it is just this that establishes the main difference between their consciousness and man's. Perfect *reflectiveness* or *circumspection* (*Besonnenheit*) rests on distinct consciousness of the past and of the eventual future *as such* and in connexion with the present. Therefore the real memory required for this is a systematic, orderly, coherent, and thinking recollection. This, however, is possible only by means of *general concepts,* whose aid is required even by what is entirely individual, so that it is recalled in its order and concatenation. For the boundless multitude of things and events of the same and similar kinds in the course of our life does not admit directly of a perceptive and individual recollection of each particular thing; for that neither the powers of the most comprehensive faculty of memory nor our time would be sufficient. Therefore all this can be preserved only by subsuming it under universal concepts and by the reference arising out of this to relatively few principles. By means of these principles we then have constantly

---

[1] This chapter, together with the following, is connected with §§ 8 and 9 of volume 1.

at our disposal a systematic, orderly, and adequate survey of our past. We can conjure up in our minds through perception only particular scenes of the past, but of the time that has since elapsed and of its content we are conscious only *in abstracto* by means of concepts of things and of numbers that now represent days and years, together with the content thereof. On the other hand, the faculty of recollection of animals, like their whole intellect, is confined to what they *perceive*. Primarily this faculty consists merely in a recurring impression that presents itself as having existed already, since the present perception revives the trace of an earlier one. Therefore their recollection is always brought about by means of something now actually present. But on this very account this stimulates anew the sensation and the mood that the earlier phenomenon had produced. Accordingly, the dog recognizes acquaintances, distinguishes friends from enemies, easily finds again the path he has once travelled, houses he has formerly visited, and is at once put into the appropriate mood by the sight of a plate or of a stick. All kinds of training depend on the use of this perceptive faculty of recollection and on force of habit, which in the case of animals is exceedingly strong. Therefore this training is just as different from human education as perceiving is from thinking. In particular cases, where memory proper breaks down, even we are confined to that merely perceptive recollection, and so can from our own experience measure the difference between the two. For example, at the sight of a person who seems known to us, without our remembering when and where we have seen him; likewise, when we visit a place where we were in early childhood, while our faculty of reason was still undeveloped, which we have therefore entirely forgotten; but now we feel the impression of what is present as of something that has already existed. All the recollections of animals are of this kind. We have only to add that, in the case of the most intelligent, this merely perceptive memory rises to a certain degree of *fantasy* which again assists it, and in virtue of which, for example, the image of his absent master floats before the dog's mind and excites a longing for him; thus, in the master's prolonged absence, the dog looks for him everywhere. His dreams also depend on this fantasy. Accordingly, the consciousness of animals is a mere succession of present events, none of which, however, exists as future before its appearance, or as past after its disappearance, this being the distinctive characteristic of human consciousness. Therefore the animals have infinitely less to *suffer* than have we, since they know no other sufferings than those directly brought about by the *present*. But the present is without extension; the future and the past, on the other hand, which contain most of the causes of our sufferings, are widely extended. To their actual content the merely possible is added, whereby an unlimited field is opened up to desire and fear. The animals, on the other hand, are undisturbed by these; they peacefully and serenely enjoy every present moment, even if it is only bearable. In this they may be approached by human beings of very limited capacity. Further, the sufferings that belong *solely* to the present can be merely physical. Animals do not really feel even death; they can get to know it only when it appears, and then they already are no more. Thus the life of the animal is a continual present. It lives on without reflection and is deeply engrossed in the present; the great majority of men, even, live with very little reflection. Another consequence of the nature of the intellect of animals, which we have discussed, is the exact agreement of their consciousness with their environment. Nothing stands between the animal and the external world; but between us and that world there are always our thoughts and ideas about it, and these often make us inaccessible to it, and it to us.. Only in the case of children and of very uneducated persons does this wall sometimes become so thin that to know what is going on within them we need only see what is going on around them. Therefore animals are not capable either of purpose or of dissimulation; they have nothing in reserve. In this respect, the dog is related to the man as a glass tumbler is to a metal one, and this greatly helps to endear the dog so much to us. It affords us great pleasure to see simply and openly displayed in him all those inclinations and emotions that in ourselves we so often conceal. In general, animals play always with their cards on the table, so to speak; we therefore contemplate with so much pleasure their behaviour towards one another, not only when they belong to the same species, but also when they are of different species. It is characterized by a certain stamp of innocence, in contrast to the conduct of human beings, which is withdrawn from the innocence of nature by the first appearance of the faculty of reason, and therewith of prudence or deliberation. Instead of this, human conduct has throughout the stamp of intention or deliberate purpose, the absence of which, and the consequent determination by the impulse of the moment, constitute the fundamental characteristic of all animal conduct. Thus no animal is capable of a purpose or intention proper; to conceive and follow out a purpose is the prerogative of man; and this has extremely important consequences. Of course an instinct like that of birds of passage or of bees, and moreover a permanent and persistent desire, a longing like that of the dog for his absent master, may produce the appearance of purpose, but it is not to be confused therewith. All this has its ultimate ground in the relation between human and animal intellect, which can be expressed as follows. The animals have only an *immediate* knowledge; we have a *mediate* knowledge in addition; and the advantage which the indirect has over the direct in many things, e.g., in trigonometry and analysis, in machine-work instead of hand-labour, and so on, occurs here also. In accordance with this, we can also say that animals have merely a *simple or single* intellect, we a *double,* a thinking as well as a perceiving intellect; and the operations of the two often take place independently of each other; we perceive one thing and think another. Again, they are often connected with each other. This characterizing of the matter enables us specially to understand the essential openness and naivety of animals above mentioned in contrast with human concealment and reserve.

However, the law *natura non facit saltus*[2] is not entirely abolished even with regard to the intellect of animals, although the step from the animal to the human intellect is indeed the greatest nature has made in the production of her creatures. Certainly in the most select individuals of the highest animal species there sometimes appears, always to our astonishment, a feeble trace of reflection, of the faculty of reason, of the understanding of words, of thought, purpose, or deliberation. The most striking features of this kind are furnished by the elephant, whose highly developed intellect is enhanced and sustained by the practice and experience of a life lasting sometimes two hundred years. He has often given unmistakable signs, recorded in well-known anecdotes, of premeditation, which always astonishes us above all else in animals. Of particular interest is the story of the tailor on whom an elephant wreaked his vengeance for having been pricked by a needle. I wish to rescue from oblivion a parallel case to this, because it has the advantage of being substantiated by judicial inquiry. On 27 August 1830, a coroner's inquest was held at Morpeth in England on Baptist Bernhard, a keeper who had been killed by his elephant. From the evidence, it appeared that two years previously he had grossly offended the elephant; and now, without any cause but at a favourable opportunity, the elephant had suddenly seized and crushed him. (See the *Spectator* and other English newspapers of those days.) For special information on the intellect of animals, I recommend the excellent book of Leroy, *Sur l'intelligence des animaux,* new ed., 1802.

---

[2] "Nature makes no leaps." [Tr.]

CHAPTER VI

On the Doctrine of Abstract Knowledge, or Knowledge of Reason

The outer impression on the senses, together with the mood that it alone and by itself evokes in us, vanishes with the presence of things. Therefore these two cannot themselves constitute *experience* proper, whose teaching is to guide our conduct for the future. The image of that impression preserved by the imagination is already weaker than the impression itself; day by day it grows weaker still, and in time becomes completely extinct. There is only one thing, *the concept,* which is not subject either to that instantaneous vanishing of the impression, or to the gradual disappearance of its image, and consequently is free from the power of time. Therefore in the concept the teaching of experience must be stored up, and it alone is suitable as a safe guide for our steps in life. Therefore Seneca rightly says: *Si vis tibi omnia subjicere, te subjice rationi* (*Ep.* 37).[1] And I add that, to be superior (*überlegen*) to others in real life, the indispensable condition is to be thoughtful and deliberate (*überlegt*), in other words, to set to work in accordance with concepts. So important an instrument of intelligence as the *concept* obviously cannot be identical with the *word,* that mere sound, which as a sense-impression passes away with the present moment, or as a phantasm of hearing will die away with time. But the concept is a representation, whose distinct consciousness and preservation are tied to the word. Therefore the Greeks called word, concept, relation, thought, idea, and reason (*Vernunft*) by the name of the first, ὁ λόγος. Yet the *concept* is entirely different not only from the *word* to which it is tied, but also from the perceptions from which it originates. It is of a nature entirely different from these sense-impressions; yet it is able to take up into itself all the results of perception, in order to give them back again unchanged and undiminished even after the longest period of time; only in this way does *experience*

---

[1] If you want to subject everything to yourself, then subject yourself to reason." [Tr.]

arise. But the concept does not preserve what is perceived or what is felt; rather it preserves what is essential thereof in an entirely altered form, yet as an adequate representative of those results. Thus, flowers cannot be preserved, but their ethereal oil, their essence, with the same smell and the same virtues, can. The conduct that has had correct concepts for its guidance will, in the result, coincide with the reality intended. We can judge the inestimable value of *concepts,* and consequently of the faculty of *reason,* if we glance at the endless multitude and variety of things and conditions coexisting and succeeding one another, and then reflect that language and writing (the signs of concepts) are nevertheless able to afford us accurate information about everything and every relation, whenever and wherever it may have been, in that comparatively *few* concepts concern and represent an infinite number of things and conditions. In our reflection, *abstraction* is a throwing off of useless luggage for the purpose of handling more easily the knowledge to be compared and manoeuvred in all directions. Thus, much that is inessential, and therefore merely confusing, in real things is omitted, and we operate with few but essential determinations conceived in the abstract. But just because universal concepts result only from thinking away and leaving out actual and existing determinations, and are therefore the emptier the more universal they are, the use of this procedure is limited to the *elaboration* of knowledge already acquired. To this elaboration belongs also the drawing of conclusions from premises contained in our knowledge. Fresh insight, on the contrary, can be drawn only from knowledge of perception with the aid of the faculty of judgement, for such knowledge alone is complete and abundant. Further, since the content and extent of concepts are in inverse relation to each other, and thus the more that is thought *under a* concept, the less is thought *in* it, concepts form a sequence, a hierarchy, from the most special to the most universal, at the lower end of which scholastic realism, and at the upper end nominalism, are almost right. For the most special concept is almost the individual and thus almost real; and the most universal concept, e.g., Being (the infinitive of the copula) is scarcely anything but a word. Therefore philosophical systems, keeping within such very universal concepts without descending to the real, are scarcely anything but a mere idle display of words. For, as all abstraction consists in mere thinking away, the farther we continue it, the less we have left. Therefore when I read those modern philosophemes that constantly move in nothing but very wide abstractions, I am soon unable to think of hardly anything more in connexion with them, in spite of all my attention, because I receive no material for thinking, but am supposed to operate with nothing but empty husks. This gives me a feeling similar to that which occurs when I attempt to throw very light bodies; the strength and exertion are there, but the object to take them up, so as to supply the other moment of motion, is lacking. Whoever wishes to experience this should read the works of Schellingians, and better still of Hegelians. *Simple* concepts would necessarily be in reality such as are irresolvable; accordingly, they could never be the subject of an analytical judgement. This I regard as impossible, for, if we think of a concept, we must be able to state its content also. What are usually quoted as examples of simple concepts are not concepts at all, but in part mere sensations of the senses, say those of a definite colour, and in part the forms of perception known to us *a priori,* and so, properly speaking, the ultimate elements of *knowledge of perception.* This itself, however, is for the system of all our ideas what granite is for geology, the final firm ground that supports everything, beyond which we cannot go. The *distinctness* of a concept requires not only that we should be able to split it up into its attributes, but also that we should be able to analyse these once more, even in the event of their being abstractions, and so on, until we reach down to knowledge of *perception,* and consequently refer to concrete things. Through the clear perception of these we verify the final abstractions, and thus assure reality to them, as also to all higher abstractions resting on them. Therefore the ordinary explanation that the concept is distinct as soon as we can state its attributes is not sufficient. For the splitting up of these attributes may possibly lead again and again only to concepts without there being that ultimate basis of perceptions which would impart reality to all those concepts. Take, for example, the concept "spirit," and analyse it into its attributes: "a thinking, willing, immaterial, simple, indestructible being, occupying no space." Nothing distinct is thought in connexion with it, because the elements of these concepts cannot be verified by perceptions, for a thinking being without a brain is like a digesting being without a stomach. Only perceptions, not concepts, are really *clear;* concepts can at best be *distinct.* Therefore, absurd as it was, "clear and confused" were put together and used as synonyms, when knowledge of perception was declared to be only confused abstract knowledge, because this latter was the only distinct knowledge. This was first done by Duns Scotus, but at bottom Leibniz also has this view, on which depends his *Identitas indiscernibilium.*[2] See Kant's refutation of it, p. 275 of the first edition of the *Critique of Pure Reason.*

[2] The principle of Leibniz according to which two things that are not discernible are identical. [Tr.]

The close connexion of the concept with the word, and thus of language with reason (*Vernunft*), which was touched on above, rests ultimately on the following. Our whole consciousness with its inward and outward apprehension has *time* as its form throughout. On the other hand, concepts have arisen through abstraction, and are wholly universal representations which differ from all particular things. In this property they have, to a certain extent, an objective existence that yet does not belong to any time-series. Therefore, to enter the immediate present of an individual consciousness, and consequently to be capable of insertion into a time-series, they must be to a certain extent brought down again to the nature of particular things, individualized, and thus linked to a representation of the senses; this is the *word*. Accordingly, this is the sensible sign of the concept, and as such is the necessary means of *fixing* it, in other words, of presenting it vividly to the consciousness that is tied to the form of time, and thus of establishing a connexion between our faculty of reason, whose objects are merely general *universalia* knowing neither place nor time, and consciousness which is tied to time, sensuous, and to this extent merely animal. Only by this means is the arbitrary reproduction, and thus the recollection and preservation of concepts, possible and open to us; and only by this means are the operations possible which are to be undertaken with concepts, namely judging, inferring, comparing, limiting, and so on. Of course, it sometimes happens that concepts occupy consciousness even without their signs, since occasionally we run through a chain of reasoning so rapidly that we could not have thought of the words in so short a time. But such cases are exceptions that assume great exercise of the faculty of reason, which it could have attained only by means of language. We see how much the use of the faculty of reason is tied to language in the case of deaf-mutes. If they have learnt no kind of language, they show hardly any more intelligence than do orang-utans and elephants; for they have the faculty of reason almost entirely *potentiâ*, not *actu*.

Word and speech, therefore, are the indispensable means to clear thinking. But just as every means, every machine, at the same time burdens and obstructs, so does language, since it forces the infinitely shaded, mobile, and modifiable idea into certain rigid, permanent forms, and by fixing the idea it at the same time fetters it. This hindrance is partly eliminated by our learning several languages; for then the thought is cast from one form into another; and in each form it alters its shape somewhat, and thus is stripped more and more of each form and covering. In this way its own proper nature comes more distinctly into consciousness, and it again obtains its original capacity for modification. The ancient languages, however, perform this service very much better than the modern, because, on account of their great difference from these, the same idea must be expressed in them in quite a different way, and so assume a very different form. In addition to this is the fact that the more perfect grammar of the ancient languages makes a more artistic and perfect construction of the ideas and of their association and relation possible. Therefore a Greek or Roman could, if need be, rest content with his own language; but the man who does not understand anything more than a single modern *patois,* will soon betray this poverty in writing and speaking, since his thinking, tied firmly to such wretched, stereotyped forms, is bound to appear stiff and monotonous. Genius, of course, makes up for this as for everything; for example, in Shakespeare.

Burke, in his *Inquiry into the Sublime and Beautiful,* p. 5, sect. 4 and 5, has given a perfectly correct and very detailed explanation of what I expounded in § 9 of the first volume, that the words of a speech are perfectly understood without giving rise to representations of perception, to pictures in our head. But from this he draws the entirely false conclusion that we hear, apprehend, and use words without associating any representation with them, whereas he should have concluded that not all representations are images of perception, but that precisely those that must be expressed by words are mere *concepts (abstract notions),* and these are by their nature not perceivable. Just because words communicate mere universal concepts which are absolutely different from the representations of perception, all the hearers will of course receive the same *concepts* during the narration of an event, for example. But if subsequently they wish to make the event clear to themselves, each will sketch in his imagination a different *picture* or *image* of it, and this differs considerably from the correct picture that only the eyewitness has. Here is to be found the primary reason (there are others as well) why every fact is necessarily distorted through further narration. The second narrator communicates concepts which he has abstracted from the picture of *his* imagination, and from these a third narrator again sketches for himself a picture or image differing still more widely, which he now converts in turn into concepts, and so the process goes on. He who is matter-of-fact enough to stick to the concepts imparted to him, and to pass these on to the next person, will be the most trustworthy reporter.

The best and most logical explanation concerning the essence and nature of concepts which I have been able to find is in Thomas Reid's *Essays on the Powers of Human Mind,* Vol. II, Essay 5, ch. 6. This has since been rejected by Dugald Stewart in his *Philosophy of the Human Mind.* In order not to waste paper on this man, I will only say briefly that he was one of the many who obtained an unmerited reputation through favour and friends. Therefore I can only recommend that not an hour be wasted over the scribblings of that shallow mind.

The princely scholastic, Pico de Mirandola, already saw that *reason* is the faculty of abstract representations, and the *understanding* the faculty of representations of perception. For in his book *De Imaginatione,* ch. 11, he carefully distinguishes understanding and reason, and explains the latter as the discursive faculty peculiar to man, and the former as the intuitive faculty akin to the angels', and indeed God's, method of knowledge. Spinoza also quite correctly characterizes reason as the faculty for forming universal concepts, *Ethics,* II, prop. 40, schol. 2. It would not be necessary to mention such things, were it not by reason of the tricks and farces that have been played in the last fifty years with the concept of *reason* by all the philosophasters of Germany. For with shameless audacity they wanted to smuggle in under this name a wholly false and fabricated faculty of immediate, metaphysical, so-called supersensuous knowledge. Actual reason, on the other hand, they called *understanding,* and understanding proper, as something very strange to them, they entirely overlooked; they ascribed its intuitive functions to sensibility.

As in the case of all things in this world, new drawbacks or disadvantages cleave at once to every expedient, every privilege, and every advantage; and thus the faculty of reason also, which gives man such great advantages over the animals, has its special disadvantages, and opens up to him paths of error into which the animal can never stray. Through the faculty of reason an entirely new species of motives, to which the animal is inaccessible, obtains power over man's will. These are the *abstract* motives, the mere thoughts or ideas, which are by no means always drawn from his own experience, but often come to him only through the talk and example of others, through tradition and the written word. Having become accessible to the *thought* or *idea,* he is at once exposed to *error.* But sooner or later every error must do harm, and this harm is all the greater, the greater the error. He who cherishes the individual error must one day atone for it, and often pay dearly for it. The same thing will hold good on a large scale as regards the common errors of whole nations. Therefore it cannot be repeated too often that, wherever we come across any error, it is to be pursued and eradicated as an enemy of mankind, and there cannot be any privileged or even sanctioned errors. The thinker should attack them, even though mankind should cry aloud, like a sick person whose ulcer is touched by the physician. The animal can never stray far from the path of nature, for its motives lie only in the world of *perception,* where only the possible, only the actual indeed, finds room. On the other hand, all that is merely imaginable or conceivable, and consequently also what is false, impossible, absurd, and senseless, enters into abstract concepts, into thoughts, ideas, and words. Now since the faculty of reason is given to all, but power of judgement to few, the consequence is that man is exposed to delusion, since he is abandoned to every conceivable chimera into which he is talked by anyone, and which, acting as motive to his willing, can induce him to commit perversities and follies of all kinds, and to indulge in the most unheard-of extravagances, even in actions most contrary to his animal nature. Real culture, where knowledge and judgement go hand in hand, can be brought to bear only on a few, and fewer still are capable of assimilating it. For the great majority of people a kind of training everywhere takes the place of culture. It is achieved by example, custom, and the very early and firm impression of certain concepts, before any experience, understanding, and power of judgement existed to disturb the work. Thus ideas are implanted which afterwards cling so firmly, and are not to be shaken by any instruction, just as if they were *innate;* and they have often been regarded as such, even by philosophers. In this way we can with equal effort impress people with what is right and rational, or with what is most absurd. For example, we can accustom them to approach this or that idol imbued with sacred awe, and, at the mention of its name, to prostrate themselves in the dust not only with their body, but also with their whole spirit; we can accustom them to stake their property and their lives willingly on words, names, and the defence of the strangest whims, to attach arbitrarily the greatest honour or the deepest disgrace to this or that, and accordingly to esteem highly or disdain everyone with inner conviction; we can accustom them to renounce all animal food, as in Hindustan, or to devour the still warm and quivering pieces cut from the living animal, as in Abyssinia; to eat human beings as in New Zealand, or to sacrifice their children to Moloch, to castrate themselves, to fling themselves voluntarily on to the funeral pile of the deceased—in a word, to do *anything we wish.* Hence the Crusades, the excesses of fanatical sects; hence Chiliasts and Flagellants, persecutions of heretics, *autos da fe,* and whatever else is offered by the long register of human perversities and absurdities. Lest it may be thought that only the dark ages afford such examples, I add a couple of more recent ones. In the year 1818 seven thousand Chiliasts moved from Würtemberg into the neighbourhood of Ararat, because the new kingdom of God, specially announced by Jung-Stilling, was to appear there.[3] Gall relates that in his time a mother killed and roasted her child, in order to cure her husband's rheumatism with its fat.[4] The tragic side of error and of prejudice lies in the practical, the comic is reserved for the theoretical. For example, if we were firmly to persuade only three persons that the sun is not the cause of daylight, we might hope to see it soon accepted as the general conviction. In Germany it was possible to proclaim Hegel, a repulsive and dull charlatan and an unparalleled scribbler of nonsense, the greatest philosopher of all time. For twenty years many thousands have stubbornly' and firmly believed this, and even outside Germany the Danish Academy denounced me in support of his fame, and wished to accept him as a *summus philosophus*. (On this see the preface to my *Grundprobleme der Ethik*.) These, then, are the disadvantages involved in the existence of the faculty of reason, on account of the rarity of the power of judgement. To them is also added the possibility of madness. Animals do not go mad, although carnivora are liable to fury, and graminivora to a kind of frenzy.

---

[3] Illgen's *Zeitschrift für historische Theologie*, 1839, first part, p. 182.
[4] Gall and Spurzheim, *Des dispositions innées*, 1811, p. 253

On the Relation of Knowledge of Perception to Abstract Knowledge

It has been shown that concepts borrow their material from knowledge of perception, and that therefore the whole structure of our world of thought rests on the world of perceptions. It must therefore be possible for us to go back from every concept, even if through intermediate stages, to the perceptions from which it has itself been directly drawn, or from which have been drawn the concepts of which it is in turn an abstraction. In other words, it must be possible for us to verify the concept with perceptions that stand to abstractions in the relation of examples. Therefore these perceptions furnish us with the real content of all our thinking, and wherever they are missing we have had in our heads not concepts, but mere words. In this respect our intellect is like a bank of issue which, if it is to be sound, must have ready money in the safe, in order to be able, on demand, to meet all the notes it has issued; the perceptions are the ready money, the concepts are the notes. In this sense the perceptions might very appropriately be called *primary* representations, the concepts, on the other hand, being *secondary*. Not quite so appropriately the scholastics, at the instance of Aristotle (*Metaphysics,* vi, 11; xi, 1), called real things *substantiae primae* and concepts *substantiae secundae*. Books communicate only secondary representations. Mere concepts of a thing without perception give a merely general knowledge of it. We have a thorough understanding of things and their relations only in so far as we are capable of representing them to ourselves in purely distinct perceptions without the aid of words. To explain words by words, to compare concepts with concepts, in which most philosophizing consists, is at bottom playing with concept-spheres and shifting them about, in order to see which goes into the other and which does not. At best, we shall in this way arrive at conclusions; but even conclusions

---

[1] This chapter is connected with § 12 of volume 1.

by no means give new knowledge. On the contrary they only show us all that lay in the knowledge already existing, and what part of this might perhaps be applicable to each particular case. On the other hand, to perceive, to allow the things themselves to speak to us, to apprehend and grasp new relations between them, and then to precipitate and deposit all this into concepts, in order to possess it with certainty; this is what gives us new knowledge. But whereas almost everyone is capable of comparing concepts with concepts, to compare concepts with perceptions is a gift of the select few. According to its degree of perfection, this gift is the condition of wit, power of judgement, sagacity, and genius. With the former faculty, on the other hand, the result is never much more than possibly rational reflections. The innermost kernel of every genuine and actual piece of knowledge is a perception; every new truth is also the fruit of such a perception. All original thinking is done in pictures or images; the imagination is therefore so necessary an instrument of thinking, and minds without imagination will never achieve anything great, unless it be in mathematics. On the other hand, merely abstract ideas, which have no kernel of perception, are like cloud formations without reality. Even writing and speaking, whether didactic or poetical, have as their ultimate aim the guidance of the reader to that knowledge of perception from which the author started; if they do not have this aim, they are bad. For this reason, the contemplation and observation of everything *actual,* as soon as it presents something new to the observer, is more instructive than all reading and hearing about it. For indeed, if we go to the bottom of the matter, all truth and wisdom, in fact the ultimate secret of things, is contained in everything actual, yet certainly only *in concreto* and like gold hidden in the ore. The question is how to extract it. From a book, on the other hand, we obtain the truth only second-hand at best, and often not at all.

With most books, quite apart from really bad ones, if they are not entirely of empirical content, it is true that the author has *thought,* but not *perceived;* he has written from reflection, not from intuition. It is just this that makes them mediocre and wearisome. For what the author has thought, the reader also could have thought, at any rate with some effort; for it is just rational ideas, more detailed explanations of what is contained *implicite* in the theme. But no really new knowledge comes into the world in this way; that is produced only at the moment of perception, of directly apprehending a new side of things. Therefore where *a perception or intuition* was the basis of an author's thinking, it is as if he wrote from a land where his reader has never been, for everything is fresh and new, since it is drawn directly from the primary source of all knowledge. I will illustrate the difference here touched on by a quite easy and simple example. Every commonplace writer will readily describe profound contemplation or petrifying astonishment by saying: "He stood like a statue"; but Cervantes says: "Like a draped statue; for the wind moved his garments" (*Don Quixote,* Bk. vi, ch. 19). In such a way have all great minds always *thought in the presence of perception,* and in their thinking kept their gaze steadily on it. We recognize this, among other things, in the fact that even the most heterogeneous of them so often agree and concur in detail, just because they all speak of the same thing which they all had before their eyes, namely the world, the actuality of perception. In fact, to a certain extent they all say the same thing, and others never believe them. It is further recognized in the appropriateness and originality of their expression, which is always exactly suited to the case, because perception has prompted that expression; it is recognized in the naivety of the statements, the freshness of the images, and the striking effect of the similes. All this without exception distinguishes the works of great minds; whereas it is always lacking in the works of others. For this reason, only trite and humdrum modes of expression and hackneyed similes are at the latter's disposal; and they never dare allow themselves to be naïve, on pain of displaying their vulgarity in all its dreary emptiness; instead of this they are affected in their style. Therefore Buffon said: *Le style est l'homme même.*[2] When ordinary minds write poetry they have a few traditional, indeed conventional, opinions, passions, noble sentiments, and the like, obtained in the abstract; and these they attribute to the heroes of their poems. In this way such heroes become a mere personification of those opinions; and hence to a certain extent they are themselves abstractions, and thus dull and wearisome. If they philosophize, they take possession of a few wide abstract concepts which they cast about in all directions, as though it were a matter of algebraical equations, and hope that something will result therefrom. At most we see that they have all read the same thing. Such casting about with abstract concepts, after the manner of algebraical equations, nowadays called dialectic, does not, like real algebra, give us sure and certain results; for here the concept, represented by the word, is not a quantity positively and precisely determined, like that denoted by the letters of algebra, but something that is wavering, ambiguous, and capable of extension and contraction. Strictly speaking, all thinking, in other words all combining of abstract concepts, has at best for its material *recollections* of what was previously

---

[2] "The style is the man himself." [Tr.]

perceived, and this indirectly, that is in so far as it constitutes the basis of all concepts. Actual, i.e., immediate knowledge, on the other hand, is perception alone, new, fresh perception itself. But the concepts that are formed by the faculty of reason and preserved by memory can never all be present in consciousness at the same time; only a very small number of them are present at one moment. On the other hand, the energy with which we apprehend what is present in perception—and in this the essential of all things in general is really always contained and represented *virtualiter*—fills the consciousness in one moment with all its force. On this rests the infinite superiority of genius to learning; they are related to each other as is the text of an ancient classical author to its commentary. Actually all truth and all wisdom ultimately lie in *perception;* but unfortunately perception cannot be either retained or communicated. At the most, the *objective* conditions for this can be presented to others purified and elucidated through the plastic and pictorial arts, and much more indirectly through poetry; but it rests just as much on *subjective* conditions that are not at everyone's disposal, and not at anyone's at all times; in fact, such conditions in the higher degrees of perfection are the advantage and privilege of only the few. Only the poorest knowledge, abstract secondary knowledge, the concept, the mere shadow of knowledge proper, is unconditionally communicable. If perceptions were communicable, there would then be a communication worth the trouble; but in the end everyone must remain within his own skin and his own skull, and no man can help another. To enrich the concept from perception is the constant endeavour of poetry and philosophy. But the essential aims of man are *practical;* and for these it is sufficient that what is apprehended in perception should leave behind traces in him, by virtue of which he again recognizes it in the next similar case; he thus becomes world-wise. Therefore, as a rule, the man of the world cannot impart his accumulated truth and wisdom, but only practise it. He rightly comprehends everything that occurs, and decides what is conformable thereto. That books do not take the place of experience, and that learning is no substitute for genius, are two kindred phenomena; their common ground is that the abstract can never take the place of the perceptive. Therefore books do not take the place of experience, because *concepts* always remain *universal,* and so do not reach down to the particular; yet it is precisely the particular that has to be dealt with in life. In addition to this is the fact that all concepts are abstracted *from* the particular and perceptive of experience; we must therefore have come to know this, in order to understand adequately even only what is universal and is communicated by books.

Learning does not take the place of genius, because it also furnishes only concepts; the knowledge of genius, however, consists in the apprehension of the (Platonic) Ideas of things, and is therefore essentially intuitive. Accordingly, with the first phenomenon, the *objective* condition for perceiving knowledge is wanting; with the second, the *subjective;* the former can be attained, but not the latter.

Wisdom and genius, those two summits of the Parnassus of human knowledge, are rooted not in the abstract and discursive, but in the perceptive faculty. Wisdom proper is something intuitive, not something abstract. It does not consist in principles and ideas which a person carries round ready in his head, as results of his own or others' investigation; it is the whole way in which the world presents itself in his head. This is so exceedingly different, that by reason of it the wise man lives in a different world from the fool, and the genius sees a world different from that of the dull-witted person. The works of the genius immeasurably surpass those of all others, and this is due simply to the fact that the world which he sees, and from which he takes his utterances, is so much clearer, more profoundly worked out, so to speak, than that in the heads of others. This world naturally contains the same objects, but it is related to the world of the genius as is a Chinese picture without shade and perspective to a finished oil-painting. The material is the same in all minds, but the difference lies in the perfection of the form it assumes in each, and on this difference ultimately rest the many varying grades of intelligence. This difference, therefore, exists already in the root, in the *perceiving* apprehension, and does not originate in the abstract. Therefore original mental superiority readily shows itself on every occasion, and is instantly felt and detested by others.

In practical affairs, the intuitive knowledge of the understanding is able to guide our action and behaviour directly, whereas the abstract knowledge of the faculty of reason can do so only by means of the memory. From this springs the superiority of intuitive knowledge for all those cases that do not allow of any time for reflection, and so for daily intercourse, in which women excel on this precise account. Only the person who intuitively knows the true nature of men as they generally are, and comprehends the individuality of the particular person before him, will understand how to deal with him correctly and with certainty. Another person may know by heart all the three hundred maxims of wisdom by Gracián, but this will not protect him from stupid blunders and mistakes, if he lacks that intuitive knowledge. For all *abstract knowledge* gives primarily only universal principles and rules; but the particular case is hardly ever shaped exactly according to the rule. Then the memory should first present the rule at the right time, and this is seldom done promptly; the *propositio minor* should be formed from the present case, and finally the conclusion should be drawn. Before all this is done, the opportunity will in most cases already have turned its back on us, and then at best those excellent principles and rules enable us to estimate, when it is too late, the magnitude of the mistake we have made. In time, of course, and with experience and practice, worldly wisdom will slowly result from this; and therefore, in connexion with these, the rules in the abstract can certainly become fruitful. On the other hand, *intuitive knowledge,* always apprehending only the particular things, is in direct relation to the present case; rule, case, and application are identical for it, and action follows immediately thereon. This explains why the scholar, whose merit lies in abundance of abstract knowledge, is so inferior to the man of the world, whose merit consists in perfect intuitive knowledge, which an original disposition has conceded to him, and a rich experience has developed. Between the two kinds of knowledge there always appears the relation of paper money to hard cash; yet just as for many cases and affairs the former is to be preferred to the latter, so there are also things and situations for which abstract is more useful than intuitive knowledge. Thus, if it is a concept that guides our action in a matter, it has the advantage, when once grasped, of being unalterable; hence under its guidance we go to work with perfect certainty and determination. But this certainty granted by the concept on the subjective side is counterbalanced by the uncertainty that accompanies it on the objective side. Thus the whole concept may be false and groundless, or the object to be dealt with may not come under it, since it may not be in any way, or indeed entirely, of its species. Now if, in the particular case, we suddenly become aware of something of the sort, we are disconcerted; if we do not become aware of it, then the result tells us. Therefore, Vauvenargues says *Personne n'est sujet à plus de fautes que ceux qui n'agissent que par réflexion.*[3] On the other hand, if it is direct perception of the objects to be dealt with and of their relations that guides our action, we easily falter at every step; for perception is usually modifiable, is ambiguous, has inexhaustible details in itself, and shows many sides in succession; we therefore act without full confidence. But this subjective uncertainty is compensated by objective certainty, for here no concept stands between the object and us; we do not lose sight of it. Therefore, if only we see correctly what we have before

---

[3] "None are so prone to make mistakes as those who act only on reflection." [Tr.]

us and what we do, we shall hit the right spot. Accordingly, our action is perfectly certain and sure only when it is guided by a concept, whose correct ground, completeness, and applicability to the existing case are quite certain. Conduct according to concepts can turn into pedantry; conduct according to the impression of perception can turn into levity and folly.

Perception is not only the *source* of all knowledge, but is itself knowledge χατ' ἐξοχήν;[4] it alone is the unconditionally true genuine knowledge, fully worthy of the name. For it alone imparts *insight* proper; it alone is actually assimilated by man, passes into his inner nature, and can quite justifiably be called *his,* whereas the concepts merely cling to him. In the fourth book we see that even virtue really comes from knowledge of perception; for only those actions which it directly calls forth, and which are consequently done from the pure impulse of our own nature, are real symptoms of our true and unalterable character; but not those which, resulting from reflection and its dogmas, are often wrung from the character, and therefore have no unalterable ground in us. But *wisdom* also, the true view of life, correct insight, and clear judgement result from the way in which man apprehends the world of perception, not from his mere abstract knowledge, not from abstract concepts. The foundation or basic content of every science does not consist in proofs or in what is proved, but in the unproved foundation of the proofs; and this is ultimately apprehended only through perception. So too the foundation of every man's real wisdom and actual insight does not consist in concepts and in abstract knowledge, but in what is perceived, and in the degree of acuteness, accuracy, and profundity with which he has apprehended this. Whoever excels in this, recognizes the (Platonic) Ideas of the world and of life; every case he has seen represents for him innumerable cases; he always apprehends every being according to its true nature, and his action, like his judgement, corresponds to his insight. By degrees, even his countenance assumes the expression of the correct glance, of true judiciousness, and when it goes far enough, of wisdom. For it is only superiority in knowledge of perception that stamps its impression even on the features, whereas superiority in abstract knowledge cannot do so. According to what has been said, we find among all classes persons of intellectual superiority, often without any learning at all. For natural understanding can take the place of almost every degree of intellectual culture, but no culture can take the place of natural understanding. The scholar certainly has the advantage of such people in an abundance of cases and facts (historical knowledge),

---

[4] *"Par excellence."* [Tr.]

and of causal determinations (natural science), everything in well arranged, easily surveyed sequence; but yet, with all this, he does not have a more accurate and profound insight into what is really essential in all those cases, facts, and causalities. The unlearned man of acuteness and penetration knows how to dispense with that abundance; we are sparing of much, we make do with little. One case from his own experience teaches him more than many a scholar is taught by a thousand cases which he *knows,* but does not really *understand.* For the little knowledge of that unlearned man is *alive,* since every fact known to him is verified by accurate and well-apprehended perception. Thus this fact is for him the representative of a thousand similar facts. On the other hand, much of the ordinary scholar's knowledge is *dead,* since, even if it does not consist of mere words, as often is the case, it nevertheless consists of nothing but abstract knowledge. Such knowledge, however, obtains its value only through the individual's knowledge of *perception,* to which it must refer, and which must ultimately realize all the concepts. Now if this knowledge of perception is very scanty, such a mind is constituted like a bank whose liabilities are ten times in excess of its cash reserve, so that it ultimately becomes bankrupt. Therefore, while the correct apprehension of the world of perception has impressed the stamp of insight and wisdom on the brow of many an unlearned man, the face of many a scholar bears no other traces of his many studies than those of exhaustion and weariness through excessive and forced straining of the memory for the unnatural accumulation of dead concepts. Such a man frequently looks so simple, silly, and sheepish, that it must be supposed that the excessive strain of the indirect faculty of knowledge, applied to the abstract, produces a direct weakening of the immediate knowledge of perception, and that the natural and correct view is dazzled more and more by the light of books. The constant influx of other people's ideas must certainly stop and stifle our own, and indeed, in the long run, paralyse the power of thought, unless it has a high degree of elasticity able to withstand that unnatural flow. Therefore incessant reading and study positively ruin the mind; this, moreover, is caused by the fact that the system of our own ideas and knowledge loses its completeness and uninterrupted continuity, when we arbitrarily upset this so often in order to gain room for an entirely foreign range of ideas. To banish my thoughts in order to make room for those of a book would seem to me to be just what Shakespeare[4a] censures in the travellers of his time, that they sell their own land in order to see those of others. However, the mania of most scholars

---

[4a] *As You Like It,* Act iv, Sc. i. [Tr.]

for reading is a kind of *fuga vacui* from the lack of ideas in their own heads, which forcibly draws in the ideas of others. To have ideas, they must read a few, just as lifeless bodies obtain movement only from outside; whereas the person who thinks for himself is like the living body that moves of itself. It is even risky to read about a subject before we ourselves have reflected on it. For with the new material, another person's view and treatment of it creep into the mind, all the more since laziness and apathy urge us to save ourselves the trouble of thinking, to accept what has already been thought, and to allow this to become current. This now gains a footing, and hereafter the thoughts and ideas on it always take the accustomed path, like small streams led into ditches; to find a new idea of one's own is then doubly difficult. This contributes much to the lack of originality in scholars. In addition to this is the fact that they imagine they must divide their time, like other people, between pleasure and work. They regard reading as their work and real occupation, and therefore gorge themselves with it beyond what they can digest. Reading no longer merely anticipates thinking, but entirely takes its place. They think of things only just so long as they are reading about them, and hence with the mind of another and not with their own. But if the book is laid aside, quite different things make much more lively claims on their interest, namely personal affairs, the theatre, card-playing, skittles, the events of the day, and gossip. The thinking mind is what it is by the fact that such things have no interest for it, whereas its problems have; and so it becomes absorbed in these by itself and without a book. It is impossible to give ourselves this interest if we do not have it; that is the point. Moreover, on this rests the fact that the former always speak only of what they have read, the latter, on the other hand, of what he has thought, and that they are, as Pope says:

"For ever reading, never to be read." [4b]

The mind is by its nature free, not a slave; only what it does by itself and willingly is successful. On the other hand, the compulsory exertion of the mind in studies that are beyond its capacity, or when it has become tired, or generally too continuously and *invita Minervâ*,[5] dulls the brain, just as reading by moonlight dulls the eyes. In particular, this comes about also by straining the immature brain in the early years of childhood. I believe that the learning of Latin and Greek grammar from the sixth to the twelfth year lays

---

[4b] *Dunciad,* iii, 194. [Tr.]

[5] "Against the will of Minerva [i.e., despite its inclination]." [Tr.]

the foundation for the subsequent dulness of most scholars. The mind certainly requires nourishment, namely material from outside. All that we eat, however, is not incorporated into the organism at once, but only in so far as it has been digested, whereby only a small part of it is actually assimilated, the remainder passing from the system, so that to eat more than we can assimilate is useless, and even injurious. It is precisely the same as regards what we read; only in so far as it gives material for thinking does it increase our insight and our knowledge proper. Therefore Heraclitus said: πολυμαθίη νόον οὐ διδάσκει (*multiscitia non dat intellectum*).[6] It seems to me that learning can be compared to a heavy suit of armour, which indeed makes the strong man quite invincible, but to the weak man is a burden under which he breaks down completely.

The detailed discussion given in our third book of the knowledge of the (Platonic) Ideas as the highest attainable by man, and at the same time as a knowledge entirely of *perception or intuition,* is a proof for us that the source of true wisdom lies not in the abstract rational knowledge, but in the correct and profound apprehension of the world in perception. Therefore wise men can live in any age, and those of antiquity remain so for all the generations to come. Learning, on the other hand, is relative; the learned men of antiquity are for the most part children as compared with us, and need indulgence.

However, for the man who studies to gain *insight,* books and studies are merely rungs of the ladder on which he climbs to the summit of knowledge. As soon as a rung has raised him one step, he leaves it behind. On the other hand, the many who study in order to fill their memory do not use the rungs of the ladder for climbing, but take them off and load themselves with them to take away, rejoicing at the increasing weight of the burden. They remain below for ever, because they bear what should have borne them.

On the truth, here discussed, that the kernel of all knowledge is *perceptive or intuitive* apprehension, rests also the correct and profound observation of Helvetius that the really characteristic and original views of which a gifted individual is capable, and the elaboration, development, and manifold use whereof are his whole work, although produced much later, originate in him only up to his thirty-fifth, or at the latest his fortieth year; in fact they are really the result of combinations made in his earliest youth. For they are not mere concatenations of abstract concepts, but the intuitive apprehension, peculiar to him, of the objective world and the nature of things. That this intuitive apprehension must have com-

---

[6] "A smattering of many things does not form the mind." [Tr.]

pleted its work by the age mentioned depends partly on the fact that, by that time, the ectypes of all the (Platonic) Ideas have presented themselves to the man. Therefore, later on, no ectype is any longer able to appear with the strength of the first impression. To some extent also the highest energy of brain-activity is demanded for this quintessence of all knowledge, for these impressions of apprehension *avant la lettre*.[7] Such energy of brain-activity is conditioned by the freshness and flexibility of the brain's fibres, and the intensity with which the arterial blood flows to the brain. But this is at its strongest only so long as the arterial system has a decided predominance over the venous; it is already declining in the early thirties, until finally, after the forty-second year, the venous system obtains the upper hand, as has been admirably and instructively explained by Cabanis. Therefore the twenties and early thirties are for the intellect what May is for the trees; only at that time do the blossoms, of which all the later fruits are the development, begin to show. The world of perception has made its impression, and thus has laid the foundation of all the subsequent ideas of the individual. By reflection this individual can make clear to himself what has been apprehended; he can still acquire much knowledge as nourishment for the fruit that has once begun to show. He can enlarge his views, correct his concepts and judgements, and really become master of the material acquired only through endless combinations. In fact, he will often produce his best works much later, just as the greatest heat begins only when the days are already growing shorter. But he has no longer any hope of new original knowledge from the only living source of perception. Byron feels this when he breaks out into the exceedingly beautiful lament:

> No more—no more— Oh! never more on me
> The freshness of the heart can fall like dew,
> Which out of all the lovely things we see
> Extracts emotions beautiful and new,
> Hived in our bosoms like the bag o' the bee:
> Think'st thou the honey with those objects grew?
> Alas! 'twas not in them, but in thy power
> To double even the sweetness of a flower.[7a]

By all that has been said so far, I hope I have placed in a clear light the important truth that, just as all abstract knowledge has sprung from knowledge of perception, so has it its whole value only

---

[7] Impressions "*avant la lettre*" are in copper-engraving the first fresh impressions taken before the insertion of the signature. [Tr.]

[7a] *Don Juan,* I, 214 [Tr.]

through its relation to this knowledge of perception, and hence through the fact that its concepts, or their partial representations, can be realized, in other words proved through perceptions; likewise that the greater part depends on the quality of these perceptions. Concepts and abstractions that do not ultimately lead to perceptions are like paths in a wood that end without any way out. Concepts have their great use in the fact that by means of them the original material of knowledge can be more easily handled, surveyed, and arranged. But however many different logical and dialectical operations are possible with them, an entirely original and new knowledge will never result from them, in other words, knowledge whose material did not already lie in perception, or was drawn from self-consciousness. This is the true meaning of the doctrine ascribed to Aristotle: *Nihil est in intellectu nisi quod antea fuerit in sensu.*[8] It is likewise the sense of Locke's philosophy that made an epoch in philosophy for all time by finally starting the serious discussion of the question of the origin of our knowledge. In the main, it is also what is taught by the *Critique of Pure Reason.* Thus it also bids us not to remain at the *concepts,* but to go back to their *origin,* that is to *perception;* only with the true and important addition that what holds good of perception itself refers also to its subjective conditions, to the forms lying predisposed in the perceiving and thinking brain as its natural functions, although these functions precede, at any rate *virtualiter,* the actual sense-perception; in other words, they are *a priori,* and so do not depend on this sense-perception, but rather this perception depends on them. For these forms, in fact, have no other purpose or use than to produce empirical perception on the stimulation of the nerves of sense which occurs, just as from the material of this perception other forms are subsequently fixed for constructing ideas in the abstract. Therefore the *Critique of Pure Reason* is related to Locke's philosophy as the analysis of the infinite is to elementary geometry; it is, however, to be regarded in every way as the *continuation of Locke's philosophy.* Accordingly, the given material of every philosophy is no other than the *empirical consciousness* which is divided into the consciousness of one's self (self-consciousness) and the consciousness of other things (external perception); for this alone is the immediate, the actually given. Every philosophy which, instead of starting from this, takes as its starting-point arbitrarily chosen abstract concepts such as, for example, the absolute, absolute substance, God, infinite, finite, absolute identity, being, essence, and so on, floats in air without any

[8] "There is nothing in the intellect that was not previously in sense-perception." [Tr.]

support, and so can never lead to a real result. However, philosophers have at all times attempted it with such material; therefore even Kant at times, according to common usage, and more from custom than consistency, defines philosophy as a science of mere concepts. But such a science would really undertake to extract from mere partial representations (for this is what the abstractions are) what is not to be found in complete representations (the perceptions), from which the former are drawn off by omission. The possibility of syllogisms leads to this error, because here the construction of judgements gives a new result, although more apparent than real, since the syllogism only brings out what already lay in the given judgements, for the conclusion, of course, cannot contain more than the premisses. Concepts are naturally the material of philosophy, but only as marble is the material of the sculptor. Philosophy is not supposed to work *out of* concepts, but *into* them, in other words, to deposit its results in them, but not to start from them as that which is given. Whoever wants to have a really glaring example of such a wrong and perverse start from mere concepts should consider the *Institutio Theologica* of Proclus, to convince himself of the futility of the whole method. There abstractions like ἕν, πλῆθος, ἀγαθόν, παράγον καὶ παραγόμενον, αὔταρκες, αἴτιον, κρεῖττον, κινητόν, ἀκίνητον, κινούμενον (*unum, multa, bonum, producens et productum, sibi sufficiens, causa, melius, mobile, immobile, motum*)[9] and so on, are raked up, but the perceptions to which alone they owe their origin and content are ignored and disregarded with an air of superiority. From those concepts a theology is then constructed, and here the goal, the θεός, is kept concealed; thus the procedure is apparently quite impartial, as if the reader, as well as the author, did not know already on the first page where all this would end. I have previously quoted a fragment of this above. Actually this production of Proclus is specially appropriate for showing how utterly unsuitable and illusory such combinations of abstract concepts are, since we can make of them whatever we like, particularly if we make use of the ambiguity of many words, such as κρεῖττον (better), for example. If such an architect of concepts were present in person, we should need only to ask him naively where all the things are of which he has so much to tell us, and whence he knows the laws from which he draws his conclusions about them. He would then soon be compelled to refer to empirical perception, in which alone the real world exhibits itself, and from which those concepts

---

[9] "One, plurality, good, producer and product, self-sufficing, cause, better, mobile, immobile, moved," are abstractions with which Proclus operates in the *Institutio Theologica*. [Tr.]

are drawn. Then we would still have merely to ask why he did not quite honestly start from the given perception of such a world, where he could verify his assertions by it at every step, instead of operating with concepts, which are nevertheless drawn only from perception, and can therefore have no further validity than that which it imparts to them. But, of course, this is just his trick. Through such concepts, in which, by virtue of abstraction, what is inseparable is thought as separated, and what cannot be united as united, he goes far beyond the perception that was their origin, and thus beyond the limits of their applicability, to an entirely different world from the one that supplied the building material, and on this very account to a world of chimeras and phantasms. I have mentioned Proclus here, just because in him this method becomes particularly clear through the open audacity with which it is carried out. But even in Plato we find some examples of this kind, although less glaring ones; and in general the philosophical literature of all times affords a whole host of such instances. That of our own time abounds in them. Consider, for example, the writings of the school of Schelling, and see the constructions that are built up from such abstractions as finite and infinite—being, non-being, other-being—activity, hindrance, product—determining, being determined, determinateness—limit, limiting, being limited—unity, plurality, multiplicity—identity, diversity, indifference—thinking, being, essence, and so on. Not only does all that we have said hold good of constructions out of such material, but because an infinite amount is thought *through* such wide abstractions, only extremely little can be thought *in* them; they are empty husks. But in this way the material of the whole of philosophizing becomes astonishingly poor and paltry; and from this results the unspeakable and tormenting tediousness characteristic of all such writings. If I were to call to mind the way in which Hegel and his companions have misused such wide and empty abstractions, I should necessarily be afraid that both the reader and I would be ill, for the most sickening and loathsome tediousness hangs over the empty bombast of this repulsive philosophaster.

That likewise in *practical* philosophy no wisdom is brought to light from mere abstract concepts is the one thing to be learnt from the moral discourses of the theologian Schleiermacher. With the delivery of these he has bored the Berlin Academy for a number of years; quite recently they have been printed and published in one volume. Only abstract concepts, such as duty, virtue, highest good, moral law, and so on, are taken as the starting-point without further introduction than that they commonly occur in moral systems, and are now treated as given realities. These are then discussed with great subtlety from all angles; but no attempt is ever made to go straight to the source of those concepts, to the thing itself, the actual life of man, to which alone those concepts refer, from which they should be drawn, and with which morality is really concerned. For this reason, these diatribes are just as unfruitful and useless as they are tedious, which is saying a great deal. Men like this theologian, who is only too fond of philosophizing, are found at all times, famous while they are alive, forgotten soon afterwards. On the other hand, I advise as to be preferred the reading of those whose fate has been the opposite of this, for time is short and valuable.

Now if, in accordance with all that has been said here, wide, abstract concepts, and in particular those that are not to be realized in any perception, can never be the source of knowledge, the starting-point or the proper material of philosophizing, nevertheless particular results of philosophy can occasionally so turn out that they can be thought merely in the abstract, but cannot be verified by any perception. Knowledge of this kind will, of course, be only half-knowledge; it indicates, so to speak, only the place where that which is to be known is found; this itself remains concealed. We should therefore be satisfied with such concepts only in the extreme case, and when we have reached the limit of the knowledge possible to our faculties. An example of this kind might possibly be the concept of an existence or being out of time, such as the proposition: The indestructibility of our true nature by death is not a continued existence of it. With concepts of this sort, the firm ground that supports the whole of our knowledge trembles, as it were. Therefore philosophizing may occasionally, and in case of necessity, extend to such knowledge, but it must never begin with it.

Operating with wide abstractions, which was censured above, to the entire neglect of knowledge of perception, from which they have been drawn, and which is therefore their permanent and natural controller, has at all times been the main source of the errors of dogmatic philosophizing. A science constructed from the mere comparison of concepts, that is, from universal principles, could be certain only if all its principles were synthetic *a priori,* as is the case with mathematics; for such principles alone admit of no exceptions. But if the principles have any empirical material, we must always keep this at hand, in order to control the universal principles. For no truths in any way drawn from experience are ever unconditionally certain. They have only an approximate universal validity, since here no rule is valid without exception. Now if I link such principles one with another by virtue of the intersection of their concept-spheres, one concept will easily touch another precisely where the exception lies. But if this has happened even only once in the course of a long chain of reasoning, the whole structure is torn from its foundation, and floats in air. For example, if I say: "Ruminants are without front incisors," and I apply this, and what follows from it, to camels, then everything becomes false, for it holds good only of horned ruminants. What Kant calls *subtle argumentation* (*Vernünfteln*) and so often condemns, is precisely what is here meant; for it consists simply in subsuming concepts under concepts without regard to their origin, and without examining the correctness and exclusiveness of such a subsumption. In this way we can arrive by a longer or shorter circuitous path at almost any result we like which we have fixed as our goal. Hence this subtle argumentation differs only in degree from sophistry proper. But sophistry in the theoretical is just what chicanery is in the practical. Yet even Plato has very frequently taken upon himself to use this subtle argumentation, and, as mentioned already, Proclus, after the manner of all imitators, carried this fault of his prototype much farther. Dionysius the Areopagite, *De Divinis Nominibus,* is also strongly affected with it. Even in the fragments of the Eleatic Melissus we find clear instances of such subtle argumentation (especially §§ 2-5 in Brandis's *Comment. Eleat.*). His method with concepts resembles blows given for the sake of appearance, which never hit the mark; these concepts never touch the reality from which they have their content, but, floating in the atmosphere of abstract universality, pass lightly over it. A further real specimen of such subtle argumentation is the little book *De Diis et Mundo* of the philosopher Sallust, especially chaps. 7, 12, and 17. A real gem of philosophical subtle argumentation, passing into decided sophistication, is the following reasoning of the Platonist Maximus Tyrius, which I will quote, as it is short. "Every injustice is the taking away of a good thing; there is no good thing other than virtue. Virtue, however, cannot be taken away, therefore it is not possible for the virtuous to suffer injustice from the wicked. It remains either that no injustice at all can be suffered, or that the wicked endures it from the wicked. But the wicked person possesses no good at all, for only virtue is such a good; therefore no good can be taken from him. Thus he also cannot suffer any injustice; hence injustice is an impossible thing." The original, which through repetitions is less concise, runs as follows: Ἀδικία ἐστὶν ἀφαίρεσις ἀγαθοῦ· τὸ δὲ ἀγαθὸν τί ἂν εἴη ἄλλο ἢ ἀρετή;—ἡ δὲ ἀρετὴ ἀναφαίρετον. Οὐκ ἀδικήσεται τοίνυν ὁ τὴν ἀρετὴν ἔχων, ἢ οὔκ ἐστιν ἀδικία ἀφαίρεσις ἀγαθοῦ· οὐδὲν γὰρ ἀγαθὸν ἀφαίρετον, οὐδ' ἀπόβλητον, οὐδ' ἐλετόν, οὐδὲ ληιστόν. Εἶεν οὖν οὐδ' ἀδικεῖται ὁ χρηστός, οὐδ' ὑπὸ τοῦ μοχθηροῦ· ἀναφαίρετος γάρ. Λείπεται τοίνυν ἢ μηδένα ἀδικεῖσθαι καθάπαξ, ἢ τὸν μοχθηρὸν ὑπὸ τοῦ ὁμοίου· ἀλλὰ τῷ μοχθηρῷ οὐδενὸς μέτεστιν ἀγαθοῦ· ἡ δὲ ἀδικία ἦν ἀγαθοῦ ἀφαίρεσις· ὁ δὲ μὴ ἔχων ὅ, τι ἀφαιρεθῇ, οὐδὲ εἰς ὅ, τι ἀδικηθῇ, ἔχει (*Sermo 2*). I will also add a modern example of such proof from abstract concepts, by which an obviously absurd proposition is set up as truth, and I take it from the works of a great man, namely Giordano Bruno. In his book *Del Infinito, Universo e Mondi* (p. 87 of the edition of A. Wagner) he makes an Aristotelian prove (with the aid and exaggeration of the passage of Aristotle's *De Coelo*, i, 5) that there can be *no space* beyond the world. Thus he says that the world is enclosed by the eight spheres of Aristotle, but that beyond these there cannot be any *space;* for if there were a body beyond these, this body would be either simple or compound. It is now sophistically proved, simply from principles that are begged, that no *simple* body can be there, and likewise no *compound* body, for that would necessarily consist of simple ones. Hence there is, in general, no body there; and so also *no space.* For space is defined as "that in which bodies can be"; but it has just been demonstrated that *no* bodies can be there. Therefore there is also *no space* there. This last is the master-stroke of that proof from abstract concepts. At bottom, it rests on the fact that the proposition: "Where no space is, there can be no bodies" is taken as a universal negative, and is accordingly simply converted: "Where no bodies can be, there is no space." But, closely considered, the former proposition is a universal affirmative, namely: "Everything spaceless is bodiless"; and so we may not convert it simply. But not every proof from abstract concepts, with a result obviously conflicting with perception (as in this case the finiteness of space), can be reduced to such a logical mistake. For what is sophistical does not always lie in the form, but often in the matter, in the premises, and in the indefiniteness of the concepts and of their range or extent. Numerous instances of this are found in Spinoza, whose method indeed it is to prove from concepts; see for example the pitiable sophisms in his *Ethica,* part iv, prop. 29-31, by means of the ambiguity of the vague and indefinite concepts *convenire* and *commune habere.* However, things like this do not prevent the Neo-Spinozists of our own day from taking all that he said for gospel. Of these the Hegelians, of whom there are actually still a few, are particularly amusing by their traditional reverence for his proposition *omnis determinatio est negatio.* At this, in accordance with the charlatan-spirit of the school, they put on a face as if it were able to shake the world to its foundations, whereas it cannot be of any use at all, since even the simplest person sees for himself that, if I limit anything by determinations, I exclude, and thus deny, in this way what lies beyond the limit.

Therefore, in all sophistical reasonings of this kind, it becomes very obvious what false paths are open to that algebra with mere concepts uncontrolled by any perception, and that consequently perception is for our intellect what the firm ground on which it stands is for our body. If we forsake perception, everything is *instabilis tellus, innabilis unda.*[10] Allowance will be made for the fulness of these explanations and examples, on account of their instructive nature. I wanted in this way to stress and demonstrate the great difference, indeed opposition, between knowledge of perception and abstract or reflected knowledge. Hitherto this difference has received too little attention, and its establishment is a fundamental feature of my philosophy; for many phenomena of our mental life can be explained only from this difference. The connecting link between these two such different kinds of knowledge forms the *power of judgement,* as I have explained in § 14 of volume one. It is true that this power of judgement is also active in the province of merely abstract knowledge, where it compares concepts only with concepts. Therefore every judgement, in the logical sense of this word, is certainly a work of the power of judgement, since here a narrower concept is always subsumed under a wider. Yet this activity of the power of judgement, where it merely compares concepts with one another, is one that is inferior to and easier than the activity by which it makes the transition from what is quite particular, thus perception, to what is essentially universal, thus the concept. Thus, as it must be possible, by analysing the concepts into their essential predicates, to decide their consistency or inconsistency in a purely logical way, for which the mere faculty of reason inherent in everyone is sufficient, so here the power of judgement is active only in shortening that process, since the person gifted with it surveys rapidly what others bring out only through a series of reflections. But its activity in the narrower sense certainly appears only where the perceptively known, and thus the real, experience is to be carried over into distinct abstract knowledge, subsumed under exactly corresponding concepts, and thus deposited in reflected rational knowledge. It is therefore this faculty which has to lay down the firm *foundations* of all the sciences which consist always in what is immediately known and what is not to be further derived. Here, therefore, in the fundamental judgements lies also the difficulty of the sciences, not in the inferences from them. To infer is easy, to judge difficult. False inferences are a rarity; false judgements are always the order of the day. No less in practical life has the power of judge-

---

[10] "Land on which we cannot stand, water in which we cannot swim" (Ovid, *Metamorphoses,* I, 16). [Tr.]

ment to turn the scale in the case of all fundamental decisions and principal determinations; for in the main, its work is like the judicial sentence. Just as the burning-glass focuses the sun's rays at one point, so with the activity of the power of judgement the intellect must bring all the data it has on a matter so close together, that it grasps them at a glance, which it correctly fixes, and then makes the result clear to itself with thoughtfulness and discernment. Moreover, the great difficulty of the judgement depends in most cases on the fact that we have to pass from the consequent to the ground or reason, and this path is always uncertain; indeed, I have shown that here lies the source of all error. Yet in all the empirical sciences, as also in the affairs of real life, this path is often the only one open to us. The experiment is an attempt to go over the path in the reverse direction; it is therefore decisive, and at any rate brings the error to light, always assuming that it is correctly chosen and honestly carried out, not as were Newton's experiments on the theory of colours. But again, even the experiment must be judged and reviewed. The complete certainty of the *a priori* sciences, logic and mathematics, depends mainly on the fact that in them the path from ground to consequent is open to us, and is always certain. This endows them with the character of purely *objective* sciences, in other words, of sciences about whose truths all must judge in common, when they understand them. This is all the more surprising, as it is precisely these that rest on the subjective forms of the intellect, whereas the empirical sciences alone have to do with what is palpably objective.

Wit and discernment are also manifestations of the power of judgement; in the former it is reflecting, in the latter subsuming. With most people, the power of judgement is present only nominally. It is a kind of irony that this power is numbered among the normal faculties of the mind, instead of being ascribed only to the *monstra per excessum*.[11] Ordinary minds show, even in the smallest affairs, a want of confidence in their own judgement, just because they know from experience that it is of no use to them. With them prejudice and following the judgement of others take its place. In this way they are kept in a state of permanent nonage, from which scarcely one in many hundreds is emancipated. Naturally this is not avowed, for even to themselves they seem to judge; yet all the time they are casting a furtive glance at the opinion of others, which remains their secret point of direction. While any of them would be ashamed to go about in a borrowed coat, hat, or cloak, none of them has anything but borrowed opinions which they eagerly scrape

---

[11] "Phenomena that are monstrous through excess." [Tr.]

up wherever they can get possession of them; and then they proudly strut around with them, giving them out as their own. Others in turn borrow these opinions from them, and do just the same thing with them. This explains the rapid and wide dissemination of errors, as well as the fame of what is bad. For the professional purveyors of opinion, such as journalists and the like, as a rule give out only false goods, just as those who hire out fancy dresses give only false jewellery.

On the Theory of the Ludicrous

My theory of the ludicrous also depends on the contrast, which I have explained in the preceding chapters and so forcibly stressed, between representations of perception and abstract representations. Therefore what is still to be said in explanation of this theory finds its place here, although, in accordance with the arrangement of the text, it should follow only later.

The problem of the origin, everywhere identical, and at the same time of the real significance of laughter was already recognized by Cicero, but was at once given up as insoluble (*De Oratore,* II, 58). The oldest attempt I am aware of at a psychological explanation of laughter is to be found in Hutcheson's *Introduction into Moral Philosophy,* Bk. I, ch. 1, § 14. A somewhat later anonymous work, *Traité des causes physiques et morales du rire,* 1768, is not without merit as a ventilation of the subject. Platner in his *Anthropology,* § 894, has collected the opinions of the philosophers from Home to Kant who attempt an explanation of that phenomenon peculiar to human nature. Kant's and Jean-Paul's theories of the ludicrous are well known. I regard it as superfluous to demonstrate their incorrectness, for anyone who attempts to refer given cases of the ludicrous to them will be at once convinced of their inadequacy in the great majority of instances.

According to my explanation, put forward in volume one, the origin of the ludicrous is always the paradoxical, and thus unexpected, subsumption of an object under a concept that is in other respects heterogeneous to it. Accordingly, the phenomenon of laughter always signifies the sudden apprehension of an incongruity between such a concept and the real object thought through it, and hence between what is abstract and what is perceptive. The greater and more unexpected this incongruity in the apprehension of the person laughing, the more violent will be his laughter. Accordingly, in everything that excites laughter it must always be possible to show

---

[1] This chapter refers to § 13 of volume 1.

a concept and a particular, that is to say, a thing or an event, which can of course be subsumed under that concept, and thus be thought through it, yet which in another and predominating respect does not belong under it at all, but differs strikingly from everything else thought through that concept. If, as is often the case especially with witticisms, instead of such a real object of perception, a species-concept appears that is subordinate to the higher or genus-concept, it will nevertheless excite laughter merely by the fact that the imagination realizes it, in other words, makes a representative of perception stand for it; and thus the conflict takes place between the conceived and the perceived. In fact, if we want to know the thing absolutely explicitly, we can refer everything ludicrous to a syllogism in the first figure, with an undisputed *major* and an unexpected *minor* maintained, to a certain extent, only by chicanery; and it is in consequence of this combination that the conclusion has the quality of the ludicrous.

In volume one I regarded it as superfluous to illustrate this theory by examples, as everyone can easily do this for himself by reflecting a little on the cases of the ludicrous which he calls to mind. However, to come to the aid of the mental inertness of those readers who always prefer to remain in a passive state, I will meet their wishes here. Indeed, in this third edition I will add more examples, so that there will be no question that here, after so many fruitless attempts, the true theory of the ludicrous is given, and the problem propounded but given up by Cicero definitely solved.

Bearing in mind that for an angle two lines meeting each other are required which when produced intersect each other; that the tangent, on the other hand, touches the circle only at one point, but at this point really runs parallel to it; and if we thus have present in our mind the abstract conviction of the impossibility of an angle between the circumference of a circle and the tangent, but yet have such an angle visibly before us on paper, all this will easily make us smile. In this case, of course, the ludicrous is extremely feeble; on the other hand, the origin of the ludicrous from the incongruity of the conceived with the perceived appears in it with unusual distinctness. According as we pass, when discovering such an incongruity, from the real, i.e., the perceptive, to the concept, or conversely from the concept to the real, the ludicrous that thus results is either a witticism or an absurdity, and in the higher degree, especially in the practical sphere, a folly, as was explained in the text. To consider examples of the first case, that is, of wit, we will first of all take the well-known anecdote of the Gascon at whom the king laughed on seeing him in the depth of winter in light summer clothes, and who said to the king: "If your Majesty had put on what I have put on, you would find it very warm"; then to the question what he had put on, replied: "My whole wardrobe." Under this latter concept is to be thought the immense wardrobe of a king as well as the single summer jacket of a poor devil, the sight of which on his freezing body appears very incongruous with the concept. The audience at a theatre in Paris once asked for the *Marseillaise* to be played, and as this was not done, they began shrieking and howling, so that in the end a police commissioner in uniform came on to the stage, and explained that for anything to be done in the theatre other than what appeared on the play-bill was not allowed. A voice then shouted: *Et vous, Monsieur, êtes-vous aussi sur l'affiche?*[2] a hit that raised universal laughter. For here the subsumption of the heterogeneous is immediately distinct and unforced. The epigram:

> "Bav is the true shepherd of whom the Bible spake:
> If his flock be asleep, he alone remains awake,"

subsumes under the concept of a shepherd watching over his sleeping flock, the tedious preacher who has sent his whole congregation to sleep, and then goes on bellowing without being heard. Analogous to this is the epitaph of a physician: "Here like a hero he lies, and those he has slain lie around him": this subsumes under the concept "lying surrounded by the slain," which is honourable to the hero, the physician who is supposed to preserve life. Very frequently the witticism consists in a single expression, through which only the concept is stated under which the case before us can be subsumed, but which is very different from everything else thought under it. Thus in *Romeo,* the vivacious Mercutio, mortally wounded but a moment previously, answers his friends who promise to visit him the next day: "Ask for me tomorrow, and you shall find me a *grave man.*" Under this concept a dead man is here subsumed; but in addition, there is in English a pun, for "a grave man" means both a serious man and a man of the grave. Of this kind is also the anecdote of the actor Unzelmann. After he had been strictly forbidden to improvise at all in the Berlin theatre, he had to appear on the stage on horseback. Just as he came on the stage, the horse dunged, and at this the audience were moved to laughter, but they laughed much more when Unzelmann said to the horse: "What are you doing? don't you know that we are forbidden to improvise?" Here the subsumption of the heterogeneous under the more general concept is very distinct, and so the witticism is exceedingly striking,

---

[2] "And you, sir, are you on the play-bill?" [Tr.]

and the ludicrous effect obtained extremely powerful. Further, to this class belongs a newspaper report from Hall of March 1851: "The band of Jewish swindlers which we have mentioned, was again delivered up to us with obbligato accompaniment." This subsuming of a police escort under a musical expression is very happy, although it approaches the mere play on words. On the other hand, it is exactly a case of the kind we are here considering when Saphir, in a pen-and-ink war with the actor Angeli, describes him as "Angeli, equally great in mind and in body." By reason of the actor's diminutive stature, well known to the town, the unusually small is presented in perception under the concept "great." So too, when the same Saphir calls the airs of a new opera "good old friends," and so brings under a concept used in other cases to praise, the very quality most to be condemned. Also, if we were to say of a lady, on whose favour presents would have an influence, that she knew how to combine the *utile* with the *dulci*. In this way we bring what is morally base under the concept of the rule that is commended by Horace in an aesthetic context. Likewise if, to signify a brothel, we were perhaps to describe it as a "modest abode of peaceful pleasures." Good society, in order to be thoroughly insipid, has banned all decided utterances, and therefore all strong expressions. To denote things that are scandalous or in any way shocking, it is in the habit of getting over the difficulty by expressing them in moderation by means of universal concepts. But in this way what is more or less heterogeneous to these is subsumed under them, and thus in a corresponding degree the effect of the ludicrous is produced. To this class belong the *utile dulci* mentioned above; also expressions such as "He has had unpleasantnesses at the ball," when he was thrashed and kicked out; or "He has done somewhat too well," when he is the worse for drink; also "The woman is said to have weak moments," when she is unfaithful to her husband, and so on. To this class also belong equivocations, namely concepts which in and by themselves contain nothing improper, yet the actual case brought under them leads to an improper conception. These are very frequent in society. But a perfect specimen of a sustained and magnificent equivocation is Shenstone's incomparable epitaph on a justice of the peace, which in its high-sounding lapidary style appears to speak of noble and sublime things, whereas under each of their concepts something quite different is to be subsumed, which appears only in the last word of all as the unexpected key to the whole, and the reader discovers with loud laughter that he has read merely a very obscene equivocation. In this smooth-combed age it is quite inadmissible to quote it here, much less to translate it. It is found in Shenstone's poetical works under the title "Inscription." Occasionally equivocations pass into mere puns, about which all that is necessary has been said in the text.

The subsumption, underlying everything ludicrous, of what is heterogeneous in one respect under a concept in other respects appropriate to it, may also take place contrary to our intention. For example, one of the free Negroes in North America, who endeavour to imitate the whites in all respects, recently placed an epitaph over his dead child, which begins: "Lovely, early broken lily." On the other hand, if with deliberate intention something real and perceptible is brought directly under the concept of its opposite, the result is plain, common irony. For example, if during heavy rain we say: "It is pleasant weather today"; or, of an ugly bride it is said: "He has found himself a lovely treasure"; or of a rogue: "This man of honour," and so on. Only children and people without any education will laugh at anything of this kind; for here the incongruity between the conceived and the perceived is total. Yet precisely in this deliberate exaggeration in the achievement of the ludicrous does its fundamental character, namely the aforesaid incongruity, appear very distinctly. This species of the ludicrous is, on account of the exaggeration and distinct intention, in some respects akin to the *parody*. The method of this consists in substituting for the incidents and words of a serious poem or drama insignificant, inferior persons, or petty motives and actions. It therefore subsumes the plain realities it sets forth under the lofty concepts given in the theme, under which in a certain respect they must now fit, whereas in other respects they are very incongruous therewith. In this way the contrast between the perceived and the conceived appears very glaring. There is no lack of well-known examples of this, and so I quote only one from the *Zobeide* of Carlo Gozzi, Act 4, Scene 3, where the famous stanza of Ariosto (*Orlando Furioso,* i, 22), *Oh gran bontà de' cavalieri antichi,* etc.,[3] is put word for word into the mouths of two clowns who have just been thrashing each other, and then, tired of this, lie quietly side by side. This is also the nature of the application, so popular in Germany, of serious verses, especially Schiller's, to trivial incidents, which obviously contains a subsumption of the heterogeneous under the universal concept expressed by the verse. Thus, for

---

[3] "Oh the great merit of the knights of old!
They were opponents and of different faith,
And after the hard and heavy blows they felt
Their whole body suffused with pains;
And yet they walk through dark forests
Together on the path without suspicion." [Tr.]

example, when anyone has displayed a really characteristic trait, someone will rarely be wanting who will say: "By that I know my man." But it was original and very witty of a man, who was fond of the bride, to address to a newly married couple (I know not how loudly) the concluding words of Schiller's ballad, *The Surety:*

> "Let me be, I pray you,
> In your bond the third."

Here the effect of the ludicrous is strong and inevitable, because under the concepts by which Schiller enables us to think of a morally noble relation, a forbidden and immoral relation is subsumed, yet correctly and without change, and is thus thought through it. In all the examples of wit here mentioned, we find that under a concept, or generally an abstract thought, a real thing is subsumed directly, or by means of a narrower concept; and strictly speaking, of course, this real thing belongs under it, yet is vastly different from the proper and original intention and tendency of the thought. Accordingly, wit as a mental faculty consists entirely in the facility for finding for every object that presents itself a concept under which it can certainly be thought, although it is very different from all the other objects that come under that concept.

The second species of the ludicrous, as we have mentioned, goes in the opposite direction, namely from the abstract concept to the real thing of perception that is thought through this concept. But this real thing now brings to light any incongruity with the concept which was overlooked; and in this way there arises an absurdity, and consequently in practice a foolish action. As the play requires action, this species of the ludicrous is essential to comedy. On this rests Voltaire's remark: *J'ai cru remarquer aux spectacles qu'il ne s'élève presque jamais de ces éclats de rire universels, qu'à l'occasion d'une MÉPRISE.* (Preface to *L'Enfant prodigue.*)[4] The following can be considered as examples of this species of the ludicrous. When someone had stated that he was fond of walking alone, an Austrian said to him: "You like to walk alone; so do I; then we can walk together." He starts from the concept "A pleasure which two people like can be enjoyed by them in common," and he subsumes under this the very case that excludes community. Again, the servant who rubs the worn sealskin in his master's box with Macassar oil, so that it may be covered with hair again. Here he starts from the concept "Macassar oil makes hair grow." The soldiers in the guardroom who let a prisoner, just brought in, take part in their game of cards, but because he cheats, a dispute occurs, and they throw

---

[4] "I think I have observed in the theatre that hardly ever is there a general burst of laughter except on the occasion of a *misapprehension*." [Tr.]

him out. They allow themselves to be guided by the general concept "Bad companions are turned out," but forget that he is at the same time under arrest, i.e., a man whom they ought to keep in custody. Two young peasants had loaded their gun with coarse shot which they wished to extract, in order to substitute fine shot for it, but without losing the powder. One of them put the mouth of the barrel into his hat, which he then took between his legs, and said to the other: "Now press the trigger quite gently, gently, gently, and then the shot will come first." He starts from the concept "Retarding the cause produces a retardation of the effect." Further, most of the actions of Don Quixote are illustrations, for he subsumes under concepts drawn from the romances of chivalry the realities he encounters, which are very different from such romances. For example, to protect the oppressed he frees the galley-slaves. Properly speaking, all Baron Münchhausen's tales also belong here, only they are not foolish actions performed, but impossible actions palmed off on the hearer as having actually happened. In them the fact is always grasped so that when thought merely in the abstract, and thus comparatively *a priori,* it appears possible and plausible. But if we afterwards come down to the perception of the individual case, and thus *a posteriori,* the impossibility of the thing, in fact the absurdity of the assumption, is brought into prominence, and excites laughter through the obvious incongruity between the perceived and the conceived. For example, when the melodies frozen in the postilion's horn thaw out in the warm room; when Münchhausen, sitting on a tree during a hard frost, draws up his knife that has fallen to the ground on the freezing water-jet of his own urine, and so on. Of this kind also is the story of the two lions who during the night break through the partition between them, and devour each other in their rage, so that nothing is found in the morning but their two tails.

There are still cases of the ludicrous where the concept under which the thing of perception is brought need not be either expressed or alluded to, but comes into consciousness of itself by virtue of the association of ideas. There is the case of the laughter into which Garrick burst in the middle of playing a tragedy, because a butcher, standing in front of the pit, had put his wig for a while on his large dog, so as to wipe the sweat from his own head. The dog was supported by his fore-feet on the pit railings, and was looking towards the stage. This laughter was occasioned by the fact that Garrick started from the concept of a spectator, which was added in his own mind. This is just the reason why certain animal forms, such as apes, kangaroos, jumping hares, and the like, sometimes appear ludicrous, because something in them resembling man causes us to subsume them under the concept of the human form, and, starting from this concept, we perceive their incongruity with it.

Now the concepts whose evident incongruity with perception moves us to laughter are either those of another, or they are our own. In the first case, we laugh at the other person; in the second case, we feel a surprise, often agreeable, or at any rate amusing. Therefore children and uneducated people laugh at the most trifling things, even at untoward events, if they were unexpected, and thus found their preconceived notion guilty of error. As a rule, laughing is a pleasant state; accordingly, the apprehension of the incongruity between what is conceived and what is perceived, i.e., reality, gives us pleasure, and we gladly give ourselves up to the spasmodic convulsion excited by this apprehension. The reason for this is the following. In the case of that suddenly appearing contrast between the perceived and the conceived, the perceived is always undoubtedly in the right, for it is in no way subject to error, and needs no confirmation from outside, but is its own advocate. Its conflict with what is thought springs ultimately from the fact that the latter, with its abstract concepts, cannot come down to the infinite multifariousness and fine shades of what is perceived. This triumph of knowledge of perception over thought gives us pleasure. For perception is the original kind of knowledge, inseparable from animal nature, in which everything that gives immediate satisfaction to the will presents itself. It is the medium of the present, of enjoyment and cheerfulness; moreover it is not associated with any exertion. With thinking the opposite holds good; it is the second power of knowledge, whose exercise always requires some, often considerable, exertion; and it is the concepts of thinking that are so often opposed to the satisfaction of our immediate desires, since, as the medium of the past, of the future, and of what is serious, they act as the vehicle of our fears, our regrets, and all our cares. It must therefore be delightful for us to see this strict, untiring, and most troublesome governess, our faculty of reason, for once convicted of inadequacy. Therefore on this account the mien or appearance of laughter is very closely related to that of joy.

Because of the lack of the faculty of reason, and thus of the lack of universal concepts, the animal is incapable of laughter as well as of speech. Laughter is therefore a prerogative and characteristic of man. Incidentally, his sole friend, the dog, also has an analogous and characteristic action peculiar to him alone, and as an advantage over all other animals, namely fawning and tail-wagging, which are so expressive, so kindly disposed, and thoroughly honest. Yet how favourably does this salutation, given to him by nature, contrast with the bows and simpering civilities of men! At any rate for the present, it is a thousand times more reliable than their assurance of close friendship and devotion.

The opposite of laughter and joking is *seriousness*. This, accordingly, consists in the consciousness of the perfect agreement and congruity of the concept, or the idea, with what is perceptive, with reality. The serious person is convinced that he conceives things as they are, and that they are as he conceives them. This is just why the transition from profound seriousness to laughter is particularly easy, and can be brought about by trifles. For the more perfect that agreement, assumed by seriousness, appears to be, the more easily is it abolished, even by a trifling incongruity unexpectedly coming to light. Therefore the more capable of complete seriousness a person is, the more heartily can he laugh. Persons whose laughter is always affected and forced are intellectually and morally of little worth, just as generally the way of laughing, and, on the other hand, the occasion of it, are very characteristic of the person. The relations of the sexes afford the readiest material for jokes always to hand and accessible even to the feeblest wit, as is shown by the frequency of obscene jests; this would be impossible if the deepest seriousness did not lie at their very root.

That the laughter of others at what we do or seriously say offends us so easily, is due to its asserting that there is a very great incongruity between our concepts and objective reality. For the same reason, the predicate "ludicrous," "ridiculous," is offensive and insulting. The real scornful laugh shouts triumphantly to the baffled adversary how incongruous were the concepts he cherished with the reality that now reveals itself to him. Our own bitter laughter when the terrible truth by which firmly cherished expectations are shown to be delusive reveals itself to us, is the vivid expression of the discovery now made of the incongruity between the thoughts entertained by us in our foolish confidence in men or in fate, and the reality unveiled.

The *intentionally* ludicrous is the *joke*. This is the effort to bring about a discrepancy between another's concepts and reality by displacing one of the two; whereas its opposite, *seriousness,* consists in the exact suitability of the two to each other which is at any rate striven after. If the joke is concealed behind seriousness, the result is *irony*. For example, when, in apparent seriousness, we assent to the opinions of another which are the opposite of our own, and pretend to share them with him, till at last the result confuses him as regards both us and them. This was the attitude of Socrates to Hippias, Protagoras, Gorgias, and other sophists, and to his collocutors generally. Accordingly, the opposite of irony would be the seriousness concealed behind a joke, and this is *humour*. It might be called the double counterpoint of irony. Explanations such as "Humour is the interpenetration of the finite and the infinite" express nothing but the total incapacity for thinking on the part of those who find satisfaction in such empty phrases. Irony is objective, and so is aimed at another; but *humour* is subjective, and thus exists primarily only for one's own self. Accordingly, we find the masterpieces of irony among the ancients, of humour among the moderns. For, more closely considered, humour depends on a subjective yet serious and sublime mood, involuntarily coming in conflict with a common external world very different from it. It cannot avoid or abandon itself to this world; hence, for a reconciliation, it attempts to think its own view and this external world through the same concepts, which in this way take on a double incongruity, now on one side now on the other, with the real thing thought through them. In this way the impression of the intentionally ludicrous, and thus of the joke, arises, yet behind this the deepest seriousness is concealed and shines through. Irony begins with a serious air and ends with a smile; with humour it is the reverse. The above-quoted expression of Mercutio may be regarded as an example of this. Similarly in *Hamlet* [Act II, Sc. 2]: *Polonius:* "My honourable lord, I will most humbly take my leave of you. *Hamlet:* You cannot, sir, take from me anything that I will more willingly part withal, except my life, except my life, except my life." Again, before the performance of the play at court, Hamlet says to Ophelia [Act III, Sc. 2]: "What should a man do but be merry? For, look you, how cheerfully my mother looks, and my father died within these two hours. *Ophelia:* Nay, 'tis twice two months, my lord. *Hamlet:* So long? Nay, then let the devil wear black, for I'll have a suit of sables." Again, in Jean-Paul's *Titan,* when Schoppe, who has become melancholy and is brooding over himself, frequently looks at his hands and says to himself: "There sits a lord in the flesh, and I in him; but who is such?" Heinrich Heine appears as a real humorist in his *Romancero;* behind all his jokes and farces we discern a deep seriousness that is ashamed to appear unveiled. Accordingly, humour depends on a special kind of mood or frame of mind (the German *Laune* is probably from *Luna*), through which concept, in all its modifications, a decided predominance of the subjective over the objective is thought in the apprehension of the external world. Moreover, every poetical or artistic presentation of a comic, or even a farcical scene, through which a serious thought yet gleams as its concealed background, is a product of humour, and thus is humorous. Such, for example, is a coloured drawing of Tischbein's, depicting an entirely empty room that obtains its illumination only from the fire blazing in the grate. Before the fire stands a man with his coat off, so that the shadow of his person starting from his feet stretches across the whole room. Tischbein commented thus: "This is a man who did not want to succeed in anything in the world, and made nothing of life; now he is glad that he can cast such a large shadow." If I were to express the seriousness concealed behind this jest, I could best do so by the following verse taken from the Persian poem of Anwari Soheili:

> "If you have lost possession of a world,
> Be not distressed, for it is nought;
> And have you gained possession of a world,
> Be not o'erjoyed, for it is nought.
> Our pains, our gains all pass away;
> Get beyond the world, for it is nought."

That at the present day "humorous" is generally used in German literature in the sense of "comic," arises from the miserable mania for giving things a more distinguished name than belongs to them, and hence the name of a class standing above them. Thus every public-house is called a hotel, every money-changer a banker, every trouper's stall a circus, every concert a musical academy, the merchant's counting-house a bureau, the potter an artist in clay,[5] and so also every clown a humorist. The word *humour* is borrowed from the English, in order to single out and denote a quite peculiar species of the ludicrous which, as was shown above, is even akin to the sublime, and was first observed by them. But it is not meant to be used as a title for any jest and buffoonery, as is now done universally in Germany without opposition from men of letters and scholars. For the true concept of that variety, of that mental tendency, of that child of the ludicrous and sublime, would be too subtle and too elevated for their public, to please whom they endeavour to make everything flat and vulgar. Well, "high words and low meaning" is generally the motto of the noble "nowadays."[6] Accordingly, what was formerly called a clown is today called a humorist.

---

[5] The German is *"Tonkünstler"* which also means *"Musician." "Ton"* means both *"tone"* and *"clay."* Perhaps an unconscious pun by Schopenhauer. [Tr.]

[6] Schopenhauer purposely uses the cacophonous word *Jetztzeit.* [Tr.]

CHAPTER IX

On Logic in General [1]

Logic, dialectic, and rhetoric belong together, since they make up the whole of a *technique of reason*. Under this title they should also be taught together, logic as the technique of our own thinking, dialectic as that of disputing with others, and rhetoric as that of speaking to many (*concionatio*); thus corresponding to the singular, dual, and plural, also to the monologue, dialogue, and panegyric.

By *dialectic* I understand, in agreement with Aristotle (*Metaphysics*, iii, 2, and *Analytica Posteriora*, i, 11), the art of conversation directed to the common investigation of truth, especially philosophical truth. But a conversation of this kind necessarily passes, more or less, into controversy; therefore *dialectic* can also be explained as the art of disputation. We have examples and models of dialectic in the Platonic dialogues; but hitherto very little has been done for the real and proper theory of it, that is for the technique of disputation, namely eristic. I have worked out an attempt of the kind, and furnished a specimen of it in volume 2 of the *Parerga and Paralipomena*. I will therefore entirely omit the discussion of this science.

The rhetorical figures are in rhetoric roughly what the syllogistic figures are in logic; in any case they are worth considering. In Aristotle's time they do not appear to have been an object of theoretical investigation, for he does not discuss them in any of his Rhetorics, and in this regard we are referred to Rutilius Lupus, the epitomizer of a later Gorgias.

All three sciences have in common the fact that we follow their rules without having learnt them; indeed these rules themselves are first abstracted from this natural practice. Therefore, in spite of much theoretical interest, they have but little practical use, partly because they give the rule indeed, but not the case of application; partly because in practice there is usually no time to recall the rules. They

---

[1] This chapter, together with the following, refers to § 9 of volume 1.

therefore teach only what everyone already knows and practises of himself; yet the abstract knowledge of this is interesting and important. *Logic* will not readily have any practical use, at any rate for our thinking; for the faults of our reasoning hardly ever lie in the conclusions or otherwise in the form, but in the judgements, and hence in the matter of thinking. On the other hand, in controversy we can occasionally derive some practical use from logic, by reducing to the strict form of regular syllogisms the opponent's argument which is deceptive from distinctly or vaguely conscious intention, and which he advances under the embellishment and cover of continuous speech. We then point out to him logical mistakes, e.g., simple conversion of universally affirmative judgements, syllogisms with four terms, conclusions from the consequent to the ground, syllogisms in the second figure from merely affirmative premisses, and many such cases.

It seems to me that the doctrine of the *laws of thought* could be simplified by our setting up only two of them, namely the law of the excluded middle, and that of sufficient reason or ground. The first law thus: "Any predicate can be either attributed to or denied of every subject." Here already in the "either, or" is the fact that both cannot occur simultaneously, and consequently the very thing expressed by the laws of identity and of contradiction. Therefore these laws would be added as corollaries of that principle, which really states that any two concept-spheres are to be thought as either united or separated, but never as both simultaneously; consequently, that where words are joined together which express the latter, such words state a process of thought that is not feasible. The awareness of this want of feasibility is the feeling of contradiction. The second law of thought, the principle of sufficient reason, would state that the above attribution or denial must be determined by something different from the judgement itself, which may be a (pure or empirical) perception, or merely another judgement. This other and different thing is then called the ground or reason of the judgement. In so far as a judgement satisfies the first law of thought, it is *thinkable;* in so far as it satisfies the second, it is *true,* at any rate logically or formally true, namely when the ground of the judgement is itself in turn only a judgement. But material or absolute truth is ultimately always only the relation between a judgement and a perception, hence between the abstract representation and the representation of perception. This relation is either an immediate one, or is brought about by means of other judgements, in other words through other abstract representations. Accordingly, it is easy to see that one truth can never overthrow another, but all must ultimately be in agreement, since in the perceptible, which is their common foundation, no contradiction is possible. Therefore no truth has anything to fear from other truths. Deception and error, on the contrary, have to fear every truth, because, through the logical concatenation of all truths, even the most remote is bound at some time to transmit its blow to every error. Accordingly this second law of thought is the point of contact between logic and that which is no longer logic, but the material of thinking. Consequently, on the side of the object, *truth,* and on the side of the subject, *knowledge,* consists in the agreement of the concepts, and thus of the abstract representation, with what is given in the representation of perception.

To express the above union or separation of two concept-spheres is the business of the copula, "is—is not." Through this every verb is expressible by means of its participle. Therefore all judging consists in the use of a verb, and *vice versa.* Accordingly, the significance of the copula is that in the subject the predicate is to be thought at the same time—nothing more. Now let us consider what the content of the infinitive of the copula *"to be"* amounts to. This is a principal theme of the professors of philosophy of the present time; yet we must not be too strict with them. Most of them do not want to express by it anything but material things, the corporeal world, to which they, as perfectly innocent realists, at the bottom of their hearts attribute the utmost reality. But to speak of bodies so unceremoniously seems to them too vulgar; they therefore say "being," which sounds more elegant and dignified, and here they picture to themselves the tables and chairs in front of them.

"For, because, why, therefore, thus, as, since, although, indeed, yet, but, if, either-or," and more like these, are really *logical particles,* their sole purpose being to express what is formal in the thought-processes. They are therefore a valuable possession of a language, and do not belong to all languages in equal number. In particular *"zwar"* (the contracted *"es ist wahr"*) seems to belong exclusively to German; it always refers to an *"aber"* that follows or is added in thought, just as *"if"* refers to *"then."*

The logical rule that *judgements, singular* as regards quantity, and hence judgements having as their subject a *singular concept* (*notio singularis*), are to be treated just like *universal judgements,* depends on the fact that they are actually universal judgements, having merely the peculiarity that their subject is a concept which can be supported only by a single real object, and which therefore contains under itself only a single thing; thus when the concept is denoted by a proper name. This is really to be taken into consideration, however, only when we go from the abstract representation to the representation of perception, and thus when we wish to realize the concepts. In thinking itself, in operating with judgements, no difference results from this, just because there is no logical difference between single concepts and universal concepts. "Immanuel Kant" signifies logically *"every* Immanuel Kant." Accordingly, the quantity of judgements is really only twofold, namely universal and particular. An *individual representation* cannot be in any way the subject of a judgement, because it is not an abstraction, is not something thought, but something of perception. Every concept, on the other hand, is essentially universal, and every judgement must have a *concept* as its subject.

The difference between *particular judgements* (*propositiones particulares*) and *universal judgements* often rests only on the external and accidental circumstance that the language has no word to express by itself the part of the universal concept here to be detached, which is the subject of such a judgement. If it had, many a particular judgement would be a universal one. For example, the particular judgement: "Some trees bear gall-nuts" becomes the universal, because for this detached part of the concept "tree" we have a special word: "All oaks bear gall-nuts." The judgement: "Some persons are black" is related in just the same way to the judgement: "All Negroes are black." Or else this difference depends on the fact that, in the mind of the person judging, the concept he makes the subject of the particular judgement has not been clearly detached from the general concept, as a part of which he denotes it; otherwise, instead of the particular judgement, he would be able to express a universal judgement. For example, instead of the judgement: "Some ruminants have upper incisors," this judgement: "All ruminants without horns have upper incisors."

The *hypothetical and disjunctive judgements* are statements about the relation to each other of two (in the case of the disjunctive even several) categorical judgements. The *hypothetical judgement* states that the truth of the second of the two categorical judgements here linked together depends on the truth of the first, and that the falsity of the first depends on the falsity of the second; hence that these two propositions are in direct alliance with regard to truth and falsity. The *disjunctive judgement,* on the other hand, states that on the truth of one of the categorical judgements here linked together depends the falsity of the remainder, and *vice versa;* hence that these propositions are in conflict with regard to truth and falsity. The *question* is a judgement, and of the three parts of this one is left open; thus either the copula: "Is Caius a Roman—or not?" or the predicate: "Is Caius a Roman—or something else?" or the subject:

"Is Caius a Roman—or is someone else a Roman?" The place of the concept left open may also remain quite empty; for example, *"What* is Caius?"—*"Who* is a Roman?"

The ἐπαγωγή, *inductio,* is with Aristotle the opposite of the ἀπαγωγή. The latter proves a proposition to be false by showing that what would follow from it is not true; that is, by the *instantia in contrarium.* The ἐπαγωγή, on the other hand, proves the truth of a proposition by showing that what would follow from it is true. Accordingly, it urges one through examples to an acceptance; the ἀπαγωγή likewise urges one away from an acceptance. Therefore the ἐπαγωγή, or induction, is an inference from the consequents to the ground, and in fact *modo ponente;* for out of many cases it establishes the rule from which these are again the consequents. On this very account it is never perfectly certain, but at most attains a high degree of probability. But this *formal* uncertainty can, through the large number of the enumerated consequents, make room for a *material* certainty, in a similar way as in mathematics irrational relations are brought infinitely near to rationality by means of decimal fractions. The ἀπαγωγή, on the other hand, is primarily the conclusion or inference from the ground to the consequents, yet subsequently it proceeds *modo tollente,* since it proves the non-existence of a necessary consequent, and thereby abolishes the truth of the assumed ground or reason. Precisely on this account it is always perfectly certain, and through a single, certain example *in contrarium,* achieves more than the induction does through innumerable examples in favour of the proposition laid down. It is so very much easier to refute than to prove, to overthrow than to set up.

CHAPTER X

On the Science of Syllogisms

Although it is very difficult to establish a new, correct, and fundamental view of a subject that has been handled by innumerable writers for more than two thousand years, one moreover that does not receive any additions through experience, this will not prevent me from presenting to the thinker for examination the following attempt at such a view.

An inference or conclusion is the operation of our faculty of reason by virtue of which, through the comparison of two judgements, a third judgement arises without the assistance of any knowledge obtained from elsewhere. The condition for this is that two such judgements should have *one* concept in common, for otherwise they are foreign to each other and without any common element. Under this condition, however, they become the father and mother of a child which has in itself something of both. Moreover, the operation aforesaid is no arbitrary act, but an act of the faculty of reason; for when reason has devoted itself to a consideration of such judgements, it performs the act of itself according to its own laws. So far the act is objective, not subjective, and is therefore amenable to the strictest rules.

Incidentally, it may be asked whether the person inferring or concluding really gets to know something new, something previously unknown to him, through the proposition that has just come into existence. Not absolutely, but yet to a certain extent. What he gets to know resided in what he knew; thus he knew it already, but did not know that he knew it. This is like a person having something, but not knowing that he has it; and this is as good as if he did not have it. That is to say, he knew it only *implicite;* now he knows it *explicite*. This difference, however, can be so great that the concluding proposition appears to him as a new truth. For example:

> All diamonds are stones;
> All diamonds are combustible;
> Therefore some stones are combustible.

Consequently, the nature of the inference or conclusion consists in our bringing to distinct consciousness the fact of having thought already in the premises the statement of the conclusion. Accordingly it is a means of becoming more distinctly conscious of our own knowledge, of getting to know more fully, or becoming aware of what we know. The knowledge afforded by the proposition of the conclusion was *latent;* it therefore had as little effect as latent heat has on the thermometer. He who has salt has also chlorine; but it is as if he did not have it, for only when it is chemically disengaged or evolved can it act as chlorine; hence only then does he actually possess it. It is just the same as regards the gain afforded by a mere conclusion from premises already known; a previously *bound* or *latent* knowledge thereby becomes *free.* It is true that these comparisons might appear somewhat overdrawn, but they are not really so. For since we draw very soon, very rapidly, and without formality many of the conclusions possible from our knowledge, so that no distinct recollection of them remains, it seems that no premises to possible conclusions long remained stored up unused, but that we had the conclusions already prepared for all the premises that lie within the sphere of our knowledge. But this is not always the case; on the contrary, two premises can have an isolated existence for a long time in a man's head, till at last an occasion brings them together. Then the conclusion suddenly springs forth, just as the spark appears from steel and stone only when they are struck together. Actually, the premises received from outside for theoretical insight as well as for motives that bring about resolves, often reside within us for a long time. Partly through half-conscious, and even inarticulate, acts of thinking they are compared with our remaining store of knowledge, ruminated on, and as it were shaken up together, till finally the right major comes across the right minor. These at once take up their proper places, and then, at one stroke the conclusion stands out like a light that has suddenly dawned on us, without any action on our part, as if it were an inspiration. Then we do not understand how we and others were so long in ignorance of it. Of course, in the happily organized mind this process will occur more rapidly and easily than in the ordinary mind; and just because it is carried out spontaneously, indeed without distinct consciousness, it cannot be acquired by study. Therefore Goethe says:

> "How easy anything is, he knows
> Who has thought it out and arrived at it." [1]

---

[1] *Westöstlicher Divan,* VI, 4. [Tr.]

We can look upon the thought-process here described as like those padlocks which consist of rings and letters. Hanging on the box of a travelling-coach, they are shaken for so long, until at last the letters of the word come together in the right order, and the lock opens. For the rest, it must be borne in mind that the syllogism consists in the line of thought itself. The words and propositions by which it is expressed indicate merely the trace of it left behind; they are related to it as the acoustic figures of sand are to the sounds whose vibrations they represent. When we wish to think over something, we bring our data together, and reduce them to actual judgements; these are all quickly brought together and compared, and in this way the conclusions possible from them are instantly separated out by the use of all three syllogistic figures. Yet on account of the great rapidity of these operations, only a few words, and sometimes none at all, are used, and only the conclusion is formally expressed. Thus it sometimes happens that, since in this manner, or even in the merely intuitive way, i.e., through a happy *aperçu,* we have brought some new truth to consciousness, we now look for the premisses to it as the conclusion, in other words, we should like to establish a proof for it; for, as a rule, knowledge exists earlier than its proofs. We then ransack our store of knowledge, in order to see whether we cannot find in it some truth in which the newly discovered truth was already implicitly contained, or two propositions, the regular joining together of which gives this truth as a result. On the other hand, every judicial proceeding furnishes the most formal and imposing syllogism, in fact in the first figure. The civil or criminal transgression complained of is the minor; it is established by the prosecutor. The law for such a case is the major, and the judgement is the conclusion which, as something necessary, is merely "pronounced" by the judge.

However, I will now attempt to give the simplest and most correct description of the real mechanism of inference.

Judging, that elementary and most important process of thinking, consists in comparing two *concepts; inference* consists in comparing two *judgements.* In text-books, however, inference is usually referred also to a comparison of *concepts,* although of *three,* since from the relation two of these concepts have to the third, the relation they have to one another would be known. Truth cannot be denied to this view, and since this gives rise to the perceptible demonstration of syllogistic relations by means of drawn concept-spheres, a method I have also commended in the text, it has the advantage of making the matter easy to understand. But it seems to me that here, as in so many cases, comprehensibility is attained at the expense of thoroughness. The real thought-process in inference, with which the three syllogistic figures and their necessity are strictly connected, is not recognized in this way. When inferring, we operate *not* with mere *concepts,* but with whole *judgements,* to which quality, lying only in the copula and not in the concepts, and also quantity are absolutely essential; and to these modality also is added. This description of the syllogism as a relation of *three concepts* is wrong in that it resolves judgements at once into their ultimate elements (the concepts). In this way the means of binding these together is lost, and that which is peculiar to the judgements *as such* and in their completeness, and which entails just that necessity of the conclusion that results from them, is lost sight of. It thus falls into an error analogous to that which organic chemistry would commit if, for example in the analysis of plants, it resolved these at once into their *ultimate* elements. It would then obtain in all plants carbon, hydrogen, and oxygen, but would lose the specific differences. To obtain these, we must stop at the *more particular* constituents, the so-called alkaloids, and must guard against analysing those alkaloids in their turn. From three given *concepts* no conclusion can as yet be drawn; for, of course, we say that the relation of two of them to the third must be given with them. But it is just the *judgements* combining those concepts that are the expression of this relation; and so *judgements,* not mere *concepts,* are the material of the syllogism. Accordingly, inferring or concluding is essentially a comparing of two *judgements.* The thought-process in our heads takes place with these judgements, with the ideas expressed by them, and not merely with three concepts, even when the process is expressed imperfectly, or not at all in words. We must take the process into consideration as such, as a bringing together of the complete, unanalysed judgements, in order properly to understand the technical procedure when inferring. From this, then, will also result the necessity of three really rational, syllogistic figures.

Just as, in the description of syllogistic science by means of *concept-spheres,* we present these to the mind in the form of circles, so, in the description by means of whole *judgements,* we have to picture these in the form of rods. For the purpose of comparison, these rods are held together now by one end, now by the other; and the different ways in which this can be done give the three figures. Now as every premiss contains its subject and its predicate, these two concepts are to be imagined as situated at the two ends of each rod. The two judgements are then compared with regard to the two *different* concepts in them; for, as already mentioned, the third concept must be the same in both. It is therefore not liable to any comparison, but is that *by which,* in other words, with reference to which, the other two are compared: it is the *middle term.* Accordingly, this is always only the means and not the main thing. On the other hand, the two dissimilar concepts are the object of reflection, and the purpose of the syllogism is to bring out their relation to each other by means of the judgements in which they are contained. Therefore the conclusion speaks only of them, not of the middle term, which was a mere means, a measuring rod that we let go as soon as we have used it. Now if this concept, *identical* in the two propositions, and thus the middle term, is the subject in *one* premiss, then the concept to be compared must be its predicate, and conversely. Here at once is established *a priori* the possibility of three cases: either the subject of *one* premiss is compared with the predicate of the *other,* or the subject of one with the subject of the other, or, finally, the predicate of one with the predicate of the other. From these arise the three syllogistic figures of Aristotle; the fourth, which was added somewhat obtrusively, is ungenuine and a spurious form. It is attributed to Galen; but this rests only on Arabian authorities. Each of the three figures in inferring or concluding exhibits an entirely different, correct, and natural thought-process of our faculty of reason.

Thus, if in the two judgements to be compared the relation between the *predicate of the one and the subject of the other* is the purpose of the comparison, the result is *the first figure.* This figure alone has the advantage that the concepts, which in the conclusion are subject and predicate, both appear already in the premisses in the same capacity, whereas in the other two figures one of them must always change its role in the conclusion. But in this way the result in the first figure always has less novelty and surprise than in the other two. That advantage of the first figure is obtained only by the predicate of the major being compared with the subject of the minor, not conversely; and so this is essential here, and involves that the middle term occupies the two positions of different names, in other words, is subject in the major and predicate in the minor. From this again follows its subordinate significance, since it figures as a mere weight that we lay arbitrarily now in one scale, now in the other. With this figure the course of thought is that the predicate of the major belongs to the subject of the minor, because the subject of the major is the minor's own predicate, or in the negative case the converse for the same reason. Here, therefore, a property is attributed to the things thought through a concept, because it belongs to another property that we already know in them; or conversely. Therefore, the guiding principle here is: *nota notae est nota rei ipsius, et repugnans notae repugnat rei ispi.*[2]

On the other hand, if we compare two judgements with the intention of bringing out the relation which the *subjects of both* may have to each other, we must take their predicate as the common measure. Accordingly, that will here be the middle term, and con sequently must be the same in the two judgements. The result of this is the *second figure.* Here the relation of the two *subjects* to each other is determined by that which they have to one and the same predicate. This relation, however, can become of significance only by the same predicate being attributed to *one* subject and denied to the other, as in this way it becomes an essential ground of distinction between the two. For if it were attributed to both subjects, this could not decide anything as to their relation to each other, since almost every predicate pertains to innumerable subjects. Still less would it decide, if the predicate were denied to both subjects. From this follows the fundamental characteristic of the second figure, namely that the two premisses must have *opposite quality;* one must affirm and the other deny. Here, then, the principal rule is: *sit altera negans,*[3] the corollary of which is: *e meris affirmativis nihil sequitur,*[4] a rule that is sometimes transgressed in a loose argument covered up by many inserted clauses. The course of thought exhibited by this figure appears distinctly from what has been said. It is the investigation of two kinds of things with the intention of distinguishing them, and hence of establishing that they are *not* of the same species. This is here decided by the fact that to one species a property is essential which the other species lacks. That this course of thought assumes the second figure entirely of its own accord, and is strongly marked only in this figure, may be shown by an example:

> All fishes have cold blood;
> No whale has cold blood:
> Therefore no whale is a fish.

On the other hand, in the first figure this thought is exhibited as something flat, feeble, forced, and ultimately patched up:

> Nothing that has cold blood is a whale;
> All fishes have cold blood:

---

[2] "A property belonging to the predicate belongs also to the subject of the predicate, and a property not belonging to the predicate also does not belong to the subject of the predicate." [Tr.]

[3] "The one premiss must be negative." [Tr.]

[4] "From two affirmative premisses nothing follows" (in the second syllogistic figure dependent on this rule). [Tr.]

> Therefore no fish is a whale,
> And consequently no whale is a fish.

Also an example with an affirmative minor:

> No Mohammedan is a Jew;
> Some Turks are Jews:
> Therefore some Turks are not Mohammedans.

As the guiding principle for this figure I therefore lay down: for the moods with negative minor: *cui repugnat nota, etiam repugnat notatum;*[5] and for the moods with affirmative minor: *notato repugnat id cui nota repugnat.*[6] Translated, these can be summarized thus: Two subjects standing in opposite relationship to a predicate have a negative relation to each other.

The third case is where we place two judgements together, in order to investigate the relation of their *predicates;* hence arises the *third figure.* Accordingly, in this figure the middle term appears in both premisses as subject. Here also it is the *tertium comparationis,*[7] the measure applied to the two concepts to be investigated, or, so to speak, a chemical reagent, by which we test both, in order to learn from their relation to it the relation that exists between themselves. Consequently the conclusion then states whether a relation of subject and predicate exists between the two, and how far this goes. Accordingly, what is exhibited in this figure is reflection on two *properties* which we are inclined to regard either as *incompatible,* or else as *inseparable,* and in order to decide this we attempt to make them the predicates of one and the same subject in two judgements. Now the result of this is either that both properties belong to one and the same thing, consequently their *compatibility;* or else that a thing has one property but not the other, consequently their *separableness.* The former in all moods with two affirmative premisses, the latter in all moods with a negative premiss: e.g.,

> Some animals can speak;
> All animals are irrational:
> Therefore some irrational beings can speak.

According to Kant (*Die falsche Spitzfindigkeit,* § 4) this syllogism would be conclusive only if we added in thought: "Therefore some irrational beings are animals." But this seems to be quite superfluous

---

[5] "The subject that is contradicted by a predicate, is also contradicted by the subject of this predicate." [Tr.]

[6] "The subject of a predicate is contradicted by every subject that that predicate contradicts." [Tr.]

[7] "What is common to two objects compared." [Tr.]

here, and by no means the natural process of thought. However, in order to carry out the same process of thought directly by means of the first figure, I should have to say:

> "All animals are irrational;
> Some beings able to speak are animals,"

which is obviously not the natural course of thought. In fact, the conclusion that then results, namely "Some beings able to speak are irrational," would have to be converted, in order to preserve the conclusion which the third figure gives of itself, and at which the whole course of thought has aimed. Let us take another example:

> All alkaline metals float in water;
> All alkaline metals are metals:
> Therefore some metals float in water.

With transposition into the first figure, the minor must be converted, and therefore runs: "Some metals are alkaline metals": consequently, it asserts merely that some metals lie in the sphere "alkaline metals," thus:

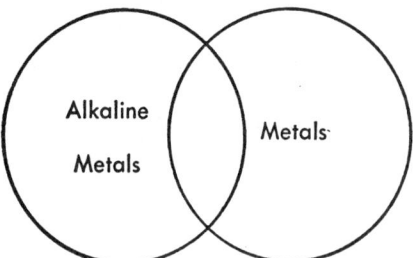

whereas our actual knowledge is that *all* alkaline metals lie in the sphere "metals," thus:

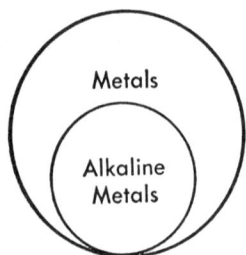

Consequently, if the first figure is to be the only normal one, in order to think naturally we should have to think less than we know, and to think indefinitely what we know definitely. This assumption has too much against it. Therefore in general it is undeniable that, when inferring or concluding in the second and third figures, we tacitly convert a proposition. On the other hand, the third figure, and the second also, exhibit just as rational a process of thought as does the first. Let us now consider another example of the other kind of the third figure, where the separableness of the two predicates is the result, on account of which one premiss must here be negative:

> No Buddhist believes in a God;
> Some Buddhists are rational:
> Therefore some rational beings do not believe in a God.

As in the above examples the *compatibility* of the two properties is the problem of reflection, so now their *separableness* is its problem; and here also this problem is decided by our comparing them with *one* subject and demonstrating in this subject *one* property without the *other*. In this way we attain our end directly, whereas through the first figure we could do so only indirectly. For in order to reduce the syllogism to the first figure, we should have to convert the minor, and therefore say: "Some rational beings are Buddhists," which would be only a faulty expression of its meaning, which is: "Some Buddhists are yet certainly rational."

Accordingly I lay down as the guiding principle of this figure: for the affirmative moods: *ejusdem rei notae, modo sit altera universalis, sibi invicem sunt notae particulares;* and for the negative moods: *nota rei competens, notae eidem repugnanti, particulariter repugnat, modo sit altera universalis.* In plain English: If two predicates are affirmed of one subject, and at least one universally, then they are also affirmed of each other particularly; on the other hand, they are particularly denied of each other as soon as one of them contradicts the subject of which the other is affirmed; only the contradiction or affirmation must be made universally.

In the *fourth figure* the subject of the major is now to be compared with the predicate of the minor; but in the conclusion both must again exchange their value and position, so that what was subject in the major appears as predicate in the conclusion, and what was predicate in the minor appears as subject in the conclusion. From this it is clear that this figure is merely the *first* wilfully turned upside down, and by no means the expression of an actual process of thought natural to our faculty of reason.

On the other hand, the first three figures are the ectype of three actual and essentially different operations of thought. These have in common the fact that they consist in the comparison of two judgements; but such a comparison becomes fruitful only when they have *one* concept in common. If we picture the premises to ourselves in the form of two rods, we can think of this concept as a tie uniting them with each other; in fact, we might make use of such rods in lecturing. On the other hand, the three figures are distinguished by the fact that those judgements are compared either with regard to their two subjects, or to their two predicates, or lastly with regard to the subject of one and to the predicate of the other. Now as every concept has the property of being subject or predicate only in so far as it is already part of a judgement, this confirms my view that in the syllogism primarily only judgements are compared, and concepts only in so far as they are parts of judgements. But in the comparison of two judgements the essential question is *in respect of what* they are compared, not *by what means* they are compared. The former is the dissimilar concepts of the judgements, the latter is the middle term, in other words, the concept identical in both. It is therefore not the right point of view which Lambert, and indeed really Aristotle and almost all the moderns have taken, to start from the *middle term* in the analysis of syllogisms, and to make it the principal thing and its position the essential characteristic of syllogisms. On the contrary, its role is only a secondary one, and its position a consequence of the logical value of the concepts really to be compared in the syllogism. These are comparable to two substances that are chemically tested, the middle term being comparable to the reagent in which they are tested. Therefore it always takes the place left vacant by the concepts to be compared, and no longer occurs in the conclusion. It is chosen according as its relation to both concepts is known, and it is suitable for the place to be occupied. Therefore in many cases we can exchange it arbitrarily for another without affecting the syllogism. For example, in the syllogism:

> All men are mortal;
> Caius is a man:

I can exchange the middle term "man" for "animal being." In the syllogism:

> All diamonds are stones;
> All diamonds are combustible:

I can exchange the middle term "diamond" for "anthracite." As an external characteristic, by which the figure of a syllogism is at once recognized, the middle term is certainly very useful. But for the fundamental characteristic of a thing to be explained, we must take what is essential to the thing. But what is essential here is whether we place two propositions together, in order to compare their predicates, or their subjects, or the predicate of the one and the subject of the other.

Therefore, in order as premisses to produce a conclusion, two judgements must have a concept in common; further, they must not be both negative or both particular; finally, in the case where the two concepts to be compared in them are their subjects, they cannot be both affirmative.

The voltaic pile can be regarded as a sensible image of the syllogism. Its point of indifference at the centre represents the middle term holding together the two premisses. By virtue of the middle term they have the power of forming a conclusion. On the other hand, the two dissimilar concepts, which are really what we have to compare, are represented by the two opposite poles of the pile. Only on these being brought together by means of their two conducting wires which represent the copulas of the two judgements does the spark leap forth on their contact—the new light of the conclusion.

CHAPTER XI[1]

On Rhetoric

Eloquence is the faculty of stirring up in others our view of a thing, or our opinion regarding it, of kindling in them our feeling about it, and thus of putting them in sympathy with us; and all this by our conducting the stream of our ideas into their heads by means of words, with such force that this stream diverts that of their own thoughts from the course already taken, and carries this away with it along its own course. The more the course of their ideas differed previously from ours, the greater will be this masterly achievement. It is easy to understand from this why a man's own conviction and passion make him eloquent, and generally why eloquence is rather the gift of nature than the work of art. Yet even here art will support nature.

In order to convince another of a truth that conflicts with an error he holds firmly, the first rule to be observed is an easy and natural one, namely: *Let the premises come first, and the conclusion follow*. This rule, however, is seldom observed, and people go to work the reverse way, since zeal, hastiness, and dogmatic positiveness urge us to shout out the conclusion loudly and noisily at the person who adheres to the opposite error. This easily makes him shy and reserved, and he then sets his will against all arguments and premisses, knowing already to what conclusion they will lead. Therefore we should rather keep the conclusion wholly concealed and give only the premises distinctly, completely, and from every point of view. If possible, we should not even express the conclusion at all. It will appear of its own accord necessarily and legitimately in the reason (*Vernunft*) of the hearers, and the conviction thus born within them will be all the more sincere; in addition, it will be accompanied by self-esteem instead of by a feeling of shame. In difficult cases, we can even assume the air of wanting to arrive at quite the opposite conclusion to the one we

---

[1] This chapter is connected with the conclusion of § 9 of volume 1.

really have in view. An example of this kind is Antony's famous speech in Shakespeare's *Julius Caesar*.

In defending a thing, many people make the mistake of confidently advancing everything imaginable that can be said in its favour, and of mixing up what is true, half true, and merely plausible. But the false is soon recognized, or at any rate felt, and then casts suspicion even on the cogent and true that is advanced along with it. Therefore let us give the cogent and true pure and alone, and guard against defending a truth with grounds and arguments that are inadequate, and are thus sophistical, in so far as they are set up as adequate. For the opponent upsets these, and thus gains the appearance of having upset also the truth itself that is supported by them; in other words he brings forward *argumenta ad hominem* as *argumenta ad rem*. Perhaps the Chinese go too far in the other direction, since they have the following maxim: "The man who is eloquent and has a sharp tongue can always leave half a sentence unspoken; and he who has right on his side can confidently yield three-tenths of his assertion."

CHAPTER XII[1]

On the Doctrine of Science

From the analysis of the various functions of our intellect, which is given in all the preceding chapters, it is clear that, for its correct and methodical use, whether for a theoretical or a practical purpose, the following are necessary: (1) the correct apprehension through perception of the real things taken into consideration, and of all their essential properties and relations, hence of all the *data.* (2) The formation from these of correct *concepts,* thus the *summarizing* of those properties under correct abstractions that then become the material of the subsequent thinking. (3) The comparison of these concepts partly with what is perceived, partly with one another, partly with the remaining store of concepts, so that correct *judgements,* appropriate to the matter, and fully comprehending and exhausting it, result from them; thus a correct *examination* or *analysis* of the matter. (4) The placing together or *combination* of these judgements for the premises of *syllogisms.* This can turn out very differently according to the choice and arrangement of the judgements, and yet the real *result* of the whole operation is primarily dependent on it. Here the principal thing is that, from so many possible combinations of these different judgements appertaining to the matter, free deliberation should hit on precisely those that serve the purpose and are decisive. But if in the first function, and thus in the apprehension through perception of things and relations, any essential point has been overlooked, then the correctness of all the subsequent operations of the mind cannot prevent the result from proving false; for there lie the *data,* the material of the whole investigation. Without the certainty that these taken together are correct and complete, we should refrain from making any definite decision in important matters.

A concept is *correct;* a judgement is *true;* a body is *real;* a relation is *evident.* A proposition of immediate certainty is an *axiom.*

---

[1] This chapter is connected with § 14 of volume 1.

Only the fundamental principles of logic and those of mathematics drawn *a priori* from intuition or perception, and finally the law of causality, have immediate certainty. A proposition of indirect certainty is a *precept* or *theorem,* and what brings about this certainty is the proof. If immediate certainty is attributed to a proposition that has no such certainty, then it is a *petitio principii.*[2] A proposition that refers directly to empirical perception is an *assertion;* confronting it with such perception demands power of judgement. Primarily, empirical perception can establish only *particular,* not universal, truths. Through manifold repetition and confirmation, such truths obtain universality as well, yet this is only comparative and precarious, because it is still always open to attack. But if a proposition has absolute, universal validity, the perception or intuition to which it refers is not empirical, but *a priori.* Accordingly, only logic and mathematics are perfectly certain sciences; but they really teach us only what we already knew beforehand. For they are mere elucidations of that of which we are *a priori* conscious, namely the forms of our own knowledge, the one being the science of the form of thinking, the other that of the form of perceiving. We therefore spin them entirely out of ourselves. All other rational knowledge is empirical.

A proof proves *too much,* if it extends to things or cases to which what is to be proved obviously does not apply; hence it is apagogically refuted by these. The *deductio ad absurdum* really consists in our taking the false assertion set up as the major, adding a correct minor, and obtaining a conclusion that contradicts facts known from experience or indubitable truths. But by a roundabout way such a conclusion is possible for every false doctrine, in so far as the advocate of this does acknowledge and admit some truth. Then the inferences from this, and again those from the false assertion, must be capable of extension so far that we arrive at two propositions directly contradicting each other. In Plato we find many examples of this beautiful artifice of genuine dialectic.

A *correct hypothesis* is nothing more than the true and complete expression of the fact before us which the originator of the hypothesis has intuitively apprehended in its real nature and inner connexion. For it tells us only what really takes place here.

The contrast of the *analytical* and *synthetical methods* is found already indicated in Aristotle, yet it is perhaps first clearly described by Proclus, who says quite correctly: Μέθοδοι δὲ παραδίδονται· καλλίστη μὲν ἡ διὰ τῆς ἀναλύσεως ἐπ' ἀρχὴν ὁμολογουμένην ἀνάγουσα τὸ ζητούμενον· ἣν καὶ Πλάτων, ὥς φασι, Λαοδάμαντι παρέδωκεν κ.τ.λ. *(Methodi traduntur sequentes: pulcherrima quidem ea, quae per*

---

[2] "Begging of the question." [Tr.]

analysin quaesitum refert ad principium, de quo jam convenit; quam etiam Plato Laodamanti tradidisse dicitur.) *In primum Euclidis librum,* Bk. iii.[3] Certainly the analytical method consists in referring the given thing to an acknowledged principle; the synthetic method, on the contrary, consists in deduction from such a principle. Therefore they are analogous to the ἐπαγωγή and ἀπαγωγή discussed in chapter IX; only that the latter is aimed not at establishing propositions, but always at overthrowing them. The analytical method goes from the facts, the particular, to the propositions, the universal, or from consequents to grounds; the other method proceeds in the reverse direction. Therefore it would be much more correct to name them the *inductive and deductive methods,* for the traditional names are unsuitable and express the matter badly.

If a philosopher tried to begin by thinking out for himself the *method* by which he wished to philosophize, he would be like a poet who first wrote for himself a system of aesthetics, in order afterwards to write poetry in accordance with it. Both would be like a person who first sang a song to himself, and afterwards danced to it. The thinking mind must find its way from original inclination. Rule and application, method and achievement, must appear inseparable, like matter and form. But after we have reached the goal, we may consider the path we have followed. By their nature, aesthetics and methodology are younger than poetry and philosophy, just as grammar is younger than language, thorough-bass younger than music, logic younger than thought.

Room may be found here for an incidental remark by which I should like to put a stop to a growing evil while there is still time. That Latin has ceased to be the language of all scientific investigation has the disadvantage that there is no longer an immediately common scientific literature for the whole of Europe, but only national literatures. In this way every scholar is primarily limited to a much smaller public, and moreover to a public steeped in national narrow views and prejudices. Then he must now learn the four principal European languages together with the two ancient languages. It will be a great relief for him that the *termini technici* of all sciences (with the exception of mineralogy) are Latin or Greek, as an inheritance from our predecessors; and so all nations wisely retain these. Only the Germans have hit upon the unfortunate idea of wanting to Germanize the *termini technici* of all the sciences. This has two great disadvantages. In the first place the foreign as well as

---

[3] "The following are handed down as methods; that method is the best which refers in an analytical way to an acknowledged principle that which it is desired to prove. It is said that Plato handed this down to Laodamas." [Tr.]

the German scholar is obliged to learn all the technical expressions of his science twice over, and, where there are many, as for example in anatomy, this is an incredibly wearisome and complicated business. If other nations were not more sensible than the Germans in this respect, we should have the trouble of learning every *terminus technicus* five times. If the Germans continue with this, foreign scholars will leave their books entirely unread; for, in addition, they are usually much too lengthy, and are written in a careless, bad, often even affected, tasteless, and inelegant style, and are frequently drawn up with an ill-mannered disregard of the reader and his requirements. In the second place, those Germanizations of the *termini technici* are almost always long, patched up, awkwardly chosen, cumbersome, hollow-sounding words that are not sharply separated from the rest of the language. Therefore such words are with difficulty impressed on the memory, whereas the Greek and Latin expressions chosen by the ancient and memorable originators of the sciences have all the opposite good qualities, and are easily impressed on the memory by their sonorous sound. For instance, how ugly and cacophonous a word is *"Stickstoff"* [nitrogen] instead of *Azot!* "Verb," "substantive," "adjective" are retained and distinguished more easily than *"Zeitwort," "Nennwort," "Beiwort,"* or even *"Umstandswort"* instead of "adverb." In anatomy it is quite intolerable; moreover, it is vulgar and savours of barber's assistants. Even *"Pulsader"* and *"Blutader"* are more readily exposed to momentary confusion than are "artery" and "vein"; but expressions like *"Fruchthälter," "Fruchtgang,"* and *"Fruchtleiter"* instead of *"uterus," "vagina,"* and *"tuba Faloppii,"* which every doctor must know, and with which he can manage in all European languages, are utterly bewildering. The same with *"Speiche"* and *"Ellenbogenröhre"* instead of *"radius"* and *"ulna,"* which the whole of Europe has understood for thousands of years. Why all this clumsy, confusing, wearisome, and silly Germanizing? No less objectionable is the translation of the technical terms in logic, where our gifted professors of philosophy are the creators of a new terminology, and almost everyone has his own. For example, with G. E. Schulze the subject is called *"Grundbegriff,"* the predicate *"Beilegungsbegriff";* then there are *"Beilegungsschlüsse," "Voraussetzungsschlüsse,"* and *"Entgegungsschlüsse";* judgements have *"Grösse," "Beschaffenheit," "Verhältnis,"* and *"Zuverlässigkeit,"* in other words, quantity, quality, relation, and modality. The same perverse influence of this Teutomania is found in all the sciences. The Latin and Greek expressions have the further advantage that they stamp the scientific concept as such, and separate it from the words of common intercourse, and the associations of ideas that cling thereto.

On the other hand, *"Speisebrei"* instead of *"chyme,"* for example, seems to speak of the food of little children, and *"Lungensack"* instead of *"pleura,"* and *"Herzbeutel"* instead of *"pericardium"* seem to have originated with butchers rather than anatomists. Finally, the most immediate necessity for learning the ancient languages is connected with the old *termini technici;* and by the use of living languages for learned investigation, the study of the ancient languages is more and more in danger of being set aside. But if it comes to this, if the spirit of the ancients tied to their languages disappears from a literary and scientific education, then coarseness, insipidity, and vulgarity will take possession of all literature. For the works of the ancients are the pole star for every artistic or literary effort; if it sets, you are lost. Even now in the pitiable and puerile style of most writers, we notice that they have never written Latin.* Devotion to the authors of antiquity is very appropriately called the *study of humanity,* for through it the student above all becomes a *human being* again, since he enters into the world that was still free from all the buffoonery and absurdities of the Middle Ages and of romanticism. Afterwards, mankind in Europe was so deeply infected with these that even now everyone comes into the world covered with them, and has first to strip them off, merely in order to become a *human being* again. Think not that your modern wisdom can ever take the place of that initiation into being a *human being;* you are not, like the Greeks and Romans, born free, unprejudiced sons of nature. In the first place, you are the sons and heirs of the crude Middle Ages and of their folly and nonsense, of infamous priestcraft, and of half brutal, half idiotic chivalry. Although both are now gradually coming to an end, you are still unable, for that reason, to stand on your own feet. Without the school of the ancients, your literature will degenerate into vulgar gossip and flat philistinism. Therefore, for all these reasons, it is my well-meant advice that we put an end without delay to the Germanizing mania censured above.

Further, I wish to take this opportunity of censuring the mischief that has been done in an unheard-of manner for some years with German orthography. Scribblers of every description have heard

---

* A principal advantage of the *study of the ancients* is that it guards us from *verbosity,* since they always take the trouble to write concisely and pregnantly, and the mistake of almost all the moderns is verbosity. The most recent of all try to make amends for this by suppressing syllables and letters. We should therefore continue to study the ancients all through our life, though limiting the time spent on this study. The ancients knew that we ought not to write as we speak. The moderns, on the other hand, even have the effrontery to print the lectures they have given.

something about brevity of expression; yet they do not know that this consists in the careful omission of everything superfluous, to which of course the whole of their scribblings belong. But they imagine they can obtain it by force by clipping words as swindlers clip coins. Every syllable that appears superfluous to them, because they do not feel its value, they nip off without more ado. For example, our ancestors said with true delicacy of feeling *"Beweis"* and *"Verweis,"* and on the other hand, *"Nachweisung."* The fine distinction, analogous to that between *"Versuch"* and *"Versuchung,"* *"Betracht"* and *"Betrachtung,"* cannot be felt by thick ears and thick skulls. They therefore invented the word *"Nachweis,"* which at once came into general use; for this only requires that an idea or notion be really crude and coarse, and an error really gross. Accordingly, the same amputation has already been made in innumerable words; for example, instead of *"Untersuchung"* people write *"Untersuch";* instead of *"allmälig,"* *"mälig";* *"nahe"* instead of *"beinahe,"* *"ständig"* instead of *"beständig."* If a Frenchman ventured to write *"près"* instead of *"presque,"* and an Englishman *"most"* instead of *"almost,"* everyone would laugh at them as fools; in Germany, however, anyone who does anything of this sort is considered to have an original mind. Chemists are already writing *"löslich"* and *"unlöslich"* instead of *"unauflöslich";* and, if the grammarians do not rap them over the knuckles, they will rob the language of a valuable word. Knots, shoe-laces, conglomerates whose cement is softened, and everything analogous to this, are *löslich* (capable of being loosened); on the other hand, whatever vanishes entirely in a liquid, like salt in water, is *auflöslich* (soluble). *"Auflösen"* (to dissolve) is the *terminus ad hoc* which states this and nothing else, separating out a definite concept. But our clever language-improvers want to pour it into the general rinsing-tub of *"lösen"* (to loosen). Then, to be consistent, they would have to use *"lösen"* also instead of *"ablösen"* (to relieve, used of guards), *"auslösen"* (to release)*,* *"einlösen"* (to redeem), and so on, and in this, as in the previous case, deprive the language of definiteness of expression. But to make the language poorer by a word is the same as making a nation's thinking poorer by a concept. This, however, has been the tendency of the united efforts of almost all our scribblers and compilers for the last ten to twenty years. For what I have here shown by *one* example could be demonstrated in a hundred others, and the meanest stinting of syllables rages like a pestilence. The wretches actually count the letters, and do not hesitate to mutilate a word, or to use one in a false sense, whenever only a couple of letters are to be gained by doing so. He who is incapable of any new ideas will at least come forward with new words, and every quill-driver regards it as his vocation to improve the language. Journalists practise this most shamelessly, and as their papers have the greatest public of all by virtue of the trivial nature of their contents, and that a public that for the most part reads nothing else, a great danger threatens the language through them. Therefore I earnestly recommend that they be subjected to an orthographical censorship, or be made to pay a fine for every unusual or mutilated word; for what could be more unworthy than that changes in language should come from the lowest branch of literature? Language, especially a relatively original language like German, is a nation's most precious heritage; it is also an exceedingly complicated work of art that is easily damaged and cannot be restored again, hence a *noli me tangere*.[4] Other nations have felt this, and have shown great reverence for their languages, though these are far less perfect than German. Thus the language of Dante and Petrarch differs only in trifles from that of today; Montaigne is still quite readable, and so also is Shakespeare in his oldest editions. For a German it is even good to have somewhat lengthy words in his mouth, for he thinks slowly, and they give him time to reflect. But that prevailing economy of language still shows itself in several characteristic phenomena. For example, contrary to all logic and grammar, they put the imperfect instead of the perfect and pluperfect; they often put the auxiliary verb in their pocket; they use the ablative instead of the genitive. To gain a pair of logical particles, they make such involved and complicated periods that we have to read them four times in order to get at the meaning; for they want to save only the paper, not the reader's time. With proper names, just like Hottentots, they do not indicate the case either by inflexion or by the article; the reader may guess it. But they are particularly fond of swindling with the double vowel and with the sound-lengthening *h,* those letters dedicated to prosody. This proceeding is precisely the same as if we were to exclude η and ω from Greek and put ε and o in their place. He who writes *Scham, Märchen, Mass, Spass,* ought also to write *Lon, Son, Stat, Sat, Jar, Al,* and so on. As writing is the copy of speech, posterity will imagine that one has to pronounce and articulate as one writes, and so of the German language there will remain only a clipped and hollow noise of consonants from a pointed snout, and all prosody will be lost. For the sake of saving a letter, the spelling *"Literatur"* instead of the correct *"Litteratur"* is very popular. In defence of this, the particle of the verb *linere* is given out as the origin of the word; but *linere*

---

4 "Touch me not." [Tr.]

means *to smear, to scribble.* Thus the favourite spelling might actually be the correct one for the greater part of German hack writing, so that we could distinguish a very small *"Litteratur"* from a very extensive *"Literatur."* To write briefly, let us improve and refine our style, and avoid all useless gossip and chatter; then we need not swindle with syllables and letters because of the cost of paper. But to write so many useless pages, useless sheets, useless books, and then seek to make up for this waste of time and paper at the expense of innocent syllables and letters—this is truly the superlative of what is called in English being penny wise and pound foolish. It is to be regretted that there exists no German academy to protect the language against literary sansculottism, especially in an age when even those who are ignorant of the ancient languages can dare to employ the press. In my *Parerga and Paralipomena,* Vol. II, chap. 23, I have expressed my opinion at greater length on the unpardonable mischief that is being done at the present day to the German language.

In my essay *On the Principle of Sufficient Reason,* § 51, I already proposed the highest *classification of the sciences* according to the form of the principle of sufficient reason prevailing in them, and touched on it again in §§ 7 and 15 of the first volume of this work. Here I will give a brief attempt; it will, of course, undoubtedly be capable of much improvement and completion.

I. Pure Sciences *a priori.*

1. The doctrine of the ground of being.
   (a) in space: Geometry.
   (b) in time: Arithmetic and Algebra.
2. The doctrine of the ground of knowing: Logic.

II. Empirical or Sciences *a posteriori.*

All according to the ground or reason of becoming, i.e., to the law of causality, and indeed to its three modes.
1. The doctrine of causes:
   (a) Universal: Mechanics, Hydrodynamics, Physics, Chemistry.
   (b) Particular: Astronomy, Mineralogy, Geology, Technology, Pharmacy.
2. The doctrine of stimuli:
   (a) Universal: Physiology of plants and animals, together with its subsidiary science, Anatomy.
   (b) Particular: Botany, Zoology, Zootomy, Comparative Physiology, Pathology, Therapeutics.

3. The doctrine of motives:
   (a) Universal: Ethics, Psychology.
   (b) Particular: Jurisprudence, History.

Philosophy or metaphysics, as the doctrine of consciousness and its contents in general, or of the whole of experience as such, does not come into the list, because it does not straightway pursue the consideration required by the principle of sufficient reason, but has as its primary object this principle itself. It is to be regarded as the thorough-bass of all the sciences, but is of a higher species than these, and is almost as much related to art as to science. Just as in music every particular period must correspond to the tonality to which thorough-bass has then advanced, so every author, according to his branch of knowledge, will bear the stamp of the philosophy prevailing in his time. In addition to this, however, every science has also its special philosophy; we therefore speak of a philosophy of botany, of zoology, of history, and so on. Reasonably speaking, nothing more is to be understood by this than the principal results of each science itself, considered and comprehended from the highest, i.e., the most universal, point of view possible within the science. These most universal results are directly associated with universal philosophy, since they furnish it with important data, and save it the trouble of looking for these in the philosophically raw material of the special sciences themselves. Accordingly, these special philosophies are intermediate between their special sciences and philosophy proper. For as philosophy proper has to give the most general information about the totality of things, it must be possible for such information to be brought down and applied to the particular of each species of things. But the philosophy of each science originates independently of general philosophy, from the data of its own branch of knowledge. Therefore it need not wait till that philosophy has at last been found, but, worked out in advance, it will in any event agree with the true, universal philosophy. On the other hand, that philosophy must be capable of receiving confirmation and elucidation from the philosophies of the individual sciences; for the most universal truth must be capable of being proved through more special truths. A fine example of the philosophy of zoology has been afforded by Goethe in his reflections on Dalton's and Pander's skeletons of rodents (*Hefte zur Morphologie*, 1824). Kielmayer, Lamarck, Geoffroy-Saint-Hilaire, Cuvier, and many others have similar merit in connexion with the same science, in so far as they have all clearly brought out the universal analogy, the inner relationship, the permanent type, and the systematic connexion of animal forms. Empirical sciences, pursued purely for their own sake and without philosophical tendency, are like a face without eyes. They are, however, a suitable occupation for people of good capacity, who nevertheless lack the highest faculties that would even be a hindrance to minute investigations of this kind. Such persons concentrate their whole strength and all their knowledge on a single limited field. Therefore in that field they can reach the most complete knowledge possible, on condition that they remain in complete ignorance of everything else, whereas the philosopher must survey all fields, and indeed to a certain extent be at home in them all. That perfection which is attained only through detail is therefore necessarily ruled out here. In this connexion, these persons are to be compared to the Geneva workmen, of whom one makes nothing but wheels, another only springs, and a third merely chains; the philosopher, on the other hand, is to be compared to the watch-maker, who from all these produces a whole that has movement and meaning. They can also be compared to the musicians in an orchestra, each of whom is master of his own instrument; and the philosopher to the conductor, who must be acquainted with the nature and method of handling every instrument, yet without playing them all, or even only one of them, with great perfection. Scotus Erigena includes all sciences under the name *scientia,* in opposition to philosophy, which he calls *sapientia.* The same distinction was made by the Pythagoreans, as is seen from Stobaeus, *Florilegium,* Vol. i, p. 24, where it is explained very clearly and neatly. But an exceedingly happy and piquant comparison of the relation of the two kinds of mental effort to each other has been repeated by the ancients so often that we no longer know to whom it belongs. Diogenes Laërtius (ii, 79) attributes it to Aristippus, Stobaeus (*Florilegium,* tit. iv, 110) to Ariston of Chios, the Scholiast of Aristotle to Aristotle (p. 8 of the Berlin edition), while Plutarch (*De Puerorum Educatione,* c. 10) attributes it to Bion, *qui aiebat, sicut Penelopes proci, quum non possent cum Penelope concumbere, rem cum ejus ancillis habuissent; ita qui philosophiam nequeunt apprehendere, eos in aliis nullius pretii disciplinis sese conterere.*[5] In our predominantly empirical and historical age it can do no harm to recall this.

---

[5] "Bion the philosopher wittily remarked that, just as the suitors associated with Penelope's maidens because they could not lie with her, so those unable to lay hold of philosophy use up their strength in other inferior branches of knowledge." [Tr.]

On the Method of Mathematics

The Euclidean method of demonstration has brought forth from its own womb its most striking parody and caricature in the famous controversy over the theory of *parallels,* and in the attempts, repeated every year, to prove the eleventh axiom. This axiom asserts, and that indeed through the indirect criterion of a third intersecting line, that two lines inclined to each other (for this is the precise meaning of "less than two right angles"), if produced far enough, must meet. Now this truth is supposed to be too complicated to pass as self-evident, and therefore needs a proof; but no such proof can be produced, just because there is nothing more immediate. This scruple of conscience reminds me of Schiller's question of law:

> "For years I have already made use of my nose for smelling:
> Then have I actually a right to it that can be demonstrated?" [2]

In fact, it seems to me that the logical method is in this way reduced to an absurdity. But it is precisely through the controversies over this, together with the futile attempts to demonstrate the *directly* certain as merely *indirectly* certain, that the independence and clearness of intuitive evidence appear in contrast with the uselessness and difficulty of logical proof, a contrast as instructive as it is amusing. The direct certainty will not be admitted here, just because it is no merely logical certainty following from the concept, and thus resting solely on the relation of predicate to subject, according to the principle of contradiction. But that axiom is a synthetic proposition *a priori,* and as such has the guarantee of pure, not empirical, perception; this perception is just as immediate and certain as is the principle of contradiction itself, from which all proofs originally derive their certainty. At bottom this holds good of every geometrical theorem, and it is arbitrary where we choose to draw the line be-

---

[1] This chapter refers to § 15 of volume 1.
[2] From Schiller's *Die Philosophen.* [Tr.]

tween what is immediately certain and what has first to be proved. It surprises me that the eighth axiom, "Figures that coincide with one another are equal to one another," is not rather attacked. For *"coinciding with one another"* is either a mere tautology, or something quite empirical, belonging not to pure intuition or perception, but to external sensuous experience. Thus it presupposes mobility of the figures, but matter alone is movable in space. Consequently, this reference to coincidence with one another forsakes pure space, the sole element of geometry, in order to pass over to the material and empirical.

The alleged inscription over the Platonic lecture-room, Ἀγεω-μέτρητος μηδεὶς εἰσίτω,[3] of which the mathematicians are so proud, was no doubt inspired by the fact that Plato regarded the geometrical figures as intermediate entities between the eternal *Ideas* and particular things, as Aristotle frequently mentions in his *Metaphysics* (especially i, c. 6, pp. 887, 998, and *Scholia*, p. 827, *ed. Berol.*). Moreover, the contrast between those eternal forms or *Ideas,* existing by themselves, and the fleeting individual things could most easily be made intelligible in geometrical figures, and in this way could be laid the foundation for the doctrine of Ideas, which is the central point of Plato's philosophy, and indeed his only serious and positive theoretical dogma. Therefore in expounding it he started from geometry. In the same sense we are told that he regarded geometry as a preliminary exercise, by which the mind of the pupils became accustomed to dealing with incorporeal objects, after this mind had hitherto in practical life had to do only with corporeal things (*Schol. in Aristot.*, pp. 12, 15). This therefore is the sense in which Plato recommended geometry to the philosophers; and so we are not justified in extending it further. On the contrary, I recommend a very thorough and informative article in the form of a review of a book by Whewell in the *Edinburgh Review* of January 1836, as an investigation of the influence of mathematics on our mental powers and of its use for scientific and literary culture in general. The author of the article, who later published it together with some other essays under his name, is Sir W. Hamilton, Professor of Logic and Metaphysics in Scotland. It has also found a German translator, and has appeared by itself under the title: *Ueber den Werth und Unwerth der Mathematik,* from the English, 1836. Its conclusion is that the value of mathematics is only indirect, and is found to be in the application to ends that are attainable only through it. In itself, however, mathematics leaves the mind where it found it; it is by no means necessary; in fact, it is a positive hindrance to the

---

[3] "Let no one enter who has not studied geometry." [Tr.]

general formation and development of the mind. This conclusion is not only proved by thorough dianoiological investigation of the mind's mathematical activity, but is also established by a very learned accumulation of examples and authorities. The only immediate use left to mathematics is that it can accustom fickle and unstable minds to fix their attention. Even Descartes, himself famous as a mathematician, held just the same opinion about mathematics. In the *Vie de Descartes* by Baillet, 1693, it is said, Bk. ii, ch. 6, p. 54: *"Sa propre expérience l'avait convaincu du peu d'utilité des mathématiques, surtout lorsqu'on ne les cultive que pour elles mêmes. . . . Il ne voyait rien de moins solide, que de s'occuper de nombres tout simples et de figures imaginaires,"*[4] and so on.

---

[4] "His own experience had convinced him of the small utility of mathematics, especially when it is pursued merely for its own sake. . . . Nothing seemed to him more pointless than to be occupied with mere numbers and imaginary figures." [Tr.]

CHAPTER XIV

On the Association of Ideas

The presence of representations and ideas in our consciousness is as strictly subject to the principle of sufficient reason or ground in its different forms as the movement of bodies is to the law of causality. It is no more possible for an idea to enter consciousness without an occasion than it is for a body to be set in motion without a cause. Now this occasion is either *external,* and thus an impression on the senses, or *internal,* and hence itself again an idea which produces another idea by virtue of *association.* This association in turn rests either on a relation of ground and consequent between the two, or on similarity, or even on mere analogy, or finally on the simultaneity of their first apprehension; and this again can have its ground in the spatial proximity of their objects. The last two cases are denoted by the words *à propos.* The predominance of one of these three bonds of association of ideas over the others is characteristic of a mind's intellectual worth. In thoughtful and profound minds the first-named will predominate, in witty, ingenious, and poetical minds the second, and in minds of limited capacity the last. No less characteristic is the degree of facility with which an idea brings about others standing in some relation to it; this constitutes the keenness of the mind. But the impossibility of a thought's entry into the mind without its sufficient occasion, even with the strongest wish to call it forth, is testified by all the cases in which we make vain efforts to *recollect* something. We then go through the whole store of our ideas, in order to find any one that may be associated with the idea we are seeking. If we find the former, the latter is there also. Whoever wishes to call up a reminiscence always looks first of all for a thread on which it hangs through the association of ideas. On this depends mnemonics; it aims at providing us with easily found occasions for all the concepts, ideas, or words to be preserved. Yet the worst of it is that even these occasions themselves must first be found again, and for this also an occasion is required. How much the occasion achieves in the case of memory can be shown by the fact that anyone who has read fifty anecdotes in a book of anecdotes, and then laid the book aside, is sometimes unable to recall even a single one immediately afterwards. But if the occasion comes, or an idea occurs to him which has any analogy with one of those anecdotes, it comes back to him at once; and so do all the fifty as opportunity offers. The same holds good of all that we read. At bottom, our immediate verbal memory, in other words our memory of words, which is not brought about by means of mnemonic artifices, and with this our whole faculty of speech, depend on the direct association of ideas. For the learning of a language consists in our linking together a concept and a word for all time, so that this word always occurs to us simultaneously with this concept, and this concept with this word. Subsequently, we have to repeat the same process when learning any new language. If, however, we learn a language merely for passive and not for active use, in other words, to read but not to speak it, as is often the case, for example, with Greek, then the concatenation is one-sided, since the concept occurs to us with the word, but the word does not usually occur to us with the concept. The same procedure as in language becomes apparent in the particular case, when we learn every new proper name. But sometimes we have no confidence in ourselves to connect directly the name of *this* person, or town, river, mountain, plant, animal, and so on, with the thought of these so firmly that it may call up each of them of itself. We then help ourselves mnemonically, and connect the image of the person or thing with any quality of perception whose name occurs in the image of that person or thing. But this is only a temporary stage for support; later on we drop it, since the association of ideas becomes an immediate support.

The search for a thread of recollection shows itself in a peculiar way, when it is a dream that we have forgotten on waking up. Here we look in vain for that which a few minutes previously occupied us with the force of the clearest and brightest present, but has now entirely vanished. We then try to seize any impression that has been left behind, and on which a slender thread hangs. By virtue of association, this thread might draw the dream back again into our consciousness. According to Kieser, *Tellurismus,* Vol. ii, § 271, recollection even from magnetic somnambulistic sleep is said to be sometimes possible through a sign perceived by the senses and found in the waking state. It depends on the same impossibility of the appearance of an idea without its occasion that, if we propose to do something at a definite time, this can happen only by our thinking of nothing else till then, or by our being *reminded* of it by something at the time in question. This may be either an external impression previously arranged for it, or an idea that is itself again brought about in a regular manner. Both then belong to the class of motives. Every morning, when we awake, our consciousness is a *tabula rasa* which is rapidly filled again. First of all, it is the environment of the previous evening which is now again entering consciousness. This environment reminds us of what we thought in these very surroundings; with this are connected the events of the previous day, and thus one idea rapidly calls forth another, until all that occupied us yesterday is present once more. On the fact that this takes place properly depends the health of the mind in contrast to madness, which, as is shown in the third book, consists in the occurrence of great gaps in the continuity of the recollection of the past. But how completely sleep breaks the thread of memory, so that it must be resumed again each morning, is seen in particular instances of the incompleteness of this operation. For example, we are sometimes unable to recall in the morning a melody that the previous evening was running through our head until we were tired of it.

An exception to what has been said seems to be afforded by those cases in which an idea or picture of the imagination suddenly comes into our mind without any conscious occasion. Yet this is in most cases a delusion resting on the fact that the occasion was so trifling, and the idea itself so bright and interesting, that the former was instantly driven out of consciousness by the latter. Yet sometimes such an instantaneous appearance of a representation may have as its cause internal bodily impressions either of the parts of the brain on one another, or of the organic nervous system on the brain.

In general, the thought-process within us is in reality not so simple as its theory, for here the whole thing is involved in a variety of ways. To make the matter clear, let us compare our consciousness to a sheet of water of some depth. Then the distinctly conscious ideas are merely the surface; on the other hand, the mass of the water is the indistinct, the feelings, the after-sensation of perceptions and intuitions and what is experienced in general, mingled with the disposition of our own will that is the kernel of our inner nature. Now this mass of the whole consciousness is more or less, in proportion to intellectual liveliness, in constant motion, and the clear pictures of the imagination, or the distinct, conscious ideas expressed in words, and the resolves of the will are what comes to the surface in consequence of this motion. The whole process of our thinking and resolving seldom lies on the surface, that is to say, seldom consists in a concatenation of clearly conceived judgements; although we aspire to this, in order to be able to give an account of it to ourselves and others. But usually the rumination of material from outside, by which it is recast into ideas, takes place in the obscure depths of the mind. This rumination goes on almost as unconsciously as the conversion of nourishment into the humours and substance of the body. Hence it is that we are often unable to give any account of the origin of our deepest thoughts; they are the offspring of our mysterious inner being. Judgements, sudden flashes of thought, resolves, rise from those depths unexpectedly and to our own astonishment. A letter brings us important news not previously expected, and in consequence our ideas and motives are thrown into confusion. For the time being we dismiss the matter from our minds, and do not think about it again. But on the next day, or on the third or fourth day, the whole situation sometimes stands distinctly before us with what we have to do in the case. Consciousness is the mere surface of our mind, and of this, as of the globe, we do not know the interior, but only the crust.

But in the last instance, or in the secret of our inner being, what puts into activity the association of ideas itself, whose laws have been explained above, is the *will*. This drives its servant, the intellect, according to its powers to link one idea on to another, to recall the similar and the simultaneous, and to recognize grounds and consequents. For it is in the interest of the will that we should generally think, so that we may be in the best possible situation for all the cases that arise. Therefore the form of the principle of sufficient reason which governs the association of ideas and keeps it active is ultimately the law of motivation. For that which rules the sensorium, and determines it to follow analogy or another association of ideas in this or that direction, is the will of the thinking subject. Now just as here the laws of the connexion of ideas exist only on the basis of the will, so in the real world the causal nexus of bodies really exists only on the basis of the will manifesting itself in the phenomena of this world. For this reason, the explanation from causes is never absolute and exhaustive, but refers back to forces of nature as their condition, and the inner being of this is just the will as thing-in-itself; here, of course, I have anticipated the following book.

Now because the *outward* (sensuous) occasions of the presence of our representations, just as much as the *inner* (of the association of ideas), and both independently of each other, are constantly affecting consciousness, there result from this the frequent interruptions of our course of thought which produce a certain cutting up and confusion of our thinking. This belongs to the imperfections of thinking which cannot be removed, and which we will now consider in a special chapter.

CHAPTER XV

On the Essential Imperfections of the Intellect

Our self-consciousness has not space as its form, but only *time;* therefore our thinking does not, like our perceiving, take place in *three* dimensions, but merely in *one,* that is, in a line, without breadth and depth. From this fact springs the greatest of our intellect's essential imperfections. We can know everything only *successively,* and are conscious of only one thing at a time, and even of that one thing only on condition that for the time being we forget, and so are absolutely unconscious of, everything else; with the consequence that, for so long, all else ceases to exist for us. In this quality, our intellect can be compared to a telescope with a very narrow field of vision, just because our consciousness is not stationary but fleeting. The intellect apprehends only successively, and to grasp one thing it must give up another, retaining nothing of it but traces which become weaker and weaker. The idea that is now vividly engrossing my attention is *bound* after a little while to have slipped entirely from my memory. Now if a good night's sleep intervenes, it may be that I shall never find the thought again, unless it is tied up with my personal interest, in other words, with my will, which is always in command of the field.

On this imperfection of the intellect depends the rhapsodical and often *fragmentary nature of the course of our thoughts,* which I already touched on at the end of the previous chapter, and from this arises the inevitable *distraction* of our thinking. Sometimes external impressions of sense throng in on it, disturbing and interrupting it, and forcing the strangest and oddest things on it at every moment; sometimes *one* idea draws in *another* by the bond of association, and is itself displaced by it; finally, even the intellect itself is not capable of sticking very long and continuously to *one* idea. On the contrary, just as the eye, when it gazes for a long time at *one* object, is soon not able to see it distinctly any longer, because the outlines run into one another, become confused, and finally everything becomes obscure, so also through long-continued rumination on *one* thing our thinking gradually becomes confused and dull, and ends in complete stupor. Therefore after a certain time, varying with the individual, we must for the time being give up every meditation or deliberation, which has fortunately remained undisturbed, but has not yet been brought to an end, even when it concerns a matter of the greatest importance and interest to us. We must dismiss from our consciousness the subject of the deliberation that interests us so much, however heavily our concern about it may weigh upon us, in order to be occupied with unimportant and indifferent matters. During this time, that important subject no longer exists for us; like the heat in cold water, it is *latent*. If we take it up again at another time, we approach it as we approach a new thing with which we become acquainted afresh, although more quickly; and its agreeable or disagreeable impression on our will also appears afresh. But we ourselves do not come back entirely unchanged. For with the physical composition of the humours and the tension of the nerves, constantly varying according to the hour, day, and season, our mood and point of view also change. Moreover, the different kinds of representations that have been there in the meantime, have left behind an echo whose tone has an influence on those that follow. Therefore the same thing often appears very different to us at different times, in the morning, in the evening, at midday, or on another day; opposing views jostle one another and increase our doubt. Therefore we speak of sleeping on a matter, and great decisions demand a long time for deliberation. Now although this quality of our intellect, as springing from its weakness, has its obvious disadvantages, nevertheless it offers the advantage that, after the distraction and physical change of mood, we return to our business as comparatively different beings, fresh and strange, and so are able to view it several times in a very varied light. From all this it is evident that human consciousness and thinking are by their nature necessarily fragmentary, and that therefore the theoretical or practical results obtained by putting such fragments together often turn out to be defective. In this our thinking consciousness is like a magic lantern, in the focus of which only one picture can appear at a time; and every picture, even when it depicts the noblest thing, must nevertheless soon vanish to make way for the most different and even most vulgar thing. In practical affairs, the most important plans and resolutions are settled in general, and others are subordinated to these as means to an end, and others in turn to these, and so on down to the individual thing to be carried out *in concreto*. But they are not put into execution in their order of dignity; on the contrary, while we are concerned with plans on a large and general scale, we have to contend with the most trifling details and with the cares of the moment. In this way our consciousness becomes still more desultory. In general, theoretical mental occupations make us unfit for practical affairs, and *vice versa.*

In consequence of the inevitably scattered and fragmentary nature of all our thinking, which has been mentioned, and of the mixing together of the most heterogeneous representations thus brought about and inherent even in the noblest human mind, we really possess only *half a consciousness.* With this we grope about in the labyrinth of our life and in the obscurity of our investigations; bright moments illuminate our path like flashes of lightning. But what is to be expected generally from heads of which even the wisest is every night the playground of the strangest and most senseless dreams, and has to take up its meditations again on emerging from these dreams? Obviously a consciousness subject to such great limitations is little fitted to explore and fathom the riddle of the world; and to beings of a higher order, whose intellect did not have time as its form, and whose thinking therefore had true completeness and unity, such an endeavour would necessarily appear strange and pitiable. In fact, it is a wonder that we are not completely confused by the extremely heterogeneous mixture of fragments of representations and of ideas of every kind which are constantly crossing one another in our heads, but that we are always able to find our way again, and to adapt and adjust everything. Obviously there must exist a simple thread on which everything is arranged side by side: but what is this? Memory alone is not enough, since it has essential limitations of which I shall shortly speak; moreover, it is extremely imperfect and treacherous. The *logical ego,* or even the *transcendental synthetic unity of apperception,* are expressions and explanations that will not readily serve to make the matter comprehensible; on the contrary, it will occur to many that

"Your wards are deftly wrought, but drive no bolts asunder."[1]

Kant's proposition: "The *I think* must accompany all our representations," is insufficient; for the "I" is an unknown quantity, in other words, it is itself a mystery and a secret. What gives unity and sequence to consciousness, since, by pervading all the representations of consciousness, it is its substratum, its permanent supporter, cannot itself be conditioned by consciousness, and therefore cannot be a representation. On the contrary, it must be the *prius* of consciousness, and the root of the tree of which consciousness is the fruit. This, I say, is the *will;* it alone is unalterable and absolutely identi-

---

[1] Goethe's *Faust,* Bayard Taylor's translation. [Tr.]

cal, and has brought forth consciousness for its own ends. It is therefore the will that gives it unity and holds all its representations and ideas together, accompanying them, as it were, like a continuous ground-bass. Without it the intellect would have no more unity of consciousness than has a mirror, in which now one thing now another presents itself in succession, or at most only as much as a convex mirror has, whose rays converge at an imaginary point behind its surface. But it is *the will* alone that is permanent and unchangeable in consciousness. It is the will that holds all ideas and representations together as means to its ends, tinges them with the colour of its character, its mood, and its interest, commands the attention, and holds the thread of motives in its hand. The influence of these motives ultimately puts into action memory and the association of ideas. Fundamentally it is the will that is spoken of whenever "I" occurs in a judgement. Therefore the will is the true and ultimate point of unity of consciousness, and the bond of all its functions and acts. It does not, however, itself belong to the intellect, but is only its root, origin, and controller.

From *the form of time and of the single dimension* of the series of representations, on account of which the intellect, in order to take up one thing, must drop everything else, there follows not only the intellect's distraction, but also its *forgetfulness*. Most of what it has dropped it never takes up again, especially as the taking up again is bound to the principle of sufficient reason, and thus requires an occasion which the association of ideas and motivation have first to provide. Yet this occasion may be the remoter and the smaller, the more our susceptibility to it is enhanced by interest in the subject. But, as I have already shown in the essay *On the Principle of Sufficient Reason*, memory is not a receptacle, but a mere faculty, acquired by practice, of bringing forth any representations at random, so that these have always to be kept in practice by repetition, otherwise they are gradually lost. Accordingly, the knowledge even of the scholarly head exists only *virtualiter* as an acquired practice in producing certain representations. *Actualiter*, on the other hand, it is restricted to one particular representation, and for the moment is conscious of this one alone. Hence there results a strange contrast between what a man knows *potentiâ* and what he knows *actu,* in other words, between his knowledge and his thinking at any moment. The former is an immense and always somewhat chaotic mass, the latter a single, distinct thought. The relation is like that between the innumerable stars of the heavens and the telescope's narrow field of vision; it stands out remarkably when, on some occasion, a man wishes to bring to distinct recollection some isolated fact from his knowledge, and time and trouble are required to look for it and pick it out of that chaos. Rapidity in doing this is a special gift, but depends very much on the day and the hour; therefore sometimes memory refuses its service, even in things which, at another time, it has ready at hand. This consideration requires us in our studies to strive after the attainment of correct insight rather than an increase of learning, and to take to heart the fact that the *quality* of knowledge is more important than its *quantity*. Quantity gives books only thickness; quality imparts thoroughness as well as style; for it is an *intensive* dimension, whereas the other is merely extensive. It consists in the distinctness and completeness of the concepts, together with the purity and accuracy of the knowledge of perception that forms their foundation. Therefore the whole of knowledge in all its parts is permeated by it, and is valuable or trifling accordingly. With a small quantity but good quality of knowledge we achieve more than with a very great quantity but bad quality.

The most perfect and satisfactory knowledge is that of perception, but this is limited to the absolutely particular, to the individual. The comprehension of the many and the various into *one* representation is possible only through the *concept,* in other words, by omitting the differences; consequently the concept is a very imperfect way of representing things. The particular, of course, can also be apprehended immediately as a universal, namely when it is raised to the (Platonic) *Idea;* but in this process, which I have analysed in the third book, the intellect passes beyond the limits of individuality and therefore of time; moreover, this is only an exception.

These inner and essential imperfections of the intellect are further increased by a disturbance to some extent external to it but yet inevitable, namely, the influence that the *will* exerts on all its operations, as soon as that will is in any way concerned in their result. Every passion, in fact every inclination or disinclination, tinges the objects of knowledge with its colour. Most common of occurrence is the falsification of knowledge brought about by desire and hope, since they show us the scarcely possible in dazzling colours as probable and well-nigh certain, and render us almost incapable of comprehending what is opposed to it. Fear acts in a similar way; every preconceived opinion, every partiality, and, as I have said, every interest, every emotion, and every predilection of the will act in an analogous manner.

Finally, to all these imperfections of the intellect we must also add the fact that it grows old with the brain; in other words, like all physiological functions, it loses its energy in later years; in this way all its imperfections are then greatly increased.

The defective nature of the intellect here described will not surprise us, however, if we look back at its origin and its destiny, as I have pointed it out in the second book. Nature has produced it for the service of an individual will; therefore it is destined to know things only in so far as they serve as the motives of such a will, not to fathom them or to comprehend their true inner essence. Human intellect is only a higher degree of the animal intellect, and just as this animal intellect is limited entirely to the present, so also does our intellect bear strong traces of this limitation. Therefore our memory and recollection are a very imperfect thing. How little are we able to recall of what we have done, experienced, learnt, or read! and even this little often only laboriously and imperfectly. For the same reason, it is very difficult for us to keep ourselves free from the impression of the present moment. Unconsciousness is the original and natural condition of all things, and therefore is also the basis from which, in particular species of beings, consciousness appears as their highest efflorescence; and for this reason, even then unconsciousness still always predominates. Accordingly, most beings are without consciousness; but yet they act according to the laws of their nature, in other words, of their will. Plants have at most an extremely feeble analogue of consciousness, the lowest animals merely a faint gleam of it. But even after it has ascended through the whole series of animals up to man and his faculty of reason, the unconsciousness of the plant, from which it started, still always remains the foundation, and this is to be observed in the necessity for sleep as well as in all the essential and great imperfections, here described, of every intellect produced through physiological functions. And of any other intellect we have no conception.

But the *essential* imperfections of the intellect here demonstrated are also always increased in the individual case by *inessential* imperfections. The intellect is never in *every* respect what it might be; the perfections possible to it are so opposed that they exclude one another. No one, therefore, can be *simultaneously* Plato and Aristotle, or Shakespeare and Newton, or Kant and Goethe. On the other hand, the imperfections of the intellect agree together very well, and therefore it often remains in reality far below what it might be. Its functions depend on so very many conditions which we can comprehend only as anatomical and physiological in the *phenomenon* in which alone they are given to us, that an intellect that positively excels even in *one* single direction is among the rarest of natural phenomena. Therefore the very productions of such an intellect are preserved for thousands of years; in fact, every relic of such a favoured individual becomes the most precious of possessions. From such an intellect down to that which approaches imbecility the gradations are innumerable. Now according to these gradations, *the mental horizon* of each of us primarily proves to be very different. It varies from the mere apprehension of the present, which even the animal has, to the horizon embracing the next hour, the day, the following day also, the week, the year, life, the centuries, thousands of years, up to the horizon of a consciousness that has almost always present, although dimly dawning, the horizon of the infinite. Therefore the thoughts and ideas of such a consciousness assume a character in keeping therewith. Further, this difference between intelligences shows itself in the *rapidity* of their thinking, which is very important, and may be as different and as finely graduated as the speed of the points in the radius of a revolving disc. The remoteness of the consequents and grounds to which anyone's thinking can reach seems to stand in a certain relation to the rapidity of the thinking, since the greatest exertion of thinking in general can last only quite a short time, yet only while it lasts could an idea be well thought out in its complete unity. It is then a question of how far the intellect can pursue the idea in such a short time, and thus what distance it can cover in that time. On the other hand, in the case of some people the rapidity may be offset by the longer duration of that time of perfectly consistent and uniform thinking. Probably slow and continuous thinking makes the mathematical mind, while rapidity of thinking makes the genius. The latter is a flight, the former a sure and certain advance step by step on firm ground. Yet even in the sciences, as soon as it is no longer a question of mere quantities but of understanding the real nature of phenomena, slow and continuous thinking is inadequate. This is proved, for example, by Newton's theory of colours, and later by Biot's drivel about colour-rings. Yet this nonsense is connected with the whole atomistic method of considering light among the French, with their *molécules de lumière,*[2] and in general with their fixed idea of wanting to reduce everything in nature to merely mechanical effects. Finally, the great individual difference between intelligences, of which we are speaking, shows itself pre-eminently in the *degree of clearness of understanding,* and accordingly in the *distinctness of the whole thinking.* What to one man is comprehension or understanding, to another is only observation to some extent; the former is already finished and at the goal while the latter is only at the beginning; what is the solution to the former is only the problem to the latter. This rests on the *quality of the thinking* and of knowledge which has been previously mentioned. Just as the degree of brightness varies

[2] "Molecules of light." [Tr.]

in rooms, so it does in minds. We notice this *quality of the whole thinking* as soon as we have read only a few pages of an author; for then we have had to comprehend directly with his understanding and in his sense. Therefore, before we know *what* he has thought, we already see *how* he thinks, and so what the *formal* nature, the *texture,* of his thinking is. This texture is always the same in everything he thinks about, and the train of thought and the style are its impression. In this we at once feel the pace, the step, the flexibility and lightness, indeed even the acceleration of his mind, or, on the contrary, its heaviness, dulness, stiffness, lameness, and leadenness. For just as a nation's language is the counterpart of its mind, so is style the immediate expression, the physiognomy, of an author's mind. Let us throw away a book when we observe that in it we enter a region that is more obscure than our own, unless we have to get from it merely facts and not ideas. Apart from this, only *that* author will be profitable whose understanding is keener and clearer than our own, and who advances our thinking instead of hindering it. It is hindered by the dull mind that wants to compel us to share in the toad-like pace of its own thinking. Thus we shall find that author profitable the occasional use of whose mind when we think affords us sensible relief, and by whom we feel ourselves borne whither we could not attain alone. Goethe once said to me that, when he read a page of Kant, he felt as if he were entering a bright room. Inferior minds are such not merely by their being distorted and thus judging falsely, but above all through the *indistinctness* of their whole thinking. This can be compared to seeing through a bad telescope, in which all the outlines appear indistinct and as if obliterated, and the different objects run into one another. The feeble understanding of such minds shrinks from the demand for distinctness of concepts; and so they themselves do not make this demand on it, but put up with haziness. To satisfy themselves with this, they gladly grasp at *words,* especially those which denote indefinite, very abstract, and unusual concepts difficult to explain, such, for example, as infinite and finite, sensuous and supersensuous, the Idea of being, Ideas of reason, the Absolute, the Idea of the good, the divine, moral freedom, power of self-generation, the absolute Idea, subject-object, and so on. They confidently make lavish use of such things, actually imagine that they express ideas, and expect everyone to be content with them. For the highest pinnacle of wisdom they can see is to have such ready-made words at hand for every possible question. The inexpressible *satisfaction in words* is thoroughly characteristic of inferior minds; it rests simply on their incapacity for distinct concepts, whenever these are to go beyond the most trivial and simple relations; consequently, it rests on the weakness and indolence of their intellect, indeed on their secret awareness thereof. In the case of scholars, this awareness is bound up with a hard necessity, early recognized, of passing themselves off as thinking beings; and to meet this demand in all cases they keep such a suitable store of ready-made words. It must be really amusing to see in the chair a professor of philosophy of this kind, who *bona fide* delivers such a display of words devoid of ideas, quite honestly under the delusion that these really are thoughts and ideas, and to see the students in front of him who, just as *bona fide,* that is to say, under the same delusion, are listening attentively and taking notes, while neither professor nor students really go beyond the words. Indeed these words, together with the audible scratching of pens, are the only realities in the whole business. This peculiar *satisfaction in words* contributes more than anything else to the perpetuation of errors. For, relying on the words and phrases received from his predecessors, each one confidently passes over obscurities or problems; and thus these are unnoticed and are propagated through the centuries from one book to another. The thinking mind, especially in youth, begins to doubt whether it is incapable of understanding these things; or whether there is really nothing intelligible in them; and similarly, whether the problem which they all slink past with such comic gravity and earnestness on the same footpath is for others no problem at all; or whether it is merely that they do not want to see it. Many truths remain undiscovered merely because no one has the courage to look the problem in the face and tackle it. In contrast to this, the distinctness of thought and clearness of concepts peculiar to eminent minds produce the effect that even well-known truths, when enunciated by *them,* acquire new light, or at any rate a fresh stimulus. If we hear or read them, it is as though we had exchanged a bad telescope for a good one. For example, let us read simply in Euler's *Briefe an eine Prinzessin* his exposition of the fundamental truths of mechanics and optics. On this is based Diderot's remark in *Le Neveu de Rameau,* that only perfect masters are capable of lecturing really well on the elements of a science, for the very reason that they alone really understand the questions, and words for them never take the place of ideas.

But we ought to know that inferior minds are the rule, good minds the exception, eminent minds extremely rare, and genius a portent. Otherwise, how could a human race consisting of some eight hundred million individuals have left so much still to be discovered, invented, thought out, and expressed after six thousand years? The intellect is calculated for the maintenance of the individual alone, and, as a rule, is barely sufficient even for this. But nature has wisely been very sparing in granting a larger measure; for the mind of limited capacity can survey the few and simple relations that lie within the range of its narrow sphere of action, and can handle the levers of these with much greater ease than the eminent mind could. Such a mind takes in an incomparably greater and richer sphere and works with long levers. Thus the insect sees everything on its little stem and leaf with the most minute accuracy and better than we can; but it is not aware of a man who stands three yards from it. On this rests the slyness of the dull and stupid, and this paradox: *Il y a un mystère dans l'esprit des gens qui n'en ont pas.*[3] For practical life genius is about as useful as an astronomer's telescope is in a theatre. Accordingly, in regard to the intellect nature is extremely *aristocratic.* The differences she has established in this respect are greater than those made in any country by birth, rank, wealth, and caste distinction. However, in nature's aristocracy as in others, there are many thousands of plebeians to one nobleman, many millions to one prince, and the great multitude are mere populace, mob, rabble, *la canaille.* There is, of course, a glaring contrast between nature's list of ranks and that of convention, and the adjustment of this difference could be hoped for only in a golden age. However, those who stand very high in the one list of ranks and those in the other have in common the fact that they generally live in exalted isolation, to which Byron refers when he says:

> To feel me in the solitude of kings,
> Without the power that makes them bear a crown.
> (*The Prophecy of Dante,* canto i, l. 166)

For the intellect is a differentiating, and consequently separating, principle. Its different gradations, much more even than those of mere culture, give everyone different concepts, in consequence of which everyone lives to a certain extent in a different world, in which he meets directly only his equals in rank, but can attempt to call to the rest and make himself intelligible to them only from a distance. Great differences in the degree, and thus the development, of the understanding open a wide gulf between one man and another, which can be crossed only by kindness of heart. This, on the other hand, is the unifying principle that identifies everyone else with one's own self. The connexion, however, remains a moral one; it cannot become intellectual. Even in the event of a fairly equal degree of culture, the conversation between a great mind and an ordinary one is like the common journey of two men, of whom one is mounted on

---

[3] "There is a mystery in the minds of those men who have none." [Tr.]

a mettlesome horse while the other is on foot. It soon becomes extremely irksome for both of them, and in the long run impossible. It is true that for a short distance the rider can dismount, in order to walk with the other, though even then his horse's impatience will give him a great deal of trouble.

The public, however, could not be benefited by anything so much as by the recognition of this *intellectual aristocracy of nature*. By virtue of such recognition it would comprehend that the normal mind is certainly sufficient where it is a question of facts, as where a report is to be made from experiments, travels, old manuscripts, historical works, and chronicles. On the other hand, where it is a case merely of *thoughts and ideas,* especially of those whose material or data are within everyone's reach, and so where it is really only a question of *thinking before* others, the public would see that decided superiority, innate eminence, bestowed only by nature and then extremely rarely, is inevitably demanded, and that no one deserves a hearing who does not give immediate proofs of this. If the public could be brought to see this for itself, it would no longer waste the time sparingly meted out to it for its culture on the productions of ordinary minds, on the innumerable bunglings in poetry and philosophy that are concocted every day. It would no longer always rush after what is newest, in the childish delusion that books, like eggs, must be enjoyed while they are fresh. On the contrary, it would stick to the achievements of the few select and celebrated minds of all ages and nations, endeavour to get to know and understand them, and thus might gradually attain to genuine culture. Then those thousands of uncalled-for productions that, like tares, impede the growth of good wheat, would soon disappear.

On the Practical Use of Our Reason and on Stoicism

I showed in the seventh chapter that, in the theoretical, to start from *concepts* is sufficient only for mediocre achievements, whereas eminent and superior achievements demand that we draw from perception itself as the primary source of all knowledge. In the practical, however, the converse is true; there, to be determined by what is perceived is the method of the animal, but is unworthy of man, who has *concepts* to guide his conduct. In this way he is emancipated from the power of the present moment existing in perception, to which the animal is unconditionally abandoned. In proportion as man asserts this prerogative, his conduct can be called *rational,* and only in *this* sense can we speak of *practical reason,* not in the *Kantian* sense, whose inadmissibility I have discussed in detail in the essay *On the Basis of Morality.*

But it is not easy to let ourselves be determined by *concepts* alone; for the directly present external world with its perceptible reality obtrudes itself forcibly even on the strongest mind. But it is just in overcoming this impression, in annihilating its deception, that man's mind shows its intrinsic worth and greatness. Thus, if inducements to pleasure and enjoyment leave it unaffected, or the threats and fury of enraged enemies do not shake it; if the entreaties of deluded friends do not cause its resolve to waver, and the deceptive forms with which preconcerted intrigues surround it leave it unmoved; if the scorn of fools and the populace does not disconcert it or perplex it as to its own worth, then it seems to be under the influence of a spirit-world visible to it alone (and this is the world of concepts), before which that perceptibly present moment, open to all, dissolves like a phantom. On the other hand, what gives the external world and visible reality their great power over the mind is their nearness and immediacy. Just as the magnetic needle, which is kept in position

---

[1] This chapter refers to § 16 of volume 1.

by the combined effect of widely distributed natural forces embracing the whole earth, can nevertheless be perturbed and set in violent oscillation by a small piece of iron, if one is brought quite close to it, so even a powerful intellect can sometimes be disconcerted and perturbed by trifling events and persons, if only they affect it very closely. The most deliberate resolution can be turned into a momentary irresolution by an insignificant but immediately present counter-motive. For the relative influence of the motives is under a law directly opposed to that by which the weights act on a balance; and in consequence of that law a very small motive that lies very close to us can outweigh a motive much stronger in itself, yet acting from a distance. But it is that quality of mind by virtue of which it may be determined in accordance with this law, and is not withdrawn therefrom by dint of the really practical reason (*Vernunft*) which the ancients expressed by *animi impotentia,*[2] which really signifies *ratio regendae voluntatis impotens.*[3] Every *emotion* (*animi perturbatio*) arises simply from the fact that a representation acting on our will comes so extremely near to us that it conceals from us everything else, and we are no longer able to see anything but it. Thus we become incapable for the moment of taking anything of a different kind into consideration. It would be a good remedy for this if we were to bring ourselves to regard the present in our imagination as if it were the past, and consequently to accustom our apperception to the epistolary style of the Romans. On the other hand, we are well able to regard what is long past as so vividly present, that old emotions long asleep are reawakened thereby to their full intensity. In the same way, no one would become indignant and disconcerted over a misfortune, a vexation, if his faculty of reason always kept before him what man really is, the most needy and helpless of creatures, daily and hourly abandoned to great and small misfortunes without number, τὸ δειλότατον ζῶον, who has therefore to live in constant care and fear. Πᾶν ἐστι ἄνθρωπος συμφορή (*Homo totus est calamitas*)[4] as Herodotus [i. 32] has it.

The first result of applying the faculty of reason to practical affairs is that it puts together again what is one-sided and piecemeal in knowledge of mere perception, and uses the contrasts presented thereby as corrections for one another; in this way the objectively correct result is obtained. For example, if we look at a man's bad action we shall condemn him; on the other hand, if we consider merely the need that induced him to perform it, we shall sympathize

---

[2] "Want of self-control." [Tr.]
[3] "Reason which is not able to control the will." [Tr.]
[4] "Man is wholly abandoned to chance." [Tr.]

with him. The faculty of reason by means of its concepts weighs the two, and leads to the result that the man must be restrained, restricted, and guided by appropriate punishment.

Here I recall once more Seneca's utterance: *"Si vis tibi omnia subjicere, te subjice rationi."* [5] Now since, as is shown in the fourth book, suffering is of a positive nature and pleasure of a negative, the man who takes abstract or rational knowledge as his rule of conduct, and accordingly always reflects on its consequences and on the future, will very frequently have to practise *sustine et abstine,* since to obtain the greatest possible painlessness in life he generally sacrifices the keenest joys and pleasures, mindful of Aristotle's ὁ φρόνιμος τὸ ἄλυπον διώκει, οὐ τὸ ἡδύ (*Quod dolore vacat, non quod suave est, persequitur vir prudens*).[6] With him, therefore, the future is always borrowing from the present instead of the present from the future as in the case of the frivolous fool, who thus becomes impoverished and ultimately bankrupt. In the case of the former the faculty of reason, of course, must often play the part of an ill-humoured mentor, and incessantly demand renunciations, without being able to promise anything in return for them except a fairly painless existence. This depends on the fact that the faculty of reason, by means of its concepts, surveys the *whole* of life, the result of which, in the happiest conceivable case, can be no other than what we have said.

When this striving after a painless existence, in so far as such an existence might be possible by applying and observing rational deliberation and acquired knowledge of the true nature of life, was carried out with strict consistency and to the utmost extreme, it produced *Cynicism,* from which *Stoicism* afterwards followed. I will discuss this briefly here, in order to establish more firmly the concluding argument of our first book.

All the moral systems of antiquity, with the single exception of Plato's, were guides to a blissful life; accordingly, virtue in them has its end in this world, and certainly not beyond death. For with them it is simply the right path to the truly happy life; for this reason it is chosen by the prudent man. Hence we get the lengthy debates preserved for us especially by Cicero, those keen and constantly renewed investigations as to whether virtue, entirely alone and of itself, is really sufficient for a happy life, or whether something external is also required for this; whether the virtuous and the prudent are happy even on the rack and wheel or in the bull of Phalaris;

---

[5] "If you wish to subject everything to yourself, then subject yourself to reason." [Tr.]

[6] "The prudent man strives for freedom from pain, not for pleasure." [*Nicomachean Ethics,* vii, 12. Tr.]

or whether it does not go as far as this. For this of course would be the touchstone of an ethical system of this kind, that the practice of it would inevitably and necessarily produce happiness immediately and unconditionally. Unless it can do this, it does not achieve what it ought, and is to be rejected. Consequently, it is as correct as it is in accordance with the Christian point of view for Augustine to preface his exposition of the moral systems of the ancients (*De Civitate Dei*, Bk. xix, c. 1) with the explanation: *Exponenda sunt nobis argumenta mortalium, quibus sibi ipsi beatitudinem facere IN HUJUS VITAE INFELICITATE moliti sunt; ut ab eorum rebus vanis spes nostra quid differat clarescat. De finibus bonorum et malorum multa inter se philosophi disputarunt; quam quaestionem maxima intentione versantes, invenire conati sunt, quid efficiat hominem beatum: illud enim est finis bonorum.*[7] I wish to place beyond doubt by a few express statements of the ancients the declared eudaemonistic purpose of the ethics of antiquity. Aristotle says in the *Magna Moralia*, i, 4: Ἡ εὐδαιμονία ἐν τῷ εὖ ζῆν ἐστιν, τὸ δὲ εὖ ζῆν ἐν τῷ κατὰ τὰς ἀρετὰς ζῆν (*Felicitas in bene vivendo posita est; verum bene vivere est in eo positum, ut secundum virtutem vivamus*),[8] and with this can be compared *Nicomachean Ethics*, i, 5; Cicero, *Tusculan Disputations*, v, 1: *Nam, quum ea causa impulerit eos, qui primi se ad philosophiae studia contulerunt, ut omnibus rebus posthabitis, totos se in optimo vitae statu exquirendo collocarent; profecto spe beate vivendi tantam in eo studio curam operamque posuerunt.*[9] According to Plutarch (*De Repugn. Stoic.*, c. 18) Chrysippus said: Τὸ κατὰ κακίαν ζῆν τῷ κακοδαιμόνως ζῆν ταὐτόν ἐστιν (*Vitiose vivere idem est, quod vivere infeliciter*).[10] *Ibid.*, c. 26: Ἡ φρόνησις οὐχ ἕτερόν ἐστι τῆς εὐδαιμονίας καθ' ἑαυτό, ἀλλ' εὐδαιμονία (*Prudentia nihil differt a felicitate, estque ipsa adeo felicitas*).[11] Stobaeus, *Eclogues*, Bk.

---

[7] "It is incumbent on us to explain the arguments by which men have attempted to obtain for themselves a supreme happiness *in the unhappiness of this life*, so that the great difference between what we hope for and their vain efforts may become all the clearer. Philosophers have disputed much among themselves over the highest good and the greatest evil, and in treating this question with the greatest zeal, have tried to find out what makes man happy, for this is what is called the highest good." [Tr.]

[8] "Happiness consists in the happy life, but the happy life consists in the virtuous life." [Tr.]

[9] "For, as this [the happy life] was the cause that first prompted those concerned with the study of philosophy to disregard everything else, and to devote themselves entirely to the investigation of the best way of conducting life, they have actually bestowed so much care and trouble on this study in the hope of attaining to a happy life in this way." [Tr.]

[10] "The immoral life is identical with the unhappy life." [Tr.]

[11] "Prudent conduct is not something different from perfect happiness, but is itself perfect happiness." [Tr.]

ii, c. 7: Τέλος δέ φασιν εἶναι τὸ εὐδαιμονεῖν, οὗ ἕνεκα πάντα πράττεται (*Finem esse dicunt felicitatem, cujus causa fiunt omnia*).[12] Εὐδαιμονίαν συνωνυμεῖν τῷ τέλει λέγουσι (*Finem bonorum et felicitatem synonyma esse dicunt*).[13] Epictetus, in Arrian, *Discourses*, i, 4: Ἡ ἀρετὴ ταύτην ἔχει τὴν ἐπαγγελίαν, εὐδαιμονίαν ποιῆσαι (*Virtus profitetur, se felicitatem praestare*).[14] Seneca, *Epistola* 90: *Ceterum* (*sapientia*) *ad beatum statum tendit, illo ducit, illo vias aperit.* Idem, *Epistola* 108: *Illud admoneo, auditionem philosophorum lectionemque ad propositum beatae vitae trahendum.*[15]

Therefore the ethics of the *Cynics* also adopted this aim of the happiest life, as is expressly testified by the Emperor Julian (*Oratio* 6): Τῆς Κυνικῆς δὲ φιλοσοφίας σκοπὸς μέν ἐστι καὶ τέλος, ὥσπερ δὴ καὶ πάσης φιλοσοφίας, τὸ εὐδαιμονεῖν· τὸ δὲ εὐδαιμονεῖν ἐν τῷ ζῆν κατὰ φύσιν, ἀλλὰ μὴ πρὸς τὰς τῶν πολλῶν δόξας (*Cynicae philosophiae, ut etiam omnis philosophiae, scopus et finis est feliciter vivere: felicitas vitae autem in eo posita est, ut secundum naturam vivatur, nec vero secundum opiniones multitudinis*).[16] Only the Cynics followed a very special path to this goal, one that is quite the opposite of the ordinary path, that, namely, of carrying privation to the farthest possible limits. Thus they started from the insight that the motions into which the will is put by the objects that stimulate and stir it, and the laborious and often frustrated efforts to attain them, or the fear of losing them when they are attained, and finally also the loss itself, produce far greater pains and sorrows than the want of all these objects ever can. Therefore, to attain to the most painless life, they chose the path of the greatest possible privation, and fled from all pleasures as snares by which one would subsequently be delivered over to pain. Then they could boldly bid defiance to happiness and its strange tricks. This is the *spirit of cynicism;* Seneca sets it forth distinctly in the eighth chapter *De Tranquillitate Animi: Cogitandum est quanto levior dolor sit, non habere, quam perdere: et intelligemus, paupertati eo minorem tormentorum quo minorem damnorum esse materiam.* And: *Tolerabilius est faciliusque non*

---

[12] "They [the Stoics] describe perfect happiness as the highest goal, for the sake of which everything is done." [Tr.]

[13] Perfect happiness and the highest end are declared to be synonymous." [Tr.]

[14] "Virtue itself promises to bring about happiness." [Tr.]

[15] "For the rest, wisdom aspires to a blissful state: it leads thereto; it opens the way thereto. . . . I remind you that hearing and reading philosophers are included in the plan for a happy life." [Tr.]

[16] "The happy life is regarded as the goal and final aim in the philosophy of the Cynics, as well as in every other philosophy. But a happy life consists in our living according to nature, and not according to the opinions of the crowd." [Tr.]

acquirere, quam amittere. . . . Diogenes effecit, ne quid sibi eripi posset, . . . qui se fortuitis omnibus exuit. . . . Videtur mihi dixisse: age tuum negotium, fortuna: nihil apud Diogenem jam tuum est.[17] The parallel passage to this last sentence is the quotation in Stobaeus (*Eclogues*, ii, 7): Διογένης ἔφη νομίζειν ὁρᾶν τὴν Τύχην ἐνορῶσαν αὐτὸν καὶ λέγουσαν· τοῦτον δ'οὐ δύναμαι βάλέειν κύνα λυσσητῆρα (*Diogenes credere se dixit videre Fortunam ipsum intuentem ac dicentem: Ast hunc non potui tetigisse canem rabiosum*).[18] The same spirit of cynicism is also testified by the epitaph of Diogenes in Suidas, under the word Φιλίσκος, and in Diogenes Laërtius, vi, 2:

Γηράσκει μὲν χαλκὸς ὑπὸ χρόνου· ἀλλὰ σὸν οὔτι
Κῦδος ὁ πᾶς αἰών, Διόγενες, καθελεῖ·
Μοῦνος ἐπεὶ βιοτῆς αὐτάρκεα δόξαν ἔδειξας
Θνητοῖς, καὶ ζωῆς οἶμον ἐλαφροτάτην.
(*Aera quidem absumit tempus, sed tempore numquam
Interitura tua est gloria, Diogenes:
Quandoquidem ad vitam miseris mortalibus aequam
Monstrata est facilis, te duce, et ampla via.*)[19]

Accordingly, the fundamental idea of cynicism is that life in its simplest and most naked form, with the hardships that naturally belong to it, is the most tolerable, and is therefore to be chosen. For every aid, comfort, enjoyment, and pleasure by which people would like to make life more agreeable, would produce only new worries and cares greater than those that originally belong to it. Therefore the following sentence may be regarded as the expression of the very core of the doctrine of cynicism: Διογένης ἐβόα πολλάκις λέγων, τὸν τῶν ἀνθρώπων βίον ῥᾴδιον ὑπὸ τῶν θεῶν δεδόσθαι, ἀποκεκρύφθαι δὲ αὐτὸν ζητούντων μελίπηκτα καὶ μύρα καὶ τὰ παραπλήσια (*Diogenes clamabat saepius, hominum vitam facilem a diis dari, verum occultari illam quaerentibus mellita cibaria, unguenta, et his similia.* Diogenes Laër-

---

[17] "We must consider how much less painful it is not to have something than to lose it; and we should understand that the poor have the less to suffer the less they have to lose. . . . It is easier and more endurable not to gain than to lose. . . . Diogenes managed so that he could not be robbed of anything. . . . [Regard him as poor or as like the gods] who has rendered himself free from everything fortuitous. It seems to me that Diogenes said: O Fate, concern yourself about your own; in Diogenes there is no longer anything that you can call yours." [Tr.]

[18] "Diogenes said that he thought he saw Fate looking at him and saying: I am not able to touch this mad dog." [Tr.]

[19] "Even brass becomes worn out in time, but never will future ages detract from your fame, Diogenes. For you alone showed the splendour of a frugal and moderate existence. You show the easiest path to the happiness of mortals." [Tr.]

tius, vi, 2).[20] And further: Δέον, ἀντὶ τῶν ἀχρήστων πόνων, τοὺς κατὰ φύσιν ἑλομένους, ζῆν εὐδαιμόνως· παρὰ τὴν ἄνοιαν κακοδαιμονοῦσι. — — — τὸν αὐτὸν χαρακτῆρα τοῦ βίου λέγων διεξάγειν, ὅνπερ καὶ Ἡρακλῆς, μηδὲν ἐλευθερίας προκρίνων (*Quum igitur, repudiatis inutilibus laboribus, naturales insequi, ac vivere beate debeamus, per summam dementiam infelices sumus. . . . eandem vitae formam, quam Hercules, se vivere affirmans, nihil libertati praeferens.* Ibid.)[21] Accordingly, the old genuine Cynics, Antisthenes, Diogenes, Crates, and their disciples, renounced every possession, all conveniences and pleasures, once for all, in order to escape for ever from the troubles and cares, the dependence and pains, that are inevitably bound up with them, and for which they are no compensation. By the bare satisfaction of the most pressing needs and the renunciation of everything superfluous, they thought they would come off best. They therefore put up with what in Athens and Corinth was to be had almost for nothing, such as lupins, water, a second-hand cloak, a knapsack, and a staff. They begged occasionally, so far as was necessary to obtain these things, but they did not work. But they accepted absolutely nothing in excess of the necessaries above-mentioned. Independence in the widest sense was their object. They spent their time in resting, walking about, talking with everyone, and in scoffing, laughing, and joking. Their characteristics were heedlessness and great cheerfulness. Now since with this way of living they had no aims of their own, no purposes and intentions to pursue, and so were lifted above human activities, and at the same time always enjoyed complete leisure, they were admirably suited, as men of proved strength of mind, to become the advisers and counsellors of others. Therefore, Apuleius says (*Florida,* iv): *Crates ut lar familiaris apud homines suae aetatis cultus est. Nulla domus ei unquam clausa erat: nec erat patrisfamilias tam absconditum secretum, quin eo tempestive Crates interveniret, litium omnium et jurgiorum inter propinquos disceptator et arbiter.*[22] Hence

---

[20] "Diogenes was in the habit of exclaiming often that it had been granted to men by the gods to live an easy life, but that this remained hidden from those who coveted sweetmeats, ointments, and the like." [Tr.]

[21] "When we endeavour merely to live naturally instead of making useless efforts, we are bound to lead a happy life; and we are unhappy only because of our folly. . . . And he maintained that his way of life was like that of Hercules, as he held nothing more dear than freedom." [Tr.]

[22] "Crates was worshipped by the men of his time as a household god. No house was ever closed to him, and no householder had a secret so hushed up that Crates would not have been let into it at the right moment, so that he might investigate and settle all disputes and quarrels between relatives." [Tr.]

in this, as in so many other things, they showed great similarity with the mendicant friars of modern times, at any rate with the better and more genuine of these, whose ideal may be seen in the Capuchin Cristoforo in Manzoni's famous novel. This similarity, however, is to be found only in the effects, not in the cause. They concur and coincide in the result, but the fundamental idea of the two is quite different. With the friars, as with the Sannyâsis who are akin to them, it is a goal transcending life; with the Cynics, however, it is only the conviction that it is easier to reduce one's desires and needs to the *minimum* than to attain to their *maximum* satisfaction; and this is even impossible, as with satisfaction desires and needs grow *ad infinitum*. Therefore to reach the goal of all ancient ethics, namely the greatest possible happiness in this life, they took the path of renunciation as the shortest and easiest: ὅθεν καὶ τὸν Κυνισμὸν εἰρήκασιν σύντομον ἐπ' ἀρετὴν ὁδόν (*unde et Cynismum dixere compendiosam ad virtutem viam.* Diogenes Laërtius, vi, 9).[23] The fundamental difference between the spirit of cynicism and that of asceticism comes out very clearly in the humility essential to asceticism, but so foreign to cynicism that the latter, on the contrary, has in view pride and disdain for all other men:

> *Sapiens uno minor est Jove, dives,*
> *Liber, honoratus, pulcher, rex denique regum.*[24]
> (Horace, *Epist.* [I.i. 106]).

On the other hand, the Cynics' view of life agrees in spirit with that of J.-J. Rousseau as he expounds it in the *Discours sur l'origine de l'inégalité;* for he too would lead us back to the crude state of nature, and regards the reduction of our needs to the minimum as the surest path to perfect happiness. For the rest, the Cynics were exclusively *practical* philosophers; at any rate, no account of their theoretical philosophy is known to me.

The Stoics proceeded from them by changing the practical into the theoretical. They were of opinion that *actual* dispensing with everything that can be discarded is not required, but that it is sufficient for us constantly to regard possession and enjoyment as *dispensable,* and as held in the hand of chance; for then the actual privation, should it eventually occur, would not be unexpected, nor would it be a burden. We can in all circumstances possess and enjoy everything, only we must always keep in mind the conviction of the worthlessness and dispensableness of such good things on the one hand, and their uncertainty and perishableness on the other; con-

---

[23] "They therefore described cynicism as the shortest path to virtue." [Tr.]

[24] "It is true that the sage is second only to Jupiter, rich and free and honoured and beautiful and a King of kings." [Tr.]

sequently, we must entirely underrate them all, and be ready at all times to give them up. In fact, the man who actually has to do without these things in order not to be moved by them, shows in this way that in his heart he considers them as really good things, which we must put entirely out of sight if we are not to hanker after them. The wise man, on the other hand, knows that they are not good things at all, but rather quite insignificant, ἀδιάφορα, or at most προηγμένα.[25] Therefore when they are offered to him, he will accept them; yet he is always ready to give them up again with the greatest indifference, if chance, to which they belong, demands them back, since they are τῶν οὐκ ἐφ᾽ ἡμῖν.[26] In this sense Epictetus (chap. vii) says that the wise man, like one who has disembarked from a ship, and so forth, will allow himself to be welcomed by his wife or little boy, but will always be ready to let them go again, as soon as the ship's master summons him. Thus the Stoics perfected the theory of equanimity and independence at the cost of practice, by reducing everything to a mental process; and by arguments like those presented in the first chapter of Epictetus, they sophisticated themselves into all the amenities of life. But in doing so they left out of account the fact that everything to which we are accustomed becomes a necessity, and therefore can be dispensed with only with pain; that the will cannot be trifled with, and cannot enjoy pleasures without becoming fond of them; that a dog does not remain indifferent when we draw through his mouth a piece of roast meat, or a sage when he is hungry; and that between desiring and renouncing there is no mean. But they believed they came to terms with their principles if, when sitting at a luxurious Roman table, they left no dish untasted; yet they assured everyone that these things were all and sundry mere προηγμένα, not ἀγαθά;[27] or in plain English, they ate, drank, and made merry, yet gave no thanks to God for it all, but rather made fastidious faces, and always bravely assured everyone that they got the devil a bit out of the whole feast! This was the expedient of the Stoics; accordingly, they were mere braggarts, and are related to the Cynics in much the same way as the well-fed Benedictines and Augustinians are to the Franciscans and Capuchins. Now the more they neglected practice, the more sharply did they bring theory to a fine point. Here I wish to add a few more isolated proofs and supplements to the explanation given at the end of our first book.

If, in the writings of the Stoics which are left to us, all of which

---

[25] "Indifferent"; "to be preferred." [Tr.]

[26] "Of the class of things that are not in our own power." [Tr.]

[27] "Preferable things"—"good things." [Tr.]

are unsystematically composed, we look for the ultimate ground of that unshakable equanimity that is constantly expected of us, we find none other than the knowledge that the course of the world is entirely independent of our will, and consequently that the evil that befalls us is inevitable. If we have regulated our claims in accordance with a correct insight into this, then mourning, rejoicing, fearing, and hoping are follies of which we are no longer capable. Here, especially in the commentaries of Arrian, it is surreptitiously assumed that all that is οὐκ ἐφ ἡμῖν (in other words, does not depend on us) would also at once be οὐ πρός ἡμᾶς (in other words, would not concern us). Yet it remains true that all the good things of life are in the power of chance, and consequently as soon as chance exercises this power and takes them away from us, we are unhappy if we have placed our happiness in them. We are supposed to be delivered from this unworthy fate by the correct use of our faculty of reason, by virtue of which we do not ever regard all these good things as our own, but only as lent to us for an indefinite time; only thus can we never really lose them. Therefore, Seneca says (*Epistola* 98): *Si quid humanarum rerum varietas possit cogitaverit, ante quam senserit,*[28] and Diogenes Laërtius (vii, 1.87): Ἴσον δέ ἐστι τὸ κατ' ἀρετὴν ζῆν τῷ κατ' ἐμπειρίαν τῶν φύσει συμβαινόντων ζῆν (*Secundum virtutem vivere idem est, quod secundum experientiam eorum, quae secundum naturam accidunt, vivere*).[29] Here the passage in Arrian's *Discourses of Epictetus*, Bk. iii, chap. 24, 84-89, is particularly relevant, and especially, as a proof of what I have said in this respect in § 16 of the first volume, the passage: Τοῦτο γάρ ἐστι τὸ αἴτιον τοῖς ἀνθρώποις πάντων τῶν κακῶν, τὸ τὰς προλήψεις τὰς κοινὰς μὴ δύνασθαι ἐφαρμόζειν ταῖς ἐπὶ μέρους, *ibid.* IV, 1.42. (*Haec enim causa est hominibus omnium malorum, quod anticipationes generales rebus singularibus accommodare non possunt.*[30] Similarly the passage in Marcus Aurelius (IV, 29): Εἰ ξένος κόσμου ὁ μὴ γνωρίζων τὰ ἐν αὐτῷ ὄντα, οὐχ ἧττον ξένος καὶ ὁ μὴ γνωρίζων τὰ γιγνόμενα, in other words: "If he is a stranger in the world who does not know what there is in it, no less of a stranger is he who does not know how things go on in it." The eleventh chapter of Seneca's *De Tranquillitate Animi* is also a complete illustration of this view. The opinion of the Stoics on the whole amounts to this, that if a man has watched the juggling

---

[28] "[But we shall then be calm and resigned] when we have reflected on what the fickleness of human things can do before we come to feel this." [Tr.]

[29] "To live according to virtue is the same as to live according to the experience of what usually happens by nature." [Tr.]

[30] "For this is the cause of all evil for men, that they are unable to apply universal concepts to particular cases." [Tr.]

illusion of happiness for a while and then uses his faculty of reason, he must recognize the rapid change of the dice as well as the intrinsic worthlessness of the counters, and must therefore henceforth remain unmoved. In general, the Stoic view can also be expressed as follows. Our suffering always springs from an incongruity between our desires and the course of the world. One of these two must therefore be changed and adapted to the other. Now as the course of things is not in our power (οὐκ ἐφ' ἡμῖν), we must regulate our wishing and desiring according to the course of things, for the will alone is ἐφ' ἡμῖν. This adaptation of willing to the course of the external world, and hence to the nature of things, is very often understood by the ambiguous κατὰ φύσιν ζῆν.[31] See Arrian, *Diss.* ii, 17, 21, 22. Seneca further expresses this view when he says (*Epistola* 119): *Nihil interest, utrum non desideres, an habeas. Summa rei in utroque est eadem: non torqueberis.*[32] Also Cicero (*Tusc.* iv, 26) by the words: *Solum habere velle, summa dementia est.*[33] Similarly Arrian (*Discourses of Epictetus*, iv, 1, 175): Οὐ γὰρ ἐκπληρώσει τῶν ἐπιθυμουμένων ἐλευθερία παρασκευάζεται, ἀλλὰ ἀνασκευῇ τῆς ἐπιθυμίας (*Non enim explendis desideriis libertas comparatur, sed tollenda cupiditate.*)[34]

The quotations collected in the *Historia Philosophiae Graeco-Romanae* of Ritter and Preller, § 398, may be regarded as proofs of what I have said in the place referred to above about the ὁμολογουμένως ζῆν[35] of the Stoics; similarly the saying of Seneca (*Ep.* 31 and again *Ep.* 74): *Perfecta virtus est aequalitas et tenor vitae per omnia consonans sibi.*[36] The spirit of the Stoa in general is clearly expressed by this passage of Seneca (*Ep.* 92): *Quid est beata vita? Securitas et perpetua tranquillitas. Hanc dabit animi magnitudo, dabit constantia bene judicati tenax.*[37] A systematic study of the Stoics will convince anyone that the aim of their ethics, like that of *Cynicism* from which it sprang, is absolutely none other than a life as painless

---

[31] "To live according to nature." [Tr.]

[32] "It comes to the same thing whether we do not crave for something or we have it. In both cases the main thing is the same, we are free from great suffering." [Tr.]

[33] "That we should wish merely to have something is the greatest folly." [Tr.]

[34] "For not by attaining to what we desire is true freedom gained, but by the suppression of desires." [Tr.]

[35] "Living harmoniously." [Tr.]

[36] "Perfect virtue consists in equableness and in a conduct of life that is at all times in harmony with itself." [Tr.]

[37] "In what does the happy life consist? In safety and unshakable peace. This is attained by greatness of soul, by a constancy that adheres to what is correctly discerned." [Tr.]

as possible, and thus as happy as possible. From this it follows that the Stoic morality is only a particular species of *eudaemonism*. It has not, like Indian, Christian, and even Platonic ethics, a metaphysical tendency, a transcendent end, but an end that is wholly immanent and attainable in this life; the imperturbability ($\dot{\alpha}\tau\alpha\rho\alpha\xi\dot{\iota}\alpha$) and unclouded, serene happiness of the sage whom nothing can assail or disturb. However, it is undeniable that the later Stoics, Arrian especially, sometimes lose sight of this aim, and betray a really ascetic tendency, to be ascribed to the Christian and, in the main, oriental spirit that was already spreading at the time. If we consider closely and seriously the goal of Stoicism, this $\dot{\alpha}\tau\alpha\rho\alpha\xi\dot{\iota}\alpha$, we find in it a mere hardening and insensibility to the blows of fate. This is attained by our always keeping in mind the shortness of life, the emptiness of pleasures, the instability of happiness, and also by our having seen that the difference between happiness and unhappiness is very much smaller than our anticipation of both is wont to make us believe. This, however, is still not a happy state or condition, but only the calm endurance of sufferings which we foresee as inevitable. Nevertheless, magnanimity and intrinsic merit are to be found in our silently and patiently bearing what is inevitable, in melancholy calm, remaining the same while others pass from jubilation to despair and from despair to jubilation. Thus we can also conceive of Stoicism as a spiritual dietetics, and in accordance with this, just as we harden the body to the influences of wind and weather, to privation and exertion, we also have to harden our mind to misfortune, danger, loss, injustice, malice, spite, treachery, arrogance, and men's folly.

I remark further that the $\varkappa\alpha\theta\tilde{\eta}\varkappa\text{o}\nu\tau\alpha$ of the Stoics, which Cicero translates *officia*, signify roughly *Obliegenheiten,* or that which it befits the occasion to do, English *incumbencies,* Italian *quel che tocca a me di fare o di lasciare,* and so in general what it *behoves* a reasonable person to do. See Diogenes Laërtius, vii, 1, 109. Finally, the *pantheism* of the Stoics, though absolutely inconsistent with so many of Arrian's exhortations, is most distinctly expressed by Seneca: *Quid est Deus? Mens universi. Quid est Deus? Quod vides totum, et quod non vides totum. Sic demum magnitudo sua illi redditur, qua nihil majus excogitari potest: si solus est omnia, opus suum et extra et intra tenet. (Quaestiones Naturales, I, praefatio, 12* [correctly, 13—Tr.])[38]

---

[38] "What is God? The soul of the universe. What is God? All that you see, and all that you do not see. Only thus is his greatness acknowledged, and nothing can be conceived greater than this. If he alone is everything, then he embraces his work and permeates it." [Tr.]

On Man's Need for Metaphysics

No beings, with the exception of man, feel surprised at their own existence, but to all of them it is so much a matter of course that they do not notice it. Yet the wisdom of nature speaks out of the peaceful glance of the animals, since in them will and intellect are not separated widely enough for them to be capable of being astonished at each other when they meet again. Thus in them the whole phenomenon is still firmly attached to the stem of nature from which it has sprung, and partakes of the unconscious omniscience of the great mother. Only after the inner being of nature (the will-to-live in its objectification) has ascended vigorously and cheerfully through the two spheres of unconscious beings, and then through the long and broad series of animals, does it finally attain to reflection for the first time with the appearance of reason (*Vernunft*), that is, in man. It then marvels at its own works, and asks itself what it itself is. And its wonder is the more serious, as here for the first time it stands consciously face to face with *death,* and besides the finiteness of all existence, the vanity and fruitlessness of all effort force themselves on it more or less. Therefore with this reflection and astonishment arises the *need for metaphysics* that is peculiar to man alone; accordingly, he is an *animal metaphysicum.* At the beginning of his consciousness, he naturally takes himself also as something that is a matter of course. This, however, does not last long, but very early, and simultaneously with the first reflection, appears that wonder which is some day to become the mother of metaphysics. In accordance with this, Aristotle says in the introduction to his *Metaphysics* [i, 982]: Διὰ γὰρ τὸ θαυμάζειν οἱ ἄνθρωποι καὶ νῦν καὶ τὸ πρῶτον ἤρξαντο φιλοσοφεῖν. (*Propter admirationem enim et nunc et primo inceperunt homines philosophari.*)[2] Moreover, the philosophical disposition properly speaking consists especially in our

---

[1] This chapter refers to § 15 of volume 1.

[2] "For on account of wonder and astonishment men now philosophize, as they began to do in the first place." [Tr.]

being capable of wondering at the commonplace thing of daily occurrence, whereby we are induced to make the *universal* of the phenomenon our problem. Investigators in the physical sciences, on the other hand, marvel only at selected and rare phenomena, and their problem is merely to refer these to phenomena better known. The lower a man is in an intellectual respect, the less puzzling and mysterious existence itself is to him; on the contrary, everything, how it is and that it is, seems to him a matter of course. This is due to the fact that his intellect remains quite true to its original destiny of being serviceable to the will as the medium of motives, and is therefore closely bound up with the world and with nature as an integral part of them. Consequently it is very far from comprehending the world purely objectively, detaching itself, so to speak, from the totality of things, facing this whole, and thus for the time being existing by itself. On the other hand, the philosophical wonder that springs from this is conditioned in the individual by higher development of intelligence, though generally not by this alone; but undoubtedly it is the knowledge of death, and therewith the consideration of the suffering and misery of life, that give the strongest impulse to philosophical reflection and metaphysical explanations of the world. If our life were without end and free from pain, it would possibly not occur to anyone to ask why the world exists, and why it does so in precisely this way, but everything would be taken purely as a matter of course. In keeping with this, we find that the interest inspired by philosophical and also religious systems has its strongest and essential point absolutely in the dogma of some future existence after death. Although the latter systems seem to make the existence of their gods the main point, and to defend this most strenuously, at bottom this is only because they have tied up their teaching on immortality therewith, and regard the one as inseparable from the other; this alone is really of importance to them. For if we could guarantee their dogma of immortality to them in some other way, the lively ardour for their gods would at once cool; and it would make way for almost complete indifference if, conversely, the absolute impossibility of any immortality were demonstrated to them. For interest in the existence of the gods would vanish with the hope of a closer acquaintance with them, down to what residue might be bound up with their possible influence on the events of the present life. But if continued existence after death could also be proved to be incompatible with the existence of gods, because, let us say, it presupposed originality of mode of existence, they would soon sacrifice these gods to their own immortality, and be eager for atheism. The fact that the really materialistic as well as the absolutely sceptical systems have never been able to obtain a general or lasting influence is attributable to the same reason.

Temples and churches, pagodas and mosques, in all countries and ages, in their splendour and spaciousness, testify to man's need for metaphysics, a need strong and ineradicable, which follows close on the physical. The man of a satirical frame of mind could of course add that this need for metaphysics is a modest fellow content with meagre fare. Sometimes it lets itself be satisfied with clumsy fables and absurd fairy-tales. If only they are imprinted early enough, they are for man adequate explanations of his existence and supports for his morality. Consider the Koran, for example; this wretched book was sufficient to start a world-religion, to satisfy the metaphysical need of countless millions for twelve hundred years, to become the basis of their morality and of a remarkable contempt for death, and also to inspire them to bloody wars and the most extensive conquests. In this book we find the saddest and poorest form of theism. Much may be lost in translation, but I have not been able to discover in it one single idea of value. Such things show that the capacity for metaphysics does not go hand in hand with the need for it. Yet it will appear that, in the early ages of the present surface of the earth, things were different, and those who stood considerably nearer to the beginning of the human race and to the original source of organic nature than do we, also possessed both greater energy of the intuitive faculty of knowledge, and a more genuine disposition of mind. They were thus capable of a purer and more direct comprehension of the inner essence of nature, and were thus in a position to satisfy the need for metaphysics in a more estimable manner. Thus there originated in those primitive ancestors of the Brahmans, the Rishis, the almost superhuman conceptions recorded in the *Upanishads* of the *Vedas*.

On the other hand, there has never been a lack of persons who have endeavoured to create their livelihood out of this need of man's for metaphysics, and to exploit it as much as possible. Therefore in all nations there are monopolists and farmers-general of it, namely the priests. But their vocation had everywhere to be assured to them by their receiving the right to impart their metaphysical dogmas to people at a very early age, before the power of judgement has been roused from its morning slumber, and hence in earliest childhood; for every dogma well implanted then, however senseless it may be, sticks for all time. If they had to wait till the power of judgement is mature, their privileges could not last.

A second, though not a numerous, class of persons, who derive their livelihood from men's need of metaphysics is constituted by those who live on *philosophy*. Among the Greeks they were called sophists; among the moderns they are called professors of philosophy. Aristotle (*Metaphysics,* ii, 2) without hesitation numbers Aristippus among the sophists. In Diogenes Laërtius (ii, 65) we find the reason for this, namely that he was the first of the Socratics to be paid for his philosophy, on which account Socrates sent him back his present. Among the moderns also those who live *by* philosophy are not only, as a rule and with the rarest exceptions, quite different from those who live *for* philosophy, but very often they are even the opponents of the latter, their secret and implacable enemies. For every genuine and important philosophical achievement will cast too great a shadow over theirs, and moreover will not adapt itself to the aims and limitations of the guild. For this reason they always endeavour to prevent such an achievement from finding favour. The customary means for this purpose, according to the times and circumstances in each case, are concealing, covering up, suppressing, hushing up, ignoring, keeping secret, or denying, disparaging, censuring, slandering, distorting, or finally denouncing and persecuting. Therefore many a great mind has had to drag itself breathlessly through life unrecognized, unhonoured, unrewarded, till finally after his death the world became undeceived as to him and as to them. In the meantime they had attained their end, had been accepted, by not allowing the man with a great mind to be accepted; and, with wife and child, they had lived *by* philosophy, while that man lived *for* it. When he is dead, however, matters are reversed; the new generation, and there always is one, now becomes heir to his achievements, trims them down to its own standard, and now lives *by* him. That Kant could nevertheless live both *by* and *for* philosophy was due to the rare circumstance that, for the first time since Divus Antoninus and Divus Julianus, a philosopher once more sat on the throne. Only under such auspices could the *Critique of Pure Reason* have seen the light. Hardly was the king dead when already we see Kant, seized with fear, because he belonged to the guild, modify, castrate, and spoil his masterpiece in the second edition, yet even so, soon run the risk of losing his post, so that Campe invited him to come to Brunswick, to live with him as the instructor of his family (Ring, *Ansichten aus Kants Leben,* p. 68). As for university philosophy, it is as a rule mere juggling and humbug. The real purpose of such philosophy is to give the students in the very depths of their thinking that mental tendency which the ministry that appoints people to professorships regards as in keeping with its views and intentions. From the statesman's point of view, the ministry may even be right, only it follows from this that such philosophy of the chair is a *nervis alienis mobile lignum*,[3] and cannot pass for serious philosophy, but only for philosophy that is a joke. Moreover, it is in any case reasonable that such a supervision or guidance should extend only to chair-philosophy, not to the real philosophy that is in earnest. For if anything in the world is desirable, so desirable that even the dull and uneducated herd in its more reflective moments would value it more than silver and gold, it is that a ray of light should fall on the obscurity of our existence, and that we should obtain some information about this enigmatical life of ours, in which nothing is clear except its misery and vanity. But supposing even that this were in itself attainable, it is made impossible by imposed and enforced solutions of the problem.

We will now, however, subject to a general consideration the different ways of satisfying this need for metaphysics that is so strong.

By *metaphysics* I understand all so-called knowledge that goes beyond the possibility of experience, and so beyond nature or the given phenomenal appearance of things, in order to give information about that by which, in some sense or other, this experience or nature is conditioned, or in popular language, about that which is hidden behind nature, and renders nature possible. But the great original difference in the powers of understanding, and also their cultivation, which requires much leisure, cause so great a variety among men that, as soon as a nation has extricated itself from the uncultured state, no *one* metaphysical system can suffice for all. Therefore in the case of civilized nations we generally come across two different kinds of metaphysics, distinguished by the fact that the one has its verification and credentials *in itself,* the other *outside itself.* As the metaphysical systems of the first kind require reflection, culture, leisure, and judgement for the recognition of their credentials, they can be accessible only to an extremely small number of persons; moreover, they can arise and maintain themselves only in the case of an advanced civilization. The systems of the second kind, on the other hand, are exclusively for the great majority of people who are not capable of thinking but only of believing, and are susceptible not to arguments, but only to authority. These systems may therefore be described as popular metaphysics, on the analogy of popular poetry and popular wisdom, by which is understood proverbs. These systems are known under the name of religions, and are to be found among all races, with the exception of the most uncivilized of all. As I have said, their evidence is external, and, as such, is called revelation, which is authenticated by signs and mira-

---

[3] "A wooden puppet moved by extraneous forces." [Tr.]

cles. Their arguments are mainly threats of eternal, and indeed also temporal evils, directed against unbelievers, and even against mere doubters. As *ultima ratio theologorum*[4] we find among many nations the stake or things like it. If they seek a different authentication or use different arguments, they make the transition into the systems of the first kind, and may degenerate into a cross between the two, which brings more danger than advantage. For their invaluable prerogative of being imparted to *children* gives them the surest guarantee of permanent possession of the mind, and in this way their dogmas grow into a kind of second inborn intellect, like the twig on the grafted tree. The systems of the first kind, on the other hand, always appeal only to adults, but in them they always find a system of the second kind already in possession of their conviction. Both kinds of metaphysics, the difference between which can be briefly indicated by the expressions doctrine of conviction and doctrine of faith, have in common the fact that every particular system of them stands in a hostile relation to all others of its kind. Between those of the first kind war is waged only with word and pen; between those of the second kind with fire and sword as well. Many of those of the second kind owe their propagation partly to this latter kind of polemic, and in the course of time all have divided the earth among themselves, and that with such decided authority that the peoples of the world are distinguished and separated rather according to them than according to nationality or government. They alone are *dominant,* each in its own province; those of the first kind, on the contrary, are at most *tolerated,* and even this only because, by reason of the small number of their adherents, they are usually not considered worth the trouble of combating with fire and sword, although, where it has seemed necessary, even these have been employed against them with success; moreover they are found only sporadically. But they have usually been tolerated only in a tamed and subjugated condition, since the system of the second kind that prevailed in the country ordered them to adapt their doctrines more or less closely to its own. Occasionally it has not only subjugated them, but made them serve its purpose, and used them as an additional horse to its coach. This, however, is a dangerous experiment, for, since those systems of the first kind are deprived of power, they believe they can assist themselves by craft and cunning; and they never entirely renounce a secret malice. This malice then occasionally comes on the scene unexpectedly, and inflicts injuries that are hard to cure. Moreover, their dangerous nature is increased by the fact that all the physical sciences, not excepting even the most innocent,

---

[4] "The ultimate argument of theologians." [Tr.]

are their secret allies against the systems of the second kind, and, without being themselves 'openly at war with these, they suddenly and unexpectedly do great harm in their province. Moreover, the attempt aimed at by the above-mentioned enlistment of the services of the systems of the first kind by those of the second, namely to give a system which originally has its authentication from outside an additional authentication from within, is by its nature perilous; for if it were capable of such an authentication, it would not have required an external one. And in general, it is always a hazardous undertaking to attempt to put a new foundation under a finished structure. Moreover, why should a religion require the suffrage of a philosophy? Indeed, it has everything on its side, revelation, documents, miracles, prophecies, government protection, the highest dignity and eminence, as is due to truth, the consent and reverence of all, a thousand temples in which it is preached and practised, hosts of sworn priests, and, more than all this, the invaluable prerogative of being allowed to imprint its doctrines on the mind at the tender age of childhood, whereby they become almost innate ideas. With such an abundance of means at its disposal, still to desire the assent of wretched philosophers it would have to be more covetous, or still to attend to their contradiction it would have to be more apprehensive, than appears compatible with a good conscience.

To the above-established distinction between metaphysics of the first kind and of the second, is still to be added the following. A system of the first kind, that is, a philosophy, makes the claim, and therefore has the obligation, to be true *sensu stricto et proprio* in all that it says, for it appeals to thought and conviction. A religion, on the other hand, has only the obligation to be true *sensu allegorico,* since it is destined for the innumerable multitude who, being incapable of investigating and thinking, would never grasp the profoundest and most difficult truths *sensu proprio*. Before the people truth cannot appear naked. A symptom of this *allegorical* nature of religions is the *mysteries,* to be found perhaps in every religion, that is, certain dogmas that cannot even be distinctly conceived, much less be literally true. In fact, it might perhaps be asserted that some absolute inconsistencies and contradictions, some actual absurdities, are an essential ingredient of a complete religion; for these are just the stamp of its *allegorical* nature, and the only suitable way of making the ordinary mind and uncultured understanding *feel* what would be incomprehensible to it, namely that religion deals at bottom with an entirely different order of things, an order of *things-in-themselves*. In the presence of such an order the laws of this phenomenal world, according to which it must speak, disappear.

Therefore, not only the contradictory but also the intelligible dogmas are really only allegories and accommodations to the human power of comprehension. It seems to me that Augustine and even Luther adhered to the mysteries of Christianity in this spirit, as opposed to Pelagianism, which seeks to reduce everything to trite and dull comprehensibility. From this point of view it is easy to understand how Tertullian could in all seriousness say: *Prorsus credibile est, quia ineptum est: . . . certum est, quia impossibile.* (*De Carne Christi,* c. 5.)[5] This *allegorical* nature of religions also exempts them from the proofs incumbent on philosophy, and in general from scrutiny and investigation. Instead of this, they demand faith, in other words, a voluntary acceptance that such is the state of affairs. Then, as faith guides conduct, and the allegory is framed so that, as regards the practical, it always leads precisely whither the truth *sensu proprio* would also lead, religion justly promises eternal bliss to those who believe. We therefore see that in the main, and for the great majority unable to devote themselves to thinking, religions fill very well the place of metaphysics in general, the need of which man feels to be imperative. They do this partly for a practical purpose as the guiding star of their action, as the public standard of integrity and virtue, as Kant admirably expresses it; partly as the indispensable consolation in the deep sorrows of life. In this they completely take the place of an objectively true system of metaphysics, since they lift man above himself and above existence in time, as well, perhaps, as such a system ever could. In this their great value, indeed their indispensability is quite clearly to be seen. For Plato rightly says: φιλόσοφον πλῆθος ἀδύνατον εἶναι (*vulgus philosophum esse impossibile est*),[6] (*Republic,* VI [494 A], p. 89 *Bip.*). On the other hand, the only stumbling-block is that religions never dare acknowledge their allegorical nature, but have to assert that they are true *sensu proprio.* In this way they encroach on the sphere of metaphysics proper, and provoke its antagonism. Therefore such antagonism is expressed at all times, when metaphysics has not been chained up. The controversy between supernaturalists and rationalists, carried on so incessantly in our own day, is due to the failure to recognize the allegorical nature of all religion. Thus, both want to have Christianity true *sensu proprio;* in this sense, the supernaturalists wish to maintain it without deduction, with skin and hair as it were; and here they have much to contend with in view of the knowledge and general culture of the age. The rationalists, on the other hand, attempt

---

[5] "It is thoroughly credible because it is absurd: . . . it is certain because it is impossible." [Tr.]

[6] "It is impossible for the crowd to be philosophically enlightened." [Tr.]

to explain away exegetically all that is characteristically Christian, whereupon they retain something that is not true either *sensu proprio* or *sensu allegorico,* but rather a mere platitude, little better than Judaism, or at most a shallow Pelagianism, and, what is worst of all, an infamous optimism, absolutely foreign to Christianity proper. Moreover, the attempt to found a religion on reason (*Vernunft*) removes it into the other class of metaphysics, namely that which has its authentication *in itself,* and thus on to a foreign soil, the soil of the philosophical systems, and consequently into the conflict these wage against one another in their own arena; and so this brings it under the rifle-fire of scepticism, and the heavy artillery of the *Critique of Pure Reason.* But for it to venture here would be downright presumption.

It would be most beneficial to both kinds of metaphysics for each to remain clearly separated from the other, and to confine itself to its own province, in order there to develop fully its true nature. Instead of this, the endeavour throughout the Christian era has been to bring about a fusion of the two by carrying over the dogmas and concepts of the one into the other, and in this way both are impaired. In our day this has been done most openly in that strange hybrid or centaur, the so-called philosophy of religion. As a kind of gnosis, this attempts to interpret the given religion, and to explain what is true *sensu allegorico* through something that is true *sensu proprio.* But for this we should have already to know the truth *sensu proprio,* and in that case interpretation would be superfluous. For to attempt first to find metaphysics, i.e., the truth *sensu proprio,* merely from religion by explanation and a fresh interpretation, would be a precarious and perilous undertaking. We could decide to do this only if it were established that truth, like iron and other base metals, could occur only in the ore, and not in the pure unalloyed state, and that it could therefore be obtained only by reduction from that ore.

Religions are necessary for the people, and are an inestimable benefit to them. But if they attempt to oppose the progress of mankind in the knowledge of truth, then with the utmost possible indulgence and forbearance they must be pushed on one side. And to require that even a great mind—a Shakespeare or a Goethe—should make the dogmas of any religion his implicit conviction, *bona fide et sensu proprio,* is like requiring a giant to put on the shoes of a dwarf.

As religions are calculated with reference to the mental capacity of the great mass of people, they can have only an indirect, not a direct truth. To demand direct truth of them is like wanting to read the type set up in a compositor's stick instead of its impression. Accordingly, the value of a religion will depend on the greater or lesser content of truth which it has in itself under the veil of allegory; next on the greater or lesser distinctness with which this content of truth is visible through the veil, and hence on that veil's transparency. It almost seems that, as the oldest languages are the most perfect, so too are the oldest religions. If I wished to take the results of my philosophy as the standard of truth, I should have to concede to Buddhism pre-eminence over the others. In any case, it must be a pleasure to me to see my doctrine in such close agreement with a religion that the majority of men on earth hold as their own, for this numbers far more followers than any other. And this agreement must be yet the more pleasing to me, inasmuch as in my philosophizing I have certainly not been under its influence. For up till 1818, when my work appeared, there were to be found in Europe only a very few accounts of Buddhism, and those extremely incomplete and inadequate, confined almost entirely to a few essays in the earlier volumes of the *Asiatic Researches,* and principally concerned with the Buddhism of the Burmese. Only since that time has fuller information about this religion gradually reached us, chiefly through the profound and instructive articles of that meritorious member of the St. Petersburg Academy, I. J. Schmidt, in the records of his Academy, and then in the course of time through several English and French scholars, so that I have been able to furnish a fairly numerous list of the best works on this religion in my book *On the Will in Nature* under the heading "Sinology." Unfortunately, Csoma Körösi, that steadfast and assiduous Hungarian, who, in order to study the language and sacred writings of Buddhism, spent many years in Tibet and particularly in Buddhist monasteries, was carried off by death just as he was beginning to work out for us the results of his investigations. But I cannot deny the pleasure with which I read in his preliminary accounts several passages taken from the *Kahgyur* itself, for example, the following discourse of the dying Buddha with Brahma who is paying him homage: "There is a description of their conversation on the subject of creation—By whom was the world made? Shakya asks several questions of Brahma—whether was it he, who made or produced such and such things, and endowed or blessed them with such and such virtues or properties,—whether was it he who caused the several revolutions in the destruction and regeneration of the world. He denies that he had ever done anything to that effect. At last he himself asks Shakya how the world was made,—by whom? Here are attributed all changes in the world to the moral works of the animal beings, and it is stated that in the world all is illusion, there is no reality in the things; all is empty. Brahma being instructed in his doctrine, becomes his follower." (*Asiatic Researches,* Vol. XX, p. 434.)

I cannot, as is generally done, put the *fundamental difference* of all religions in the question whether they are monotheistic, polytheistic, pantheistic, or atheistic, but only in the question whether they are optimistic or pessimistic, in other words, whether they present the existence of this world as justified by itself, and consequently praise and commend it, or consider it as something which can be conceived only as the consequence of our guilt, and thus really ought not to be, in that they recognize that pain and death cannot lie in the eternal, original, and immutable order of things, that which in every respect ought to be. The power by virtue of which Christianity was able to overcome first Judaism, and then the paganism of Greece and Rome, is to be found solely in its pessimism, in the confession that our condition is both exceedingly sorrowful and sinful, whereas Judaism and paganism were optimistic. That truth, profoundly and painfully felt by everyone, took effect, and entailed the need for redemption.

I turn to a general consideration of the other kind of metaphysics, that which has its authentication in itself, and is called *philosophy.* I remind the reader of its previously mentioned origin from a *wonder or astonishment* about the world and our own existence, since these obtrude themselves on the intellect as a riddle, whose solution then occupies mankind without intermission. Here I would first of all draw attention to the fact that this could not be the case if, in Spinoza's sense, so often put forth again in our own day under modern forms and descriptions as pantheism, the world were an *"absolute substance,"* and consequently a *positively necessary mode of existence.* For this implies that it exists with a necessity so great, that beside it every other necessity conceivable as such to our understanding must look like an accident or contingency. Thus it would then be something that embraced not only every actual, but also any possible, existence in such a way that, as indeed Spinoza states, its possibility and its actuality would be absolutely one. Therefore its non-being would be impossibility itself, and so it would be something whose non-being or other-being would inevitably be wholly inconceivable, and could in consequence be just as little thought away as can, for instance, time or space. Further, since *we ourselves* would be parts, modes, attributes, or accidents of such an absolute substance, which would be the only thing capable in any sense of existing at any time and in any place, our existence and its, together with its properties, would necessarily be very far from presenting themselves to us as surprising, remarkable, problematical, in fact as the unfathomable and ever-disquieting riddle; on the contrary, they would of necessity be even more self-evident and a matter of course than the fact that two and two make four. For we should necessarily be quite incapable of thinking anything else than that the world is, and is as it is; consequently, we should inevitably be just as little conscious of its existence *as such,* that is to say, as a problem for reflection, as we are of our planet's incredibly rapid motion.

Now all this is by no means the case. Only to the animal lacking thoughts or ideas do the world and existence appear to be a matter of course. To man, on the contrary, they are a problem, of which even the most uncultured and narrow-minded person is at certain more lucid moments vividly aware, but which enters the more distinctly and permanently into everyone's consciousness, the brighter and more reflective that consciousness is, and the more material for thinking he has acquired through culture. Finally, in minds adapted to philosophizing, all this is raised to Plato's θαυμάζειν, μάλα φιλοσοφι-κὸν πάθος (*mirari, valde philosophicus affectus*),[7] that is, to that *wonder or astonishment* which comprehends in all its magnitude the problem that incessantly occupies the nobler portion of mankind in every age and in every country, and allows it no rest. In fact, the balance wheel which maintains in motion the watch of metaphysics that never runs down, is the clear knowledge that this world's non-existence is just as possible as is its existence. Therefore, Spinoza's view of the world as an absolutely necessary mode of existence, in other words, as something that positively and in every sense ought to and must be, is a false one. Even simple theism in its cosmological proof tacitly starts from the fact that it infers the world's previous non-existence from its existence; thus, it assumes in advance that the world is something contingent. What is more, in fact, we very soon look upon the world as something whose non-existence is not only conceivable, but even preferable to its existence. Therefore our astonishment at it easily passes into a brooding over that *fatality* which could nevertheless bring about its existence, and by virtue of which such an immense force as is demanded for the production and maintenance of such a world could be directed so much against its own interest and advantage. Accordingly, philosophical astonishment is at bottom one that is dismayed and distressed; philosophy, like the overture to *Don Juan,* starts with a minor chord. It follows from this that philosophy cannot be either Spinozism or optimism. The more specific character, just mentioned, of the astonishment that urges us to philosophize, obviously springs from the sight of the *evil and wickedness* in the world. Even if these were

---

[7] "Astonishment as a very philosophical emotion." [*Theaetetus,* 155 D. Tr.]

in the most equal ratio to each other, and were also far outweighed by the good, yet they are something that absolutely and in general ought not to be. But as nothing can come out of nothing, they too must have their germ in the origin or the kernel of the world itself. It is hard for us to assume this when we look at the size, the order, and the completeness of the physical world, since we imagine that what had the power to produce such a world must also have been well able to avoid the evil and the wickedness. It is easy to understand that this assumption (the truest expression of which is Ormuzd and Ahriman) is hardest of all for theism. Therefore, the freedom of the will was invented in the first place to dispose of *wickedness;* this, however, is only a disguised way of making something out of nothing, since it assumes an *operari* that resulted from no *esse* (see *Die beiden Grundprobleme der Ethik,* pp. 58 *et seq.;* 2nd ed., pp. 57 *et seq.*). Then the attempt was made to get rid of *evil* by imputing it to matter, or even to an unavoidable necessity, and here the devil, who is really the *expediens ad hoc,*[8] was reluctantly set aside. To evil *death* also belongs; but *wickedness* is merely the shifting of the evil that exists in each case from oneself on to another. Hence, as we have said above, it is wickedness, evil, and death that qualify and intensify philosophical astonishment. Not merely that the world exists, but still more that it is such a miserable and melancholy world, is the *punctum pruriens*[9] of metaphysics, the problem awakening in mankind an unrest that cannot be quieted either by scepticism or criticism.

We also find *physics,* in the widest sense of the word, concerned with the explanation of phenomena in the world; but it lies already in the nature of the explanations themselves that they cannot be sufficient. *Physics* is unable to stand on its own feet, but needs a *metaphysics* on which to support itself, whatever fine airs it may assume towards the latter. For it explains phenomena by something still more unknown than are they, namely by laws of nature resting on forces of nature, one of which is also the vital force. Certainly the whole present condition of all things in the world or in nature must necessarily be capable of explanation from purely physical causes. But such an explanation—supposing one actually succeeded so far as to be able to give it—must always just as necessarily be burdened with two essential imperfections (as it were with two sore points, or like Achilles with the vulnerable heel, or the devil with the cloven foot). On account of these imperfections, everything so explained would still really remain unexplained. The first imperfec-

---

[8] "Means to this end." [Tr.]
[9] "Tormenting problem." [Tr.]

tion is that the *beginning* of the chain of causes and effects that explains everything, in other words, of the connected and continuous changes, can positively *never* be reached, but, just like the limits of the world in space and time, recedes incessantly and *in infinitum*. The second imperfection is that all the efficient causes from which everything is explained always rest on something wholly inexplicable, that is, on the original *qualities* of things and the *natural forces* that make their appearance in them. By virtue of such forces they produce a definite effect, e.g., weight, hardness, impact, elasticity, heat, electricity, chemical forces, and so on, and such forces remain in every given explanation like an unknown quantity, not to be eliminated at all, in an otherwise perfectly solved algebraical equation. Accordingly there is not a fragment of clay, however little its value, that is not entirely composed of inexplicable qualities. Therefore these two inevitable defects in every purely physical, i.e., causal, explanation indicate that such an explanation can be only *relatively* true, and that its whole method and nature cannot be the only, the ultimate and hence sufficient one, in other words, cannot be the method that will ever be able to lead to the satisfactory solution of the difficult riddle of things, and to the true understanding of the world and of existence; but that the *physical* explanation, in general and as such, still requires one that is *metaphysical,* which would furnish the key to all its assumptions, but for that very reason would have to follow quite a different path. The first step to this is that we should bring to distinct consciousness and firmly retain the distinction between the two, that is, the difference between *physics* and *metaphysics*. In general this difference rests on the Kantian distinction between *phenomenon* and *thing-in-itself.* Just because Kant declared the thing-in-itself to be absolutely unknowable, there was, according to him, no *metaphysics* at all, but merely immanent knowledge, in other words mere *physics,* which can always speak only of phenomena, and together with this a critique of reason which aspires to metaphysics. However, to show the true point of contact between my philosophy and Kant's, I will here anticipate the second book, and stress the fact that, in his fine explanation of the compatibility of freedom with necessity (*Critique of Pure Reason,* first edition, pp. 532-554, and *Critique of Practical Reason,* pp. 224-231 of the Rosenkranz edition), Kant demonstrates how one and the same action can be perfectly explained on the one hand as necessarily arising from the man's character, from the influence he has undergone in the course of his life, and from the motives now present to him, and yet on the other hand must be regarded as the work of his free will. In the same sense he says, § 53 of the *Prolegomena*:

"It is true that natural necessity will attach to all connexion of cause and effect in the world of sense, yet, on the other hand, freedom is conceded to that cause which is itself no phenomenon (although forming the foundation of the phenomenon). Hence nature and freedom can without contradiction be attributed to the same thing, but in a different reference; at one time as phenomenon, at another as a thing-in-itself." Now what Kant teaches about the phenomenon of man and his actions is extended by my teaching to *all* the phenomena in nature, since it makes their foundation the *will* as thing-in-itself. This procedure is justified first of all by the fact that it must not be assumed that man is specifically, *toto genere,* and radically different from the rest of the beings and things in nature, but rather that he is different only in degree. From this anticipatory digression, I turn back to our consideration of the inadequacy of physics to give us the ultimate explanation of things. I say, therefore, that everything is certainly physical, yet not explainable. As for the motion of the projected bullet, so also for the thinking of the brain, a physical explanation in itself must ultimately be possible which would make the latter just as comprehensible as the former. But the former, which we imagine we understand so perfectly, is at bottom just as obscure to us as the latter; for whatever the inner nature of expansion in space, of impenetrability, mobility, hardness, elasticity, and gravity may be—it remains, after all physical explanations, just as much a mystery as thinking does. But because in the case of thought the inexplicable stands out most immediately, a jump was at once made here from physics to metaphysics, and a substance of quite a different kind from everything corporeal was hypostatized; a soul was set up in the brain. Yet if we were not so dull as to be capable of being struck only by the most remarkable phenomenon, we should have to explain digestion by a soul in the stomach, vegetation by a soul in the plant, elective affinity by a soul in the reagents, in fact the falling of a stone by a soul in the stone. For the quality of every inorganic body is just as mysterious as is life in the living body. Therefore in the same way, physical explanation everywhere comes across what is metaphysical, and by this is reduced to nought, in other words, ceases to be explanation. Strictly speaking, it could be asserted that all natural science at bottom achieves nothing more than what is also achieved by botany, namely the bringing together of things that are homogeneous, classification. A system of physics which asserted that its explanations of things— in the particular from causes and in general from forces—were actually sufficient, and therefore exhausted the inner essence of the world, would be *naturalism* proper. From Leucippus, Democritus, and Epicurus down to the *Système de la nature,* and then to La-marck, Cabanis, and the materialism cooked up again in the last few years, we can follow the unceasing attempt to set up a *system of physics without metaphysics,* in other words, a doctrine that would make the phenomenon into the thing-in-itself. But all their explanations try to conceal from the explainers themselves and from others that they assume the principal thing without more ado. They endeavour to show that all phenomena are physical, even those of the mind; and rightly so, only they do not see that everything physical is, on the other hand, metaphysical also. Without Kant, how-ever, this is difficult to see, for it presupposes the distinction of the phenomenon from the thing-in-itself. Yet even without this, Aristotle, much inclined to empiricism as he was, and far removed as he was from Platonic hyperphysics, kept himself free from this limited view. He says: Εἰ μὲν οὖν μὴ ἐστί τις ἑτέρα οὐσία παρὰ τὰς φύσει συνεστη-κυίας, ἡ φυσικὴ ἂν εἴη πρώτη ἐπιστήμη· εἰ δέ ἐστί τις οὐσία ἀκίνητος, αὕτη προτέρα καὶ φιλοσοφία πρώτη, καὶ καθόλου οὕτως, ὅτι πρώτη· καὶ περὶ τοῦ ὄντος ᾗ ὄν, ταύτης ἂν εἴη θεωρῆσαι. (*Si igitur non est aliqua alia substantia praeter eas quae natura consistunt, physica profecto prima scientia esset: quodsi autem est aliqua substantia immobilis, haec prior et philosophia prima, et universalis sic, quod prima; et de ente, prout ens est, speculari hujus est.*) *Metaphysics,* v [vi], 1 [1026a].[10] Such an *absolute system of physics* as described above, which would leave no room for any *metaphysics,* would make *natura naturata* (created nature) into *natura naturans* (creative nature); it would be physics seated on the throne of metaphysics. But in this high position it would look almost like Holberg's theatri-cal pot-house politician who was made burgomaster. Even behind the reproach of atheism, in itself absurd and often spiteful, there lies, as its inner meaning and truth that gives it strength, the obscure conception of such an absolute system of physics without meta-physics. Certainly such a system would necessarily be destructive for ethics, and just as theism has been falsely regarded as inseparable from morality, this is really true only of a *system of metaphysics in general,* in other words, of the knowledge that the order of nature is not the only and absolute order of things. We can therefore set this up as the necessary *credo* of all righteous and good men: "I believe in a system of metaphysics." In this respect it is important

---

[10] "Now if there is no other entity except those existing by nature, physics would be the first science; but if there is any immutable entity, then this is the earlier science, and philosophy from it is the first and therefore the most universal science, because it is the first, and its problem would be to enquire after that which is as such." [Tr.]

and necessary for us to be convinced of the untenable nature of an *absolute system of physics,* the more so as such a system, namely *naturalism* proper, is a view that of its own accord and ever anew forces itself on man, and can be done away with only by deeper speculation. In this respect, all kinds of systems and doctrines of faith, in so far and as long as they are held in esteem, certainly also serve as a substitute for such speculation. But that a fundamentally false view thrusts itself automatically on man, and must first be ingeniously removed, is to be explained by the fact that the intellect is not originally destined to enlighten us on the nature of things, but only to show us their relations in reference to our will. As we shall find in the second book, the intellect is the mere medium of motives. Now that the world is schematized in the intellect in a manner presenting quite a different order of things from the absolutely true one, because it shows us not their kernel but only their outer shell, happens accidentally, and cannot be used as a reproach to the intellect; the less so, as the intellect indeed finds within itself the means for rectifying that error. Thus it arrives at the distinction between phenomenon and the being-in-itself of things. At bottom, this distinction existed at all times, only it was often brought to consciousness very imperfectly, was therefore inadequately expressed, and indeed often appeared in strange disguise. For example, the Christian mystics, by calling the intellect the *light of nature,* declare it to be inadequate for comprehending the true inner nature of things. The intellect is, so to speak, a mere superficial force, like electricity, and does not penetrate into the very essence of things.

The inadequacy of pure naturalism, as I have said, first appears on the empirical path itself, from the fact that every physical explanation explains the particular from its cause; but the chain of these causes, as we know *a priori,* and consequently with perfect certainty, runs back into infinity, so that absolutely no cause could ever be the first. But then the effectiveness of every cause is referred to a law of nature, and this law in the end to a force of nature, which remains as the absolutely inexplicable. This inexplicable, however, to which all the phenomena of this so clearly given and so naturally explainable world, from the highest to the lowest, are referred, just betrays that the whole nature of such explanation is only conditional, only *ex concessis* so to speak, and is by no means the real and sufficient one. I therefore said above that physically everything and nothing is explainable. That absolutely inexplicable something which pervades all phenomena, which is most striking in the highest, e.g., in generation, yet is just as much present in the lowest, e.g., in the mechanical, points to an order of things of an entirely different kind lying at the foundation of the physical order, and this is just what Kant calls the order of things-in-themselves, and is the goal of metaphysics. But secondly, the inadequacy of pure naturalism is evident from that fundamental philosophical truth which we considered at length in the first half of this book, and which is the theme of the *Critique of Pure Reason*—the truth that every *object,* according to its objective existence in general and also to the mode and manner (the formal) of this existence, is conditioned throughout by the knowing *subject,* and consequently is mere phenomenon, not thing-in-itself. This is explained in § 7 of the first volume, where it was shown that nothing can be more clumsy than for us, after the manner of all materialists, blindly to take the objective as absolutely given, in order to derive everything from it without paying any regard to the subjective. By means of this subjective, in fact in it alone, the objective exists. Specimens of this procedure are most readily afforded us by the fashionable materialism of our own day, which has thus become a real philosophy for barbers' and druggists' apprentices. In its innocence, matter, which without hesitation is taken as absolutely real, is for it a thing-in-itself, and impulsive force is the only quality or faculty of a thing-in-itself, since all other qualities can be only phenomena thereof.

Accordingly, naturalism, or the purely physical way of considering things, will never be sufficient; it is like a sum in arithmetic that never comes out. Beginningless and endless causal series, inscrutable fundamental forces, endless space, beginningless time, infinite divisibility of matter, and all this further conditioned by a knowing brain, in which alone it exists just like a dream and without which it vanishes—all these things constitute the labyrinth in which naturalism leads us incessantly round and round. The height to which the natural sciences have risen in our time puts all the previous centuries entirely in the shade in this respect, and is a summit reached by mankind for the first time. But however great the advances which *physics* (understood in the wide sense of the ancients) may make, not the smallest step towards *metaphysics* will be made in this way, just as a surface never attains cubical contents however far its extension is carried. For such advances will always supplement only knowledge of the *phenomenon,* whereas *metaphysics* strives to pass beyond the phenomenal appearance to that which appears; and even if we had in addition an entire and complete experience, matters would not be advanced in this way as regards the main point. In fact, even if a man wandered through all the planets of all the fixed stars, he would still not have made one step in *metaphysics.* On the contrary, the greatest advances in *physics* will only make the need for a system of *metaphysics* felt more and more, since the corrected, extended, and more thorough knowledge of nature is the very knowledge that always undermines and finally overthrows the metaphysical assumptions that till then have prevailed. On the other hand, such knowledge presents the problem of metaphysics itself more distinctly, correctly, and completely, and separates it more clearly from all that is merely physical. In addition, the more perfectly and accurately known intrinsic essence of individual things demands more pressingly the explanation of the whole and the universal, and this whole only presents itself as the more puzzling and mysterious, the more accurately, thoroughly, and completely it is known empirically. Of course, the individual simple investigator of nature in a separate branch of physics is not clearly aware of all this at once. On the contrary, he sleeps comfortably with his chosen maid in the house of Odysseus, banishing all thoughts of Penelope (see chap. 12, end). Therefore at the present day we see the *husk of nature* most accurately and exhaustively investigated, the intestines of intestinal worms and the vermin of vermin known to a nicety. But if anyone, such as myself for instance, comes along and speaks of the *kernel of nature,* they do not listen; they just think that this has nothing to do with the matter, and go on sifting their husks. One feels tempted to apply to these excessively microscopical and micrological investigators of nature the name of nature's meddlers. But those who imagine crucibles and retorts to be the true and only source of all wisdom are in their way just as wrong-headed as their antipodes the scholastics were previously. Thus, just as the scholastics, captivated entirely by their concepts, used these as their weapons, neither knowing nor investigating anything besides them, so the investigators of nature, captivated entirely by their empiricism, accept nothing but what their eyes see. With this they imagine they arrive at the ultimate ground of things, not suspecting that between the phenomenon and that which manifests itself therein, namely the thing-in-itself, there is a deep gulf, a radical difference. This difference can be cleared up only by the knowledge and accurate delimitation of the subjective element of the phenomenon, and by the insight that the ultimate and most important information about the inner nature of things can be drawn only from self-consciousness. Without all this, we cannot go one step beyond what is given immediately to the senses, and thus do no more than arrive at the problem. On the other hand, it must be noted that the most complete knowledge of nature possible is the corrected *statement of the problem* of metaphysics. No one, therefore, should venture on this without having previously acquired a knowledge of all the branches of natural science which, though only general, is yet thorough, clear, and connected. For the problem must come before the solution; but then the investigator must turn his glance inwards, for intellectual and ethical phenomena are more important than physical, to the same extent that animal magnetism, for example, is an incomparably more important phenomenon than mineral magnetism. Man carries the ultimate fundamental secrets within himself, and this fact is accessible to him in the most immediate way. Here only, therefore, can he hope to find the key to the riddle of the world, and obtain a clue to the inner nature of all things. Thus the very special province of *metaphysics* certainly lies in what has been called mental philosophy.

> "The ranks of living creatures thou dost lead
> Before me, teaching me to know my brothers
> In air and water and the silent wood: . . .
> Then to the cave secure thou leadest me,
> Then show'st me mine own self, and in my breast
> The deep, mysterious miracles unfold." [11]

Finally, as regards the *source or fount* of metaphysical knowledge, I have already declared myself opposed to the assumption, repeated even by Kant, that it must lie in *mere concepts*. In no knowledge can concepts be the first thing, for they are always drawn from some perception. But what led to that assumption was probably the example of mathematics. Leaving perception entirely, as happens in algebra, trigonometry, and analysis, mathematics can operate with pure abstract concepts, indeed with concepts represented only by signs instead of words, and yet arrive at a perfectly certain result which is still so remote that no one continuing on the firm ground of perception could have reached it. But the possibility of this depends, as Kant has sufficiently shown, on the fact that the concepts of mathematics are drawn from the most certain and definite of all perceptions, the *a priori,* yet intuitively known, relations of quantity. Therefore the concepts of mathematics can always be once more realized and controlled by these relations of quantity, either arithmetically, by performing the calculations that those signs merely indicate, or geometrically, by means of what Kant calls the construction of concepts. On the other hand, this advantage is not possessed by the concepts from which it had been imagined that metaphysics could be built up, such as for example essence, being, substance, perfection, necessity, reality, finite, infinite, absolute, reason, ground, and so on. For concepts of this kind are by no means original, as though

---

[11] From Bayard Taylor's translation of *Faust.* [Tr.]

fallen from heaven, or even innate; but they also, like all concepts, are drawn from perceptions; and as they do not, like mathematical concepts, contain the merely formal part of perception, but something more, empirical perceptions lie at their foundation. Therefore nothing can be drawn from them which empirical perception did not also contain, in other words, which was not a matter of experience, and which, since these concepts are very wide abstractions, would be obtained from experience with much greater certainty and at first hand. For from concepts nothing more can ever be drawn than is contained in the perceptions from which they are drawn. If we want *pure* concepts, in other words concepts having no empirical origin, then only those can be produced which concern space and time, i.e., the merely formal part of perception, consequently only the mathematical concepts, or at most also the concept of causality. This concept, it is true, has not sprung from experience, but yet it comes into consciousness only by means of experience (first in sense-perception). Therefore experience is indeed possible only through the concept of causality, but this concept is also valid only in the realm of experience. For this reason Kant has shown that it merely serves to give sequence and continuity to experience, but not to soar beyond it; that it therefore admits merely of physical, not of metaphysical application. Of course, only its *a priori* origin can give to any knowledge apodictic certainty; but this very origin limits it to what is merely *formal* of experience in general, since it shows that experience is conditioned by the subjective nature of the intellect. Therefore such knowledge, far from leading us beyond experience, gives only a *part* of this experience itself, namely the *formal* part that belongs to it throughout and is thus universal, consequently mere form without content. Now since metaphysics can least of all be limited to this, it too must have *empirical* sources of knowledge; consequently, the preconceived idea of a system of metaphysics to be found purely *a priori* is necessarily vain and fruitless. It is actually a *petitio principii*[12] of Kant, which he expresses most clearly in § 1 of the *Prolegomena,* that metaphysics may not draw its fundamental concepts and principles from experience. Here it is assumed in advance that only what we know *prior* to all experience can extend beyond possible experience. Supported by this, Kant then comes and shows that all such knowledge is nothing more than the form of the intellect for the purpose of experience, and that in consequence it cannot lead beyond experience, and from this he then rightly infers the impossibility of all metaphysics. But does it not rather seem positively wrong-headed that, in order to solve the

_____
[12] "Begging of the question." [Tr.]

riddle of experience, in other words, of the world which alone lies before us, we should close our eyes to it, ignore its contents, and take and use for our material merely the empty forms of which we are *a priori* conscious? Is it not rather in keeping with the matter that the *science of experience in general* and as such should draw also from experience? Its problem is itself given to it empirically; why should not its solution also call in the assistance of experience? Is it not inconsistent and absurd that he who speaks of the nature of things should not look at the things themselves, but stick only to certain abstract concepts? It is true that the task of metaphysics is not the observation of particular experiences; but yet it is the correct explanation of experience as a whole. Its foundation, therefore, must certainly be of an empirical nature. Indeed even the *a priori nature* of a part of human knowledge is apprehended by it as a given *fact,* from which it infers the subjective origin of that part. Only in so far as the consciousness of its *a priori* nature accompanies it is it called by Kant *transcendental,* as distinguished from *transcendent,* which signifies "passing beyond all possibility of experience," and has as its opposite *immanent,* which means remaining within the bounds of that possibility. I like to recall the original meaning of these expressions introduced by Kant, with which, as also with that of *category* and many others, the apes of philosophy carry on their game at the present day. In addition to this, the source of the knowledge of metaphysics is not only *outer* experience, but also *inner.* In fact, its most peculiar characteristic, whereby the decisive step alone capable of solving the great question becomes possible for it, consists in its combining at the right place outer experience with inner, and making the latter the key to the former. This I have explained thoroughly and fully in the essay *On the Will in Nature* under the heading "Physical Astronomy."

The origin of metaphysics from empirical sources of knowledge, which is here discussed and which cannot honestly be denied, does of course deprive it of the kind of apodictic certainty that is possible only through knowledge *a priori.* This remains the property of logic and mathematics, but these sciences really teach only what everyone knows already as a matter of course, though not distinctly. At most the primary elements of natural science can be derived from knowledge *a priori.* By this admission, metaphysics gives up only an old claim, which, as appears from what has been said above, rested on misunderstanding, and against which the great diversity and changeable nature of metaphysical systems, and also the constantly accompanying scepticism, have at all times testified. However, this changeable nature cannot be asserted against the possibility of metaphysics in general, for it affects just as much all branches of natural science, chemistry, physics, geology, zoology, and so on; and even history has not remained exempt from it. But when once a correct system of metaphysics has been found, in so far as the limits of the human intellect allow it, then the unchangeable nature of an *a priori* known science will indeed belong to it, since its foundation can be only *experience in general,* not the particular individual experiences. Through these, on the other hand, the natural sciences are always being modified, and new material is constantly being provided for history. For experience, in general and as a whole, will never change its character for a new one.

The next question is how a science drawn from experience can lead beyond it, and thus merit the name of *metaphysics.* It cannot perhaps do so in the way in which we find from three proportional numbers the fourth, or a triangle from two sides and an angle. This was the way of pre-Kantian dogmatics, which, according to certain laws known to us *a priori,* tried to infer the not-given from the given, the ground from the consequent, and thus that which could not possibly be given in any experience from experience. Kant proved the impossibility of a system of metaphysics on this path by showing that, although those laws were not drawn from experience, they had validity only for experience. Therefore he rightly teaches that we cannot soar in such a way beyond the possibility of all experience; but there are still other paths to metaphysics. The whole of experience is like a cryptograph, and philosophy is like the deciphering of it, and the correctness of this is confirmed by the continuity and connexion that appear everywhere. If only this whole is grasped in sufficient depth, and inner experience is connected to outer, it must be capable of being *interpreted, explained* from itself. After Kant has irrefutably proved to us that experience in general arises from two elements, the forms of knowledge and the being-in-itself of things, and that these two can be distinguished from each other in experience, namely what we are conscious of *a priori* and what has been added *a posteriori,* it can be stated, at any rate in general, what in the given experience (primarily mere *phenomenon*) belongs to this phenomenon's *form* conditioned by the intellect, and what remains over for the *thing-in-itself* after the withdrawal of the intellect. And although no one can recognize the thing-in-itself through the veil of the forms of perception, on the other hand everyone carries this within himself, in fact he himself is it; hence in self-consciousness it must be in some way accessible to him, although still only conditionally. Thus the bridge on which metaphysics passes beyond experience is nothing but just that analysis of experience into phenomenon and thing-in-itself in which I have placed Kant's greatest merit. For it contains the proof of a kernel of the phenomenon different from the phenomenon itself. It is true that this kernel can never be entirely separated from the phenomenon, and be regarded by itself as an *ens extramundanum;* but it is known always only in its relations and references to the phenomenon itself. The interpretation and explanation of the phenomenon, however, in relation to its inner kernel can give us information about it which does not otherwise come into consciousness. Therefore in this sense metaphysics goes beyond the phenomenon, i.e., nature, to what is concealed in or behind it (τὸ μετὰ τὸ φυσικόν), yet always regarding it only as that which appears in the phenomenon, not independently of all phenomenon. Metaphysics thus remains immanent, and does not become transcendent; for it never tears itself entirely from experience, but remains the mere interpretation and explanation thereof, as it never speaks of the thing-in-itself otherwise than in its relation to the phenomenon. This, at any rate, is the sense in which I have attempted to solve the problem of metaphysics, taking into general consideration the limits of human knowledge which have been demonstrated by Kant. Therefore I approve and accept his *Prolegomena* to every metaphysical system as valid for mine also. Accordingly, this never really goes beyond experience, but discloses only the true understanding of the world lying before it in experience. According to the definition of metaphysics repeated also by Kant, it is neither a science of mere concepts nor a system of inferences and deductions from *a priori* principles, the uselessness of which for the purpose of metaphysics Kant has demonstrated. On the contrary, it is a rational knowledge (*Wissen*) drawn from perception of the external actual world and from the information about this furnished by the most intimate fact of self-consciousness, deposited in distinct concepts. Accordingly, it is the science of experience; but the universal and the whole of all experience are its subject and its source. I admit entirely Kant's doctrine that the world of experience is mere phenomenon, and that knowledge *a priori* is valid only in reference thereto; but I add that, precisely as phenomenal appearance, it is the manifestation of that which appears, and with him I call that which appears the thing-in-itself. Therefore, this thing-in-itself must express its inner nature and character in the world of experience; consequently it must be possible to interpret these from it, and indeed from the material, not from the mere form, of experience. Accordingly, philosophy is nothing but the correct and universal understanding of experience itself, the true interpretation of its meaning and content. This is the metaphysical, in other words, that which is merely clothed in the phenomenon and veiled in its forms, that which is related to the phenomenon as the thought or idea is to the words.

Such a deciphering of the world with reference to what appears in it must receive its confirmation from itself through the agreement in which it places the many different phenomena of the world with one another, and which we do not perceive without it. If we find a document the script of which is unknown, we continue trying to interpret it until we hit upon a hypothesis as to the meaning of the letters by which they form intelligible words and connected sentences. Then there remains no doubt as to the correctness of the deciphering, since it is not possible for the agreement and consistency, in which all the signs of that writing are placed by this explanation, to be merely accidental; nor is it possible for us, by giving the letters an entirely different value, to recognize words and sentences in this new arrangement of them. Similarly, the deciphering of the world must be completely confirmed from itself. It must spread a uniform light over all the phenomena of the world, and bring even the most heterogeneous into agreement, so that the contradiction may be removed even between those that contrast most. This confirmation from itself is the characteristic stamp of its genuineness; for every false deciphering, even though it suits some phenomena, will all the more glaringly contradict the remainder. Thus, for example, the optimism of Leibniz conflicts with the obvious misery of existence; Spinoza's doctrine that the world is the only possible and absolutely necessary substance is incompatible with our wonder and astonishment at its existence and essential nature; Wolff's doctrine that man has his *existentia* and *essentia* from a will foreign to him runs counter to our moral responsibility for actions resulting with strict necessity from these in conflict with the motives. The oft-repeated doctrine of a progressive development of mankind to an ever higher perfection, or generally of any kind of becoming by means of the world-process, is opposed to the *a priori* view that, up to any given point of time, an infinite time has already elapsed, and consequently that all that is supposed to come with time is bound to have existed already. In this way, an interminable list of the contradictions of dogmatic assumptions with the given reality of things could be compiled. But I must deny that any doctrine of my philosophy could honestly be added to such a list, just because each one has been thought out in the presence of perceived reality, and none has its root in abstract concepts alone. However, as there is in it a fundamental idea that is applied to all the phenomena of the world as their key, this idea proves to be the correct alphabet, and by its application all words and sentences have sense and significance. The discovered answer to a riddle shows itself as the right one by the fact that all the statements of the riddle are consistent with it. Thus my teaching enables us to perceive agreement and consistency in the contrasting confusion of the phenomena of this world, and solves the innumerable contradictions which, seen from every other point of view, are presented by it. Therefore it is, to this extent, like an arithmetical sum that comes out, although by no means in the sense that it leaves no problem still to be solved, no possible question unanswered. To assert anything of the kind would be a presumptuous denial of the limits of human knowledge in general. Whatever torch we kindle, and whatever space it may illuminate, our horizon will always remain encircled by the depth of night. For the ultimate solution of the riddle of the world would necessarily have to speak merely of things-in-themselves, no longer of phenomena. All our forms of knowledge, however, are intended precisely for phenomena alone; hence we must comprehend everything through coexistence, succession, and relations of causality. But these forms have sense and significance merely with reference to the phenomenon; the things-in-themselves and their possible relations cannot be grasped through them. Therefore the actual, positive solution to the riddle of the world must be something that the human intellect is wholly incapable of grasping and conceiving; so that if a being of a higher order came and took all the trouble to impart it to us, we should be quite unable to understand any part of his disclosures. Accordingly, those who profess to know the ultimate, i.e., the first grounds of things, thus a primordial being, an Absolute, or whatever else they choose to call it, together with the process, the reasons, grounds, motives, or anything else, in consequence of which the world results from them, or emanates, or falls, or is produced, set in existence, "discharged" and ushered out, are playing the fool, are vain boasters, if indeed they are not charlatans.

I regard it as a great merit of my philosophy that all its truths have been found independently of one another, through a consideration of the real world; but their unity and agreement, about which I did not concern myself, have always appeared subsequently of themselves. For this reason also it is rich, and has wide-spreading roots in the soil of the reality of perception from which all the nourishment of abstract truths springs. Again, therefore, it is not wearisome and tedious—a quality that might otherwise be regarded as essential to philosophy, to judge from the philosophical writings of the last fifty years. On the other hand, if all the doctrines of a philosophy are derived merely one from another, and ultimately indeed even from one first principle, it must prove to be poor and meagre, and consequently wearisome, for nothing more can follow from a proposition than what in reality it already states itself. Moreover, everything then depends on the correctness of *one* proposition, and by a single mistake in the deduction, the truth of the whole would be endangered. Even less guarantee is given by the systems that start from an intellectual intuition, i.e., a kind of ecstasy or clairvoyance. All knowledge so gained must be rejected as subjective, individual, and consequently problematical. Even if it actually existed, it would not be communicable, for only the normal knowledge of the brain is communicable; if it is abstract knowledge, through concepts and words; if it is knowledge of mere perception, through works of art.

If, as so often happens, metaphysics is reproached with having made so little progress in the course of so many centuries, it should also be borne in mind that no other science has grown up like it under constant oppression, none has been so hampered and hindered from without as it has been at all times by the religion of every country. Everywhere in possession of a monopoly of metaphysical knowledge, religion regards metaphysics as a weed growing by its side, as an unauthorized worker, as a horde of gypsies. As a rule, it tolerates metaphysics only on condition that the latter accommodates itself to serve and emulate it. For where has there ever been true freedom of thought? People have boasted of it often enough, but as soon as it tried to do more than to differ from the religion of the country about some subordinate dogmas, a holy shudder at its audacity seized the proclaimers of tolerance, and they said; "Not a step farther!" What progress in metaphysics was possible under such oppression? Indeed, that pressure or coercion exercised by the privileged metaphysics extends not only to the *communication* of thoughts, but to *thinking* itself. This is brought about by its dogmas being so firmly impressed with studied, solemn, and serious airs on the tender, docile, trusting, and thoughtless age of childhood, that henceforth they grow up with the brain, and assume almost the nature of inborn ideas. Therefore some philosophers have considered them to be such, and there are still several who pretend so to regard them. But nothing can so firmly oppose the comprehension of even the *problem* of metaphysics as a previous solution to it forced on the mind, and early implanted in it. For the necessary starting-point of all genuine philosophizing is the deep feeling of the Socratic: "This one thing I know, that I know nothing." In this respect also the ancients had the advantage over us; for it is true that their national religions somewhat restricted the communication of what was thought, but they did not encroach on the freedom of thought itself, because they were not formally and solemnly impressed on children, and in general were not taken so seriously. Therefore the ancients are still our teachers in metaphysics.

Whenever metaphysics is reproached with its slight progress, and with never having yet reached its goal in spite of such constant efforts, we should further reflect that in the meanwhile it has always performed the invaluable service of limiting the infinite claims of the privileged metaphysics, and yet at the same time working against naturalism and materialism proper, which are brought about by this very metaphysics as an inevitable reaction. Consider to what a pitch of arrogance and insolence the priesthood of every religion would go, if belief in its doctrines were as firm and blind as they really wish. Look back also at all the wars, riots, rebellions, and revolutions in Europe from the eighth to the eighteenth century; how few will be found that have not had as their essence or pretext some controversy about beliefs, that is, metaphysical problems, which became the occasion for making trouble between nations. That whole period of a thousand years is indeed one of constant massacre and murder, now on the battlefield, now on the scaffold, now in the streets—all over metaphysical questions! I wish I had an authentic list of all the crimes that Christianity has actually prevented, and of all the good deeds that it has actually performed, in order to be able to put them in the other pan of the balance.

Finally, as regards the *obligations* of metaphysics, it has but one, for it is one that tolerates no other beside it, namely the obligation to be *true*. If we wished to impose on it other obligations besides this one, such as that it must be spiritualistic, optimistic, monotheistic, or even only moral, we cannot know beforehand whether this would be opposed to the fulfilment of that first obligation, without which all its other achievements would of necessity be obviously worthless. Accordingly, a given philosophy has no other standard of its value than that of truth. For the rest, philosophy is essentially *world-wisdom;* its problem is the world. With this alone it has to do, and it leaves the gods in peace; but in return for this, it expects them to leave it in peace also.

"Ihr folget falscher Spur,
Denkt nicht, wir scherzen!
Ist nicht der Kern der Natur
Menschen im Herzen?"

Goethe

("You follow a false trail,
Think not that we jest!
Is not the core of nature
In the heart of men?" [Tr.])

On the Possibility of Knowing the Thing-in-Itself

In 1836, under the title *Ueber den Willen in der Natur* (second edition, 1854), I already published the really essential supplement to this book, which contains the most characteristic and important step of my philosophy, namely the transition from the phenomenon to the thing-in-itself, given up by Kant as impossible. We should make a great mistake if we tried to regard the statements of others, with which I have there associated my explanations, as the real and proper material and subject of that work, a work small in volume but important as regards its contents. On the contrary, those statements are merely the occasion from which I have started, and I have there discussed that fundamental truth of my teaching with greater distinctness than anywhere else, and brought it down to the empirical knowledge of nature. This has been done most exhaustively and stringently under the heading "Physical Astronomy"; so that I cannot hope ever to find a more correct and accurate expression of that core of my philosophy than what is there recorded. Whoever wishes to know my philosophy thoroughly and investigate it seriously must first take that chapter into consideration. Therefore all that is said in that small work would in general constitute the main subject-matter of the present supplements, if it had not to be excluded as having preceded them; whereas I here assume it to be known, since otherwise what is best would be missing.

First of all, I will make a few preliminary observations from a more general point of view as to the sense in which we can speak of a knowledge of the thing-in-itself, and of the necessary limitation of this sense.

What is *knowledge?* It is above all else and essentially *representation.* What is *representation?* A very complicated *physiological* occurrence in an animal's brain, whose result is the consciousness of a *picture or image* at that very spot. Obviously the relation of such a picture to something entirely different from the animal in whose

---

[1] This chapter refers to § 18 of volume 1.

brain it exists can only be a very indirect one. This is perhaps the simplest and most intelligible way of disclosing the *deep gulf between the ideal and the real.* This is one of the things of which, like the earth's motion, we are not immediately aware; the ancients, therefore, did not notice it, just as they did not observe the earth's motion. On the other hand, once first demonstrated by Descartes, it has ever since given philosophers no rest. But after Kant had at last shown most thoroughly the complete diversity of the ideal and the real, it was an attempt as bold as it was absurd, yet quite correctly calculated with regard to the power of judgement of the philosophical public in Germany and thus crowned with brilliant success, to try to assert the *absolute identity* of the two by dogmatic utterances referring to a so-called intellectual intuition. On the contrary, a subjective and an objective existence, a being for self and a being for others, a consciousness of one's own self and a consciousness of other things, are in truth given to us immediately, and the two are given in such a fundamentally different way that no other difference compares with this. About *himself* everyone knows directly, about everything else only very indirectly. This is the fact and the problem.

On the other hand, it is no longer the essential point here, but one of secondary importance, whether, through further processes in the interior of the brain, universal concepts (*universalia*) are abstracted from the representations or pictures of perception that have arisen in the brain, for the purpose of further combinations, whereby knowledge becomes *rational,* and is then called *thinking.* For all such *concepts* borrow their contents only from the representation of perception, which is therefore *primary knowledge,* and thus is alone taken into consideration when we investigate the relation between the ideal and the real. Accordingly, it is evidence of a complete ignorance of the problem, or at any rate it is very inept, to want to describe this relation as that between *being* and *thinking.* In the first place, *thinking* has a relation only to *perceiving,* but *perceiving* has a relation to the *being-in-itself* of what is perceived, and this last is the great problem with which we are here concerned. On the other hand, empirical being, as it lies before us, is simply nothing but being-given in perception; but the relation of this to *thinking* is no riddle, for the concepts, and hence the immediate material of thinking, are obviously *abstracted* from perception, as no reasonable person can doubt. Incidentally, we can see how important the choice of expressions in philosophy is from the fact that the inept expression censured above, and the misunderstanding that has arisen from it, have become the foundation of the whole Hegelian pseudo-philosophy that has engrossed the attention of the German public for twenty-five years.

But if it should be said that "perception is already knowledge of the thing-in-itself, for it is the effect of that which exists outside us, and as this *acts,* so it *is;* its action is just its being"; then to this we reply: (1) that the law of causality, as has been sufficiently proved, is of subjective origin, as is also the sensation of the senses from which the perception comes; (2) that time and space, in which the object presents itself, are likewise of subjective origin; (3) that, if the being of the object consists merely in its acting, this means that it consists merely in the changes produced by it in others; consequently, itself and in itself it is nothing at all. Only of *matter* is it true, as I have said in the text and discussed in the essay *On the Principle of Sufficient Reason* at the end of § 21, that its being consists in its acting, that it is through and through only causality, and thus is causality itself objectively perceived, but that it is thus nothing in itself (ἡ ὕλη τὸ ἀληθινὸν ψεῦδος, *materia mendacium verax*);[2] on the contrary, as an ingredient of the perceived object it is a mere abstraction, which by itself alone cannot be given in any experience. It will be fully considered later on in a chapter to itself. Yet the perceived object must be something *in itself,* and not merely *something for others;* for otherwise it would be positively only representation, and we should have an absolute idealism that in the end would become theoretical egoism, in which all reality disappears, and the world becomes a mere subjective phantasm. However, if, without questioning further, we stop altogether at the *world as representation,* then of course it is immaterial whether I declare objects to be representations in my head or phenomena that exhibit themselves in time and space, since time and space themselves are only in my head. In this sense, then, an identity of the ideal and the real might still be affirmed; yet since Kant, this would be to say nothing new. Moreover, the inner nature of things and of the phenomenal world would obviously not be exhausted in this way, but with it we should still always be only on the *ideal* side. The *real* side must be something *toto genere* different from the *world as representation,* namely that which things are *in themselves;* and it is this complete diversity between the ideal and the real that Kant has demonstrated most thoroughly.

Locke had denied knowledge of things as they are in themselves to the senses; but Kant denied it also to the perceiving *understanding.* Under this name I embrace here what he calls *pure* sensibility and the law of causality that brings about empirical perception, in

---

[2] "Matter is a lie and yet true." [Tr.]

so far as this law is given *a priori*. Not only are both right, but it can also be seen quite directly that there is a contradiction in the assertion that a thing is known according to what it is in and by itself, in other words, outside our knowledge. For, as I have said, all knowing is essentially a making of representations; but my making of representations, just because it is mine, can never be identical with the being-in-itself of the thing outside me. The being in and by itself of every thing must necessarily be *subjective*. But in the representation of another, it exists just as necessarily as something *objective*, a difference that can never be entirely reconciled. For through this the whole mode of its existence is fundamentally changed; as something objective, it presupposes a foreign subject, and exists as the representation of that subject; moreover, as Kant has shown, it has entered forms foreign to its own nature, just because they belong to that foreign subject whose knowledge becomes possible only through them. If, absorbed in this reflection, I perceive, let us say, lifeless bodies of easily observable size and regular comprehensible form, and then attempt to conceive this spatial existence in its three dimensions as their being-in-itself, and consequently as the existence that is subjective to the things, then I at once feel the impossibility of the thing, since I can never think of those objective forms as the being that is subjective to the things. On the contrary, I become directly conscious that what I represent there is a picture or image, brought about in my brain and existing only for me as the knowing subject, and that this picture cannot constitute the ultimate, and therefore subjective, being-in-and-by-itself of even these lifeless bodies. On the other hand, I cannot assume that even these lifeless bodies exist simply and solely in my representation, but as they have unfathomable properties, and, by virtue of these, activity, I must concede them a *being-in-itself* of some kind. But this very inscrutability of the properties, pointing as it certainly does on the one hand to something existing independently of our knowledge, on the other hand gives the empirical proof that, because our knowledge consists only in the *framing of representations* by means of subjective forms, such knowledge always furnishes mere *phenomena,* not the being-in-itself of things. From this it can be explained that in all we know, a certain something remains hidden from us as being quite unfathomable, and we must confess that we are unable to understand even the commonest and simplest phenomena. For not merely do the highest productions of nature, namely living beings, or the *complicated* phenomena of the inorganic world remain inscrutable to us, but even every rock-crystal, even iron pyrites, are, by virtue of their crystallographical, optical, chemical, and electrical properties, an abyss of incomprehensibilities and mysteries for our searching consideration and investigation. This could not be so if we knew things as they are in themselves; for then at any rate the simpler phenomena, the path to whose properties was not barred to us by ignorance, would of necessity be thoroughly intelligible to us, and their whole being and inner nature could not fail to pass over into knowledge. Therefore it lies not in the defectiveness of our acquaintance with things, but in the very nature of knowledge itself. For if our perception, and thus the whole empirical apprehension of the things that present themselves to us, is already determined essentially and principally by our cognitive faculty and by its forms and functions, then it must be that things exhibit themselves in a manner quite different from their own inner nature, and that therefore they appear as through a mask. This mask enables us always merely to assume, never to know, what is hidden beneath it; and this something then gleams through as an inscrutable mystery. Never can the nature of anything pass over into knowledge wholly and without reserve; but still less can anything real be constructed *a priori*, like something mathematical. Therefore the empirical inscrutability of all the beings of nature is an *a posteriori* proof of the ideality, and merely phenomenal actuality, of their empirical existence.

In consequence of all this, on the path of *objective knowledge*, thus starting from the *representation*, we shall never get beyond the representation, i.e., the phenomenon. We shall therefore remain at the outside of things; we shall never be able to penetrate into their inner nature, and investigate what they are in themselves, in other words, what they may be by themselves. So far I agree with Kant. But now, as the counterpoise to this truth, I have stressed that other truth that we are not merely the *knowing subject*, but that *we ourselves* are also among those realities or entities we require to know, that *we ourselves are the thing-in-itself*. Consequently, a way *from within* stands open to us to that real inner nature of things to which we cannot penetrate *from without*. It is, so to speak, a subterranean passage, a secret alliance, which, as if by treachery, places us all at once in the fortress that could not be taken by attack from without. Precisely as such, the *thing-in-itself* can come into consciousness only quite directly, namely by *it itself being conscious of itself;* to try to know it objectively is to desire something contradictory. Everything objective is representation, consequently appearance, in fact mere phenomenon of the brain.

Kant's principal result may be summarized in its essence as follows: "All concepts which do not have as their basis a perception in space and time (sensuous perception), or in other words, have not been drawn from such a perception, are absolutely empty, that is to say, they give us no knowledge. But as perception can furnish only *phenomena,* not things-in-themselves, we too have absolutely no knowledge of things-in-themselves." I admit this of everything, but not of the knowledge everyone has of his own *willing.* This is neither a perception (for all perception is spatial), nor is it empty; on the contrary, it is more real than any other knowledge. Further, it is not *a priori,* like merely formal knowledge, but entirely *a posteriori;* hence we are unable to anticipate it in the particular case, but in this are often guilty of error concerning ourselves. In fact, our *willing* is the only opportunity we have of understanding simultaneously from within any event that outwardly manifests itself; consequently, it is the one thing known to us *immediately,* and not given to us merely in the representation, as all else is. Here, therefore, lies the datum alone capable of becoming the key to everything else, or, as I have said, the only narrow gateway to truth. Accordingly, we must learn to understand nature from ourselves, not ourselves from nature. What is directly known to us must give us the explanation of what is only indirectly known, not conversely. Do we understand, let us say, the rolling away of a ball when it has received an impulse more thoroughly than we understand our own movement when we have perceived a motive? Many may think so, but I say that the reverse is the case. However, we shall arrive at the insight that in both the occurrences just mentioned what is essential is identical, although identical in the same way as the lowest audible note of harmony is identical with the note of the same name ten octaves higher.

Meanwhile it is to be carefully noted, and I have always kept it in mind, that even the inward observation we have of our own will still does not by any means furnish an exhaustive and adequate knowledge of the thing-in-itself. It would do so if it were a wholly immediate observation. But such observation is brought about by the will, with and by means of corporization, providing itself also with an intellect (for the purpose of its relations with the external world), and then through this intellect knowing itself in self-consciousness (the necessary reverse of the external world); but this knowledge of the thing-in-itself is not wholly adequate. In the first place, such knowledge is tied to the form of the representation; it is perception or observation, and as such falls apart into subject and object. For even in self-consciousness, the I is not absolutely simple, but consists of a knower (intellect) and a known (will); the former is not known and the latter is not knowing, although the two flow together into the consciousness of an I. But on this very account, this I is not *intimate* with itself through and through, does not shine through so to speak, but is opaque, and therefore remains a riddle to itself. Hence even in inner knowledge there still occurs a difference between the being-in-itself of its object and the observation or perception of this object in the knowing subject. But the inner knowledge is free from two forms belonging to outer knowledge, the form of *space* and the form of *causality* which brings about all sense-perception. On the other hand, there still remains the form of *time,* as well as that of being known and of knowing in general. Accordingly, in this inner knowledge the thing-in-itself has indeed to a great extent cast off its veils, but still does not appear quite naked. In consequence of the form of time which still adheres to it, everyone knows his *will* only in its successive individual *acts,* not as a whole, in and by itself. Hence no one knows his character *a priori,* but he becomes acquainted with it only by way of experience and always imperfectly. Yet the apprehension in which we know the stirrings and acts of our own will is far more immediate than is any other. It is the point where the thing-in-itself enters the phenomenon most immediately, and is most closely examined by the knowing subject; therefore the event thus intimately known is simply and solely calculated to become the interpreter of every other.

For in the case of every emergence of an act of will from the obscure depths of our inner being into the knowing consciousness, there occurs a direct transition into the phenomenon of the thing-in-itself that lies outside time. Accordingly, the act of will is indeed only the nearest and clearest *phenomenon* of the thing-in-itself; yet it follows from this that, if all the other phenomena could be known by us just as immediately and intimately, we should be obliged to regard them precisely as that which the will is in us. Therefore in this sense I teach that the inner nature of every thing is *will,* and I call the will the thing-in-itself. In this way, Kant's doctrine of the inability to know the thing-in-itself is modified to the extent that the thing-in-itself is merely not absolutely and completely knowable; that nevertheless by far the most immediate of its phenomena, distinguished *toto genere* from all the rest by this immediateness, is its representative for us. Accordingly we have to refer the whole world of phenomena to that one in which the thing-in-itself is manifested under the lightest of all veils, and still remains phenomenon only in so far as my intellect, the only thing capable of knowledge, still always remains distinguished from me as the one who wills, and does not cast off the knowledge-form of *time,* even with *inner* perception.

Accordingly, even after this last and extreme step, the question may still be raised what that will, which manifests itself in the world and as the world, is ultimately and absolutely in itself; in other words, what it is, quite apart from the fact that it manifests itself as *will,* or in general *appears,* that is to say, *is known* in general. This question can *never* be answered, because, as I have said, being-known of itself contradicts being-in-itself, and everything that is known is as such only phenomenon. But the possibility of this question shows that the thing-in-itself, which we know most immediately in the will, may have, entirely outside all possible phenomenon, determinations, qualities, and modes of existence which for us are absolutely unknowable and incomprehensible, and which then remain as the inner nature of the thing-in-itself, when this, as explained in the fourth book, has freely abolished itself as *will,* has thus stepped out of the phenomenon entirely, and as regards our knowledge, that is to say as regards the world of phenomena, has passed over into empty nothingness. If the will were positively and absolutely the thing-in-itself, then this nothing would be *absolute,* instead of which it expressly appears to us there only as a *relative* nothing.

I now proceed to supplement by a few relevant observations the establishment, given in our second book as well as in the work *On the Will in Nature,* of the doctrine that what makes itself known in the most immediate knowledge as will is precisely that which objectifies itself at different grades in all the phenomena of this world. I shall begin by producing a series of psychological facts proving first of all that in our own consciousness the *will* always appears as the primary and fundamental thing, and throughout asserts its pre-eminence over the intellect; that, on the other hand, the intellect generally turns out to be what is secondary, subordinate, and conditioned. This proof is the more necessary as all philosophers before me, from the first to the last, place the true and real inner nature or kernel of man in the *knowing* consciousness. Accordingly, they have conceived and explained the I, or in the case of many of them its transcendent hypostasis called soul, as primarily and essentially *knowing,* in fact *thinking,* and only in consequence of this, secondarily and derivatively, as *willing.* This extremely old, universal, and fundamental error, this colossal πρῶτον ψεῦδος and fundamental ὕστερον πρότερον,[3] must first of all be set aside, and instead of it the

---

[3] "The first false step." "Confusion of the earlier with the later, or of ground with consequent." [Tr.]

true state of the case must be brought to perfectly distinct consciousness. However, as this is done for the first time here after thousands of years of philosophizing, some detailed account will not be out of place. The remarkable phenomenon that in this fundamental and essential point all philosophers have erred, in fact have completely reversed the truth, might be partly explained, especially in the case of the philosophers of the Christian era, from the fact that all of them aimed at presenting man as differing as widely as possible from the animal. Yet they felt vaguely that the difference between the two was to be found in the intellect and not in the will. From this arose in them unconsciously the tendency to make the intellect the essential and principal thing, in fact to describe willing as a mere function of the intellect. Therefore the concept of a *soul,* as transcendent hypostasis, is not only inadmissible, as is established by the *Critique of Pure Reason,* but it becomes the source of irremediable errors by its establishing beforehand in its "simple substance" an indivisible unity of knowledge and of the will, the separation of which is precisely the path to truth. Therefore that concept can no longer occur in philosophy, but is to be left to German medical men and physiologists, who, laying aside scalpel and scoop, venture to philosophize with concepts they received when they were confirmed. They might perhaps try their luck with them in England. The French physiologists and zootomists have (till recently) kept themselves entirely free from this reproach.

The first consequence of their common fundamental error, which is very inconvenient to all these philosophers, is that, since in death the knowing consciousness obviously perishes, either they must admit death to be the annihilation of man, against which our inner nature revolts, or resort to the assumption of a continued existence of the knowing consciousness. For this a strong faith is required, since everyone's own experience has abundantly demonstrated to him the complete and general dependence of the knowing consciousness on the brain, and one can just as easily believe in a digestion without a stomach as in a knowing consciousness without a brain. My philosophy alone leads us out of this dilemma; in the first place it puts man's real inner nature not in consciousness, but in the will. This will is not essentially united with consciousness, but is related to consciousness, in other words to knowledge, as substance to accident, as something illuminated to light, as the string to the sounding-board; it comes into consciousness from within just as the corporeal world comes from without. Now we can grasp the indestructibility of this real kernel and true inner being that is ours, in spite of the obvious extinction of consciousness in death and its corresponding non-existence before birth. For the intellect is as fleeting and as perishable as is the brain, and is the brain's product, or rather its activity. But the brain, like the whole organism, is the product or phenomenon of, in short a secondary thing to, the will, and it is the will alone that is imperishable.

CHAPTER XIX[1]

On the Primacy of the Will in Self-Consciousness

The will, as the thing-in-itself, constitutes the inner, true, and indestructible nature of man; yet in itself it is without consciousness. For consciousness is conditioned by the intellect, and the intellect is a mere accident of our being, for it is a function of the brain. The brain, together with the nerves and spinal cord attached to it, is a mere fruit, a product, in fact a parasite, of the rest of the organism, in so far as it is not directly geared to the organism's inner working, but serves the purpose of self-preservation by regulating its relations with the external world. On the other hand, the organism itself is the visibility, the objectivity, of the individual will, its image, as this image presents itself in that very brain (which in the first book we learned to recognize as the condition of the objective world in general). Therefore, this image is brought about by the brain's forms of knowledge, namely space, time, and causality; consequently it presents itself as something extended, successively acting, and material, in other words, operative or effective. The parts of the body are both directly felt and perceived by means of the senses only in the brain. In consequence of this, it can be said that the intellect is the secondary phenomenon, the organism the primary, that is, the immediate phenomenal appearance of the will; the will is metaphysical, the intellect physical; the intellect, like its objects, is mere phenomenon, the will alone is thing-in-itself. Then, in a more and more *figurative* sense, and so by way of comparison, it can be said that the will is the substance of man, the intellect the accident; the will is the matter, the intellect the form; the will is heat, the intellect light.

We will now first of all verify, and at the same time elucidate, this thesis by the following facts appertaining to the inner life of man. Perhaps, on this occasion, more will be gained for knowledge of the inner man than is to be found in many systematic psychologies.

1. Not only the consciousness of other things, i.e., the appre-

---

[1] This chapter refers to § 19 of volume 1.

hension of the external world, but also *self-consciousness,* as already mentioned, contains a knower and a known, otherwise it would not be a *consciousness.* For *consciousness* consists in knowing, but knowing requires a knower and a known. Therefore self-consciousness could not exist if there were not in it a known opposed to the knower and different therefrom. Thus, just as there can be no object without a subject, so there can be no subject without an object, in other words, no knower without something different from this that is known. Therefore, a consciousness that was through and through pure intelligence would be impossible. The intelligence is like the sun that does not illuminate space unless an object exists by which its rays are reflected. The knower himself, precisely as such, cannot be known, otherwise he would be the *known* of another knower. But as the *known* in self-consciousness we find exclusively the *will.* For not only willing and deciding in the narrowest sense, but also all striving, wishing, shunning, hoping, fearing, loving, hating, in short all that directly constitutes our own weal and woe, desire and disinclination, is obviously only affection of the will, is a stirring, a modification, of willing and not-willing, is just that which, when it operates outwards, exhibits itself as an act of will proper.[2] But in all knowledge the known, not the knower, is the first and essential thing, inasmuch as the former is the πρωτότυπος, the latter the ἔκτυπος.[3] Therefore in self-consciousness the known, consequently the will, must be the first and original thing; the knower, on the other hand, must be only the secondary thing, that which has been added, the mirror. They are related somewhat as the self-luminous is to the reflecting body; or as the vibrating strings are to the sounding-board, where the resulting note would then be consciousness. We can also consider the plant as such a symbol of consciousness. As we know, it has two poles, root and corona; the former reaching down into darkness, moisture and cold, and the latter up into brightness, dryness and warmth; then as the point of indifference of the two poles

---

[2] It is remarkable that Augustine already knew this. Thus in the fourteenth book *De Civitate Dei,* c. 6, he speaks of the *affectiones animi* that in the previous book he brought under four categories, namely *cupiditas, timor, laetitia, tristitia,* and he says: *voluntas est quippe in omnibus, imo omnes nihil aliud, quam voluntates sunt: nam quid est cupiditas et laetitia, nisi voluntas in eorum consensionem, quae volumus? et quid est metus atque tristitia, nisi voluntas in dissensionem ab his, quae nolumus?*

"In them all [desire, fear, joy, sadness] the will is to be found; in fact they are all nothing but affections of the will. For what are desire and joy but the will to consent to what we want? And what are fear and sadness but the will not to consent to what we do not want?" [Tr.]

[3] "Prototype"; "copy," "ectype." [Tr.]

where they part from each other close to the ground, the collum or root-stock (*rhizoma, le collet*). The root is what is essential, original, perennial, whose death entails the death of the corona; it is therefore primary. The corona, on the other hand, is the ostensible, that which has sprouted forth, that which passes away without the root dying; it is therefore the secondary. The root represents the will, the corona the intellect, and the point of indifference of the two, namely the collum, would be the *I*, which, as their common extreme point, belongs to both. This I is the *pro tempore* identical subject of knowing and willing, whose identity I call in my very first essay (*On the Principle of Sufficient Reason*) and in my first philosophical astonishment, the miracle κατ' ἐξοχήν.[4] It is the point of departure and of contact of the whole phenomenon, in other words, of the objectification of the will; it is true that it conditions the phenomenon, but the phenomenon also conditions it. The comparison here given can be carried even as far as the individual character and nature of men. Thus, just as usually a large corona springs only from a large root, so the greatest mental abilities are found only with a vehement and passionate will. A genius of phlegmatic character and feeble passions would be like succulent plants that have very small roots in spite of an imposing corona consisting of thick leaves; yet he will not be found. Vehemence of the will and passionate ardour of the character are a condition of enhanced intelligence, and this is shown physiologically through the brain's activity being conditioned by the movement communicated to it with every pulsation through the great arteries running up to the *basis cerebri*. Therefore an energetic pulse, and even, according to Bichat, a short neck are necessary for great activity of the brain. But the opposite of the above is of course found; that is, vehement desires, passionate, violent character, with weak intellect, in other words, with a small brain of inferior conformation in a thick skull. This is a phenomenon as common as it is repulsive; it might perhaps be compared to the beetroot.

2. But in order not merely to describe consciousness figuratively, but to know it thoroughly, we have first to find out what exists in every consciousness in the same manner, and what therefore will be, as the common and constant element, that which is essential. We shall then consider what distinguishes one consciousness from another, and this accordingly will be the accidental and secondary element.

Consciousness is known to us positively only as a property of animal nature; consequently we may not, indeed we cannot, think of it otherwise than as *animal consciousness,* so that this expression

---

[4] "*Par excellence.*" [Tr.]

is in fact tautological. Therefore what is always to be found in *every* animal consciousness, even the most imperfect and feeblest, in fact what is always its foundation, is the immediate awareness of a *longing,* and of its alternate satisfaction and non-satisfaction in very different degrees. To a certain extent we know this *a priori,* For amazingly varied as the innumerable species of animals may be, and strange as some new form of them, never previously seen, may appear to us, we nevertheless assume beforehand with certainty its innermost nature as something well known, and indeed wholly familiar to us. Thus we know that the animal *wills,* indeed even *what* it wills, namely existence, well-being, life, and propagation. Since we here presuppose with perfect certainty an identity with ourselves, we have no hesitation in attributing to it unchanged all the affections of will known to us in ourselves; and we speak positively and plainly of its desire, aversion, fear, anger, hatred, love, joy, sorrow, longing, and so on. On the other hand, as soon as we come to speak of phenomena of mere knowledge, we run into uncertainty. We do not venture to say that the animal conceives, thinks, judges, or knows; we attribute to it with certainty only representations in general, since without these its *will* could not be stirred or agitated in the ways previously mentioned. But as regards the animals' definite way of knowing, and its precise limits in a given species, we have only indefinite concepts, and make conjectures. Therefore understanding between us and them is often difficult, and is brought about ingeniously only in consequence of experience and practice. Here, then, are to be found distinctions of consciousness. On the other hand, longing, craving, willing, or aversion, shunning, and not-willing, are peculiar to every consciousness; man has them in common with the polyp. Accordingly, this is the essential and the basis of every consciousness. The difference of its manifestations in the various species of animal beings depends on the different extension of their spheres of knowledge in which the motives of those manifestations are to be found. Directly from our own nature we understand all the actions and attitudes of animals that express stirrings and agitations of the will; and so to this extent we sympathize with them in many different ways. On the other hand, the gulf between us and them arises simply and solely from a difference of intellect. The gulf between a very intelligent animal and a man of very limited capacity is possibly not much greater than that between a blockhead and a genius. Therefore here also, the resemblance between them in another aspect, springing from the likeness of their inclinations and emotions and again assimilating both, sometimes stands out surprisingly, and excites astonishment. This consideration makes it clear that in all animal beings the *will* is the primary and substantial thing; the *intellect,* on the other hand, is something secondary and additional, in fact a mere tool in the service of the will, which is more or less complete and complicated according to the requirements of this service. Just as a species of animals appears equipped with hoofs, claws, hands, wings, horns, or teeth according to the aims of its will, so is it furnished with a more or less developed brain, whose function is the intelligence requisite for its continued existence. Thus the more complicated the organization becomes in the ascending series of animals, the more manifold do its needs become, and the more varied and specially determined the objects capable of satisfying them, consequently the more tortuous and lengthy the paths for arriving at these, which must now all be known and found. Therefore, to the same extent, the animal's representations must also be more versatile, accurate, definite, and connected, and its attention more eager, more continuous, and more easily roused; consequently its intellect must be more developed and complete. Accordingly we see the organ of intelligence, the cerebral system, together with the organs of sense, keep pace with an increase of needs and wants, and with the complication of the organism. We see the increase of the *representing* part of consciousness (as opposed to the *willing* part) bodily manifesting itself in the ever-increasing proportion of the brain in general to the rest of the nervous system, and of the cerebrum to the cerebellum. For (according to Flourens) the former is the workshop of representations, while the latter is the guide and regulator of movements. But the last step taken by nature in this respect is disproportionately great. For in man not only does the power of representation in *perception,* which hitherto has existed alone, reach the highest degree of perfection, but the *abstract* representation, thinking, i.e., *reason (Vernunft)* is added, and with it reflection. Through this important enhancement of the intellect, and hence of the secondary part of consciousness, it obtains a preponderance over the primary part in so far as it becomes from now on the predominantly active part. Thus, whereas in the case of the animal the immediate awareness of its satisfied or unsatisfied desire constitutes by far the principal part of its consciousness, and indeed the more so the lower the animal stands, so that the lowest animals are distinguished from plants only by the addition of a dull representation, with man the opposite is the case. Intense as his desires may be, more intense even than those of any animal and rising to the level of passions, his consciousness nevertheless remains continuously and predominantly concerned and engrossed with representations and ideas. Undoubtedly this is mainly what has given rise to that fundamental error of all philosophers, by virtue of which they make thinking the essential and primary element of the so-called soul, in other words, of man's inner or spiritual life, always putting it first, but regard willing as a mere product of thinking, and as something secondary, additional, and subsequent. But if willing resulted merely from knowing, how could the animals, even the lowest of them, manifest a will that is often so indomitable and vehement, in spite of such extremely limited knowledge? Accordingly, since that fundamental error of the philosophers makes, so to speak, the accident into the substance, it leads them on to wrong paths from which there is no longer a way out. Therefore that relative predominance of the *knowing* consciousness over the *desiring,* and consequently of the secondary part over the primary, which appears in man, can in certain abnormally favoured individuals go so far that, in moments of supreme enhancement, the secondary or knowing part of consciousness is entirely detached from the willing part, and passes by itself into free activity, in other words, into an activity not stimulated by the will, and therefore no longer serving it. Thus the knowing part of consciousness becomes purely objective and the clear mirror of the world, and from this the conceptions of *genius* arise, which are the subject of our third book.

3. If we descend through the series of grades of animals, we see the intellect becoming weaker and weaker and more and more imperfect; but we certainly do not observe a corresponding degradation of the will. On the contrary, the will everywhere retains its identical nature, and shows itself as a great attachment to life, care for the individual and for the species, egoism and lack of consideration for all others, together with the emotions springing therefrom. Even in the smallest insect the will is present complete and entire; it wills what it wills as decidedly and completely as does man. The difference lies merely in *what* it wills, that is to say, in the motives; but these are the business of the intellect. As that which is secondary and tied to bodily organs, the intellect naturally has innumerable degrees of perfection, and in general is essentially limited and imperfect. The *will,* on the other hand, as that which is original and the thing-in-itself, can never be imperfect, but every act of will is wholly what it can be. By virtue of the simplicity belonging to the will as the thing-in-itself, as the metaphysical in the phenomenon, its *essential nature* admits of no degrees, but is always entirely itself. Only its *stimulation or excitement* has degrees, from the feeblest inclination up to passion, and also its excitability, and thus its vehemence, from the phlegmatic to the choleric temperament. On the other hand, the *intellect* has not merely degrees of *excitement,* from sleepi-

ness up to the mood and inspiration, but also degrees of its *real nature,* of the completeness thereof; accordingly, this rises gradually from the lowest animal which perceives only obscurely up to man, and in man again from the blockhead to the genius. The *will* alone is everywhere entirely itself, for its function is of the greatest simplicity; for this consists in willing and in not-willing, which operates with the greatest ease and without effort, and requires no practice. On the other hand, knowing has many different functions, and never takes place entirely without effort, which it requires for fixing the attention and making the object clear, and at a higher degree, also for thinking and deliberation; it is therefore capable of great improvement through practice and training. If the intellect holds out to the will something simple and perceptible, the will at once expresses its approval or disapproval. This is the case even when the intellect has laboriously pondered and ruminated, in order finally to produce from numerous data by means of difficult combinations the result that seems most in agreement with the interests of the will. Meanwhile, the will has been idly resting; after the result is reached, it enters, as the sultan does on the divan, merely to express again its monotonous approval or disapproval. It is true that this can turn out different in degree, but in essence it remains always the same.

This fundamentally different nature of the will and the intellect, the simplicity and originality essential in the former in contrast to the complicated and secondary character of the latter, become even clearer to us when we observe their strange interplay within us, and see in a particular case how the images and ideas arising in the intellect set the will in motion, and how entirely separated and different are the roles of the two. Now it is true that we can already observe this in the case of actual events that vividly excite the will, whereas primarily and in themselves they are merely objects of the intellect. But, to some extent, it is not so obvious here that this reality as such primarily exists only in the intellect; and again, the change generally does not occur as rapidly as is necessary, if the thing is to be easily seen at a glance, and thus really comprehensible. On the other hand, both these are the case if it is mere ideas and fantasies that we allow to act on the will. If, for example, we are alone, and think over our personal affairs, and then vividly picture to ourselves, say, the menace of an actually present danger, and the possibility of an unfortunate outcome, anxiety at once compresses the heart, and the blood ceases to flow. But if the intellect then passes to the possibility of the opposite outcome, and allows the imagination to picture the happiness long hoped-for as thereby attained, all the pulses at once quicken with joy, and the heart feels as light as a feather, until the intellect wakes up from its dream. But then let some occasion lead the memory to an insult or injury suffered long ago, and anger and resentment at once storm through the breast that a moment before was at peace. Then let the image of a long-lost love arise, called up by accident, with which is connected a whole romance with its magic scenes, and this anger will at once give place to profound longing and sadness. Finally, if there occur to us some former humiliating incident, we shrivel up, would like to be swallowed up, blush with shame, and often try to divert and distract ourselves forcibly from it by some loud exclamation, scaring away evil spirits as it were. We see that the intellect strikes up the tune, and the will must dance to it; in fact, the intellect causes it to play the part of a child whom its nurse at her pleasure puts into the most different moods by chatter and tales alternating between pleasant and melancholy things. This is due to the fact that the will in itself is without knowledge, but the understanding associated with it is without will. Therefore the will behaves like a body that is moved, the understanding like the causes that set it in motion, for it is the medium of motives. Yet with all this, the primacy of the will becomes clear again when this will, that becomes, as we have shown, the sport of the intellect as soon as it allows the intellect to control it, once makes its supremacy felt in the last resort. This it does by prohibiting the intellect from having certain representations, by absolutely preventing certain trains of thought from arising, because it knows, or in other words experiences from the self-same intellect, that they would arouse in it any one of the emotions previously described. It then curbs and restrains the intellect, and forces it to turn to other things. However difficult this often is, it is bound to succeed the moment the will is in earnest about it; for the resistance then comes not from the intellect, which always remains indifferent, but from the will itself; and the will has an inclination in one respect for a representation it abhors in another. Thus the representation is in itself interesting to the will, just because it excites it. At the same time, however, abstract knowledge tells the will that this representation will cause it a shock of painful and unworthy emotion to no purpose. The will then decides in accordance with this last knowledge, and forces the intellect to obey. This is called "being master of oneself"; here obviously the master is the will, the servant the intellect, for in the last instance the will is always in command, and therefore constitutes the real core, the being-in-itself, of man. In this respect Ἡγεμονικόν[5] would be a fitting title for the *will;* yet again this title seems to apply to

---

[5] "The principal faculty" (a Stoic term). [Tr.]

the *intellect,* in so far as that is the guide and leader, like the footman who walks in front of the stranger. In truth, however, the most striking figure for the relation of the two is that of the strong blind man carrying the sighted lame man on his shoulders.

The relation of the will to the intellect here described can further be recognized in the fact that the intellect is originally quite foreign to the decisions of the will. It furnishes the will with motives; but only subsequently, and thus wholly *a posteriori,* does it learn how these have acted, just as a man making a chemical experiment applies the reagents, and then waits for the result. In fact, the intellect remains so much excluded from the real resolutions and secret decisions of its own will that sometimes it can only get to know them, like those of a stranger, by spying out and taking unawares; and it must surprise the will in the act of expressing itself, in order merely to discover its real intentions. For example, I have devised a plan, but I still have some scruple regarding it; on the other hand, the feasibility of the plan, as regards its possibility, is completely uncertain, since it depends on external circumstances that are still undecided. Therefore at all events it is unnecessary for the present to come to a decision about it, and so for the time being I let the matter rest. Now I often do not know how firmly I am already attached in secret to this plan, and how much I desire that it be carried into effect, in spite of the scruple; in other words, my intellect does not know this. But only let a favourable report reach me as to its feasibility, and at once there arises within me a jubilant, irresistible gladness, diffused over my whole being and taking permanent possession of it, to my own astonishment. For only now does my intellect learn how firmly my will had already laid hold of the plan, and how entirely it was in agreement therewith, whereas the intellect had still regarded it as entirely problematical and hardly a match for that scruple. Or in another case, I have entered very eagerly into a mutual obligation that I believe to be very much in accordance with my wishes. As the matter progresses, the disadvantages and hardships make themselves felt, and I begin to suspect that I even repent of what I pursued so eagerly. However, I rid myself of this suspicion by assuring myself that, even if I were not bound, I should continue on the same course. But then the obligation is unexpectedly broken and dissolved by the other party, and I observe with astonishment that this happens to my great joy and relief. We often do not know what we desire or fear. For years we can have a desire without admitting it to ourselves or even letting it come to clear consciousness, because the intellect is not to know anything about it, since the good opinion we have of ourselves would inevitably suffer thereby. But if the wish is fulfilled, we get to know from our joy, not without a feeling of shame, that this is what we desired; for example, the death of a near relation whose heir we are. Sometimes we do not know what we really fear, because we lack the courage to bring it to clear consciousness. In fact, we are often entirely mistaken as to the real motive from which we do or omit to do something, till finally some accident discloses the secret to us, and we know that our real motive was not what we thought of it as being, but some other that we were unwilling to admit to ourselves, because it was by no means in keeping with our good opinion of ourselves. For example, as we imagine we omit to do something for purely moral reasons; yet we learn subsequently that we were deterred merely by fear, since we do it as soon as all danger is removed. In individual cases this may go so far that a man does not even guess the real motive of his action, in fact does not regard himself as capable of being influenced by such a motive; yet it is the real motive of his action. Incidentally, we have in all this a confirmation and illustration of the rule of La Rochefoucauld: *"L'amour-propre est plus habile que le plus habile homme du monde,"*[6] in fact even a commentary on the Delphic γνῶθι σαυτόν[6a] and its difficulty. Now if, on the other hand, as all philosophers imagine, the intellect constituted our true inner nature, and the decisions of the will were a mere result of knowledge, then precisely *that* motive alone, from which we *imagined* we acted, would necessarily be decisive for our moral worth, on the analogy that the intention, not the result, is decisive in this respect. But then the distinction between imagined and actual motive would really be impossible. Therefore, all cases described here, and moreover the analogous cases which anyone who is attentive can observe in himself, enable us to see how the intellect is such a stranger to the will that occasionally it is even mystified thereby. For it is true that it furnishes the will with motives; but it does not penetrate into the secret workshop of the will's decisions. It is, of course, a confidant of the will, yet a confidant that does not get to know everything. A confirmation of this is also afforded by the fact that occasionally the intellect does not really trust the will; and at some time or other almost everyone will have an opportunity of observing this in himself. Thus, if we have formed some great and bold resolution— which, however, as such is only a promise given by the will to the intellect—there often remains within us a slight, unconfessed doubt whether we are quite in earnest about it, whether, in carrying it out,

---

[6] "Self-esteem is cleverer than the cleverest man of the world." [Tr.]
[6a] "Know yourself." [Tr.]

we shall not waver or flinch, but shall have firmness and determination enough to carry it through. It therefore requires the deed to convince us of the sincerity of the resolve.

All these facts are evidence of the complete difference between the will and the intellect, and demonstrate the former's primacy and the latter's subordinate position.

4. The *intellect* grows tired; the *will* is untiring. After continuous work with the head, we feel fatigue of the brain, just as we feel fatigue of the arm after continuous bodily work. All *knowing* is associated with effort and exertion; *willing,* on the contrary, is our very nature, whose manifestations occur without any weariness and entirely of their own accord. Therefore, if our *will* is strongly excited, as in all emotions such as anger, fear, desire, grief, and so on, and we are then called upon to *know,* perhaps with the intention of correcting the motives of those emotions, then the violence we must do to ourselves for this purpose is evidence of the transition from the original, natural activity proper to us to the activity that is derived, indirect, and forced. For the will alone is αὐτόματος and therefore ἀκάματος καὶ ἀγήρατος ἤματα πάντα (*lassitudinis et senii expers in sempiternum*).[7] It alone is active, unbidden and of its own accord, and hence often too early and too much; and it knows no weariness. Infants, who show scarcely the first feeble trace of intelligence, are already full of self-will; through uncontrollable, aimless storming and screaming, they show the pressure of will with which they are full to overflowing, whereas their willing as yet has no object, in other words, they will without knowing what they will. The remarks of Cabanis are to the point here: *Toutes ces passions, qui se succèdent d'une manière si rapide, et se peignent avec tant de naïveté, sur le visage mobile des enfans. Tandis que les faibles muscles de leurs bras et de leurs jambes savent encore à peine former quelques mouvemens indécis, les muscles de la face expriment déjà par des mouvemens distincts presque toute la suite des affections générales propres à la nature humaine: et l'observateur attentif reconnait facilement dans ce tableau les traits caractéristiques de l'homme futur.*[8] (*Rapports du physique et moral,* Vol. I, p. 123.) The intellect, on the contrary, develops slowly, following on the completion of the

---

[7] "Self-moving"; "untiring and not growing old for ever." [Tr.]

[8] "All these passions which follow one another so rapidly and are portrayed with such ingenuousness on the mobile features of children. Whereas the feeble muscles of their arms and legs are as yet scarcely able to perform a few undecided movements, the muscles of the face already express by distinct movements almost the whole range of general emotions peculiar to human nature; and the attentive observer easily recognizes in this picture the characteristic features of the future man." [Tr.]

brain and the maturity of the whole organism. These are the conditions of the intellect, just because it is only a somatic function. Because the brain has already attained its full size in the seventh year, children after that age become remarkably intelligent, inquisitive, and sensible. But then comes puberty; to a certain extent, it affords a support to the brain, or a sounding-board, and all at once raises the intellect by a large step, by an octave as it were, corresponding to the lowering of the voice by a like amount. But at the same time the animal desires and passions that now appear oppose the reasonableness that has hitherto prevailed, and this is progressive. Further evidence of the indefatigable nature of the will is afforded by the fault more or less peculiar to all people by nature, and overcome only by training—*precipitancy* or *rashness*. This consists in the will's hurrying prematurely to its business. This is the purely active and executive part that should appear only after the exploratory, deliberate, and thus the knowing part has thoroughly completed its business; but rarely does one actually wait for this time. Scarcely are a few data superficially comprehended and hastily gathered up by knowledge concerning the circumstances before us, or the event that has occurred, or the opinion of someone else that is conveyed to us, when from the depths of our nature the will, always ready and never tired, steps forth unbidden. It shows itself as terror, fear, hope, joy, desire, envy, grief, zeal, anger, or courage, and leads to hasty words or actions. These are often followed by repentance, after time has taught us that the hegemonikon, namely the intellect, has not been able to finish even half its business of comprehending the circumstances, reflecting on their connexion, and deciding what is advisable. This is because the will did not wait for it, but sprang forward long before its time with "Now it is my turn!" and at once took up an active part without the intellect's offering any resistance. But as a mere slave and bondman of the will, the intellect is not, like it, αὐτόματος, or active from its own power and its own impulse. It is therefore easily pushed aside by the will, and brought to silence by a nod therefrom; whereas on its own part it is hardly able, even with the greatest effort, to bring the will even to a brief pause, in order to get a word in edgeways. This is why people are so rare, and are found almost exclusively among Spaniards, Turks, and possibly Englishmen, who, even in the most provocative circumstances, *keep their heads*. Imperturbably they continue to comprehend and investigate the state of affairs, and where others would already be beside themselves, ask a further question *con mucho sosiego*.[9] This is something quite different from the composure

---

• "With much composure." [Tr.]

and unconcern, based on indolence and apathy, of many Germans and Dutchmen. Iffland used to give an incomparable illustration of this admirable quality when taking the part of Hetman of the Cossacks in Benyowski. When the conspirators enticed him into their tent, they held a rifle at his head, intimating that it would be fired the moment he uttered a cry; Iffland blew into the muzzle of the rifle to test whether it was loaded. Of ten things that annoy us, nine could not do so if we thoroughly understood them from their causes, and so knew their necessity and true nature; but we should do this much oftener if we made them the object of reflection before making them the object of indignation and annoyance. For what bridle and bit are to an unmanageable horse, the intellect is to the will in man; it must be led by this bridle by means of instruction, exhortation, training, and so on; for in itself the will is as wild and impetuous an impulse as is the force appearing in the plunging waterfall; in fact, it is, as we know, ultimately identical therewith. In the height of anger, in intoxication, in despair, the will has taken the bit between its teeth; it has bolted, and follows its original nature. In *mania sine delirio*,[10] it has completely lost bridle and bit, and then shows most clearly its original and essential nature, and that the intellect is as different from it as the bridle is from the horse. In this state it can also be compared to a clock that runs down without a stop after a certain screw is removed.

This consideration, therefore, also shows us the will as something original and thus metaphysical, but the intellect as something secondary and physical. For as such the intellect, like everything physical, is subject to *vis inertiae*,[11] and is therefore active only when it is put in motion by something else, by the will; and this will rules it, guides it, incites it to further effort, in short imparts to it the activity that is not originally inherent in it. Therefore it willingly rests as soon as it is allowed to do so, and often declares itself to be *indolent* and disinclined to activity. Through continued effort it becomes tired to the point of complete dulness; it is exhausted just as the voltaic pile is through repeated shocks. Therefore all continuous mental work requires pauses and rest, otherwise stupidity and incapacity are the result. Of course these are at first only temporary; but if this rest is constantly denied to the intellect, it becomes excessively and perpetually strained. The consequence is that it becomes permanently dull, and in old age this dulness can pass into complete incapacity, childishness, imbecility, and madness. It is not to be ascribed to old age in and by itself, but to long-continued tyrannical

[10] "Madness without delirium." [Tr.]
[11] "Force of inertia." [Tr.]

overstraining of the intellect or the brain, when these disorders appear in the last years of life. From this can be explained the fact that Swift became mad, Kant childish, Sir Walter Scott, and also Wordsworth, Southey, and many of less eminence, dull and incapable. Goethe to the end remained clear, and mentally vigorous and active, because he, who was always a man of the world and a courtier, never pursued his mental occupations with self-compulsion. The same holds good of Wieland and the ninety-one-year-old Knebel, as well as Voltaire. But all this proves how very secondary and physical the intellect is, what a mere tool it is. For this reason it needs, for almost a third of its life, the entire suspension of its activity in sleep, in resting the brain. The intellect is the mere function of the brain, which therefore precedes it just as the stomach precedes digestion, or as bodies precede their impact, and together with which it flags and becomes exhausted in old age. The *will,* on the contrary, as thing-in-itself, is never indolent, is absolutely untiring. Its activity is its essence; it never ceases to will, and when, during deep sleep, it is forsaken by the intellect, and is therefore unable to act outwardly from motives, it is active as vital force, looks after the inner economy of the organism with the less interruption, and, as *vis naturae medicatrix,*[12] again sets in order the irregularities that had found their way into it. For it is not, like the intellect, a function of the body, but *the body is its function;* therefore *ordine rerum* it is prior to that body, as it is the metaphysical substratum of that body, the in-itself of that body's phenomenal appearance. For the duration of life it communicates its indefatigability to the *heart,* that *primum mobile* of the organism, which has therefore become its symbol and synonym. Moreover it does not disappear in old age, but still goes on willing what it has willed. It becomes, in fact, firmer and more inflexible than it was in youth, more irreconcilable, implacable, self-willed, and intractable, because the intellect has become less responsive and susceptible. Therefore we can perhaps get the better of a person in old age only by taking advantage of the weakness of his intellect.

The usual *weakness* and *imperfection* of the intellect, as shown in the want of judgement, narrow-mindedness, perversity, and folly of the great majority, would also be quite inexplicable if the intellect were not something secondary, adventitious, and merely instrumental, but the immediate and original essence of the so-called soul, or in general of the inner man, as was formerly assumed by all philosophers. For how could the original inner nature err and fail so frequently in its immediate and characteristic function? That which is

---

[12] "The healing power of nature." [Tr.]

actually original in human consciousness, namely *willing,* goes on all the time with perfect success; every being wills incessantly, vigorously, and decidedly. To regard the immoral element in the will as an imperfection of it would be a fundamentally false point of view; on the contrary, morality has a source that really lies beyond nature; hence it is in contradiction with the utterances of nature. For this reason, morality is directly opposed to the natural will, which in itself is absolutely egoistic; in fact, to pursue the path of morality leads to the abolition of the will. On this point I refer to our fourth book and to my essay *On the Basis of Morality.*

5. That the *will* is what is real and essential in man, whereas the *intellect* is only the secondary, the conditioned, and the produced, becomes clear from the fact that the intellect can fulfil its function quite properly and correctly only so long as the will is silent and pauses. On the other hand, the function of the intellect is disturbed by every observable excitement of the will, and its result is falsified by the will's interference; but the converse, namely that the intellect is in a similar manner a hindrance to the will, does not hold. Thus the moon cannot produce any effect when the sun is in the heavens; yet the moon in the heavens does not prevent the sun from shining.

A great *fright* often deprives us of our senses to such an extent that we become petrified, or do the most preposterous things; for example, when a fire has broken out, we run right into the flames. *Anger* makes us no longer know what we do, still less what we say. *Rashness,* for this reason called blind, makes us incapable of carefully considering the arguments of others, or even of picking out and putting in order our own. *Joy* makes us inconsiderate, thoughtless, and foolhardy; *desire* acts in almost the same way. *Fear* prevents us from seeing and seizing the resources that still exist, and are often close at hand. Therefore *equanimity, composure,* and *presence of mind* are the most essential qualifications for overcoming sudden dangers, and also for contending with enemies and opponents. Composure consists in the silence of the will, so that the intellect can act; presence of mind consists in the undisturbed activity of the intellect under the pressure of events that act on the will. Therefore composure is the condition of presence of mind, and the two are closely related; they are rare, and exist always only in a limited degree. But they are of inestimable advantage, because they allow of the use of the intellect just at those times when we are most in need of it; and in this way they confer decided superiority. He who does not possess them knows what he ought to have done or said only after the opportunity has passed. It is very appropriately said of him who is violently moved, in other words whose will is so strongly excited as to destroy the purity of the intellect's function, that he is *disarmed;*[13] for the correct knowledge of circumstances and relations is our defence and weapon in the conflict with events and people. In this sense, Balthasar Gracián says: *Es la pasión enemiga declarada de la cordura* (Passion is the declared enemy of prudence). Now if the intellect were not something completely different from the will, but, as has hitherto been supposed, knowing and willing were radically one, and were equally original functions of an absolutely simple substance, then with the rousing and heightening of the will, in which emotion consists, the intellect also would of necessity be heightened. But, as we have seen, it is rather hindered and depressed by this; and for this reason, the ancients called emotion *animi perturbatio.* The intellect is really like the mirror-surface of water, the water itself being like the will; the agitation of the water therefore destroys at once the purity of that mirror and the distinctness of its images. The *organism* is the will itself, embodied will, in other words, *will* objectively perceived in the brain. For this reason many of its functions, such as respiration, blood circulation, bile secretion, and muscular force, are enhanced and accelerated by the pleasant, and generally robust, emotions. The *intellect,* on the other hand, is the mere function of the *brain,* which is nourished and sustained by the organism only parasitically. Therefore every perturbation of the *will,* and with it of the *organism,* must disturb or paralyse the function of the brain, a function existing by itself, and knowing no other needs than simply those of rest and nourishment.

But this disturbing influence of the will's activity on the intellect can be shown not only in the perturbations produced by the emotions, but also in many other more gradual, and therefore more lasting, falsifications of thought through our inclinations and tendencies. *Hope* makes us regard what we desire, and *fear* what we are afraid of, as being probable and near, and both magnify their object. Plato (according to Aelian, *Variae Historiae,* 13, 28) has very finely called *hope* the dream of him who is awake. Its nature lies in the fact that the will, when its servant, the *intellect,* is unable to produce the thing desired, compels this servant at any rate to picture this thing to it, and generally to undertake the role of comforter, to pacify its lord and master, as a nurse does a child, with fairy-tales, and to deck these out so that they obtain an appearance of verisimilitude. Here the intellect is bound to do violence to its own nature, which is aimed at truth, since it is compelled, contrary to its own laws, to regard as true things that are neither true nor probable, and often

---

[13] The German word *"entrüstet"* also means "in anger." [Tr.]

scarcely possible, merely in order to pacify, soothe, and send to sleep for a while the restless and unmanageable *will*. We clearly see here who is master and who is servant. Indeed, many may have made the observation that, if a matter of importance to them admits of several courses of development, and they have brought all these into one disjunctive judgement that in their opinion is complete, the outcome is nevertheless quite different and wholly unexpected by them. But possibly they will not have noticed that this result was then almost always the one most unfavourable to them. This can be explained from the fact that, while their *intellect* imagined that it surveyed the possibilities completely, the worst of all remained quite invisible to it, because the *will*, so to speak, kept this covered with its hand; in other words, the will so mastered the intellect that it was quite incapable of glancing at the worst case of all, although, this case was the most probable, since it actually came to pass. However, in decidedly melancholy dispositions, or those which have grown wiser through like experience, the process is indeed reversed, since apprehension and misgiving in them play the part formerly played by hope. The first appearance of a danger puts them into a state of groundless anxiety. If the intellect begins to investigate matters, it is rejected as incompetent, in fact as a deceptive sophist, because the heart is to be believed. The heart's timidity and nervousness are now actually allowed to pass as arguments for the reality and magnitude of the danger. So then the intellect is not at all allowed to look for counter-arguments that it would soon recognize if left to itself, but is forced to picture to them at once the most unfortunate issue, even when it itself can conceive this as scarcely possible:

> Such as we know is false, yet dread in sooth,
> Because the worst is ever nearest truth.
> (Byron, *Lara*, i, 28)

Love and *hatred* entirely falsify our judgement; in our enemies we see nothing but shortcomings, in our favourites nothing but merits and good points, and even their defects seem amiable to us. Our *advantage,* of whatever kind it may be, exercises a similar secret power over our judgement; what is in agreement with it at once seems to us fair, just, and reasonable; what runs counter to it is presented to us in all seriousness as unjust and outrageous, or inexpedient and absurd. Hence so many prejudices of social position, rank, profession, nationality, sect, and religion. A hypothesis, conceived and formed, makes us lynx-eyed for everything that confirms it, and blind to everything that contradicts it. What is opposed to our party, our plan, our wish, or our hope often cannot possibly be grasped and comprehended by us, whereas it is clear to the eyes of everyone else; on the other hand, what is favourable to these leaps to our eyes from afar. What opposes the heart is not admitted by the head. All through life we cling to many errors, and take care never to examine their ground, merely from a fear, of which we ourselves are unconscious, of possibly making the discovery that we have so long and so often believed and maintained what is false. Thus is our intellect daily befooled and corrupted by the deceptions of inclination and liking. This has been finely expressed by Bacon in the following words: *Intellectus LUMINIS SICCI non est; sed recipit infusionem a voluntate et affectibus: id quod generat ad quod vult scientias: quod enim mavult homo, id potius credit. Innumeris modis, iisque interdum imperceptibilibus, affectus intellectum imbuit et inficit* (*Novum Organum*, I, 49).[14] Obviously, it is also this that opposes all new fundamental views in the sciences and all refutations of sanctioned errors; for no one will readily see the correctness of that which convicts him of incredible want of thought. From this alone can be explained the fact that the truths of Goethe's colour theory, so clear and simple, are still denied by the physicists; and thus even he had to learn from experience how much more difficult is the position of one who promises people instruction rather than entertainment. It is therefore much more fortunate to have been born a poet than a philosopher. On the other hand, the more obstinately an error has been held, the more mortifying does the convincing proof subsequently become. With a system that is overthrown, as with a beaten army, the most prudent is he who runs away from it first.

A trifling and ridiculous, but striking example of the mysterious and immediate power exercised by the will over the intellect is that, when doing accounts, we make mistakes more frequently to our advantage than to our disadvantage, and this indeed without the least intention of dishonesty, but merely through the unconscious tendency to diminish our *debit* and increase our *credit*.

Finally, the fact is also relevant here that, in the case when any advice is to be given, the slightest aim or purpose in the adviser generally outweighs his insight, however great this may be. Therefore we dare not assume that he speaks from insight when we sus-

---

[14] "The intellect is no *light that would burn dry* (*without oil*), but receives its supply from the will and from the passions; and this produces knowledge according as we desire to have it. For man prefers most of all to believe what he would like to. Passion influences and infects the intellect in innumerable ways that are sometimes imperceptible." [Tr.]

pect intention. How little absolute sincerity is to be expected, even from persons otherwise honest, whenever their interest in any way bears on a matter, can be judged from the fact that we so often deceive ourselves where hope bribes us, or fear befools us, or suspicion torments us, or vanity flatters us, or a hypothesis infatuates and blinds us, or a small purpose close at hand interferes with one greater but more distant. In these we see the direct, unconscious, and disadvantageous influence of the will on knowledge. Accordingly it ought not to surprise us if, when advice is asked, the will of the person asked immediately dictates the answer, even before the question could penetrate to the forum of his judgement.

Here I wish to point out in a word what is fully discussed in the following book, namely that the most perfect knowledge, the purely objective apprehension of the world, that is, the apprehension of the genius, is conditioned by a silencing of the will so profound that, so long as it lasts, even the individuality disappears from consciousness, and the man remains *pure subject of knowing,* which is the correlative of the Idea.

The disturbing influence of the will on the intellect, as all these phenomena prove, and, on the other hand, the intellect's frailty and feebleness, by virtue of which it is incapable of operating correctly whenever the will is in any way set in motion, give us yet another proof that the will is the radical part of our real nature, and acts with original force, whereas the intellect, as something adventitious and in many ways conditioned, can act only in a secondary and conditional manner.

There is no immediate disturbance of the will by knowledge, corresponding to the disturbance and clouding of knowledge by the will which has been discussed; in fact, we cannot really form any conception of such a thing. No one will try to explain it by saying that falsely interpreted motives lead the will astray, for this is a fault of the intellect in its own function. This fault is committed purely within the province of the intellect, and its influence on the will is wholly indirect. It would be more plausible to attribute *irresolution* to this, as in its case, through the conflict of the motives presented by the intellect to the will, the latter is brought to a standstill, and is therefore impeded. But on closer consideration it becomes very clear that the cause of this hindrance is to be sought not in the activity of the *intellect* as such, but simply and solely in the *external objects* brought about by this activity. The objects stand for once precisely in such a relation to the will, which is here interested, that they pull it in different directions with nearly equal force. This real cause acts merely *through* the intellect as the medium of motives, although, of course, only on the assumption that the intellect is keen enough to comprehend the objects and their manifold relations exactly. Indecision as a trait of character is conditioned just as much by qualities of the will as by those of the intellect. It is, of course, not peculiar to extremely limited minds, because their feeble understanding does not enable them to discover so many different qualities and relations in things. Moreover, their understanding is so little fitted for the effort of reflecting on and pondering over those things, and so over the probable consequences of each step, that they prefer to decide at once in accordance with the first impression or some simple rule of conduct. The converse of this occurs in the case of people of considerable understanding. Therefore, whenever these have in addition a tender care for their own well-being, in other words, a very sensitive egoism that certainly does not want to come off too badly and wants to be always safe and secure, this produces at every step a certain uneasiness, and hence indecision. Therefore this quality points in every way to a want not of understanding, but of courage. Yet very eminent minds survey the relations and their probable developments with such rapidity and certainty that, if only they are supported by some courage, they thus acquire that quick peremptoriness and resoluteness which fits them to play an important role in world affairs, provided that times and circumstances afford the opportunity for so doing.

The only decided, direct hindrance and disturbance that the will can suffer from the intellect as such, may indeed be quite exceptional. This is the consequence of an abnormally predominant development of the intellect, and hence of that high endowment described as genius. Such a gift is indeed a decided hindrance to the energy of the character, and consequently to the power of action. Therefore it is not the really great minds that make historical characters, since such characters, capable of bridling and governing the mass of mankind, struggle with world-affairs. On the contrary, men of much less mental capacity are suitable for this, when they have great firmness, resolution, and inflexibility of will, such as cannot exist at all with very high intelligence. Accordingly, with such high intelligence a case actually occurs where the intellect directly impedes the will.

6. In contrast to the obstacles and hindrances mentioned, which the intellect suffers from the will, I wish now to show by a few examples how, conversely, the functions of the intellect are sometimes aided and enhanced by the incentive and spur of the will, so that here also we may recognize the primary nature of the one and the secondary nature of the other, and that it may become clear that the intellect stands to the will in the relation of a tool.

A powerfully acting motive, such as a yearning desire or pressing need, sometimes raises the intellect to a degree of which we had never previously believed it capable. Difficult circumstances, imposing on us the necessity of certain achievements, develop entirely new talents in us, the germs of which had remained hidden from us, and for which we did not credit ourselves with any capacity. The understanding of the stupidest person becomes keen when it is a question of objects that closely concern his willing. He now observes, notices, and distinguishes with great subtlety and refinement even the smallest circumstances that have reference to his desires or fears. This has much to do with that cunning of half-witted persons which is often observed with surprise. For this reason, Isaiah rightly says: *vexatio dat intellectum*,[15] which is therefore also used as a proverb: akin to it is the German proverb *"Die Not ist die Mutter der Künste"* (Necessity is the mother of the arts); the fine arts, however, must form an exception, since the kernel of every one of their works, namely the conception, must result from a perfectly will-less, and only thus a purely objective, perception, if they are to be genuine. Even the understanding of animals is considerably enhanced through necessity, so that in difficult cases they achieve things at which we are astonished. For example, almost all of them reckon that it is safer not to run away when they believe they are not seen; thus the hare lies still in the furrow of the field and lets the hunter pass close to it; if insects cannot escape, they pretend to be dead, and so on. We become more closely acquainted with this influence from the special story of the wolf's self-training under the spur of the great difficulty of its position in civilized Europe, to be found in the second letter of Leroy's excellent book *Lettres sur l'intelligence et la perfectibilité des animaux*. Immediately afterwards, in the third letter, there follows the high school of the fox; in an equally difficult position, he has far less physical strength, but in his case greater understanding compensates for this. Yet this understanding reaches the high degree of cunning, which distinguishes him especially in old age, only through constant struggle with want on the one hand and danger on the other, and thus under the spur of the will. In all these enhancements of the intellect, the will plays the part of the rider urging his horse with the spur beyond the natural measure of its strength.

In just the same way, *memory* is enhanced by pressure of the will. Even when otherwise weak, it preserves completely what is of value to the ruling passion. The lover forgets no opportunity favourable to him, the man of ambition no circumstance that suits his

---

[15] "Vexation bestows intellect." Isa. 28:19, Vulg. [Tr.]

plans, the miser never forgets the loss he has suffered, the proud man never forgets an injury to his honour, the vain person remembers every word of praise and even the smallest distinction that falls to his lot. This also extends to the animals; the horse stops at the inn where it was once fed a long time ago; dogs have an excellent memory for all occasions, times, and places that have afforded them dainty morsels, and foxes for the various hiding-places in which they have stored their plunder.

An examination of ourselves gives us an opportunity for finer observations in this respect. Through an interruption or disturbance, what I was just thinking about, or even the news that I have just come to hear, sometimes slips entirely from my memory. Now, if the matter had in any way a personal interest, however remote, there remains the after-effect of the impression thus made by it on the *will*. Thus I am still quite conscious how far it affected me agreeably or disagreeably, and also of the special way in which this happened, thus whether, although in a feeble degree, it offended me, or made me anxious, or irritated me, or grieved me, or else produced the opposite of these affections. Hence the mere relation of the thing to my will has been retained in the memory, after the thing itself has vanished from me; and this relation in turn often becomes the clue for returning to the thing itself. The sight of a person sometimes affects us in an analogous way, since only in general do we remember having had something to do with him, without knowing where, when, and what it was, or who he is. On the other hand, the sight of him still recalls pretty accurately the feeling or frame of mind formerly roused in us by our dealings with him, that is, whether it was agreeable or disagreeable, and to what degree and in what way it was so. Therefore the memory has preserved merely the approval or disapproval of the *will,* not what called it forth. We might call that which is the foundation of this course of events the memory of the heart; this is much more intimate than that of the head. Yet at bottom the connexion of the two is so far-reaching that, if we reflect deeply on the matter, we shall reach the conclusion that memory in general requires the foundation of a will as a point of contact, or rather as a thread on which the recollections range themselves, and which holds them firmly together, or that the will is, so to speak, the ground on which the individual recollections stick, and without which they could not be fixed. We shall therefore reach the conclusion that a memory cannot really be conceived in a pure intelligence, in other words in a merely knowing and absolutely will-less being. Accordingly, the above-mentioned enhancement of the memory through the spur of the ruling passion is only the higher degree of what takes place in all retention and recollection, since its basis and condition is always the will. Hence in all this also, it becomes clear how very much more intimate to us the will is than the intellect. The following facts may also serve to confirm this.

The intellect often obeys the will; for example, if we wish to remember something, and after some effort succeed; as also if we wish to think over something accurately and deliberately, and in many such cases. Again, the intellect sometimes refuses to obey the will, e.g., when we strive in vain to fix on something, or vainly demand back from the memory something entrusted to it. The anger of the will towards the intellect on such occasions makes its relation to the intellect and the difference between the two very easy to recognize. Indeed the intellect, vexed by this anger, officiously supplies what was asked of it sometimes hours later, or even on the following morning, quite unexpectedly and at the wrong time. On the other hand, the will, properly speaking, never obeys the intellect, but the intellect is merely the cabinet council of that sovereign. It lays before the will all kinds of things, and in accordance with these the will selects what is in conformity with its true nature, although in doing so it determines itself with necessity, because this inner nature is firm and unchangeable, and the motives now lie before it. For this reason, no system of ethics which would mould and improve the will itself is possible. For all teaching affects only *knowledge,* and knowledge never determines the will itself, in other words, the *fundamental character* of willing, but merely its application to the circumstances in question. Rectified knowledge can modify conduct only in so far as it demonstrates more accurately and enables one to judge more correctly the objects of the will's choice which are accessible to the will. In this way the will estimates more correctly its relation to things, sees more distinctly what it wills, and in consequence is less subject to error in its choice. Over willing itself, however, over its main tendency or fundamental maxim, the intellect has no power. To believe that knowledge really and radically determines the *will* is like believing that the lantern a man carries at night is the *primum mobile* of his steps. He who, taught by experience or by the exhortations of others, recognizes and deplores a fundamental defect in his character, firmly and honestly forms the resolution to improve himself and to get rid of the defect; but in spite of this, the defect obtains full play on the very next occasion. New regrets, new resolutions, new transgressions. When this is gone through several times, he becomes aware that he cannot mend his ways, that the defect lies in his nature and personality, is in fact identical with these. He will then disapprove of and condemn his nature and personality; he will have a painful feeling that may rise to qualms of conscience; but change these he cannot. Here we see distinctly separated that which condemns and that which is condemned. We see the former as a merely theoretical faculty, picturing and presenting the praiseworthy and therefore desirable course of life, and the other as something real and unalterably present, taking quite a different course, in spite of the former. Then again, we see the former left behind with useless and ineffective complaints about the nature of the latter, with which it again identifies itself through this very grief and distress. Will and intellect here separate out very distinctly; but the will shows itself as that which is the stronger, the invincible, the unalterable, the primitive, and at the same time the essential, that on which everything depends, since the intellect deplores the will's defects, and finds no consolation in the correctness of the *knowledge* as its own function. Therefore the intellect shows itself as entirely secondary, now as the spectator of another's deeds, accompanying them with ineffective praise or blame, now as determinable from without, since, enlightened by experience, it draws up and modifies its precepts. Special illustrations of this subject are found in the *Parerga,* Vol. II, § 118. Accordingly, a comparison of our way of thinking at different periods of our life will present us with a strange mixture of constancy and inconstancy. On the one hand, the moral tendency of the man in his prime and of the old man is still the same as was that of the boy. On the other hand, much has become so strange to him that he no longer knows himself, and wonders how he was once able to do or say this or that. In the first half of life, to-day often laughs at yesterday, in fact even looks down on it with contempt; in the second half, on the other hand, it looks back on it more and more with envy. On closer investigation, however, it will be found that the changeable element was the *intellect* with its functions of insight and knowledge. These every day assimilate fresh material from outside, and present a constantly altered system of ideas, whereas the intellect itself rises and sinks with the rise and decline of the organism. On the other hand, the will, the very basis of the organism, and thus the inclinations, passions, emotions, character, show themselves as that which is unalterable in consciousness. Yet we must take into account the modifications depending on the physical capacities for enjoyment, and thus on age. For example, the keen desire for sensual pleasure will appear in boyhood as a fondness for dainties, in youth and manhood as a tendency to voluptuousness, and in old age once more as a fondness for dainties.

7. If, as is generally assumed, the will proceeded from knowledge

as its result or product, then where there is much will there would necessarily be much knowledge, insight, and understanding. This, however, is by no means the case; on the contrary, we find in many men a strong, i.e., decided, resolute, persistent, inflexible, obstinate, and vehement will associated with a very feeble and incompetent understanding. Thus whoever has dealings with them is reduced to despair, since their will remains inaccessible to all arguments and representations, and is not to be got at, so that it is, so to speak, hidden in a sack out of which it *wills* blindly. Animals have less understanding by far in spite of a will that is often violent and stubborn. Finally, plants have mere will without any knowledge at all.

If willing sprang merely from knowledge, our *anger* would inevitably be exactly proportionate to its cause or occasion in each case, or at any rate to our understanding thereof, since it too would be nothing more than the result of the present knowledge. But it very rarely turns out like this; on the contrary, anger usually goes far beyond the occasion. Our fury and rage, the *furor brevis,* often with trifling occasions and without error in regard to them, are like the storming of an evil demon, which, having been shut up, only waited for the opportunity to dare to break loose, and now rejoices at having found it. This could not be the case if the ground of our true nature were a *knower,* and willing were a mere result of *knowledge;* for how could anything come into the result which did not lie in the elements thereof? The conclusion cannot contain more than is contained in the premisses. Thus here also the will shows itself as an essence which is entirely different from knowledge, and makes use of knowledge merely for communication with the outside world. But then it follows the laws of its own nature without taking from knowledge anything more than the occasion.

The intellect, as the will's mere tool, is as different from it as is the hammer from the smith. So long as the intellect alone is active in a conversation, that conversation remains *cold;* it is almost as though the man himself were not there. Moreover, he cannot then really compromise himself, but can at most make himself ridiculous. Only when the will comes into play is the man really present; he now becomes *warm,* in fact matters often become *hot.* It is always the *will* to which we ascribe the warmth of life; on the other hand, we speak of the *cold* understanding, or to investigate a thing *coolly,* in other words, to think without the influence of the will. If we attempt to reverse the relation, and consider the will as the tool of the intellect, it is as if we were to make the smith the tool of the hammer.

Nothing is more tiresome and annoying than when we argue with a person with reasons and explanations, and take all the trouble to convince him, under the impression that we have to deal only with his *understanding,* and then finally discover that he *will* not understand; that we therefore had to deal with his *will,* which pays no heed to the truth, but brings into action wilful misunderstandings, chicaneries, and sophisms, entrenching itself behind its understanding and its supposed want of insight. Then he is of course not to be got at in this way, for *arguments and proofs applied against the will* are like the blows of a concave mirror's phantom against a solid body. Hence the oft-repeated saying: *Stat pro ratione voluntas.*[16] Proofs enough of what has been said are furnished by ordinary, everyday life; but unfortunately they are also to be found on the path of the sciences. Acknowledgement of the most important truths, of the rarest achievements, will be expected in vain from those who have an interest in not allowing them to be accepted. Such an interest springs either from the fact that such truths contradict what they themselves teach every day, or from their not daring to make use of it and afterwards teach it; or, even if all this is not the case, they do not acknowledge such truths, because the watchword of mediocrities will always be: *Si quelqu'un excelle parmi nous, qu'il aille exceller ailleurs,*[17] as Helvetius has delightfully rendered the saying of the Ephesians in Cicero (*Tusc.* v, c. 36); or as a saying of the Abyssinian Fit Arari has it: "Among quartzes the diamond is outlawed." Therefore whoever expects from this always numerous band a just appreciation of his achievements will find himself very much deceived; and perhaps for a while he will not be able to understand their behaviour at all, until at last he finds out that, whereas he appealed to *knowledge,* he had to do with the *will.* Thus he finds himself entirely in the position above described; in fact, he is really like the man who brings his case before a court all of whose members are bribed. In individual cases, however, he will obtain the most conclusive proof that he was opposed by their *will* and not by their *insight,* when one or the other of them makes up his mind to plagiarize. He will then see with astonishment what shrewd judges they are, what an accurate judgement they have of the merit of others, and how well they are able to discover the best, like sparrows that never miss the ripest cherries.

The opposite of the will's victorious resistance to knowledge which I here describe, is seen when, in expounding our arguments and

---

[16] "My will [to do something] is my reason [for doing it]." [Tr.]

[17] "If anyone makes his mark among us, let him go and do so elsewhere." [Tr.]

proofs, we have on our side the will of the persons addressed. All are then equally convinced, all arguments are striking, and the matter is at once as clear as daylight. Popular speakers know this. In the one case as in the other, the will shows itself as that which has original force, against which the intellect can do nothing.

8. But now we will take into consideration the individual qualities, the merits and defects of the will and character on the one hand, and of the intellect on the other, in order to bring out clearly in their relation to each other and their relative worth the complete difference of the two fundamental faculties. History and experience teach that the two appear quite independently of each other. That the greatest eminence of mind is not easily found combined with an equal eminence of character is sufficiently explained from the extraordinary rarity of both, whereas their opposites are generally the order of the day; hence we daily find these opposites in combination. But we never infer a good will from a superior mind, or the latter from the former, or the opposite from the opposite; but every unprejudiced person accepts them as wholly separate qualities, whose existence, each by itself, is to be determined through experience. Great narrowness of mind can coexist with great goodness of heart, and I do not believe that Balthasar Gracián is right in saying (*Discreto,* p. 406): *No hay simple que no sea malicioso* (There is no simpleton who is not malicious), although he has on his side the Spanish proverb: *Nunca la necedad anduvo sin malicia* (Stupidity is never without malice). Yet it may be that many a stupid person becomes malicious for the same reason that many a hunchback does, namely from irritation at the slight he has suffered from nature; for he imagines he can occasionally make up for what he lacks in understanding through malicious tricks, seeking in this a brief triumph. Incidentally, it is easy to understand from this why almost everyone readily becomes malicious in the presence of a very superior mind. Again, stupid people very often have a reputation for special kindness of heart; yet this is so rarely confirmed, that I could not help wondering how they obtained such a reputation, until I could flatter myself that I had found the key to it in what follows. Moved by a secret inclination, everyone likes best to choose for his most intimate acquaintance someone to whom he is a little superior in understanding, for only with such a person does he feel at ease, since according to Hobbes, *omnis animi voluptas, omnisque alacritas in eo sita est, quod quis habeat, quibuscum conferens se, possit magnifice sentire de se ipso* (*De Cive,* I, 5).[18] For the same reason, everyone

---

[18] "All the delights of the heart and every cheerful frame of mind depend on our having someone with whom we can compare ourselves and think highly of ourselves." [Tr.]

avoids a person who is superior to him; and therefore Lichtenberg quite rightly observes that "To certain persons a man of mind is a more odious creature than the most pronounced rogue."[18a] Likewise, Helvetius says: *Les gens médiocres ont un instinct sûr et prompt pour connaître et fuir les gens d'esprit;*[19] and Dr. Johnson assures us that "There is nothing by which a man exasperates most people more, than by displaying a superior ability of brilliancy in conversation. They seem pleased at the time; but their envy makes them curse him at their hearts." (Boswell; *aet. anno* 74). To bring to light even more relentlessly this truth so generally and carefully concealed, I quote the expression of it by Merck, the celebrated friend of Goethe's youth, from his narrative *Lindor:* "He possessed talents given to him by nature and acquired by him through knowledge, and these enabled him at most parties to leave the worthy members of them far behind. If, at the moment of delight in seeing an extraordinary man, the public swallows these excellent points without actually putting at once a bad construction on them, nevertheless a certain impression of this phenomenon is left behind. If this impression is often repeated, it may on serious occasions have unpleasant consequences in the future for the person guilty of it. Without anyone consciously taking particular notice of the fact that on this occasion he was insulted, on the quiet he is not unwilling to stand in the way of this man's advancement." Therefore, on this account, great mental superiority isolates a person more than does anything else, and makes him hated, at any rate secretly. Now it is the opposite that makes stupid people so universally liked, especially as many a person can find only in them what he is bound to look for in accordance with the above-mentioned law of his nature. Yet no one will confess to himself, still less to others, this real reason for such an inclination; and so, as a plausible pretext for it, he will impute to the person of his choice a special goodness of heart, which, as I have said, actually exists very rarely indeed, and only accidentally in combination with weakness of intellect. Accordingly, want of understanding is by no means favourable or akin to goodness of character. On the other hand, it cannot be asserted that great understanding is so; on the contrary, there has never really been any scoundrel without such understanding. In fact, even the highest intellectual eminence can coexist with the greatest moral depravity. An example of this was afforded by Bacon. Ungrateful, filled with lust for power, wicked and base, he ultimately went so far that, as Lord Chancellor

---

[18a] [*Vermischte Schriften*, Göttingen, 1844, Vol. 2, p. 177.—Tr.]

[19] "Mediocrities have a sure and ready instinct for discovering and avoiding persons of intellect." [*De L'Esprit*, Disc. II, chap. 3.—Tr.]

and the highest judge of the realm, he frequently allowed himself to be bribed in civil actions. Impeached before his peers, he pleaded guilty, was expelled from the House of Lords, and condemned to a fine of forty thousand pounds and to imprisonment in the Tower. (See the review of the new edition of Bacon's works in the *Edinburgh Review*, August 1837.) For this reason Pope calls him "the wisest, brightest, meanest of mankind" (*Essay on Man,* iv, 282). A similar example is afforded by the historian Guicciardini, of whom Rosini says in the *Notizie Storiche,* drawn from good contemporary sources and given in his historical novel *Luisa Strozzi: Da coloro che pongono l'ingegno e il sapere al di sopra di tutte le umane qualità, questo uomo sarà riguardato come fra i più grandi del suo secolo: ma da quelli che reputano la virtù dovere andare innanzi a tutto, non potra esecrarsi abbastanza la sua memoria. Esso fu il più crudele fra i cittadini a perseguitare, uccidere e confinare,* etc.[20]

Now if it is said of one person that "he has a good heart, though a bad head," but of another that "he has a very good head, yet a bad heart," everyone feels that in the former case the praise far outweighs the blame, and in the latter the reverse. Accordingly we see that, when anyone has done a bad deed, his friends and he himself try to shift the blame from the *will* on to the *intellect,* and to make out the faults of the heart to be faults of the head. They will call mean tricks *erratic courses;* they will say it was mere want of understanding, thoughtlessness, levity, folly; in fact, if need be, they will plead a paroxysm, a momentary mental derangement, and if it is a question of a grave crime, even madness, merely in order to exonerate the *will* from blame. In just the same way, when we ourselves have caused a misfortune or injury, we most readily impeach our *stultitia* before others and before ourselves, merely in order to avoid the reproach of *malitia.* Accordingly, in the case of an equally unjust decision of the judge, the difference is immense whether he made a mistake or was bribed. All this is evidence enough that the *will* alone is the real and essential, the kernel of man, and the intellect merely its tool, which may always be faulty without the will being concerned. The accusation of want of understanding is, at the moral judgement-seat, no accusation at all; on the contrary, it even gives privileges. In just the same way, before the courts of the world, it is everywhere sufficient, in order to exonerate an offender

---

[20] "By those who place mind and learning above all other human qualities, this man will be reckoned among the greatest of his century. But by those who think that virtue should take precedence of everything else, his memory can never be sufficiently execrated. He was the cruellest of the citizens in persecuting, putting to death, and banishing." [Tr.]

from all punishment, for the guilt to be shifted from his will to his *intellect,* by demonstrating either unavoidable error or mental derangement. For then it is of no more consequence than if hand or foot had slipped contrary to the will. I have discussed this fully in the Appendix "On Intellectual Freedom" to my essay *On the Freedom of the Will,* and to this I refer so as not to repeat myself.

Everywhere those who promote the appearance of any piece of work appeal, in the event of its turning out unsatisfactorily, to their good will, of which there was no lack. In this way they believe they safeguard the essential, that for which they are properly responsible, and their true self. The inadequacy of their faculties, on the other hand, is regarded by them as the want of a suitable tool.

If a person is *stupid,* we excuse him by saying that he cannot help it; but if we attempted to excuse in precisely the same way the person who is *bad,* we should be laughed at. And yet the one quality, like the other, is inborn. This proves that the will is the man proper, the intellect its mere tool.

Therefore it is always only our *willing* that is regarded as dependent on us, in other words, the expression of our real inner nature, for which we are therefore made responsible. For this reason it is absurd and unjust when anyone tries to take us to task for our beliefs, and so for our knowledge; for we are obliged to regard this as something that, although it rules within us, is as little within our power as are the events of the external world. Therefore here also it is clear that the *will* alone is man's own inner nature; that the *intellect,* on the other hand, with its operations which occur regularly like the external world, is related to the will as something external, as a mere tool.

High intellectual faculties have always been regarded as a *gift* of nature or of the gods; thus they have been called *Gaben, Begabung, ingenii dotes,* gifts (a man highly gifted), and have been regarded as something different from man himself, as something that has fallen to his lot by favour. On the other hand, no one has ever taken the same view with regard to moral excellences, though they too are inborn; on the contrary, these have always been regarded as something coming from the man himself, belonging to him essentially, in fact constituting his own true self. Now it follows from this that the will is man's real inner nature, while the intellect, on the other hand, is secondary, a tool, an endowment.

In accordance with this, all religions promise a reward beyond this life in eternity for excellences of the *will* or of the heart, but none for excellences of the head, of the understanding. Virtue expects its reward in the next world; prudence hopes for it in this;

genius neither in this world nor in the next; for it is its own reward. Accordingly the will is the eternal part, the intellect the temporal.

Association, community, intercourse between persons is based as a rule on relations concerning the *will,* rarely on such as concern the *intellect.* The first kind of community may be called the *material,* the other the *formal.* Of the former kind are the bonds of family and relationship, as well as all connexions and associations that rest on any common aim or interest, such as that of trade, profession, social position, a corporation, party, faction, and so on. With these it is a question merely of the disposition, the intention, and there may exist the greatest diversity of intellectual faculties and of their development. Therefore everyone can not only live with everyone else in peace and harmony, but co-operate with him and be allied to him for the common good of both. Marriage also is a union of hearts, not of heads. Matters are different, however, with merely *formal* community that aims only at an exchange of ideas; this requires a certain equality of intellectual faculties and of culture. Great differences in this respect place an impassable gulf between one man and another; such a gulf lies, for example, between a great mind and a blockhead, a scholar and a peasant, a courtier and a sailor. Therefore such heterogeneous beings have difficulty in making themselves understood, so long as it is a question of communicating ideas, notions, and views. Nevertheless, close *material* friendship can exist between them, and they can be faithful allies, conspirators, and persons under a pledge. For in all that concerns the *will* alone, which includes friendship, enmity, honesty, fidelity, falseness, and treachery, they are quite homogeneous, formed of the same clay, and neither mind nor culture makes any difference to this; in fact, in this respect the uncultured man often puts the scholar to shame, and the sailor the courtier. For in spite of the most varied degrees of culture there exist the same virtues and vices, emotions and passions; and although somewhat modified in their expression, they very soon recognize one another, even in the most heterogeneous individuals, whereupon those who are like-minded come together, and those of contrary opinion show enmity to one another.

Brilliant qualities of the mind earn admiration, not affection; that is reserved for moral qualities, qualities of character. Everyone will much rather choose as his friend the honest, the kind-hearted, and even the complaisant, easy-going person who readily concurs, than one who is merely witty or clever. Many a man will be preferred to one who is clever, even through insignificant, accidental, and external qualities that are exactly in keeping with the inclinations of someone else. Only the man who himself possesses great intellect will want a clever man for his companion; on the other hand, his friendship will depend on moral qualities, for on these rests his real estimation of a person, in which a single good trait of character covers up and effaces great defects of understanding. The known goodness of a character makes us patient and accommodating to weaknesses of understanding as well as to the obtuseness and child-ishness of old age. A decidedly noble character, in spite of a com-plete lack of intellectual merits and culture, stands out as one that lacks nothing; on the other hand, the greatest mind, if tainted by strong moral defects, will nevertheless always seem blameworthy. For just as torches and fireworks become pale and insignificant in the presence of the sun, so intellect, even genius, and beauty like-wise, are outshone and eclipsed by goodness of heart. Where such goodness appears in a high degree, it can compensate for the lack of those qualities to such an extent that we are ashamed of having regretted their absence. Even the most limited understanding and grotesque ugliness, whenever extraordinary goodness of heart has proclaimed itself as their accompaniment, become transfigured, as it were, enwrapped in rays of a beauty of a more exalted kind, since now a wisdom speaks out of them in whose presence all other wis-dom must be reduced to silence. For goodness of heart is a tran-scendent quality; it belongs to an order of things reaching beyond this life, and is incommensurable with any other perfection. Where it is present in a high degree, it makes the heart so large that this embraces the world, so that everything now lies within it, no longer outside. For goodness of heart identifies all beings with its own na-ture. It then extends to others the boundless indulgence that every-one ordinarily bestows only on himself. Such a man is not capable of becoming angry; even when his own intellectual or physical de-fects have provoked the malicious sneers and jeers of others, in his heart he reproaches himself alone for having been the occasion of such expressions. He therefore continues, without imposing restric-tions on himself, to treat those persons in the kindest manner, con-fidently hoping that they will turn from their error in his regard, and will recognize themselves also in him. What are wit and genius in comparison with this? What is Bacon?

A consideration of the estimation of our own selves leads also to the same result that we have here obtained from considering our estimation of others. How fundamentally different is the self-satis-faction which occurs in a moral respect from that which occurs in an intellectual! The former arises from our looking back on our conduct and seeing that we have practised fidelity and honesty with heavy sacrifices, that we have helped many, forgiven many, have been better to others than they have been to us, so that we can say with King Lear: "I am a man more sinn'd against than sinning"; and it arises to the fullest extent when possibly even some noble deed shines in our memory. A profound seriousness will accompany the peaceful bliss that such an examination affords us; and if we see others inferior to us in this respect, this will not cause us any rejoicing; on the contrary, we shall deplore it and sincerely wish that they were as we are. How entirely differently, on the other hand, does the knowledge of our intellectual superiority affect us! Its ground-bass is really the above-quoted saying of Hobbes: *Omnis animi voluptas, omnisque alacritas in eo sita est, quod quis habeat, quibuscum conferens se, possit magnifice sentire de se ipso.*[21] Arrogant, triumphant vanity, a proud, scornful, contemptuous disdain of others, inordinate delight in the consciousness of decided and considerable superiority, akin to pride of physical advantages—this is the result here. This contrast between the two kinds of self-satisfaction shows that the one concerns our true inner and eternal nature, the other a more external, merely temporal, indeed scarcely more than a mere physical advantage. In fact, the *intellect* is a mere function of the brain; the *will,* on the contrary, is that whose function is the whole man, according to his being and inner nature.

If, glancing outwards, we reflect that ὁ βίος βραχύς, ἡ δὲ τέχνη μακρά (*vita brevis, ars longa*),[22] and consider how the greatest and finest minds, often when they have scarcely reached the zenith of their productive power, and likewise great scholars, when they have only just attained a thorough insight into their branch of knowledge, are snatched away by death, then this also confirms that the meaning and purpose of life are not intellectual, but moral.

The complete difference between mental and moral qualities shows itself lastly in the fact that the intellect undergoes extremely important changes with time, whereas the will and character remain untouched thereby. The new-born child has as yet no use at all for its understanding; yet it acquires this within the first two months to the extent of perceiving and apprehending things in the external world, a process I have more fully explained in the essay *Ueber das Sehn und die Farben* (p. 10 of the second edition). The development of reason (*Vernunft*) to the point of speech, and hence of thought, follows this first and most important step much more slowly, generally only in the third year. Nevertheless, early childhood remains irrevocably abandoned to silliness and stupidity, primarily because the brain still lacks physical completeness, which is attained,

---

[21] See note 18, p. 227. [Tr.]
[22] "Life is short, art is long." [Hippocrates, *Aphorismata,* I, 1. Tr.]

as regards both size and texture, only in the seventh year. But for its energetic activity the antagonism of the genital system is still required; hence that activity begins only with puberty. Through this, however, the intellect has then attained only the mere *capacity* for its psychic development; the capacity itself can be acquired only through practice, experience, and instruction. Therefore, as soon as the mind has been delivered from the silliness of childhood, it falls into the snares of innumerable errors, prejudices, and chimeras, sometimes of the absurdest and crassest kind. It wilfully and obstinately sticks firmly to these, till experience gradually rescues it from them; many also are imperceptibly lost. All this happens only in the course of many years, so that we grant to the mind its coming of age soon after the twentieth year, but put full maturity, years of discretion, only at the fortieth. But while this *psychic* development, resting on help from outside, is still in process of growth, the inner *physical* energy of the brain is already beginning to sink again. So, on account of this energy's dependence on blood-pressure and on the pulse's effect on the brain, and thus again on the preponderance of the arterial system over the venous, as well as on the fresh delicacy or softness of the brain-filaments, and also through the energy of the genital system, such energy has its real culminating point at about the thirtieth year. After the thirty-fifth year a slight decrease of this physical energy is already noticeable. Through the gradually approaching preponderance of the venous over the arterial system, as well as through the consistency of the brain-filaments which is always becoming firmer and drier, this decrease of energy occurs more and more. It would be much more noticeable if the *psychic* improvement through practice, experience, increase of knowledge, and the acquired skill in handling this did not counteract it. Fortunately, this antagonism lasts to an advanced age, since the brain can be compared more and more to a played-out instrument. But yet the decrease of the intellect's original energy, which depends entirely on organic conditions, continues, slowly it is true, but irresistibly. The faculty of original conception, the imagination, the suppleness, plasticity, and memory become noticeably more feeble; and so it goes on, step by step, downwards into old age, which is garrulous, without memory, half-unconscious, and finally quite childish.

On the other hand, the *will* is not simultaneously affected by all this growth, development, change, and alteration, but from beginning to end is unalterably the same. Willing does not need to be learnt like knowing, but succeeds perfectly at once. The new-born child moves violently, screams and cries; it wills most vehemently, although it does not yet know what it wills. For the medium of motives, the intellect, is still quite undeveloped. The will is in the dark concerning the external world in which its objects lie; and it rages like a prisoner against the walls and bars of his dungeon. Light, however, gradually comes; at once the fundamental traits of universal human willing, and at the same time their individual modification that is here to be found, show themselves. The character, already emerging, appears, it is true, only in feeble and uncertain outline, on account of the defective functioning of the intellect that has to present it with motives. But to the attentive observer the character soon announces its complete presence, and this soon becomes unmistakable. The traits of character make their appearance, and last for life; the main tendencies of the will, the easily stirred emotions, the ruling passion express themselves. Therefore events at school are for the most part related to those of the future course of life, as the dumb-show in *Hamlet,* preceding the play to be performed at court and foretelling its contents in the form of pantomime, is to the play itself. However, it is by no means possible to predict the future intellectual capacities of the man from those appearing in the boy. On the contrary, *ingenia praecocia,* youthful prodigies, as a rule become blockheads; genius, on the other hand, is often in childhood of slow conception, and comprehends with difficulty, just because it comprehends deeply. Accordingly, everyone relates with a laugh and without reserve the follies and stupidities of his childhood; e.g., Goethe, how he threw all the kitchen-utensils out of the window (*Poetry and Truth,* Vol. i, p. 7); for we know that all this concerns only what is changeable. On the other hand, a prudent man will not favour us with the bad features, the malicious and treacherous tricks, of his youth, for he feels that they still bear witness to his present character. It has been reported to me that when Gall, the phrenologist and investigator of man, had to form an association with someone as yet unknown to him, he got him to speak of his youthful years and tricks, in order, if possible, to discover from these the traits of his character, because this was bound to be still the same. On this rests the fact that, while we are indifferent to, and indeed look back with smiling satisfaction on, the follies and want of understanding of our youthful years, the bad features of character of that period, the malicious actions and misdeeds committed at the time, exist even in advanced age as inextinguishable reproaches, and disturb our conscience. Therefore, just as the character now appears complete, so it remains unaltered right into old age. The assaults of old age, gradually consuming the intellectual powers, leave the moral qualities untouched. Goodness of heart still makes the old man honoured and loved, when his head already shows the weaknesses that are beginning to bring him to his second childhood. Gentleness, patience, honesty, truthfulness, unselfishness, philanthropy, and so on are maintained throughout life, and are not lost through the weakness of old age. In every clear moment of the decrepit old man, they stand out undiminished, like the sun from the winter clouds. On the other hand, malice, spite, avarice, hardheartedness, duplicity, egoism, and baseness of every kind remain undiminished to the most advanced age. We would not believe anyone, but would laugh at him, if he were to say that "In former years I was a malicious rogue, but now I am an honest and noble-minded man." Therefore Sir Walter Scott, in *The Fortunes of Nigel,* has shown very beautifully how, in the case of the old moneylender, burning greed, egoism, and dishonesty are still in full bloom, like the poisonous plants in autumn, and still powerfully express themselves, even after the intellect has become childish. The only alterations that take place in our likings and inclinations are those that are direct consequences of a decrease in our physical strength, and therewith in our capacities for enjoyment. Thus voluptuousness will make way for intemperance, love of splendour for avarice, and vanity for ambition, like the man who, before he had a beard, stuck on a false one, and who will later on dye brown his own beard that has become grey. Therefore, while all the organic forces, muscular strength, the senses, memory, wit, understanding, genius, become worn out and dull in old age, the will alone remains unimpaired and unaltered; the pressure and tendency of willing remain the same. Indeed, in many respects the will shows itself even more decided in old age, e.g., in its attachment to life, which, as we know, grows stronger; also in its firmness and tenacity with regard to what it has once seized, in obstinacy. This can be explained from the fact that the susceptibility of the intellect to other impressions, and thus the excitability of the will through motives that stream in on it, have grown weaker. Hence the implacability of the anger and hatred of old people:

> The young man's wrath is like light straw on fire;
> But like red-hot steel is the old man's ire.
> (*Old Ballad.*)

From all these considerations it is unmistakable to our deeper glance that, while the *intellect* has to run through a long series of gradual developments, and then, like everything physical, falls into decline, the *will* takes no part in this, except in so far as it has to contend at first with the imperfection of its tool, the intellect, and ultimately again with its worn-out condition. The will itself, however, appears as something finished and perfect, and remains unchanged, not subject to the laws of time and of becoming and passing away in time. In this way it makes itself known as something metaphysical, as not itself belonging to the world of phenomena.

9. The universally used and generally very well understood expressions *heart* and *head* have sprung from a correct feeling of the fundamental distinction in question. They are therefore significant and to the point, and are found again and again in all languages. *Nec cor nec caput habet,*[23] says Seneca of the Emperor Claudius (*Ludus de morte Claudii Caesaris,* c. 8). The *heart,* that *primum mobile* of animal life, has quite rightly been chosen as the symbol, indeed the synonym, of the *will,* the primary kernel of our phenomenon; and it denotes this in contrast with the *intellect* which is exactly identical with the *head.* All that which is the business of the *will* in the widest sense, such as desire, passion, joy, pain, kindness, goodness, wickedness, and also that which is usually understood by the term *"Gemüt"* (disposition, feeling), and what Homer expresses by φίλον ἦτορ,[24] is attributed to the *heart.* Accordingly, we say: He has a bad heart; his heart is in this business; it comes from his heart; it cut him to the heart; it breaks his heart; his heart bleeds; the heart leaps for joy; who can read a man's heart? it is heart-rending, heart-crushing, heart-breaking, heart-inspiring, heart-stirring; he is good-hearted, hard-hearted; heartless, stout-hearted, faint-hearted, and so on. Quite especially, however, love affairs are called affairs of the heart, *affaires du cœur;*[25] because the sexual impulse is the focus of the will, and the selection with reference thereto constitutes the principal concern of natural, human willing, the ground of which I shall discuss at length in a chapter supplementary to the fourth book. In *Don Juan* (canto 11, v. 34) Byron is satirical about love being to women an affair of the head instead of an affair of the heart. On the other hand, the *head* denotes everything that is the business of *knowledge.* Hence a man of brains, a good head, a clever head, a fine head, a bad head, to lose one's head, to keep one's head, and so on. Heart and head indicate the whole person. But the head is always the secondary, the derived; for it is not the centre of the body, but its highest efflorescence. When a hero dies, his heart is embalmed, not his brain. On the other hand, we like to preserve the skulls of poets, artists, and philosophers. Thus Raphael's skull

---

[23] "He has neither heart nor head." [Tr.]

[24] "The beloved heart." [*Iliad,* V, 250.—Tr.]

[25] "Affairs of the heart." [Tr.]

was preserved in the Accademia di S. Luca in Rome, though recently it was shown to be not genuine; in 1820 Descartes' skull was sold by auction in Stockholm.[26]

A certain feeling of the true relation between will, intellect, and life is also expressed in the Latin language. The intellect is *mens*, νοῦς; the will, on the other hand, is *animus,* which comes from *anima,* and this from ἄνεμος. *Anima* is life itself, the breath, ψυχή; but *animus* is the life-giving principle and at the same time the will, the subject of inclinations, likings, purposes, passions, and emotions; hence also *est mihi animus, fert animus,* for "I feel inclined to," "I should like to," as well as *animi causa,* and so on; it is the Greek θυμός, the German *Gemüt,* and thus heart, not head. *Animi perturbatio* is emotion; *mentis perturbatio* would signify madness or craziness. The predicate *immortalis* is attributed to *animus,* not to *mens.* All this is the rule based on the great majority of passages, although, with concepts so closely related, it is bound to happen that the words are sometimes confused. By ψυχή the Greeks appear primarily and originally to have understood the vital force, the life-giving principle. In this way there at once arose the divination that it must be something metaphysical, consequently something that would not be touched by death. This is proved, among other things, by the investigations of the relation between νοῦς and ψυχή preserved by Stobaeus (*Eclogues,* Bk. I, c. 51, §§ 7, 8).

10. On what does the *identity of the person* depend? Not on the matter of the body; this becomes different after a few years. Not on the form of the body, which changes as a whole and in all its parts, except in the expression of the glance, by which we still recognize a man even after many years. This proves that, in spite of all the changes produced in him by time, there yet remains in him something wholly untouched by it. It is just this by which we recognize him once more, even after the longest intervals of time, and again find the former person unimpaired. It is the same with ourselves, for, however old we become, we yet feel within ourselves that we are absolutely the same as we were when we were young, indeed when we were still children. This thing which is unaltered and always remains absolutely the same, which does not grow old with us, is just the kernel of our inner nature, and that does not lie in time. It is assumed that the identity of the person rests on that of consciousness. If, however, we understand by this merely the continuous recollection of the course of life, then it is not enough. We know, it is true, something more of the course of our life than of a novel we have formerly read, yet only very little indeed. The principal

---

[26] *The Times,* 18 October, 1845; from the *Athenaeum.*

events, the interesting scenes, have been impressed on us; for the rest, a thousand events are forgotten for one that has been retained. The older we become, the more does everything pass us by without leaving a trace. Great age, illness, injury to the brain, madness, can deprive a man entirely of memory, but the identity of his person has not in this way been lost. That rests on the identical *will* and on its unalterable character; it is also just this that makes the expression of the glance unalterable. In the *heart* is the man to be found, not in the head. It is true that, in consequence of our relation to the external world, we are accustomed to regard the subject of knowing, the knowing I, as our real self which becomes tired in the evening, vanishes in sleep, and in the morning shines more brightly with renewed strength. This, however, is the mere function of the brain, and is not our real self. Our true self, the kernel of our inner nature, is that which is to be found behind this, and which really knows nothing but willing and not-willing, being contented and not contented, with all the modifications of the thing called feelings, emotions, and passions. This it is which produces that other thing, which does not sleep with it when it sleeps, which also remains unimpaired when that other thing becomes extinct in death. On the other hand, everything related to *knowledge* is exposed to oblivion; even actions of moral significance sometimes cannot be completely recalled by us years after, and we no longer know exactly and in detail how we behaved in a critical case. The *character itself,* however, to which the deeds merely testify, we cannot forget; it is still exactly the same now as then. The will itself, alone and by itself, endures; for it alone is unchangeable, indestructible, does not grow old, is not physical but metaphysical, does not belong to the phenomenal appearance, but to the thing itself that appears. How the identity of consciousness, so far as it goes, depends on the will, I have already shown in chapter 15; therefore I need not dwell on it here.

11. Incidentally, Aristotle says in the book on the comparison of the desirable: "To live well is better than to live" (βέλτιον τοῦ ζῆν τὸ εὖ ζῆν, *Topica,* iii, 2). From this it might be inferred, by twofold contraposition, that not to live is better than to live badly. This is evident to the intellect; yet the great majority live very badly rather than not at all. Therefore this attachment to life cannot have its ground in its own *object,* for life, as was shown in the fourth book, is really a constant suffering, or at any rate, as will be shown later in chapter 28, a business that does not cover the cost; hence that attachment can be founded only in its own *subject.* But it is not founded in the *intellect,* it is no result of reflection, and generally is not a matter of choice; on the contrary, this willing of life is some-

thing that is taken for granted; it is a *prius* of the *intellect* itself. We ourselves are the will-to-live; hence we must live, well or badly. Only from the fact that this attachment or clinging to a life so little worthy of it is entirely *a priori* and not *a posteriori,* can we explain the excessive fear of death inherent in every living thing. La Rochefoucauld expressed this fear with rare frankness and naivety in his last reflection; on it ultimately rests the effectiveness of all tragedies and heroic deeds. Such effectiveness would be lost if we assessed life only according to its objective worth. On this inexpressible *horror mortis* rests also the favourite principle of all ordinary minds that whoever takes his own life must be insane; yet no less is the astonishment, mingled with a certain admiration, which this action always provokes even in thinking minds, since such action is so much opposed to the nature of every living thing that in a certain sense we are forced to admire the man who is able to perform it. Indeed, we even find a certain consolation in the fact that, in the worst cases, this way out is actually open to us, and we might doubt it if it were not confirmed by experience. For suicide comes from a resolve of the intellect, but our willing of life is a *prius* of the intellect. Therefore this consideration, that will be discussed in detail in chapter 28, also confirms the primacy of the *will* in self-consciousness.

12. On the other hand, nothing more clearly demonstrates the *intellect's* secondary, dependent, and conditioned nature than its periodical intermission. In deep sleep all knowing and forming of representations entirely ceases; but the kernel of our true being, its metaphysical part, necessarily presupposed by the organic functions as their *primum mobile,* never dares to pause, if life is not to cease; moreover, as something metaphysical, and consequently incorporeal, it needs no rest. Therefore the philosophers who set up a *soul,* i.e., an originally and essentially *knowing* being, as this metaphysical kernel, saw themselves forced to the assertion that this soul is quite untiring in its representing and knowing, and consequently continues these even in the deepest sleep; only after waking up we are left with no recollection of this. However, the falsity of this assertion was easy to see, as soon as that *soul* had been set aside in consequence of Kant's teaching. For sleep and waking show the unprejudiced mind in the clearest manner that knowing is a secondary function, and is conditioned by the organism, just as is any other function. The *heart* alone is untiring, because its beating and the circulation of the blood are not conditioned directly by the nerves, but are just the original expression of the will. All other physiological functions, governed merely by the ganglionic nerves that have only a very

indirect and remote connexion with the brain, also continue in sleep, although the secretions take place more slowly. Even the beating of the heart, on account of its dependence on respiration which is conditioned by the cerebral system (*medulla oblongata*), becomes a little slower with this. The stomach is perhaps most active in sleep; this is to be ascribed to its special consensus with the brain that is now resting from its labours, such consensus causing mutual disturbances. The *brain* alone, and with it knowledge, pause completely in deep sleep; for it is merely the ministry of foreign affairs, just as the ganglionic system is the ministry of home affairs. The brain with its function of knowing is nothing more than a *guard* mounted by the will for its aims and ends that lie outside. Up in the watch-tower of the head this guard looks round through the windows of the senses, and watches the point from which mischief threatens and advantage is to be observed, and the will decides in accordance with its report. This *guard,* like everyone engaged on active service, is in a state of close attention and exertion, and therefore is glad when it is again relieved after discharging its duties of watching, just as every sentry likes to be withdrawn from his post. This withdrawal is falling asleep, which for that reason is so sweet and agreeable, and to which we are so ready to yield. On the other hand, being roused from sleep is unwelcome, because it suddenly recalls the *guard* to its post. Here we feel generally the reappearance of the hard and difficult diastole after the beneficent systole, the separation once more of the intellect from the will. On the other hand, a so-called *soul* that was originally and radically a *knowing* being would of necessity on waking up feel like a fish put back into water. In sleep, where only the vegetative life is carried on, the will alone operates according to its original and essential nature, undisturbed from outside, with no deduction from its force through activity of the brain and the exertion of knowing. Knowledge is the heaviest organic function, but is for the organism merely a means, not an end; therefore in sleep the whole force of the will is directed to the maintenance, and where necessary to the repair, of the organism. For this reason, all healing, all salutary and wholesome crises, take place in sleep, since the *vis naturae medicatrix*[27] has free play only when it is relieved of the burden of the function of knowledge. Therefore the embryo, that still has to form the body, sleeps continuously, and so for the greatest part of its time does the new-born child. In this sense Burdach (*Physiologie,* vol. III, p. 484) quite rightly declares sleep to be the *original state.*

With regard to the brain itself, I account in more detail for the

---

[27] "The healing power of nature." [Tr.]

necessity of sleep through a hypothesis that appears to have been advanced first in Neumann's book *Von den Krankheiten des Menschen,* 1834, vol. IV, § 216. This is that the nutrition of the brain, and hence the renewal of its substance from the blood, cannot take place while we are awake, since the highly eminent, organic function of knowing and thinking would be disturbed and abolished by the function of nutrition, low and material as it is. By this is explained the fact that sleep is not a purely negative state, a mere pausing of the brain's activity, but exhibits at the same time a positive character. This is seen from the fact that between sleep and waking there is no mere difference of degree, but a fixed boundary which, as soon as sleep intervenes, declares itself through dream-apparitions that are completely heterogeneous from our immediately preceding thoughts. A further proof of this is that, when we have dreams that frighten us, we try in vain to cry out, or to ward off attacks, or to shake off sleep, so that it is as if the connecting link between the brain and the motor nerves, or between the cerebrum and the cerebellum (as the regulator of movements), were abolished; for the brain remains in its isolation, and sleep holds us firmly as with brazen claws. Finally, the positive character of sleep is seen in the fact that a certain degree of strength is required for sleeping; therefore too much fatigue as well as natural weakness prevent us from seizing it, *capere somnum.* This can be explained from the fact that the *process of nutrition* must be introduced if sleep is to ensue; the brain must, so to speak, begin to take nourishment. Moreover, the increased flow of blood into the brain during sleep can be explained by the process of nutrition, as also the instinctively assumed position of the arms, which are laid together above the head because it promotes this process. This is also why children require a great deal of sleep, as long as the brain is still growing; whereas in old age, when a certain atrophy of the brain, as of all parts, occurs, sleep becomes scanty; and finally why excessive sleep produces a certain dulness of consciousness, in consequence of a temporary hypertrophy of the brain, which, in the case of habitual excess of sleep, can become permanent and produce imbecility: ἀνίη καὶ πολὺς ὕπνος (*noxae est etiam multus somnus*).[28] [*Odyssey,* 15, 394.] The need for sleep is accordingly directly proportional to the intensity of the brain-life, and thus to clearness of consciousness. Those animals whose brain-life is feeble and dull, reptiles and fishes for instance, sleep little and lightly. Here I remind the reader that the winter-sleep is a sleep almost in name only, since it is not an inactivity of the brain alone, but of the whole organism, and so a kind

---

[28] "Even copious sleep is a burden and a misery." [Tr.]

of suspended animation. Animals of considerable intelligence sleep soundly and long. Even human beings require more sleep the more developed, as regards quantity and quality, and the more active their brain is. Montaigne relates of himself that he had always been a heavy sleeper; that he had spent a large part of his life in sleeping; and that at an advanced age he still slept from eight to nine hours at a stretch (Bk. iii, ch. 13). It is also reported of Descartes that he slept a great deal (Baillet, *Vie de Descartes* (1693), p. 288). Kant allowed himself seven hours for sleep, but it became so difficult for him to manage with this that he ordered his servant to force him, against his will and without listening to his remonstrances, to get up at a fixed time (Jachmann, *Immanuel Kant,* p. 162). For the more completely awake a man is, in other words the clearer and more wide-awake his consciousness, the greater is his necessity for sleep, and thus the more soundly and longer he sleeps. Accordingly, much thinking or strenuous head-work will increase the need for sleep. That sustained muscular exertion also makes us sleepy can be explained from the fact that in such exertion the brain, by means of the *medulla oblongata,* the spinal marrow, and the motor nerves, continuously imparts to the muscles the stimulus affecting their irritability, and in this way its strength is exhausted. Accordingly the fatigue we feel in our arms and legs has its real seat in the brain, just as the pain felt in these parts is really experienced in the brain; for the brain is connected with the motor nerves just as it is with the nerves of sense. The muscles not actuated by the brain, e.g., those of the heart, therefore do not become tired. From the same reason we can explain why we cannot think acutely either during or after great muscular exertion. That we have far less mental energy in summer than in winter is partly explained by the fact that in summer we sleep less; for the more soundly we have slept, the more completely wakeful, the more wide awake are we afterwards. But this must not lead us astray into lengthening our sleep unduly, since it then loses in intension, in other words, in depth and in soundness, what it gains in extension, and thus it becomes a mere waste of time. Goethe means this when he says (in the second part of *Faust*) of morning slumber: "Sleep's a shell, to break and spurn!"[29] In general, therefore, the phenomenon of sleep most admirably confirms that consciousness, apprehension, perception, knowing, and thinking are not something original in us, but a conditioned, secondary state. It is a luxury of nature, and indeed her highest, which she is therefore the less able to continue without interruption, the higher the pitch to which it has been brought. It is the product, the efflores-

---

[29] Bayard Taylor's translation. [Tr.]

cence, of the cerebral nerve-system, which is itself nourished like a parasite by the rest of the organism. This is also connected with what is shown in our third book, that knowing is the purer and more perfect the more it has freed and severed itself from willing, whereby the purely objective, the aesthetic apprehension appears. In just the same way, an extract is so much the purer, the more it has been separated from that from which it has been extracted, and the more it has been refined and clarified of all sediment. The contrast is shown by the *will,* whose most immediate manifestation is the whole organic life, and primarily the untiring heart.

This last consideration is related to the theme of the following chapter, to which it therefore makes the transition; yet there is still the following observation connected with it. In magnetic somnambulism consciousness is doubled; two ranges of knowledge arise, each continuous and coherent in itself, but quite separate from the other; the waking consciousness knows nothing of the somnambulent. But in both the will retains the same character, and remains absolutely identical; it expresses the same inclinations and disinclinations in both. For the function can be doubled, but not the true being-in-itself.

Objectification of the Will
in the Animal Organism

By *objectification* I understand self-presentation or self-exhibition in the real corporeal world. But this world itself, as was fully shown in the first book and its supplements, is throughout conditioned by the knowing subject, by the intellect; consequently it is absolutely inconceivable as such outside the knowledge of this knowing subject. For primarily it is only representation of perception, and as such is a phenomenon of the brain. After its elimination, the thing-in-itself would remain. That this is the *will* is the theme of the second book; and it is there first of all demonstrated in the human and animal organism.

The knowledge of the external world can also be described as the *consciousness of other things* as distinct from *self-consciousness*. Now after finding in self-consciousness the will as its real object or substance, we shall, with the same purpose, take into consideration the consciousness of other things, hence objective knowledge. Here my thesis is this: *that which in self-consciousness, and hence subjectively, is the intellect, presents itself in the consciousness of other things, and hence objectively, as the brain; and that which in self-consciousness, and hence subjectively, is the will, presents itself in the consciousness of other things, and hence objectively, as the entire organism.*

I add the following supplements and illustrations to the proofs in support of this proposition which have been furnished in our second book and in the first two chapters of the essay *On the Will in Nature.*

Nearly all that is necessary for establishing the first part of this thesis has already been stated in the preceding chapter, since in the necessity for sleep, the changes through age, and the difference of anatomical conformation, it was demonstrated that the intellect,

---

[1] This chapter refers to § 20 of volume 1.

being of a secondary nature, is absolutely dependent on a single organ, the brain, and that it is the function of the brain, just as grasping is the function of the hand; consequently, that it is physical like digestion, not metaphysical like the will. Just as good digestion requires a healthy, strong stomach, or athletic prowess muscular, sinewy arms, so extraordinary intelligence requires an unusually developed, finely formed brain, conspicuous for its fine texture, and animated by an energetic and vigorous pulse. The nature of the will, on the other hand, is not dependent on any organ, and is not to be prognosticated from any. The greatest error in Gall's phrenology is that he sets up organs of the brain even for moral qualities. Head injuries with loss of brain-substance have as a rule a very detrimental effect on the intellect; they result in complete or partial imbecility, or forgetfulness of language permanent or temporary, though sometimes of only one language out of several that were known; sometimes again only of proper names, and likewise the loss of other knowledge that had been possessed, and so on. On the other hand we never read that, after an accident of this kind, the *character* has undergone a change; that the person has possibly become morally worse or better, or has lost certain inclinations or passions, or has even assumed new ones; never. For the will does not have its seat in the brain; moreover, as the metaphysical, it is the *prius* of the brain, as well as of the whole body, and therefore cannot be altered through injuries to the brain. According to an experiment made by Spallanzani and repeated by Voltaire,[2] a snail that has had its head cut off remains alive, and after a few weeks a new head grows, together with horns. With this head consciousness and representation appear again, whereas till then the animal exhibited through unregulated movements mere blind will. Therefore we here find the will as the substance that persists, but the intellect conditioned by its organ, as the changing accident. It can be described as the regulator of the will.

Perhaps it was Tiedemann who first compared the cerebral nerve-system to a *parasite* (Tiedemann and Treviranus' *Journal für Physiologie,* Vol. I, p. 62). The comparison is striking and to the point, in so far as the brain, together with the spinal cord and nerves attached to it, is, so to speak, implanted in the organism and nourished by it, without on its part *directly* contributing anything to the maintenance of the organism's economy. Therefore life can exist without a brain, as in the case of brainless abortions, and of tortoises that still live

---

[2] Spallanzani, "Risultati di esperienze sopra la riproduzione della testa nelle lumache terrestri," in the *Memorie di matematica e fisica della Società Italiana,* vol. I, p. 581.—Voltaire, *Les Colimaçons du révérend père l'escarbotier.*

for three weeks after their heads have been cut off; only the *medulla oblongata,* as the organ of respiration, must be spared. A hen also lived for ten months and grew, after Flourens had cut away the whole of its cerebrum. Even in the case of man, the destruction of the brain does not produce death directly, but only through the medium of the lungs and then of the heart (Bichat, *Sur la vie et la mort,* Part II, art. 11, § 1). On the other hand, the brain controls the relations with the external world; this alone is its office, and in this way it discharges its debt to the organism that nourishes it, since the latter's existence is conditioned by the external relations. Accordingly the brain alone, of all parts, requires sleep, because its *activity* is entirely separate from its *maintenance;* the former merely consumes strength and substance, the latter is achieved by the remainder of the organism as the nurse of the brain. Therefore, since its activity contributes nothing to its existence, that activity becomes exhausted, and only when this pauses in sleep does the brain's nourishment go on unhindered.

The second part of our above-stated thesis will require a more detailed discussion, even after all that I have already said about it in the works mentioned. I have already shown in chapter 18 that the thing-in-itself, which must be the foundation of every phenomenon and so of our own also, casts off in self-consciousness one of its phenomenal forms, space, and retains only the other, time. For this reason it makes itself known here more immediately than anywhere else, and we declare it to be will in accordance with this most undisguised phenomenon of it. But no *enduring substance,* such as matter, can exhibit itself in mere time alone, since such a substance, as was shown in § 4 of volume one, becomes possible only through the intimate union of space with time. Therefore in self-consciousness the will is not perceived as the permanent substratum of its emotions and impulses, and therefore not as enduring substance; merely its individual acts, stirrings, and states, such as resolves, desires, and emotions, are known successively and, during the time they last, immediately, yet not by way of perception. Accordingly the knowledge of the will in self-consciousness is not a *perception* of it, but an absolutely immediate awareness of its successive impulses or stirrings. On the other hand we have the knowledge that is directed *outwards,* brought about by the senses, and perfected in the understanding. Besides time, this knowledge has space also for its form, and it connects these two in the most intimate way through the function of the understanding, causality, whereby exactly it becomes *perception.* The same thing that in inner immediate apprehension was grasped as *will,* is *perceptibly* presented to this *outwardly* directed knowledge as *organic body*. The individual movements of this body visibly present to us the acts, its parts and forms visibly present the permanent tendencies, the basic character, of the individually given will. In fact the pain and comfort of this body are absolutely immediate affections of this will itself.

We first become aware of this identity of the body with the will in the individual actions of the two, for in these what is known in self-consciousness as immediate, real act of will exhibits itself outwardly, at the same time and unseparated, as movement of the body; and everyone perceives at once from the instantaneous appearance of the motives the appearance, equally instantaneous, of his resolves of will in an equal number of actions of his body which are copied as faithfully as are these last in that body's shadow. From this there arises for the unprejudiced person in the simplest manner the insight that his body is merely the outward appearance of his will, in other words, the mode and manner in which his will exhibits itself in his perceiving intellect, or his will itself under the form of the representation. Only when we forcibly deprive ourselves of this original and simple information are we able for a short time to marvel at the process of our own bodily action as a miracle. This miracle then rests on the fact that there is actually no causal connexion between the act of will and the action of the body, for they are directly *identical*. Their apparent difference arises solely from the fact that one and the same thing is here apprehended or perceived under two different modes of knowledge, the outer and the inner. Thus actual willing is inseparable from doing, and, in the narrowest sense, that alone is an act of will which is stamped as such by the deed. On the other hand, mere resolves of the will, until they are carried out, are only intentions, and therefore a matter of the intellect alone. As such, they have their place merely in the brain, and are nothing more than the completed calculations of the relative strength of the different opposing motives. It is true, therefore, that they have great probability, but never infallibility. Thus they may prove false not only through an alteration in the circumstances, but also through the possibility that the estimate of the respective effect of the motives on the will proper may be inaccurate. This then shows itself by the deed's not being true to the intention; hence no resolve is certain before the carrying out of the deed. Therefore the *will itself* is active only in real action, consequently in muscular action, hence in *irritability;* thus the *will* proper objectifies itself therein. The cerebrum is the place of motives, and through these the will here becomes free choice (*Willkür*), in other words, more closely determined by motives. These motives are representations, and, on the occasion of external stimuli of the sense-organs, these representations arise by means of the brain's functions, and are elaborated into concepts, and then into resolves. When it comes to the real act of will, these motives, whose factory is the cerebrum, act through the medium of the cerebellum on the spinal cord and the nerves that issue from it; these nerves then act on the muscles, yet merely as *stimuli* of their irritability. For galvanic, chemical, and even mechanical stimuli can also effect the same contraction that is produced by the motor nerve. Thus what was *motive* in the brain acts as mere *stimulus* when it reaches the muscle through the nerves. Sensibility in itself is quite incapable of contracting a muscle; only the muscle itself can do this, its ability to do so being called *irritability,* in other words, *susceptibility to stimulus.* This is an exclusive property of the muscle, just as sensibility is an exclusive property of the nerve. The nerve indeed gives the muscle the *occasion* for its contraction; but it is by no means the nerve which in some mechanical way might contract the muscle; on the contrary, this takes place simply and solely by virtue of *irritability,* which is a power of the muscle itself. Apprehended from without, this is a *qualitas occulta,* and only self-consciousness reveals it as the *will.* In the causal chain here briefly set forth, from the impression of the motive lying outside up to the contraction of the muscle, the will does not in some way come in as the last link of the chain, but is the metaphysical substratum of the irritability of the muscle. Therefore it plays exactly the same role here as is played by the mysterious forces of nature which underlie the course of events in a physical or chemical causal chain. As such, these forces are not themselves involved as links in the causal chain, but impart to all its links the capacity to act; this I have explained at length in § 26 of volume one. We should therefore attribute to the contraction of the muscle a mysterious natural force of this kind, were this contraction not disclosed to us through an entirely different source of knowledge, namely self-consciousness, as *will.* Hence, as we said above, if we start from the will, our own muscular movement seems to us a miracle, since certainly a strict causal chain extends from the external motive up to the muscular action; yet the will itself is not included as a link in the chain, but, as the metaphysical substratum of the possibility of the muscle's actuation through brain and nerve, it is the foundation of the muscular action in question. This action, therefore, is really not its *effect,* but its *phenomenal appearance.* As such, it appears in the world of representation, whose form is the law of causality, a world entirely different from the *will-in-itself.* If we start from the *will,* this phenomenal appearance looks like a miracle to the person who attentively reflects; but to the one who investigates more deeply, it affords the most direct verification of the great truth that what appears in the phenomenon as body and as action of the phenomenon, is in itself *will.* Now if, say, the motor nerve leading to my hand is severed, my will can no longer move it. But this is not because the hand has ceased to be, like every part of my body, the objectivity, the mere visibility, of my will, or in other words, because the irritability has vanished, but because the impression of the motive, in consequence of which alone I can move my hand, cannot reach it and act on its muscles as a stimulus, for the line connecting it with the brain is broken. Hence in this part my will is really deprived only of the impression of the motive. The will objectifies itself directly in irritability, not in sensibility.

To prevent all misunderstandings on this important point, particularly those that arise from physiology pursued in a purely empirical way, I will explain the whole course of events somewhat more thoroughly. My teaching asserts that the whole body is the will itself, exhibiting itself in the perception of the brain; consequently as having entered the knowledge-forms of the brain. From this it follows that the will is everywhere equally and uniformly present in the whole body, as is also demonstrably the case, for the organic functions are just as much its work as are the animal functions. But how are we to reconcile this with the fact that the *arbitrary and voluntary* actions, those most undeniable expressions of the will, obviously come from the *brain,* and reach the nerve fibres only through the spinal cord, those fibres finally setting the limbs in motion, and the paralysis or severing of them destroying the possibility of arbitrary or voluntary movement? According to this, one would think that the will, like the intellect, had its seat in the brain, and, also like the intellect, was a mere function of the brain.

Yet this is not so; but the whole body is and remains the presentation of the will in perception, and hence the will itself objectively perceived by virtue of the brain's functions. But in the case of acts of will, that process rests on the fact that the will, which manifests itself, according to my teaching, in every phenomenon of nature, even of vegetable and inorganic nature, appears in the human and animal body as a *conscious will.* But a *consciousness* is essentially something uniform and united, and therefore always requires a central point of unity. As I have often explained, the necessity of consciousness is brought about by the fact that, in consequence of an organism's enhanced complication and thus of its more manifold and varied needs, the acts of its will must be guided by *motives,* no longer by mere stimuli, as at the lower stages. For this purpose it had now to appear furnished with a knowing consciousness, and so with an intellect as the medium and place of the motives. When this intellect is itself objectively perceived, it exhibits itself as the brain with its appendages, the spinal cord and the nerves. Now it is the intellect in which the representations arise on the occasion of external impressions, and such representations become motives for the will. In the *rational* intellect, however, they undergo besides this a still further elaboration through reflection and deliberation. Therefore such an intellect must first of all unite in *one* point all impressions together with their elaboration through its functions, whether for mere perception or for concepts. This point becomes, as it were, the focus of all its rays, so that there may arise that unity of consciousness which is the *theoretical ego,* the supporter of the whole consciousness. In this consciousness itself, the theoretical ego presents itself as identical with the *willing ego,* of which it is the mere function of knowledge. That point of unity of consciousness, or the theoretical ego, is exactly Kant's synthetic unity of apperception on which all representations are ranged as pearls on a string, and by virtue of which the "I think," as the thread of the string of pearls, "must be capable of accompanying all our representations."* Therefore this meeting-point of the motives, where their entrance into the uniform focus of consciousness takes place, is the brain. Here in the nonrational consciousness they are merely perceived; in the *rational* consciousness they are elucidated through concepts, and so are first of all thought in the abstract and compared; whereupon the will decides in accordance with its individual and unalterable character. Thus the *resolve* follows, which then sets the external limbs in motion by means of the cerebellum, the spinal cord, and the nerve fibres. For although the will is quite directly present in these, since they are its mere phenomenon, yet where it has to move according to *motives* or even according to reflection, it needed such an apparatus for the apprehension and elaboration of representations into such motives, in conformity with which its acts here appear as resolves. In just the same way, the nourishment of the blood through chyle requires a stomach and intestines in which this is prepared, and then flows as such into the blood through the thoracic duct. This duct plays here the part played in the other case by the spinal cord. The matter may be grasped most simply and generally as follows: the will is immediately present as irritability in all the muscular fibres of the whole body, as a continual striving for activity in general. But if this striving is to realize itself, and thus manifest itself as movement, then this movement, precisely as such, must have some direction;

* Cf. chap. 22.

but this direction must be *determined* by something, in other words, it requires a guide; this guide is the nervous system. For to mere irritability, as it lies in the muscular fibre and in itself is pure will, all directions are alike; hence it does not decide on a direction, but behaves like a body drawn equally in all directions; it remains at rest. With the intervention of nervous activity as motive (or in the case of reflex movements as stimulus), the striving force, i.e., the irritability, receives a definite direction, and then produces the movements. But those external acts of will, which require no motives, and so no elaboration of mere stimuli into representations in the brain, such representations giving rise to motives, but which follow immediately on mere stimuli, mostly inner stimuli, are the reflex movements coming from the mere spinal cord, as, for example, spasms and convulsions. In these the will acts without the brain taking any part. In an analogous way, the will carries on organic life likewise on a nerve stimulus that does not come from the brain. Thus the will appears in every muscle as irritability, and consequently is of itself in a position to contract this muscle, yet only *in general.* For a definite contraction to ensue at a given moment, a cause is needed, as everywhere, which in this case must be a stimulus. Everywhere this stimulus is given by the nerve that enters the muscle. If this nerve is connected with the brain, the contraction is a conscious act of will; in other words, it takes place from motives that, in consequence of *external* impression, have arisen in the brain as representations. If the nerve is *not* connected with the brain, but with the *sympathicus maximus,* the contraction is involuntary and unconscious, and thus an act serving organic life; and the nerve-stimulus for it is occasioned by *inner* impression, e.g., by the pressure on the stomach of food that has been ingested, or by the chyme on the intestines, or by the inflowing blood on the walls of the heart. Accordingly, it is the process of digestion in the stomach, or peristaltic movements, or beating of the heart, and so on.

But if we go back a step farther with this process, we find that the muscles are the product and work of the blood's solidification; in fact they are, to a certain extent, only blood that has become congealed, or as it were clotted or crystallized, since they have assimilated its fibrin (*cruor*) and pigment almost unchanged (Burdach, *Physiologie,* Vol. V, p. 686). But the force that formed the muscle from the blood cannot be assumed to be different from the force which subsequently moves this muscle as irritability through nerve-stimulus supplied by the brain. In this case, the force then announces itself to self-consciousness as what we call *will.* Moreover, the close connexion between the blood and irritability is shown also by the fact that where, on account of the defective nature of the lesser blood circulation, a part of the blood goes back unoxidized to the heart, irritability is at once extraordinarily feeble, as in the amphibians. The movement of the blood, like that of the muscle, is also independent and original; it does not even require, like irritability, the influence of the nerve, and is independent of the heart also. This is shown most clearly by the return of the blood through the veins to the heart; for in this case it is not propelled by a *vis a tergo*,[3] as in arterial circulation; and all the other mechanical explanations also, such as a force of suction of the heart's right ventricle, are quite inadequate. (See Burdach's *Physiologie*, Vol. IV, § 763, and Rösch, *Ueber die Bedeutung des Bluts*, p. 11 *seq.*) It is remarkable to see how the French, who know of nothing but mechanical forces, are at variance with one another with insufficient grounds on both sides, and how Bichat ascribes the flowing back of the blood through the veins to the pressure of the walls of the capillary vessels, whereas Magendie ascribes it to the ever-acting impulse of the heart. (*Précis de physiologie* by Magendie, vol. II, p. 389.) That the movement of the blood is also independent of the nervous system, at any rate of the cerebral nervous system, is shown by foetuses, which are (according to Müller's *Physiologie*) without brain or spinal cord, but yet have blood circulation. And Flourens also says: *Le mouvement du cœur, pris en soi, et abstraction faite de tout ce qui n'est pas essentiellement lui, comme sa durée, sa régularité, son énergie, ne dépend ni immédiatement, ni coinstantanément, du système nerveux central, et conséquemment c'est dans tout autre point de ce système que dans les centres nerveux eux-mêmes, qu'il faut chercher le principe primitif et immédiat de ce mouvement*[4] (*Annales des sciences naturelles*, by Audouin et Brongniard, 1828, Vol. 13). Cuvier also says: *La circulation survit à la destruction de tout l'encéphale et de toute la moëlle épiniaire*[5] (*Mémoires de l'académie des sciences*, 1823, Vol. 6; *Histoire de l'académie*, by Cuvier, p. cxxx). *Cor primum vivens et ultimum moriens*,[6] says Haller. The beating of the heart ultimately ceases in death. The blood has made the vessels

---

[3] "A force impelling from behind." [Tr.]

[4] "The movement of the heart, taken by itself and apart from all that is not essential to it, as for example its duration, its regularity, and its vigour, does not depend either directly or indirectly on the central nervous system. Consequently the original and immediate principle of this movement must be sought at a point in this system quite different from the nerve-centres themselves." [Tr.]

[5] "The circulation survives the destruction of the entire brain and of the whole spinal cord." [Tr.]

[6] "The heart is that which is the first to live and the last to die." [Tr.]

themselves, for it appears in the ovum before they do; they are only its paths, voluntarily taken, then rendered smooth, and finally by degrees condensed and closed up; this is taught by Caspar Wolff, *Theorie der Generation,* §§ 30-35. The motion of the heart, inseparable from that of the blood, although occasioned by the necessity of sending blood into the lung, is also an original motion, in so far as it is independent of the nervous system and of sensibility, as is fully shown by Burdach. "In the heart," he says, "there appears with the maximum of irritability a minimum of sensibility" (*op. cit.,* § 769). The heart belongs to the muscular system as well as to the blood or vascular system; here, once again, it is clear that the two are closely related, are in fact one whole. Now as the metaphysical substratum of the force moving the muscle, and thus of irritability, is the *will,* this will must also be the metaphysical substratum of that force which underlies the movement and formation of the blood by which the muscle has been produced. The course of the arteries, moreover, determines the shape and size of all the limbs; consequently, the whole form of the body is determined by the course of the blood. Therefore, just as the blood nourishes all the parts of the body, so, as the primary fluid of the organism, it has produced and formed these parts originally out of itself; and the nourishment of the parts, which admittedly constitutes the principal function of the blood, is only the continuation of that original formation of them. This truth is found thoroughly and admirably explained in the above-mentioned work of Rösch, *Ueber die Bedeutung des Bluts* (1839). He shows that it is the blood that is the first thing to be vivified or animated, and that it is the source of both the existence and the maintenance of all the parts. He shows also that all the organs have been separated out from it by secretion, and simultaneously with them, for the guidance of their functions, the nervous system. This system appears now as *plastic,* arranging and guiding the life of the particular parts within, now as *cerebral,* arranging and controlling the relation to the external world. "The blood," he says on page 25, "was flesh and nerve at the same time; and at the same moment when the muscle was detached from it, the nerve, separated in like manner, remained opposed to the flesh." It goes without saying that, before those solid parts are separated out from the blood, it has also a character somewhat different from what it has subsequently. It is then, as Rösch describes it, the chaotic, animated, mucous, primary fluid, an organic emulsion, so to speak, in which all the subsequent parts are contained *implicite;* moreover, at the very beginning it has not the red colour. This disposes of the objection that might be raised from the fact that the brain and spinal cord begin to form before the circulation of the blood is visible, or the heart comes into existence. In this sense, Schultz also says (*System der Cirkulation,* p. 297): "We do not believe that Baumgärtner's view, according to which the nervous system is formed before the blood, can be maintained, for Baumgärtner reckons the origin of the blood only from the formation of the vesicles, whereas in the embryo and in the series of animals, blood already appears much earlier in the form of pure plasma." The blood of invertebrates, however, never assumes the red colour; yet we do not on that account deny that they have blood, as does Aristotle. It is worth noting that, according to the account of Justinus Kerner (*Geschichte zweier Somnambulen,* p. 78) a somnambulist with a very high degree of clairvoyance says: "I am as deep within myself as ever a person can be led into himself; the force of my earthly life seems to me to have its origin in the blood. In this way the force is communicated through circulation in the veins by means of the nerves to the whole body, and the noblest part of this above itself to the brain."

From all this it follows that the will objectifies itself most immediately in the *blood* as that which originally creates and forms the organism, perfects and completes it through growth, and afterwards continues to maintain it both by the regular renewal of all the parts and· by the extraordinary restoration of such as happen to be injured. The first products of the blood are its own vessels, and then the muscles, in the irritability of which the will makes itself known to self-consciousness; also with these the heart, which is at the same time vessel and muscle, and is therefore the true centre and *primum mobile* of all life. But for individual life and continued existence in the external world, the will requires two subsidiary systems, *one* to govern and order its inner and outer activity, and the *other* constantly to renew the mass of the blood; it thus requires a controller and a sustainer. Therefore the will creates for itself the nervous and the intestinal systems. Hence the *functiones animales* and the *functiones naturales* are associated in a subsidiary way with the *functiones vitales,* which are the most original and essential. Accordingly, in the *nervous system* the will objectifies itself only in an indirect and secondary way, in so far as this system appears as a mere subsidiary organ, a contrivance or arrangement, by means of which the will arrives at a knowledge of those causes or occasions, partly internal and partly external, on which it has to express itself in accordance with its aims. The *internal* occasions are received by the *plastic* nervous system, hence by the sympathetic nerve, that *cerebrum abdominale,* as mere stimuli, and the will reacts to them on the spot without the brain's being conscious of the fact. The *ex-*

ternal occasions are received by the *brain* as *motives,* and the will reacts to them through conscious actions directed outwards. Consequently, the whole nervous system constitutes, so to speak, the antennae of the will, which it extends and spreads inwards and outwards. The nerves of the brain and the spinal cord are divided at their roots into sensory and motor. The sensory nerves receive information from outside, which is then collected in the central seat of the brain and elaborated there; from it representations arise primarily as motives. The motor nerves, however, like couriers, inform the muscle of the result of the brain-function; this result, as stimulus, acts on the muscle, whose irritability is the immediate phenomenon of the will. Presumably the plastic nerves are likewise divided into sensory and motor, although on a subordinate scale. We must think of the role played by the ganglia in the organism as a diminutive brain-role, so that the one becomes the elucidation of the other. The ganglia lie wherever the organic functions of the vegetative system require supervision. It is as if the will were not able to manage there with its direct and simple action, in order to carry its aims into effect, but needed some guidance and hence control of this action; just as when in a business a man's own memory is not sufficient, but he must at all times take notes of what he does. For this purpose, mere knots of nerves are sufficient for the interior of the organism, just because everything goes on within the organism's own sphere. But for the exterior a very complicated arrangement of the same kind was required. This is the brain, with its tentacles or feelers, the nerves of sense that it stretches and extends into the external world. Even in the organs communicating with this great nerve centre, however, the matter need not in very simple cases be brought before the highest authority, but a subordinate one is sufficient to decide what is necessary. Such an authority is the spinal cord, in the reflex movements discovered by Marshall Hall, such as sneezing, yawning, vomiting, the second part of swallowing, and so on. The will itself is present in the whole organism, for this is its mere visibility. The nervous system exists everywhere, merely in order to make possible a *direction* of the will's action by a control thereof, to serve, so to speak, as a mirror for the will, so that it may see what it does, just as we make use of a mirror when shaving. In this way, small sensoria, namely the ganglia, arise in the interior for special and therefore simple functions, but the chief sensorium, the brain, is the great and cunningly devised apparatus for the complicated and varied functions that relate to the ceaselessly and irregularly changing external world. Wherever in the organism the nerve-threads run together into a ganglion, there, to a certain extent, an animal exists on its own and is complete and isolated. By means of the ganglion it has a kind of feeble knowledge; but the sphere of that knowledge is limited to the parts from which these nerves directly come. But what actuates these parts to such quasi-knowledge is obviously *will;* indeed, we are quite unable even to conceive it otherwise. On this rest the *vita propria* of each part, and in the case of insects, that have, instead of the spinal cord, a double cord of nerves with ganglia at regular intervals, the ability of each part to live for days after it has been severed from the head and the rest of the trunk; finally, those actions also that in the last resort do not receive their motives from the brain, i.e., instinct and mechanical skill. Marshall Hall, whose discovery of reflex movements I mentioned above, has really given us here the *theory of involuntary movements.* Some of these are normal or physiological, such as the closing of the body's places of ingress and egress, e.g. of the *sphincteres vesicae et ani* (coming from the nerves of the spinal cord), the closing of the eyelids in sleep (from the fifth pair of nerves), of the larynx (from *N. vagus*) when food passes it or carbonic acid tries to enter; then swallowing from the pharynx, yawning, sneezing, respiration, wholly in sleep, partially when we are awake; finally, erection, ejaculation, and also conception, and many more. Some again are abnormal or pathological, such as stuttering, hiccoughing, vomiting, as also cramps and convulsions of every kind, especially in epilepsy, tetanus, hydrophobia and otherwise; finally, the jerkings and twitchings produced by galvanic or other stimuli, and taking place without feeling or consciousness in paralysed limbs, that is to say, limbs put out of touch with the brain; likewise the twitchings of decapitated animals; and finally, all the movements and actions of children born without brains. All spasms and convulsions are a rebellion of the nerves of the limbs against the sovereignty of the brain; the normal reflex movements, on the other hand, are the legitimate autocracy of the subordinate officials. All these movements are therefore involuntary, because they do not come from the brain, and thus take place not on motives, but on mere stimuli. The stimuli occasioning them extend only to the spinal cord or the *medulla oblongata,* and from there the reaction immediately takes place which brings about the movement. The spinal cord has the same relation to these involuntary movements as the brain has to motive and action; and what the sentient and voluntary nerve is for the latter, the incident and motor nerve is for the former. That in the one as in the other what really moves is nevertheless the *will,* is brought all the more clearly to light, as the involuntarily moved muscles are for the most part the same as those which are moved from the brain in other circumstances in the voluntary actions where their *primum mobile* is intimately known to us through self-consciousness as *will*. Marshall Hall's excellent book *On the Diseases of the Nervous System* is very well calculated to bring out clearly the difference between free choice (*Willkür*) and will, and to confirm the truth of my fundamental teaching.

To illustrate all that has been said here, let us now call to mind the origination of an organism highly accessible to our observation. Who makes the little chicken in the egg? Some power and skill coming from outside and penetrating the shell? No! The little chicken makes itself, and the very force that carries out and perfects this task, so inexpressibly complicated, so well calculated and fitted for the purpose, breaks through the shell as soon as it is ready, and performs the external actions of the chicken under the name of *will*. It could not achieve both at once; previously, concerned with the elaboration of the organism, it had no attention directed outwards. But after the elaboration of the organism is completed, attention directed outwards now appears under the guidance of the brain and its tentacles or feelers, namely the senses, as a tool prepared beforehand for this purpose. The service of this tool begins only when it wakes in self-consciousness as intellect; this is the lantern of the will's steps, its ἡγεμονικόν,[7] and at the same time the supporter of the objective outside world, however limited the horizon of this may be in the consciousness of a hen. But what the hen is now able to achieve in the external world through the medium of this organ, is, as that which is brought about by something secondary, infinitely less important than what it achieved in its primordial nature, for it made itself.

We became acquainted previously with the cerebral nervous system as a *subsidiary organ* of the will, in which therefore the will objectifies itself in a *secondary* way. Hence the cerebral system, although it takes no direct part in the sphere of the vital functions of the organism, but only guides its relations to the outer world, nevertheless has the organism as its basis, and is nourished by it as a reward for its services; thus the cerebral or animal life is to be regarded as the product of the organic. As this is the case, the brain and its functions, thus knowledge, and hence the intellect, belong in an indirect and secondary way to the phenomenon of the *will*. The will also objectifies itself therein, and that indeed as will to perceive or to apprehend the external world, hence as a *will-to-know*. Therefore, however great and fundamental in us is the difference between willing and knowing, the ultimate substratum of the two nevertheless

---

[7] "Principal faculty" [from the Stoics. Tr.].

remains the same, namely the *will* as the being-in-itself of the whole phenomenon. But knowing, and thus the intellect, presenting itself in self-consciousness wholly as the secondary element, is to be regarded not merely as the will's accident, but also as its work; knowledge is thus by a roundabout way traceable again to the will. Just as the intellect presents itself physiologically as the function of an organ of the body, so is it to be regarded metaphysically as a work of the will, the objectification or visibility of which is the whole body. Therefore the *will-to-know,* objectively perceived, is the brain, just as the *will-to-walk,* objectively perceived, is the foot; the *will-to-grasp,* the hand; the *will-to-digest,* the stomach; the *will-to-procreate,* the genitals, and so on. This whole objectification, of course, exists ultimately only for the brain, as its perception; in such perception the will exhibits itself as organized body. But in so far as the brain *knows,* it is not *itself* known, but is the *knower,* the subject of all knowledge. But in so far as it *is known* in objective perception, that is to say, in the consciousness *of other things,* and thus secondarily, it belongs, as organ of the body, to the objectification of the will. For the whole process is the *self-knowledge of the will;* it starts from and returns to the will, and constitutes what Kant called the *phenomenon* as opposed to the thing-in-itself. Therefore what *becomes known,* what *becomes representation,* is the *will;* and this representation is what we call the *body.* As something spatially extended and moving in time, the body exists only by means of the brain's functions, hence only in the brain. On the other hand, what *knows,* what *has that representation,* is the *brain;* yet this brain does not know itself, but becomes conscious of itself only as intellect, in other words as *knower,* and thus only subjectively. That which, seen from within, is the faculty of knowledge, is, seen from without, the brain. This brain is a part of that body, just because it itself belongs to the objectification of the *will;* thus the will's *will-to-know,* its tendency towards the external world, is objectified in the brain. Accordingly the brain, and hence the intellect, is certainly conditioned directly by the body, as the body again is by the brain, yet only indirectly, namely as something spatial and corporeal, in the world of perception, but not in itself, in other words, as will. Thus the whole is ultimately the will that itself becomes representation; it is the unity that we express by I. In so far as the brain *is represented*—thus in the consciousness of other things, and consequently secondarily—it is only representation. In itself, however, and in so far as it *represents,* it is the will, for this is the real substratum of the whole phenomenon; its will-to-know objectifies itself as brain and brain-functions. We can regard the voltaic pile as a comparison, imperfect it is true, yet to some extent illustrating the inner nature of the human phenomenon, as we consider it. The metals together with the fluid would be the body; the chemical action, as the basis of the whole operation, the will, and the resultant electric tension producing shock and spark the intellect. However, *omne simile claudicat.*[8]

Quite recently, the *physiatric* standpoint has at last asserted itself in pathology. Seen from this standpoint, diseases are themselves a healing process of nature, which she introduces in order to eliminate some disorder that has taken root in the organism by overcoming its causes. Here in the decisive struggle, in the crisis, nature either gains the victory and attains her end, or else is defeated. This view obtains its complete rationality only from our standpoint, which enables us to see the *will* in the vital force that here appears as *vis naturae medicatrix.*[9] In the healthy state, the will lies at the foundation of all organic functions; but with the appearance of disorders that threaten its whole work, it is vested with dictatorial power, in order to subdue the rebellious forces by quite extraordinary measures and wholly abnormal operations (the disease), and to lead everything back on to the right track. On the other hand, it is a gross misconception to say that the *will itself* is sick, as Brandis repeatedly has it in the passage of his book *Ueber die Anwendung der Kälte,* which I have quoted in the first part of my essay *On the Will in Nature.* I ponder over this, and at the same time observe that Brandis in his earlier book, *Ueber die Lebenskraft,* of 1795, betrayed no inkling that this force is in itself the *will.* On the contrary, he says on p. 13: "Vital force cannot possibly be the inner nature that we know only through our consciousness, as most movements occur without our consciousness. The assertion that this inner nature, of which the only characteristic known to us is consciousness, also affects the body without consciousness, is at least quite arbitrary and unproven"; and on p. 14: "Haller's objections to the opinion that all living movement is the effect of the soul are, I believe, irrefutable." Further, I bear in mind that he wrote his book, *Ueber die Anwendung der Kälte,* in his seventieth year, at an age when as yet no one has conceived original and fundamental ideas for the first time; and that in this book the will appears decidedly all at once as vital force. Further, I take into account the fact that he makes use of my exact expressions "will and representation," but not of the expressions "appetitive faculty" and "cognitive faculty" which elsewhere are much more common. When I reflect on all these

---

[8] "No comparison runs exactly on all fours." [Tr.]
[9] "Healing power of nature." [Tr.]

points, I am now convinced, contrary to my previous assumption, that he borrowed his fundamental idea from me, and, with the usual honesty prevailing in the learned world at the present day, said nothing about it. The particulars about this are found in the second (and third) edition of the work *On the Will in Nature*, p. 14.

Nothing is more calculated to confirm and illustrate the thesis that engages our attention in the present chapter than Bichat's justly celebrated book *Sur la vie et la mort*. His reflections and mine mutually support each other, since his are the physiological commentary on mine, and mine the philosophical commentary on his; and we shall be best understood by being read together side by side. This refers particularly to the first half of his work entitled *Recherches physiologiques sur la vie*. He makes the basis of his explanations the contrast between *organic* and *animal* life, corresponding to mine between will and intellect. He who looks at the sense, not at the words, will not be put out by Bichat's ascribing the will to animal life, for by this, as usual, he understands merely conscious, free choice. This certainly proceeds from the brain, where, however, as shown above, it is not as yet an actual willing, but the mere deliberation on and estimation of the motives whose conclusion or product ultimately appears as an act of will. All that I ascribe to the *will* proper he attributes to *organic* life, and all that I conceive as *intellect* is with him the *animal* life. For him animal life has its seat only in the brain together with its appendages; and organic life in the whole of the rest of the organism. The general mutual opposition in which he shows the two corresponds to the contrast existing with me between will and intellect. As anatomist and physiologist, he starts from the objective, in other words, from the consciousness of other things; as philosopher, I start from the subjective, from self-consciousness; it is a pleasure to see how, like the two voices in a duet, we advance in harmony with each other, although each of us has something different to say. Therefore anyone who wants to understand me should read him, and anyone who wants to understand him more thoroughly than he understood himself, should read me. For in article 4 Bichat shows us that *organic* life begins before and ends after *animal* life; consequently, as the latter rests in sleep, the former has nearly twice as long a duration. And in articles 8 and 9, he shows that organic life performs everything perfectly at once and automatically; animal life, on the other hand, requires long practice and education. But he is most interesting in the sixth article, where he shows that *animal* life is restricted entirely to the intellectual operations, and therefore takes place coldly and indifferently, whereas the emotions and passions have their seat in *organic* life, although the occasions for these lie in animal, i.e., cerebral life. Here he has ten valuable pages which I should like to copy out in full. On page 50 he says: *Il est sans doute étonnant, que les passions n'ayent jamais leur terme ni leur origine dans les divers organes de la vie animale; qu'au contraire les parties servant aux fonctions internes, soient constamment affectées par elles, et même les déterminent suivant l'état où elles se trouvent. Tel est cependant ce que la stricte observation nous prouve. Je dis d'abord que l'effet de toute espèce de passion, constamment étranger à la vie animale, est de faire naître un changement, une altération quelconque dans la vie organique.*[10] Then he explains how anger acts on the blood circulation and the beating of the heart; then how joy acts, and lastly how fear; next, how the lungs, the stomach, the intestines, liver, glands, and pancreas are affected by these and kindred emotions, and how grief and affliction impair nutrition; then how animal, in other words, brain-life remains untouched by all this, and calmly continues its course. He refers also to the fact that, to indicate intellectual operations, we put our hand to our head, whereas we lay our hand on the heart, stomach, or intestines when we wish to express love, joy, sadness, or hatred. He remarks that a person would inevitably be a bad actor who, when he spoke of his grief, touched his head, and, when he spoke of his mental exertion, touched his heart. He also says that, whereas the learned represent the so-called soul as residing in the head, ordinary people always describe by the right expressions the clearly felt difference between intellect and affections of the will. Thus, for example, we speak of a capable, shrewd, and fine head, but of a good heart, a heart full of feeling; and we say that "his blood boils with anger," "anger stirs up my bile," "my stomach leaps for joy," "jealousy poisons my blood," and so on. *Les chants sont le langage des passions, de la vie organique, comme la parole ordinaire est celui de l'entendement, de la vie animale: la déclamation tient le milieu, elle anime la langue froide du cerveau, par la langue expressive des organes intérieurs, du cœur, du foie, de l'estomac etc.*[11] His result

---

[10] "It is undoubtedly astonishing that the passions never have either their end or their origin in the various organs of animal life. On the contrary, those parts that serve the internal functions are constantly affected by them and even determine them according to the state in which they happen to be. And yet this is what strict observation demonstrates to us. In the first place, I assert that the effect of all kinds of passion is permanently foreign to animal life, and consists in bringing about a change, some kind of alteration in organic life." [Tr.]

[11] "Songs are the language of the passions, of organic life, just as the ordinary spoken word is the language of the understanding, of animal life.

is that *la vie organique est le terme où aboutissent, et le centre d'où partent les passions.*[12] Nothing is better calculated than this admirable and thorough book to confirm and bring out clearly that the body is only the *will* itself embodied (i.e., perceived by means of the brain-functions, time, space, and causality). From this it follows that the will is primary and original, but that the intellect, on the other hand, as mere brain-function, is secondary and derived. But in Bichat's train of thought, the most admirable, and to me most gratifying, thing is that this great anatomist actually gets so far on the path of his purely physiological investigations as to explain the unalterable nature of the *moral character*. This he does by saying that only *animal* life, and hence the function of the brain, is subject to the influence of education, practice, culture, and habit; but the *moral character* belongs to *organic* life, in other words, to all the other parts, incapable of modification from outside. I cannot refrain from quoting the passage: it is in article 9, § 2. *Telle est donc la grande différence des deux vies de l'animal* (cerebral or animal and organic life) *par rapport à l'inégalité de perfection des divers systèmes de fonctions, dont chacune résulte; savoir, que dans l'une la prédominance ou l'infériorité d'un système, relativement aux autres, tient presque toujours à l'activité ou à l'inertie plus grandes de ce système, à l'habitude d'agir ou de ne pas agir; que dans l'autre, au contraire, cette prédominance ou cette infériorité sont immédiatement liées à la texture des organes, et jamais à leur éducation. Voilà pourquoi le tempérament physique et le CARACTÈRE MORAL ne sont point susceptibles de changer par l'éducation, qui modifie si prodigieusement les actes de la vie animale; car, comme nous l'avons vu, tous deux APPARTIENNENT À LA VIE ORGANIQUE. Le caractère est, si je puis m'exprimer ainsi, la physionomie des passions; le tempérament est celle des fonctions internes; or les unes et les autres étant toujours les mêmes, ayant une direction que l'habitude et l'exercice ne dérangent jamais, il est manifeste que le tempérament et le caractère doivent être aussi soustraits à l'empire de l'éducation. Elle peut modérer l'influence du second, perfectionner assez le jugement et la réflexion, pour rendre leur empire supérieur au sien, fortifier la vie animale, afin qu'elle résiste aux impulsions de l'organique. Mais vouloir par elle dénaturer le caractère, adoucir ou exalter les passions dont il est l'expression habituelle, agrandir ou resserrer leur sphère,*

Declamation holds the mean; it animates the cold language of the brain through the expressive language of the internal organs, the heart, the liver, the stomach, and so on." [Tr.]

[12] "Organic life is the final point where the passions end, and the centre from which they start." [Tr.]

c'est une entreprise analogue à celle d'un médecin qui essaierait d'élever ou d'abaisser de quelques degrés, et pour toute la vie, la force de contraction ordinaire au cœur dans l'état de santé, de précipiter ou de ralentir habituellement le mouvement naturel aux artères, et qui est nécessaire à leur action etc. Nous observerions à ce médecin, que la circulation, la respiration etc. ne sont point sous le domaine de la volonté (free choice), *qu'elles ne peuvent être modifiées par l'homme, sans passer à l'état maladif etc. Faisons la même observation à ceux qui croient qu'on change le caractère, et par-là même LES PASSIONS, puisque celles-ci sont UN PRODUIT DE L'ACTION DE TOUS LES ORGANES INTERNES, ou qu'elles y ont au moins spécialement leur siège.*[13] The reader familiar with my philosophy can imagine how great was my delight when I discovered, so to speak, the proof of my own conclusions in those obtained in an entirely different field by this distinguished man who was snatched from the world at so early an age.

A special proof of the truth that the organism is the mere visi-

---

[13] "This, then, is the great difference in the two lives of the animal with regard to the inequality of the perfection of the different systems of functions from which each results. Thus in the one the predominance or inferiority of a system, relatively to others, depends almost always on the greater or lesser activity or inertia of that system, on the habit of acting or of not acting. In the other, on the contrary, this predominance or inferiority is directly connected with the texture of the organs and never with their training. This is the reason why the physical constitution and the *moral character* are not at all susceptible of a change through training, which modifies so extraordinarily the actions of animal life; for, as we have seen, the two *belong to organic life*. The character is, if I may so express myself, the physiognomy of the passions; the constitution that of the internal functions. Now as both always remain the same and have a tendency that can never be upset by habit or exercise, it is clear that the constitution and the character must also remain withdrawn from the influence of training. This can certainly moderate the influence of the character, can appreciably perfect judgement and reflection, in order to render their influence superior to that of the character. Moreover, it can strengthen animal life so that this resists the impulses of organic life. But to try through training to alter the nature of the character, to allay or enhance the passions of which the character is the regular expression, to widen or restrict their sphere, is an undertaking somewhat similar to that of a physician who would attempt to raise or to lower by several degrees, and for the whole of life, the force of contraction peculiar to the heart in a healthy state; to accelerate or to retard permanently the motion natural to the arteries and necessary for their action. We should point out to this physician that circulation, respiration, and so on are certainly not under the control of free choice, and that they cannot be modified by man without his falling into a morbid state, and so on. We can make the same observations to those who think that the character, and through this even the *passions,* can be changed. For these are a *product of the action of all the internal organs,* or at any rate have their special seat there." [Tr.]

bility of the will is given to us also by the fact that, if dogs, cats, domestic cocks, and in fact other animals, bite when most violently angry, the wound can be fatal; in fact, coming from a dog, it can produce hydrophobia in the person bitten, without the dog being mad or afterwards becoming so. For extreme anger is only the most decided and vehement will to annihilate its object. This appears here in the fact that the saliva then assumes instantaneously a pernicious force which is, to a certain extent, magically effective, and which proves that will and organism are indeed one. This is also evident from the fact that violent anger can rapidly impart so pernicious a quality to the mother's milk that the infant at once dies in convulsions (Most, *Ueber sympathetische Mittel*, p. 16).

* * *

NOTE ON WHAT IS SAID ABOUT BICHAT.

As shown above, Bichat cast a deep glance into human nature, and, in consequence, gave an exceedingly admirable explanation that is one of the most profoundly conceived works in the whole of French literature. Now, sixty years later, M. Flourens suddenly appears with a polemic against it in his *De la vie et de l'intelligence.* He has the effrontery summarily to declare false all that Bichat brought to light on this subject, one quite peculiarly his own. And what does he bring against him? Counter-arguments? No, counter-assertions[14] and authorities that are indeed as inadmissible as they are strange, namely Descartes—and Gall! By conviction M. Flourens is a Cartesian, and for him, even in the year 1858, Descartes is *"le philosophe par excellence."* Now Descartes was certainly a great man, yet only as a pioneer; in the whole of his dogmas, on the other hand, there is not a word of truth, and to appeal to these as authorities at this time of day is positively absurd. For in the nineteenth century a Cartesian is in philosophy what a follower of Ptolemy would be in astronomy, or a follower of Stahl in chemistry. But for M. Flourens the dogmas of Descartes are articles of faith. Descartes taught that *les volontés sont des pensées,*[15] therefore it is so, although

---

[14] *"Tout ce qui est relatif à l'entendement appartient à la vie animale,"* dit Bichat, *et jusque-là point de doute; "tout ce qui est relatif aux passions appartient à la vie organique"—et ceci est absolument faux.* ('All that relates to the understanding belongs to animal life,' says Bichat, and so far he is undoubtedly right; 'all that relates to the passions belongs to organic life' —and this is absolutely untrue. [Tr.]) Indeed?—*decrevit Florentius magnus.* ("Thus has the great Flourens decreed." Tr.)

[15] "Acts of will are thoughts." [Tr.]

everyone feels within himself that willing and thinking differ from each other as white from black. Therefore, in chapter 19 above, I have been able to demonstrate and elucidate this fully and thoroughly, and always under the guidance of experience. But first of all there are, according to Descartes, the oracle of M. Flourens, two fundamentally different substances, body and soul. Consequently, as an orthodox Cartesian, M. Flourens says: *Le premier point est de séparer, même par les mots, ce qui est du corps de ce qui est de l'âme* (i, 72).[16] Further, he informs us that this *âme réside uniquement et exclusivement dans le cerveau*[17] (ii, 137); from here, according to a passage of Descartes, it sends the *spiritus animales* as couriers to the muscles, yet it itself can be affected by the brain alone. The passions, therefore, have their seat (*siège*) in the heart, as that which is altered by them; yet they have their place (*place*) in the brain. Thus does the oracle of M. Flourens actually speak; he is so much edified by it, that he even repeats it mechanically twice over (ii, 33 and ii, 135) for an unfailing triumph over the ignorant Bichat, who knows neither soul nor body, but merely an animal life and an organic life. He then patronizingly informs Bichat that we must thoroughly distinguish the parts where the passions have their *seat* (*siègent*) from those which they *affect*. Accordingly, the passions *act* in one place, while they *are* in another. Corporeal things usually act only where they are, but with an immaterial soul the case may be different. What in general can he and his oracle have really pictured to themselves by this distinction of *place* and *siège, siéger* and *affecter*? The fundamental error of M. Flourens and of his Descartes really springs from the fact that they confuse the motives or occasions of the passions, which certainly lie as representations in the intellect, i.e., the brain, with the passions themselves, that, as stirrings of the will, lie in the whole body; and this (as we know) is the perceived will itself. As I have said, the second authority of M. Flourens is Gall. At the beginning of this twentieth chapter (and indeed even in the earlier edition) I did say, of course, that "the greatest error in Gall's phrenology is that he sets up organs of the brain even for moral qualities." But what I censure and reject is precisely what M. Flourens praises and admires, for he bears in his heart Descartes' doctrine that *les volontés sont des pensées*. Accordingly, he says on p. 144: *Le premier service que Gall a rendu à la PHYSIOLOGIE* (?) *a été de ramener le moral à l'intellectuel, et de faire voir que les facultés morales et les facultés intellectuelles sont*

---

[16] "The first thing is to separate, even in words, what belongs to the body from what belongs to the soul." [Tr.]

[17] "This soul resides uniquely and exclusively in the brain." [Tr.]

des facultés du même ordre, et de les placer toutes, autant les unes que les autres, uniquement et exclusivement dans le cerveau.[18] To a certain extent my whole philosophy, and especially chapter 19 of this volume, consists in the refutation of this fundamental error. M. Flourens, on the other hand, is never tired of extolling this as a great truth and Gall as its discoverer; e.g., on p. 147: *Si j'en étais à classer les services que nous a rendu Gall, je dirais que le premier a été de ramener les qualités morales au cerveau. . . .* p. 153: *Le cerveau seul est l'organe de l'âme, et de l'âme dans toute la plénitude de ses fonctions* (we see the Cartesian simple *soul* always in the background, as the kernel of the matter); *il est le siège de toutes les facultés morales, comme de toutes les facultés intellectuelles. . . . Gall a ramené le MORAL à L'INTELLECTUEL, il a ramené les qualités morales au même siège, au même organe, que les facultés intellectuelles.*[19] Oh, how ashamed of ourselves Bichat and I must be in the presence of such wisdom! But, seriously speaking, what can be more depressing, or rather more shocking, than to see the true and profound rejected, and the false and absurd praised and commended? What is more disheartening than to live to see important truths that have been deeply concealed and gained with difficulty at a late hour once more torn down, and to see the old, stale, recently overthrown error put once more in their place; in fact to be reduced to the fear that, through such a procedure, the very difficult advances in human knowledge will again be turned into steps in the reverse direction? But let us calm ourselves, for *magna est vis veritatis et praevalebit.*[20] M. Flourens is unquestionably a man of much merit, but he has acquired it principally on the path of experiment. But these most important truths cannot be drawn from experiment, but only from meditation and penetration. Thus by his meditation and profound insight Bichat brought to light a truth which is one of those that remain inaccessible to the experimental efforts of M. Flourens, even if he, as a genuine and consistent Cartesian,

---

[18] "The first service rendered by Gall to *physiology* was to reduce the moral to the intellectual, and to show that moral and intellectual faculties are faculties of the same order, and to place them all, moral as well as intellectual, uniquely and exclusively in the brain." [Tr.]

[19] "If I had to enumerate the services rendered to us by Gall, I would say that the first was to reduce moral qualities to the brain. . . . The brain alone is the organ of the soul, and of the soul in all the fulness of its functions; . . . it is the seat of all the moral as well as of all the intellectual faculties . . . Gall has reduced the *moral* to the *intellectual;* he has traced moral qualities to the same seat, the same organ, as intellectual faculties." [Tr.]

[20] "Great is the power of truth, and it will prevail." [Tr.]

tortures a hundred more animals to death. But he should have observed and thought something about this before it was too late:
"Take care, my friend; it burns." Now the audacity and self-conceit,
such as are imparted only by superficiality combined with a false
presumption, with which M. Flourens nevertheless undertakes to
refute a thinker like Bichat by mere counter-assertions, old women's
conclusions, and futile authorities, even to reprimand and admonish
him, indeed almost to scoff at him, have their origin in the business
of the Academy and its *fauteuils* or seats. Enthroned on these, and
greeting one another as *illustre confrère*,[21] the gentlemen cannot
possibly help putting themselves on an equality with the best who
have ever lived, regarding themselves as oracles, and decreeing accordingly what shall be false and what true. This impels and en-
titles me to say quite plainly for once that the really superior and
privileged minds, who are born now and then for the enlightenment
of the rest, and among whom Bichat certainly belongs, are so "by
the grace of God." Accordingly, they are related to the Academies
(in which they have generally occupied only the forty-first *fauteuil*)[22]
and to their *illustres confrères* as princes by birth are to the numerous representatives of the people chosen from the mob. Therefore
a secret awe should warn these gentlemen of the Academy (who
always exist by the score) before they pick a quarrel with such a
man—unless they have the most valid reasons to offer, not mere
counter-assertions and appeals to *placita* of Descartes; at the present
day this is positively ludicrous.

---

[21] "Illustrious colleague." [Tr.]
[22] The French Academy has only forty seats. [Tr.]

CHAPTER XXI

Retrospect and More General Consideration

If the *intellect* were not of a secondary nature, as the two preceding chapters show, then everything that takes place without it, in other words, without intervention of the representation, such, for example, as generation, procreation, the development and preservation of the organism, the healing of wounds, the restoration or vicarious repair of mutilated parts, the salutary crisis in diseases, the works of animal mechanical skill, and the activity of instinct in general, would not turn out so infinitely better and more perfect than what takes place with the aid of the intellect, namely all the conscious and intended achievements and works of men. Such works and achievements, when compared with those others, are mere botching and bungling. Generally, *nature* signifies that which operates, urges, and creates without the intervention of the intellect. That this is really identical with what we find in ourselves as *will* is the sole and exclusive theme of this second book, as also of the essay *On the Will in Nature*. The possibility of this fundamental knowledge rests on the fact that the same thing is immediately illuminated *in us* by the intellect, here appearing as self-consciousness; otherwise we should just as little arrive at a fuller knowledge of it in ourselves as outside ourselves, and we should have to stop for ever in the presence of inscrutable natural forces. We have to think away the assistance of the *intellect,* if we wish to comprehend the true essence of the will-in-itself, and thus, as far as possible, to penetrate into nature's inner being.

Incidentally, for this reason, my direct antipode among the philosophers is Anaxagoras; for he arbitrarily assumed a νοῦς, an intelligence, a creator of representations, as the first and original thing, from which everything proceeds; and he is looked upon as the first to have advanced such a view. According to this view, the world had existed earlier in the mere representation than in itself, whereas with me it is the *will*-without-knowledge that is the foundation of the reality of things; and their development must have already gone a good way before representation and intelligence were reached in animal consciousness, so that with me thinking appears as the last thing of all. But according to the testimony of Aristotle (*Metaphysics*, i, 4), Anaxagoras himself did not very well know how to begin with νοῦς, but merely set it up, and then left it standing, like a painted saint at the entrance, without making use of it for his elucidations of nature, except in cases of need, when he did not know how to help himself otherwise. All physico-theology is a perpetration of the error opposed to the truth (expressed at the beginning of this chapter), the error that the most perfect manner of origin of things is that through the medium of an *intellect*. This, therefore, puts a stop to all deeper investigation of nature.

From the time of Socrates down to our own, we find that a principal subject of the interminable disputations of philosophers is that *ens rationis* called *soul*. We see most of them assert its immortality, which means its metaphysical nature; yet we see others, supported by facts that incontestably show the intellect's complete dependence on bodily organs, unweariedly maintain the opposite. By all and above all, that *soul* was taken to be *absolutely simple;* for precisely from this were its metaphysical nature, its immateriality, and its immortality demonstrated, although these by no means necessarily follow from it. For although we can conceive the destruction of a formed body only through its decomposition into its parts, it does not follow from this that the destruction of a simple substance or entity, of which, moreover, we have no conception, may not be possible in some other way, perhaps by its gradually vanishing. I, on the other hand, start by doing away with the presupposed simplicity of our subjectively conscious nature or of the ego, since I show that the manifestations from which this simplicity was inferred have two very different sources, and that in any case the *intellect* is physically conditioned, the function of a material organ, and therefore dependent on it; and that without such an organ it is just as impossible as it is to grasp without a hand. Accordingly with me the intellect belongs to the mere phenomenon, and therefore shares its fate; the *will,* on the contrary, is tied to no special organ, but is everywhere present, is everywhere that which really moves and forms, and consequently conditions, the whole organism. In fact, the will constitutes the metaphysical substratum of the whole phenomenon, and thus is not, like the intellect, a *posterius,* but the *prius,* of the phenomenon; the phenomenon depends on it, not it on the phenomenon. The body, however, is reduced even to a mere representation, since it is only the way in which the *will* exhibits itself in the perception of the intellect or brain. On the other hand, the *will,* which appears as one of the last results in all previous systems, so different in other respects, is with me the very first. As mere function of the brain, the *intellect* is affected by the destruction of the body; the *will,* on the contrary, is by no means so affected. From this heterogeneity of the two, together with the secondary nature of the intellect, it is easy to understand that, in the depths of his self-consciousness, man feels himself to be eternal and indestructible; but that nevertheless he can have no memory, either *a parte ante* or *a parte post,*[1] beyond the duration of his life. I do not want to anticipate here the discussion of the true indestructibility of our inner nature, which has its place in the fourth book; I wish only to indicate the place with which it is connected.

But in an expression certainly one-sided yet from our point of view true, the body is called a mere representation. This is due to the fact that an existence in space as something extended and in time as something changing, yet more closely determined in both by the causal nexus, is possible only in the *representation.* For those determinations together rest on the forms of the representation, and hence in a brain, in which such an existence accordingly appears as something objective, in other words as foreign. Therefore even our own body can have this kind of existence only in a brain. For the knowledge I have of my body as extended, as filling space, and as movable, is merely *indirect;* it is a picture in my brain which is brought about by means of the senses and the understanding. The body is given to me *directly* only in muscular action and in pain or pleasure, both of which primarily and immediately belong to the will. But bringing together these two different kinds of knowledge of my own body afterwards gives me the further insight that all other things, which have also the aforesaid objective existence that is primarily only in my brain, that all other things, I say, are not therefore absolutely non-existent apart from this brain, but that they too *in themselves* must ultimately be what makes itself known to self-consciousness as *will.*

---

[1] "On the side of the past or of the future." [Tr.]

Objective View of the Intellect

There are two fundamentally different ways of considering the intellect, which depend on the difference of point of view; and much as they are in consequence opposed to each other, they must yet be brought into agreement. One is the *subjective* way, which, starting from *within,* and taking *consciousness* as what is given, shows us by what mechanism the world exhibits itself in this consciousness, and how from materials furnished by the senses and the understanding the world is built up in it. We must regard Locke as the originator of this method of consideration; Kant brought it to an incomparably higher perfection, and our first book, together with its supplements, is devoted to this method.

The opposite to this way of considering the intellect is the *objective* method. Starting from *outside,* it takes as its object not our own consciousness, but the beings that are given in external experience, and are conscious of themselves and the world. It then investigates what relation their intellect has to their other qualities, how this intellect has become possible, how it has become necessary, and what it achieves for them. The standpoint of this method of consideration is the empirical; it takes the world and the animal beings in it as absolutely given, since it starts from them. Accordingly, it is primarily zoological, anatomical, physiological, and becomes philosophical only through connexion with that first method of consideration, and from the higher point of view obtained thereby. We are indebted to zootomists and physiologists, mostly French, for the only foundation to it hitherto given. In particular, Cabanis is to be mentioned here; his excellent work, *Des rapports du physique au moral,* is a pioneer work on the path of physiology for this method of consideration. The celebrated Bichat was a contemporary of his, but his theme was much more comprehensive. Even Gall may be mentioned here, although his principal aim was missed. Ignorance and prejudice have brought the accusation of materialism against

---

[1] This chapter refers to the last half of § 27 of volume 1.

this method of consideration, because, adhering simply to experience, it does not know the immaterial substance, namely soul. The most recent advances in the physiology of the nervous system by Sir Charles Bell, Magendie, Marshall Hall, and others have also enriched and corrected the subject-matter of this method of consideration. A philosophy like the Kantian, that entirely ignores this point of view for the intellect, is one-sided, and therefore inadequate. It leaves an immense gulf between our philosophical and physiological knowledge, with which we can never be satisfied.

Although what I have said in the two preceding chapters on the life and activity of the brain belongs to this method of consideration, and in the same way all the explanations given under the heading "Physiology of Plants" in the essay *On the Will in Nature,* and also a part of those to be found under the heading "Comparative Anatomy" are devoted to it, the following statement of its results in general will certainly not be superfluous.

We shall become most vividly aware of the glaring contrast between the two methods of considering the intellect which in the above remarks are clearly opposed, if we carry the matter to the extreme, and realize that what the one as reflective thought and vivid perception immediately takes up and makes its material, is for the other nothing more than the physiological function of an internal organ, the brain. In fact, we are justified in asserting that the whole of the objective world, so boundless in space, so infinite in time, so unfathomable in its perfection, is really only a certain movement or affection of the pulpy mass in the skull. We then ask in astonishment what this brain is, whose function produces such a phenomenon of all phenomena. What is this matter that can be refined and potentiated to such a pulpy mass, that the stimulation of a few of its particles becomes the conditional supporter of the existence of an objective world? The dread of such questions drove men to the hypothesis of the simple substance of an immaterial soul, which merely dwelt in the brain. We say fearlessly that this pulpy mass, like every vegetable or animal part, is also an organic structure, like all its humbler relations in the inferior dwelling-place of our irrational brothers' heads, down to the humblest that scarcely apprehends. Nevertheless, that organic pulpy mass is nature's final product, which presupposes all the rest. In itself, however, and outside the representation, the brain too, like everything else, is *will. To-exist-for-another is to-be-represented; being-in-itself is to will.* Precisely to this is due the fact that, on the purely *objective* path, we never attain to the inner nature of things, but if we attempt to find their inner nature from outside and empirically, this inner always becomes an outer in our hands; the pith of the tree as well as its bark; the heart of the animal as well as its hide; the white and the yolk of an egg as well as its shell. On the *subjective* path, however, the inner nature is at every moment accessible to us, for we find it as the *will* primarily within ourselves; and with the clue of the analogy with our own inner nature, it must be possible for us to unravel the rest, since we attain to the insight that a being-in-itself, independent of being known, that is, of exhibiting itself in an intellect, is conceivable only as a *willing*.

Now if in the *objective* comprehension of the intellect we go back as far as we can, we shall find that the necessity or need of *knowledge in general* arises from the plurality and *separate* existence of beings, from individuation. For let us imagine that there exists only a *single* being, then such a being needs no knowledge, because there would not then exist anything different from that being itself,—anything whose existence such a being would therefore have to take up into itself only indirectly through knowledge, in other words, through picture and concept. It would already *itself* be all in all; consequently there would remain nothing for it to know, in other words, nothing foreign that could be apprehended as object. On the other hand, with the plurality of beings, every individual finds itself in a state of isolation from all the rest, and from this arises the necessity for knowledge. The nervous system, by means of which the animal individual first of all becomes conscious of itself, is bounded by a skin; yet in the brain raised to intellect, it crosses this boundary by means of its form of knowledge, causality, and in this way perception arises for it as a consciousness of *other* things, as a picture or image of beings in space and time, which change in accordance with causality. In this sense it would be more correct to say "Only the different is known by the different," than, as Empedocles said, "Only the like is known by the like," which was a very indefinite and ambiguous proposition; although points of view may well be expressed from which it is true; as, for instance, that of Helvetius, when he observes beautifully and strikingly: *Il n'y a que l'esprit qui sente l'esprit: c'est une corde qui ne frémit qu'à l'unison;*[2] this corresponds to Xenophanes' σοφὸν εἶναι δεῖ τὸν ἐπιγνωσόμενον τὸν σοφόν (*sapientem esse oportet eum qui sapientem agniturus sit*),[3] and is a great and bitter grief. But we know again from the other side that, conversely, plurality of the homogeneous becomes possible only through time and space, i.e., through the forms of our knowledge. Space first arises

---

[2] "The mind alone is capable of understanding the mind; it is a string that vibrates only in harmony with another." [Tr.]

[3] "One must be a sage to recognize a sage." [Tr.]

by the knowing subject seeing outwards; it is the manner in which the subject apprehends something as different from itself. But we just now saw that knowledge in general is conditioned by plurality and difference. Therefore knowledge and plurality, or individuation, stand and fall together, for they condition each other. It is to be concluded from this that, beyond the phenomenon, in the true being-in-itself of all things, to which time and space, and therefore plurality, must be foreign, there cannot exist any knowledge. Buddhism describes this as Prajna Paramita, i.e., that which is beyond all knowledge. (See I. J. Schmidt, *On the Mahayana and Prachna-Paramita.*) Accordingly, a "knowledge of things-in-themselves" in the strictest sense of the word, would be impossible, because where the being-in-itself of things begins, knowledge ceases, and all knowledge primarily and essentially concerns merely phenomena. For it springs from a limitation, by which it is rendered necessary, in order to extend the limits.

For the objective consideration, the brain is the efflorescence of the organism; therefore only where the organism has reached its highest perfection and complexity does the brain appear in its greatest development. But in the preceding chapter we recognized the organism as the objectification of the will; hence the brain, as part of the organism, must belong to this objectification. Further, from the fact that the organism is only the visibility of the will, and thus in itself is this will, I have deduced that every affection of the *organism* simultaneously and immediately affects the *will,* in other words, is felt pleasantly or painfully. Yet through the enhancement of sensibility, with the higher development of the nervous system, there arises the possibility that in the nobler, i.e., *objective,* sense-organs (sight and hearing), the extremely delicate affections appropriate to them are felt without affecting the will immediately and in themselves, in other words, without being painful or pleasant; and that in consequence they appear in consciousness as in themselves indifferent, merely *perceived,* sensations. But in the brain this enhancement of sensibility reaches such a high degree that on received sense-impressions there even occurs a reaction. This reaction does not come directly from the will, but is primarily a spontaneity of the function of understanding, a function that makes the transition from the directly perceived sensation of the senses to the *cause* of this sensation. In this way there arises the perception or intuition of an *external object,* since here the brain simultaneously produces the form of space. We can therefore regard as the boundary between the world as will and the world as representation, or even as the birth-place of the latter, the point where, from the sensation on the retina, still a mere affection of the body and to that extent of the will, the understanding makes the transition to the *cause* of that sensation. The understanding projects the sensation, by means of its form of space, as something external and different from its own person. But with man the spontaneity of the brain's activity, conferred of course in the last instance by the will, goes farther than mere *perception* and immediate apprehension of causal relations. It extends to the formation of abstract concepts from those perceptions, and to operating with them, in other words, to *thinking,* as that in which man's *reason (Vernunft)* consists. The *ideas,* therefore, are farthest removed from the affections of the body, and since this body is the objectification of the will, these can pass at once into pain through intensification, even in the organs of sense. In accordance with what we have said, representation and idea can also be regarded as the efflorescence of the will, in so far as they spring from the highest perfection and enhancement of the organism; but, in itself and apart from the representation, this organism is the *will.* In my explanation, the existence of the body certainly presupposes the world of representation, in so far as it also, as body or real object, is only in this world. On the other hand, the representation itself just as much presupposes the body, for it arises only through the function of an organ of the body. That which lies at the foundation of the whole phenomenon, that in it which alone is being-in-itself and is original, is exclusively the *will;* for it is the will which, through this very process, assumes the form of the *representation,* in other words, enters into the secondary existence of an objective world, the sphere of the knowable. The philosophers before Kant, with few exceptions, attempted from the wrong side to explain how our knowledge comes about. They started from a so-called soul, an entity whose inner nature and peculiar function consisted in thinking, indeed quite specially in abstract thinking, with mere concepts; and these belonged to it the more completely the farther they lay from all perceptibility. (Here I request the reader to look up the note at the end of § 6 in my essay *On the Basis of Morality.*) This soul is supposed to have come into the body in some inconceivable way, and there suffers only disturbances in its pure thinking first from sense-impressions and perceptions, still more from the desires that these excite, and finally from the emotions, in fact the passions, into which these desires develop. On the other hand, this soul's own and original element is said to be pure, abstract thinking; left to this, it has only universals, inborn concepts, and *aeternae veritates* for its objects, and leaves everything of perception lying far below it. Hence arises the contempt with which even now "sensibility" and the "sensible" or "sensuous" are referred to, and are even made by the professors of philosophy the chief source of immorality; whereas because the senses, in combination with the *a priori* functions of the intellect, produce *perception,* it is precisely these that are the pure and innocent source of all our knowledge, from which all thinking first borrows its contents. We might really suppose that, in speaking of sensibility, these gentlemen always thought only of the pretended sixth sense of the French. Therefore, as previously stated, in the process of knowledge, its ultimate product, namely abstract thinking, was made the first and original thing, and accordingly, as I have said, the matter was tackled from the wrong end. According to my account, the intellect springs from the organism, and thus from the will, and so without this could not exist. Without the will, it would find no material and nothing to occupy it, since everything knowable is just the objectification of the will.

But not only is perception of the external world, or the consciousness of other things, conditioned by the brain and its functions, but so is self-consciousness also. The will in itself is without consciousness, and in the greatest part of its phenomena remains so. The secondary world of the representation must be added for the will to become conscious of itself, just as light becomes visible only through the bodies that reflect it, and otherwise loses itself ineffectually in darkness. Since the will, for the purpose of comprehending its relations with the external world, produces in the animal individual a brain, the consciousness of itself first arises in this by means of the subject of knowledge, and this subject comprehends things as existing and the I or *ego* as willing. Thus the sensibility, enhanced to the highest degree in the brain and yet spread through its different parts, must first of all bring together all the rays of its activity, concentrate them, so to speak, in a focus; yet this focal point lies not without, as with concave mirrors, but within, as with convex. With this point, sensibility first of all describes the line of time on which everything represented by it must exhibit itself, and which is the first and most essential form of all knowing, or the form of the inner sense. This focal point of the whole activity of the brain is what Kant called the synthetic unity of apperception.* Only by means of this does the will become conscious of itself, since this focus of the brain's activity, or that which knows, apprehends itself as identical with its own basis from which it has sprung, i.e., with what wills, and thus arises the *ego.* Nevertheless, this focus of brain-activity remains primarily a mere subject of knowing, and, as such, capable of being the cold

---

* Cf. p. 251.

and indifferent spectator, the mere guide and counsellor of the will, and also of comprehending the external world purely objectively, regardless of the will and of its weal or woe. But as soon as it is directed inwards, it recognizes the will as the basis of its own phenomenon, and therefore merges with this will into the consciousness of an *ego*. That focus of brain-activity (or the subject of knowledge) is indeed, as an indivisible point, simple, yet it is not on that account a substance (soul), but a mere condition or state. That of which it itself is a state or condition can be known by it only indirectly, through reflection as it were. But the cessation of the state or condition cannot be regarded as the annihilation of that of which it is a state or condition. This *knowing* and conscious *ego* is related to the will, which is the basis of its phenomenal appearance, as the image in the focus of the concave mirror is to that mirror itself; and, like that image, it has only a conditioned, in fact, properly speaking, a merely apparent reality. Far from being the absolutely first thing (as Fichte taught, for example), it is at bottom tertiary, since it presupposes the organism, and the organism presupposes the will. I admit that everything said here is really only metaphor and figure of speech, in part even hypothetical; but we stand at a point which thoughts and ideas, much less proofs, scarcely reach. I therefore ask the reader to compare it with what I have set forth at length on this subject in chapter 20.

Now, although the true being-in-itself of every existing thing consists in its will, and knowledge together with consciousness is added only as something secondary at the higher stages of the phenomenon, we find nevertheless that the difference placed between one being and another by the presence and different degree of consciousness and intellect is exceedingly great, and has important results. We must picture to ourselves the subjective existence of the plant as a weak analogue, a mere shadow of comfortable and uncomfortable feeling; and even in this extremely weak degree, the plant knows only of itself, not of anything outside it. On the other hand, even the lowest animal that stands next to it is induced by enhanced and more definitely specified needs to extend the sphere of its existence beyond the limit of its own body. This takes place through knowledge. It has a dull perception of its immediate surroundings out of which motives for its action arise for the purpose of its maintenance and support. Accordingly, the *medium of motives* appears in this way, and this is—the world standing out objectively in time and space, the *world as representation*, however feeble, dull, and dimly dawning this first and lowest specimen of it may be. Yet it is marked more and more distinctly, more and more widely and deeply, in proportion as the brain is more and more perfectly produced in the ascending series of animal organizations. But this enhancement of brain-development, and hence of the intellect and of the clearness of the representation, at each of these ever higher stages, is brought about by the ever-increasing and more complicated *need* of these phenomena of the will. This need must always first give rise to it, for without need or want nature (in other words, the will objectifying itself therein) produces nothing, least of all the most difficult of her productions, a more perfect brain, in consequence of her *lex parsimoniae: Natura nihil agit frustra et nihil facit supervacaneum.*[4] She has equipped every animal with the organs necessary for its maintenance and support, with the weapons necessary for its conflict, as I have explained at length in the work *On the Will in Nature* under the heading "Comparative Anatomy." Therefore by the same standard, she has imparted to each the most important of the organs directed outwards, namely the brain with its function, i.e., the intellect. Thus the more complicated its organization became through higher development, the more manifold and specially determined became its needs; consequently, the more difficult and dependent on opportunity became the procuring of what satisfies them. Therefore, a wider range of vision, a more accurate comprehension, a more correct distinction of things in the external world in all their circumstances and relations were here required. Accordingly, we see the powers of representation and their organs, brain, nerves, and organs of sense, appear more and more perfect, the higher we ascend in the scale of animals; and in proportion as the cerebral system develops, does the external world appear in consciousness ever more distinct, many-sided, and complete. The comprehension of the world now demands more and more attention, and ultimately to such an extent that at times its relation to the will must be momentarily lost sight of, so that it may occur the more purely and correctly. This quite definitely appears first in the case of man; only with him does a *pure separation of knowing from willing* occur. This is an important point that I merely touch on here, to indicate its place, so as to be able to take it up again later on. But this last step in extending and perfecting the brain, and thus increasing the powers of knowledge, is taken by nature, like all the rest, merely in consequence of the increased *needs,* and hence in the service of the *will.* What this will aims at and attains in man is indeed essentially the

---

[4] "Law of parsimony: Nature does nothing in vain, and creates nothing superfluous." [Tr.]

same as, and not more than, what its goal is in the animal, nourishment and propagation. But through the organization of man the requirements for the attainment of that goal were so greatly increased, enhanced, and specified, that an incomparably more important enhancement of the intellect than that offered by previous stages was necessary, or at any rate was the easiest means of attaining the end. But as the intellect, in consequence of its very essence, is a tool of exceedingly varied and extensive uses, and is equally applicable to the most heterogeneous aims and objects, nature, true to her spirit of parsimony, could now meet through it alone all the demands of the wants and needs that had become so manifold. Therefore she sent man forth without clothing, without natural weapons of defence or of attack, indeed with relatively little muscular strength, great weakness, and little endurance against adverse influences and deficiencies. This she did in reliance on that one great tool, for which she had to retain only the hands of the next stage below him, the ape. But through the preponderating intellect that here appears, not only are the comprehension of the motives, their multiplicity and variety, and generally the horizon of the aims infinitely increased, but the distinctness with which the will is conscious *of itself* is also enhanced in the highest degree, in consequence of the clearness of the whole consciousness which has come about. This clearness, supported by the capacity for abstract knowledge, now reaches complete reflectiveness. But in this way, as also through the vehemence of the will, necessarily presupposed as the supporter of so enhanced an intellect, there appeared a heightening of all the *emotions,* indeed the possibility of *passions,* which, in the proper sense, are unknown to the animal. For the vehemence of the will keeps pace with the enhancement of the intelligence, just because in reality this enhancement always springs from the will's increased needs and more pressing demands; but in addition to this, the two mutually support each other. Thus the vehemence of the character is connected with greater energy of heart-beat and of blood circulation, which physically heightens the activity of the brain. On the other hand, clearness of intelligence again heightens the emotions produced through external circumstances by means of the more lively apprehension of them. Therefore young calves, for example, calmly allow themselves to be packed into a cart and dragged off; but young lions, if only separated from their mother, remain permanently restless and roar incessantly from morning till night; children in such a situation would cry and worry themselves almost to death. The liveliness and impetuosity of the ape are connected precisely with its greatly developed intelligence. It depends precisely on this reciprocal relationship that man is generally capable of much greater sorrows than is the animal, but also of greater joy in satisfied and happy emotions. In just the same way, enhanced intellect makes him more susceptible to boredom than the animal; but, if it is individually very complete, it also becomes a perennial source of diversion and entertainment. Thus on the whole, the phenomenal appearance of the will in man is related to that in the animal of a higher species as a note that is struck is to its fifth pitched two or three octaves lower. But even between the different species of animals, the differences of intellect and therefore of consciousness are great and endlessly graduated. The mere analogue of consciousness, which we must ascribe to the plant, will be related to the still far duller subjective inner being of an inorganic body in much the same way as the consciousness of the lowest animal is related to this quasi-consciousness of the plant. We can picture to ourselves the innumerable gradations in degree of consciousness from the illustration of the different velocity of points on a disc which are situated at different distances from the centre. But the most correct, and indeed, as our third book teaches, the natural illustration of that gradation is afforded by the musical scale in its whole range from the lowest audible note to the highest. But it is the degree of consciousness that determines the degree of a being's existence. For all immediate existence is subjective; objective existence is present in the consciousness of another, and hence is only for this other; consequently it is quite indirect. Through the degree of consciousness beings are as different as through the will they are alike, in so far as this will is what is common to them all.

However, what we have now considered as between plant and animal, and again between the different species of animals, also occurs between one man and another. Thus what is secondary, namely the intellect, here sets up, by means of the clearness of consciousness and the distinctness of knowledge dependent on it, a fundamental and immeasurably great difference in the whole mode, and thus in the degree, of existence. The higher the consciousness has risen, the more distinct and connected are the thoughts and ideas, the clearer the perceptions, the deeper and profounder the sensations. In this way everything gains more depth: emotion, sadness, joy, and sorrow. Ordinary shallow minds are not even capable of real joy; they live on in dull insensibility. Whereas one man's consciousness presents to him only his own existence, together with the motives that must be apprehended for the purpose of sustaining and enlivening it, in a bare and inadequate apprehension of the external world, to another person his own consciousness is a *camera obscura* in which the macrocosm exhibits itself:

> He feels he holds a little world
> Brooding in his brain,
> That it begins to act and live,
> That it from himself he fain would give.[5]

The difference of the whole mode of existence established between one man and another by the extremes of gradation of intellectual abilities is so great, that that between a king and an artisan seems small by comparison. Here also, as in the case of animal species, a connexion can be shown between the vehemence of the will and the enhancement of the intellect. Genius is conditioned by a passionate temperament, and a phlegmatic genius is inconceivable. It seems that an exceedingly vehement and hence strongly desiring will must exist, if nature is to provide an abnormally heightened intellect as appropriate to it, whilst the merely physical account of this points to the greater energy with which the arteries of the head move the brain and increase its turgescence. But the quantity, quality, and form of the brain itself are of course the other and incomparably rarer condition of genius. On the other hand, phlegmatic persons are as a rule of very moderate mental powers, and so the northern, cold-blooded, and phlegmatic nations are in general noticeably inferior in mind to the southern, vivacious, and passionate races; although, as Bacon has most strikingly observed,[6] when once a northerner is highly gifted by nature, he can reach a degree never attained by a southerner. Accordingly, it is as absurd as it is common to take the great minds of the different nations as the standard for comparing those nations' mental powers; for this is equivalent to trying to establish the rule through the exceptions. On the contrary, it is the great majority of every nation that we have to consider; for one swallow does not make a summer. It has still to be observed here that the very passionateness that is a condition of genius, and is bound up with the genius's vivid apprehension of things, produces in practical life, where the will comes into play, especially in sudden emergencies, so great an excitement of the emotions that it disturbs and confuses the intellect. The phlegmatic man, on the other hand, still retains the full use of his mental powers, although these are much more limited; and then he achieves far more with these than the greatest genius can. Accordingly, a passionate temperament is favourable to the original quality of the intellect; but a phlegmatic one is favourable to its use. Therefore genius proper is only for theoretical achievements, for which it can choose and bide

---

[5] From Goethe's *Miscellaneous Poems*. [Tr.]
[6] *De Augmentis Scientiarum*, Bk. vi, c. 3.

its time. This time will be precisely when the will is entirely at rest, and no wave disturbs the clear mirror of the world-view. Genius, on the other hand, is unqualified and unserviceable for practical life, and is therefore often unlucky and unhappy. Goethe's *Tasso* is written in this sense. Now just as genius proper rests on the *absolute* strength and vigour of the intellect, which must be paid for by a correspondingly excessive vehemence of disposition, so great pre-eminence in practical life, which makes generals and statesmen, rests on the *relative* strength of the intellect, on the highest degree of it which can be attained without too great an excitability of the emotions, together with too great a vehemence of character, and which therefore holds its own even in the storm. Here great firmness of will and imperturbability of mind, together with a capable and fine understanding, are sufficient; and what goes beyond this has a detrimental effect, for too great a development of intelligence stands right in the way of firmness of character and resoluteness of will. Accordingly this kind of eminence is not so abnormal, and is a hundred times less rare than that other; and so we see great generals and great ministers appear at all times, whenever external circumstances are favourable to their activity. On the other hand, great poets and philosophers are centuries in coming; yet humanity may rest content with even this rare appearance of them, for their works remain, and do not exist merely for the present, as do the achievements of those others. It is also wholly in accordance with the above-mentioned law of the parsimony of nature that she bestows intellectual eminence generally on extremely few, and genius only as the rarest of all exceptions. She equips the great mass of the human race, however, with no more mental powers than are required for the maintenance of the individual and the species. For the great needs of the human race are constantly increased by their very satisfaction, and make it necessary for the large majority to spend their lives in rough physical and wholly mechanical work. For what would be the use to such persons of a lively mind, a glowing imagination, a subtle understanding, or a profound and penetrating discrimination? Such qualities would merely make them misfits and unhappy. Nature has therefore dealt with the most precious of all her productions in the least extravagant way. In order not to judge unfairly, we should also definitely settle our expectations of the mental achievements of people generally from this point of view. For example, as even scholars have, as a rule, become such merely through external causes, we should regard them primarily as men who are really destined by nature for farming and wood-cutting. In fact, even professors of philosophy should be estimated according to this standard, and then their achievements will be found to come up to all reasonable expectations. It is noteworthy that in the south, where the cares of life weigh less heavily on the human race and more leisure is given it, the mental faculties even of the mob at once become more active and acute. Physiologically, it is remarkable that the preponderance of the mass of the brain over that of the spinal cord and nerves, which according to Sömmering's clever discovery affords the true and closest measure of the degree of intelligence both in animal species and in individual men, at the same time increases the direct mobility, the agility, of the limbs. For through the great inequality of the relation, the dependence of all the motor nerves on the brain becomes more decided. In addition to this, we have the fact that the cerebellum, that primary controller of movement, shares the qualitative perfection of the cerebrum. Therefore through both, all arbitrary movements gain greater facility, rapidity, and manageableness; and through the concentration of the starting-point of all activity there arises what Lichtenberg praises in Garrick, namely that "he appeared wholly present in the muscles of his body." Heaviness in the movement of the body, therefore, indicates heaviness in the movement of thoughts and ideas; and it is regarded as a sign of dulness and stupidity both in individuals and in nations, just as are flabbiness of the facial features and feebleness of the glance. Another symptom of the physiological facts of the case referred to is the circumstance that many people have at once to stand still, as soon as their conversation with anyone accompanying them begins to have some connexion. For as soon as their brain has to link a few ideas together, it no longer has as much force left over as is required to keep the legs in motion through the motor nerves; with them everything is so fine and close-cut.

The result of the whole of this objective consideration of the intellect and of its origin is the fact that it is designed for comprehending those ends on the attainment of which depend individual life and its propagation. But such an intellect is by no means destined to interpret the inner essence-in-itself of things and of the world, which exists independently of the knower. What susceptibility to light, in consequence of which it guides its growth in the direction of the light, is to the plant is the same in kind as knowledge to the animal, in fact even to man, although it is enhanced in degree in proportion as the needs of each of these beings demand. With all of them, perception or apprehension remains a mere awareness of their relation to other things, and is by no means intended to present once again the true, absolutely real inner nature of these things in the consciousness of the knower. On the contrary, as springing from the will, the intellect is designed for the will's service, and hence for the comprehension of motives; to this it is adapted, and so it is thoroughly practical in tendency. This also holds good in so far as we conceive the metaphysical significance of life as ethical; for in this sense too, we find man a knower only with a view to his conduct. Such a faculty of knowledge, existing exclusively for practical ends, will by its nature always comprehend only the relations of things to one another, not their inner nature as it is in itself. But to regard the complex of these relations as the inner being of the world, which exists absolutely and in itself, and the manner in which they necessarily exhibit themselves according to laws preformed in the brain as the eternal laws of the existence of all things, and then to construct ontology, cosmology, and theology on this pattern—all this was really the ancient fundamental error, which Kant's teaching brought to an end. Here, then, our consideration of the intellect, objective and thus for the most part physiological, meets *his* transcendental consideration; in fact, in a sense, it even appears as an *a priori* insight into it, since, from an external standpoint that we have taken, our objective consideration enables us to know genetically, and thus as *necessary,* what the transcendental consideration, starting from facts of consciousness, presents only as a matter of fact. For in consequence of our objective consideration of the intellect, the world as representation, as it exists extended in space and time and continues to move regularly according to the strict rule of causality, is primarily only a physiological phenomenon, a function of the brain that brings this about on the occasion of certain external stimuli, it is true, but yet in accordance with its own laws. Accordingly, it is already a matter of course that what goes on in this function itself, and consequently through it and for it, cannot possibly be regarded as the quality or nature of *things-in-themselves* that exist independently of and are entirely different from it; but primarily exhibits merely the mode and manner of this function itself. This can always receive only a very minor modification through that which exists wholly independent of it, and as stimulus sets it in motion. Accordingly, just as Locke claimed for the organs of sense all that comes into perception or apprehension by means of *sensation,* in order to deny it to things-in-themselves, so Kant, with the same purpose and pursuing the same path, showed everything that makes real *perception* possible, namely space, time, and causality, to be brain-function. He refrained, however, from using this physiological expression, to which our present method of consideration necessarily leads us, coming as it does from the opposite, the real side. On his analytical path, Kant reached the result that what we know is mere *phenomena*. What this puzzling expression really means becomes clear from our objective and genetic consideration of the intellect. The phenomena are the motives for the purposes and aims of an individual will, as they exhibit themselves in the intellect produced by the will for this purpose (this intellect itself *appears* objectively as brain); and when they are comprehended as far as we can follow their concatenation, they furnish in their continuity and sequence the world extending itself in time and space, which I call the world as representation. Moreover, from our point of view, the objectionable element to be found in the *Kantian* doctrine disappears. This element arises from the fact that, since the intellect knows mere phenomena instead of things as they are in themselves, and in fact in consequence of them is led astray into paralogisms and unfounded hypostases by means of "sophistications, not of persons but of reason itself, from which even the wisest cannot rid himself, and when perhaps after much effort he is able to prevent error, he can never get rid of the delusion that incessantly worries and mocks him"—this element, I say, makes it appear as if our intellect were intentionally designed to lead us into error. For the objective view of the intellect here given, which contains a genesis of it, makes it conceivable that, being destined exclusively for practical ends, the intellect is the mere *medium of motives*. Consequently, it fulfils its mission by correctly presenting these, and if we undertake to construct the true nature of things-in-themselves from the complex and conformity to law of the phenomena that objectively present themselves to us here, it is done at our own peril and on our own responsibility. Thus we have recognized that the inner force of nature, originally without knowledge and working in the dark, which, if it has worked its way up to self-consciousness, reveals itself thereto as *will,* reaches this stage only by the production of an animal brain and of knowledge as the function thereof, whereupon there arises in this brain the phenomenon of the world of perception. But to declare this mere brain-phenomenon, with the conformity to law that invariably belongs to its functions, to be the objective being-in-itself of the world and of the things in it—a being-in-itself that exists independently of this phenomenon, before it and after it—is obviously a leap that nothing warrants us in taking. From this *mundus phaenomenon,* however, from this perception arising under such a variety of conditions, all our concepts are drawn; they have all their content only from it, indeed only in relation to it. Therefore, as Kant says, they are only for immanent, not for transcendent use; in other words, these concepts of ours, this first material of thinking, and so still more the judgements resulting from their combination, are unsuitable for the task of reflecting on the inner essence of things-in-themselves and on the true connexion of the world and of existence. Indeed, to undertake this is analogous to expressing the cubical contents of a body in square inches. For our intellect, originally intended only to present to an individual will its paltry aims, accordingly comprehends mere *relations* of things, and does not penetrate to their inner being, their true nature. Accordingly it is a mere superficial force, clinging to the surface of things, and grasping mere *species transitivae*,[7] not their true being. The result is that we cannot understand and grasp a single thing, even the simplest and smallest, through and through, but in everything there is something left over that remains entirely inexplicable to us. Just because the intellect is a product of nature, and is therefore adapted only for her aims and ends, the Christian mystics have very aptly called it the "light of nature," and have kept it within bounds; for nature is the object to which it alone is the subject. The idea from which the *Critique of Pure Reason* sprang is really at the root of this expression. That we cannot comprehend the world on the direct path, in other words, through the uncritical, direct application of the intellect and its data, but are ever more deeply involved in insoluble riddles when we reflect on it, points to the fact that the intellect, and so knowledge itself, is already something secondary, a mere product. It is brought about by the development of the inner being of the world, which consequently till then preceded it; and it finally appeared as a breaking through into the light from the obscure depths of the striving without knowledge, and the true nature of such striving exhibits itself as *will* in the self-consciousness that simultaneously arises in this way. That which precedes knowledge as its condition, whereby that knowledge first of all became possible, and hence its own basis, cannot be immediately grasped by knowledge, just as the eye cannot see itself. On the contrary, the relations that exhibit themselves on the surface of things between one being and another are its sole concern, and are so only by means of the apparatus of the intellect, that is, its forms, time, space, causality. Just because the world has made itself without the aid of knowledge, its whole inner being does not enter into knowledge, but knowledge presupposes the existence of the world, and for this reason the origin of the world's existence does not lie within the province of knowledge. Accordingly, knowledge is limited to the relations between existing things, and is thus sufficient for the individual will, for whose service alone it arose. For, as has been shown,

---

[7] "Fleeting phenomena" [an expression of the scholastics. Tr.].

the intellect is conditioned by nature, resides therein, belongs thereto, and therefore cannot be set up in opposition to nature as something entirely foreign to it, in order thus to assimilate absolutely, objectively, and thoroughly nature's whole inner essence. With the help of good fortune, the intellect can understand everything *in* nature, but not nature itself, at any rate not immediately.

However discouraging for metaphysics this essential limitation of the intellect may be, resulting as it does from the intellect's nature and origin, there is yet another very consoling side to it. It deprives the direct utterances of nature of their unconditional validity, in the assertion of which *naturalism* proper consists. Thus nature presents to us every living thing as arising out of nothing, and, after an ephemeral existence, returning for ever into nothing again; and she seems to take a delight in ceaselessly creating afresh, in order to be able ceaselessly to destroy. On the other hand, she is unable to bring to light anything lasting or enduring. Accordingly we have to recognize *matter* as the only permanent thing, as that which never originated and never passes away, which brings forth everything from its womb; for this reason, its name seems to have come from *mater rerum*. Along with matter we have to recognize, as the father of things, *form,* which, just as fleeting as matter is permanent, really changes every moment, and can maintain itself only so long as it clings parasitically to matter (now to one part thereof, now to another). But when once form entirely loses its hold, it ceases to exist, as is testified by the palaeotherium and the ichthyosaurus. If we consider all this, we must indeed recognize it as the direct and genuine utterance of nature; but, on account of the origin of the intellect previously explained, and of the *nature of the intellect* that results from this origin, we cannot grant an *unconditional truth* to this utterance, but in general only a *conditional,* which Kant has strikingly indicated as such by calling it the *phenomenon* as opposed to the *thing-in-itself.*

If, in spite of this essential limitation of the intellect, it becomes possible in a roundabout way, by means of widely pursued reflection and by the ingenious connexion of outwardly directed objective knowledge with the data of self-consciousness, to arrive at a certain understanding of the world and the inner essence of things, this will nevertheless be only a very limited, entirely indirect, and relative understanding, a parabolic translation into the forms of knowledge, hence a *quadam prodire tenus,*[8] which must leave many problems still unsolved. On the other hand, the fundamental mistake of the old *dogmatism* in all its forms, which Kant destroyed, was that it

---

[8] "Advance up to a certain limit." [Tr.]

started absolutely *from knowledge,* i.e., *from the world as representation,* in order to deduce and construct being in general from the laws of knowledge. Such dogmatism took that world of the representation, together with its laws, to be something positively existing and absolutely real; whereas the whole existence of that world is fundamentally relative, and a mere result or phenomenon of the true being-in-itself that lies at its root; or in other words, dogmatism constructed an ontology where it had material only for a dianoiology. Kant discovered the subjectively conditioned, and thus positively immanent, nature of *knowledge,* in other words, its unsuitability for transcendent use, from this knowledge's own conformity to law. He therefore very appropriately called his teaching the *Critique of Reason.* He carried this out partly by showing the considerable and universally *a priori* portion of all knowledge, which, as being absolutely subjective, vitiates all objectivity; and partly by ostensibly proving that the principles of knowledge, taken as purely objective, led to contradictions when followed out to the end. But he had too hastily assumed that, apart from *objective* knowledge, in other words, apart from the world as *representation,* nothing is given to us except perhaps conscience. From this he constructed the little of metaphysics that still remained, namely moral theology, to which, however, he granted positively only a practical, certainly not a theoretical, validity. He had overlooked the fact that, although objective knowledge, or the world as representation, certainly affords nothing but phenomena, together with their phenomenal connexion and regressus, our own inner being nevertheless belongs of necessity to the world of things-in-themselves, since this inner being must be rooted in such a world. From this, however, even if the root cannot be directly brought to light, it must yet be possible to lay hold of some data for explaining the connexion between the world of phenomena and the being-in-itself of things. Here, therefore, lies the path on which I have gone beyond Kant and the limit he set. But in doing this, I have always stood on the ground of reflection, consequently of honesty, and hence without the vain pretension of intellectual intuition or absolute thought that characterizes the period of pseudo-philosophy between Kant and myself. In his proof of the inadequacy of rational knowledge for fathoming the inner nature of the world, Kant started from knowledge as a *fact* furnished by our consciousness; thus in this sense, he proceeded *a posteriori.* In this chapter, however, as well as in my work *On the Will in Nature,* I have tried to show what knowledge is according to its *essence and origin,* that is, something secondary destined for individual ends. From this it follows that knowledge is *bound to be* inadequate for fathoming the true nature of the world; and so to this extent I have reached the same goal *a priori*. But we do not know anything wholly and completely until we have gone right round it, and have arrived back at the starting-point from the other side. Therefore, in the case of the important fundamental knowledge considered here, we must also go not merely from intellect to knowledge of the world, as Kant did, but also, as I have undertaken to do here, from the world, taken as given, to the intellect. Then in the wider sense this physiological consideration becomes the supplement to that ideological, as the French say, or more accurately transcendental, consideration.

In order not to break the thread of the discussion, I have in the above remarks postponed the explanation of one point I have touched on. This was that, in proportion as the intellect appears more and more developed and complete in the ascending series of animals, *knowing* is more and more distinctly *separated from willing,* and thereby becomes purer. What is essential on this point is to be found in my work *On the Will in Nature* under the heading "Physiology of Plants" (pp. 68-72 of the second edition), and to that I refer, in order to avoid repetition; here I add only a few remarks. Since the plant possesses neither irritability nor sensibility, but in it the will objectifies itself only as plasticity or reproductive force, it has neither muscle nor nerve. At the lowest stages of the animal kingdom, in the zoophytes, especially the polyps, we are still unable to recognize distinctly the separation of these two constituent parts, yet we assume their existence, although in a state of fusion, since we perceive movements occurring, not on mere stimuli like those of the plant, but on motives, in other words, in consequence of a kind of perception or apprehension. Now in the ascending series of animals, the nervous and muscular systems *separate* ever more distinctly from each other, till in the vertebrates, and most completely in man, the nervous system is divided into an organic and a cerebral nervous system. This cerebral nervous system, again, is developed to the extremely complicated apparatus of the cerebrum and cerebellum, the spinal cord, cerebral and spinal nerves, sensory and motor nerve-fascicles. Of these only the cerebrum, together with the sensory nerves attached to it, and the posterior spinal nerve-fascicles are intended to *take up* the motives from the external world. All the other parts, on the other hand, are intended only to *transmit* the motives to the muscles in which the will directly manifests itself. Bearing the above separation in mind, we see the *motive separated* to the same extent more and more distinctly *in consciousness* from the *act of will* it calls forth, as is the *representation* from the *will*.

Now in this way the *objectivity* of consciousness is constantly increasing, since in it the representations exhibit themselves more and more distinctly and purely. However, the two *separations* are really only one and the same, considered here from two sides, the objective and the subjective, or first in the consciousness of other things and then in self-consciousness. On the degree of this separation ultimately depend the difference and gradation of the intellectual abilities between the various species of animals, as well as between individual human beings; hence it gives the standard for their intellectual perfection. For on it depends clearness of consciousness of the external world, the objectivity of perception. In the passage referred to above, I have shown that the animal perceives things only in so far as they are *motives* for its will, and that even the most intelligent animals scarcely go beyond this limit, since their intellect is still too firmly attached to the will from which it has sprung. On the other hand, even the stupidest person comprehends things to some extent *objectively,* since he recognizes in them not merely what they are with reference to him, but also something of what they are with reference to themselves and other things. Yet in the case of very few does this reach such a degree that they are able to examine and judge of anything purely objectively, but their goal is "This must I do, this must I say, this must I believe"; and on every occasion their thinking hurries in a straight line to this goal where their understanding at once finds welcome relaxation. For thinking is as intolerable to the feeble head as lifting a load is to the weak arm; both hasten to put it down. The objectivity of knowledge, and above all of knowledge of perception, has innumerable degrees, depending on the energy of the intellect and its separation from the will. The highest degree is *genius,* in which the comprehension of the external world becomes so pure and objective that to it even more is directly revealed in the individual things than these things themselves, namely the true nature of their whole *species,* i.e., their Platonic *Idea.* This is conditioned by the fact that the will here vanishes entirely from consciousness. This is the point where the present consideration, starting from physiological foundations, is connected with the subject of our third book, the metaphysics of the beautiful. Really aesthetic comprehension, in the higher degree peculiar only to genius, is fully considered there as the state or condition of pure, that is to say wholly will-less, knowledge, which on this account is completely objective. In accordance with what has been said, the enhancement of intelligence from the dullest animal consciousness to that of man is a progressive *loosening of the intellect from the will,* which appears complete, although only by way of exception, in *genius*. Genius can therefore be defined as the highest degree of the *objectivity* of knowledge. The condition for this, which exists so rarely, is a decidedly greater measure of intelligence than is required for the service of the will which constitutes its foundation. Accordingly, it is only this surplus or excess becoming free that really and truly becomes aware of the world, in other words, comprehends it perfectly *objectively,* and then paints, writes poetry, and thinks in accordance with this comprehension.

On the Objectification of the Will in Nature without Knowledge

The first step in the fundamental knowledge of my metaphysics is that the will we find within us does not, as philosophy previously assumed, proceed first of all from knowledge; that it is not, in fact, a mere modification of knowledge, and thus something secondary, derived, and, like knowledge itself, conditioned by the brain; but that it is the *prius* of knowledge, the kernel of our true being. The will is that primary and original force itself, which forms and maintains the animal body, in that it carries out that body's unconscious as well as conscious functions. Paradoxical as it appears to many even now that the will-in-itself is without knowledge, yet the scholastics already recognized and saw it to some extent, for Jul. Caes. Vaninus (that well-known victim of fanaticism and priestly wrath), who was thoroughly versed in their philosophy, says in his *Amphitheatrum,* p. 181; *Voluntas potentia caeca est, ex scholasticorum opinione.*[2] Further, it is the same will that in the plant forms the bud, in order to develop from it leaf or flower; in fact the regular form of the crystal is only the trace of its momentary striving left behind. Generally, as the true and only αὐτόματον in the proper sense of the word, it underlies all the forces of inorganic nature, plays and acts in all their manifold phenomena, endows their laws with force, and, even in the crudest mass, manifests itself as gravity. This insight is the second step in that fundamental knowledge, and is brought about by further reflection. It would, however, be the grossest of all misunderstandings to imagine that this is a question only of a *word* for denoting an unknown quantity. On the contrary, it is the most real of all real knowledge that is here expressed in language. For it is the tracing back of that which is wholly inaccessible to our immediate knowledge, hence of that which is essentially foreign and un-

---

[1] This chapter refers to § 23 of volume 1.

[2] "According to the view of the scholastics, the will is a blind power." [Tr.]

known to us, which we denote by the words *force of nature,* to that which is known to us most accurately and intimately, yet is immediately accessible to us only in our own inner being; it must therefore be transferred from this to other phenomena. It is the insight that what is inward and original in all the changes and movements of bodies, however varied and different they may be, is essentially identical; that we nevertheless have only *one* opportunity of becoming more closely and immediately acquainted with it, namely in the movements of our own body; and in consequence of this knowledge, we must call it *will.* It is the insight that what acts and drives in nature, and manifests itself in ever more perfect phenomena, after working itself up to such a height that the light of knowledge immediately falls on it—in other words, after getting as far as the state or condition of self-consciousness—now stands out as that *will.* It is the will which is what we know most intimately, and is therefore not to be explained further by anything else; on the contrary, it furnishes the explanation for all else. Accordingly, it is the *thing-in-itself,* in so far as this can in any way be reached by knowledge. Consequently, it is what must express itself in some way in everything in the world; for it is the true inner being of the world and the kernel of all phenomena.

As my essay *On the Will in Nature* is specially devoted to the subject of this chapter, and furnishes the evidence of unprejudiced empiricists for this principal point of my teaching, I have here to add only a few supplementary remarks to what was said in that work; and these are therefore strung together somewhat piecemeal.

First, therefore, in regard to plant life; I draw attention to the remarkable first two chapters of Aristotle's work on plants. As is so often the case with Aristotle, what is most interesting in them are the opinions of the earlier and profounder philosophers he quotes. There we see that Anaxagoras and Empedocles quite rightly taught that plants have the motion of their growth by virtue of their indwelling *desire* (ἐπιθυμία); in fact that they attributed to them even pleasure and pain, and consequently sensation. Plato, however, attributed to them *only desires,* and that on account of their appetite for nutrition (cf. *Timaeus,* p. 403 *Bip.*). On the other hand, true to his customary method, Aristotle glides over the surface of things, sticks to isolated characteristics and concepts fixed by current expressions, and asserts that there can be no desire without sensation, whereas plants have no sensation. However, as his confused words testify, he is considerably embarrassed, until here also "where concepts fail, a word appears on the scene at the right moment," namely τό θρεπτικόν, the faculty of nourishing. He asserts that plants have this, and hence a part of the so-called soul, according to his favourite division into *anima vegetativa, sensitiva, et intellectiva.* But this is just a scholastic *quidditas,* and says: *Plantae nutriuntur, quia habent facultatem nutritivam.*[3] Consequently it is a bad substitute for the deeper enquiry of his predecessors whom he criticizes. We see also in the second chapter that Empedocles had recognized even the sexuality of plants. Aristotle finds fault with this, and conceals his lack of real practical knowledge behind general principles, such as that plants could not have the two sexes in combination, for then they would be more complete than animals. By a wholly analogous procedure, he set aside the correct astronomical system of the universe propounded by the Pythagoreans; and by his absurd fundamental principles, explained in detail in his books *De Coelo,* he introduced the system of Ptolemy. In this way, mankind was once more deprived for almost two thousand years of an already discovered truth of the highest importance.

I cannot refrain from giving here the saying of an excellent biologist of our own time who fully agrees with my teaching: G. R. Treviranus, who in his work *Ueber die Erscheinungen und Gesetze des organischen Lebens* (1832, Vol. II, Part 1, p. 49), says: "A form of life is, however, conceivable where the effect of the external on the internal gives rise to mere feelings of inclination and aversion, and in consequence of these to *cravings* or *desires.* Such a form is *plant life.* In the higher forms of *animal* life the external is felt as something objective." Here Treviranus speaks from a pure and unprejudiced comprehension of nature, and is as little aware of the metaphysical importance of his utterance as he is of the *contradictio in adjecto* that lies in the concept of something "felt as objective," a thing that he even works out at great length. He does not know that all feeling is essentially subjective, and that everything objective is perception, and consequently a product of the understanding. But this does not detract from the truth and importance of his statement.

Indeed, the truth that the will can exist without knowledge is apparent, we might say palpably recognizable, in plant life. For in it we see a decided striving, determined by needs, modified in many different ways, and adapting itself to the variety of circumstances— yet clearly without knowledge. And just because the plant is without knowledge, it ostentatiously displays its organs of generation in complete innocence; it knows nothing of them. On the other hand, as soon as knowledge appears in the series of beings, the genitals are shifted to a concealed spot. But man, with whom this is less the case, covers them up deliberately; he is ashamed of them.

---

[3] "Plants are nourished, because they have a faculty of nourishing." [Tr.]

Primarily, therefore, the vital force is identical with the will; but so also are all the other forces of nature, though this is less apparent. Therefore, if we find the recognition of a desire, in other words of a will, as the basis of *plant life* expressed at all times with more or less distinctness of conception, then the reference of the forces of *inorganic* nature to the same foundation is rarer to the extent that their remoteness from our own inner being is greater. In fact, the boundary between the organic and the inorganic is the most sharply drawn in the whole of nature, and is probably the only one admitting of no transitions, so that here the saying *Natura non facit saltus*[4] seems to meet with an exception. Although many crystallizations display an external form resembling the vegetable, yet even between the smallest lichen, the lowest fungus, and everything inorganic there remains a fundamental and essential difference. In the *inorganic* body the essential and permanent element, that on which its identity and integrity rest, is the material, is *matter;* the inessential and changeable, on the other hand, is the *form.* With the *organic* body the case is the very opposite; for its life, in other words its existence as something organic, consists simply in the constant change of the *material* with persistence of the *form;* thus its essence and identity lie in the *form* alone. Therefore the *inorganic* body has its continued existence through *repose* and isolation from external influences; only in this way is its existence preserved; and if this state or condition is perfect, such a body lasts for ever. On the other hand, the *organic* body has its continued existence precisely through incessant *movement* and the constant reception of external influences. As soon as these cease, and movement in it comes to a standstill, it is dead, and thus ceases to be organic, although the trace of the organism that existed still for a while continues. Accordingly, the talk, so fashionable in our day, of the life of the inorganic, and even of the globe, and that this globe as well as the planetary system is an organism, is absolutely inadmissible. The predicate life belongs only to what is organic. However, every organism is organic through and through, is so in all its parts, and nowhere are these, even in their smallest particles, composed by aggregation from what is inorganic. Therefore, if the earth were an organism, all mountains and rocks and the whole interior of their mass would necessarily be organic. Properly speaking, therefore, absolutely nothing inorganic would exist; consequently, the whole conception of the inorganic would be wanting.

On the other hand, an essential point of my teaching is that the

---

[4] "Nature makes no jumps." [Law of continuity first propounded by Aristotle. Tr.]

phenomenal appearance of a *will* is as little tied to life and organization as it is to knowledge, and that therefore the inorganic also has a will, whose manifestations are all its fundamental qualities that are incapable of further explanation; although the trace of such an idea is to be found far more rarely in the writers who have preceded me than is that of the will in plants, where such a will is still without knowledge.

In the formation of the crystal we see, as it were, a tendency to life, an attempt thereat, though it does not attain to it, because the fluidity of which, like a living thing, it consists at the moment of that movement, is not enclosed in a *skin,* as with a living thing is always the case; accordingly, it does not have *vessels* in which that movement could continue, nor does anything separate it from the outside world. Therefore, coagulation at once seizes that momentary movement, of which only the trace remains as crystal.

Even Goethe's *Elective Affinities,* as its title itself indicates, although he was unaware of this, has as its foundation the idea that the *will,* which constitutes the basis of our own inner being, is the same will that manifests itself in the lowest, inorganic phenomena; for this reason, the conformity to law of both phenomena exhibits a complete analogy.

Mechanics and *astronomy* really show us how this *will* conducts itself in so far as it appears at the lowest stage of its phenomenon merely as gravity, rigidity, and inertia. *Hydraulics* shows us the same thing where rigidity is abolished, and the fluid material is abandoned without restraint to its prevailing passion, gravity. In this sense, hydraulics can be conceived as a description of the character of water, in that it states for us the manifestations of will to which water is moved by gravity. These always correspond exactly to the external influences, for in the case of all non-individual modes of existence, no particular character exists along with the general one; thus they can easily be referred to fixed fundamental characteristics, which we call laws, and learn by observing the experience of water. These laws state exactly how water will behave in different circumstances of every kind by reason of its weight, the unconditioned mobility of its parts, and its want of elasticity. Hydrostatics teaches how it is brought to rest through gravity; hydrodynamics, how it is set in motion. This last has to take into consideration also the hindrances that adhesion opposes to the will of the water; the two together constitute *hydraulics.* In the same way, *chemistry* teaches us how the will behaves when the inner qualities of the elements obtain free play through the bringing about of a state of fluidity. There now appear that wonderful seeking and shunning, separating and combining, the giving up of one thing in order to seize another, that is testified by every precipitate, and all this is expressed as *elective affinity* (an expression borrowed entirely from the conscious will). But *anatomy* and *physiology* enable us to see how the will behaves, in order to bring about the phenomenon of life and maintain it for a while. Finally, the *poet* shows us how the will conducts itself under the influence of motives and of reflection. Therefore he generally exhibits it in the most perfect of its phenomena, rational beings, whose character is individual, and whose actions and sufferings he presents as drama, epic, romance, and so on. The more correct, the more strictly in accordance with the laws of nature, the presentation of his characters proves to be, the greater is his fame; hence Shakespeare stands at the head. The point of view here adopted corresponds at bottom to the spirit in which Goethe pursued and loved the natural sciences, although he was not conscious of the matter in the abstract. I know this from his personal statements even more than it appears from his works.

If we consider the will where no one denies it, namely in knowing beings, we find everywhere, as its fundamental effort, the *self-preservation* of every being: *Omnis natura vult esse conservatrix sui.*[5] But all manifestations of this fundamental effort can always be traced back to a seeking or pursuing, an avoiding, shunning, or fleeing, according to the occasion. This can still be demonstrated even at the lowest of all the stages of nature, and hence of the objectification of the will, namely where bodies still act only as bodies in general, that is, where they are the objects of *mechanics,* and are considered merely according to their manifestations of impenetrability, cohesion, rigidity, elasticity, and weight. Here also the *seeking* shows itself as gravitation, the *fleeing* as reception of motion; and the *mobility* of bodies by pressure or impact, which constitutes the basis of mechanics, is at bottom a manifestation of the effort after *self-preservation* which dwells also in them. Since as bodies they are impenetrable, this is the sole means of preserving their cohesion, and so their continued existence in each case. The body that is pushed or pressed would be pulverized by what pushes or presses it, if it did not withdraw itself from its power through flight, in order to preserve its cohesion; and where it is deprived of flight, this actually happens. In fact, we can regard *elastic* bodies as the *more courageous,* which try to repel the enemy, or at least to deny him further pursuit. Thus we see in the only secret which (apart from gravity) is left by mechanics, which is otherwise so clear, namely the communicability of motion, a manifestation of the

---

[5] "Every being in nature endeavours to preserve itself." [Tr.]

will's fundamental effort in all its phenomena, the impulse to self-preservation, which shows itself as the essential element even at the lowest stage.

In inorganic nature the will objectifies itself primarily in the universal forces, and only by their means in the phenomena of individual things brought about by causes. In § 26 of volume one I adequately explained the relation between cause, force of nature, and will as thing-in-itself. It is seen from this that metaphysics never interrupts the course of physics, but only takes up the thread where physics leaves it, that is, at the original forces in which all causal explanation has its limits. Only here begins the metaphysical explanation from the will as thing-in-itself. In the case of every physical phenomenon, every *change* of material things, its *cause* is first of all to be indicated, and this is just such a particular *change* appearing immediately before it. Then the original *force of nature,* by virtue of which this cause was capable of acting, is to be indicated; and the *will* is to be recognized primarily as this force's being-in-itself, in contrast to its phenomenon. Yet the will proclaims itself just as directly in the fall of a stone as in the action of man. The difference is only that its particular manifestation is brought about in the one case by a motive, in the other by a mechanically acting cause, e.g., the removal of the stone's support, yet in both cases with equal necessity; and that in the one case it depends on an individual character, in the other on a universal force of nature. This identity of what is fundamentally essential even becomes obvious when, for instance, we attentively observe a body that has lost its equilibrium. By virtue of its special shape, it rolls backwards and forwards for a long time, till it again finds its centre of gravity; a certain appearance of life then forces itself on us, and we feel directly that something analogous to the basis of life is active here also. This, of course, is the universal force of nature, which, in itself identical with the *will,* becomes here, so to speak, the soul of a very brief quasi-life. Thus what is identical in the two extremes of the will's phenomenon makes itself faintly known even to direct perception, since this raises a feeling in us that here also something entirely original, such as we know only from the acts of our own will, attains directly to the phenomenon.

We can arrive at an intuitive knowledge of the existence and activity of the will in inorganic nature in quite a different and majestic way, if we carefully study the problem of the three bodies, and therefore become somewhat more accurately and specially acquainted with the course of the moon round the earth. Through the different combinations produced by the constant change of the position of these three heavenly bodies relative to one another, the course of the moon is now accelerated, now retarded, and now approaches, now recedes from the earth. Again, this is different at the perihelion of the earth from what it is at the aphelion; and all this together introduces such an irregularity into the moon's course, that it acquires a really capricious appearance, since even Kepler's second law no longer remains constantly valid, but the moon sweeps out unequal areas in equal times. The consideration of this course is a small and separate chapter of celestial mechanics. Such mechanics differs from the terrestrial in a sublime way by the absence of all impact and pressure, and hence of the *vis a tergo*[6] which appears so intelligible to us, and even of the actually completed case, since besides the *vis inertiae*[7] it knows no other moving and directing force but gravitation, that longing of bodies for union which emerges from their true inner being. Now if in this given case we picture to ourselves down to the smallest detail the working of gravitation, we recognize distinctly and directly in the force that moves here just that which is given to us in self-consciousness as will. For the alterations in the course of the earth and the moon, according as one of them is by its position now more, now less exposed to the sun's influence, have an obvious analogy to the influence of newly appearing motives on the will, and to the modifications of our action according to them.

The following is an illustrative example of another kind. Liebig (*Chemie in Anwendung auf Agrikultur,* p. 501), says: "If we bring damp copper into air containing carbonic acid, the affinity of the metal for the oxygen of the air is raised by contact with this acid to such a degree that the two combine with each other. The surface of the copper is covered with green carbonic oxide of copper. But two bodies which have the capacity to combine assume opposite states of electricity the moment they come in contact with each other. Therefore, if we touch the copper with iron by arousing a particular state of electricity, the capacity of the copper to enter into combination with the oxygen is destroyed; even under the above conditions it remains bright." The fact is well known and of use in technology. I quote it, in order to say that here the will of the copper, claimed and preoccupied by the electrical opposition to the iron, leaves unused the opportunity that presents itself for its chemical affinity for oxygen and carbonic acid. Accordingly, it behaves exactly as the will does in a person who abstains from an action to which

---

[6] "Force impelling from behind." [Tr.]

[7] "Force of inertia." [Tr.]

he would otherwise feel moved, in order to perform another to which he is urged by a stronger motive.

In volume one I have shown that the forces of nature lie outside the chain of causes and effects, since they constitute their universal condition, their metaphysical foundation. They therefore prove to be eternal and omnipresent, in other words independent of time and space. Even in the undisputed truth that the essential point of a *cause,* as such, consists in its producing at any future time the same effect as it does now, there is already contained the fact that there lies in the cause something independent of the course of time, something outside all time; this is the force of nature that manifests itself therein. We can even convince ourselves, to a certain extent empirically and as a matter of fact, of the mere *ideality* of this form of our perception by fixing our eye on the powerlessness of *time* in face of the forces of nature. For example, if by some external cause a planet is put into a rotatory motion, this will go on for ever if no new cause comes along to stop it. This could not be so if time were something in itself, and had an objective, real existence; for then it would inevitably produce some effect. Therefore we here see that the forces of nature, which manifest themselves in that rotation, and when once it is begun continue it for ever, without themselves growing weary or dying out, prove to be eternal or timeless, and thus positively real and existing in themselves. On the other hand, we see *time* as something that consists in the mode and manner in which *we* apprehend that phenomenon, since it exerts no power and no influence on the phenomenon itself; for that which does not *act,* likewise does not *exist.*

We have a natural tendency to explain, whenever possible, every natural phenomenon *mechanically,* doubtless because mechanics calls in the assistance of the fewest original, and therefore inexplicable, forces, and again because it contains much which is *a priori* knowable and therefore depends on the forms of our intellect. That which is *a priori* knowable, precisely as such, carries with it the highest degree of intelligibility and clearness. However, in the *Metaphysical Rudiments of Natural Science,* Kant traces mechanical activity itself back to a dynamic activity. On the other hand, the application of mechanical hypotheses of explanation beyond the demonstrably mechanical, to which acoustics, for example, still belongs, is entirely unjustified, and I shall never believe that even the simplest chemical combination, or even the difference of the three states of aggregation, will ever be capable of mechanical explanation, much less the properties of light, heat, and electricity. These will always admit of only a dynamic explanation, in other words, of one that explains the phenomenon from original forces entirely different from those of impact, pressure, weight, and so on, and thus of a higher order, that is to say, most distinct objectifications of the will that attains to visibility in all things. I am of the opinion that light is neither an emanation nor a vibration; both views are akin to that which explains transparency from pores, the obvious falsity of which proves that light is not amenable to any mechanical laws. To obtain the most direct conviction of this, we need only look at the effects of a strong gale, which bends, upsets, and scatters everything, but during which a ray of light shooting down from a gap in the clouds stands out entirely unmoved and is firmer than a rock. Thus it directly proclaims that it belongs to an order of things other than the mechanical; it stands there motionless like a ghost. But the constructions of light from molecules and atoms which have come from the French are a revolting absurdity. We can regard as a flagrant expression of this absurdity, as of the whole atomistic theory in general, an article by Ampère, otherwise so clear-sighted, on light and heat to be found in the issue of the *Annales de chimie et de physique* for April 1835. There the solid, fluid, and elastic consist of the same atoms, and all differences spring solely from their aggregation. In fact, it is said that space is infinitely divisible, but not matter, because, if the division has been carried as far as the atoms, further division must fall into the spaces between the atoms! Light and heat, then, are vibrations of atoms; sound, on the other hand, is a vibration of the molecules compounded from the atoms. But in truth the atoms are a fixed idea of French savants, who therefore talk about them just as if they had seen them. Besides, we cannot help marvelling that such a matter-of-fact nation, holding such empirical views, as the French, can stick so firmly to a wholly transcendent hypothesis that soars beyond all possibility of experience, and confidently build on it at random. This is just a consequence of the backward state of the metaphysics which they avoid so much, and which is poorly represented by M. Cousin. In spite of his good will, this man is superficial and very scantily endowed with power of judgement. Fundamentally they are still followers of Locke through the earlier influence of Condillac. To them, therefore, the *thing-in-itself* is really *matter,* from whose fundamental properties, such as impenetrability, form, shape, hardness, and the other primary qualities, everything in the world must be ultimately capable of explanation. They will not be talked out of this, and their tacit assumption is that matter can be moved by mechanical forces alone. In

Germany Kant's teaching has prevented the continuance of the absurdities of the atomistic and purely mechanical physics, although even here, at the present moment, such views prevail. This is a consequence of the shallowness, lack of culture and of knowledge brought about by Hegel. It is undeniable, however, that not only the obviously porous nature of natural bodies, but also two special doctrines of modern physics, have apparently supported the atomic mischief. Thus Hauy's crystallography, which traces every crystal back to its kernel-form that is something ultimate, yet only *relatively* indivisible; and Berzelius's doctrine of *chemical* atoms, which are nevertheless mere expressions of the ratios of combination, and thus only arithmetical quantities, and at bottom nothing more than counters. On the other hand, Kant's thesis in the second antinomy, set up, of course, only for dialectical purposes and in defence of atoms, is, as I have demonstrated in the criticism of his philosophy, a mere sophism; and our understanding itself certainly does not lead us necessarily to the assumption of atoms. For I am not obliged to think of the slow but constant and uniform *motion* of a body, which occurs in my presence, as consisting of innumerable motions that are absolutely rapid, but are broken off and interrupted by just as many absolutely short moments of rest. On the contrary, I know quite well that the stone that is thrown flies more slowly, of course, than the projected bullet, but that on its path it does not rest for a moment. In just the same way, I am no more obliged to think of the mass of a body as consisting of atoms and of the spaces between them, in other words, of absolute density and absolute vacuum, but I comprehend without difficulty those two phenomena as constant *continua,* one of which *uniformly fills time,* and the other *space.* But just as *one* motion can be *quicker* than another, in other words, run through more space in equal time, so can one body be specifically heavier than another, in other words, contain more matter in equal space. In both cases, the difference depends on the intensity of the operating force, for Kant (after the example of Priestley) has quite rightly reduced matter to forces. But even if we did not admit as valid the analogy here set up, but tried to insist that the difference of specific gravity can always have its ground only in porosity, then this assumption would still not lead to atoms, but only to a perfectly dense matter unequally distributed in different bodies. Therefore this matter could certainly not be further *compressed,* where pores no longer run through it, yet, like the space it fills, it would always remain infinitely *divisible.* For the fact that it would be without pores certainly does not mean that no possible force could do away with the continuity of its spatial parts. It is an entirely arbitrary assertion to say that this is everywhere possible only by extending the already existing interstices.

The assumption of atoms rests on the two phenomena mentioned, namely the difference of the specific gravity of bodies, and that of their compressibility, as both are conveniently explained by the assumption of atoms. But then both would also have to be present in equal measure; which is by no means the case. Water, for instance, has a far lower specific gravity than have all the metals properly so called; it would therefore necessarily have fewer atoms and greater interstices between them, and so would inevitably be very compressible; but it is almost entirely incompressible.

The defence of atoms could be conducted by our starting from porosity and saying something like this: all bodies have pores, and so too have all the parts of a body; if this were continued to infinity, then there would ultimately be nothing left of a body but pores. The refutation would be that what remained would certainly have to be assumed as without pores, and to this extent as absolutely dense, yet still not on that account as consisting of absolutely indivisible particles or atoms. Nevertheless it would be absolutely incompressible, but not absolutely indivisible; for we should have to try to assert that the division of a body is possible only by penetrating into its pores; but this is entirely unproved. Yet if we assume it, then, of course, we have atoms, in other words, absolutely indivisible bodies, that is, bodies with such strong cohesion of their spatial parts that no possible power can separate them. But then we can just as well assume such bodies to be large as small, and an atom might be as large as an ox, if only it resisted every possible attack.

Imagine two extremely heterogeneous bodies rendered entirely free from all pores by compression, say by means of hammering or by pulverization; would their specific gravity then be the same? This would be the criterion of dynamics.

CHAPTER XXIV

On Matter

Matter was discussed in chapter 4 of the supplements to the first book, when we were considering that part of our knowledge of which we are *a priori* conscious. Yet it could be considered there only from a one-sided point of view, because we had in mind its relation merely to the forms of the intellect, not to the thing-in-itself. Consequently we investigated it only from the subjective side, in so far as it is our representation, and not from the objective side, according to what it may be in itself. In the first respect, our conclusion was that it is *activity* in general, conceived objectively yet without further definition; therefore it occupies the position of *causality* in the table of our *a priori* knowledge given in that chapter. For what is material is that which *acts* (the actual) in general, apart from the specific nature of its acting. Therefore, merely as such, matter is not an object of *perception,* but only of *thinking,* and is thus really an abstraction. On the other hand, it occurs in perception only in combination with form and quality, as body, in other words, as a quite definite mode of acting. Only by abstracting from this closer determination do we think of *matter* as such, that is to say, as separated from form and quality. Consequently, under matter we think of *acting* positively and in general, and hence of *activity* in the abstract. We then comprehend the more closely *determined* acting as the *accident* of matter; only by means of this accident does matter become *perceptible,* in other words, exhibit itself as body and object of experience. Pure matter, on the other hand, which alone, as I have shown in the Criticism of the Kantian Philosophy, constitutes the actual and legitimate content of the concept *substance,* is *causality* itself, thought of objectively, consequently as in space, and therefore as filling space. Accordingly, the whole essence of matter consists in *acting;* only through this does it fill space and endure in time; it is through and through pure causality. Therefore wherever there is action there is matter, and the material is in general that which acts. But causality itself is the form of our *understanding,* for we are conscious of it *a priori,* just as we are of space and time. Therefore matter, *so far* and up to this point, belongs also to the *formal* part of our knowledge, and is accordingly the understanding's form of *causality* itself, a form that is combined with space and time, and thus objectified, in other words, conceived as that which fills space. (The fuller explanation of this doctrine is found in the second edition of the essay *On the Principle of Sufficient Reason,* p. 77.) So far, however, matter is, properly speaking, not the *object* but the *condition* of experience, just as is the pure understanding itself, whose function to this extent it is. Of pure matter, therefore, there is only a concept, no perception; it enters into every external experience as a necessary constituent part thereof; yet it cannot be given in any experience; on the contrary, it is only *thought,* and thought indeed as what is absolutely inert, inactive, formless, and without qualities, but is nevertheless the supporter of all forms, qualities, and effects. Accordingly, of all fleeting phenomena, and so of all the manifestations of natural forces and all living beings, matter is the permanent *substratum,* necessarily produced by the forms of our intellect, in which the world as *representation* exhibits itself. As such, and as having sprung from the forms of the intellect, its behaviour towards those phenomena themselves is one of absolute *indifference,* that is to say, it is just as ready to be the supporter of one natural force as of another, whenever under the guidance of causality the conditions for this have appeared. On the other hand, matter itself, just because its existence is really only *formal,* in other words, is grounded in the *intellect,* must be conceived as that which under all that change endures and persists absolutely, hence as that which is without beginning and end in time. This is why we cannot give up the idea that anything can come out of anything, for example gold out of lead, since this would merely require that we should find out and bring to pass the intermediate states that matter, in itself indifferent, would have to pass through on that path. For *a priori,* we can never see why the same matter that is now the supporter of the quality lead might not one day become the supporter of the quality gold. Matter, as what is merely *thought a priori,* is indeed distinguished from the *a priori intuitions or perceptions* proper by the fact that we are able to think it away entirely, but space and time we are never able to think away. But this means simply that we can form a mental picture or representation of space and time even without matter. For the matter that is once put into them, and is accordingly conceived as *existing,* can no longer be absolutely thought away by us, in other words, pictured by us as having vanished and been annihilated; on the contrary, we can always picture it only as moved into another space. Therefore to this extent matter is connected with our faculty of knowledge just as inseparably as are space and time themselves. Yet the difference that matter must first be voluntarily posited as existing, in itself indicates that it does not belong so entirely and in every respect to the *formal* part of our knowledge as do space and time, but that simultaneously it contains an element that is given only *a posteriori*. In fact, it is the point of connexion of the empirical part of our knowledge with the pure and *a priori* part, and consequently the special and characteristic foundation-stone of the world of experience.

Only where all *a priori* assertions cease, and consequently in the *entirely empirical* part of our knowledge of bodies, hence in their form, quality, and definite mode of acting, does that *will* reveal itself which we have already recognized and established as the being-in-itself of things. But these forms and qualities always appear only as properties and manifestations of that *matter,* whose existence and essence depend on the subjective forms of our intellect; in other words, they become visible only in it, and so by means of it. For whatever exhibits itself to us is always only *matter* acting in some specially determined way. Every definite mode of acting of given bodies results from the inner properties of such matter, properties incapable of further explanation; and yet matter itself is never perceived, only those effects and the definite properties that underlie them. After the separation and setting aside of those properties, matter, as what still remains over, is necessarily added by us in thought; for, in accord with the explanations given above, it is objectified *causality* itself. Consequently, matter is that whereby the *will,* which constitutes the inner essence of things, enters into perceptibility, becomes perceptible or *visible*. Therefore in this sense matter is the mere visibility of the will, or the bond between the world as will and the world as representation. It belongs to the *latter* in so far as it is the product of the intellect's functions; to the *former,* in so far as that which manifests itself in all material beings, i.e., in phenomena, is the *will*. Therefore, every object as thing-in-itself is will, and as phenomenon is matter. If we could divest any given matter of all properties that come to it *a priori,* in other words, of all the forms of our perception and apprehension, we should be left with the thing-in-itself, that which, by means of those forms, appears as the purely empirical in matter, but would then itself no longer appear as something extended and acting; that is to say, we should no longer have before us any matter, but the will. This very thing-in-itself, or the will, by becoming the phenomenon, by entering the forms of our intellect, appears as *matter,* that is to say, as the supporter, itself invisible but necessarily assumed, of properties visible only through it. Therefore in this sense, matter is the visibility of the *will*. Accordingly, Plotinus and Giordano Bruno were right, not in their sense only but also in ours, when they made the paradoxical statement already mentioned in chapter 4, that matter itself is not extended, and consequently is incorporeal. For space, which is our form of intuition or perception, endows matter with extension, and corporeality consists in acting, and acting depends on causality, consequently on the form of our understanding. On the other hand, every definite quality or property, and thus everything empirical in matter, even gravity, rests on that which becomes visible only *by means of* matter, on the thing-in-itself, on the will. But gravity is the lowest of all the grades of the will's objectification; it therefore shows itself in *all* matter without exception; thus it is inseparable from matter in general. Yet, just because it is already manifestation of will, it belongs to knowledge *a posteriori,* not to knowledge *a priori.* Therefore, we can perhaps picture matter to ourselves without weight, but not without extension, force of repulsion, and persistence; for it would then be without impenetrability, and consequently without space-occupation, that is to say, without the *power of acting.* But the essence of matter, as such, consists precisely in *acting,* that is to say, in causality in general; and causality rests on the *a priori* form of our understanding, and therefore cannot be thought away.

Accordingly, matter is the *will* itself, yet no longer in itself, but in so far as it is *perceived,* that is to say, assumes the form of the objective representation; thus what objectively is matter, subjectively is will. Wholly in keeping with this, as was shown above, our body is only the visibility, the objectivity of our will; and in just the same way, each body is the objectivity of the will at one of its stages. As soon as the will exhibits itself to objective knowledge, it enters into the intellect's forms of perception, into time, space, and causality. But it at once stands out as a *material* object by virtue of these forms. We can picture to ourselves form without matter, but not matter without form, because matter, divested of form, would be the *will* itself. The will, however, becomes objective only by entering our intellect's mode of perception, and therefore only by means of the assumption of *form.* Space is the perception-form of matter, because space is the substance (*Stoff*) of mere form, but matter can appear only in the form.

Since the will becomes objective, that is to say, passes over into the representation, matter is the universal substratum of this objectification, or rather the objectification itself taken in the abstract, that is, apart from all form. Matter is accordingly the *visibility* of the will in general, whereas the character of its definite phenomena has its expression in *form* and quality. Hence that which in the phenomenon, in other words for the representation, is *matter,* is in itself *will.* Therefore, under the conditions of experience and perception, everything holds good of it that holds good of the will in itself, and it gives again in the image of time all the relations and properties of the will. Accordingly it is the *substance* of the world of perception, just as the *will* is the being-in-itself of all things. The shapes and forms are innumerable: matter is one, just as the will is one in all its objectifications. Just as the will never objectifies itself as something general, in other words, as will absolutely, but always as something particular, that is to say, under special determinations and a given character, so matter never appears as such, but always in combination with some particular form and quality. In the phenomenon or objectification of the will, matter represents the totality and entirety of the will, the will itself that in all things is one, just as matter in all bodies is one. Just as the will is the innermost kernel of all phenomenal beings, so is matter the substance left over after the elimination of all accidents. Just as the will is the absolutely indestructible in all that exists, so is matter that which is imperishable in time and endures through all changes. That matter by itself, separated from form, cannot be perceived or represented, rests on the fact that, in itself and as that which is the purely substantial of bodies, it is really the *will* itself. But the will cannot be apprehended objectively or perceived in itself, but only under all the conditions of the *representation,* and thus only as *phenomenon.* Under these conditions, however, it exhibits itself forthwith as body, that is, as matter clothed in form and quality; but form is conditioned by space, and quality or activity by causality; and so both rest on the functions of the intellect. Matter without them would be just the thing-in-itself, i.e., the will itself. Therefore, as has been said, Plotinus and Giordano Bruno could only be brought on the completely objective path to the assertion that matter in and by itself is without extension, consequently without spatiality, and hence without corporeality.

Therefore, since matter is the visibility of the will, and every force in itself is will, no force can appear without a material substratum, and conversely no body can exist without forces dwelling in it which constitute its quality. Thus a body is the union of matter and form which is called substance (*Stoff*). Force and substance are inseparable, because at bottom they are one; for, as Kant has shown, matter itself is given to us only as the union of two forces, that of expansion and that of attraction. Therefore there exists no opposition between force and substance; on the contrary, they are precisely one.

Led by the course of our consideration to this standpoint and having arrived at this metaphysical view of matter, we shall readily confess that the temporal *origin* of forms, shapes, or species cannot reasonably be sought elsewhere than in matter. At one time they must have burst forth from matter, just because it is the mere *visibility of the will* that constitutes the being-in-itself of all phenomena. Since the will becomes phenomenon, that is to say, *objectively* exhibits itself to the intellect, matter, as its visibility, assumes *form* by means of the functions of the intellect. Therefore the scholastics said: *Materia appetit formam.*[1] That such was the origin of all forms of living things is not to be doubted; we cannot even conceive it otherwise. But whether even now, as the paths to perpetuating the forms are open, and are secured and maintained by nature with boundless care and eagerness, *generatio aequivoca* takes place, is to be decided only by experience, especially since the saying *natura nihil facit frustra*[2] might be used as a valid argument against it with reference to the paths of regular propagation. Yet, despite the most recent objections to it, I regard *generatio aequivoca* as extremely probable at very low stages, and above all in the case of entozoa and epizoa, particularly those which appear in consequence of special cachexia of the animal organisms. For the conditions for their life occur only by way of exception; thus their form cannot propagate itself in the regular way, and therefore has to arise anew when the opportunity offers. Therefore, as soon as the conditions for life of epizoa have appeared, as a result of certain chronic diseases or cachexia, there arise according to them, entirely automatically and without any egg, *pediculus capitis,* or *pubis,* or *corporis,* however complicated the structure of these insects may be. For the putrefaction of a living animal body affords material for higher productions than those of hay in water, which gives rise only to infusoria. Or do we prefer to think even that the eggs of the epizoa are constantly floating about in the air full of hope? (Terrible thought!) Let us rather call to mind the disease of phthiriasis, which is found even now. An analogous case occurs when, through special circumstances, the life-conditions appear for a species that was till then foreign to the *locality.* Thus in Brazil, August Saint-Hilaire, after the burning of a primeval forest, saw a number of plants grow up out of the ashes, as soon as they had become cool; and far and wide this species of plant was not to be found. Quite recently, Admiral Petit-Thouars informed the *Académie des Sciences* that on the newly forming coral

---

[1] "Matter strives for form." [Tr.]

[2] "Nature does nothing in vain." [Tr.]

islands in Polynesia a soil is being gradually deposited, now dry, now lying in water. Vegetation at once takes possession of this soil, producing trees that are quite exclusively peculiar to these islands (*Comptes Rendus,* 17 Jan. 1859, p. 147). Wherever putrefaction occurs, mould, fungi, and, in liquids, infusoria appear. The assumption, now in favour, that spores and eggs of the innumerable species of all those kinds of animal are floating everywhere in the air, waiting long years for a favourable opportunity, is more paradoxical than that of *generatio aequivoca.* Putrefaction is the decomposition of an organic body first into its *more immediate* chemical constituents. Now since in all living beings these are more or less of the same nature, the omnipresent will-to-live can at such a moment take possession of them, in order, according to the circumstances, to produce new beings from them. Forming and shaping themselves appropriately, in other words, objectifying the will's volition in each case, these new beings coagulate out of the chemical constituents just as the chicken does out of the fluid part of the egg. But if this does not take place, the putrefying substances are decomposed into their *more remote* constituent parts which are the chemical elements, and they then pass over into the great circulation of nature. The war that has been waged for the last ten or fifteen years against *generatio aequivoca,* with its premature shouts of victory, was the prelude to the denial of vital force, and is related thereto. But let us not be deceived by dogmatic utterances and brazen assurances that these matters are decided, settled, and generally admitted. On the contrary, the entire mechanical and atomistic view of nature is approaching bankruptcy, and its advocates have to learn that something more is concealed behind nature than thrust and counter-thrust. The reality of *generatio aequivoca* and the unreality of the fantastic assumption that everywhere and always in the atmosphere billions of seeds of all possible fungi and eggs of all possible infusoria are floating about, until first one and then another by chance finds the medium suitable to it, have been thoroughly and triumphantly demonstrated quite recently (1859) by Pouchet before the French Academy, to the great annoyance of its other members.

Our astonishment at the idea of the origination of forms from matter is at bottom like that of the savage who looks in a mirror for the first time, and marvels at his own image facing him. For our own inner nature is the *will,* the mere *visibility* whereof is matter. Yet matter never appears otherwise than with the *visible,* that is to say, under the veil of form and quality; therefore it is never immediately apprehended, but is always only added in thought as that which is identical in all things under every variety of quality and form, as that which is precisely substantial, properly speaking, in all of them. For this reason, it is rather a metaphysical than a merely physical principle of explanation of things, and to represent all beings as springing from it is really equivalent to explaining them by something that is very mysterious. This is recognized as such by all except those who confuse undertaking something with understanding it. In truth, the ultimate and exhaustive explanation of things is by no means to be looked for in matter; but of course the temporal origin of both inorganic forms and organic beings is certainly to be sought in it. But it seems that the original generation of organic forms, the production of the species themselves, is almost as difficult for nature to effect as for us to comprehend. This is indicated by nature's entirely extravagant provision for the maintenance of the species that now exist. Yet on the present surface of this planet the will-to-live has played through the scale of its objectification three times, quite independently of one another, in a different mode, but also in very varied perfection and completeness. Thus, as is well known, the Old World, America, and Australia have each its own characteristic series of animals, independent of and entirely different from those of the other two. On each of these great continents the species are different in every way; but yet they have a thorough analogy with one another which runs parallel through them, since all three belong to the same planet; therefore the *genera* are for the most part the same. In Australia this analogy can be followed only very imperfectly, since its fauna is very poor in mammalia, and has neither beasts of prey nor apes. On the other hand, between the Old World and America this analogy is obvious, in fact in such a way that in mammalia America shows always the worse analogue, but in birds and reptiles the better. Thus it certainly has the advantage in the condor, the macaw, the humming-bird, and in the largest amphibians and reptiles; on the other hand, it has, for example, only the tapir instead of the elephant, the puma instead of the lion, the jaguar instead of the tiger, the llama instead of the camel, and only long-tailed monkeys instead of apes proper. It may be concluded from this last defect that in America nature was unable to rise to the production of man; for even from the nearest stage below man, namely the chimpanzee and the orang-utan or pongo, the step to man was exceedingly great. In keeping with this, we find that the three races of men, which on physiological as well as on linguistic grounds are not to be doubted and are equally original, namely the Caucasian, the Mongolian, and the Ethiopian, are at home only in the Old World. America, on the other hand, is populated by a mixed or climatically modified Mongolian race that must have come over from Asia. On the surface of the earth which immediately preceded the present surface, nature in places got as far as apes, but not as far as man.

From this standpoint of our consideration, which enables us to recognize matter as the immediate visibility of the will appearing in all things, and even regards matter as the origin of things for the merely physical investigation that follows the guidance of time and causality, we are easily led to the question whether, even in philosophy, we could not just as well start from the objective as from the subjective side, and accordingly set up as the fundamental truth the proposition: "In general there is nothing but matter and the forces inherent in it." But with these "inherent forces," here spoken of so readily, it must at once be remembered that to assume them reduces every explanation to a wholly incomprehensible miracle, and then lets it stop at this, or rather begin from it. For every definite and inexplicable force of nature, lying at the root of the different kinds of effects of an inorganic body, no less than the vital force that manifests itself in every organic body, is indeed such an incomprehensible miracle. I have fully explained this in chapter 17, and have there shown that physics can never be set on the throne of metaphysics, just because it leaves the assumption mentioned, and also many others, quite untouched. In this way it renounces at the outset the claim to give the ultimate explanation of things. Further, I must remind the reader of the proof of the inadmissibility of materialism given towards the end of chapter 1, in so far as materialism, as stated in that chapter, is the philosophy of the subject who forgets himself in his calculation. But all these truths rest on the fact that everything *objective,* everything external, as it is always only something apprehended, something known, always remains only indirect and secondary; and thus it can never possibly become the ultimate ground of the explanation of things or the starting-point of philosophy. Thus philosophy necessarily requires for its starting-point that which is absolutely immediate; but obviously such an absolutely immediate thing is only that which is given to *self-consciousness,* that which is within, the *subjective.* It is therefore a most eminent merit of Descartes that he was the first to make philosophy start from self-consciousness. This path the genuine philosophers, particularly Locke, Berkeley, and Kant, have since continued to follow, each in his own way; and in consequence of their investigations, I was led to recognize and make use not of *one,* but of *two* wholly different data of immediate knowledge in self-consciousness, the representation and the will. By the combined application of these we go farther in philosophy, to the same extent that we can achieve more in an algebraical problem when two known quantities are given instead of only one.

In agreement with what has been said, the inevitably false element in *materialism* consists primarily in its starting from a *petitio principii*,[3] which, more closely considered, proves to be even a πρῶτον ψεῦδος.[4] It starts from the assumption that matter is something positively and unconditionally given, something that exists independently of the knowledge of the subject, and thus really a thing-in-itself. It attributes to matter (and also to its presuppositions, time and space) an existence that is *absolute,* that is to say, independent of the perceiving subject; this is its fundamental mistake. If it intends to go to work honestly, it must leave unexplained and start from the qualities inherent in the given materials, hence in the substances, together with the natural forces that manifest themselves therein, and finally even vital force, as unfathomable *qualitates occultae* of matter. Physics and physiology actually do this, just because they make no claim to be the ultimate explanation of things. But precisely in order to avoid this, materialism does *not* go to work honestly, at any rate as it has been seen hitherto. Thus it flatly denies all those original forces, since it ostensibly and apparently reduces them all, and in the last resort even vital force, to the merely mechanical activity of matter, and thus to manifestations of impenetrability, form, cohesion, impact, inertia, gravity, and so on. Of course, these qualities have in themselves that which is least inexplicable, just because they rest partly on what is *a priori* certain, consequently on the forms of our own intellect, which are the principle of all ease of comprehension. But the intellect, as the condition of every object, and thus of the entire phenomenon, is totally ignored by materialism. Its purpose is to reduce everything qualitative to something merely quantitative, since it refers the qualitative to mere *form* in contrast to *matter* proper. Of the really *empirical* qualities it leaves to matter only gravity, because this already appears in itself as something quantitative, as the sole measure of the quantity of matter. This path necessarily leads materialism to the fiction of atoms, which now become the material out of which it intends to construct the very mysterious manifestations of all the original forces. Here it is really no longer concerned at all with empirically *given* matter, but with a matter which is not to be found *in rerum natura,* which is rather a mere abstraction of that actual matter. Thus it is concerned with a matter that would have absolutely none other than those *mechanical* qualities; and, with the exception of gravity, these can be pretty well

---

[3] "Begging of the question." [Tr.]
[4] "A first false step" (in the premiss of a syllogism). [Tr.]

construed *a priori,* just because they depend on the forms of space, time, and causality, and consequently on our intellect. Materialism, therefore, sees itself reduced to this miserable stuff in the erection of its castle in the air.

Here it inevitably becomes *atomism,* as happened to it in its childhood at the hands of Leucippus and Democritus, and as happens to it again now that it has reached its second childhood through age; thus at the hands of the French, because they have never known the Kantian philosophy, and of the Germans, because they have forgotten it. In fact, it behaves even more strangely in its second childhood than in its first; not merely are *solid* bodies said to consist of atoms, but also *fluids,* water, even air, gases, and light. This last is said to be the undulations of a wholly hypothetical and entirely undemonstrated ether consisting of atoms, and colours are said to be caused by their varying velocity. This is a hypothesis that starts, like Newton's seven-colour hypothesis of old, from an analogy with music which is quite arbitrarily assumed and then forcibly carried through. One must really be credulous to an unheard-of extent, to allow oneself to be persuaded that the infinitely varied ether-vibrations, arising from the endless variety and multiplicity of coloured surfaces in this many-coloured world, could constantly, each at a different speed, run through one another in all directions, and cross one another everywhere, without disturbing one another, but would, on the contrary, through such tumult and confusion produce the profoundly peaceful aspect of illuminated nature and art. *Credat Judaeus Apella!* [5] The nature of light is certainly a mystery, but it is better to confess this than to bar the way to future knowledge by bad theories. That light is something quite different from a merely mechanical movement, undulation, or vibration and tremor, indeed that it is material, is shown by its chemical effects, a beautiful series of which was recently laid before the *Académie des Sciences* by Chevreul, who caused sunlight to act on materials of different colours. The most beautiful thing here is that a white roll of paper which has been exposed to sunlight produces the same effects, in fact does so even after six months, if during this time it has been kept in a firmly closed metal tube. Has the tremor, then, paused for some six months, and does it join in again *a tempo?* (*Comptes Rendus* of 20 December 1858.) This whole ether-atom-tremor-hypothesis is not only a chimera, but in crude clownishness equals Democritus at his worst; yet it is shameless enough to give itself out at the present day as an established fact. The result of all this is that this hypothesis is repeated mechanically and in an orthodox manner, and believed in

[5] "The Jew Apella may believe it!" [Horace, *Satires,* I, v, 100. Tr.]

as gospel by a thousand stupid scribblers of all branches of knowledge, who know nothing of such things. But the doctrine of atoms in general goes even farther; and soon it will be a case of *Spartam, quam nactus es, orna!* [6] Different perpetual motions, revolving, vibrating, and so on, are then ascribed to all the atoms according to their function. Similarly, each atom has its atmosphere of ether, or something else, and whatever other fancies of this kind there are. The fancies of Schelling's philosophy of nature and of its followers were indeed often ingenious, lively, or at any rate witty; but these other fancies are dull, crude, clumsy, insipid, paltry, and clownish. They are the offspring of minds incapable, in the first place, of conceiving any reality other than a fabulous matter devoid of qualities, a matter that would thus be an absolute object, an object without subject, and, in the second place, of conceiving any activity other than motion and impact. These two things alone are intelligible to them, and their *a priori* assumption is that everything runs back to these; for these are their *thing-in-itself*. To attain this goal, vital force is reduced to chemical forces (insidiously and unjustifiably called molecular forces), and all processes of inorganic nature are reduced to mechanism, to thrust and counter-thrust. And so in the end, the whole world with all the things in it would be merely a mechanical conjuring-trick, like the toys driven by levers, wheels, and sand, which represent a mine or the work on a farm. The source of the evil is that, through the large amount of hand-work in experimenting, the head-work of thinking has got out of practice. Crucibles and voltaic piles are supposed to take over the functions of thinking; hence the deep aversion to all philosophy.

But the case could also be presented in such a way as this by saying that materialism, as it has appeared hitherto, has failed, merely because it has not adequately *known* the *matter* out of which it thought to construct the world, and has therefore dealt not with matter itself, but with a false conception of it devoid of qualities. On the other hand, if instead of this materialism had taken the actual and *empirically* given matter (in other words, material substance or rather substances), endowed as it is with all the physical, chemical, electrical properties, and also with properties spontaneously producing life out of matter itself, hence the true *mater rerum,* from the obscure womb of which all phenomena and forms come forth to fall at some time back into it again, then from this, that is to say, from matter fully comprehended and exhaustively known, a world could have been constructed of which materialism need not have been ashamed. Quite right: only the trick would then have consisted

* "Sparta is the place you belong to; be a credit to it!" [Tr.]

in our putting the *quaesita* in the *data,* since we should take as given, and make the starting-point of the deductions, ostensibly mere matter, but actually all the mysterious forces of nature that cling to it, or more correctly, that become visible to us by its means; much the same as when we understand by the word dish that which lies on it. For actually matter is for our knowledge merely the *vehicle* of the qualities and natural forces that appear as its accidents; and just because I have traced these back to the will, I call matter the mere *visibility of the will.* Stripped of all these qualities, however, matter remains behind as that which is devoid of qualities, the *caput mortuum* of nature, out of which nothing can honestly be made. On the other hand, if, in the manner mentioned, we *leave* to it all those qualities, we have committed a concealed *petitio principii,* since we have caused the *quaesita* to be given to us in advance as *data.* What is brought about by *this* will no longer be a *materialism* proper, but mere *naturalism,* that is to say, an absolute system of *physics,* which, as shown in chapter 17, can never occupy and fill the place of metaphysics, just because it begins only after so many assumptions, and so never once undertakes to explain things from the very bottom. Therefore mere naturalism is based essentially on nothing but *qualitates occultae,* and we can never get beyond these, except, as I have done, by calling in the aid of the *subjective* source of knowledge. This, then, naturally leads to the long and toilsome roundabout way of metaphysics, since it presupposes the complete analysis of self-consciousness and of the intellect and will that are given in it. However, to start from the *objective,* the basis of which is *external perception,* so distinct and comprehensible, is a path that is so natural, and presents itself of its own accord to man, that *naturalism,* and consequently *materialism,* because it cannot satisfy as not being exhaustive, are systems to which speculative reason must necessarily come, in fact before everything else. We therefore see naturalism appear at the very beginning of the history of philosophy in the systems of the Ionic philosophers, and then materialism in the teaching of Leucippus and Democritus; and indeed even later we see them always renewed from time to time.

CHAPTER XXV

Transcendent Considerations on the Will as Thing-in-Itself

The merely empirical consideration of nature already recognizes a constant transition from the simplest and most necessary manifestation of some universal force of nature up to the life and consciousness of man, through easy gradations and with merely relative, indeed often vague and indefinite, boundaries. Reflection, following this view and penetrating into it somewhat more deeply, is soon led to the conviction that in all these phenomena the inner essence, that which manifests itself, that which appears, is one and the same thing standing out more and more distinctly. Accordingly, that which exhibits itself in a million forms of endless variety and diversity, and thus performs the most variegated and grotesque play without beginning and end, is this one essence. It is so closely concealed behind all these masks that it does not recognize itself again, and thus often treats itself harshly. Therefore the great doctrine of the ἓν καὶ πᾶν[1] appeared early in the East as well as in the West; and in spite of every contradiction it has asserted itself, or has been constantly renewed. But now we are let more deeply into the secret, since, by what has been said hitherto, we have been led to the insight that, when in any particular phenomenon a *knowing consciousness* is added to that inner being that underlies all phenomena, a consciousness that in its direction inward becomes *self-consciousness,* then that inner being exhibits itself to this self-consciousness as that which is so familiar and mysterious, and is denoted by the word *will.* Consequently, we have called that universal fundamental essence of all phenomena *the will,* according to the manifestation in which it appears most unveiled. Accordingly, by the word *will* we express anything but an unknown x; on the contrary, we express that which, at any rate from *one* side, is infinitely better known and more intimate than anything else.

Now let us call to mind a truth whose fullest and most thorough

---

[1] "One and all" [Tr.]

proof is found in my essay *On the Freedom of the Will,* namely that, by virtue of the absolutely universal validity of the law of causality, the conduct or action of all beings in this world appears always strictly *necessitated* by the causes that in each case call it forth. It makes no difference in this respect whether such conduct or action has been called forth by causes in the narrowest sense of the word, or by stimuli, or finally by motives, since these differences refer only to the degree of susceptibility of the different kinds of beings. We must have no illusion on this point: the law of causality knows of no exceptions, but everything, from the movement of a mote in a sunbeam to the well-considered action of man, is subject to it with equal strictness. Therefore, in the whole course of the world, a mote in a sunbeam could never describe any line in its flight other than the one it has described, nor could a man ever act in any way different from that in which he has acted. No truth is more certain than this, namely that all that happens, be it great or small, happens with complete *necessity.* Consequently, at every given moment of time the whole state or condition of all things is firmly and accurately determined by the state or condition that has just preceded it; and so it is with the stream of time back to infinity and on to infinity. Consequently, the course of the world is like that of a clock after it has been put together and wound up; hence, from this undeniable point of view, it is a mere machine, whose purpose we do not see. Even if we were to assume a first beginning, quite without justification and also despite all conceivability with its conformity to law, nothing would be essentially changed thereby. For the first condition of things arbitrarily assumed would have irrevocably determined and fixed at their origin the condition immediately following it, as a whole and down to the smallest detail; this state again would have determined the next following, and so on *per saecula saeculorum.* For the chain of causality with its universal strictness—that brazen bond of necessity and fate—produces every phenomenon irrevocably and unalterably, just as it is. The difference would be merely that, in the case of the one assumption, we should have before us a piece of clockwork once wound up, in the case of the other a *perpetuum mobile;* but the necessity of the course would remain the same. In the essay already quoted, I have irrefutably proved that man's action can form no exception, since I have shown how it results every time with strict necessity from two factors, his character and the motives that present themselves. The character is inborn and unalterable, the motives are necessarily produced under the guidance of causality by the strictly determined course of the world.

Accordingly, from one point of view, which we cannot possibly avoid, because it is established by world-laws valid objectively and *a priori,* the world with everything in it appears as a purposeless, and therefore incomprehensible, play of an eternal necessity, an unfathomable and inexorable 'Ανάγκη.[2] But the shocking, indeed revolting, thing about this inevitable and irrefutable view of the world cannot be thoroughly eliminated by any assumption except the one that, as every being in the world is on the one hand phenomenon and is necessarily determined by the laws of the phenomenon, it is on the other in itself *will,* indeed absolutely *free will.* For all necessity arises only through the forms that belong entirely to the phenomenon, namely the principle of sufficient reason in its different aspects. But then *aseity*[3] must also belong to such a will, for as free, in other words, as thing-in-itself and thus not subordinate to the principle of sufficient reason, it can no more depend on another thing in its being and essence than it can in its doing and acting. By this assumption alone, as much *freedom* is supposed as is necessary to counterbalance the inevitable strict *necessity* that governs the course of the world. Accordingly, we really have only the choice either of seeing the world as a mere machine of necessity running down, or of recognizing a free will as the world's essence-in-itself, whose manifestation is not directly the action, but primarily the *existence and essence* of things. This freedom is therefore transcendental, and is just as compatible with empirical necessity as the transcendental ideality of phenomena is with their empirical reality. I have shown in the essay *On the Freedom of the Will* that only on its assumption is a person's action nevertheless *his own,* in spite of the necessity with which it follows from his character and from the motives; but here *aseity* is attributed to his true being. Now the same relation holds good of all things in the world. The strictest *necessity,* honestly carried out with rigid consistency, and the most perfect *freedom,* raised to omnipotence, had to appear simultaneously and together in philosophy. But without doing violence to truth, this could come about only by putting the whole necessity in the *acting and doing* (*operari*), and the whole *freedom,* on the other hand, in the *being and essence* (*esse*). In this way a riddle is solved which is as old as the world, just because hitherto it had always been held upside down, and freedom was positively looked for in the *operari,* and necessity in the *esse.* On the other hand, I say that every being without exception *acts* with strict necessity, but *exists* and is what it

---

[2] "Compulsion, necessity." [Tr.]
[3] "Being by and of itself." [Tr.]

is by virtue of its *freedom*. Therefore with me, freedom and necessity are to be met with neither more nor less than in any previous system; although now one and now the other must appear, according as we take umbrage at the fact that the *will* is attributed to natural events hitherto explained from pure necessity, or at the fact that the same strict necessity is attributed to motivation as to mechanical causality. The two have merely changed places; freedom has been shifted to the *esse,* and necessity limited to the *operari.*

In short, *determinism* stands firm; for fifteen hundred years attempts to undermine it have been made in vain. They have been urged by certain queer ideas which we know quite well, but dare not call entirely by their name. In consequence of it, however, the world becomes a puppet show worked by wires (motives) without its even being possible to see for whose amusement. If the piece has a plan, then a *fate* is the director; if it has no plan, blind necessity is the director. There is no escape from this absurdity other than the knowledge that the *being and essence* of all things are the phenomenon of a really *free will* that knows itself precisely in them; for their *doing and acting* are not to be delivered from necessity. To save freedom from fate or chance, it had to be transferred from the action to the existence.

Accordingly, as *necessity* belongs only to the phenomenon, not to the thing-in-itself, in other words, not to the true nature of the world, so also does *plurality;* this is sufficiently explained in § 25 of volume one. Here I have to add merely a few remarks confirming and illustrating this truth.

Everyone knows only *one* being quite immediately, namely his own will in self-consciousness. He knows everything else only mediately, and then judges it by analogy with that one being; according to the degree of his power of reflection, this analogy is carried further. Even this springs ultimately and fundamentally from the fact that there is really *only one being;* the illusion of plurality (*Maya*), resulting from the forms of external, objective apprehension, could not penetrate right into the inner, simple consciousness; hence this always meets with only one being.

We contemplate perfection in the works of nature, which can never be sufficiently admired, and which, even in the lowest and smallest organisms, e.g., fertilizing parts of plants or the internal structure of insects, is carried out with such infinite care and unwearied labour, as though the work of nature before us had been her only one, on which she was therefore able to lavish all her skill and power. Nevertheless, we find the same thing repeated an infinite number of times in each one of innumerable individuals of every kind, and no less carefully perfected in the one whose dwelling-place is the loneliest and most neglected spot to which no eye has yet penetrated. We now follow out the combination of the parts of every organism as far as we can; and yet we never come across anything that is quite simple and therefore ultimate, not to mention anything that is inorganic. Finally, we lose ourselves in estimating the appropriateness of all those parts of the organism for the stability of the whole, by virtue of which every living thing is perfect and complete in and by itself. At the same time, we reflect that each of these masterpieces, itself of short duration, has already been produced afresh an infinite number of times, and that nevertheless each specimen of its kind, every insect, every flower, every leaf, still appears just as carefully perfected as was the first of its species. We therefore observe that nature by no means wearies or begins to bungle, but that with equally patient master-hand she perfects the last as the first. If we bear all this in mind, we become aware first that all human art or skill is completely different, not merely in degree but in kind, from the creation of nature, and also that the operating, original force, the *natura naturans*,[4] is *immediately present whole and undivided* in each of its innumerable works, in the smallest as in the largest, in the last as in the first. From this it follows that the *natura naturans,* as such and in itself, knows nothing of space and time. Further, we bear in mind that the production of those hyperboles of all the works of skill nevertheless costs nature absolutely nothing, so that, with inconceivable prodigality, she creates millions of organisms that never reach maturity. Every living thing is unsparingly exposed to a thousand different hazards and chances; on the other hand, if favoured by accident or directed by human purpose, it readily affords millions of specimens of a kind of which there was hitherto only one; consequently, millions cost her no more effort than one. All this leads to the insight that the plurality of things has its root in the subject's manner of knowledge, but is foreign to the thing-in-itself, to the inner primary force manifesting itself in things; consequently, that space and time, on which rests the possibility of all plurality, are mere forms of our perception or intuition. In fact, even that wholly inconceivable ingenuity of structure, associated with the most reckless prodigality of the works on which it has been lavished, at bottom springs only from the way in which we apprehend things, since, when the simple and indivisible original striving of the will as thing-in-itself exhibits itself as object in our cerebral knowledge, it must appear as an

---

[4] "Creative nature." [Tr.]

ingenious concatenation of separate parts, as means and ends of one another, carried out with exceeding perfection.

The *unity of that will* here alluded to, which lies beyond the phenomenon, and in which we have recognized the inner being of the phenomenal world, is a metaphysical unity. Consequently, knowledge of it is transcendent; that is to say, it does not rest on the functions of our intellect, and is therefore not to be really grasped with them. The result is that this unity opens to the consideration an abyss whose depth no longer grants an entirely clear and systematically connected insight, but only isolated glances that enable us to recognize this unity in this or that relation of things, now in the subjective, now in the objective. In this way new problems are again raised, and I do not undertake to solve all these, but rather appeal here to the words *est quadam prodire tenus,*[5] more concerned not to set up anything false or arbitrarily invented than to give a thorough account of everything; at the risk of furnishing here only a fragmentary statement.

If we picture to ourselves and clearly go over in our minds the very ingenious theory of the origin of the planetary system, advanced first by Kant and later by Laplace, whose correctness can scarcely be doubted, we see the lowest, crudest, and blindest forces of nature, bound to the most rigid conformity to law, bring about the fundamental framework of the world, the future dwelling-place suitably adapted for innumerable living beings. This they do by means of their conflict in one and the same given matter and of the accidental consequences this conflict produces. This framework of the world is produced as a system of order and harmony at which, the more distinctly and accurately we learn to understand it, the more are we astonished. For example, we see that every planet with its present velocity can maintain itself only exactly where it has its place, since if it were brought nearer to the sun it would inevitably fall into it, or if placed farther from it would necessarily fly away from it. Conversely, if we take its place as given, it can remain there only with its present velocity and with no other, since by going more rapidly it would inevitably fly away from the sun, and by going more slowly it would necessarily fall into it; hence we see that only *one* definite place is suitable to each definite velocity of a planet. We then see this problem solved by the fact that the same physical cause, necessarily and blindly operating, which assigned it its place, at the same time and precisely in this way imparted to it the exact velocity suitable to this place alone, in consequence of the natural law that a body moving in a circle increases its velocity in proportion

---

[5] "Advance up to a certain limit." [Tr.]

as that circle becomes smaller. Moreover, we understand finally how an endless duration is assured to the whole system by the fact that all the mutual disturbances that inevitably occur in the course of the planets must in time adjust themselves again. We then see how precisely the irrationality of the periods of revolution of Jupiter and Saturn in respect to each other prevents their mutual perturbations from repeating themselves at one spot, whereby they would become dangerous. The result of this irrationality is that, appearing rarely and always at a different place, such perturbations must again balance each other; this is comparable to the dissonances in music which resolve themselves once more into harmony. By means of such considerations, we recognize a suitability and perfection such as could have been brought about only by the freest arbitrary will guided by the most searching understanding and the keenest and most acute calculation. And yet, under the guidance of that cosmogony of Laplace which is so well thought out and so accurately calculated, we cannot refrain from seeing that wholly blind forces of nature, acting according to immutable natural laws, could, through their conflict and in their purposeless play with one another, produce nothing but just this fundamental framework of the world, which is equal to the work of a hyperbolically enhanced combination. Instead of dragging in here, after the manner of Anaxagoras, the aid of an *intelligence,* known to us from animal nature alone and calculated only for such a nature, an intelligence that, coming from outside, had cunningly made use of the forces of nature and their laws once existing and given, in order to carry out its aims that are really foreign to these—we recognize in those lowest natural forces themselves that same one will, which has its first manifestation in them. Already striving towards its goal in this manifestation and through its original laws themselves, the will works towards its final aim; and therefore everything that happens according to blind laws of nature must serve and be in keeping with this aim. Indeed, it cannot turn out otherwise, in so far as everything material is nothing but the phenomenon, the visibility, the objectivity of the will-to-live, which is one. Thus the lowest natural forces themselves are already animated by this same will that afterwards, in individual beings endowed with intelligence, marvels at its own work; just as in the morning the somnambulist is astonished at what he did in his sleep; or, more correctly, like one who is astonished at his own form when he sees it in the mirror. This unity, here demonstrated, of the accidental with the intentional, of the necessary with the free, by virtue of which the blindest chances, resting on universal laws of nature, are, so to speak, the keys on which the world-spirit plays its melodies so fraught with meaning—this unity, as I have said, is an abyss for our consideration into which not even philosophy can throw a full light, but only a glimmer.

I now turn to a *subjective* consideration that belongs here; yet I can give even less distinctness to it than to the objective consideration just discussed, for I shall be able to express it only by image and simile. Why is our consciousness brighter and more distinct the farther it reaches outwards, so that its greatest clearness lies in sense perception, which already half belongs to things outside us; and, on the other hand, becomes more obscure as we go inwards, and leads, when followed to its innermost recesses, into a darkness in which all knowledge ceases? Because, I say, consciousness presupposes *individuality;* but this belongs to the mere phenomenon, since, as the plurality of the homogeneous, it is conditioned by the forms of the phenomenon, time and space. On the other hand, our inner nature has its root in what is no longer phenomenon but thing-in-itself, to which therefore the forms of the phenomenon do not reach; and in this way, the chief conditions of individuality are wanting, and distinct consciousness ceases therewith. In this root-point of existence the difference of beings ceases, just as that of the radii of a sphere ceases at the centre. As in the sphere the surface is produced by the radii ending and breaking off, so consciousness is possible only where the true inner being runs out into the phenomenon. Through the forms of the phenomenon separate individuality becomes possible, and on this individuality rests consciousness, which is on this account confined to phenomena. Therefore everything distinct and really intelligible in our consciousness always lies only outwards on this surface of the sphere. But as soon as we withdraw entirely from this, consciousness forsakes us—in sleep, in death, and to a certain extent also in magnetic or magic activity; for all these lead through the centre. But just because distinct consciousness, as being conditioned by the surface of the sphere, is not directed towards the centre, it recognizes other individuals certainly as of the same kind, but not as identical, which, however, they are in themselves. Immortality of the individual could be compared to the flying off at a tangent of a point on the surface; but immortality, by virtue of the eternity of the true inner being of the whole phenomenon, is comparable to the return of that point on the radius to the centre, whose mere extension is the surface. The will as thing-in-itself is entire and undivided in every being, just as the centre is an integral part of every radius; whereas the peripheral end of this radius is in the most rapid revolution with the surface that represents time and its content, the other end at the centre where eternity lies, remains in profoundest peace, because the centre is the point whose rising half is no different from the sinking half. Therefore, it is said also in the *Bhagavad-Gita: Haud distributum animantibus, et quasi distributum tamen insidens, animantiumque sustentaculum id cognoscendum, edax et rursus genitale* (xiii, 16, trans. Schlegel).[6] Here, of course, we fall into mystical and metaphorical language, but it is the only language in which anything can be said about this wholly transcendent theme. Thus even this simile also may pass, that the human race can be figuratively represented as an *animal compositum*, a form of life of which examples are furnished by many polyps, especially those that swim, such as *Veretillum, Funiculina,* and others. Just as in the case of these, the head portion isolates each individual animal, but the lower portion with the common stomach combines them all into the unity of one life process, so the brain with its consciousness isolates human individuals. On the other hand, the unconscious part, namely the vegetative life with its ganglionic system, into which brain consciousness disappears in sleep, like the lotus nightly submerged in the flood, is a common life of all. By means of it they can even communicate in exceptional cases, as occurs, for example, when dreams are directly communicated, the thoughts of the mesmerizer pass over into the somnambulist, and finally in the magnetic or generally magical influence coming from intentional willing. Thus, when such an influence takes place, it is *toto genere* different from any other that takes place through the *influxus physicus,* since it is a real *actio in distans,* which the will, proceeding indeed from the individual, nevertheless performs in its metaphysical capacity as the omnipresent substratum of the whole of nature. It might also be said that, just as in *generatio aequivoca,* sometimes and by way of exception there appears a feeble remnant of the will's *creative power* that has done its work in the existing forms of nature and in these is extinguished, so by way of exception there can become active in such magical influences a surplus, so to speak, of the will's original *omnipotence* that completes its work, and is used up in the production and maintenance of the organism. I have spoken at length of this magical property of the will in the essay *On the Will in Nature;* and here I gladly pass over considerations that of necessity refer to uncertain facts, which cannot, however, be entirely ignored or denied.

---

[6] "Undivided it dwells in beings, and yet as it were divided; it is to be known as the sustainer, annihilator, and producer of beings." [Tr.]

CHAPTER XXVI[1]

On Teleology

The universal suitability of organic nature relating to the continued existence of every being, together with the appropriateness of organic nature to inorganic, cannot be easily associated with any philosophical system except that which makes a *will* the basis of every natural being's existence, a will that accordingly expresses its true being and tendency not merely in the actions, but also in the *form and shape,* of the organism that appears. In the preceding chapter I merely hinted at the account of this subject which our line of thought suggests, having already discussed it in the passage of volume one referred to below, and with special clearness and fullness in the essay *On the Will in Nature* under the heading "Comparative Anatomy." To this I now add the following remarks.

The astonished admiration that usually seizes us when we contemplate the endless appropriateness in the structure of organic beings, rests at bottom on the certainly natural yet false assumption that that *agreement or harmony* of the parts with one another, with the whole of the organism, and with its aims in the external world, as we comprehend and judge of it by means of *knowledge,* and thus on the path of the *representation,* has also come into being on the same path; hence that, as it exists *for* the intellect, it was also brought about *through* the intellect. *We,* of course, can bring about something regular and conforming to law, such as is, for example, every crystal, only under the guidance of the law and the rule; in just the same way, we can bring about something appropriate and to the purpose only under the guidance of the concept of an end or aim. We are in no way justified, however, in imputing this limitation of ours to nature; for nature herself is a *prius* of all intellect, and, as was stated in the previous chapter, her acting differs from ours in its whole manner. She achieves without reflection, and without conception of an end, that which appears so appropriate and so deliberate, because she does so without representation, which is entirely of sec-

---

[1] This and the following chapter refer to § 28 of volume 1.

ondary origin. Let us first consider that which is merely regular, not yet fitted for an end. The six equal radii of a snowflake separating out at equal angles are not measured beforehand by any knowledge; on the contrary, it is the simple tendency of the original will thus exhibiting itself for knowledge, when knowledge supervenes. Now just as the will here brings about the regular figure without mathematics, so does it bring about without physiology the form that is organic and organized with supreme suitability. The regular form in space exists only for perception, the perception-form of which is space; so the appropriateness of the organism exists merely for our knowing faculty of reason, the reflection of which is tied to the concepts of end and means. If a direct insight into the working of nature were possible, we should of necessity recognize that the above-mentioned teleological astonishment was analogous to what that savage, whom Kant mentions in his explanation of the ludicrous, felt, when he saw froth irresistibly gushing out of a newly-opened bottle of beer. He expressed his astonishment not at the froth coming out, but at how anyone could have put it into the bottle. For we too assume that the appropriateness of the products of nature has entered on the path on which it comes out for us. Therefore our teleological astonishment can also be compared to that which the first products of the art of printing excited in those who considered them on the supposition that they were works of the pen, and accordingly resorted to the assumption of a devil's assistance in order to explain them. For, let it be said here once more, it is our intellect that by means of its own forms, space, time, and causality, apprehends as object the act of will, in itself metaphysical and indivisible, and exhibiting itself in the phenomenon of an animal; it is our intellect which first produces the plurality and variety of the parts and their functions, and is then struck with amazement at their perfect agreement and conspiracy that result from the original unity; here, then, in a sense, it admires its own work.

If we give ourselves up to the contemplation of the inexpressibly and infinitely ingenious structure of any animal, be it only the commonest insect, and lose ourselves in admiration of it, and it then occurs to us that nature recklessly exposes this exceedingly ingenious and highly complicated organism daily and in thousands to destruction by accident, animal rapacity, and human wantonness, this immense prodigality fills us with amazement. But this amazement rests on an amphiboly of the concepts, since we have in mind here the human work of art which is brought about through the agency of the intellect and by overcoming a foreign and resistant material, and in consequence certainly costs much trouble. On the other hand, nature's works, however ingenious, cost her absolutely no trouble, since here the will to work is the work in itself, for, as already stated, the organism is merely the visibility of the will here existing, which is brought about in the brain.

In consequence of the constitution of organic beings which has been explained, teleology, as the assumption of the suitability of every part, is a perfectly safe guide when we consider the whole of organic nature. On the other hand, in a metaphysical regard, for the explanation of nature beyond the possibility of experience, it can be looked upon as valid only in a secondary and subsidiary manner for confirming principles of explanation established in a different way; for then it belongs to those problems of which an account is to be given. Accordingly, if in an animal a part is found for which we do not see any purpose, we must never venture to presume that nature has produced it aimlessly, perhaps in play and out of mere caprice. At the most, something of the kind could be conceived as possible on the assumption of Anaxagoras that nature had obtained her disposition and structure by means of an organizing and regulating understanding that serves as such a foreign arbitrary will, but not on the assumption that the being-in-itself (in other words, outside our representation) of every organism is simply and solely *its own will.* For then the existence of every part is conditioned by the fact that, in some way, it serves the will that here underlies it, expresses and realizes some tendency in it, and consequently contributes somehow to the maintenance of this organism. For, apart from the *will manifesting itself in it,* and apart from the conditions of the external world under which this has voluntarily undertaken to live, and for the conflict with which, therefore, its whole form and structure are already intended, nothing can have had any influence on it, and have determined its form and parts, hence no arbitrary power, no caprice. For this reason, everything in it *must* be suitable for the purpose; therefore, *final causes* (*causae finales*) are the clue to the understanding of organic nature, just as efficient causes (*causae efficientes*) are to that of inorganic nature. It is due to this that, if in anatomy or zoology we cannot find the end or aim of an existing part, our understanding receives therefrom a shock similar to that which in physics must be given by an effect whose cause remains concealed. We assume as necessary both this cause and that part, and therefore go on looking for it, however often this may have been done in vain. This is so, for instance, as regards the spleen, concerning the purpose of which men never cease to invent hypotheses, until some day one of these proves to be correct. It is just the same with the large, spiral-formed teeth of the babirussa, the horn-shaped excrescences of a few caterpillars, and other things of this kind. Negative cases we also judge according to the same rule; for example, that in a class on the whole so uniform as that of the saurians, so important a part as the bladder is present in many species, while in others it is missing; likewise that dolphins and some cetacea related to them are entirely without olfactory nerves, whereas the remaining cetacea and even fishes have them; this must be determined by some reason or ground.

Actual isolated exceptions to this universal law of suitability in organic nature have certainly been discovered, and with great astonishment; yet the words *exceptio firmat regulam*[2] find application in those cases, since an account of them can be given in a different way. Thus it is that the tadpoles of the Surinam toad have tails and gills, although they do not swim like all other tadpoles, but await their metamorphosis on the mother's back; that the male kangaroo has a rudiment of the bone which in the female carries the pouch; that even male mammals have nipples; that *Mus typhlus,* a rat, has eyes, although tiny ones, without an opening for them in the outer skin, which, covered with hair, therefore passes over them; and that the mole of the Apennines and also two kinds of fish, namely *Murena caecilia* and *Gastrobranchus caecus,* are in the same case; *Proteus anguinus* is of the same kind. These rare and surprising exceptions to the rule of nature, otherwise so rigid, these contradictions with herself into which she falls, must be explained from the inner connexion the different kinds of her phenomena have with one another, by virtue of the unity of that which manifests itself in them. In consequence of such connexion, nature must suggest something in one phenomenon, merely because another connected therewith actually has it. Accordingly, the male animal has a rudiment of an organ which in the female is actually present. As the difference of the *sexes* here cannot abolish the type of the *species,* so the type of a whole *class,* of the amphibians for instance, asserts itself where in a particular species (Surinam toad) one of its determinations becomes superfluous. Still less can nature allow a determination (eyes) belonging to the type of a whole *fundamental class (Vertebrata)*, to vanish entirely without a trace, even if it should atrophy in a particular species as being superfluous (*Mus typhlus*). On the contrary, here also she must indicate, at least in a rudimentary way, what she carries out in all the rest.

Even from this point of view it can be seen to a certain extent on what rests that *homology* in the skeleton firstly of mammals and in a wider sense of all vertebrates, which has been discussed at such

---

[2] "The exception confirms the rule." [Tr.]

length, especially by Richard Owen in his *Ostéologie comparée*. By virtue of this homology, for example, all mammals have seven cervical vertebrae; every bone of the human hand and arm finds its analogue in the fin of the whale; the skull of the bird in the egg has precisely as many bones as has that of the human foetus, and so on. Thus all this points to a principle that is independent of teleology. Yet this principle is the foundation on which teleology builds, or the material given in advance for its works, and is just what Geoffroy Saint-Hilaire has explained as the "anatomical element." It is the *unité de plan*,[3] the primary and basic type of the higher animal world, the arbitrarily chosen key, so to speak, on which nature here plays her tune.

The difference between the efficient cause (*causa efficiens*) and the final cause (*causa finalis*) has been correctly described by Aristotle (*De partibus animalium*, I, 1) in these words: Δύο τρόποι τῆς αἰτίας, τὸ οὗ ἕνεκα καὶ τὸ ἐξ ἀνάγκης, καὶ δεῖ λέγοντας τυγχάνειν μάλιστα μὲν ἀμφοῖν. (*Duo sunt causae modi: alter cujus gratia, et alter e necessitate; ac potissimum utrumque eruere oportet.*)[4] The *efficient* cause is that *by which* a thing is; the final cause is that *on account of which* a thing is. The phenomenon to be explained has in time the former *behind* it and the latter *before* it. Merely in the case of the arbitrary actions of animal beings do the two directly coincide, since in them the final cause, the end or aim, appears as *motive*. Such a motive, however, is always the true and real *cause* of the action, is wholly and solely the cause that *brings about or occasions* the action, the change preceding it which calls it into existence, by virtue of which it *necessarily* appears, and without which it could not happen, as I have shown in my essay on freedom. For whatever we should like to insert physiologically between the act of will and the bodily movement, here the *will* always remains admittedly that which moves, and what moves *it* is the *motive* coming from outside, and thus the *causa finalis,* that consequently appears here as *causa efficiens.* Moreover, we know from our previous remarks that the bodily movement is at bottom identical with the act of will, as its mere appearance or phenomenon in cerebral perception. This coincidence of the *causa finalis* with the efficient cause in the one and only phenomenon *intimately* known to us, which therefore remains throughout our primary phenomenon, must be firmly retained; for it leads precisely to the conclusion that, at any rate in organic nature, the

---

[3] "Unity of plan." [Tr.]

[4] "There are two kinds of causes, the final cause and the necessary efficient cause; and in what we have to say we must take both into consideration as much as possible." [Tr.]

knowledge of which has throughout final causes for its clue, a *will* is that which forms or shapes. In fact we cannot clearly conceive a final cause except as an intended aim or end, i.e., as a motive. Indeed, if we carefully consider the final cause in nature, in order to express its transcendent character, we must not shrink from a contradiction, and boldly state that the final cause is a motive that acts on a being by whom it is not known. For the nests of termites are certainly the motive that has called into existence the toothless jaw of the ant-eater, together with its long, thread-like, and glutinous tongue. The hard egg-shell, holding the chicken a prisoner, is certainly the motive for the horny point with which its beak is provided, in order with it to break through that shell; after this, the chicken casts it off as of no further use. In the same way, the laws of the reflection and refraction of light are the motive for that excessively ingenious and complicated optical instrument, the human eye, which has the transparency of its cornea, the different density of its three aqueous humours, the shape of its lens, the blackness of its choroid, the sensitiveness of its retina, the power of contraction of its pupil, and its muscular system, accurately calculated according to those laws. But those motives already operated before they were apprehended; it is not otherwise, however contradictory it may sound. For here is the transition of the physical into the metaphysical; but the latter we have recognized in the *will;* therefore we are bound to see that the will that extends the elephant's trunk to an object is also the same will that, anticipating objects, has pushed the trunk forth and shaped it.

It is in conformity with this that, in the investigation of *organic* nature, we are referred entirely to *final causes;* we look for *these* everywhere, and explain everything from *them.* The *efficient causes,* on the other hand, here occupy only quite a subordinate position as the mere tools of the final causes, and, just as in the case of the arbitrary movement of the limbs which is admittedly produced by external motives, they are assumed rather than demonstrated. With the explanation of the physiological *functions,* we certainly look about for efficient causes, though for the most part in vain. But with the explanation of the *origin of the parts* we no longer look for them at all, but are satisfied with the final causes alone. At most, we have here some such general principle as that the larger a part is to be, the stronger must be the artery that supplies it with blood; but we know absolutely nothing of the really *efficient* causes that bring about, for example, the eye, the ear, or the brain. In fact, even with the explanation of the mere *functions,* the *final cause* is far more important and to the point than is the *efficient cause.* Therefore, if the former alone is known, we are generally speaking instructed and satisfied; while the efficient cause by itself gives us little help. For example, if we actually knew the *efficient cause* of blood circulation —for we really do not, and are still looking for it—this would afford us little help without the *final cause,* namely that the blood must go into the lungs for oxidation, and flow back again for the purpose of nutrition. On the other hand, by the final cause, even without the efficient cause, we are greatly enlightened. For the rest, as I have said, I am of opinion that blood circulation has no really efficient cause at all, but that the will is just as directly active in it as it is in muscular movement, where motives determine it by means of nerve-conduction. Therefore here also the movement is immediately called into existence by the final cause, that is, by the need for oxidation in the lungs, that need here acting on the blood to a certain extent as motive, yet in such a way that the mediation of knowledge is wanting, since everything takes place in the interior of the organism. The so-called metamorphosis of plants, an idea lightly sketched by Caspar Wolff, which, under this hyperbolic title, Goethe pompously and with solemn delivery expounds as his own production, belongs to those explanations of the organic from the *efficient* cause. At bottom, however, he merely states that nature does not in the case of every production begin at the beginning and create out of nothing, but continuing to write, so to speak, in the same style, she adds on to what exists, makes use of previous forms, develops them and raises them to a higher power, to carry her work farther, just as she has done in the ascending series of animals, entirely in accordance with the rule: *Natura non facit saltus, et quod commodissimum in omnibus suis operationibus sequitur* (Aristotle, *De Incessu Animalium,* c. 2 and 8).[5] In fact, to explain the blossom by demonstrating in all its parts the form of the leaf seems to me almost like explaining the structure of a house by showing that all its parts, storeys, balconies, and attics are composed only of bricks and are a mere repetition of the original unity of the brick. And not much better, yet much more problematical, seems the explanation of the skull from the vertebrae, though here too it is self-evident that the case or covering of the brain will not be absolutely different and entirely disparate from the case or covering of the spinal cord, of which it is the continuation and terminal knob, but that it will rather be a continuation in the same manner. This whole method of consideration belongs to the above-mentioned homology of Richard Owen. But the following explanation of the true nature of the flower from its *final cause,* attributable to an Italian whose name has slipped my memory, seems to me to

---

[5] "Nature makes no leaps, and in all her operations follows the most convenient path." [Tr.]

give a much more satisfactory account. The aim of the *corolla* is (1) protection of the pistil and of the stamens; (2) by its means the refined saps are prepared which are concentrated in the *pollen* and *germen;* (3) from the glands of its base is separated the essential or volatile oil which, often as a fragrant vapour surrounding anthers and pistil, protects it to some extent from the influence of damp air. It is also one of the advantages of final causes that every *efficient* cause ultimately rests always on something mysterious and inscrutable, a force of nature, i.e., a *qualitas occulta,* and can therefore give only a *relative* explanation, whereas the final cause, within its province, furnishes a satisfactory and complete explanation. We are entirely satisfied, of course, only when we know simultaneously and yet separately the two, namely the efficient cause, also called by Aristotle ἡ αἰτία ἐξ ἀνάγκης,[6] and the final cause, ἡ χάριν τοῦ βελτίονος,[7] as their concurrence, their marvellous conspiracy, surprises us, and by virtue thereof, the best appears as something entirely necessary, and the necessary again as though it were merely the best and not necessary. For there arises in us the instinctive feeling that, however different their origin, the two causes are yet connected in the root, the inner essence of the thing-in-itself. Yet such a twofold knowledge is seldom attainable, in *organic* nature because the *efficient* cause is seldom known to us, in *inorganic* nature because the *final* cause remains problematical. In the meantime I wish to illustrate this by a couple of examples as good as I can find in the range of my physiological knowledge, for which physiologists may substitute clearer and more striking ones. The louse of the Negro is black; final cause: its own safety. Efficient cause: because its nourishment is the Negro's black *rete Malpighi.* The extremely varied, brilliant and vivid colouring of the plumage of tropical birds is explained, though only very generally, by the strong effect of light in the tropics, as its efficient cause. As final cause, I would state that those brilliant feathers are the gorgeous uniform in which the individuals of the innumerable species, often belonging to the same genus, recognize one another, so that every male finds his female. The same holds good of the butterflies of different zones and latitudes. It has been observed that consumptive women readily become pregnant in the last stage of their illness, that during pregnancy the disease stops, but that after confinement it appears again worse than before, and often results in death; similarly that consumptive men often beget another child in the last days of their life. The *final cause* here is that nature, everywhere so anxiously concerned for the maintenance of the spe-

---

[6] "The cause from necessity." [Tr.]

[7] "The cause with a view to the better." [Tr.]

cies, tries to replace rapidly by a new individual the approaching loss of one in the prime of life. On the other hand, the *efficient cause* is the unusually excited state of the nervous system which appears in the last period of consumption. From the same final cause is to be explained the analogous phenomenon that (according to Oken, *Die Zeugung,* p. 65) a fly poisoned with arsenic still mates from an unexplained impulse, and dies in copulation. The *final cause* of the *pubes* in both sexes, and of the *mons Veneris* in the female, is that, even in the case of very slender subjects, the *ossa pubis* shall not be felt during copulation, for it might excite aversion. The *efficient cause,* on the other hand, is to be sought in the fact that, wherever the mucous membrane passes over to the outer skin, hair grows in the vicinity; also in the fact that head and genitals are, to a certain extent, opposite poles of each other. They therefore have many different relations and analogies to each other, one of which is that of being covered with hair. The same *efficient* cause also holds good of men's beards; I imagine that the *final* cause of the beard is the fact that what is pathognomonic, and thus the rapid change in the features of the face which betrays every hidden movement of the mind, becomes visible mainly in the mouth and its vicinity. Therefore, to conceal this from the prying glance of an adversary as something that is often dangerous in negotiations or in sudden emergencies, nature (knowing that *homo homini lupus*) gave man the beard. Woman, on the other hand, could dispense with it, for with her dissimulation and self-control (*contenance*) are inborn. As I have said, it must be possible to find far more apt and striking examples, to show how the completely blind working of nature coincides in the result with the apparently intentional, or, as Kant puts it, the mechanism of nature with her technique. This points to the fact that both have beyond this difference their common origin in the will as thing-in-itself. Much would be achieved for the elucidation of this point of view if, for example, we could find the *efficient* cause which conveys the driftwood to the treeless polar regions, or even that which has concentrated the dry land of our planet principally in the northern hemisphere, while it is to be regarded as the final cause of this that the winter of that half turns out to be eight days shorter and is thus also milder, because it occurs at the perihelion that accelerates the course of the earth. Yet when *inorganic* nature is considered, the final cause is always ambiguous, and leaves us in doubt, especially when the *efficient* cause is found, as to whether it is not a merely subjective view, an aspect of things conditioned by our point of view. But in this respect it is comparable to many works of art, e.g., coarse mosaics, theatre decorations, and the Apennine god at Pratolino near Florence, which is composed of large masses of rock. All these are effective only at a distance, but vanish when we are close to them, since instead of them the *efficient* cause of their appearance then becomes visible; but yet the forms actually exist and are no mere delusion or fancy. Analogous to this, therefore, are the final causes in inorganic nature, when the *efficient* causes appear. In fact, whoever has a wide view of things would perhaps admit it, if we added that something similar is the cause with omens.

For the rest, if anyone wishes to misuse the *external* appropriateness that always remains ambiguous, as I have said, for physico-theological demonstrations, as is still done at the present day, though it is to be hoped only by Englishmen, then there are in this class enough examples *in contrarium,* thus ateleologies, to upset his conception. One of the strongest is presented to us by the fact that sea-water is undrinkable, in consequence of which man is nowhere more exposed to the danger of dying of thirst than in the very midst of the largest mass of water of his planet. Let us ask our Englishman: "For what purpose need the sea be salt?"

In *inorganic* nature, the final causes withdraw entirely into the background, so that an explanation given from them alone is no longer valid; on the contrary, the *efficient* causes are indispensable. This depends on the fact that the will, objectifying itself in inorganic nature, no longer appears here in individuals who by themselves constitute a whole, but in natural forces and their action. In this way, end and means are too widely separated for their relation to be clear, and for us to be able to recognize in them a manifestation of will. This already occurs in a certain degree even in *organic* nature, namely where the appropriateness is an *external* one, where the end lies in *one* individual, the means in *another.* Yet here also it still remains unquestionable, so long as the two belong to the same species; in fact, it then becomes the more striking. Here may be reckoned first of all the mutually adapted organization of the genitals of the two sexes; and then also much that assists procreation, for example, in the case of *Lampyris noctiluca* (the glow-worm) the circumstance that only the male, which does not emit light, has wings to enable it to seek out the female; on the other hand, as they come out only in the evening, the wingless female possesses phosphorescent light, so that she can be found by the male. Yet in the case of *Lampyris italica,* both sexes emit light, which is an instance of the natural luxury of the south. However, a striking, because quite special, example of the kind of appropriateness here discussed is afforded by the fine discovery, made by Geoffroy Saint-Hilaire in the last years of his life, of the more exact nature of the sucking apparatus of the cetacea. Thus, as all sucking demands the activity of respiration, it can take place only in the respirable medium itself, but not under water, where the suckling of the whale nevertheless hangs on to the mother's teats. To meet this, the whole mammary apparatus of the cetacea is so modified that it has become an injection-organ; and, placed in the suckling's mouth, it squirts the milk into it without the young having to suck. On the other hand, where the individual which affords essential help to another belongs to an entirely different species, even another kingdom of nature, we shall doubt this external appropriateness just as we do in the case of inorganic nature, unless the maintenance of the species obviously depends on it. This, however, is the case with many plants, whose fertilization takes place only by means of insects that either bear the pollen to the stigma or bend the stamens to the pistil. The common barberry, many kinds of iris, and *Aristolochia clematitis* cannot fertilize themselves at all without the help of insects. (C. C. Sprengel, *Entdecktes Geheimniss* etc., 1793; Wildenow, *Grundriss der Kräuterkunde,* 353.) In the same case are very many dioecia, monoecia, and polygamia, for example cucumbers and melons. The mutual support that plant and insect worlds receive from each other is admirably described in Burdach's large *Physiologie,* Vol. I, § 263. Very beautifully he adds: "This is no mechanical assistance, no makeshift, as though nature had formed the plants yesterday, and thus made a mistake which through the insect she tried to correct today; on the contrary, it is a more deep-lying sympathy between plant and animal worlds. The identity of the two ought to be revealed. Children of *one* mother, the two ought to subsist with and through each other." And farther on: "But the organic world is in such a sympathy even with the inorganic," and so on. A proof of this *consensus naturae* is also given by the observation, communicated in volume 2 of the *Introduction into Entomology* by Kirby and Spence, that the insect eggs that hibernate attached to the branches of the trees that serve as nourishment for their larvae, are hatched at the very time when the branch buds; thus for example, the aphis of the birch a month earlier than that of the ash; similarly that the insects of perennial plants hibernate on these as eggs, but since those of mere annuals cannot do this, they hibernate in the pupal state.

Three great men have entirely rejected teleology or the explanation from final causes; and many small men have echoed them. These are Lucretius, Bacon, and Spinoza. In the case of all three we know clearly enough the source of this aversion, namely that they regarded teleology as inseparable from speculative theology. But they entertained so great a fear of theology (which Bacon indeed prudently tries to conceal), that they wanted to give it a wide berth. We also find Leibniz labouring entirely under that prejudice, since with characteristic naivety he expresses it as something self-evident in his *Lettre à M. Nicaise* (Spinoza, *Opera,* ed. Paulus, Vol. II, p. 672): *Les causes finales, ou ce qui est LA MÊME CHOSE, la considération de la sagesse divine dans l'ordre des choses.*[8] (The devil also, *même chose!*) Indeed, we find at the same point of view even Englishmen of the present day, namely the Bridgewater Treatise men. Lord Brougham, and so on. In fact, even Richard Owen in his *Ostéologie comparée* thinks exactly as Leibniz does, and I have already censured this in my first volume. To all these teleology is at once also theology, and at every appropriateness or suitability they recognize in nature, instead of thinking and learning to understand nature, they at once break out into a childish cry of "Design! design!" They then strike up the refrain of their old women's philosophy, and stop their ears against all rational arguments such as the great Hume advanced against them.[9] Ignorance of the Kantian philosophy, which now after seventy years is a real disgrace to Englishmen of learning, is mainly responsible for the whole of this miserable and pitiful state of the English. Again, this ignorance depends, at any rate to a great extent, on the deplorable influence of that infamous English clergy, with whom stultification of every kind is a thing after their own hearts, so that they may be able still to keep the English nation, otherwise so intelligent, labouring under the most degrading bigotry. Therefore, inspired by the basest obscurantism, they oppose public instruction, the investigation of nature, in fact the advancement of all human knowledge in general, with all their might. They do this by means of their connexions, as well as by means of their scandalous, unwarrantable wealth that increases the misery of the people. Their influence extends even to university scholars and authors, who accordingly (e.g., Thomas Brown, *On Cause and Effect*) resort to suppressions and distortions of every kind, simply in order not to oppose, be it only remotely, that "cold

---

[8] "The final causes, or what is *the same thing,* the consideration of the divine wisdom in the order of things." [Tr.]

[9] Incidentally, it should here be noted that, to judge from German literature since Kant, we should be obliged to think that the whole of Hume's wisdom consisted in his palpably false scepticism with regard to the law of causality, as this alone is discussed everywhere. To know Hume, we must read his *Natural History of Religion* and the *Dialogues on Natural Religion.* There we see him in his greatness, and these, together with Essay 20 *On National Character,* are the works on account of which—I can think of nothing better to say for his fame—he is hated above all by the English clergy even at the present day.

superstition" (as Pückler very happily describes their religion), or the current arguments in its favour.

On the other hand, as the three great men we are discussing lived long before the dawn of the Kantian philosophy, their fear of teleology, on account of its origin, is pardonable; yet even Voltaire regarded the physico-theological proof as irrefutable. But to go into this somewhat more fully; first of all, the polemic of Lucretius (iv, 824-858) against teleology is so crass and crude, that it refutes itself and convinces us of the opposite. But as to Bacon (*De Augmentis Scientiarum,* III, 4), in the first place he makes no distinction, with reference to the use of final causes, between organic and inorganic nature (which is the very main point in question), since, in his examples of them, he mixes the two together. He then banishes final causes from physics to metaphysics; but for him, as for many even at the present day, metaphysics is identical with speculative theology. He therefore regards final causes as inseparable from this, and goes so far in this respect as to blame Aristotle, because that philosopher made vigorous use of final causes (a thing which in a moment I shall specially praise), yet without ever connecting them with speculative theology. Finally, Spinoza (*Ethics,* I, *prop.* 36, *appendix*) makes it very clear that he identifies teleology so entirely with physico-theology, against which he expresses himself with bitterness, that he explains: *Natura nihil frustra agere: hoc est, quod in usum hominum non sit;* similarly: *Omnia naturalia tanquam ad suum utile media considerant, et credunt aliquem alium esse, qui illa media paraverit;* and also: *hinc statuerunt, Deos omnia in usum hominum fecisse et dirigere.*[10] On this he then bases his assertion: *Natura finem nullum sibi praefixum habere et omnes causas finales nihil nisi humana esse figmenta.*[11] He was merely concerned with barring the way to theism; but he had quite rightly recognized the physico-theological proof as its strongest weapon. But it was reserved for Kant actually to refute this proof, and for me to give the correct explanation of its subject-matter; in this way I have satisfied the maxim *Est enim verum index sui et falsi.*[12] But Spinoza did not know how to help himself except by the desperate stroke of denying teleology itself, thus denying the appropriateness or suitability in the works of nature, an assertion

---

[10] "Nature does nothing in vain, in other words, that does not serve the purpose of mankind; . . . they regard all natural things as a means for their benefit, and believe that there is another who has prepared these means; . . . from this they have concluded that the gods have created and directed everything for the benefit of mankind." [Tr.]

[11] "Nature has not set herself an aim or end, and all final causes are nothing more than human fictions and inventions." [Tr.]

[12] "For the true bears evidence of itself and of the false." [Tr.]

whose monstrous character is at once apparent to anyone who has in any way acquired a more accurate knowledge of organic nature. This limited viewpoint of Spinoza, together with his complete ignorance of nature, is sufficient evidence of his total incompetence in this matter, and of the silliness of those who, on his authority, think they must judge disdainfully of final causes.

Aristotle, who here shows his brilliant side, contrasts very advantageously with these philosophers of modern times. Without prejudice he goes to nature, knows nothing of a physico-theology, such a thing never entered his head, and has never looked at the world to see whether it was something made. In his heart, he is free from all this, for he advances hypotheses (*De Generatione Animalium*, iii, 11) on the origin of animals and human beings without running into the physico-theological train of thought. He always says ἡ φύσις ποιεῖ (*natura facit*), never ἡ φύσις πεποίηται (*natura facta est*). However, after studying nature honestly and carefully, he finds that everywhere she goes to work appropriately, and he says: Μάτην ὁρῶμεν οὐδὲν ποιοῦσαν τὴν φύσιν (*Naturam nihil frustra facere cernimus*);[13] *De Respiratione*, c. 10, and in the books *De Partibus Animalium* which are a comparative anatomy: Οὐδὲ περίεργον οὐδέν, οὔτε μάτην ἡ φύσις ποιεῖ. . . . Ἡ φύσις ἕνεκά του ποιεῖ πάντα. . . . Πανταχοῦ δὲ λέγομεν τόδε τοῦδε ἕνεκα, ὅπου ἂν φαίνηται τέλος τι, πρὸς ὃ ἡ κίνησις περαίνει· ὥστε εἶναι φανερόν, ὃ δὴ καὶ τι τοιοῦτον, ὃ δὴ καὶ καλοῦμεν φύσιν. . . . Ἐπεὶ τὸ σῶμα ὄργανον· ἕνεκά τινος γὰρ ἕκαστον τῶν μορίων, ὁμοίως τε καὶ τὸ ὅλον. (*Nihil supervacaneum, nihil frustra natura facit. . . . Natura rei alicujus gratia facit omnia. . . . Rem autem hanc esse illius gratia asserere ubique solemus, quoties finem intelligimus aliquem, in quem motus terminetur: quocirca ejusmodi aliquid esse constat, quod Naturam vocamus. . . . Est enim corpus instrumentum: nam membrum unumquodque rei alicujus gratia est, tum vero totum ipsum.*[14] In more detail on pp. 645 and 663 of the Berlin quarto edition, as also *De Incessu Animalium* c. 2: Ἡ φύσις οὐδὲν ποιεῖ μάτην, ἀλλ' ἀεί, ἐκ τῶν ἐνδεχομένων τῇ οὐσίᾳ, περὶ ἕκαστον γένος ζῴου, τὸ ἄριστον. (*Natura nihil frustra facit, sed semper ex iis, quae cuique animalium generis essentiae contingunt, id quod optimum*

---

[13] "We see that nature does nothing in vain." [Tr.]

[14] "Nature does nothing superfluous and nothing in vain. . . . Nature does everything for the sake of an end. . . . But everywhere we say that this is done for the sake of that, where an end or aim is visible in which the movement terminates, so that it is clear that there is something we call nature. . . . For the body is an instrument; for each of its parts serves an end, and so also does the whole." [Tr.]

est.)[15] But he expressly recommends teleology at the end of the books *De Generatione Animalium,* and blames Democritus for having denied it; and this is precisely what Bacon in his narrow-mindedness praises in that thinker. But particularly in *Physica,* ii, 8, p. 198, Aristotle speaks *ex professo* of final causes, and sets them up as the true principle of the investigation of nature. Indeed, every good and normal mind, when considering organic nature, must hit upon teleology; yet, unless it is determined by preconceived opinions, it will not by any means hit either on physico-theology or on the anthropo-teleology censured by Spinoza. As regards Aristotle generally, I still wish to draw attention here to the fact that his teachings, in so far as they concern *inorganic* nature, are extremely defective and useless, since in the fundamental concepts of mechanics and physics he subscribes to the crudest errors. This is the less pardonable, as before him the Pythagoreans and Empedocles had already been on the right path, and had taught much better. Indeed, as we see from Aristotle's second book *De Coelo* (i, p. 284) Empedocles had already grasped the concept of a tangential force which arises through rotation, and counteracts gravity, a concept which Aristotle in turn rejects. Aristotle's attitude to a consideration of *organic* nature is quite the opposite; here is his field; here the abundance of his knowledge, his keen observation, and occasionally deep insight, astonish us. Thus, to quote only *one* instance, he had already recognized in ruminants the antagonism in which the horns and the teeth of the upper jaw stand to each other, by virtue of which the latter are wanting where the former are found, and *vice versa* (*De Partibus Animalium,* iii, 2). Hence also his correct estimation of final causes.

[15] "Nature does nothing in vain, but always that which is the best of what is possible for each animal species." [Tr.]

CHAPTER XXVII

On Instinct and Mechanical Tendency

It is as if, in the mechanical tendencies of animals, nature had wished to supply the investigator with an illustrative commentary on her works according to final causes and the admirable appropriateness of her organic productions which is thus brought about. For these mechanical tendencies show us most clearly that creatures can work with the greatest decision and certainty towards an end they do not know, of which, indeed, they have no notion. Such, for instance, is the bird's nest, the spider's web, the ant-lion's pitfall, the very ingenious beehive, the marvellous termite structure, and so on, at any rate for those individual animals that carry out such things for the first time; for neither the form of the work that is to be completed nor its use can be known to them. But it is precisely in this way that *organizing nature* works; for this reason, I gave in the previous chapter the paradoxical explanation of the final cause, namely that it is a motive that acts without being known. And just as in working from mechanical tendency what is active therein is obviously and admittedly the *will,* so also it is really the will that is active in the working of organizing nature.

It might be said that the will of animal creatures is set in motion in two different ways, either by motivation or by instinct, and hence from without or from within, by an external occasion or by an inner impulse; the former is explicable, because it lies without, before us, the latter is inexplicable, because it is merely internal. More closely considered, however, the contrast between the two is not so sharp; in fact, ultimately it runs back to a difference of degree. The motive also acts only on the assumption of an inner impulse, that is to say, of a definite disposition or quality of the will, called its *character*. The motive in each case gives this only a decided direction; individualizes it for the concrete case. In just the same way, although instinct is a decided impulse of the will, it does not act entirely from within, like a spring, but it too waits for an external circumstance necessarily required for this action, and that circumstance determines the moment of the instinct's manifestation.

Such is the season of the year for the migratory bird; the fertilization that has occurred and the material at its disposal, for the bird building its nest. For the bee it is, for beginning the structure, the basket or the hollow tree, and for the operations that follow, many circumstances that appear individually. For the spider it is a suitable and convenient corner; for the caterpillar, the suitable leaf; for the egg-laying insect, the place, in most cases very specially determined and often unusual, where the larvae on being hatched will at once find their nourishment; and there are other instances. It follows from this that, in works of mechanical tendency, the instinct is active in the first place, yet the intellect of these animals is also active in a subordinate way. Thus the instinct gives the universal, the rule; the intellect gives the particular, the application, since it directs the detail of the execution in which the work of these animals therefore obviously adapts itself to the circumstances in each case. In accordance with all this, the difference between instinct and mere character is to be settled by saying that instinct is a character set in motion only by a *quite specially determined* motive, and therefore the action resulting from it proves to be always of exactly the same kind; whereas the character, as possessed by every animal species and every human individual, is certainly also a permanent and unalterable quality of will. Yet this quality can be set in motion by very different motives, and adapts itself to them. For this reason the action resulting from it can, according to its material quality, turn out very different, yet it will always bear the stamp of the same character. It will therefore express and reveal this character; consequently, for the knowledge of this, the material quality of the action in which the character appears is essentially a matter of indifference. Accordingly, we might declare *instinct* to be an excessively *one-sided* and *strictly determined character*. It follows from this statement that to be determined by mere *motivation* presupposes a certain width of the sphere of knowledge, and consequently a more perfectly developed intellect. It is therefore peculiar to the higher animals, and quite specially to man. On the other hand, to be determined by *instinct* demands only as much intellect as is necessary to apprehend the one quite specially determined motive that alone and exclusively becomes the occasion for the instinct's manifestation. For this reason, it occurs in the case of an extremely limited sphere of knowledge, and therefore, as a rule and in the highest degree, only in the case of animals of the inferior classes, particularly insects. Accordingly, as the actions of these animals require only an extremely simple and limited motivation from outside, the medium of this, the intellect or brain, is developed in them only feebly, and their external actions are for the most part under the same guidance as are the internal physiological functions occurring on mere stimuli, hence as is the ganglionic system. In them, therefore, this is developed to an exceedingly high degree; their principal nerve-stem runs in the form of two cords under the belly, and with every limb of the body these form a ganglion often only a little inferior in size to the brain. According to Cuvier, this nerve-stem is an analogue not so much of the spinal cord as of the great sympathetic nerve. As a result of all this, instinct and guidance through mere motivation stand in a certain antagonism, in consequence of which the former reaches its maximum in insects, the latter in man. The actuation of all the other animals lies between the two in many different gradations, according as the cerebral or the ganglionic system is predominantly developed in each. If we regard the instinctive actions and skilful operations of insects as coming only from the brain, and try to explain them accordingly, we run into absurdities, in that we then apply a false key, because they are directed mainly from the ganglionic system. But the same circumstance gives to their actions a remarkable similarity to those of somnambulists. Indeed, this is also explained from the fact that, instead of the brain, the sympathetic nerve has taken over the direction of the external actions as well. Accordingly, insects are to a certain extent natural somnambulists. Things that we cannot get at directly must be made intelligible to us through an analogy. The one just touched on will achieve this in a high degree, if we make use here of the fact that in Kieser's *Tellurismus* (Vol. II, p. 250) a case is mentioned "where the order of the mesmerizer to the somnambulist to perform a definite action in the waking state was carried out by her when she had woken up, without her clearly recalling the order." Thus to her it was as though she had to perform that action without really knowing why. This certainly has the greatest resemblance to what happens in the case of the mechanical tendencies in insects. The young spider feels as if it had to spin its web, although it neither knows nor understands its purpose. Here we are also reminded of the daemon of Socrates, by virtue of which he had the feeling that he must leave undone an action expected of him or lying near him, without his knowing why; for his prophetic dream about it was forgotten. We have quite well-authenticated cases analogous to this in our own day; I therefore call these to mind only briefly. One person had booked his passage in a ship, but when it was about to sail he positively would not go on board, and was not aware of any ground or reason; the ship went down. Another goes with companions to a powder-magazine; when he arrives in its vicinity, he absolutely refuses to go any farther, but quickly turns round; he is seized with fear without knowing why; the magazine blew up. A third person at sea feels induced one evening, without any ground or reason, not to undress. He lies down in his clothes and boots, and even with his spectacles on. In the night the ship catches fire, and he is one of the few who are saved in the boat. All this depends on the dull after-effect of forgotten fatidical dreams, and gives us the key to an analogous understanding of instinct and mechanical tendencies.

On the other hand, as I have said, the mechanical tendencies of insects reflect much light on the working of the will-without-knowledge in the inner mechanism of the organism and its formation. For we can see quite easily and naturally in the ant-hill or in the beehive the picture of an organism explained and brought to the light of knowledge. In this sense, Burdach says (*Physiologie,* Vol. II, p. 22): "The formation and laying of the eggs is the queen's part; the insemination and care for their development fall to the workers; in the former the ovary, in the latter the uterus, have, so to speak, become individual." In the insect society, as in the animal organism, the *vita propria* of each part is subordinated to the life of the whole, and the care for the whole precedes that for the particular or specific existence; the latter, in fact, is willed only conditionally, the former unconditionally. Therefore the individuals are occasionally even sacrificed to the whole, just as we have a limb removed in order to save the whole body. Thus, for example, if the way is barred to a column of ants by water, the foremost ants boldly throw themselves in, until their corpses have been heaped up into a dam for those that follow. When the drones have become useless, they are stung to death. Two queens in the hive are surrounded, and must fight with each other until one of them loses its life. The mother-ant bites off her own wings after the business of impregnation is over; they would be only a hindrance to her in the actual business of tending under the earth the new family she is to start. (Kirby and Spence, Vol. I.) The liver will do nothing more than secrete bile for the service of digestion; in fact, it exists merely for this purpose, and every other part is just the same. So also the workers will do nothing more than collect honey, separate wax, and build cells for the brood of the queen; the drones will do nothing more than fertilize, the queen nothing more than lay eggs. Thus all the parts work merely for the continued existence of the whole, which alone is the unconditional aim or end, exactly like the parts of the organism. The difference is merely that in the organism the will acts quite blindly in its primary and original nature; on the other hand, in the insect society the thing goes on in the light of knowledge. But a decided co-operation and even some choice are left to this knowledge only in the accidents of detail, where it gives assistance and adapts to the circumstances what is to be carried out. The insects, however, will the end as a whole without knowing it, just as organic nature works according to final causes. Even the choice of the means as a whole is not left to their knowledge, but only the more detailed ordering of these separately. Yet just on this account their action is by no means mechanical, and this becomes most clearly visible when we put obstacles in the way of their movements. For example, the caterpillar spins itself in leaves without knowing the purpose; but if we destroy the web, it skilfully mends it. To begin with, bees adapt their hive to circumstances as they find them, and subsequent mishaps, such as intentional destruction, are remedied by them in the way most suitable to the particular case. (Kirby and Spence, *Introduction to Entomology;* Huber, *Des abeilles.*) Such things excite our admiration, because the apprehension of the circumstances and the adaptation to them are obviously a matter of knowledge, whereas we credit them once for all with the most ingenious foresight for the coming generation and the remote future, well knowing that in this they are not guided by knowledge; for a foresight of this kind proceeding from knowledge demands a brain-activity raised to the level of the faculty of reason. On the other hand, even the intellect of the lower animals is equal to modifying and arranging the individual case according to existing or supervening circumstances, since, guided by instinct, it has only to fill up the gaps left thereby. Thus we see ants drag away their larvae as soon as the place becomes too damp, and again as soon as it becomes too dry. They do not know the purpose of this; hence in this they are not guided by knowledge, but the choice of the moment when the place is no longer suitable for the larvae, and the choice of another place to which they then bring them, are left to their knowledge. Here I wish to mention a fact that someone related to me verbally from his own experience, although I have since found that Burdach quotes it as coming from Gleditsch. To test the burying-beetle (*Necrophorus vespillo*), the former had tied a dead frog lying on the ground to a string fastened at the upper end to a stick inserted obliquely in the ground. After several burying-beetles had, according to their custom, undermined the frog, it could not sink into the ground, as they expected; after much perplexed running about, they also undermined the stick. In the organism, we find the *healing power* of nature analogous to this assistance rendered to instinct, and to that repairing of the works of mechanical tendency. This healing power not only closes up and heals wounds, thus replacing even bone and nerve substance, but also, if a connexion is interrupted through loss of a vein branch or nerve branch, opens a new connexion by means of an enlargement of other veins or nerves, possibly even by pushing out new branches. Further, it causes another part or function to take the place of one that is diseased; on the loss of an eye, it sharpens the other, and on the loss of one sense, it sharpens all the rest. Sometimes it closes even an intestinal wound, in itself fatal, by adhesion of the mesentery or the peritoneum; in short, it tries to cope with every injury and disturbance in the most ingenious manner. On the other hand, if the injury is quite incurable, it expedites death, and indeed the more so the higher the species, thus the more sensitive the organism. Even this has its analogue in the instinct of insects; thus wasps who have reared their larvae throughout the whole summer with great trouble and labour on the produce of their plundering, but then see the last generation of these face starvation in October, sting them to death. (Kirby and Spence, Vol. I, p. 374.) In fact, even stranger and more special analogies may be found; for example, if the female bumble-bee (*Apis terrestris, bombylius*) lays eggs, the working bumble-bees are seized with an urge to devour them. This lasts from six to eight hours, and is satisfied, unless the mother keeps them off, and carefully guards the eggs. After this time, however, the working bumble-bees show absolutely no desire to eat the eggs, even when they are offered to them. On the contrary, they now become the zealous fosterers and sustainers of the larvae that are being hatched. This may be taken quite naturally as an analogue of children's complaints, especially of teething, where it is just the future nourishers of the organism that make on it an attack that so frequently costs it its life. The consideration of all these analogies between organic life and instinct, together with the mechanical tendency of the lower animals, serves to strengthen more and more the conviction that the *will* is the basis of the one as of the other, since here it also shows the subordinate role of knowledge in the working of the will, a role that is sometimes more restricted, sometimes less, and sometimes entirely wanting.

But in yet another respect instincts and the animal organization mutually illustrate each other, namely through the *anticipation of the future* which appears in both. By means of instincts and mechanical tendencies, animals provide for the satisfaction of needs they do not yet feel, indeed not only their own needs, but even those of their future offspring. Hence they work for a purpose still unknown to them. As I have illustrated in my work *On the Will in Nature*, p. 45 (second edition) by the example of the *Bombex*, this goes to the extent that they pursue and kill in advance the enemies of their future eggs. In just the same way, we see in the whole corporization of an animal its future needs, its prospective aims, anticipated by the organic implements for their attainment and satisfaction. From this there results that perfect fitness of every animal's structure to its mode of life, that equipping of it with the weapons necessary for it to attack its prey and to ward off its enemies, and that calculation of its whole shape and form with regard to the element and environment in which it has to appear as a pursuer. I have fully described this in my work *On the Will in Nature* under the heading "Comparative Anatomy." All these anticipations, appearing in instinct as well as in the organization of animals, could be brought under the concept of knowledge *a priori,* if a *knowledge* in general were the basis of them. But this, as I have shown, is not the case; their origin lies deeper than the sphere of knowledge, namely in the will as the thing-in-itself. This as such remains free even from the *forms* of knowledge; therefore with reference to it *time* has no significance, and consequently the future is just as near to it as the present.

CHAPTER XXVIII[1]

Characterization of the Will-to-Live

Our second book ends with the question as to the aim and purpose of this will that has proved to be the inner nature of all things in the world. The following remarks serve to supplement the answer to this question which is given there in general terms, since they explain the character of that will in general.

Such a characterization is possible, since we have recognized as the inner being of the world something thoroughly actual and empirically given. On the other hand, the name "world-soul," by which many have expressed that inner being, gives, instead of this, a mere *ens rationis*. For "soul" signifies an individual unity of consciousness which obviously does not belong to that inner being; and generally, since the concept "soul" supposes knowing and willing to be in inseparable connexion, and yet independent of the animal organism, it is not to be justified, and therefore not to be used. The word should never be applied except in a metaphorical sense, for it is by no means as simple and natural as ψυχή or *anima,* which mean breath.

Even much more unsuitable is the method of expression of the so-called pantheists; their whole philosophy consists principally in their giving the title "God" to the inner nature of the world which is unknown to them, and by this they imagine they have achieved a great deal. Accordingly, the world would be a theophany. But let us merely look at it; this world of constantly needy creatures who continue for a time merely by devouring one another, pass their existence in anxiety and want, and often endure terrible afflictions, until they fall at last into the arms of death. He who has this clearly in view will allow that Aristotle is right when he says: ἡ φύσις δαιμονία ἀλλ' οὐ θεία ἐστι (*natura daemonia est, non divina;*[2] *De Divinatione,* c. 2, p. 463); in fact he will have to admit that a God who should presume to transform himself into such a world would certainly have

---

[1] This chapter refers to § 29 of volume 1.
[2] "Nature is not divine, but demon-like." [Tr.]

been inevitably troubled and tormented by the devil. I know quite well that the would-be philosophers of this century emulate Spinoza, and consider themselves justified in so doing. But Spinoza had special reasons for calling his sole and exclusive substance God, namely to preserve at least the word, if not the thing. The stake of Giordano Bruno and Vanini was still fresh in the memory; these also had been sacrificed to that God, in whose honour incomparably more human sacrifices have bled than have been offered on the altars of all the heathen gods of both hemispheres together. Therefore, when Spinoza calls the world God, it is only exactly the same thing as when Rousseau, in the *Contrat social,* constantly and throughout describes the people by the word *souverain.* We might also compare it with this, that once a prince, who intended to abolish the nobility in his country, hit on the idea of ennobling all his subjects, in order not to deprive anyone of his property. Those wise men of our day have of course yet another reason for the nomenclature we are speaking of, but it is no more valid. Thus in their philosophizing, they all start not from the world or from our consciousness thereof, but from God as something given and known; he is not their *quaesitum* but their *datum.* If they were boys, I would explain to them that this is a *petitio principii;* but they know this as well as I do. But after Kant had shown that the path of the earlier dogmatism proceeding honestly, namely the path from the world to a God, does not lead there, these gentlemen imagined they had found a fine way out, and did it cunningly. I hope the reader of later times will forgive me for talking about persons with whom he is not acquainted.

Every glance at the world, to explain which is the task of the philosopher, confirms and establishes that the *will-to-live,* far from being an arbitrary hypostasis or even an empty expression, is the only true description of the world's innermost nature. Everything presses and pushes towards *existence,* if possible towards *organic existence,* i.e., *life,* and then to the highest possible degree thereof. In animal nature, it then becomes obvious that *will-to-live* is the keynote of its being, its only unchangeable and unconditioned quality. Let us consider this universal craving for life, and see the infinite eagerness, ease, and exuberance with which the will-to-live presses impetuously into existence under millions of forms everywhere and at every moment by means of fertilizations and germs, and indeed, where these are lacking, by means of *generatio aequivoca,* seizing every opportunity, greedily grasping for itself every material capable of life; and then again, let us cast a glance at its awful alarm and wild rebellion, when in any individual phenomenon it is to pass out of existence, especially where this occurs with distinct consciousness.

Then it is precisely the same as if in this single phenomenon the whole world were to be annihilated for ever; and the entire inner nature of a living being thus threatened is at once transformed into the most desperate struggle against, and resistance to, death. Let us see, for example, the incredible anxiety of a person in danger of his life, the quick and serious sympathy of every witness to this, and the boundless rejoicing after he has been saved. Look at the rigid terror with which a sentence of death is heard, the profound dread with which we view the preparations for carrying it out, and the heartrending pity that seizes us at the execution itself. We might then imagine that it was a question of something quite different from merely a few years less of an empty, sad existence embittered by worries and troubles of every kind, and always uncertain. On the contrary, we could not fail to be amazed that it should be of any consequence whether a person reached a few years earlier the place where after an ephemeral existence he has to be for billions of years. Therefore in such phenomena it becomes evident that I have rightly declared the *will-to-live* to be that which is incapable of further explanation, but is the basis of every explanation; and that, far from being an empty-sounding word, like the Absolute, the infinite, the idea, and other similar expressions, it is the most real thing we know, in fact the kernel of reality itself.

But if we abstract for a while from this interpretation that is drawn from our inner being, and confront nature as strangers, in order to comprehend her objectively, we find that, from the grade of organic life upwards, she has only *one* purpose, namely that of *maintaining all the species*. She works towards this through the immense surplus of seeds and germs, through the pressing intensity of the sexual impulse, through the eagerness of this impulse to adapt itself to all circumstances and opportunities, even to the production of bastards, and through that instinctive maternal affection whose strength is so great that in many kinds of animals it outweighs self-love, so that the mother sacrifices her own life in order to save that of her young. On the other hand, the individual has for nature only an indirect value, in so far as it is a means for maintaining the species. Apart from this, its existence is a matter of indifference to nature; in fact, nature herself leads it to destruction as soon as it ceases to be fit for that purpose. For what purpose the individual exists is therefore clear; but for what purpose does the species itself exist? This is a question to which nature makes no reply, when she is considered merely objectively. For when we contemplate her, we try in vain to discover a purpose for this restless bustle and activity, this impetuous pressing into existence, this anxious care for the maintenance of species. The strength and time of individuals are consumed in the effort to procure sustenance for themselves and their young, and they are only just sufficient, sometimes even quite insufficient, for this. But although, here and there, a surplus of strength, and thus of ease and comfort—and of knowledge also in the case of the *one* rational species—remains, this is much too insignificant to be capable of being regarded as the end and purpose of that whole process of nature. Thus regarded purely objectively, and even as extraneous to us, the whole thing looks just as if nature were concerned only that, of all her (Platonic) Ideas, i.e., permanent forms, none should be lost. Accordingly, it looks as if she had so thoroughly satisfied herself in the fortunate invention and combination of these Ideas (for which the three preceding animal populations of the earth's surface were the preliminary practice), that her only concern now was that any one of these fine fancies might be lost, in other words, that any one of those forms might disappear from time and the causal series. For the individuals are fleeting, like the water in the stream; the Ideas, on the other hand, are permanent, like its eddies; only the drying up of the water would destroy these. We should have to stop at this puzzling view if nature were given to us only from outside, and thus merely *objectively;* we should have to accept it as it is comprehended by knowledge, also as sprung from knowledge, i.e., in the sphere of the representation, and accordingly should have to keep to this sphere when unravelling nature. But the case is otherwise, and a glance into the *interior of nature* is certainly granted to us, in so far as this is nothing but *our own inner being.* It is precisely here that nature, having arrived at the highest stage up to which her activity could work, is immediately found in self-consciousness by the light of knowledge. Here the *will* shows itself to us as something *toto genere* different from the *representation,* in which nature stood out, unfolded to all her (Platonic) Ideas. It now gives us at one stroke the explanation that was never to be found on the merely *objective* path of the *representation.* Therefore the subjective here gives the key to the explanation of the objective.

In order to recognize, as something original and unconditioned, that exceedingly strong tendency of all animals and human beings to maintain life and continue it as long as possible—a tendency that was described above as the characterization of this subjective, or of the will—we are still required to make it clear that this tendency is by no means the result of any objective *knowledge* of the value of life, but is independent of all knowledge; or, in other words, that those beings exhibit themselves not as drawn from the front, but as driven from behind.

With this purpose, we first of all review the immense series of animals, and consider the infinite variety of their forms, as they exhibit themselves always differently modified, according to the element and mode of life. At the same time we reflect on the unattainable ingenuity of their structure and mechanism, carried out in each individual with equal perfection. Finally, we take into consideration the incredible expenditure of strength, skill, shrewdness, and activity every animal has to undertake incessantly throughout its life. Going into the matter more closely, for example, we contemplate the restless industry of wretched little ants, the marvellous and ingenious diligence of bees, or observe how a single burying-beetle (*Necrophorus vespillo*) buries a mole forty times its own size in two days, in order to lay its eggs in it, and to ensure nourishment for the future offspring (Gleditsch, *Physik. Bot. Oekon.*, Art. III, 220). In this connexion, we call to mind how in general the life of most insects is nothing but a restless labour for preparing nourishment and dwelling for the future offspring that will come from their eggs. After the offspring have consumed the nourishment and have turned into the chrysalis stage, they enter into life merely to begin the same task again from the beginning. We then reflect how, in a similar manner, the life of birds is taken up with their distant and wearisome migration, then with the building of the nest and the procuring of food for the offspring, and how these themselves have to play the same role in the following year; and thus all work constantly for the future that afterwards becomes bankrupt. If we consider the foregoing, we cannot help looking round for the reward of all this skill and exertion, for the end or aim which the animals have before their eyes, and to which they aspire so restlessly; in short, we cannot help asking what comes of all this, and what is attained by animal existence that demands such immense preparations. And there is nothing to show but the satisfaction of hunger and sexual passion, and in any case a little momentary gratification, such as falls to the lot of every individual animal, now and then, between its endless needs and exertions. If we put the two together, the inexpressible ingenuity of the preparations, the untold abundance of the means, and the inadequacy of what is thus aimed at and attained, we are driven to the view that life is a business whose returns are far from covering the cost. This becomes most evident in many animals of a particularly simple mode of life. For example, consider that indefatigable worker the mole; to dig strenuously with its enormous shovel-paws is the business of its whole life; permanent night surrounds it; it has its embryo eyes merely to avoid the light. It alone is a true *animal nocturnum*, not cats, owls, and bats which see by night. What does it attain by this course of life that is full of trouble and devoid of pleasure? Nourishment and procreation, that is, only the means for continuing and beginning again in the new individual the same melancholy course. In such examples it becomes clear that the cares and troubles of life are out of all proportion to the yield or profit from it. The consciousness of the world of perception, however, gives an appearance of objective worth of existence to the life of those animals that see, although such consciousness is with them entirely subjective and limited to the influence of motives. The *blind* mole, however, with its perfect organization and restless activity, limited to the alternation of insect larvae and starvation, makes obvious the disproportion of the means to the end. In this respect, the consideration of the animal world left to itself in countries uninhabited by human beings is also particularly instructive. A fine picture of such a world, and of the sufferings nature herself prepares for it without the interference of man, is given by Humboldt in his *Ansichten der Natur,* second edition, pp. 30 *seq.;* nor does he neglect on page 44 to cast a glance at the analogous suffering of the human race, always and everywhere at variance with itself. But the futility and fruitlessness of the struggle of the whole phenomenon are more readily grasped in the simple and easily observable life of animals. The variety and multiplicity of the organizations, the ingenuity of the means by which each is adapted to its element and to its prey, here contrast clearly with the absence of any lasting final aim. Instead of this, we see only momentary gratification, fleeting pleasure conditioned by wants, much and long suffering, constant struggle, *bellum omnium,* everything a hunter and everything hunted, pressure, want, need, and anxiety, shrieking and howling; and this goes on *in saecula saeculorum,* or until once again the crust of the planet breaks. Junghuhn relates that in Java he saw an immense field entirely covered with skeletons, and took it to be a battle-field. However, they were nothing but skeletons of large turtles five feet long, three feet broad, and of equal height. These turtles come this way from the sea, in order to lay their eggs, and are then seized by wild dogs (*Canis rutilans*); with their united strength, these dogs lay them on their backs, tear open their lower armour, the small scales of the belly, and devour them alive. But then a tiger often pounces on the dogs. Now all this misery is repeated thousands and thousands of times, year in year out. For this, then, are these turtles born. For what offence must they suffer this agony? What is the point of this whole scene of horror? The only answer is that the *will-to-live* thus objectifies itself.*

---

* In the *Siècle* of 10 April 1859 there is a very finely written story of a squirrel that was *magically* drawn by a snake right into its jaws: "*Un voy-*

Let us fully consider it, and comprehend it in all its objectifications, and we shall then arrive at an understanding of its true nature and of

---

ageur qui vient de parcourir plusieurs provinces de l'île de Java cite un exemple remarquable du pouvoir fascinateur des serpens. Le voyageur dont il est question commençait à gravir le Junjind, un des monts appelés par les Hollandais Pepergebergte. Après avoir pénétré dans une épaisse forêt, il aperçut sur les branches d'un kijatile un écureuil de Java à tête blanche, folâtrant avec la grâce et l'agilité qui distinguent cette charmante espèce de rongeurs. Un nid sphérique, formé de brins flexibles et de mousse, placé dans les parties les plus élevées de l'arbre, à l'enfourchure de deux branches et une cavité dans le tronc, semblaient les points de mire de ses yeux. A peine s'en était-il éloigné qu'il y revenait avec une ardeur extrême. On était dans le mois de juillet et probablement l'écureuil avait en haut ses petits, et dans le bas le magasin à fruits. Bientôt il fut comme saisi d'effroi, ses mouvemens devinrent désordonnés, on eut dit qu'il cherchait toujours à mettre un obstacle entre lui et certaines parties de l'arbre: puis il se tapit et resta immobile entre deux branches. Le voyageur eut le sentiment d'un danger pour l'innocente bête, mais il ne pouvait deviner lequel. Il approcha, et un examen attentif lui fit découvrir dans un creux du tronc une couleuvre lien, dardant ses yeux fixes dans la direction de l'écureuil. . . . Notre voyageur trembla pour le pauvre écureuil.—L'appareil destiné à la perception des sons est peu parfait chez les serpens et ils ne paraissent pas avoir l'ouïe très fine. La couleuvre était d'ailleurs si attentive à sa proie qu'elle ne semblait nullement remarquer la présence d'un homme. Notre voyageur, qui était armé, aurait donc pu venir en aide à l'infortuné rongeur en tuant le serpent. Mais la science l'emporta sur la pitié, et il voulut voir quelle issue aurait le drame. Le dénoûment fut tragique. L'écureuil ne tarda point à pousser un cri plaintif qui, pour tous ceux qui le connaissent, dénote le voisinage d'un serpent. Il avança un peu, essaya de reculer, revint encore en avant, tâcha de retourner en arrière, mais s'approcha toujours plus du reptile. La couleuvre, roulée en spirale, la tête au-dessus des anneaux, et immobile comme un morceau de bois, ne le quittait pas du regard. L'écureuil, de branche en branche, et descendant toujours plus bas, arriva jusqu'à la partie nue du tronc. Alors le pauvre animal ne tenta même plus de fuir le danger. Attiré par une puissance invincible, et comme poussé par le vertige, il se précipita dans la gueule du serpent, qui s'ouvrit tout à coup démesurément pour le recevoir. Autant la couleuvre avait été inerte jusque là, autant elle devint active dès qu'elle fut en possession de sa proie. Déroulant ses anneaux et prenant sa course de bas en haut avec une agilité inconcevable, sa reptation la porta en un clin d'œil au sommet de l'arbre où elle alla sans doute digérer et dormir."

["A traveller, who recently journeyed through several provinces of the island of Java, quotes a remarkable instance of the fascinating power of snakes. The traveller in question began to ascend the Junjind, one of the mountains called Pepergebergte by the Dutch. After he had penetrated the dense jungle, he noticed on the branches of a kijatile a Javanese squirrel with a white head. It was sporting and frisking about with the grace and agility that distinguish this charming species of rodents. A spherical nest, formed of flexible twigs and moss and set in the higher part of the tree at the fork of two branches, and a cavity in the trunk, seemed to be the two goals of its eyes. No sooner was it at a distance from them than it returned the world; but we shall not do so, if we frame general concepts and build houses of cards out of these. Comprehending the great drama of the objectification of the *will-to-live* and the characterization of its true nature certainly demands a somewhat more accurate consideration and greater thoroughness than simply disposing of the world by attributing to it the name of God, or, with a silliness such as only the German Fatherland offers and is able to delight in, by explaining that it is the "Idea in its being otherwise." The simpletons of my time have for twenty years found in this their unutterable delight.

to them with the greatest eagerness. It was the month of July, and probably the squirrel had its young in the nest and its storehouse of fruit in the cavity. Suddenly it appeared to be seized with terror and its movements became irregular; it was as if it were trying always to place an obstacle between itself and certain parts of the tree. Finally it crouched and remained motionless between two branches. The traveller had the impression that danger threatened the innocent little animal, but he could not tell what was the nature of the peril. He approached, and a careful examination enabled him to discover in a hollow of the trunk a ribbon snake fixing its eyes in the direction of the squirrel. . . . Our traveller trembled for the poor little squirrel. The mechanism intended for the hearing of sounds is little developed in snakes, and they do not appear to have a very fine sense of hearing. Moreover, the snake was so preoccupied with its prey that it did not appear at all to notice the presence of a human being. Our traveller, who was armed, could have come to the assistance of the unfortunate rodent and killed the snake. But science was stronger than pity, and he wanted to see how the drama would end. The outcome was tragic. The squirrel certainly did not fail to utter a plaintive cry which, for all who know it, indicates the presence of a snake. It went forward a step, attempted to retreat, went forward again, and tried to turn back, but came ever nearer to the reptile. The snake, coiled up and with its head above its coils, was as motionless as a piece of wood, and did not take its eyes off the squirrel. The squirrel descended from branch to branch until it reached a bare part of the trunk. The poor animal now made no further attempt to avoid the danger. Attracted by an invincible power and seized as it were by dizziness, it rushed headlong into the jaws of the snake which were suddenly opened as wide as possible in order to receive it. Up till then the snake had been quite motionless, but now it became just as active as soon as it was in possession of its prey. Uncoiling itself and pursuing its course upwards with incredible agility, it reached the top of the tree in an instant, where no doubt it digested its prey and went to sleep." Tr.]

In this example we see what spirit animates nature, since it reveals itself in this, and how very true is the above-quoted saying of Aristotle. This story is important not merely in a magic regard, but also as an argument for *pessimism*. That an animal is suddenly attacked and devoured by another is bad, yet we can reconcile ourselves to this; but that such a poor innocent squirrel, sitting by its nest with its young, is compelled, step by step, reluctantly, struggling with itself and lamenting, to approach the snake's wide, open jaws and hurl itself consciously into these, is so revolting and atrocious, that we feel how right Aristotle is in saying ἡ φύσις δαιμονία μέν ἐστι, οὐ δὲ θεία. How frightful is this nature to which we belong!

According to pantheism or Spinozism, of which those systems of our century are mere travesties, all this of course actually reels itself off without end, straight on through all eternity. For then the world is a God, *ens perfectissimum;* that is to say, there can be nothing better, nor can anything better be conceived. Hence there is no need of deliverance from it, consequently there is none; but no one has the remotest idea why the whole tragi-comedy exists, for it has no spectators, and the actors themselves undergo endless worry and trouble with little and merely negative enjoyment.

Let us now add a consideration of the human race; the matter indeed becomes more complicated, and assumes a certain seriousness of aspect, yet the fundamental character remains unchanged. Here too life by no means presents itself as a gift to be enjoyed, but as a task, a drudgery, to be worked through. According to this we see, on a large scale as well as on a small, universal need, restless exertion, constant pressure, endless strife, forced activity, with extreme exertion of all bodily and mental powers. Many millions, united into nations, strive for the common good, each individual for his own sake; but many thousands fall a sacrifice to it. Now senseless delusion, now intriguing politics, incite them to wars with one another; then the sweat and blood of the great multitude must flow, to carry through the ideas of individuals, or to atone for their shortcomings. In peace industry and trade are active, inventions work miracles, seas are navigated, delicacies are collected from all the ends of the earth, the waves engulf thousands. All push and drive, some plotting and planning, others acting; the tumult is indescribable. But what is the ultimate aim of it all? To sustain ephemeral and harassed individuals through a short span of time, in the most fortunate case with endurable want and comparative painlessness, yet boredom is at once on the lookout for this; then the propagation of this race and of its activities. With this evident want of proportion between the effort and the reward, the will-to-live, taken objectively, appears to us from this point of view as a fool, or taken subjectively, as a delusion. Seized by this, every living thing works with the utmost exertion of its strength for something that has no value. But on closer consideration, we shall find here also that it is rather a blind urge, an impulse wholly without ground and motive.

As was discussed in § 29 of volume 1, the law of motivation extends only to particular actions, not to willing *as a whole and in general.* It depends on this that, if we conceive the human race and its activities *as a whole and universally,* it does not present itself to us, as when we have in view individual actions, like a puppet-show, the dolls of which are pulled by external strings in the ordinary way.

On the contrary, from this point of view, it presents itself as puppets that are set in motion by an internal clockwork. For if we compare, as was done just now, the restless, serious, and laborious efforts of men with what they get from them, in fact with what they ever can get, the disproportion we have pointed out becomes apparent, since we recognize that what is to be attained, taken as motive power, is wholly inadequate to explain that movement and that restless activity. Thus, what are a short postponement of death, a small alleviation of need and want, a deferment of pain, a momentary satisfaction of desire, with the frequent and certain victory of death over them all? Taken as actual causes of movement of the human race, what could such advantages achieve? This human race is innumerable through its being constantly renewed; it is incessantly astir, pushes, presses, worries, struggles, and performs the whole tragi-comedy of world-history. In fact, what says more than anything else, everyone *perseveres* in such a mock existence as long as he possibly can. Obviously, all this is not to be explained, if we look for the moving causes outside the figures, and conceive the human race as striving, in consequence of a rational reflection or of something analogous thereto (as pulling strings), after the good things which are presented to it and whose attainment would be an adequate reward for its restless efforts and troubles. If the matter were taken thus, everyone would rather have said long ago *Le jeu ne vaut pas la chandelle,*[3] and would have passed out. On the contrary, everyone guards and protects his life like a precious pledge entrusted to him under a heavy responsibility, under infinite care and daily necessity; and under these life is just tolerable. Naturally, he does not see the why and the wherefore, the reward for this, but has accepted the value of that pledge in good faith and on trust without looking into it; and he does not know in what this value consists. Therefore I have said that those puppets are not pulled from outside, but that each of them bears in itself the clockwork from which its movements result. This is the *will-to-live* manifesting itself as an untiring mechanism, as an irrational impulse, which does not have its sufficient ground or reason in the external world. It holds the individuals firmly on this scene, and is the *primum mobile* of their movements; whereas the external objects, the motives, determine merely the direction of these movements in the particular case, otherwise the cause would not be in any way appropriate to the effect. For, just as every manifestation of a force of nature has a cause, but the force of nature itself has none, so has every individual act of will a motive, but the will in

---

[3] "The game is not worth the candle." [Tr.]

general, none; in fact, at bottom these two are one and the same. The will, as the metaphysical, is everywhere the boundary-stone of every investigation, beyond which this cannot go anywhere. From the original and unconditioned nature of the will, which has been demonstrated, it is easy to explain that man loves above everything else an existence which is full of want, misery, trouble, pain, anxiety, and then again full of boredom, and which, were it pondered over and considered purely objectively, he would of necessity abhor; and that he fears above everything else the end of this existence, which is nevertheless for him the one and only thing certain.[4] Accordingly, we often see a miserable figure, deformed and bent with age, want, and disease, appeal to us from the bottom of his heart for help for the prolongation of an existence, whose end would necessarily appear as altogether desirable, if it were an objective judgement that was the determining factor. Therefore, instead of this, it is the blind will appearing as the tendency to life, the love of life, vital energy; it is the same thing that makes the plant grow. This vital energy can be compared to a rope, stretched above the puppet-show of the world of men, on which the puppets hang by means of invisible threads, while they are *only apparently* supported by the ground beneath them (the objective value of life). But if once this rope becomes weak, the puppet sinks; if it breaks, the puppet must fall, for the ground under it supports it only in appearance; in other words, the weakening of that love of life shows itself as hypochondria, spleen, melancholy; the complete exhaustion of that love of life shows itself as an inclination to suicide. This then occurs on the slightest occasion, in fact on one that is merely imaginary, since the person, so to speak, now picks a quarrel with himself, in order to shoot himself dead, as many a person does to another for a similar purpose; in fact, in an emergency, suicide is resorted to without any special occasion. (Proofs of this are found in Esquirol, *Des maladies mentales,* 1838.) And as it is with the persistence in life, so is it also with its action and movement. This is not something freely chosen; but whereas everyone would really like to rest, want and boredom are the whips that keep the top spinning. Therefore the whole and each individual bear the stamp of a forced condition. Since everyone is inwardly indolent and longs for rest, but must nevertheless go forward, he is like his planet, that does not fall into the sun only because a force driving it forward does not allow this to happen. Thus everything is in permanent tension and forced movement, and the course of the world goes on, to

---

[4] Augustine, *The City of God,* xi, c. 27, deserves to be compared as an interesting commentary on what is said here.

use an expression of Aristotle (*De Coelo,* ii, 13), οὐ φύσει, ἀλλὰ βίᾳ (*motu non naturali, sed violento*).[5] Only apparently are people drawn from in front; in reality they are pushed from behind. It is not life that entices them on, but want and trouble that drive them forward. Like all causality, the law of motivation is a mere form of the phenomenon. Incidentally, here is to be found the origin of the comical, the burlesque, the grotesque, the ridiculous side of life; for, driven forward against his will, everyone bears himself as best he can, and the resultant perplexity and embarrassment often present a ludicrous effect, however serious may be the care and worry underlying them.

From all these considerations it thus becomes clear to us that the will-to-live is not a consequence of the knowledge of life, is in no way a *conclusio ex praemissis,* and in general is nothing secondary. On the contrary, it is that which is first and unconditioned, the premiss of all premisses, and for this reason that from which philosophy has to *start,* since the will-to-live does not appear in consequence of the world, but the world appears in consequence of the will-to-live.

I need hardly draw attention to the fact that the considerations with which we here conclude the second book point forcibly to the serious theme of the fourth. In fact, they would pass directly into that fourth book, if my architectonics did not make it necessary for our third book with its bright and fair contents to come in between as a second consideration of the *world as representation.* The conclusion of this third book, however, points once more in the same direction.

---

[5] "Not naturally, but violently." [Tr.]

Et is similis spectatori est, quod ab omni separatus spectaculum videt.

Oupnekhat, Vol. I, p. 304.

["And he is like a spectator, because, separated from everything, he beholds a drama."—Tr.]

On Knowledge of the Ideas

The intellect, which hitherto had been considered only in its original and natural condition of servitude under the will, appears in the third book in its deliverance from that servitude. Here, however, it must at once be observed that it is not a question of a lasting emancipation, but merely of a brief hour of rest, of an exceptional, and in fact only momentary, release from the service of the will. As this subject has been dealt with in sufficient detail in volume one, I have to add here only a few supplementary remarks.

Thus, as we explained in § 33 of volume one, the intellect in its activity in the service of the will, that is, in its natural function, really knows mere *relations* of things, primarily their relations to the will itself, to which it belongs, whereby they become motives of the will, but also, with a view to the completeness of this knowledge, the relations of things to one another. This latter knowledge first appears in some volume and significance in the human intellect; in the case of animals, on the other hand, it appears only within very narrow limits, even where their intellect is already considerably developed. Clearly the apprehension of the relations that things have *to one another* takes place only *indirectly* in the service of the will. It therefore forms the transition to the purely objective knowledge that is entirely independent of the will; it is scientific knowledge, the latter being artistic knowledge. Thus, if many and varied relations of an object are immediately apprehended, its peculiar and proper nature then appears from these more and more distinctly, and is thus gradually constructed out of mere relations, although it itself is entirely different from them. With this method of apprehension, the subjection of the intellect to the will at the same time becomes more and more indirect and limited. If the intellect has strength enough to gain the ascendancy, and to abandon entirely the relations of things to the will, in order to apprehend instead of them the purely objective nature of a phenomenon that expresses itself through all relations,

---

[1] This chapter refers to §§ 30-32 of volume 1.

then, simultaneously with the service of the will, it also forsakes the apprehension of mere relations, and with this also really that of the individual thing as such. The intellect then freely soars aloft and no longer belongs to a will. In the particular thing, it knows merely the *essential,* and therefore its whole *species;* consequently, it now has for its object the *Ideas,* in my sense, which agrees with the original Platonic meaning, of this grossly misused word. Thus it has the permanent, unchangeable *forms,* independent of the temporal existence of individual beings, the *species rerum,* which really constitute the purely objective element of phenomena. An *Idea* thus apprehended is, of course, not as yet the essence of the thing-in-itself, for the very reason that it has sprung from knowledge of mere relations. Nevertheless, as the result of the sum of all relations, it is the peculiar *character* of the thing, and thus the complete expression of the essence that exhibits itself to perception as object, apprehended not in relation to an individual will, but as it expresses itself spontaneously. In this way, it determines all its relations which alone were known till then. The Idea is the root point of all these relations, and thus the complete and perfect *phenomenon,* or, as I have expressed it in the text, the adequate objectivity of the will at this stage of its phenomenal appearance. At bottom, even form and colour, which are what is immediate in the apprehension of the Idea through perception, do not belong to the Idea, but are only the medium of its expression; for, strictly speaking, space is as foreign to it as is time. In this sense, the Neo-Platonist Olympiodorus said in his commentary to Plato's *Alcibiades* (Kreuzer's edition of Proclus and Olympiodorus, Vol. II, p. 82): τὸ εἶδος μεταδέδωκε μὲν τῆς μορφῆς τῇ ὕλῃ· ἀμερὲς δὲ ὂν μετελάβεν ἐξ αὖτης τοῦ διαστάτου, in other words, the Idea, in itself unextended, certainly imparted the form to matter, but first assumed extension from it. Hence, as I have said, the Ideas still do not reveal the being-in-itself of things, but only their objective character, and thus always only the phenomenon. And we should not understand even this character, if the inner essence of things were not otherwise known to us, at least obscurely and in feeling. Thus this essence itself cannot be understood from the Ideas, and in general not through any merely *objective* knowledge; therefore it would remain eternally a secret, unless we had access to it from an entirely different side. Only in so far as every knowing being is at the same time an individual and thus a part of nature, does the approach to the interior of nature stand open to him, namely in his own self-consciousness. Here it manifests itself most immediately, and then, as we found, as *will.*

Now what the Platonic *Idea* is, considered as merely objective image, mere form, and thereby lifted out of time as well as out of all relations, is the *species* or kind taken empirically and in time; this, then, is the empirical correlative of the Idea. The Idea is really eternal, but the species is of endless duration, although its phenomenal appearance on a planet can become extinct. Even the names of the two pass over into each other: ἰδέα, εἶδος, *species,* kind. The Idea is *species,* but not *genus;* therefore the *species* are the work of nature, the *genera* the work of man; thus they are mere concepts. There are *species naturales,* but only *genera logica.* Of manufactured articles there are no Ideas, but mere concepts, therefore *genera logica,* and their subspecies are *species logicae.* To what has been said in this respect in volume one, § 41 I wish to add that Aristotle states (*Metaphysics,* i, 9 and xiii, 5) that the Platonists did not admit any Ideas of manufactured articles, οἷον οἰκία, καὶ δακτύλιος, ὧν οὔ φασιν εἶναι εἴδη (*ut domus et annulus, quorum ideas dari negant*).[2] Compare with this the Scholiast, pp. 562, 563 of the Berlin quarto edition. Further, Aristotle says (*Metaphysics,* xi, 3): ἀλλ' εἴπερ (*supple* εἴδη ἐστι) ἐπὶ τῶν φύσει (ἐστι)· διὸ δὴ οὐ κακῶς ὁ Πλάτων ἔφη, ὅτι εἴδη ἐστὶν ὁπόσα φύσει (*Si quidem ideae sunt, in iis sunt, quae natura fiunt: propter quod non male Plato dixit, quod species eorum sunt, quae natura sunt*).[3] On this the Scholiast remarks, p. 800: καὶ τοῦτο ἀρέσκει καὶ αὐτοῖς τοῖς τὰς ἰδέας θεμένοις· τῶν γὰρ ὑπὸ τέχνης γινομένων ἰδέας εἶναι οὐκ ἔλεγον ἀλλὰ τῶν ὑπὸ φύσεως (*Hoc etiam ipsis ideas statuentibus placet: non enim arte factorum ideas dari aiebant, sed natura procreatorum*).[4] For the rest, the doctrine of the Ideas came originally from Pythagoras, that is, if we do not propose to question Plutarch's statement in the book *De Placitis Philosophorum,* i, c. 3.

The individual is rooted in the species, and time in eternity; and just as every individual is such only by its having the essence of its species in itself, so does it have duration in time only by its being simultaneously in eternity. In the following book a special chapter is devoted to the life of the species.

In § 49 of volume one, I sufficiently emphasized the *difference* between the Idea and the concept. Their *similarity,* on the other hand, rests on the following. The original and essential unity of an Idea is dispersed into the plurality of individual things by the sensu-

---

[2] "For example, house and ring, of which they do not say there are Ideas." [Tr.]

[3] "But if in general Ideas are to be assumed, then this is only of the things of nature; hence Plato was not wrong in saying that there are as many Ideas as there are species in nature." [Tr.]

[4] "And those who accept Ideas also teach this; for they said that there are no Ideas of the products of art, but only of the products of nature." [Tr.]

ously and cerebrally conditioned perception of the knowing individual. But that unity is then restored again through the reflection of the faculty of reason, yet only *in abstracto,* as concept, *universale,* which is indeed equal to the Idea in *extension,* but has assumed quite a different *form.* In this way, however, it has lost perceptibility and thus its general definiteness and distinctness. In this sense (yet in no other) we might, in the language of the scholastics, describe the Ideas as *universalia ante rem,* and the concepts as *universalia post rem.* Individual things stand between the two, and even the animal has knowledge thereof. The realism of the scholastics has certainly arisen from the confusion of the Platonic Ideas, to which an objective, real existence can of course be attributed, as they are at the same time the species, with the mere concepts, to which the Realists wished to attribute such an existence, and thereby brought about the triumphant opposition of Nominalism.

On the Pure Subject of Knowing

Apprehension of an Idea, its entry into our consciousness, comes about only by means of a change in us, which might also be regarded as an act of self-denial. To this extent it consists in knowledge turning away entirely from our own will, and thus leaving entirely out of sight the precious pledge entrusted to it, and considering things as though they could never in any way concern the will. For only thus does knowledge become the pure mirror of the objective inner nature of things. A knowledge so conditioned must be the basis of every genuine work of art as its origin. The change in the subject required for this, just because it consists in the elimination of all willing, cannot proceed from the will, and hence cannot be an arbitrary act of will, in other words, cannot rest with us. On the contrary, it springs only from a temporary preponderance of the intellect over the will, or, physiologically considered, from a strong excitation of the brain's perceptive activity, without any excitation of inclinations or emotions. To explain this somewhat more accurately, I remind the reader that our consciousness has two sides; in part it is consciousness of *our own selves,* which is the *will,* and in part consciousness of *other things,* and as such primarily knowledge of the external world *through perception,* apprehension of objects. Now the more one side of the whole consciousness comes to the front, the more does the other withdraw. Accordingly, the consciousness *of other things,* or knowledge of perception, becomes the more perfect, in other words the more objective, the less conscious of ourselves we are during it. Here an antagonism actually occurs. The more conscious we are of the object, the less conscious we are of the subject; on the other hand, the more this occupies consciousness, the weaker and less perfect is our perception of the external world. The state required for pure objectivity of perception has in part permanent conditions in the perfection of the brain and of the physiological quality generally favourable to its activity; in

---

[1] This chapter refers to §§ 33, 34 of volume 1.

part temporary conditions, in so far as this state is favoured by everything that increases the attention and enhances the susceptibility of
the cerebral nervous system, yet without the excitation of any passion. Let us not think here of alcoholic drinks or of opium; on the
contrary, what is required is a peaceful night's sleep, a cold bath,
and everything that furnishes brain-activity with an unforced ascendancy by a calming down of the blood circulation and of the passionate nature. It is especially these natural means of promoting
cerebral nervous activity which have the effect, the better, of course,
the more developed and energetic the brain is in general, of making
the object more and more detached from the subject, and which
finally produce that state of pure objectivity of perception. Such a
state of itself eliminates the will from consciousness, and in it all
things stand before us with enhanced clearness and distinctness,
so that we are aware almost alone *of them* and hardly at all *of ourselves*. Therefore our whole consciousness is hardly anything more
than the medium through which the perceived object appears in the
world as representation. Thus pure will-less knowledge is reached
by the consciousness of other things being raised to so high a
potential that the consciousness of our own selves vanishes. For we
apprehend the world purely objectively, only when we no longer
know that we belong to it; and all things appear the more beautiful,
the more we are conscious merely of them, and the less we are
conscious of ourselves. Now as all suffering proceeds from the will
that constitutes the real self, all possibility of suffering is abolished
simultaneously with the withdrawal of this side of consciousness. In
this way, the state of pure objectivity of perception becomes one
that makes us feel positively happy. I have therefore shown in it
one of the two constituent elements of aesthetic enjoyment. On
the other hand, as soon as the consciousness of one's own self, and
thus subjectivity, i.e., the will, again obtains the ascendancy, a
degree of discomfort or disquiet appears in keeping therewith; of
discomfort, in so far as corporeality (the organism that in itself
is will) again makes itself felt; of disquiet, in so far as the will, on
the intellectual path, again fills our consciousness by desires,
emotions, passions, and cares. For the will, as the principle of
subjectivity, is everywhere the opposite, indeed the antagonist, of
knowledge. The greatest concentration of subjectivity consists in the
act of will proper, and in this therefore we have the clearest consciousness of our own selves. All other excitements of the will are
only preparations for this; the act itself is for subjectivity what the
jumping of the spark is for the electrical apparatus. Every bodily
sensation is in itself excitement of the will, and more often indeed of

the *noluntas* than of the *voluntas*. The excitement of the will on the intellectual path is that which occurs by means of motives; thus subjectivity is here awakened and brought into play by objectivity itself. This occurs the moment any object is no longer apprehended purely objectively, and so disinterestedly, but excites, directly or indirectly, desire or aversion, even if only by means of a recollection; for then it already acts as motive in the widest sense of this word.

Here I observe that abstract thinking and reading, that are connected with words, do indeed belong in the wider sense to the consciousness *of other things,* and so to the objective employment of the mind, yet only indirectly, namely by means of concepts. These, however, are the artificial product of our faculty of reason, and so are already a work of deliberation. In all abstract employment of the mind, the will is also the ruler. According to its intentions, the will imparts direction to the employment of the mind, and also fixes the attention; therefore this is always associated with some exertion; but such exertion presupposes activity of the will. Therefore complete objectivity of consciousness does not occur with this kind of mental activity in the same way as it accompanies, as its condition, aesthetic contemplation, i.e., a knowledge of the Ideas.

In accordance with the above, the pure objectivity of perception, by virtue of which we know no longer the individual thing as such, but the Idea of its species, is conditioned by the fact that one is conscious no longer of oneself, but only of the perceived objects, hence that one's own consciousness has been left merely as the supporter of the objective existence of those objects. What makes this state difficult and therefore rare is that in it the accident (the intellect), so to speak, subdues and eliminates the substance (the will), although only for a short time. Here also are to be found the analogy and even relationship of this with the denial of the will, discussed at the end of the following book. Thus although, as was shown in the previous book, knowledge has sprung from the will, and is rooted in the phenomenon of the will, that is in the organism, it is nevertheless vitiated by the will, just as the flame is by its combustible material and its smoke. It is due to this that we can apprehend the purely objective inner nature of things, namely the *Ideas* appearing in them, only when we ourselves have no interest in them, in that they stand in no relation to our will. It arises from this, again, that the Ideas of things appeal to us more easily from the work of art than from reality. For what we behold only in the picture or in the poem stands outside all possibility of any relation to our will; for already in itself it exists merely for *knowledge* and directly appeals to that alone. On the other hand, apprehension of the Ideas from *reality* presupposes to a certain extent an abstraction from our own will, an exaltation above its interests, which demands a special energy and elasticity on the part of the intellect. In a high degree and with some duration, this is characteristic only of genius. Genius consists precisely in the existence of a greater measure of the power of knowledge than the service of an individual will requires. This surplus becomes free, and then apprehends the world without reference to the will. Thus the *work of art* so greatly facilitates the apprehension of the Ideas in which aesthetic enjoyment consists; and this is due not merely to the fact that art presents things more clearly and characteristically by emphasizing the essential and eliminating the inessential, but just as much to the fact that the absolute silence of the will, required for the purely objective apprehension of the true nature of things, is attained with the greatest certainty. Such silence is attained by the perceived object itself lying entirely outside the province of things capable of reference to the will, in that it is nothing actual but a mere picture or image. This holds good not only of the works of plastic and pictorial art, but of poetry also. The effect of this is also conditioned by disinterested, will-less, and thus purely objective apprehension. It is precisely this that causes a perceived object to appear *picturesque,* and an event of real life to seem *poetical,* since this alone spreads over the objects of reality the magic gleam that in the case of sensibly perceived objects is called the picturesque, and in the case of those viewed only in the imagination the poetical. When poets sing of a bright morning, of a beautiful evening, of a still moonlight night, and of many such things, the real object of their glorification is, unknown to them, the pure subject of knowing, called forth by those beauties of nature. On its appearance the will vanishes from consciousness, and in this way there enters that peace of heart which is otherwise unattainable in the world. For example, how otherwise could the verse

> *Nox erat, et coelo fulgebat luna sereno,*
> *Inter minora sidera*[2]

affect us so delightfully and beneficially, in fact so enchantingly? Further, the stranger, or the mere passing traveller, feels the effect of the picturesque or poetical from objects unable to produce this effect on those who live among them. This is explained by the fact that even the novelty and strangeness of the objects of such a dis-interested and purely objective apprehension is favourable thereto. For example, the sight of a wholly strange town often makes on the

---

[2] "It was night, and the moon was shining in the serene heavens garlanded by small stars." [Horace, *Epod.* 15, 1. Tr.]

traveller an unusually agreeable impression, which is certainly not produced on the person living in the town; for that impression springs from the fact that the traveller, being out of all relation to the town and its inhabitants, perceives it purely objectively. The pleasure of travelling is in part due to this. This also appears to be the reason why attempts are made to enhance the effect of narrative or dramatic works by shifting the scene to distant times and countries, in Germany to Italy and Spain, in Italy to Germany, Poland, and even Holland. Now if wholly objective, intuitive apprehension, purified of all willing, is the condition for the *enjoyment* of aesthetic objects, even more so is it for their *production*. Every good painting, every genuine poem, bears the stamp of the frame of mind it depicts. For only what has sprung from perception, indeed from purely objective perception, or is directly stimulated by it, contains the living germ from which genuine and original achievements can result, not only in the plastic and pictorial arts, but also in poetry, and even in philosophy. The *punctum saliens* of every beautiful work, every great and profound thought, is an entirely objective perception. But such a perception is absolutely conditioned by a complete silencing of the will which leaves the person as pure subject of knowing. The aptitude for the prevalence of this state is simply genius.

With the disappearance of willing from consciousness, the individuality is really abolished also, and with it its suffering and sorrow. I have therefore described the pure subject of knowing, which then remains over as the eternal world-eye. This eye looks out from all living beings, though with very different degrees of clearness, and is untouched by their arising and passing away. It is thus identical with itself, constantly one and the same, and the supporter of the world of permanent Ideas, i.e., of the adequate objectivity of the will. On the other hand, the individual subject, clouded in his knowledge by the individuality that springs from the will, has as object only particular things, and is as transient and fleeting as these themselves are. In the sense here indicated, we can attribute to everyone a twofold existence. As will, and therefore as individual, he is only one, and that one exclusively, which gives him plenty to do and to suffer. As that which makes a purely objective representation he is the pure subject of knowledge, and only in the consciousness of this does the objective world have its existence. As such he is *all things,* in so far as he perceives them, and in him their existence is without burden and hardship. Thus it is *his* existence in so far as it exists in *his* representation; but then it is without will. On the other hand, in so far as it is will, it is not in him. It is well for everyone in that state where he is all things; it is woeful where he is exclusively one. Every state or condition, every person, every scene of life, needs to be apprehended only purely objectively, and made the object of a description or sketch, whether with brush or with words, in order to appear interesting, delightful, and enviable. However, if one is in it, if one is oneself it, then (as is often said) may the devil endure it. Therefore Goethe says:

> What in life does us annoy,
> We in picture do enjoy.

There was a period in the years of my youth when I was constantly at pains to see myself and my actions from outside, and to picture them to myself; probably in order to make them enjoyable to me.

As the matter here considered has never come under discussion before me, I wish to add a few psychological illustrations of it.

In the immediate perception of the world and of life, we consider things as a rule merely in their relations, and consequently according to their relative, not their absolute, essence and existence. For example, we regard houses, ships, machines, and the like with the idea of their purpose and their suitability therefor; human beings with the idea of their relation to us, if they have any, and then of their relation to one another, whether in their present actions or according to their position and vocation, perhaps judging their fitness for it, and so on. We can pursue such a consideration of the relations more or less to the most distant links of their concatenation. In this way the consideration will gain in accuracy and extent, but remains the same as regards its quality and nature. It is the consideration of things in their relations, in fact *by means of* these, and hence according to the principle of sufficient reason. In most cases and as a rule, everyone is abandoned to this method of consideration; I believe even that most people are incapable of any other. But if, by way of exception, it happens that we experience a momentary enhancement of the intensity of our intuitive intelligence, we at once see things with entirely different eyes, for we now apprehend them no longer according to their relations, but according to what they are in and by themselves; and then, in addition to their relative existence, we suddenly perceive their absolute existence as well. Every individual at once represents its species; accordingly, we now apprehend the universal in beings. What we know in such a way are the *Ideas* of things; but from these there now speaks a higher wisdom than that which knows of mere relations. We ourselves have also stepped out of relations, and have thereby become the pure subject of knowing. But what produces this state or condition by way of exception must be internal physiological processes, which purify and enhance the activity of the brain to such a degree that such a sudden spring-tide of this activity arises. This state is conditioned from outside by our remaining wholly foreign to, and detached from, the scene to be contemplated, and not being at all actively involved in it.

In order to see that a purely objective, and therefore correct, apprehension of things is possible only when we consider them without any personal participation in them, and thus under the complete silence of the will, let us picture to ourselves how much every emotion or passion obscures and falsifies knowledge, in fact how every inclination or disinclination twists, colours, and distorts not merely the judgement, but even the original perception of things. Let us recall how, when we are delighted by a successful outcome, the whole world at once assumes a bright colour and a smiling aspect, and on the other hand looks dark and gloomy when care and sorrow weigh on us. Let us then see how even an inanimate thing, which is yet to become the instrument for some event we abhor, appears to have a hideous physiognomy; for example the scaffold, the fortress to which we are taken, the surgeon's case of instruments, the travelling coach of loved ones, and so on; indeed, numbers, letters, seals can grin at us horribly and affect us like fearful monsters. On the other hand, the instruments for fulfilling our wishes immediately look pleasant and agreeable; for example, the old woman with a hump who carries a love-letter, the Jew with the *louis d'ors,* the rope-ladder for escape, and so on. Now just as here, in the case of decided aversion or affection, the falsification of the representation by the will is unmistakable, so is it present in a lesser degree in the case of every object that has only some remote relation to our will, in other words, to our inclination or disinclination. Only when the will with its interests has forsaken consciousness, and the intellect freely follows its own laws, and as pure subject mirrors the objective world, yet from its own impulse is in the highest state of tension and activity, goaded by no willing, only then do the colour and form of things stand out in their true and full significance. Only from such an apprehension, therefore, can genuine works of art result, whose permanent value and constantly renewed approval spring from the very fact that they alone exhibit what is purely objective. This is the foundation of the various subjective, and thus distorted, perceptions, as that which is common to them all and alone stands fast; it shines through them as the common theme to all those subjective variations. For the nature displayed before our eyes certainly exhibits itself very differently in different minds; and just as each sees it, so alone can he reproduce it whether by brush or chisel, or in words, or through gestures on the stage. Objectivity alone qualifies one for becoming an artist; but it is possible only by the intellect being detached from its root, the will, by its being free to move, and being nevertheless active with the highest degree of energy.

To the youth, whose perceiving intellect still acts with fresh energy, nature often exhibits herself with complete objectivity and therefore in full beauty. But the pleasure of such a glance is sometimes marred by the distressing reflection that the objects present and exhibiting themselves in such beauty do not also stand in a personal relation to him, by virtue of which they could interest and delight him. Thus he expects his life to take the form of an interesting work of fiction. "Behind that prominent cliff there must be waiting the well-mounted band of my friends; at that waterfall my beloved must be resting; this beautifully lighted building must be her dwelling and that ivy-clad window hers; but this beautiful world is for me a desert!" and so on. Melancholy reveries of youth like these really demand something precisely self-contradictory. For the beauty with which those objects present themselves rests precisely on the pure objectivity, i.e., disinterestedness, of their perception, and it would therefore be abolished at once by the relation to his own will which the youth painfully misses. Consequently the whole charm which now affords him a pleasure, although alloyed with a mixture of pain, would not exist at all. Moreover, the same thing holds good of every age and in every connexion; the beauty of the objects of a landscape, which now delights us, would have vanished, if we stood to them in personal relations of which we always remain conscious. Everything is beautiful only so long as it does not concern us. (Here it is not a case of the passion of love, but of aesthetic enjoyment.) Life is *never* beautiful, but only the pictures of it, namely in the transfiguring mirror of art or of poetry, particularly in youth, when we do not yet know it. Many a youth would obtain great composure if one could help him to gain this insight.

Why does the sight of the full moon have such a beneficent, soothing, and exalting effect? Because the moon is an object of perception, never of willing:

> The stars not coveted by us
> Delight us with their splendour.
> [Goethe]

Further, it is *sublime,* in other words, it induces in us a sublime mood, because, without any reference to us, it moves along eternally foreign to earthly life and activity, and sees everything, but takes part in nothing. Therefore at the sight of it the will, with its constant care and sorrow, vanishes from consciousness, and leaves it behind as a purely knowing consciousness. Possibly there is also mingled a feeling that we share this sight with millions whose individual differences are extinguished in it, so that in this perception they are one, and this likewise enhances the impression of the sublime. Finally, this impression is also increased by the fact that the moon shines without warming; and here certainly is to be found the reason why it has been called chaste and identified with Diana. In consequence of this whole beneficent impression on our feeling, the moon gradually becomes our bosom friend. On the other hand, the sun never does this; it is like a boundless benefactor whom we are quite incapable of looking in the face.

The following remark may find a place here as an addition to what was said in § 38 of volume 1 on the aesthetic enjoyment afforded by light, reflection, and colours. The wholly immediate, unreflective, yet also inexpressible, pleasure that is excited in us by the impression of colours, which is strengthened by metallic lustre, and still more by transparency, as for example in stained glass windows, and even more by means of clouds and their reflection at sunset—this pleasure, I say, ultimately rests on the fact that in the easiest manner, in a manner that is almost physically necessary, the whole of our interest is here won for knowledge without any excitement of our will. We thus enter into the state of pure knowing, although in the main this consists in this case in a mere sensation of the retina's affection. But as this sensation is in itself wholly free from pain or pleasure, it is without any direct excitement of the will, and thus belongs to pure knowledge.

CHAPTER XXXI[1]

On Genius

What is properly denoted by the name genius is the predominant capacity for the kind of knowledge described in the two previous chapters, from which all genuine works of the arts, of poetry, and even of philosophy, spring. Accordingly, as this has for its object the (Platonic) *Ideas,* these being apprehended, however, not in the abstract but only *in perception,* the true nature of genius must lie in the completeness and energy of the knowledge of *perception.* In accordance with this, we hear described most decidedly as works of genius those which start from, and appeal to, perception, hence those of the plastic and pictorial arts, and then those of poetry which brings about its perceptions through the imagination. Here too the difference between genius and mere talent becomes marked. Talent is a merit to be found in the greater versatility and acuteness of discursive rather than of intuitive knowledge. The person endowed with talent thinks more rapidly and accurately than do the rest; on the other hand, the genius perceives a world different from them all, though only by looking more deeply into the world that lies before them also, since it presents itself in his mind more objectively, consequently more purely and distinctly.

By its destiny, the intellect is merely the medium of motives; and so it apprehends originally in things nothing but their relations to the will, the direct, the indirect, the possible. In the case of the animals, where it remains almost entirely at the direct relations, the matter is on that account most apparent. That which has no reference to their will does not exist for them. For this reason we occasionally see with surprise that even clever animals do not at all notice something conspicuous in itself; for instance, they express no surprise at obvious alterations in our person or environment. In the case of the normal person, the indirect, in fact the possible, relations to the will are added, and the sum of these constitutes the whole of useful knowledge; but even here knowledge remains confined to *relations.*

---

[1] This chapter refers to § 36 of volume 1.

Therefore an entirely pure and objective picture of things is not reached in the normal mind, because its power of perception at once becomes tired and inactive, as soon as this is not spurred on and set in motion by the will. For it has not enough energy to apprehend the world purely objectively from its own elasticity and *without a purpose.* On the other hand, where this happens, where the brain's power of forming representations has such a surplus that a pure, distinct, objective picture of the external world exhibits itself *without a purpose* as something useless for the intentions of the will, which is even disturbing in the higher degrees, and can even become injurious to them—then there already exists at least the natural disposition for that abnormality. This is denoted by the name of *genius,* which indicates that something foreign to the will, i.e., to the I or ego proper, a *genius* added from outside so to speak, seems to become active here. To speak without metaphor, however, genius consists in the knowing faculty having received a considerably more powerful development than is required by the *service of the will,* for which alone it originally came into being. Therefore, strictly speaking, physiology could to a certain extent class such a surplus of brain-activity, and with this of the brain itself, among the *monstra per excessum,* which, as we know, are co-ordinated by it with the *monstra per defectum* and the *monstra per situm mutatum.*[2] Genius, therefore, consists in an abnormal excess of intellect which can find its use only by being employed on the universal of existence. In this way it then applies itself to the service of the whole human race, just as does the normal intellect to that of the individual. To make the matter really intelligible, we might say that, if the normal person consists of two-thirds will and one-third intellect, the genius, on the contrary, has two-thirds intellect and one-third will. This could again be illustrated by a chemical simile; the base and the acid of a neutral salt are distinguished by the fact that in each of the two the radical has a ratio to oxygen which is the inverse of that in the other. Thus the base or the alkali is what it is because in it the radical predominates with reference to the oxygen, and the acid is what it is because in it the oxygen predominates. Now in just the same way are the normal person and the genius related as regards will and intellect. From this arises a fundamental difference between them, visible already in their whole nature and activity, but which really comes to light in their achievements. We might still add as a distinction that, whereas that total contrast between the chemical materials establishes the strongest affinity and attraction to each

[2] "Deformities through excess, through defect, and through wrong position." [Tr.]

other, in the case of the human race it is rather the opposite that is usually seen.

The first manifestation occasioned by such a surplus of the power of knowledge shows itself for the most part in the really original and fundamentally essential knowledge, i.e., knowledge of *perception,* and brings about the repetition of this in a picture or image; hence arise the painter and the sculptor. Accordingly, with these the path from the apprehension of genius to the artistic production is the shortest; therefore the form in which genius and its activity are exhibited in them is the simplest, and its description the easiest. Yet it is just here that the source is seen from which all genuine productions in every art, even poetry and philosophy, have their origin, though in these cases the process is not so simple.

Let us here recall the result obtained in the first book, that all perception is intellectual, and not merely of the senses. If we now add to this the explanation given here, and at the same time fairly take into consideration that the philosophy of the eighteenth century denoted the perceiving faculty of knowledge by the name "lower powers of the soul," we shall not find it so utterly absurd, or so worthy of the bitter scorn with which Jean-Paul mentions it in his *Vorschule der Aesthetik,* that Adelung, having to speak the language of his time, placed genius in "a marked strength of the lower powers of the soul." However great the merits possessed by this admirable man's above-menitoned work, I must nevertheless remark that, wherever a theoretical discussion and instruction in general are the end in view, the method of presentation which indulges in displays of wit and strides along in mere similes cannot be appropriate.

But it is *perception* above all to which the real and true nature of things discloses and reveals itself, although still in a limited way. All concepts, all things that are thought, are indeed only abstractions, and consequently partial representations from perception, and have arisen merely through our thinking something away. All profound knowledge, even wisdom proper, is rooted in the *perceptive* apprehension of things. We have considered this fully in the supplements to the first book. A *perceptive* apprehension has always been the process of generation in which every genuine work of art, every immortal idea, received the spark of life. All original and primary thinking takes place figuratively. On the other hand, from *concepts* arise the works of mere talent, merely rational ideas, imitations, and generally everything calculated only for the present need and for contemporary events.

But if our perception were always tied to the real presence of things, its material would be entirely under the dominion of chance, which rarely produces things at the right time, seldom arranges them appropriately, and often presents them to us in very defective copies. For this reason *imagination* is needed, in order to complete, arrange, amplify, fix, retain, and repeat at pleasure all the significant pictures of life, according as the aims of a profoundly penetrating knowledge and of the significant work by which it is to be communicated may require. On this rests the high value of imagination as an indispensable instrument of genius. For only by virtue of imagination can genius present to itself each object or event in a vivid image, according to the requirements of the connexion of its painting, poetry, or thinking, and thus always draw fresh nourishment from the primary source of all knowledge, perception. The man gifted with imagination is able, so to speak, to call up spirits revealing to him at the right time truths that the bare reality of things exhibits only feebly, rarely, and often at the wrong time. Therefore the man without imagination is related to him as the mussel fastened to its rock, compelled to wait for what chance brings it, is to the freely moving or even winged animal. For such a man knows no other perception than the actual perception of the senses; until it comes, he nibbles at concepts and abstractions which are nevertheless only shells and husks, not the kernel of knowledge. He will never achieve anything great, unless it be in arithmetic and mathematics. The works of the plastic and pictorial arts and of poetry, likewise the achievements of mimicry, can also be regarded as the means by which those who have no imagination may make up for this defect as far as possible, and those gifted with imagination may facilitate the use of it.

Accordingly, although the peculiar and essential kind of knowledge of genius is that of *perception,* particular things do not by any means constitute its real object; this is rather the (Platonic) Ideas expressing themselves therein, as the apprehension of them was analysed in chapter 29. Always to see the universal in the particular is precisely the fundamental characteristic of genius, whereas the normal man recognizes in the particular only the particular as such; for only as such does it belong to reality, which alone has interest for him, has reference to his *will.* The degree in which everyone not so much conceives as actually perceives in the particular thing only the particular, or something more or less universal up to the most universal of the species, is the measure of his approach to genius. In accordance with this, the real object of genius is only the essential nature of things in general, the universal in them, the totality. The investigation of individual phenomena is the field of the talents, in the modern sciences, whose object in reality is always only the relations of things to one another.

What was shown at length in the previous chapter, namely that the apprehension of the *Ideas* is conditioned by the fact that the knower is the *pure subject* of knowledge, and that the will vanishes entirely from consciousness, is here present to our minds. The pleasure we enjoy in many of Goethe's songs which bring the landscape before our eyes, or in Jean-Paul's descriptions of nature, rests on our thus participating in the objectivity of those minds, that is to say, in the purity with which in them the world as representation had been separated from the world as will, and had been as it were entirely detached therefrom. The kind of knowledge of the genius is essentially purified of all willing and of references to the will; and it also follows from this that the works of genius do not result from intention or arbitrary choice, but that genius is here guided by a kind of instinctive necessity. What is called the awakening of genius, the hour of inspiration, the moment of rapture or exaltation, is nothing but the intellect's becoming free, when, relieved for a while from its service under the will, it does not sink into inactivity or apathy, but is active for a short time, entirely alone and of its own accord. The intellect is then of the greatest purity, and becomes the clear mirror of the world; for, wholly separated from its origin, that is, from the will, it is now the world as representation itself concentrated in *one* consciousness. At such moments is the soul of immortal works, so to speak, begotten. On the other hand, in the case of all intentional reflection the intellect is not free, for the will in fact guides it, and prescribes its theme.

The stamp of commonness, the expression of vulgarity, impressed on the great majority of faces, really consists in this, that there becomes visible in them the strict subordination of their knowing to their willing, the firm chain linking the two together, and the impossibility that follows from this of apprehending things save in reference to the will and its aims. On the other hand, the expression of genius, which constitutes the evident family likeness of all highly gifted men, lies in our distinctly reading in it the intellect's liberation, manumission, from the service of the will, the predominance of knowing over willing. Because all suffering proceeds from willing, while knowing on the other hand is in and by itself painless and serene, this gives to their lofty brows and to their clear, perceptive glance, which are not subject to the service of the will and its needs, the appearance of great, as it were supernatural, unearthly serenity. At times this breaks through, and is quite consistent with the melancholy of the other features of the face, especially the mouth; in this connexion it can be aptly described by the motto of Giordano Bruno: *In tristitia hilaris, in hilaritate tristis.*[3]

The will that is the root of the intellect is opposed to every activity of the intellect which is directed to anything other than its own aims. Therefore the intellect is capable of a purely objective and profound apprehension of the external world only when it has detached itself, for a while at any rate, from this its root. So long as it still remains bound to the will, it is quite incapable of any activity from its own resources; it sleeps in stupor, whenever the will (the interest) does not awaken it and set it in motion. If this happens, however, it is then very suitable for recognizing the relations of things according to the interest of the will. This is done by the prudent mind that must also be always awakened, in other words, by a mind that is vividly aroused by willing; but, on this very account, it is incapable of comprehending the purely objective nature of things. For willing and aims make it so one-sided, that it sees in things only what refers to these, and the rest partly disappears, partly enters consciousness in an adulterated form. For example, a traveller who is anxious and in a hurry, will see the Rhine and its banks only as a dash or stroke, and the bridge over it only as a line intersecting that stroke. In the head of the man filled with his own aims, the world appears just as a beautiful landscape does on the plan of a battlefield. These, of course, are extremes taken for the sake of clarity; but even every slight excitement of the will will have as its consequence a slight, yet always analogous, falsification of knowledge. The world can appear in its true colour and form, in its complete and correct significance, only when the intellect, freed from willing, moves freely over objects, and yet is energetically active without being spurred on by the will. This is certainly contrary to the nature and destiny of the intellect; thus it is to a certain extent unnatural, and for this reason exceedingly rare. But it is precisely in this that the true nature of *genius* lies; and in this alone does that state occur in a high degree and for some time, whereas in the rest it appears only approximately and exceptionally. I take it in the sense here discussed, when Jean-Paul (*Vorschule der Aesthetik,* § 12) puts the essence of genius in *reflectiveness.* Thus the normal person is immersed in the whirl and tumult of life, to which he belongs through his will; his intellect is filled with the things and events of life, but he does not in the least become aware of these things and of life in their objective significance; just as the merchant on the Amsterdam exchange hears and understands perfectly what his neighbour says,

---

[3] "Cheerful in sadness, sad in cheerfulness." [Tr.]

but does not hear at all the continual humming of the whole exchange, which is like the roaring of the sea, and which astonishes the distant observer. On the other hand, the intellect of the genius is detached from the will and so from the person, and what concerns these does not conceal from him the world and things themselves; on the contrary, he becomes distinctly conscious of them, and apprehends them in objective perception in and by themselves; in this sense he is *reflective*.

It is this *reflectiveness* that enables the painter to reproduce faithfully on canvas the nature he has before his eyes, and the poet accurately to call up again by means of abstract concepts the perceptive present by expressing it, and thus bringing it to distinct consciousness; likewise to express in words everything that others merely feel. The animal lives without any reflectiveness. It has consciousness, that is to say, it knows itself and its weal and woe, and in addition the objects that occasion these. Its knowledge, however, always remains subjective; it never becomes objective. Everything occurring therein seems to the animal to be a matter of course, and can therefore never become for it the matter to be dealt with (object of description) or the problem (object of meditation). Its consciousness is therefore entirely *immanent*. The consciousness of the common type of man is of course not of the same kind, but yet is of a kindred nature, since his apprehension of things and of the world is also chiefly subjective, and remains predominantly immanent. It apprehends the things in the world, but not the world; its own actions and sufferings, but not itself. Now as the distinctness of consciousness is enhanced in infinite gradations, reflectiveness appears more and more; in this way it gradually comes about that occasionally, though rarely and again with extremely different degrees of distinctness, the question passes through the mind like a flash: "What is all this?" or: *"How* is it really constituted?" If the first question attains to great distinctness and is continuously present, it will make the philosopher; and in just the same way the other question will make the artist or the poet. Therefore the high calling of these two has its root in the reflectiveness which springs primarily from the distinctness with which they are conscious of the world and of themselves, and thus come to reflect on these. But the whole process springs from the fact that, through its preponderance, the intellect frees itself for a time from the will to which it was originally subject.

These considerations concerning genius are connected as supplements to the exposition, contained in chapter 22, of the *ever wider separation between the will and the intellect* which is observable in the whole range of beings. This reaches its highest degree precisely in genius, where it attains to the complete detachment of the intellect from its root, the will, so that here the intellect becomes wholly free, whereby the *world as representation* first of all attains to complete objectification.

Now a few more remarks concerning the individuality of genius. According to Cicero (*Tusc.*, I, 33), Aristotle already remarked *omnes ingeniosos melancholicos esse;*[4] this undoubtedly refers to the passage in Aristotle's *Problemata,* 30, 1. Goethe also says:

> My poetic fire was very low
> So long as I encountered good;
> Whereas it was all aflame,
> When I fled from imminent evil.
> The delicate verse like a rainbow
> Is drawn only on a dark ground,
> Hence the poet's genius relishes
> The element of melancholy.

This is explained by the fact that, as the will constantly reasserts its original mastery over the intellect, the latter withdraws more easily from such mastery in unfavourable personal circumstances, because it readily turns from adverse circumstances in order to divert itself to a certain extent. It then directs itself with all the greater energy to the foreign external world, and thus more easily becomes purely objective. Favourable personal circumstances have the opposite effect. On the whole, however, the melancholy accompanying genius rests on the fact that, the brighter the intellect enlightening the will-to-live, the more distinctly does it perceive the wretchedness of its condition. The gloomy disposition of highly gifted minds, so frequently observed, has its emblem in Mont Blanc, whose summit is often hidden in the clouds. But when on occasion, especially in the early morning, the veil of clouds is rent, and the mountain, red in the sunlight, looks down on Chamonix from its celestial height above the clouds, it is then a sight at which the heart of everyone is most deeply stirred. So also does the genius, who is often melancholy, display at times that characteristic serenity already described, which is possible in him alone, and springs from the most perfect objectivity of the mind. It floats like a radiant gleam of light on his lofty brow; *in tristitia hilaris, in hilaritate tristis.*[5]

All bunglers are what they are ultimately because their intellect, still too firmly tied to the will, becomes active only under the will's

---

[4] "All men of genius are melancholy." [Tr.]

[5] "Cheerful in sadness, sad in cheerfulness." [Tr.]

spur, and therefore remains entirely in its service. Accordingly they are capable of none other than personal aims. In keeping with this they produce bad paintings, dull and spiritless poems, shallow, absurd, and very often dishonest philosophemes, when, that is, it is of importance to them to recommend themselves to higher authorities through pious dishonesty. Thus all their thoughts and actions are personal; and so they succeed at most in appropriating as mannerisms what is external, accidental, and arbitrary in the genuine works of others. They seize the shell instead of the kernel, and yet imagine they have reached everything, indeed have surpassed those works. If the failure becomes obvious, many hope nevertheless to attain success in the end through their good will. But it is precisely this good will that makes it impossible, since this leads only to personal ends; with these, however, neither art, nor poetry, nor philosophy can ever be taken seriously. Therefore the expression that they stand in their own light is quite peculiarly applicable to such men. They have no idea that it is only the intellect, torn from the mastery of the will and from all its projects and thus freely active, that makes one capable of genuine productions, because it alone imparts true seriousness; and for them this is a good thing, otherwise they would jump into the water. In *morality* the *good will* is everything, but in *art* it is nothing; for, as the word (*Kunst*) already indicates, *ability* (*Können*) alone is of any consequence. Ultimately it is all a question of where the man's real *seriousness* is to be found. In the case of almost all, it is to be found exclusively in their own well-being and that of their families. They are therefore in a position to promote this and nothing else, since no resolution, no arbitrary and intentional effort, imparts, or makes up for, or more correctly furnishes, true, profound seriousness proper. For it always remains where nature has placed it; but without it everything can be only half performed. For the same reason, therefore, individuals of genius often give very little attention to their own welfare. Just as a leaden pendulum always brings a body back into the position required by the centre of gravity determined by such a pendulum, so man's true seriousness always draws the force and attention of his intellect back to *where it lies;* everything else is pursued by him *without true seriousness.* Therefore only extremely rare and abnormal men, whose true seriousness lies not in the personal and practical, but in the objective and theoretical, are in a position to apprehend the essential element of things and of the world, and hence the highest truths, and in some way to reproduce them. For such a seriousness of the individual, falling outside him in the *objective,* is something foreign to human nature, something unnatural, properly speaking supernatural. But only through it is a man *great;* and accordingly, what he produces or creates is then ascribed to a *genius* different from him, which takes possession of him. For such a man, his painting, poetry, or thinking is an *end;* for the other it is a *means.* These others look in it for *their own interest* and, as a rule, know quite well how to promote it, for they insinuate themselves into the favour of contemporaries, and are ready to serve their wants and whims. They therefore usually live in happy circumstances; whereas the genius often exists under very wretched conditions. For he sacrifices his personal welfare to the *objective* end; he simply cannot do otherwise, because there lies his seriousness. They act conversely; therefore they are *small,* but he is *great.* His work, accordingly, is for all times and ages, but its recognition usually begins only with posterity; *they* live and die with their time. In general, he alone is *great* who in his work, be it practical or theoretical, *seeks not his own interest,* but pursues only an *objective* end. However, he is such even when in the practical this aim or end is misunderstood, and even when, in consequence of this, it should be a crime. What makes him *great* in all circumstances is the fact that *he does not seek himself and his own interest.* On the other hand, all action or effort directed to personal ends or aims is *small,* since he who is moved to activity in this way knows and finds himself only in his own evanescent and trifling person. On the other hand, he who is *great* recognizes himself in all and thus in the whole; he does not live, like others, only in the microcosm, but still more in the macrocosm. For this reason, the whole concerns him, and he tries to grasp it, in order to present it, or explain it, or act on it in practice. For to him it is not strange; he feels that it concerns him. On account of this extension of his sphere, he is called *great.* Accordingly, that sublime predicate belongs by right only to the true hero in any sense and to the genius; it signifies that, contrary to human nature, they have not sought their own interest, and have lived not for themselves, but for all. Now just as the great majority must obviously be *always* small, and can *never* be great, the converse is not possible, namely that a person should be great in every way, that is to say, constantly and at every moment:

> For man is made of common clay,
> And custom he calls his nurse.
> [Schiller]

Thus every great man must nevertheless often be only the individual, have in view only *himself;* and this means he must be *small.* On this rests the very true remark that no man is a hero to his valet, not on the fact that the valet does not know how to appreciate the hero; Goethe in the *Elective Affinities* (vol. II, chap. 5) serves this up as an idea that occurred to Ottilie.

Genius is its own reward; for the best that one is, one must necessarily be for oneself. "Whoever is born *with* a talent, *to* a talent, finds his fairest existence therein," says Goethe. When we look back at a great man of former times, we do not think, "How lucky he is to be still admired by us all!" but, "How lucky he must have been in the immediate enjoyment of a mind, with the remaining traces of which centuries regale themselves!" Not in fame, but in that by which it is attained, lies the value, and in the production of immortal children lies the pleasure. Therefore those who attempt to demonstrate the vanity of posthumous fame from the fact that he who acquires it has no experience of it, is to be compared to the wiseacre who very sagely tried to demonstrate the utter uselessness of a heap of oyster-shells to a man casting envious glances at one in his neighbour's yard.

In accordance with the description we have given of the true nature of genius, it is contrary to nature in so far as it consists in the intellect, whose real destiny is the service of the will, emancipating itself from that service in order to be active on its own account. Accordingly, genius is an intellect that has become unfaithful to its destiny; on this rest the *disadvantages* connected with it. We now prepare the way for a consideration of these by comparing genius with the less decided preponderance of the intellect.

The intellect of the normal man, strictly bound to the service of his will, and thus in reality occupied only with the reception and taking up of motives, may be regarded as the complex system of wires with which each of these puppets is set in motion on the stage of the world-theatre. From this springs the dry, grave seriousness of most people, which is surpassed only by that of the animals, which never laugh. On the other hand, the genius, with his unfettered intellect, could be compared to a living person playing among the large puppets of the famous Milan puppet-show. This person would be the only one among them who would perceive everything, and would therefore gladly quit the stage for a while in order to enjoy the play from the boxes; this is the reflectiveness of genius. But even the extremely intelligent and rational man, whom we might almost call wise, is very different from the genius; and indeed he is so because his intellect retains a *practical* tendency. It is concerned with the choice of the best of all ends and means; it therefore remains in the service of the will, and accordingly is occupied really and truly in conformity with nature. The firm, practical seriousness of life, described by the Romans as *gravitas,* presupposes that the intellect does *not* forsake the service of the will, in order to wander away after what does not concern this. It therefore does not admit of that separation of the will and the intellect which is the condition of genius. The able, indeed the eminent man, fitted for great achievements in the practical sphere, is as he is precisely through objects that keenly rouse his will, and spur it on to the restless investigation of their connexions and relations. Thus his intellect has grown up firmly connected with his will. On the other hand, there floats before the mind of the genius, in its objective apprehension, the phenomenon of the world as something foreign to him, as an object of contemplation, expelling his willing from consciousness. On this point hinges the difference between the capacity for *deeds* and that for *works.* The latter demands an objectivity and depth of knowledge that presuppose the complete separation of the intellect from the will. The former, on the other hand, demands the application of knowledge, presence of mind, and resoluteness, and these require that the intellect shall constantly carry out the service of the will. Where the bond between intellect and will is loosened, the intellect, diverted from its natural destiny, will neglect the service of the will. For example, even in the emergency of the moment, it will still maintain its emancipation, and possibly will have no choice but to apprehend the environment, according to the picturesque impression thereof, from which the present danger threatens the individual. On the other hand, the intellect of the man of reason and understanding is always at its post, is directed to the circumstances and their requirements. Therefore such a man will in all cases determine and carry out what is appropriate to the matter. Consequently he will certainly not run into those eccentricities, personal slips, and even follies, to which the genius is exposed. The genius does this because his intellect does not remain exclusively the guide and guardian of his will, but is engrossed more or less in what is purely objective. In the contrast between Tasso and Antonio, Goethe has given us an illustration of the opposition in which the two entirely different kinds of capacity, here described in the abstract, stand to each other. The frequently observed kinship of genius with madness rests chiefly on that very separation of the intellect from the will, essential to genius yet contrary to nature. But this separation itself is not in any way to be ascribed to the fact that genius is accompanied by less intensity of the will, for it is rather conditioned by a vehement and passionate character; on the contrary, it is to be explained from the fact that the practically eminent man, the man of deeds, has merely the whole, full measure of intellect required for an energetic will, whereas most men lack even this. Genius, however, consists in a wholly abnormal, actual excess of intellect, such as is not required for the service of any will. For this reason, the men of genuine works are a thousand times rarer than the men of deeds. It is just that abnormal excess of intellect, by virtue of which it obtains the decided preponderance, emancipates itself from the will, and, forgetful of its origin, is freely active from its own force and elasticity. It is from this that the creations of genius result.

Further, genius consists in the working of the free intellect, that is, of the intellect emancipated from the service of the will; and a consequence of this very fact is that the productions of genius serve no useful purpose. The work of genius may be music, philosophy, painting, or poetry; it is nothing for use or profit. To be useless and unprofitable is one of the characteristics of the works of genius; it is their patent of nobility. All other human works exist only for the maintenance or relief of our existence; only those here discussed do not; they alone exist for their own sake, and are to be regarded in this sense as the flower or the net profit of existence. Our heart is therefore gladdened at the enjoyment of them, for we rise out of the heavy earthly atmosphere of need and want. Moreover, analogous to this, we rarely see the beautiful united with the useful. Tall and fine trees bear no fruit; fruit trees are small, ugly, and stunted. The double garden rose is not fruitful, but the small, wild, almost scentless rose is. The most beautiful buildings are not the useful ones; a temple is not a dwelling-house. A person of high, rare mental gifts, compelled to attend to a merely useful piece of business for which the most ordinary person would be fitted, is like a valuable vase decorated with the most beautiful painting, which is used as a kitchen-pot; and to compare useful men with men of genius is like comparing bricks with diamonds.

The merely practical man, therefore, uses his intellect for that for which nature destined it, namely for comprehending the relations of things partly to one another, partly to the will of the knowing individual. The genius, on the other hand, uses his intellect contrary to its destiny, for comprehending the objective nature of things. His mind therefore belongs not to himself, but to the world, to the elucidation of which it will in some sense contribute. From this, *disadvantages* of many kinds are bound to arise to the individual favoured with genius. For in general, his intellect will show the faults that are usually bound to appear in the case of every tool that is used for a purpose for which it is not made. In the first place, it will be, so to speak, the servant of two masters, since at every opportunity it emancipates itself from the service in keeping with its destiny, in order to follow its own ends. In this way it often leaves the will very inopportunely in the lurch; and accordingly, the individual so gifted becomes more or less useless for life; in fact, by his conduct we are sometimes reminded of madness. Then, by virtue of its enhanced power of knowledge, it will see in things more of the universal than of the particular, whereas the service of the will mainly requires knowledge of the particular. And again, when that entire, abnormally enhanced power of knowledge occasionally directs itself suddenly with all its energy to the affairs and miseries of the will, it will readily apprehend these too vividly, will view everything in too glaring colours, in too bright a light, and in a monstrously exaggerated form; and in this way the individual falls into mere extremes. The following may help to explain this in even greater detail. All great theoretical achievements, be they of what kind they may, are brought about by their author directing all the forces of his mind to one point. He causes them to be united at this point and concentrates them so vigorously, firmly, and exclusively, that all the rest of the world vanishes for him, and his object for him fills all reality. It is just this great and powerful concentration, forming one of the privileges of genius, which sometimes appears for it, even in the case of objects of reality and of the events of everyday life. Brought under such a focus, these are then magnified to such monstrous proportions that they appear like the flea that under the solar microscope assumes the stature of an elephant. The result of this is that, by trifles, highly gifted individuals are sometimes thrown into emotions of the most varied kind. To others such emotions are incomprehensible, for they see these individuals reduced to grief, joy, care, fear, anger, and so on by things that would leave the ordinary man quite unruffled. Therefore the genius lacks *coolness or soberness,* which consists simply in our seeing in things nothing more than actually belongs to them, especially in respect of our possible aims; hence no cool or sober man can be a genius. With the disadvantages just mentioned is also associated an excessive sensibility entailed by an abnormally enhanced nervous and cerebral life; we see it, in fact, associated with the vehemence and passionateness of willing, which is likewise a condition of genius, and which manifests itself physically as energy of the heart's pulsation. From all this very readily arise that extravagance of disposition, that vehemence of the emotions, that quick change of mood under prevailing melancholy, which Goethe has presented to us in *Tasso.* What reasonableness, quiet composure, comprehensive survey, complete certainty and regularity of conduct are shown by the well-equipped normal man in comparison with the now dreamy and brooding absorption and now passionate excitement of the genius, whose inner affliction is the womb of immortal works! With all this there is also the fact that the genius lives essentially alone. He is too rare to be capable of easily coming across his like, and too different from the rest to be their companion. With them it is willing, with him it is knowing, that prevails; hence their joys and pleasures are not his, nor his theirs. They are only moral beings, and have merely personal relations; he is at the same time a pure intellect that as such belongs to the whole of mankind. The train of thought of the intellect which is detached from its maternal soil, the will, and which only periodically returns thereto, will soon differ in every way from that of the normal intellect which still cleaves to its stem. For this reason, and on account of the inequality of the pace, the detached intellect is not adapted to thinking in common, that is to say, to conversation with others; they will have as little pleasure in him and his oppressive superiority as he will have in them. They will therefore feel more at ease with their equals, and he will prefer conversation with his equals, although as a rule this is possible only through the works they have left behind. Therefore Chamfort says very rightly: *Il y a peu de vices qui empêchent un homme d'avoir beaucoup d'amis, autant que peuvent le faire de trop grandes qualités.*[6] The happiest lot that can befall the genius is to be released from action, which is not his element, and to have leisure for production. From all this it follows that, although genius may highly favour the person gifted with it in the hours in which, devoted to it, he revels unhindered in its enjoyment, yet it is by no means calculated to procure for him a happy course of life; rather the contrary. This is also confirmed by the experience recorded in biographies. In addition there is an external incongruity, since in his efforts and achievements themselves, the genius is often in contradiction and conflict with his times. Mere men of talent always come at the right time; for, as they are roused by the spirit of their age and are called into being by its needs, they are only just capable of satisfying them. They therefore go hand in hand with the advancing culture of their contemporaries, or with the gradual advancement of a special science; for this they reap reward and approbation. But to the next generation their works are no longer enjoyable; they must be replaced by others; and these do not fail to appear. The genius, on the other hand, lights on his age like a comet into the paths of the planets, to whose well-regulated and comprehensible arrangement its wholly eccentric course is foreign. Accordingly, he cannot go hand in hand

---

[6] "Few vices are as capable of preventing a man from having many friends as is the possession of qualities that are too great." [Tr.]

with the regular course of the culture of the times as found; on the contrary, he casts his works far out on to the path in front (just as the emperor, giving himself up to death, flings his spear among the enemy), on which time has first to overtake them. His relation to the culminating men of talent during his time might be expressed in the words of the Evangelist: Ὁ καιρὸς ὁ ἐμὸς οὔπω πάρεστιν· ὁ δὲ καιρὸς ὁ ὑμέτερος πάντοτέ ἐστιν ἕτοιμος (John vii, 6).[7] *Talent* is able to achieve what is beyond other people's capacity to achieve, yet not what is beyond their capacity of apprehension; therefore it at once finds its appreciators. The achievement of *genius*, on the other hand, transcends not only others' capacity of achievement, but also their capacity of apprehension; therefore they do not become immediately aware of it. Talent is like the marksman who hits a target which others cannot reach; genius is like the marksman who hits a target, as far as which others cannot even see. Therefore these others obtain information about genius only indirectly, and thus tardily, and even this they accept only on trust and faith. Accordingly, Goethe says in a didactic epistle: "Imitation is inborn in us; what is to be imitated is not easily recognized. Rarely is the excellent found, more rarely is it appreciated." And Chamfort says: *Il en est de la valeur des hommes comme de celle des diamans, qui, à une certaine mesure de grosseur, de pureté, de perfection, ont un prix fixe et marqué, mais qui, par-delà cette mesure, restent sans prix, et ne trouvent point d'acheteurs.*[8] Bacon has also expressed it: *Infimarum virtutum, apud vulgus, laus est, mediarum admiratio, supremarum sensus nullus* (*De Augm. Sc.*, L. vi., c. 3).[9] Indeed, one would perhaps like to retort, *apud vulgus!* However, I must come to his assistance with Machiavelli's assurance: *Nel mondo non è se non volgo.*[10] Thilo (*Über den Ruhm*) also observes that usually there belongs to the vulgar herd one more than each of us believes. It is a consequence of this late recognition of the works of genius that they are rarely enjoyed by their contemporaries, and accordingly in the freshness of colour imparted by contemporaneousness and presence; on the contrary, like figs and dates, they are enjoyed much more in the dry state than in the fresh.

Finally, if we now consider genius from the somatic angle, we

---

[7] "My time is not yet come: but your time is alway ready." [Tr.]

[8] "It is the same with the value of men as it is with that of diamonds, which, up to a certain degree of size, purity, and perfection, have a fixed and definite price, but beyond that degree remain without price and find no buyers at all." [Tr.]

[9] "The lowest virtues meet with applause from the people, the intermediate admiration, and the highest no appreciation." [Tr.]

[10] "There is nothing else in the world but the vulgar." [Tr.]

find it conditioned by several anatomical and physiological qualities, which individually are rarely present in perfection, and even more rarely complete together, but all of which are nevertheless indispensably required; and this explains why genius occurs only as a wholly isolated and almost portentous exception. The fundamental condition is an abnormal preponderance of sensibility over irritability and reproductive power; in fact, what makes the matter more difficult is that this must occur in a male body. (Women can have remarkable talent, but not genius, for they always remain subjective.) Similarly, the cerebral system must be clearly separated from the ganglionic by total isolation, so that it stands in complete opposition thereto, whereby the brain leads its parasitic life on the organism in a very decided, isolated, powerful, and independent manner. Naturally, it will thus have a hostile effect on the rest of the organism, and by its enhanced life and restless activity will prematurely exhaust it, unless it is also of energetic vital force and of good constitution; this latter, therefore, is also one of the conditions. In fact, even a good stomach is a condition, on account of the special and close agreement of this part with the brain. Mainly the brain, however, must be of unusual development and size, especially broad and lofty; on the other hand, its dimension in depth will be inferior, and the cerebrum will preponderate abnormally in proportion to the cerebellum. Very much depends undoubtedly on the shape and formation of the brain as a whole and in its parts, but our knowledge is not yet sufficient to determine this accurately, although we easily recognize the form of a skull that proclaims a noble and exalted intelligence. The texture of the mass of the brain must be of extreme fineness and perfection, and must consist of the purest, most clarified, delicate, and sensitive nerve-substance. The quantitative proportion of white to grey matter certainly has a decided influence; and this we are likewise still unable to measure. The report of the post-mortem examination on the body of Byron,[11] however, states that in his case the white matter was in unusually large proportion to the grey, and that his brain weighed six pounds. Cuvier's brain weighed five pounds; the normal weight is three. In contrast to the preponderance of the brain, the spinal cord and nerves must be unusually slender. A finely arched, lofty, and broad skull of thin bone must protect the brain without in any way cramping it. The whole of this quality of the brain and nervous system is the inheritance from the mother; we shall return to this in the following book. But this is quite inadequate for producing the phenomenon of genius, unless

---

[11] In Medwin's *Conversations of Lord Byron*, p. 333.

there is added as the inheritance from the father a lively, passionate temperament, manifesting itself somatically as unusual energy of the heart, and consequently of the blood circulation, especially towards the head. For in the first place, that turgescence peculiar to the brain is increased in this way, and by virtue of it the brain presses against its walls. Therefore the brain oozes out of every opening in these which has been caused by injury. In the second place, the brain receives through the requisite strength of the heart that inner movement which is different from its constant rising and sinking at every breath, consisting in an agitation of the whole mass of the brain at every pulsation of the four cerebral arteries, and the energy of which must correspond to the quantity of the brain increased here, just as this movement in general is an indispensable condition of the brain's activity. For this reason a small stature and especially a short neck are also favourable to such activity, because on the shorter path the blood reaches the brain with more energy; therefore great minds seldom have a large body. This shortness of the path, however, is not indispensable; Goethe, for example, was of more than average height. But if the whole condition, affecting the blood circulation and thus coming from the father, is lacking, the favourable quality of the brain originating from the mother will at most produce a talent, a fine understanding, supported by the phlegmatic temperament that then appears; but a phlegmatic genius is impossible. This condition of genius coming from the father explains many of the temperamental defects of genius previously described. On the other hand, if this condition is present without the former, and so with an ordinarily or even badly constituted brain, it gives vivacity without mind, heat without light; it produces madcaps, persons of insufferable restlessness and petulance. Of two brothers only one has genius, and then often the elder, as was the case, for example, with Kant. This can be explained above all from the fact that only when *he* was begotten was his father at the age of strength and ardour, although the other condition also originating from the mother can be ruined by unfavourable circumstances.

I have still to add here a special remark on the *childlike* character of genius, on a certain resemblance between genius and the age of childhood. Thus in childhood, as in the case of genius, the cerebral and nervous systems are decidedly predominant, for their development hurries far in advance of that of the rest of the organism, so that even by the seventh year the brain has attained its full extension and mass. Therefore Bichat says: *Dans l'enfance le système nerveux, comparé au musculaire, est proportionnellement plus considérable que dans tous les âges suivans, tandis que, par la suite, la pluspart des autres systèmes prédominent sur celui-ci. On sait que, pour bien voir les nerfs, on choisit toujours les enfans.*[12] (*De la vie et de la mort,* Art. 8, § 6.) On the other hand, the development of the genital system begins last, and only at the age of manhood are irritability, reproduction, and the genital function in full force; then, as a rule, they have the ascendancy over the brain-function. From this it can be explained why children in general are so sensible, reasonable, eager to learn, and easy to teach, in fact are on the whole more disposed to and suitable for all theoretical occupations than are grown-up people. Thus in consequence of that process of development they have more intellect than will, in other words than inclination, craving, and passion. For intellect and brain are one; and in just the same way, the genital system is one with the most vehement of all desires. I have therefore called this the focus of the will. Just because the terrible activity of this system still slumbers, while that of the brain already has full briskness, childhood is the time of innocence and happiness, the paradise of life, the lost Eden, on which we look back longingly through the whole remaining course of our life. But the basis of that happiness is that in childhood our whole existence lies much more in knowing than in willing. This state or condition is also supported from outside by the novelty of all objects. Thus in the morning sunshine of life, the world lies before us so fresh, so magically gleaming, so attractive. The little desires, the uncertain inclinations, and the trifling cares of childhood are only a feeble counterpoise to that predominance of the activity of knowledge. The innocent and clear glance of children, at which we revive ourselves, and which sometimes in particular cases reaches the sublime, contemplative expression with which Raphael has adorned his cherubs, is to be explained from what we have said. Accordingly, mental powers develop much earlier than the needs they are destined to serve, and here, as everywhere, nature proceeds very appropriately. For in this period of predominant intelligence, man gathers a great store of knowledge for future needs that at the time are still foreign to him. Now incessantly active, his intellect therefore eagerly apprehends all phenomena, broods over them, and carefully stores them up for the coming time, like the bee which gathers far more honey than it can consume, in anticipation of future needs. It is certain that what man gains in insight and knowledge up

---

[12] "In childhood the nervous system, compared with the muscular, is proportionately more considerable than in all the ages that follow, whilst later on most of the other systems predominate over this. It is well known that, for a thorough study of the nerves, one always chooses children." [Tr.]

to the age of puberty is, taken as a whole, more than all that he learns subsequently, however learned he may become; for it is the foundation of all human knowledge. Up till the same time, plasticity predominates in the child's body, and after this plasticity has completed its work, its forces later apply themselves through a metastasis to the system of generation. In this way the sexual impulse appears with puberty, and the will gradually gains the upper hand. Childhood, which is predominantly theoretical and eager to learn, is then followed by the restless age of youth, now boisterous and impetuous, now dejected and melancholy, and this passes subsequently into the vigorous and earnest age of manhood. Just because that impulse, pregnant with evil, is lacking in the child, its willing is so moderate and is subordinated to knowing; and from this arises that character of innocence, intelligence, and reasonableness which is peculiar to the age of childhood. I need hardly state further on what the resemblance of childhood to genius depends; it is to be found in the surplus of the powers of knowledge over the needs of the will, and in the predominance of the activity of pure knowledge that springs therefrom. In fact, every child is to a certain extent a genius, and every genius to a certain extent a child. The relationship between the two shows itself primarily in the naivety and sublime ingenuousness that are a fundamental characteristic of true genius. Moreover it comes to light in several features, so that a certain childlike nature does indeed form part of the character of genius. In Riemer's *Mitteilungen über Goethe* (Vol. I, p. 184) it is related that Herder and others found fault with Goethe, saying that he was always like a big child; they were certainly right in what they said, only they were not right in finding fault. It was also said of Mozart that he remained a child all his life. (Nissen's Biography of Mozart, pp. 2 and 529.) Schlichtegroll's Necrology (for 1791, Vol. II, p. 109) says of him: "In his art he early became a man, but in all other respects he invariably remained a child." Therefore every genius is already a big child, since he looks out into the world as into something strange and foreign, a drama, and thus with purely objective interest. Accordingly, just like the child, he does not have the dull gravity and earnestness of ordinary men, who, being capable of nothing but subjective interests, always see in things merely motives for their actions. He who throughout his life does not, to a certain extent, remain a big child, but becomes an earnest, sober, thoroughly composed and rational man, can be a very useful and capable citizen of this world; but he will never be a genius. In fact, the genius is such through that preponderance of the sensible system and of the activity of knowledge, natural to the age of childhood, maintaining itself in him in an abnormal manner throughout his whole life, and so becoming perennial. A trace of this certainly continues in many an ordinary person right into the age of youth; thus, for example, a purely intellectual tendency and an eccentricity suggestive of genius are still unmistakable in many a student. But nature returns to her track; these assume the chrysalis form, and reappear at the age of manhood as Philistines incarnate, at whom we are horrified when we meet them again in later years. Goethe's fine remark depends on all that has been discussed here. He says: "Children do not keep their promise; young people very seldom, and if they do keep their word, the world does not keep its word with them." (*Elective Affinities,* I, chap. 10.) Thus he means the world that afterwards bestows the crowns, which it holds aloft for merit, on those who become the instruments of its low aims, or who know how to dupe it. In accordance with what we have said, just as there is a mere beauty of youth, possessed at some time by almost everyone (*beauté du diable*),[13] so is there also a mere intellectuality of youth, a certain mental nature disposed and adapted to apprehending, understanding, and learning, which everyone has in childhood, and some still have in youth, but which is subsequently lost, just as that beauty is. Only with extremely few, with the elect, does the one, like the other, last throughout life, so that even in old age a trace of it still remains visible; these are the truly beautiful and the men of true genius.

The predominance of the cerebral nervous system and of the intelligence in childhood, which we are considering, together with its decline in mature age, finds an important illustration and confirmation in the fact that in the species of animals closest to man, the apes, the same relation occurs in a striking degree. Gradually, it has become certain that the extremely intelligent orang-utan is a young pongo. When it is grown up, it loses the marked human resemblance of the countenance, and at the same time its astonishing intelligence, for the lower, animal part of the face increases in size, the forehead recedes, large *cristae* for muscular development give the skull an animal form; the activity of the nervous system diminishes, and in its place is developed an extraordinary muscular strength. As this strength is sufficient for the animal's preservation, it renders any great intelligence superfluous. Of special importance is what F. Cuvier has said in this respect, and Flourens has explained in a review of the former's *Histoire naturelle.* It is to be found in the September, 1839, issue of the *Journal des Savans,* and also separately

---

[13] "Beauty of the devil." [Tr.]

printed with a few additions under the title: *Résumé analytique des observations de Fr. Cuvier sur l'instinct et l'intelligence des animaux, p. Flourens,* 1841. On page 50 it is said: *L'intelligence de l'orang-outang, cette intelligence si développée, et développée de si bonne heure, décroit avec l'âge. L'orang-outang, lorsqu'il est jeune, nous étonne par sa pénétration, par sa ruse, par son adresse; l'orang-outang, devenu adulte, n'est plus qu'un animal grossier, brutal, intraitable. Et il en est de tous les singes comme de l'orang-outang. Dans tous, l'intelligence décroit à mesure que les forces s'accroissent. L'animal qui a le plus d'intelligence, n'a toute cette intelligence que dans le jeune âge.* Further, on p. 87: *Les singes de tous les genres offrent ce rapport inverse de l'âge et de l'intelligence. Ainsi, par exemple, l'Entelle (espèce de guenon du sous-genre des Semnopithèques et l'un des singes vénérés dans la religion des Brames) a, dans le jeune âge, le front large, le museau peu saillant, le crâne élevé, arrondi, etc. Avec l'âge le front disparaît, recule, le museau proémine; et le moral ne change pas moins que le physique: l'apathie, la violence, le besoin de solitude, remplacent la pénétration, la docilité, la confiance. Ces différences sont si grandes, dit Mr. Fréd. Cuvier, que dans l'habitude où nous sommes de juger des actions des animaux par les nôtres, nous prendrions le jeune animal pour un individu de l'âge, où toutes les qualités morales de l'espèce sont acquises, et l'Entelle adulte pour un individu qui n'aurait encore que ses forces physiques. Mais la nature n'en agit pas ainsi avec ces animaux, qui ne doivent pas sortir de la sphère étroite, qui leur est fixée, et à qui il suffit en quelque sorte de pouvoir veiller à leur conservation. Pour cela l'intelligence était nécessaire, quand la force n'existait pas, et quand celle-ci est acquise, toute autre puissance perd de son utilité.* And on p. 118: *La conservation des espèces ne repose pas moins sur les qualités intellectuelles des animaux, que sur leurs qualités organiques.*[14] This last confirms my principle that the

---

[14] "The intelligence of the orang-utan, which is highly developed at such an early age, declines as he grows older. The orang-utan when young astonishes us with his mental acuteness, his wiliness, and his cleverness; but when he is grown up, he is nothing but a coarse, brutal, and intractable animal. And it is just the same with all the apes as with the orang-utan. In all of them the intelligence declines in proportion as their strength increases. The animal that has the highest intelligence has the whole of this intelligence only in his youth. . . . Apes of all species show us this inverse ratio of age and intelligence. For example, the entellus (a monkey of the sub-genus *Semnopithecus* and one of the apes worshipped in the religion of the Brahmans as Hanuman) has in its youth a broad forehead, a not very prominent muzzle, and a lofty round skull. With advancing age the forehead disappears and recedes, the muzzle becomes more prominent, and the moral qualities

intellect, like the claws and teeth, is nothing but a tool for the service of the will.

---

change like the physical. Apathy, violence, and the need for solitude replace mental acuteness, docility, and trust. These differences are so great, says Cuvier, that, according to our habit of judging the actions of animals by our own, we should regard the young animal as an individual at the age when all the moral qualities of the species have been acquired, and the adult entellus as an individual who still has only its physical strength. But nature does not act in this way with these animals; they cannot go outside the narrow sphere which is fixed for them and is just sufficient in some way for looking after their preservation. For this purpose the intelligence was necessary when the strength did not exist; and when this is acquired, every other faculty loses its use. . . . The preservation of the species is conditioned just as much by the intellectual qualities of animals as by their organic qualities." [Tr.]

On Madness

Real soundness of mind consists in perfect recollection. Naturally this is not to be understood as meaning that our memory preserves everything. For the past course of our life shrinks up in time just as that of the wanderer who looks back shrinks up in space. Sometimes it is difficult for us to distinguish particular years; the days often become indistinguishable. But really only exactly similar events, recurring innumerable times, whose images are, so to speak, identical in all respects, are supposed to run together in the memory, so that individually they become indistinguishable. On the other hand, if the intellect is normal, powerful, and quite healthy, it must be possible to find again in memory any event that is characteristic or significant. In the text I have described *madness* as the *broken* thread of this memory which nevertheless continues to run uniformly, although with constantly decreasing fulness and distinctness. The following consideration may help to confirm this.

The memory of a healthy person affords certainty as to an event of which he was a witness; and this certainty is regarded as just as firm and sure as is his actual apprehension of a thing. Therefore, when the event is confirmed by him on oath, it is thereby established before a court of law. On the other hand, the mere suspicion of madness will at once weaken a witness's statement. Here, then, is to be found the criterion between soundness of mind and insanity. The moment I doubt whether an event, which I recollect, actually took place, I bring on myself the suspicion of madness, unless it is that I am uncertain whether it was not a mere dream. If another person doubts the reality of an event recounted by me as an eyewitness, and does not distrust my honesty, he regards me as insane. Whoever, through frequently recounting an event that he originally fabricated, comes at last to believe in it himself, is really already insane on this one point. We can credit an insane person

---

[1] This chapter refers to the second half of § 36 of volume 1.

with flashes of wit, isolated shrewd ideas, even correct judgements, but we shall not attach any validity to his testimony as to past events. In the *Lalita-Vistara*, well known as the life story of the Buddha Sakyamuni, it is related that, at the moment of his birth, all the sick throughout the world became well, all the blind saw, all the deaf heard, and all the insane "recovered their memory." This last is even mentioned in two passages.[2]

My own experience of many years has led me to the conjecture that madness occurs in most frequent proportion among actors. But what an abuse these men make of their memory! Every day they have to learn a new part by heart, or brush up an old one; but these parts are entirely without connexion; in fact, they are in contradiction and contrast with one another, and every evening the actor strives to forget himself entirely, in order to be quite a different person. Things like this pave the way to madness.

The description of the origin of madness given in the text will become easier to understand, if we remember how reluctantly we think of things that powerfully prejudice our interests, wound our pride, or interfere with our wishes; with what difficulty we decide to lay such things before our own intellect for accurate and serious investigation; how easily, on the other hand, we unconsciously break away or sneak off from them again; how, on the contrary, pleasant affairs come into our minds entirely of their own accord, and, if driven away, always creep on us once more, so that we dwell on them for hours. In this resistance on the part of the will to allow what is contrary to it to come under the examination of the intellect is to be found the place where madness can break in on the mind. Every new adverse event must be assimilated by the intellect, in other words, must receive a place in the system of truths connected with our will and its interests, whatever it may have to displace that is more satisfactory. As soon as this is done, it pains us much less; but this operation itself is often very painful, and in most cases takes place only slowly and with reluctance. But soundness of mind can continue only in so far as this operation has been correctly carried out each time. On the other hand, if, in a particular case, the resistance and opposition of the will to the assimilation of some knowledge reaches such a degree that that operation is not clearly carried through; accordingly, if certain events or circumstances are wholly suppressed for the intellect, because the will cannot bear the sight of them; and then, if the resultant gaps are arbitrarily filled up for the sake of the necessary connexion; we then have madness. For

---

[2] *Rgya Tcher Rol Pa, Hist. de Bouddha Chakya Mouni,* translated from the Tibetan by Foucaux, 1848, pp. 91 and 99.

the intellect has given up its nature to please the will; the person then imagines what does not exist. But the resultant madness then becomes the Lethe of unbearable sufferings; it was the last resource of worried and tormented nature, i.e., of the will.

I may here mention incidentally a proof of my view which is worthy of notice. Carlo Gozzi in the *Mostro turchino,* Act I, Scene 2, presents us with a person who has drunk a magic potion that produces forgetfulness; this person appears to be exactly like a madman.

In accordance with the above discussion, we can regard the origin of madness as a violent "casting out of one's mind" of something; yet this is possible only by a "putting into the head" of something else. The reverse process is rarer, namely that the "putting into the head" is the first thing, and the "casting out of the mind" the second. It takes place, however, in cases where a person keeps constantly present to his mind, and cannot get rid of, the cause of his insanity; thus, for example, in the case of many who have gone mad from love, erotomaniacs, where the cause is constantly longed for; also in the case of madness that has resulted from horror at a sudden, frightful occurrence. Such patients cling convulsively, so to speak, to the conceived idea, so that no other, at any rate none that opposes it, can arise. But in the two processes, what is essential to madness remains the same, namely the impossibility of a uniformly coherent recollection, such as is the basis of our healthy and rational reflection. Perhaps the contrast, here described, in the manner of origin might, if applied with judgement, afford a sharp and fundamental principle of division of delusion proper.

But I have taken into consideration only the psychic origin of madness, that is, of madness produced by external, objective occasions. Yet it depends more often on purely somatic causes, on malformations or partial disorganizations of the brain or its membranes, also on the influence exercised on the brain by other parts affected with disease. Mainly in the last kind of madness, false sense-perceptions, hallucinations, may arise. Each of the two causes of madness, however, will often have some of the characteristics of the other, particularly the psychic of the somatic. It is the same as with suicide; rarely can this be brought about by the external occasion alone, but a certain bodily discomfort underlies it, and according to the degree reached by this discomfort a greater or smaller external occasion is required. Only in the case of the highest degree of discomfort is no external occasion required at all. Therefore no misfortune is so great that it would induce everyone to commit suicide; and none so small that one like it may not already have led to suicide. I have discussed the psychic origin of madness, as brought about, at least according to all appearance, in the sound mind by a great misfortune. In the case of the person already strongly disposed to it somatically, a very trifling vexation will be sufficient to induce it. For example, I remember a man in a lunatic asylum who had been a soldier and had gone out of his mind because his officer had addressed him as *Er*.[3] In the case of marked bodily disposition, no occasion is required at all, when such a disposition has reached maturity. The madness that has sprung from merely psychic causes can possibly bring about, through the violent inversion of the course of thought that produces it, even a kind of paralysis or other depravation of some parts of the brain; and if this is not soon removed, it becomes permanent. Therefore madness is curable only at its beginning, not after a long time.

Pinel taught that there is a *mania sine delirio,* a frenzy without insanity; Esquirol disputed this, and since then much has been said both for and against it. The question can be decided only empirically. However, if such a state actually occurs, it is to be explained by the fact that the will periodically withdraws itself entirely from the government and guidance of the intellect, and consequently of the motives. In this way it then appears as a blind, impetuous, destructive force of nature, and accordingly manifests itself as the mania to annihilate everything that comes in its way. The will thus let loose is then like the river that has broken through the dam, the horse that has thrown its rider, the clock from which the checking screws are taken out. But only the faculty of reason, or *reflective* knowledge, is affected by this suspension, not *intuitive* knowledge, otherwise the will would remain entirely without guidance, and consequently the person would remain immovable. On the contrary, the man in a frenzy perceives objects, for he breaks loose on them; he is also conscious of his present action and remembers it afterwards. He is, however, entirely without reflection, and hence without any guidance through his faculty of reason. Consequently he is quite incapable of any consideration or regard for the absent, the past, and the future. When the attack is over, and his faculty of reason has regained its command, its functioning is correct and methodical, for its own activity is not deranged or damaged, only the will has found the means for withdrawing itself entirely from it for a while.

---

[3] *Er* was formerly used as a form of address to subordinates. [Tr.]

Isolated Remarks on Natural Beauty

What contributes among other things to make the sight of a beautiful landscape so exceedingly delightful, is the universal *truth and consistency* of nature. Here, of course, nature does not follow the guiding line of logic in the sequence and connexions of the grounds of knowledge, of antecedent and consequent clauses, of premises and conclusions; yet she follows the analogous line of the law of causality in the visible connexion of causes and effects. Every modification, even the slightest, which an object receives through its position, foreshortening, concealment, distance, distribution of light and shade, linear and atmospheric perspective, and so on, is unerringly given through its effect on the eye, and is accurately taken into account. Here the Indian proverb "Every grain of rice casts its shadow" finds its confirmation. Therefore everything here shows itself so universally consistent and logical, exactly correct and methodical, coherent and connected, and scrupulously right; there are no shifts or subterfuges here. Now if we take into consideration the sight of a beautiful view merely as *brain-phenomenon,* then it is the only one of the complicated brain-phenomena which is always quite regular, methodical, faultless, unexceptionable, and perfect. For all the rest, especially our own operations of thought, are in the formal or material more or less affected with defects or inaccuracies. From this excellent quality of the sight of the beauties of nature is to be explained first the harmonious and thoroughly satisfying character of its impression, and then the favourable effect it has on the whole of our thinking. In this way our thinking becomes in its formal part more accurately disposed, and to a certain extent is purified, since that brain-phenomenon which alone is entirely faultless puts the brain generally into a wholly normal action, and the thinking now attempts to follow in the consistency, connexion, regularity, and harmony of all its processes that method of nature, after

---

[1] This chapter refers to § 38 of volume 1.

it has been brought thereby into the right inspiration. A beautiful view is therefore a cathartic of the mind, just as music is of one's feelings, according to Aristotle; and in its presence a person will think most correctly.

That the sight of a *mountain range* suddenly appearing before us so easily puts us into a serious, and even sublime, mood, may be due partly to the fact that the form of the mountains, and the outline of the range that results therefrom, are the only *permanent* line of the landscape; for the mountains alone defy the deterioration and dissolution that rapidly sweep away everything else, especially our own ephemeral person. Not that all this would appear in our clear consciousness at the sight of the mountain range, but an obscure feeling of it becomes the fundamental note of our mood.

I should like to know why it is that, whereas for the human form and countenance illumination from above is absolutely the most advantageous and that from below the most unfavourable, the very opposite holds good in respect of landscape nature.

Yet how aesthetic nature is! Every little spot entirely uncultivated and wild, in other words, left free to nature herself, however small it may be, if only man's paws leave it alone, is at once decorated by her in the most tasteful manner, is draped with plants, flowers, and shrubs, whose easy unforced manner, natural grace, and delightful grouping testify that they have not grown up under the rod of correction of the great egoist, but that nature has here been freely active. Every neglected little place at once becomes beautiful. On this rests the principle of English gardens, which is to conceal art as much as possible, so that it may look as if nature had been freely active. For only then is nature perfectly beautiful, in other words, shows in the greatest distinctness the objectification of the will-to-live that is still without knowledge. This will unfolds itself here in the greatest naivety, since the forms are not determined, as in the animal world, by external aims and ends, but only immediately by soil, climate, and a mysterious third something, by virtue of which so many plants that have sprung originally from the same soil and climate nevertheless show such varied forms and characters.

The immense difference between English, or more correctly Chinese, gardens and old French gardens, which are now becoming more and more rare, but still exist in a few splendid specimens, ultimately rests on the fact that the former are laid out in an objective, the latter in a subjective spirit. Thus, in the former the will of nature, as it objectifies itself in tree, shrub, mountain, and stretch of water, is brought to the purest possible expression of these its Ideas, and thus of its own inner being. In French gardens, on the other hand, only the will of the possessor is mirrored. It has subdued nature, so that, instead of her Ideas, she bears, as tokens of her slavery, forms in keeping with it, and forcibly imposed on her, such as clipped hedges, trees cut into all kinds of shapes, straight avenues, arcades, arches, and the like.

On the Inner Nature of Art

Not merely philosophy but also the fine arts work at bottom towards the solution of the problem of existence. For in every mind which once gives itself up to the purely objective contemplation of the world, a desire has been awakened, however concealed and unconscious, to comprehend the true nature of things, of life, and of existence. For this alone is of interest to the intellect as such, in other words, to the subject of knowing which has become free from the aims of the will and is therefore pure; just as for the subject, knowing as mere individual, only the aims and ends of the will have interest. For this reason the result of every purely objective, and so of every artistic, apprehension of things is an expression more of the true nature of life and of existence, more an answer to the question, "What is life?" Every genuine and successful work of art answers this question in its own way quite calmly and serenely. But all the arts speak only the naïve and childlike language of *perception,* not the abstract and serious language of *reflection;* their answer is thus a fleeting image, not a permanent universal knowledge. Thus for *perception,* every work of art answers that question, every painting, every statue, every poem, every scene on the stage. Music also answers it, more profoundly indeed than do all the others, since in a language intelligible with absolute directness, yet not capable of translation into that of our faculty of reason, it expresses the innermost nature of all life and existence. Thus all the other arts together hold before the questioner an image or picture of perception and say: "Look here; this is life!" However correct their answer may be, it will yet always afford only a temporary, not a complete and final satisfaction. For they always give only a fragment, an example instead of the rule, not the whole which can be given only in the universality of the *concept.* Therefore it is the task of philosophy to give for the concept, and hence for reflection and in the abstract, a reply to that question, which on that very account is permanent and

---

satisfactory for all time. Moreover we see here on what the relationship between philosophy and the fine arts rests, and can conclude from this to what extent the capacity for the two, though very different in its tendency and in secondary matters, is yet radically the same.

Accordingly, every work of art really endeavours to show us life and things as they are in reality; but these cannot be grasped directly by everyone through the mist of objective and subjective contingencies. Art takes away this mist.

The works of poets, sculptors, and pictorial or graphic artists generally contain an acknowledged treasure of profound wisdom, just because the wisdom of the nature of things themselves speaks from them. They interpret the utterances of things merely by elucidation and purer repetition. Therefore everyone who reads the poem or contemplates the work of art must of course contribute from his own resources towards bringing that wisdom to light. Consequently, he grasps only so much of the work as his capacity and culture allow, just as every sailor in a deep sea lets down the sounding-lead as far as the length of its line will reach. Everyone has to stand before a picture as before a prince, waiting to see whether it will speak and what it will say to him; and, as with the prince, so he himself must not address it, for then he would hear only himself. It follows from all this that all wisdom is certainly contained in the works of the pictorial or graphic arts, yet only *virtualiter* or *implicite*. Philosophy, on the other hand, endeavours to furnish the same wisdom *actualiter* and *explicite;* in this sense philosophy is related to these arts as wine is to grapes. What it promises to supply would be, so to speak, a clear gain already realized, a firm and abiding possession, whereas that which comes from the achievements and works of art is only one that is always to be produced afresh. But for this it makes discouraging demands, hard to fulfil not merely for those who are to produce its works, but also for those who are to enjoy them. Therefore its public remains small, while that of the arts is large.

The above-mentioned co-operation of the beholder, required for the enjoyment of a work of art, rests partly on the fact that every work of art can act only through the medium of the imagination. It must therefore excite the imagination, which can never be left out of the question and remain inactive. This is a condition of aesthetic effect, and therefore a fundamental law of all the fine arts. But it follows from this that not everything can be given directly to the senses through the work of art, but only as much as is required to lead the imagination on to the right path. Something, and indeed the final thing, must always be left over for it to do. Even the author must always leave something over for the reader to think; for Voltaire has very rightly said: *Le secret d'être ennuyeux, c'est de tout dire.*[2] But in addition to this, the very best in art is too spiritual to be given directly to the senses; it must be born in the beholder's imagination, though it must be begotten by the work of art. It is due to this that the sketches of great masters are often more effective than their finished paintings. Of course another advantage contributes to this, namely that they are completed at one stroke in the moment of conception, whereas the finished painting is brought about only through continued effort by means of clever deliberation and persistent premeditation, for the inspiration cannot last until the painting is completed. From the fundamental aesthetic law we are considering, it can also be explained why *wax figures* can never produce an aesthetic effect, and are therefore not real works of fine art, although it is precisely in them that the imitation of nature can reach the highest degree. For they leave nothing over for the imagination. Thus sculpture gives the mere form without the colour; painting gives the colour, but the mere appearance of the form; therefore both appeal to the imagination of the beholder. The wax figure, on the contrary, gives everything, form and colour at the same time; from this arises the appearance of reality, and the imagination is left out of account. On the other hand, *poetry* appeals indeed to the imagination alone, and makes it active by means of mere words.

An arbitrary playing with the means of art without proper knowledge of the end is in every art the fundamental characteristic of bungling. Such bungling shows itself in the supports that carry nothing, in the purposeless volutes, prominences, and projections of bad architecture, in the meaningless runs and figures together with the aimless noise of bad music, in the jingling rhymes of verses with little or no meaning, and so on.

It follows from the previous chapter and from my whole view of art that its object is to facilitate knowledge of the *Ideas* of the world (in the Platonic sense, the only one which I recognize for the word *Idea*). But the *Ideas* are essentially something of perception, and therefore, in its fuller determinations, something inexhaustible. The communication of such a thing can therefore take place only on the path of perception, which is that of art. Therefore, whoever is imbued with the apprehension of an *Idea* is justified when he chooses art as the medium of his communication. The mere *concept,* on the other hand, is something completely determinable, hence something to be exhausted, something distinctly thought, which can be, accord-

_____

[2] "The secret of being dull and tedious consists in our saying everything." [Tr.]

ing to its whole content, communicated coldly and dispassionately by words. Now to wish to communicate such a thing through *a work of art* is a very useless indirect course; in fact, it belongs to that playing with the means of art without knowledge of the end which I have just censured. Therefore, a work of art, the conception of which has resulted from mere, distinct concepts, is always ungenuine. If, when considering a work of plastic art, or reading a poem, or listening to a piece of music (which aims at describing something definite), we see the distinct, limited, cold, dispassionate concept glimmer and finally appear through all the rich resources of art, the concept which was the kernel of this work, the whole conception of the work having therefore consisted only in clearly thinking this concept, and accordingly being completely exhausted by its communication, then we feel disgust and indignation, for we see ourselves deceived and cheated of our interest and attention. We are entirely satisfied by the impression of a work of art only when it leaves behind something that, in spite of all our reflection on it, we cannot bring down to the distinctness of a concept. The mark of that hybrid origin from mere concepts is that the author of a work of art should have been able, before setting about it, to state in distinct words what he intended to present; for then it would have been possible to attain his whole end through these words themselves. It is therefore an undertaking as unworthy as it is absurd when, as has often been attempted at the present day, one tries to reduce a poem of Shakespeare or Goethe to an abstract truth, the communication whereof would have been the aim of the poem. Naturally the artist should think when arranging his work, but only *that* idea which was *perceived* before it was thought has suggestive and stimulating force when it is communicated, and thereby becomes immortal and imperishable. Hence we will not refrain from remarking that the work done at one stroke, like the previously mentioned sketches of painters, perfected in the inspiration of the first conception and drawn unconsciously as it were; likewise the melody that comes entirely without reflection and wholly as if by inspiration; finally also the lyrical poem proper, the mere song, in which the deeply felt mood of the present and the impression of the surroundings flow forth as if involuntarily in words, whose metre and rhyme are realized automatically—that all these, I say, have the great merit of being the pure work of the rapture of the moment, of the inspiration, of the free impulse of genius, without any admixture of deliberation and reflection. They are therefore delightful and enjoyable through and through, without shell and kernel, and their effect is much more infallible than is that of the greatest works of art of slow and deliberate execution. In all these, e.g., in great historical paintings, long epic poems, great operas, and so on, reflection, intention, and deliberate selection play an important part. Understanding, technical skill, and routine must fill up here the gaps left by the conception and inspiration of genius, and all kinds of necessary subsidiary work must run through the really only genuine and brilliant parts as their cement. This explains why all such works, with the sole exception of the most perfect masterpieces of the very greatest masters (such as *Hamlet, Faust,* the opera *Don Juan* for example), inevitably contain an admixture of something insipid and tedious that restricts the enjoyment of them to some extent. Proofs of this are the *Messiad, Gerusalemme Liberata,* even *Paradise Lost* and the *Aeneid;* and Horace makes the bold remark: *Quandoque dormitat bonus Homerus.*[3] But that this is the case is a consequence of the limitation of human powers in general.

The mother of the useful arts is necessity; that of the fine arts superfluity and abundance. As their father, the former have understanding, the latter genius, which is itself a kind of superfluity, that of the power of knowledge beyond the measure required for the service of the will.

---

[3] "[I am mortified] whenever the great Homer sleeps." (*Ars Poetica,* 359.) [Tr.]

On the Aesthetics of Architecture

In accordance with the derivation, given in the text, of the pure aesthetics of architecture from the lowest grades of the will's objectification, or of nature, whose Ideas it attempts to bring to distinct perceptibility, its sole and constant theme is *support and load*. Its fundamental law is that no load may be without sufficient support, and no support without a suitable load; consequently, that the relation between these two may be the exactly appropriate one. The purest execution of this theme is column and entablature; hence the order of columns has become, so to speak, the thorough-bass of the whole of architecture. In column and entablature, support and load are *completely separated,* and in this way the reciprocal effect of the two and their relation to each other become apparent. For even every plain and simple wall certainly contains support and load, but there the two are still amalgamated. Everything is support and everything load; and so there is no aesthetic effect. This first appears through *separation,* and turns out according to the degree of such separation. For there are many intermediate stages between the row of columns and the plain wall. In breaking through the wall of a house merely for windows and doors, we attempt at least to indicate that separation by flat projecting pilasters (antae) with capitals, which are substituted for the moulding, and are, if need be, represented by mere painting, in order to express somehow the entablature and an order of columns. Actual pillars, as well as consoles and supports of various kinds, further realize that pure separation of support and load to which architecture in general aspires. In this respect the vault with the pillar stands nearest to the column with the entablature, but as a characteristic construction that does not imitate them. The former, of course, are far from attaining the aesthetic effect of the latter, because in them support and load are not yet *clearly separated,* but pass over and merge into each other. In the vault itself, every stone is simultaneously load and support, and even the

---

[1] This chapter refers to § 43 of volume 1.

pillars, especially in the groined vault, are maintained in their position, apparently at least, by the pressure of opposite arches; and also, just on account of this lateral pressure, not only vaults, but even mere arches should not rest on columns; rather they require the more massive, four-cornered pillars. Only in the row of columns is the separation complete, since the entablature appears here as pure load, and the column as pure support. Accordingly, the relation of the colonnade to the plain wall is comparable to that which would exist between a scale ascending at regular intervals, and a tone ascending little by little and without gradations from the same depth to the same height, which would produce a mere howl. For in the one as in the other the material is the same, and the immense difference results only from the *pure separation*.

Moreover, the support is not *adequate* to the load when it is only just sufficient to carry it, but when it is able to do this so comfortably and abundantly that at the first glance we are perfectly at ease about it. Even this excess of support, however, may not surpass a certain degree, otherwise we perceive support without load, and this is opposed to the aesthetic aim. For determining that degree, the ancients devised as a rule the *line of equilibrium*. This is obtained by continuing the gradual diminution of the thickness of the column as we go from the bottom to the top, until it runs out into an acute angle. In this way the column becomes a cone; any cross-section will now leave the lower part so strong that it is sufficient to carry the upper part cut off. But buildings are constructed with a stability factor of twenty, that is to say, on every support is laid only one-twentieth of what it could carry as a maximum. A glaring example of load without support is presented to the eye by the balconies that stick out at the corners of many houses built in the "elegant" style of today. We do not see what carries them; they appear suspended, and disturb the mind.

In Italy even the simplest and plainest buildings make an aesthetic impression, but in Germany they do not; this is due mainly to the fact that in Italy the roofs are very flat. A high roof is neither support nor load, for its two halves mutually support each other, but the whole has no weight corresponding to its extension. It therefore presents to the eye an extended mass; this is wholly foreign to the aesthetic end, serves a merely useful purpose, and consequently disturbs the aesthetic, the theme of which is always support and load alone.

The form of the column has its basis solely in that it affords the simplest and most suitable support. In the twisted column unsuitability appears as if intentionally defiant, and thus shamelessly; therefore at the first glance good taste condemns it. The four-cornered pillar has unequal dimensions of thickness, as the diagonal exceeds the sides. These dimensions have no aim or end as their motive, but are occasioned by a feasibility that happens to be easier; and on this very account, the four-cornered pillar pleases us very much less than the column does. Even the hexagonal or octagonal pillar is more agreeable, because it approximates more closely to the round column; for the form of the column alone is determined exclusively by the aim or end. But it is so determined in all its other proportions, above all in the relation of its thickness to its height, within the limits allowed by the difference of the three orders of columns. Then its tapering off from the first third of its height upwards, and also a slight swelling at this very spot (*entasis Vitr.*) rest on the pressure of the load being greatest there. Formerly it was thought that this swelling was peculiar to Ionic and Corinthian columns, but recent measurements have shown it also in Doric, even at Paestum. Thus everything in the column, its quite definite form, the proportion of its height to its thickness, of both to the intervals between the columns, and that of the whole row to the entablature and the load resting on it, all are the accurately calculated result from the ratio of the necessary support to the given load. Because the load is uniformly distributed, so must the supports be; for this reason, groups of columns are in bad taste. On the other hand, in the best Doric temples the corner column comes somewhat nearer to the next one, because the meeting of the entablatures at the corner increases the load. But in this way the principle of architecture clearly expresses itself, namely that the structural proportions, i.e., those between support and load, are the essentials, to which those of symmetry, as being subordinate, must at once give way. According to the weight of the whole load generally, the Doric or the two lighter orders of columns will be chosen, for the first order is calculated for heavier loads, not only through its greater thickness, but also through the closer arrangement of the columns essential to it, and even the almost crude simplicity of its capital is suitable for this purpose. The capitals generally are intended to show visibly that the columns carry the entablature, and are not stuck in like pins; at the same time they increase the bearing surface by means of their abacus. Now all the laws of columnar arrangement, and consequently the form and proportion of the column in all its parts and dimensions down to the smallest detail, follow from the conception of the adequately appropriate support to a given load, a conception well understood and consistently followed out; therefore to this extent they are determined *a priori*. It is then clear how absurd is the idea, so often repeated, that the trunks of trees or even the human form (as unfortunately stated even by Vitruvius, iv, 1) were the prototype of the column. The form of the column would then be for architecture a purely accidental one taken from outside; but such a form could not appeal to us so harmoniously and satisfactorily, whenever we behold it in its proper symmetry; nor, on the other hand, could even every slight disproportion in it be felt at once by the fine and cultivated sense as disagreeable and disturbing, like a false note in music. On the contrary, this is possible only by all the rest being determined essentially *a priori,* according to the given end and means, just as in music the whole harmony is essentially determined according to the given melody and key. And, like music, architecture generally is also not an imitative art, although both have often been falsely regarded as such.

As was fully discussed in the text, aesthetic satisfaction everywhere rests on the apprehension of a (Platonic) Idea. For architecture, considered only as *fine* art, the Ideas of the lowest grades of nature, that is, gravity, rigidity, and cohesion, are the proper theme, but not, as has been assumed hitherto, merely regular form, proportion, and symmetry. These are something purely geometrical, properties of space, not Ideas; therefore they cannot be the theme of a fine art. Thus they are also in architecture of only secondary origin, and have a subordinate significance that I shall now bring out. If it were the task of architecture as a fine art simply to exhibit these, the model would of necessity produce the same effect as the finished work. But this is by no means the case; on the contrary, to have an aesthetic effect, works of architecture must throughout be of considerable size; indeed, they can never be too large, but they can easily be too small. In fact, *ceteris paribus,* the aesthetic effect is in direct proportion to the size of the buildings, because only great masses make the effectiveness of gravitation apparent and impressive in a high degree. This once more confirms my view that the tendency and antagonism of those fundamental forces of nature constitute the proper aesthetic material of architecture; and by its nature, such material requires large masses, in order to become visible, and indeed to be capable of being felt. As was shown above in the case of the column, the forms in architecture are primarily determined by the immediate structural purpose of each part. But in so far as this leaves anything undetermined, the law of the most perfect perceptibility, hence of the easiest comprehensibility, comes in; for architecture has its existence primarily in our spatial perception, and accordingly appeals to our *a priori* faculty for this. This comprehensibility, however, always results from the greatest regularity of the forms and the rationality of their proportions. Accordingly, beautiful architecture selects nothing but regular figures, made from straight lines or regular curves, and likewise the bodies that result from these, such as cubes, parallelepipeds, cylinders, spheres, pyramids, and cones; as openings, however, sometimes circles or ellipses, yet as a rule squares, and even more often rectangles, the latter of extremely rational and quite easily intelligible proportion of their sides (not, for instance, as 6:7, but as 1:2, 2:3); finally also recesses or niches of regular and intelligible proportion. For the same reason, it will readily give to the buildings themselves and their large parts a rational and easily intelligible relation of height to width. For example, it will let the height of a façade be half the width, and place the columns so that every three or four of them with their intervals will measure a line equal to the height, and thus form a square. The same principle of perceptibility and ready comprehensibility also requires that a building should be easily visible at a glance. This produces *symmetry* which is also necessary to mark out the work as a whole, and to distinguish its essential from its accidental limitation. For example, sometimes it is only under the guidance of symmetry that we know whether we have before us three buildings standing side by side or only one. Thus only by means of symmetry does a work of architecture announce itself at once as an individual unity, and as the development of a main idea.

Now although, as was shown above in passing, architecture has not by any means to imitate the *forms* of nature, such as tree-trunks or even human figures and forms, it should nevertheless create in the *spirit* of nature, especially by making its own the law that *natura nihil agit frustra, nihilque supervacaneum, et quod commodissimum in omnibus suis operationibus sequitur*.[2] Accordingly it avoids everything purposeless, even when it is only apparently so, and it attains the end in view, whether this be purely architectural, i.e., structural, or one that concerns usefulness, always by the shortest and most natural path; thus it openly exhibits this end or aim through the work itself. In this way it attains a certain grace, analogous to that which in living creatures consists in the nimbleness and suitability of every movement and position to its purpose. Accordingly, we see in the good antique style of architecture every part, whether pillar, column, arch, entablature, or door, window, staircase, or balcony, attain its end in the simplest and most direct way, at the same time openly and naively displaying it, just as is done by organic nature in its works. On the other hand, the tasteless style of architecture looks in every-

---

[2] "Nature does nothing in vain and nothing superfluous, and in all her operations she follows the most convenient path." [Tr.]

thing for useless roundabout ways, and delights in arbitrary methods. In this way it hits upon aimlessly broken entablatures running in and out, grouped columns, fragmentary cornices on door arches and gables, senseless volutes, spirals, and the like. It plays with the means of art without understanding the ends, just as children play with the implements of adults; and this was described above as the characteristic of bungling. Of this kind is every interruption of a straight line, every alteration in the sweep of a curve, without apparent purpose. On the other hand, it is just that naïve simplicity in the presentation and attainment of the end in view, corresponding to the spirit in which nature creates and fashions, which imparts to ancient earthenware vessels such beauty and grace of form that we are always astonished at them afresh. This is because it contrasts so nobly in original taste with our modern vessels which bear the stamp of vulgarity, it matters not whether they are formed from porcelain or from coarse potter's clay. When looking at the vessels and implements of the ancients we feel that, if nature had wanted to fashion such things, she would have done so in these forms. Therefore, as we see the beauty of architecture arise from the undisguised presentation of the ends and from their attainment in the shortest and most natural way, my theory here comes into direct contradiction with Kant's. His theory places the essence of everything beautiful in an apparent appropriateness without purpose.

The sole theme of architecture here stated, namely support and load, is so very simple that, on this very account, this art, in so far as it is a *fine* art (but not in so far as it serves useful ends), has been perfect and complete in essential matters since the best Greek period; at any rate, it has no longer been capable of any important enrichment. On the other hand, the modern architect cannot noticeably depart from the rules and models of the ancients without being on the path of degeneration. Therefore there is nothing left for him to do but to apply the art handed down by the ancients, and to carry out its rules in so far as this is possible under the limitations inevitably imposed on him by want, need, climate, age, and his country. For in this art, as in sculpture, to aspire to the ideal is identical with imitating the ancients.

I scarcely need remind the reader that, in all these discussions on architecture, I have had only the architectural style of the ancients in view, and not the so-called Gothic style, which is of Saracen origin, and was introduced to the rest of Europe by the Goths in Spain. Perhaps a certain beauty of its kind is not to be totally denied even to this style; for it to undertake to set itself up, however, as the equal in status of the ancient style, is a barbarous presumption that must not for one moment be allowed. After we have contemplated such Gothic magnificence, how wholesome is the effect on the mind of looking at a building correctly carried out in the style of the ancients! We at once feel that this alone is right and true. If we could bring an ancient Greek before our most famous Gothic cathedrals, what would he say to them? βάρβαροι! Our pleasure in Gothic works certainly rests for the most part on the association of ideas and on historical reminiscences, and hence on a feeling foreign to art. All that I have said about the really aesthetic aim, about the meaning and theme of architecture, loses its validity in the case of these works. For the freely lying entablature has vanished, and the column with it; support and load, arranged and distributed in order to make clear the conflict between rigidity and gravity, are no longer the theme. Moreover, the universal, pure rationality, by virtue of which everything admits of strict account, in fact already presents it to the thoughtful beholder as a matter of course, and which belongs to the character of the ancient style of architecture, is no longer to be found here. We soon become conscious that, instead of it, an arbitrary will has ruled, guided by extraneous concepts; and so much remains unexplained to us. For only the ancient style of architecture is conceived in a purely *objective* sense; the Gothic is more in the subjective. We have recognized the real, aesthetic, fundamental idea of ancient architecture to be the unfolding of the conflict between rigidity and gravity; but if we try to discover an analogous fundamental idea in Gothic architecture, it will have to be that the entire subjugation and conquest of gravity by rigidity are there to be exhibited. For according to this the horizontal line, which is that of the load, has almost entirely vanished, and the action of gravity appears only indirectly, disguised in arches and vaults; whereas the vertical line, which is that of the support, alone prevails, and renders palpable to the senses the victorious action of rigidity in excessively high buttresses, towers, turrets, and spires without number, rising unencumbered. Whereas in ancient architecture the tendency and pressure from above downwards are represented and exhibited just as well as those from below upwards, in Gothic architecture the latter decidedly predominate. From this arises that often-observed analogy with the crystal, whose formation also takes place with the overcoming of gravity. Now if we attributed this meaning and fundamental idea to Gothic architecture, and thereby tried to set it up as the equally justified antithesis to ancient architecture, it would have to be remembered that the conflict between rigidity and gravity, so openly and naively displayed by ancient architecture, is an actual and true one established in nature. On the other hand, the entire subjugation of gravity by rigidity remains a mere pretence, a fiction testified by illusion. Everyone will easily be able to see clearly how the mysterious and hyperphysical character attributed to Gothic architecture arises from the fundamental idea here expressed, and from the above-mentioned peculiarities of this architecture. As already mentioned, it arises mainly from the fact that the arbitrary has here taken the place of the purely rational, proclaiming itself as the thorough appropriateness of the means to the end. The many really purposeless things that are nevertheless so carefully perfected give rise to the assumption of unknown, inscrutable, secret ends, i.e., of the appearance of mystery. On the other hand, the brilliant side of Gothic churches is the interior, because there the effect of the groined vault impresses the mind. This vault is borne by slender, crystalline, aspiring pillars, and, with the disappearance of the load, promises eternal security. But most of the drawbacks mentioned are to be found on the outside. In ancient buildings the external side is the more advantageous, because support and load are seen better there; in the interior, on the other hand, the flat ceiling always retains something depressing and prosaic. In spite of many large outworks, the actual interior in the temples of the ancients was for the most part small. A more sublime touch was obtained by the spherical vault of a cupola, as in the Pantheon. The Italians, building in this style, have therefore made the most extensive use of this. In agreement with this is the fact that the ancients, as southern races, lived more in the open than the northern nations, who preferred Gothic architecture. But he who wishes to admit Gothic architecture as an essential and justified form may, if he is at the same time fond of analogies, call it the negative pole of architecture, or even its minor key. In the interest of good taste, I am bound to wish that great wealth be devoted to what is objectively, i.e., actually, good and right, to what in itself is beautiful, not to that whose value rests merely on the association of ideas. Now when I see how this unbelieving age so diligently finishes the Gothic churches left uncompleted by the believing Middle Ages, it seems to me as if it were desired to embalm a Christianity that has expired.

Isolated Remarks on the Aesthetics of the Plastic and Pictorial Arts

In sculpture beauty and grace are the main thing; but in painting expression, passion, and character predominate; therefore just so much of the claims of beauty must be given up. For a universal beauty of all forms, such as sculpture demands, would detract from the characteristic, and would also weary through monotony. Accordingly painting may depict even ugly faces and emaciated figures; sculpture, on the contrary, demands beauty, though not always perfect, but in every way strength and fulness of the figures. Consequently, an emaciated Christ on the cross, a dying St. Jerome wasted through age and disease, like the masterpiece of Domenichino, is a suitable subject for painting. But Donatello's marble figure of John the Baptist reduced to skin and bone through fasting, which is in the gallery at Florence, has a repulsive effect, in spite of its masterly execution. From this point of view, sculpture appears to be suitable for the affirmation of the will-to-live, painting for its denial; and we might explain from this why sculpture was the art of the ancients, painting that of Christian times.

In connexion with the explanation given in § 45 of volume one, that discovering, recognizing, and fixing the type of human beauty rest on a certain anticipation of it, and are therefore established partly *a priori,* I find I have still to emphasize the fact that this anticipation nevertheless requires experience, in order to be roused by it. This is analogous to the instinct of animals, which, although guiding the action *a priori,* nevertheless requires in its particulars the determination through motives. Experience and reality thus present human forms to the artist's intellect, and in these forms nature has been more or less successful in one part or another. He is asked, as it were, for his judgement of them, and experience and reality, according to the Socratic method, call forth the distinct and definite knowledge of the ideal from that obscure anticipation. Therefore it

---

[1] This chapter refers to §§ 44-50 of volume 1.

was certainly of great assistance to the Greek sculptors that the climate and custom of the country gave them throughout the day an opportunity to see half-nude forms, and in the gymnasia even completely nude ones. In this way, every limb invited their plastic sense to a criticism and comparison of it with the ideal that lay undeveloped in their consciousness. Thus they constantly exercised their judgement in all forms and limbs down to their finest shades of difference. In this way, their anticipation of the ideal of human beauty, originally only a dull one, could gradually be raised to such distinct consciousness that they become capable of objectifying it in the work of art. In an entirely analogous way the poet's own experience is useful and necessary to him for the presentation of characters. For although he does not work according to experience and empirical notes, but according to the clear consciousness of the true nature of mankind, as he finds this within himself, experience nevertheless serves this consciousness as the pattern, and gives it stimulation and practice. Therefore his knowledge of human nature and of its varieties, although proceeding mainly *a priori* and by anticipation, nevertheless first obtains life, precision, and range through experience. But taking our stand on the previous book and on chapter 44 of the following, we can go still more to the root of that marvellous sense of beauty of the Greeks, which enabled them alone of all nations on earth to discover the true normal type of the human form, and accordingly to set up for the imitation of all ages the standards of beauty and grace; and we can say that that which, if it remains unseparated from the *will,* gives sexual impulse with its discriminating selection, i.e., *sexual love* (which, as we know, was subject to great aberrations among the Greeks), becomes the *objective sense of beauty* for the human form, when, by reason of the presence of an abnormally preponderating intellect, it detaches itself from the will, and yet remains active. This sense shows itself primarily as a critical sense of art, but it can rise to the discovery and presentation of the pattern of all parts and proportions, as was the case in Phidias, Praxiteles, Scopas, and others. Then is fulfilled what Goethe represents the artist as saying:

> That I with mind divine
> And human hand
> May be able to form
> What with my wife
> As animal I can and must.

And once again, analogous to this, just that which, if it remained unseparated from the *will,* would in the *poet* give mere *worldly pru-*

dence, becomes, when it separates itself from the will through abnormal preponderance of the intellect, the capacity for objective, dramatic *presentation.*

Whatever modern sculpture may achieve, it is yet analogous to modern Latin poetry, and like this it is a child of imitation, sprung from reminiscences. If it presumes to try to be original, it at once goes astray, especially on the fatal path of forming in accordance with nature as it is found, instead of in accordance with the proportions of the ancients. Canova, Thorwaldsen, and many others are to be compared with Johannes Secundus and Owenus. It is just the same with architecture, but there it is founded in the art itself, whose purely aesthetic part is of small extent, and was already exhausted by the ancients. Therefore the modern architect can distinguish himself only in its wise application; and he ought to know that he always departs from good taste, inasmuch as he removes himself from the style and standard of the Greeks.

Considered only in so far as it aims at producing the appearance of reality, the art of the *painter* is ultimately reducible to the fact that he knows how to *separate* clearly what in vision or seeing is the mere sensation, that is, the affection of the retina, i.e., the only directly given *effect,* from its *cause,* i.e., from the objects of the external world, the perception whereof first of all originates in the understanding from this effect. If there is technical skill in addition, he is then in a position to produce the same effect in the eye through an entirely different cause, by laying on patches of colour. The same perception then arises again from this in the understanding of the beholder through the inevitable reference to the ordinary cause.

When we consider how something so entirely primary, so thoroughly original, is to be found in every *human countenance,* and how this reveals an entirety that can belong only to a unity consisting of nothing but necessary parts, by virtue of which we again recognize a known individual out of so many thousands, even after many years, although the possible varieties of human facial features, especially of *one* race, lie within extremely narrow limits, we cannot help doubting whether anything of such essential unity and of such great originality could ever arise from any other source than the mysterious depths of the inner being of nature. But it would follow from this that no artist would be capable of actually devising the original peculiarity of a human countenance, or even putting it together from reminiscences in accordance with nature. Accordingly, what he brought about in this way would always be only a half true, perhaps indeed an impossible, combination; for how could he put together an actual physiognomical unity, when the principle of that unity is really unknown to him? Accordingly, in the case of every face that is merely devised by an artist, we must doubt whether it is in fact a possible face, and whether nature, as the master of all masters, would not declare it to be a piece of bungling by demonstrating absolute contradictions in it. This would certainly lead to the principle that in historical pictures only portraits should always figure; these would then have to be selected with the greatest care, and would have to some extent to be idealized. It is well known that great artists have always gladly painted from living models, and have made many portraits.

Although, as stated in the text, the real purpose of painting, as of art generally, is to facilitate for us the comprehension of the (Platonic) Ideas of the nature of this world, whereby we are at the same time put into the state of pure, i.e., will-less, knowing, there yet belongs to it in addition a separate beauty independent of this. That beauty is produced by the mere harmony of the colours, the agreeable aspect of the grouping, the favourable distribution of light and shade, and the tone of the whole picture. This accompanying and subordinate kind of beauty promotes the condition of pure knowing, and is in painting what diction, metre, and rhyme are in poetry; thus both are not what is essential, but what acts first and immediately.

I produce a few more proofs in support of my judgement, given in § 50 of volume one, concerning the inadmissibility of *allegory* in painting. In the Palazzo Borghese in Rome, we find this picture by Michelangelo Caravaggio. Jesus, as a child of about ten, treads on the head of a snake, but entirely without fear and with the greatest calmness; and his mother who accompanies him remains equally unconcerned. Close by stands St. Elizabeth, solemnly and tragically looking up to heaven. Now what could be thought of this kyriological hieroglyphic by a person who had never heard anything about the seed of the woman that was to bruise the serpent's head? In Florence, in the library of the Palazzo Riccardi, we find an allegory painted on the ceiling by Luca Giordano. It is supposed to signify Science freeing the understanding from the bonds of ignorance. The understanding is a strong man bound with cords that are just falling off; one nymph holds a mirror in front of him, and another offers him a large detached wing. Above them Science sits on a globe, and beside her the naked Truth with a globe in her hand. At Ludwigsburg near Stuttgart, a picture shows us Time, as Saturn, cutting off Cupid's wings with a pair of shears. If this is supposed to signify that, when we grow old, instability in love declares itself, then this no doubt is quite true.

The following may serve to strengthen my solution of the problem why Laocoon does not cry out. As a matter of fact, we can convince ourselves of the unsuitable effect of representing shrieking in the works of plastic and pictorial art, which are essentially mute, in the Massacre of the Innocents by Guido Reni, which is to be found in the Academy of Arts in Bologna, where this great artist has made the mistake of painting six shrieking gaping mouths. Let anyone who wishes to have this even more distinct, think of a pantomimic performance on the stage, with an urgent occasion in one of the scenes for one of the players to shriek. Now if the dancer representing this part wished to express the shriek by standing for a while with his mouth wide open, the loud laughter of the whole house would testify to the thing's absurdity. As Laocoon's shrieking had to be omitted, for reasons to be found not in the object to be presented, but in the nature of the art presenting it, the problem accordingly arose how the artist could present the motive of this not-shrieking in such a way as to make it plausible to us that a person in such a position would not shriek. He solved this problem by representing the bite of the snake not as having already taken place, or even as still threatening, but as happening just at the moment, and in fact in the side. For in this way the abdomen is drawn in, and shrieking is therefore made impossible. This first, but really only secondary and subordinate, reason was correctly discovered by Goethe, and explained by him at the end of the eleventh book of his autobiography, as well as in the essay on Laocoon in the first part of the *Propylaea;* but the more distant and primary reason that conditions this one is that which I expound. I cannot refrain from remarking that here again I stand in the same relation to Goethe as I did with regard to the theory of colour. In the collection of the Duke of Aremberg in Brussels there is an antique head of Laocoon which was discovered later. But the head in the world-famous group is not a restored one, as may be concluded from Goethe's special table of all the restorations of this group, which is found at the end of volume one of the *Propylaea;* moreover, this is confirmed by the fact that the head found later is very much like the head of the group. We must therefore assume that yet another antique repetition of the group existed, to which the Aremberg head belonged. In my opinion this head surpasses that of the group in both beauty and expression. It has the mouth considerably more wide open than has the head in the group, yet not to the extent of really shrieking.

CHAPTER XXXVII[1]

On the Aesthetics of Poetry

I would like to lay down, as the simplest and most correct definition of poetry, that it is the art of bringing into play the power of imagination through words. I have stated in § 51 of volume one how it brings this about. A special confirmation of what is there said is afforded by the following passage from a letter which Wieland wrote to Merck, and which has since been published: "I have spent two and a half days on a single stanza, where at bottom the whole thing rested on a single word that I needed and could not find. I turned and twisted the thing and my brain in all directions, because, where it is a question of graphic description, I should naturally like to bring the same definite vision that floated before my mind, before the mind of my readers also, and for this, *ut nosti*,[2] everything often depends on a single touch, or relief, or reflex." (*Briefe an Merck,* ed. Wagner, 1835, p. 193.) As the reader's imagination is the material in which poetry presents its pictures, this has the advantage that the more detailed development and finer touches take place in the imagination of everyone as is most appropriate to his individuality, his sphere of knowledge, and his frame of mind; and so it moves him most vividly. Instead of this, the plastic and pictorial arts cannot adapt themselves in this way, but here *one* picture or *one* form is to satisfy all. But this will always bear in some respect the stamp of the individuality of the artist or his model, as a subjective or accidental, yet not effective, addition; though this will be less the case, the more objective, in other words the more of a genius, the artist is. This partly explains why the works of poetry exercise a much stronger, deeper, and more universal effect than pictures and statues do. These often leave ordinary people quite cold, and in general it is the plastic arts that have the weakest effect. A curious proof of this is afforded by the frequent discovery of pictures by great masters in private houses and in all kinds of

---

[1] This chapter refers to § 51 of volume 1.
[2] "As you know." [Tr.]

localities, where they have been hanging for many generations, not exactly buried and concealed, but merely unheeded, and so without effect. In my own time in Florence (1823), even a Madonna by Raphael was discovered which had hung for a great number of years on the wall of the servants' hall of a palace (in the Quartiere di S. Spirito); and this happens among Italians, who beyond all other nations are gifted with a sense of the beautiful. It shows how little direct and sudden effect the works of the plastic and pictorial arts have, and that an appreciation of them requires far more culture and knowledge than is required for all the other arts. On the other hand, how unfailingly a beautiful melody, which touches the heart, makes its journey round the world, and how an excellent poem travels from one nation to another! The great and the wealthy devote their most powerful support to the plastic and pictorial arts, and spend considerable sums only on *their* works; indeed, at the present day, an idolatry in the proper sense sacrifices the value of a large estate for a picture of a celebrated old master. This rests mainly on the rarity of the masterpieces, the possession of which therefore gratifies pride; and on the fact that their enjoyment demands very little time and effort, and is ready at any moment for a moment; whereas poetry and even music lay down incomparably more onerous conditions. Accordingly, the plastic and pictorial arts may be dispensed with; whole peoples, for example the Mohammedans, are without them; but no people is without music and poetry.

But the intention with which the poet sets our imagination in motion is to reveal to us the Ideas, in other words, to show in an example what life is, what the world is. For this the first condition is that he himself should have known it; according as this has been the case profoundly or superficially, so will his poem turn out. Therefore, just as there are innumerable degrees of depth and clearness in the comprehension of things, so are there of poets. Yet each of these must regard himself as excellent in so far as he has correctly presented what *he* knew, and his picture corresponds to *his* original. He must put himself on a level with the best, since in the picture of the best he does not recognize more than in his own, namely as much as in nature herself; for his glance does not now penetrate more deeply. But the best person recognizes himself as such in the fact that he sees how shallow was the glance of others, how much still lay behind this which they were unable to reproduce, because they did not see it, and how much farther his glance and picture reach. If he understood the shallow and superficial as little as they understand him, he would of necessity despair; for just because it requires an extraordinary man to do him justice, but inferior poets are as little able to appreciate him as he them, he too has to live for a long time on his own approbation, before that of the world follows. However, he is deprived even of his own approbation, since he is expected to be pleasantly modest. But it is just as impossible for a man who has merits, and knows what they cost, to be himself blind to them, as it is for a man six feet tall not to notice that he towers above others. If it is three hundred feet from the base of a tower to its summit, then it is certainly just as much from the summit to the base. Horace, Lucretius, Ovid, and almost all the ancients spoke of themselves with pride, and so did Dante, Shakespeare, Bacon, and many others. That a man can have a great mind without his noticing something of it is an absurdity of which only hopeless incompetence can persuade itself, in order that it may also regard as modesty the feeling of its own insignificance. An Englishman has wittily and correctly observed that *merit* and *modesty* have nothing in common but the initial letter.* I always suspect modest celebrities that they may well be right; and Corneille says plainly:

> *La fausse humilité ne met plus en crédit:*
> *Je sçais ce que je vaux, et crois ce qu'on m'en dit.*[3]

Finally, Goethe has frankly said that "only knaves and wretches are modest." But even more unerring would have been the assertion that those who so eagerly demand modesty from others, insist on modesty, and are for ever exclaiming "Only be modest, for God's sake, only be modest!" *are certainly knaves and wretches.* In other words, they are creatures wholly without merit, nature's manufactured articles, ordinary members of the rabble of humanity. For he who has merits himself does not question merits—genuine and real ones of course. But he who himself lacks all merits and points of excellence, wishes there were none. The sight of them in others racks and torments him; pale, green, yellow envy consumes his heart; he would like to annihilate and exterminate all who are personally favoured. But if, alas!, he must let them live, it must be only on condition that they conceal, wholly deny, and even renounce their merits. This, then, is the root of the frequent eulogizing of modesty. And if those who deliver such eulogies have the opportunity to stifle merit at birth, or at any rate to prevent it from showing itself,

---

* Lichtenberg (*Vermischte Schriften,* new edition, Göttingen 1844, Vol. III, p. 19) quotes Stanislaus Leszczynski as having said: *"La modestie devroit être la vertu de ceux, à qui les autres manquent."* ("Modesty ought to be the virtue of those who are wanting in the other virtues." [Tr.]

[3] "False humility no longer brings me credit; I know my worth and believe what I am told of it." [Tr.]

from becoming known, who will doubt that they will do it? For this is their theory in practice.

Now, although the poet, like every artist, always presents us only with the particular, the individual, yet what *he* knew and wants through his work to let us know is the (Platonic) Idea, the whole species. Therefore in his pictures or images, as it were, the type of human characters and situations will be strongly marked. The narrative as well as the dramatic poet takes from life that which is quite particular and individual, and describes it accurately in its individuality; but in this way he reveals the whole of human existence, since, though he appears to be concerned with the particular, he is actually concerned with that which is everywhere and at all times. From this it arises that sentences, especially of the dramatic poets, even without being general apophthegms, find frequent application in real life. Poetry is related to philosophy as experience is to empirical science. Thus experience makes us acquainted with the phenomenon in the particular and by way of example; science embraces the totality of the phenomenon by means of universal concepts. Thus poetry tries to make us acquainted with the (Platonic) Ideas of beings by means of the particular and by way of example. Philosophy aims at making us acquainted with the inner nature of things that expresses itself in these. Here we see that poetry bears more the character of youth, philosophy that of age. In fact, the gift of poetry really flourishes only in youth; also in youth susceptibility to poetry is often passionate. The young man delights in verses as such, and is often satisfied with modest wares. This tendency gradually diminishes with the years, and in old age prose is preferred. Through this poetical tendency of youth the sense for reality is then easily impaired. For poetry differs from reality by the fact that in it life flows by interesting and yet painless; in reality, on the contrary, life is uninteresting so long as it is painless; but as soon as it becomes interesting, it does not remain without pain. The youth who has been initiated into poetry before being initiated into reality, now demands from the latter that which only the former can achieve. This is a principal source of the discontent that oppresses the most gifted youths.

Metre and rhyme are a fetter, but also a veil which the poet casts round himself, and under which he is permitted to speak as otherwise he would not dare to do; and this is what delights us. Thus he is only half responsible for all that he says; metre and rhyme must answer for the other half. Metre or measure, as mere rhythm, has its essence only in *time,* which is a pure intuition *a priori;* hence, in the language of Kant, it belongs merely to *pure* sensibility. Rhyme, on the other hand, is a matter of sensation in the organ of hearing, and thus of *empirical* sensibility. Therefore rhythm is a much nobler and worthier expedient than rhyme, which the ancients accordingly despised, and which found its origin in the imperfect languages resulting from the corruption of the earlier languages of barbarous times. The poorness of French poetry is due mainly to its being restricted to rhyme alone without metre; and it is increased by the fact that, in order to conceal its want of means, it has made rhyming more difficult through a number of pedantic regulations. For example, there is the rule that only syllables written in the same way rhyme, as if it were for the eye and not for the ear; that hiatus is forbidden; that a large number of words may not be used, and many others, to all of which the modern school of French poetry is trying to put a stop. But in no language, at any rate for me, does rhyme make so pleasant and powerful an impression as in Latin; the rhymed Latin poems of the Middle Ages have a peculiar charm. This is to be explained from the fact that the Latin language is incomparably more perfect, more beautiful, and more noble than any modern language, and that it moves along so gracefully in the ornaments and spangles which really belong to the latter, and it itself originally disdained.

To serious reflection, it might appear to be almost high treason against our faculty of reason, when even the smallest violence is done to an idea or to its correct and pure expression, with the childish intention that, after a few syllables, the same word-sound may again be heard, or even that these syllables themselves may present a certain hop and jump. But without such violence, very few verses would result, for to this it must be ascribed that in foreign languages verses are very much harder to understand than prose. If we could see into the secret workshop of the poets, we should find that the idea is sought for the rhyme ten times more often than the rhyme for the idea; and even in the latter case, it does not come off easily without flexibility on the part of the idea. But the art of verse bids defiance to these considerations; moreover, it has on its side all ages and nations, so great is the power that metre and rhyme exercise on the feelings, and so effective the mysterious *lenocinium*[4] peculiar to them. I might explain this from the fact that a happily rhymed verse, through its indescribably emphatic effect, excites the feeling as if the idea expressed in it already lay predestined, or even preformed, in the language, and the poet had only to discover it. Even trivial flashes of thought obtain through rhythm and rhyme a touch of importance, and cut a figure in these flourishes, just as among girls

---

[4] "Seductive charm." [Tr.]

plain faces attract the eye through elegant attire. In fact, even distorted and false ideas gain an appearance of truth through versification. On the other hand, even famous passages from famous poets shrink up again and become insignificant when they are faithfully reproduced in prose. If only the true is beautiful, and the most cherished adornment of truth is nakedness, then an idea which appears great and beautiful in prose will have more true worth than one that has the same effect in verse. It is very surprising and well worth investigation that such trifling, and indeed apparently childish, means as metre and rhyme produce so powerful an effect. I explain it in the following way: that which is immediately given to the sense of hearing, the mere word-sound, obtains through rhythm and rhyme a certain completeness and significance in itself, since thereby it becomes a kind of music. It therefore appears now to exist for its own sake, and no longer as a mere means, a mere sign of something signified, namely the meaning of the words. To please the ear by its sound seems to be its whole destiny, and therefore with this everything seems to be attained, and all claims appear to be satisfied. But at the same time it contains a meaning, expresses an idea, presents itself as an unexpected extra, like the words to music, as an unexpected gift that agreeably surprises us, and therefore, since we made no demands of this kind at all, it very easily satisfies us. Now if this idea is such that, in itself, and so in prose, it would be significant, then we are delighted. I remember from early childhood that I was delighted by the melodious sound of verses long before I made the discovery that generally they also contained meaning and ideas. Accordingly, there is indeed in all languages a mere doggerel poetry, almost entirely devoid of meaning. Davis, the sinologist, observes in the preface to his translation of the *Laou-sang-urh* or *An Heir in Old Age* (London, 1817) that Chinese dramas consist partly of verses that are sung, and he adds: "The meaning of them is often obscure, and according to the statements of the Chinese themselves, the end of these verses is especially to flatter the ear, and the sense is neglected, and even entirely sacrificed to the harmony." Who is not reminded here of the choruses of many Greek tragedies which are often so hard to make out?

The sign by which we recognize most immediately the genuine poet, of the higher as well as of the lower species, is the easy and unforced nature of his rhymes. They have occurred automatically as if by divine decree; his ideas come to him already in rhyme. On the other hand, the homely, prosaic person seeks the rhyme for the idea; the bungler seeks the idea for the rhyme. We can very often find out from a couple of rhymed verses which of the two has the idea as its father, and which the rhyme. The art consists in concealing the latter, so that such verses do not appear almost as mere stuffed-out *bouts-rimés*.[5]

According to my feeling (proofs are not possible here) rhyme is, by its nature, merely binary; its effectiveness is limited to one single recurrence of the same sound, and is not strengthened by more frequent repetition. Therefore, as soon as a final syllable has received the one that rhymes with it, its effect is exhausted. The third occurrence of the sound acts merely as a repeated rhyme that accidentally hits on the same note, without enhancing the effect. It links itself on to the present rhyme, yet without combining with it to produce a stronger impression. For the first note does not sound through the second on to the third; and so this is an aesthetic pleonasm, a double courage, that does not help. Least of all, therefore, do such accumulations of rhymes merit the heavy sacrifices that they cost in the octave rhyme, the terza rima, and sonnet. Such accumulations are the cause of the spiritual and mental torture with which we sometimes read these productions; for under such severe mental effort poetical pleasure is impossible. That the great poetic mind can sometimes overcome even those forms and their difficulties, and move about in them with ease and grace, does not conduce to a recommendation of the forms themselves; for in themselves they are just as ineffective as they are tedious. And even when good poets make use of these forms, we frequently see in them the conflict between the rhyme and the idea, in which now the one and then the other gains the victory. Thus either the idea is stunted for the sake of the rhyme, or else the rhyme has to be satisfied with a feeble *à peu près*.[6] This being so, I do not regard it as a proof of ignorance, but of good taste, that Shakespeare in his sonnets has provided different rhymes in each of the quatrains. In any case their acoustic effect is not in the least diminished in this way, and the idea comes much more into its own right than it could have done if it had had to be laced up in the conventional Spanish boots.

For the poetry of a language, it is a disadvantage if it has many words that are not commonly used in prose, and, on the other hand, if it dare not use certain words of prose. The former is often the case in Latin and Italian, and the latter in French, where it was recently very aptly called *la bégueulerie de la langue française;*[7] both are to be found less in English, and least in German. Thus, the words that belong exclusively to poetry remain foreign to our heart,

---

[5] Verses composed to set rhymes. [Tr.]

[6] "Approximation." [Tr.]

[7] "The silly airs and graces of the French language." [Tr.]

do not speak directly to us, and therefore leave us cold. They are a poetical language of convention, and are, so to speak, merely painted instead of real sensations; they exclude warmth and genuine feeling.

The distinction, so often discussed in our day, between *classic* and *romantic* poetry seems to me to rest ultimately on the fact that the former knows none but purely human, actual, and natural motives; the latter, on the other hand, maintains as effective also motives that are pretended, conventional, and imaginary. Among such motives are those springing from the Christian myth, then those of the chivalrous, exaggerated, extravagant, and fantastic principle of honour, and further those of the absurd and ridiculous Christian-Germanic veneration of women, and finally those of doting and moonstruck hyperphysical amorousness. But even in the best poets of the romantic sort, e.g., Calderón, we can see to what ridiculous distortion of human relations and human nature these motives lead. Not to speak at all of the Autos, I refer merely to pieces like *No siempre el peor es cierto* (*The Worst is not always Certain*) and *El postrero duelo en España* (*The Last Duel in Spain*), and similar comedies *en capa y espada.*[7a] Associated with these elements is the scholastic subtlety that often appears in the conversation which at that time was part of the mental culture of the upper classes. On the other hand, how decidedly advantageous is the position of the poetry of the ancients, which always remains true to nature! The result of this is that classical poetry has an unconditional truth and exactness, romantic poetry only a conditional, analogous to Greek and Gothic architecture. On the other hand, it is to be noted that all dramatic or narrative poems which transfer their scene of action to ancient Greece or Rome suffer a disadvantage through the fact that our knowledge of antiquity, especially as regards the details of life, is inadequate, fragmentary, and not drawn from perception. This therefore forces the poet to avoid a great deal and to be content with generalities; in this way he falls into the abstract, and his work loses that perceptibility and individualization that are absolutely essential to poetry. It is this that gives all such works their characteristic appearance of emptiness and tediousness. Only Shakespeare's presentations of this kind are free from it, since he without hesitation under the names of Greeks and Romans presented Englishmen of his own time.

It has been objected to many masterpieces of *lyrical* poetry, especially to a few Odes of Horace (see, for example, the second ode of the third book), and to several of Goethe's songs (e.g., the *Shepherd's Lament*), that they lack proper sequence and connexion,

[7a] Of cloak and sword. [Tr.]

and are full of gaps in the thought. But here the logical sequence is intentionally neglected, in order that the unity of the fundamental sensation and mood expressed in them may take its place; and precisely in this way does this unity stand out more clearly, since it runs like a thread through the separate pearls, and brings about the rapid change of the objects of contemplation, just as in music the transition from one key to another is brought about by the chord of the seventh, through which the fundamental note still sounding in it becomes the dominant of the new key. The quality here described is found most distinctly, even to the point of exaggeration, in the Canzone of Petrarch which begins: *Mai non vo' più cantar, com' io soleva.*[8]

Accordingly, just as in lyrical poetry the subjective element predominates, so in the drama, on the other hand, the objective element is solely and exclusively present. Between the two, epic poetry in all its forms and modifications, from narrative romance to epic proper, has a broad middle path. For although it is mainly objective, it yet contains a subjective element, standing out more or less, which finds its expression in the tone and form of the delivery, as well as in reflections interspersed in it. We do not lose sight of the poet so entirely as we do in the drama.

The purpose of the drama generally is to show us in an example what are the nature and existence of man. Here the sad or bright side of these, or even their transitions, can be turned to us. But the expression, "nature and existence of man" already contains the germ of the controversy as to whether the nature, i.e., the characters, or the existence, i.e., the fate, the event, the action, is the main thing. Moreover, the two have grown together so firmly that they can certainly be separated in conception, but not in their presentation. For only the circumstances, fates, and events make the characters manifest their true nature, and only from the characters does the action arise from which the events proceed. Of course, in the presentation the one or the other can be rendered more prominent, and in this respect the two extremes are formed by the play of the characters and by that of the plot.

The purpose common to the drama and to the epic, namely to present in significant characters placed in significant situations the extraordinary actions brought about by both, will be most completely attained by the poet if he first introduces the characters to us in a state of calm. In this state only their general tone or complexion becomes visible, but it then introduces a motive producing an action

---

[8] "Never more do I wish to sing as I was wont." [Tr.]

from which a new and stronger motive arises. This again brings about a more significant action that again gives birth to new and ever more powerful motives. Then, at the point of time appropriate to the form, passionate excitement takes the place of the original calm, and in this excitement significant actions occur in which the qualities that previously slumbered in the characters together with the course of the world appear in a bright light.

Great poets transform themselves entirely into each of the persons to be presented, and speak out of each of them like ventriloquists; now out of the hero, and immediately afterwards out of the young innocent girl, with equal truth and naturalness; thus Shakespeare and Goethe. Poets of the second rank transform into themselves the principal person to be presented; thus Byron. In this case the other persons often remain without life, as even the principal person does in the works of mediocre poets.

Our pleasure in the *tragedy* belongs not to the feeling of the beautiful, but to that of the sublime; it is, in fact, the highest degree of this feeling. For, just as at the sight of the sublime in nature we turn away from the interest of the will, in order to behave in a purely perceptive way, so in the tragic catastrophe we turn away from the will-to-live itself. Thus in the tragedy the terrible side of life is presented to us, the wailing and lamentation of mankind, the dominion of chance and error, the fall of the righteous, the triumph of the wicked; and so that aspect of the world is brought before our eyes which directly opposes our will. At this sight we feel ourselves urged to turn our will away from life, to give up willing and loving life. But precisely in this way we become aware that there is still left in us something different that we cannot possibly know positively, but only negatively, as that which does *not* will life. Just as the chord of the seventh demands the fundamental chord; just as a red colour demands green, and even produces it in the eye; so every tragedy demands an existence of an entirely different kind, a different world, the knowledge of which can always be given to us only indirectly, as here by such a demand. At the moment of the tragic catastrophe, we become convinced more clearly than ever that life is a bad dream from which we have to awake. To this extent, the effect of the tragedy is analogous to that of the dynamically sublime, since, like this, it raises us above the will and its interest, and puts us in such a mood that we find pleasure in the sight of what directly opposes the will. What gives to everything tragic, whatever the form in which it appears, the characteristic tendency to the sublime, is the dawning of the knowledge that the world and life can afford us no true satisfaction, and are therefore not worth our attachment to them. In this the tragic spirit consists; accordingly, it leads to resignation.

I admit that rarely in the tragedy of the ancients is this spirit of resignation seen and directly expressed. Oedipus Colonus certainly dies resigned and docile; yet he is comforted by the revenge on his native land. Iphigenia at Aulis is quite ready to die, yet it is the thought of the welfare of Greece that consoles her and brings about her change of mind. By virtue of this change she readily takes upon herself the death she at first sought by every means to avoid. Cassandra, in the *Agamemnon* of the great Aeschylus (1306), willingly dies, ἀρκείτω βίος;[9] but she too is comforted by the thought of revenge. Hercules in the *Trachiniae* yields to necessity, and dies composed, but not resigned. Likewise the Hippolytus of Euripides, in whose case it surprises us that Artemis, appearing to comfort him, promises him temples and fame, but certainly does not point to an existence beyond life, and abandons him in death, just as all the gods forsake the dying; in Christianity they come to him, and likewise in Brahmanism and Buddhism, though in the latter the gods are really exotic. Thus Hippolytus, like almost all the tragic heroes of the ancients, displays submission to inevitable fate and the inflexible will of the gods, but no surrender of the will-to-live itself. Stoic equanimity is fundamentally distinguished from Christian resignation by the fact that it teaches only calm endurance and unruffled expectation of unalterably necessary evils, but Christianity teaches renunciation, the giving up of willing. In just the same way the tragic heroes of the ancients show resolute and stoical subjection under the unavoidable blows of fate; the Christian tragedy, on the other hand, shows the giving up of the whole will-to-live, cheerful abandonment of the world in the consciousness of its worthlessness and vanity. But I am fully of opinion that the tragedy of the moderns is at a higher level than that of the ancients. Shakespeare is much greater than Sophocles; compared with Goethe's *Iphigenia,* that of Euripides might be found almost crude and vulgar. The *Bacchae* of Euripides is a revolting piece of work in favour of the heathen priests. Many ancient pieces have no tragic tendency at all, like *Alcestis* and *Iphigenia in Tauris* of Euripides; some have unpleasant, or even disgusting, motives, like *Antigone* and *Philoctetes*. Almost all show the human race under the dreadful dominion of chance and error, but not the resignation these bring about which redeems us from them. All this was because the ancients had not yet reached the

---

[9] "Enough of life!" [Tr.]

summit and goal of tragedy, or indeed of the view of life generally.

Therefore, if the ancients displayed little of the spirit of resignation, little of the turning away of the will from life, in their tragic heroes themselves as their frame of mind, the characteristic tendency and effect of the tragedy nevertheless continue to be the awakening of that spirit in the spectator, the calling up, although only temporarily, of that frame of mind. The horrors on the stage hold up to him the bitterness and worthlessness of life, and so the vanity of all its efforts and endeavours. The effect of this impression must be that he becomes aware, although only in an obscure feeling, that it is better to tear his heart away from life, to turn his willing away from it, not to love the world and life. Thus in the depth of his being the consciousness is then stirred that for a different kind of willing there must be a different kind of existence also. For if this were not so, if this rising above all the aims and good things of life, this turning away from life and its temptations, and the turning, already to be found here, to an existence of a different kind, although wholly inconceivable to us, were not the tendency of tragedy, then how would it be possible generally for the presentation of the terrible side of life, brought before our eyes in the most glaring light, to be capable of affecting us so beneficially, and of affording us an exalted pleasure? Fear and sympathy, in the stimulation of which Aristotle puts the ultimate aim of tragedy, certainly do not in themselves belong to the agreeable sensations; therefore they cannot be the end, but only the means. Thus the summons to turn away the will from life remains the true tendency of tragedy, the ultimate purpose of the intentional presentation of the sufferings of mankind; consequently it exists even where this resigned exaltation of the mind is not shown in the hero himself, but is only stimulated in the spectator at the sight of great unmerited, or indeed even merited, suffering. Like the ancients, many of the moderns are also content to put the spectator into the mood just described by the objective presentation of human misfortune on a large scale, whereas others exhibit this through the change of mind in the hero himself, effected by suffering. The former give, so to speak, only the premises, and leave the conclusion to the spectator; while the latter give the conclusion, or the moral of the fable, as the conversion of the hero's frame of mind, also as an observation in the mouth of the chorus, for example, in Schiller's *The Bride of Messina:* "Life is not the greatest good." It should here be mentioned that the genuinely tragic effect of the catastrophe, the hero's resignation and spiritual exaltation produced by it, seldom appear so purely motivated and distinctly expressed as in the opera *Norma,* where it comes in the duet *Qual cor tradisti, qual cor perdesti.*[10] Here the conversion of the will is clearly indicated by the quietness suddenly introduced into the music. Quite apart from its excellent music, and from the diction that can only be that of a libretto, and considered only according to its motives and to its interior economy, this piece is in general a tragedy of extreme perfection, a true model of the tragic disposition of the motives, of the tragic progress of the action, and of tragic development, together with the effect of these on the frame of mind of the heroes, which surmounts the world. This effect then passes on to the spectator; in fact, the effect here reached is the more natural and simple and the more characteristic of the true nature of tragedy, as no Christians or even Christian sentiments appear in it.

The neglect of the unity of time and place, with which the moderns are so often reproached, becomes a fault only when it goes so far as to abolish the unity of action, where only the unity of the principal character then remains, as, for example, in Shakespeare's *Henry VIII.* But the unity of action need not go so far that the same thing is spoken of throughout, as in French tragedies. These, in general, observe it so strictly, that the course of the drama is like a geometrical line without breadth. There the order is always to "Get on! *Pensez à votre affaire!*"[11] and the affair is expedited and despatched in a thoroughly business-like manner, without anyone stopping over trivialities that do not belong to it, or looking to the right or left. On the other hand, the Shakespearian tragedy is like a line that has breadth; it gives itself sufficient time, *exspatiatur;* speeches and even whole scenes occur which do not advance the action and do not even really concern it. But through these we get to know the characters or their circumstances more fully; and accordingly we then more thoroughly understand the action. This, of course, remains the principal thing, yet not so exclusively as for us to forget that, in the last instance, the presentation of human nature and existence in general is intended.

The dramatic or epic poet should know that he is fate, and therefore should be, like this, inexorable; likewise that he is the mirror of the human race, and ought therefore to represent very many bad and sometimes wicked characters, as well as many fools, eccentrics, and simpletons; now and again a person who is reasonable, prudent, honest, or good, and only as the rarest exception someone magnanimous. In my opinion, no really magnanimous character is presented in the whole of Homer, although many are good and

---

[10] "What a heart you betrayed, what a heart you lost." [Tr.]
[11] "Think of your own affairs!" [Tr.]

honest. In the whole of Shakespeare it may be possible to find at most a couple of noble, though by no means exceedingly noble, characters; perhaps Cordelia, Coriolanus, hardly any more; on the other hand, his works abound with the species indicated above. Iffland's and Kotzebue's pieces, however, have many magnanimous characters, whereas Goldoni has done as I recommended above, thus showing that he stands at a higher level. On the other hand, Lessing's *Minna von Barnhelm* labours under too much and too universal magnanimity; but even so much magnanimity as is displayed by the one Marquis Posa is not to be found in the whole of Goethe's works. There is, however, a small German piece called *Duty for Duty's Sake* (a title that sounds as if it were taken from the *Critique of Practical Reason*), which has only three characters, yet all three of exceeding magnanimity.

For the heroes of their tragedies the Greeks generally took royal persons, and the moderns for the most part have done the same. This is certainly not because rank gives more dignity to the person who acts or suffers; and as it is merely a question of setting human passions in play, the relative worth of the objects by which this is done is a matter of indifference, and farms achieve as much as is achieved by kingdoms. Moreover, simple, civic tragedy is by no means to be unconditionally rejected. Persons of great power and prestige are nevertheless best adapted for tragedy, because the misfortune in which we should recognize the fate of human life must have sufficient magnitude, in order to appear terrible to the spectator, be he who he may. Euripides himself says: φεῦ, φεῦ, τὰ μεγάλα, μεγάλα καὶ πάσχει κακά (Stobaeus, *Florilegium*, Vol. II, p. 299).[12] But the circumstances that plunge a bourgeois family into want and despair are in the eyes of the great or wealthy often very insignificant, and can be removed by human aid, sometimes indeed by a trifle; therefore such spectators cannot be tragically shaken by them. On the other hand, the misfortunes of the great and powerful are unconditionally terrible, and are inaccessible even to help from outside; for kings must either help themselves through their own power, or be ruined. In addition to this is the fact that the fall is greatest from a height. Bourgeois characters lack the height from which to fall.

Now if we have found the tendency and ultimate intention of *tragedy* to be a turning towards resignation, to the denial of the will-to-live, we shall easily recognize in its opposite, *comedy,* an invitation to the continued affirmation of this will. It is true that even comedy must bring before our eyes sufferings and reverses of

---

[12] "Alas, alas, that the great also have to suffer greatly!" [Tr.]

fortune, as every presentation of human life inevitably must; but it exhibits them to us as fleeting, resolving themselves into joy generally mingled with success, triumph, and hope that predominate in the end. Moreover, it brings out the inexhaustible material for laughter, with which life and even its very adversities are filled, and which should keep us in all circumstances in a good mood. In the result, it therefore declares that life on the whole is quite good, and in particular is generally amusing. But it must of course hasten to drop the curtain at the moment of delight, so that we do not see what follows, whereas the tragedy, as a rule, ends so that nothing can follow. Moreover, when once we contemplate somewhat seriously that burlesque side of life, as it shows itself in the naïve utterances and gestures that petty embarrassment, personal fear, momentary anger, secret envy, and many similar emotions force on the forms of reality that here mirrors itself, forms that deviate considerably from the type of beauty, then even from this aspect, and thus in an unexpected way, the thoughtful contemplator may become convinced that the existence and action of such beings cannot themselves be an end; that, on the contrary, they could arrive at existence only by a wrong path, and that what exhibits itself thus is something that really had better not be.

On History

In the passage of the first volume referred to below I have shown in detail that more is achieved for knowledge of the true nature of mankind by poetry than by history, and I have shown why this is so, inasmuch as more real instruction is to be expected from the former than from the latter. Aristotle also has admitted this, for he says: καὶ φιλοσοφώτερον καὶ σπουδαιότερον ποίησις ἱστορίας ἐστίν (*et res magis philosophica et melior poësis est, quam historia. Poetics,* c. 9).[2] But I will state my ideas on the value of history, so as to avoid causing any misunderstanding about it.

In every class and species of things the facts are innumerable, the individual beings infinite in number, and the multiplicity and variety of their differences beyond our reach. With one look at all this, the curious and inquisitive mind is in a whirl; however much it investigates, it sees itself condemned to ignorance. But then comes *science;* it separates out the innumerable many, collects them under generic concepts, and these in turn under specific concepts, and so opens the way to a knowledge of the general and the particular. This knowledge comprehends the innumerable individuals, since it holds good of all without our having to consider each one by itself. In this way it promises satisfaction to the inquiring mind. All the sciences then put themselves together and over the real world of individual things which they have parcelled out among themselves. But philosophy excels them all as the most universal, and thus the most important, knowledge, promising information for which the others have only prepared the way. *History* alone cannot properly enter into this series, since it cannot boast of the same advantage as the others, for it lacks the fundamental characteristic of science, the subordina-

---

[1] This chapter refers to § 51 of volume 1.

[2] "Poetry is more philosophical and valuable than history." [Tr.]

Incidentally, it should here be observed that from this contrast of ποίησις and ἱστορία the origin, and thus the real meaning, of the former word appear with unusual distinctness. It signifies what is made, imagined, in contrast to what is found by enquiry.

tion of what is known; instead of this it boasts of the mere co-ordination of what is known. Therefore there is no system of history, as there is of every other branch of knowledge; accordingly, it is rational knowledge indeed, but, not a science. For nowhere does it know the particular by means of the universal, but it must comprehend the particular directly, and continue to creep along the ground of experience, so to speak. The real sciences, on the other hand, excel it, since they have attained to comprehensive concepts by means of which they command and control the particular, and, at any rate within certain limits, foresee the possibility of things within their province, so that they can be reassured even about what is still to come. As the sciences are systems of concepts, they always speak of species; history speaks of individuals. History would accordingly be a science of individual things, which implies a contradiction. It follows also from the first statement that the sciences all speak of that which always is; history, on the other hand, speaks of that which is only once, and then no more. Further, as history has to do with the absolutely particular and with individuals, which by their nature are inexhaustible, it knows everything only imperfectly and partially. At the same time, it must allow itself to be taught by the triviality of every new day that which as yet it did not know at all. If it should be objected that in history subordination of the particular under the universal also takes place, since the periods of time, the governments, and the other main and political changes, in short, everything to be found in historical tables, are the universal to which the special is subordinated, this would rest on a false understanding of the concept of the universal. For the universal here referred to is in history merely *subjective,* that is to say, its generality springs merely from the inadequacy of the individual *knowledge* of things; it is not *objective,* in other words, a concept in which the things would actually be thought together. Even the most universal in history is in itself only something individual and particular, namely a long epoch or a principal event. Hence the particular is related to this as the part to the whole, but not as the case to the rule, as occurs, on the other hand, in all the sciences proper, because they furnish concepts, not mere facts. Therefore, through correct knowledge of the universal, we can in these sciences determine with certainty the particular case that arises. For example, if I know the laws of the triangle in general, I can accordingly also state what must be the properties of the triangle before me. What holds good of all mammals, for example, that they have double ventricles of the heart, exactly seven cervical vertebrae, lungs, diaphragm, bladder, five senses, and so on, I can assert also of the strange bat that has just been caught, before it is dissected. But this is not the case in history, where the universal is not an objective universal of concepts, but merely a subjective universal of my knowledge, that can be called universal only in so far as it is superficial. Thus I may know in general about the Thirty Years' War, namely that it was a religious war waged in the seventeenth century; but this general knowledge does not enable me to state anything more detailed about its course. The same contrast also holds good in the fact that, in the actual sciences, it is the special and the individual that is the most certain, for it rests on immediate apprehension; universal truths, on the other hand, are first abstracted from it, and therefore something can more readily be erroneously assumed in these. Conversely, in history the most universal is the most certain; for example, the periods of time, the succession of kings, revolutions, wars, and treaties of peace; on the other hand, the particular of the events and of their connexion is more uncertain, and becomes always more so the deeper we go into details. History is therefore the more interesting the more special it is, but also the less trustworthy; and thus it approximates in all respects to a work of fiction. For the rest, he will best be able to judge what importance is to be attached to the boasted pragmatism of history, who remembers that at times it was only after twenty years that he understood the events of his own life in their true connexion, although the data for these were completely before him, so difficult is the combination of the action of motives under the constant interference of chance and the concealment of intentions. Now in so far as history always has for its object only the particular, the individual fact, and regards this as the exclusively real, it is the direct opposite and counterpart of philosophy, which considers things from the most universal point of view, and has the universal as its express object. In every particular this universal remains identical; thus in the former philosophy always sees only the latter, and recognizes as inessential the change in its phenomenal appearance: φιλοκαθόλου γὰρ ὁ φιλόσοφος (*generalium amator philosophus*).[3] Whereas history teaches us that at each time something different has been, philosophy endeavours to assist us to the insight that at all times exactly the same was, is, and will be. In truth, the essence of human life, as of nature everywhere, exists complete in every present time, and therefore requires only depth of comprehension in order to be exhaustively known. History, however, hopes to make up for depth by length and breadth; every present time is for it only a fragment that must be supplemented by the past. But the length of the past is

[3] "The philosopher is a friend of the universal." [Tr.]

infinite, and joined to it again is an infinite future. On this rests the opposition between philosophical and historical minds; the former want to fathom and find out, the latter try to narrate to the end. History shows on every side only the same thing under different forms; but he who does not recognize such a thing in one or a few forms, will hardly attain to a knowledge of it by running through all the forms. The chapters of the history of nations are at bottom different only through the names and dates; the really essential content is everywhere the same.

Therefore, in so far as the material of art is the *Idea,* and the material of science the *concept,* we see both occupied with that which always exists at all times in the same way, but not with something which now is and then is not, which now is thus and then otherwise. For this reason, both are concerned with what Plato posited exclusively as the object of actual rational knowledge. The material of history, on the other hand, is the individual thing in its individuality and contingency; this thing exists once, and then exists no more for ever. The material of history is the transient complexities of a human world moving like clouds in the wind, which are often entirely transformed by the most trifling accident. From this point of view, the material of history appears to us as scarcely an object worthy of the serious and arduous consideration of the human mind. Just because it is so transitory, the human mind should select for its consideration that which is destined never to pass away.

Finally, as regards the attempt specially introduced by the Hegelian pseudo-philosophy that is everywhere so pernicious and stupefying to the mind, the attempt, namely, to comprehend the history of the world as a planned whole, or, as they call it, "to construct it organically," a crude and shallow *realism* is actually at the root of this. Such realism regards the *phenomenon* as the *being-in-itself* of the world, and imagines that it is a question of this phenomenon and of its forms and events. It is still secretly supported in this by certain, mythological, fundamental views which it tacitly assumes; otherwise it might be asked for what spectator such a comedy was really being enacted. For since only the individual, not the human race, has actual, immediate unity of consciousness, the unity of this race's course of life is a mere fiction. Moreover, as in nature only the species are real and the genera mere abstractions, so in the human race only the individuals and their course of life are real, the nations and their lives being mere abstractions. Finally, constructive histories, guided by a shallow optimism, always ultimately end in a comfortable, substantial, fat State with a well-regulated constitution, good justice and police, useful arts and industries, and at most intellectual perfection, since this is in fact the only possible perfection, for that which is moral remains essentially unaltered. But according to the testimony of our innermost consciousness, it is the moral element on which everything depends; and this lies only in the individual as the tendency of his will. In reality, only the life-course of each individual has unity, connexion, and true significance; it is to be regarded as an instruction, and the significance of this is a moral one. Only the events of our *inner* life, in so far as they concern the *will,* have true reality and are actual occurrences, since the will alone is the thing-in-itself. In every microcosm lies the macrocosm, and the latter contains nothing more than is contained in the former. Plurality is phenomenon, and external events are mere configurations of the phenomenal world; they therefore have neither reality nor significance directly, but only indirectly, through their relation to the will of the individuals. Accordingly, the attempt to explain and expound them is like the attempt to see groups of persons and animals in the forms of clouds. What history relates is in fact only the long, heavy, and confused dream of mankind.

The Hegelians, who regard the philosophy of history as even the main purpose of all philosophy, should be referred to Plato, who untiringly repeats that the object of philosophy is the unchangeable and ever permanent, not that which now is thus and then otherwise. All who set up such constructions of the course of the world, or, as they call it, of history, have not grasped the principal truth of all philosophy, that that which is is at all times the same, that all becoming and arising are only apparent, that the Ideas alone are permanent, that time is ideal. This is what Plato means, this is what Kant means. Accordingly, we should try to understand what *exists,* what actually *is,* today and always, in other words, to know the *Ideas* (in Plato's sense). On the other hand, fools imagine that something is supposed to come into existence. They therefore concede to history a principal place in their philosophy, and construct this on an assumed plan of the world, according to which everything is managed for the best. This is then supposed to appear *finaliter,* and will be a great and glorious thing. Accordingly, they take the world to be perfectly real, and set its purpose in miserable earthly happiness. Even when it is greatly cherished by man and favoured by fate, such happiness is yet a hollow, deceptive, frail, and wretched thing, out of which neither constitutions, legal systems, steam-engines, nor telegraphs can ever make anything that is essentially better. Accordingly, the aforesaid philosophers and glorifiers of history are simple realists, and also optimists and eudaemonists, and consequently shallow fellows and Philistines incarnate. In addition, they are really bad Christians, for the true spirit and kernel of Christianity, as of Brahmanism and Buddhism also, is the knowledge of the vanity of all earthly happiness, complete contempt for it, and the turning away to an existence of quite a different, indeed an opposite, kind. This, I say, is the spirit and purpose of Christianity, the true "humour of the matter"; but it is not, as they imagine, monotheism. Therefore, atheistic Buddhism is much more closely akin to Christianity than are optimistic Judaism and its variety, Islam.

Therefore, a real philosophy of history should not consider, as do all these, that which is always *becoming* and never *is* (to use Plato's language), and regard this as the real nature of things. On the contrary, it should keep in view that which always is, and never becomes or passes away. Thus it does not consist in our raising the temporal aims of men to eternal and absolute aims, and then constructing with ingenuity and imagination their progress to these through every intricacy and perplexity. It consists in the insight that history is untruthful not only in its arrangement, but also in its very nature, since, speaking of mere individuals and particular events, it always pretends to relate something different, whereas from beginning to end it constantly repeats only the same thing under a different name and in a different cloak. The true philosophy of history thus consists in the insight that, in spite of all these endless changes and their chaos and confusion, we yet always have before us only the same, identical, unchangeable essence, acting in the same way today as it did yesterday and always. The true philosophy of history should therefore recognize the identical in all events, of ancient as of modern times, of the East as of the West, and should see everywhere the same humanity, in spite of all difference in the special circumstances, in costume and customs. This identical element, persisting under every change, consists in the fundamental qualities of the human heart and head, many bad, few good. The motto of history in general should run: *Eadem, sed aliter*.[4] If we have read Herodotus, we have already studied enough history from a philosophical point of view. For everything which constitutes the subsequent history of the world is already there, namely the efforts, actions, sufferings, and fate of the human race, as it results from the aforesaid qualities and from its physical earthly lot.

If, in what has been said so far, we have recognized that history, considered as a means of knowing the true nature of mankind, is inferior to poetry; and again, that it is not a science in the proper sense; and finally, that the attempt to construct it as a whole with

---

[4] "The same, but otherwise." [Tr.]

beginning, middle, and end, together with a connexion fraught with meaning, is vain and is based on misunderstanding; then it would appear as though we wished to deny it all value, unless we showed in what its value consists. Actually, however, there remains for it, after this conquest of art and rejection by science, a province which is quite peculiar and different from both, and in which it exists most honourably.

What the faculty of reason is to the individual, history is to the human race. By virtue of this faculty, man is not, like the animal, restricted to the narrow present of perception, but knows also the incomparably more extended past with which it is connected, and out of which it has emerged. But only in this way does he have a proper understanding of the present itself, and can he also draw conclusions as to the future. On the other hand, the animal, whose knowledge, devoid of reflection, is restricted to perception, and therefore to the present, moves about among persons ignorant, dull, stupid, helpless, and dependent, even when tamed. Now analogous to this is a nation which does not know its own history, and is restricted to the present time of the generation now living. It therefore does not understand itself and its own present, because it is unable to refer this to a past, and to explain it from such a past; still less can it anticipate the future. Only through history does a nation become completely conscious of itself. Accordingly, history is to be regarded as the rational self-consciousness of the human race; it is to the race what the reflected and connected consciousness, conditioned by the faculty of reason, is to the individual. Through lack of such a consciousness, the animal remains confined to the narrow present of perception. Every gap in history is therefore like a gap in a person's recollecting self-consciousness; and before a monument of extreme antiquity that has outlived its own knowledge and information, as, for example, the Pyramids, the temples and palaces of Yucatan, we stand as senseless and stupid as an animal does in the presence of human actions in which it is involved as a servant, or as a man before an old cipher of his own to which he has forgotten the key; in fact, as a somnambulist does who in the morning finds in front of him what he did in his sleep. In this sense, therefore, history is to be regarded as the faculty of reason, or the reflected consciousness of the human race; and it takes the place of a self-consciousness directly common to the whole race; so that only by virtue of history does this actually become a whole, a humanity. This is the true value of history, and accordingly the universal and predominant interest in it rests mainly on its being a personal concern of the human race. Now what *language* is for the reasoning faculty of individuals, as an indispensable condition for its use, *writing* is for the reasoning faculty of the whole race which is indicated here; for only with writing does the actual existence of this faculty of reason begin, just as the existence of the individual's reason first begins with language. Thus writing serves to restore to unity the consciousness of the human race, which is incessantly interrupted by death, and is accordingly piecemeal and fragmentary; so that the idea that arose in the ancestor is thought out to the end by his remote descendant. Writing remedies the breaking up of the human race and its consciousness into an immense number of ephemeral individuals, and thus bids defiance to irresistibly hurrying time, in whose hands goes oblivion. Written as well as *stone* monuments are to be regarded as an attempt to achieve this; to some extent the latter are older than the former. For who will believe that those who, at incalculable cost, set in motion the human powers of many thousands throughout many years, in order to erect pyramids, monoliths, rock tombs, obelisks, temples, and palaces, which still stand after thousands of years, could have had in view only themselves, the short span of their own life, too short to enable them to see the end of the construction, or even the ostensible purpose which the uncultured state of the masses required them to use as a pretext? Obviously the real purpose was to speak to their latest descendants, to enter into relationship with these, and thus to restore to unity the consciousness of mankind. The buildings of the Hindus, Egyptians, even of the Greeks and Romans, were calculated to last for several thousand years, because, through higher culture, their horizon was broader. On the other hand, the buildings of the Middle Ages and of modern times were intended to last a few centuries at most. This is due also to the fact that more confidence was placed in writing, after its use had become more general, and even more after the art of printing had been born from its womb. Yet even in the buildings of more recent times we see the urge to speak to posterity; it is therefore scandalous when they are destroyed or disfigured, to let them serve base, utilitarian purposes. Written monuments have less to fear from the elements, but more from barbarians, than have stone monuments; they achieve much more. The Egyptians sought to unite both kinds by covering their stone monuments with hieroglyphs; indeed, they added paintings in case the hieroglyphs should no longer be understood.

On the Metaphysics of Music

The outcome of my discussion of the real significance of this wonderful art, which is given in the passage of volume 1 referred to below, and is here present in the mind of the reader, was that there is indeed of necessity no resemblance between its productions and the world as representation, i.e., nature, but that there must be a distinct *parallelism,* which was then also demonstrated. I have still to add some fuller particulars of this parallelism which are worth noting. The four voices or parts of all harmony, that is, bass, tenor, alto, and soprano, or fundamental note, third, fifth, and octave, correspond to the four grades in the series of existences, hence to the mineral, plant, and animal kingdoms, and to man. This obtains an additional and striking confirmation in the fundamental rule of music, which states that the bass should remain at a much greater interval below the three upper voices or parts than these have between themselves, so that it may never approach nearer to them than an octave at most, but often remains even further below them. Accordingly, the correct triad has its place in the third octave from the fundamental note. In keeping with this, the effect of *extended* harmony, where the bass remains at a distance from the other parts, is much more powerful and beautiful than that of close harmony, where the bass is moved up nearer to them. Such close harmony is introduced only on account of the limited range of the instruments. This whole rule, however, is by no means arbitrary, but has its root in the natural origin of the tonal system, namely in so far as the shortest harmonic intervals, which sound in unison by means of the secondary vibrations, are the octave and its fifth. In this rule we recognize the musical analogue of the fundamental disposition of nature, by virtue of which organic beings are much more closely related among themselves than they are to the inanimate, inorganic mass of the mineral kingdom. Between this and them are placed the most decided boundary and the widest gulf in the whole of

---

[1] This chapter refers to § 52 of volume 1.

nature. The high voice, singing the melody, is of course at the same time an integral part of the harmony, and in this is connected even with the deepest ground-bass. This may be regarded as the analogue of the fact that *the same* matter that in a human organism is the supporter of the Idea of man must nevertheless at the same time manifest and support the Ideas of gravity and of chemical properties, hence the Ideas of the lowest grades of the will's objectification.

Because music does not, like all the other arts, exhibit the *Ideas* or grades of the will's objectification, but directly the *will itself,* we can also explain that it acts directly on the will, i.e., the feelings, passions, and emotions of the hearer, so that it quickly raises these or even alters them.

Far from being a mere aid to poetry, music is certainly an independent art; in fact, it is the most powerful of all the arts, and therefore attains its ends entirely from its own resources. Just as certainly, it does not require the words of a song or the action of an opera. Music as such knows only the tones or notes, not the causes that produce them. Accordingly, even the *vox humana* is for it originally and essentially nothing but a modified tone, just like that of an instrument; and like every other tone, it has the characteristic advantages and disadvantages that are a consequence of the instrument producing it. Now in this case it is an accidental circumstance that this very instrument serves in a different way as the organ of speech for the communication of concepts, and incidentally, of course, music can make use of this circumstance in order to enter into a relationship with poetry. But it must never make this the main thing, and be entirely concerned only with the expression of what are often, indeed essentially, silly and insipid verses (as Diderot gives us to understand in *Le Neveu de Rameau*). The words are and remain for the music a foreign extra of secondary value, as the effect of the tones is incomparably more powerful, more infallible, and more rapid than that of the words. If these are incorporated in the music, therefore, they must of course occupy only an entirely subordinate position, and adapt themselves completely to it. But the relation assumes the opposite aspect in regard to the given poetry, and hence to the song or libretto of an opera, to which a piece of music is added. For in these the musical art at once shows its power and superior capacity, since it gives the most profound, ultimate, and secret information on the feeling expressed in the words, or the action presented in the opera. It expresses their real and true nature, and makes us acquainted with the innermost soul of the events and occurrences, the mere cloak and body of which are presented on the stage. With regard to this superiority of music, and in so far as it stands to the text and the action in the relation of universal to particular, of rule to example, it might perhaps appear more suitable for the text to be written for the music than for the music to be composed for the text. With the usual method, however, the words and actions of the text lead the composer to the affections of the will that underlie them, and call up in him the feelings to be expressed; consequently they act as a means for exciting his musical imagination. Moreover, that the addition of poetry to music is so welcome, and a song with intelligible words gives such profound joy, is due to the fact that our most direct and most indirect methods of knowledge are here stimulated simultaneously and in union. Thus the most direct is that for which music expresses the stirrings of the will itself, but the most indirect that of the concepts denoted by words. With the language of the feelings, our faculty of reason does not willingly sit in complete idleness. From its own resources, music is certainly able to express every movement of the will, every feeling; but through the addition of the words, we receive also their objects, the motives that give rise to that feeling. The music of an opera, as presented in the score, has a wholly independent, separate, and as it were abstract existence by itself, to which the incidents and characters of the piece are foreign, and which follows its own unchangeable rules; it can therefore be completely effective even without the text. But as this music was composed with respect to the drama, it is, so to speak, the soul of this, since, in its connexion with the incidents, characters, and words, it becomes the expression of the inner significance of all those incidents, and of their ultimate and secret necessity that rests on this significance. Unless the spectator is a mere gaper, his pleasure really depends on an obscure feeling of this. Yet in opera, music shows its heterogeneous nature and its superior intrinsic virtue by its complete indifference to everything material in the incidents; and in consequence of this, it expresses the storm of the passions and the pathos of the feelings everywhere in the same way, and accompanies these with the same pomp of its tones, whether Agamemnon and Achilles or the dissensions of an ordinary family furnish the material of the piece. For only the passions, the movements of the will, exist for it, and, like God, it sees only the heart. It never assimilates the material, and therefore, when it accompanies even the most ludicrous and extravagant farces of comic opera, it still preserves its essential beauty, purity, and sublimity; and its fusion with those incidents cannot drag it down from its height to which everything ludicrous is really foreign. Thus the deep and serious significance of our existence hangs over the farce and the endless miseries of human life, and does not leave it for a moment.

Now if we cast a glance at purely instrumental music, a symphony of Beethoven presents us with the greatest confusion which yet has the most perfect order as its foundation; with the most vehement conflict which is transformed the next moment into the most beautiful harmony. It is *rerum concordia discors*,[2] a true and complete picture of the nature of the world, which rolls on in the boundless confusion of innumerable forms, and maintains itself by constant destruction. But at the same time, all the human passions and emotions speak from this symphony; joy, grief, love, hatred, terror, hope, and so on in innumerable shades, yet all, as it were, only in the abstract and without any particularization; it is their mere form without the material, like a mere spirit world without matter. We certainly have an inclination to realize it while we listen, to clothe it in the imagination with flesh and bone, and to see in it all the different scenes of life and nature. On the whole, however, this does not promote an understanding or enjoyment of it, but rather gives it a strange and arbitrary addition. It is therefore better to interpret it purely and in its immediacy.

After considering music, in the foregoing remarks as well as in the text, from the metaphysical aspect only, and thus with regard to the inner significance of its achievements, it is appropriate for me to subject to a general consideration the means by which, acting on our mind, it brings these about, and consequently to show the connexion of that metaphysical aspect of music with the physical, which has been adequately investigated and is well known. I start from the theory, generally known and by no means overthrown by recent objections, that all harmony of the tones rests on the coincidence of the vibrations. When two tones sound simultaneously, this coincidence occurs perhaps at every second, or third, or fourth vibration, according to which they are the octave, the fifth, or the fourth of one another, and so on. Thus, so long as the vibrations of two tones have a rational relation to one another, expressible in small numbers, they can be taken together in our apprehension through their constantly recurring coincidence; the tones are blended and are thus in harmony. On the other hand, if that relation is an irrational one, or one expressible only in large numbers, no intelligible coincidence of the vibrations occurs, but *obstrepunt sibi perpetuo*,[3] and in this way they resist being taken together in our apprehension, and accordingly are called a dissonance. As a result of this theory, music is a means of making intelligible rational and irrational numerical relations, not, like arithmetic, with the aid of the concept, but by bringing them to a knowl-

---

[2] "The discordant concord of the world." [Tr.]

[3] "They clamour incessantly against one another." [Tr.]

edge that is quite direct and simultaneously affects the senses. The connexion of the metaphysical significance of music with this its physical and arithmetical basis rests on the fact that what resists our *apprehension,* namely the irrational relation or dissonance, becomes the natural image of what resists our *will;* and, conversely, the consonance or the rational relation, by easily adapting itself to our *apprehension,* becomes the image of the satisfaction of the *will.* Now as that rational and irrational element in the numerical relations of the vibrations admits of innumerable degrees, nuances, sequences, and variations, music by means of it becomes the material in which all movements of the human heart, i.e., of the will, movements whose essential nature is always satisfaction and dissatisfaction, although in innumerable degrees, can be faithfully portrayed and reproduced in all their finest shades and modifications; and this takes place by means of the invention of the melody. Thus we here see the movements of the will tinted with the province of the mere *representation* that is the exclusive scene of the achievements of all the fine arts. For these positively demand that the *will itself* be left out of account, and that we behave in every way as purely *knowing* beings. Therefore the affections of the will itself, and hence actual pain and actual pleasure, must not be excited, but only their substitutes, that which is in conformity with the *intellect* as a *picture or image* of the will's satisfaction, and that which more or less opposes it as a *picture or image* of greater or lesser pain. Only in this way does music never cause us actual suffering, but still remains pleasant even in its most painful chords; and we like to hear in its language the secret history of our will and of all its stirrings and strivings with their many different delays, postponements, hindrances, and afflictions, even in the most sorrowful melodies. On the other hand, where in real life and its terrors our *will itself* is that which is roused and tormented, we are then not concerned with tones and their numerical relations; on the contrary, we ourselves are now the vibrating string that is stretched and plucked.

Further, since, in consequence of the underlying physical theory, the really musical quality of the notes is to be found in the proportion of the rapidity of their vibrations, but not in their relative strength, the musical ear always prefers to follow in harmony the highest note, not the strongest. Therefore, even in the most powerful orchestral accompaniment, the soprano stands out, and thus obtains a natural right to deliver the melody. At the same time this is supported by the great flexibility of the soprano, which depends on the same rapidity of the vibrations, as is seen in the ornate passages and movements. In this way the soprano becomes the suitable representative of the enhanced sensibility that is susceptible to the slightest impression and determinable through this, and consequently of the most highly developed consciousness that stands at the highest stage of the scale of beings. From opposite causes, the contrast to the soprano is formed by the bass, which moves heavily, rises and falls only by large intervals, thirds, fourths, and fifths, and is guided here by fixed rules in each of its steps. It is therefore the natural represent- ative of the inorganic kingdom of nature, which is devoid of feeling, is inaccessible to fine impressions, and is determinable only according to universal laws. It can never rise by *one* tone, e.g., from a fourth to a fifth, for this produces in the upper voices or parts the incorrect fifth or octave sequence. Therefore, originally and in its own nature, the bass can never present the melody. But if the melody is assigned to it, this is done by means of counterpoint, in other words, it is a bass *transposed,* that is to say, one of the upper voices or parts is lowered and disguised as a bass. It then really requires a second fun- damental bass for its accompaniment. This unnaturalness of a mel- ody in the bass is the reason why bass airs with full accompaniment never afford us the pure and perfect delight of the soprano air. In the connexion of the harmony, the soprano air alone is natural. Incidentally, such a melodious bass, forcibly obtained by transposi- tion, might be compared, in the sense of our metaphysics of music, to a block of marble on which the human form has been impressed. For this reason it is wonderfully appropriate to the stone guest in *Don Juan.*

But we will now go somewhat nearer to the root of the *genesis* of melody. This can be effected by analysing melody into its constituent parts; and in any case, this will afford us the pleasure that arises from our once bringing to abstract and distinct consciousness things of which everyone is aware in the concrete, whereby they gain the appearance of novelty.

Melody consists of two elements, a rhythmical and a harmonious; the former can also be described as the quantitative element, the latter as the qualitative, since the first concerns the duration of the notes, the second their pitch and depth. In writing music, the former belongs to the perpendicular lines, the latter to the horizontal. Purely arithmetical relations, hence those of time, are the basis of both; in the one case, the relative duration of the notes, in the other, the relative rapidity of their vibrations. The rhythmical element is the most essential, for by itself alone and without the other element it can present a kind of melody, as is done, for example, on the drum; yet complete melody requires both elements. Thus it consists in an alternating *discord* and *reconciliation* of them, as I shall show in a moment; but as the harmonious element has been discussed in what has been said already, I will consider somewhat more closely the rhythmical element.

Rhythm is in time what *symmetry* is in space, namely division into equal parts corresponding to one another, and first into larger parts that are again divisible into smaller parts subordinate to the former. In the series of arts furnished by me, *architecture* and *music* form the two extremes. Moreover, they are the most heterogeneous, in fact the true antipodes, according to their inner nature, their power, the range of their spheres, and their significance. This contrast extends even to the form of their appearance, since architecture is in *space* alone, without any reference to time, and music is in *time* alone without any reference to space.[4] From this springs their sole analogy, namely that as in architecture it is *symmetry* that arranges and holds together, in music it is *rhythm;* and thus we also have confirmation here that *les extrêmes se touchent.*[5] As the ultimate constituent elements of a building are the exactly similar stones, so the ultimate constituent elements of a piece of music are the exactly similar measures of time. But through arsis and thesis, or in general through the numerical fraction denoting the time, these are divided into equal parts that may perhaps be compared to the dimensions of the stone. The musical period consists of several bars, and also has two equal halves, one rising, aspiring, often going to the dominant, and one sinking, calming, and finding again the fundamental note. Two or even several periods constitute a part that is often doubled, likewise symmetrically, by the sign of repetition. From two parts we get a smaller piece of music, or only a movement of a larger piece; and thus a concerto or sonata usually consists of three movements, a symphony of four, and a mass of five. We therefore see the piece of music combined and rounded off as a whole by symmetrical distribution and repeated division, down to the beats and their fractions with general subordination, superordination, and co-ordination of its members, exactly as a building is by its symmetry; only that what with the latter is exclusively in space is with the former exclusively in time. The mere feeling of this analogy has occasioned the bold witticism, often repeated in the last thirty years, that architecture is

---

[4] It would be a false objection to say that sculpture and painting are also merely in space; for their works are connected with time, not directly of course, but indirectly, since they depict life, movement, action. It would be just as false to say that poetry, as speech, belongs only to time. This is also true only indirectly of the words; its material is everything that exists, hence the spatial.

[5] "Extremes meet." [Tr.]

frozen music. The origin of this can be traced to Goethe, for, according to Eckermann's *Conversations,* Vol. II, p. 88, he said: "Among my papers I have found a sheet on which I call architecture a congealed music, and actually there is something in it; the mood arising from architecture approximates to the effect of music." He probably uttered that witticism much earlier in the conversation, and in that case we know quite well that there was never a lack of people to glean what he dropped, in order to go about subsequently dressed up in it. For the rest, whatever Goethe may have said, the analogy of music with architecture, which I refer to its sole ground, namely the analogy of rhythm with symmetry, accordingly extends only to the outer form, and by no means to the inner nature of the two arts, which is vastly different. Indeed, it would be ridiculous to try to put the most limited and feeble of all the arts on an equal footing in essential respects with the most extensive and effective. As an amplification of the analogy pointed out it might also be added that when music, in a sudden urge for independence, so to speak, seizes the opportunity of a pause, in order to free itself from the control of rhythm, to launch out into the free fancy of an ornate cadenza, such a piece of music, divested of rhythm, is analogous to the ruin divested of symmetry. Accordingly, in the daring language of that witticism, such a ruin may be called a frozen cadenza.

After this discussion of *rhythm,* I have now to show how the true nature of melody consists in the constantly renewed *discord and reconciliation* of its rhythmical with its harmonious element. Its harmonious element has as its assumption the fundamental note, just as the rhythmical element has the measure of time, and it consists in a deviation from this through all the notes of the scale, until, by longer or shorter detours, it reaches a harmonious stage, often the dominant or subdominant that affords it an incomplete satisfaction. But then there follows on an equally long path its return to the fundamental note, with which appears complete satisfaction. But the two must now take place in such a way that reaching the aforesaid stage and finding the fundamental note once more coincide with certain favourite points of time in the *rhythm,* as otherwise it does not work. Therefore, just as the harmonious sequence of sounds requires certain *notes,* first of all the tonic, then the dominant, and so on, so rhythm on its part requires certain *points of time,* certain numbered bars, and certain parts of these bars, which are called heavy or good beats, or the accented parts of the bar, as opposed to the light or bad beats, or unaccented parts of the bar. The *discord* of those two fundamental elements consists in the fact that, by the demand of the one being satisfied, that of the other is not. But *reconciliation* consists in the two being satisfied simultaneously and at once. Thus the wandering of the sequence of notes, until the attainment of a more or less harmonious stage, must hit upon this only after a definite number of bars, but then on a *good* part of the bar, whereby this becomes for it a certain point of rest. In just the same way, the return to the tonic must again find this after an equal number of bars, and likewise on a *good* part of the bar, whereby complete satisfaction then occurs. So long as this required coincidence of the satisfactions of the two elements is not attained, the rhythm, on the one hand, may follow its regular course, and on the other hand the required notes occur often enough; yet they will remain entirely without that effect through which the melody originates. The following extremely simple example may serve to illustrate this:

Here the harmonious sequence of notes strikes the tonic right at the end of the first bar, but does not thereby obtain any satisfaction, because the rhythm is conceived in the worst part of the bar. Immediately afterwards in the second bar, the rhythm has the good part of the bar, but the sequence of notes has arrived at the seventh. Here, therefore, the two elements of the melody are entirely *disunited,* and we feel disquieted. In the second half of the period everything is reversed, and in the last note they are *reconciled.* This kind of proceeding can be demonstrated in every melody, though generally in a much more extended form. Now the constant *discord and reconciliation* of its two elements which occurs here is, metaphysically considered, the copy of the origination of new desires, and then of their satisfaction. Precisely in this way, the music penetrates our hearts by flattery, so that it always holds out to us the complete satisfaction of our desires. More closely considered, we see in this procedure of the melody a condition to a certain extent *inward* (the harmonious) meet with an *outward* condition (the rhythmical) as if by an *accident;* which is of course produced by the composer, and to this extent may be compared to the rhyme in poetry. This, however, is just the copy of the meeting of our desires with the favourable external circumstances independent of them, and is thus the picture of happiness. The effect of the *suspension* also deserves to be considered here. It is a dissonance delaying the final consonance that is with certainty awaited; in this way the longing for it is strengthened, and its appearance affords the greater satisfaction. This is clearly an analogue of the satisfaction of the will which is enhanced through delay. The complete cadence requires the preceding chord of the seventh on the dominant, because the most deeply felt satisfaction and complete relief can follow only the most pressing desire. Therefore music consists generally in a constant succession of chords more or less disquieting, i.e., of chords exciting desire, with chords more or less quieting and satisfying; just as the life of the heart (the will) is a constant succession of greater or lesser disquietude through desire or fear with composure in degrees just as varied. Accordingly the harmonious progress of notes consists of the alternation of dissonance and consonance which conforms to the rules of art. A sequence of merely consonant chords would be satiating, tedious, and empty, like the languor produced by the satisfaction of all desires. Therefore, although dissonances are disquieting and have an almost painful effect, they must be introduced, but only in order to be resolved again into consonances with proper preparation. In fact, in the whole of music there are only two fundamental chords, the dissonant chord of the seventh and the harmonious triad, and all chords that are met with can be referred to these two. This is precisely in keeping with the fact that there are for the will at bottom only dissatisfaction and satisfaction, however many and varied the forms in which these are presented may be. And just as there are two universal and fundamental moods of the mind, serenity, or at any rate vigour, and sadness, or even anguish, so music has two general keys, the major and the minor, corresponding to those moods, and it must always be found in the one or in the other. But it is indeed amazing that there is a sign of pain, namely the minor, which is neither physically painful nor even conventional, yet is at once pleasing and unmistakable. From this we can estimate how deeply music is rooted in the real nature of things and of man. With northern nations, whose life is subject to hard conditions, especially with the Russians, the minor prevails, even in church music. Allegro in the minor is very frequent in French music, and is characteristic; it is as if a man danced while his shoe pinched him.

I add a couple of secondary observations. Under a change of the tonic or key-note, and with it of the value of all the intervals, in consequence of which the same note figures as the second, the third, the fourth, and so on, the notes of the scale are analogous to actors who have to assume now one role now another, while their person remains the same. The fact that this person is often not exactly suited to that role may be compared to the unavoidable impurity of every harmonic system (mentioned at the end of § 52 of volume 1) which has been produced by the equally hovering temperament.

Perhaps some might take umbrage at the fact that, according to the present metaphysics of music, whereas it so often exalts our minds and seems to speak of worlds different from and better than ours, it nevertheless flatters only the will-to-live, since it depicts the true nature of the will, gives it a glowing account of its success, and at the end expresses its satisfaction and contentment. The following passage from the *Veda* may serve to set at rest such doubts: *Et Anand sroup, quod forma gaudii est,* τον *pram Atma ex hoc dicunt, quod quocunque loco gaudium est, particula e gaudio ejus est* (*Oupnekhat*, Vol. I, p. 405, and again Vol. II, p. 215).[6]

---

[6] "And that rapturous which is a kind of delight is called the highest Atman, because wherever there is a desire, this is a part of its delight." [Tr.]

SUPPLEMENTS TO THE FOURTH BOOK.

*Tous les hommes désirent uniquement de se délivrer de la mort:
ils ne savent pas se délivrer de la vie.*
Lao-tse, *Tao-te-king,* ed. Stanislas Julien, p. 184.

["All men desire solely to free themselves from death; they do not know
how to free themselves from life."—Tr.]

CHAPTER XL

Preface

The supplements to this fourth book would be very considerable, were it not that two of their principal subjects specially in need of a supplement, the freedom of the will and the foundation of morality, were fully discussed by me in the form of a monograph, and offered to the public in the year 1841 under the title *The Two Fundamental Problems of Ethics,* on the occasion of prize-questions set by two Scandinavian Academies. Accordingly I assume on the part of my readers an acquaintance with the work just mentioned, just as unconditionally as in the case of the supplements to Book II I assumed an acquaintance with the work *On the Will in Nature.* In general, I make the demand that whoever wishes to make himself acquainted with my philosophy shall read every line of me. For I am not a prolific writer, a fabricator of compendiums, an earner of fees, a person who aims with his writings at the approbation and assent of a minister; in a word, one whose pen is under the influence of personal ends. I aspire to nothing but the truth, and I write as the ancients wrote with the sole object of preserving my thoughts, so that they may one day benefit those who know how to meditate on them and appreciate them. I have therefore written little, but this little with reflection and at *long* intervals; accordingly, I have also confined within the smallest possible limits the repetitions, sometimes unavoidable in philosophical works on account of continuity and sequence, from which no single philosopher is free, so that most of what I have to say is to be found only in one place. Therefore, whoever wants to learn from me and to understand me must not leave unread anything that I have written. Yet without this people can criticize and condemn me, as experience has shown; and for this also I further wish them much pleasure.

However, the space gained in this fourth book of supplements by the aforesaid elimination of two main subjects will be welcome. For as those explanations which are above all close to man's heart, and therefore form in every system, as ultimate results, the culminating point of its pyramid, are also concentrated in my last book, a larger space will gladly be granted to every more solid and positive proof, or to its more detailed discussion. Moreover, we have been able to introduce here a discussion which belongs to the doctrine of the "affirmation of the will-to-live," and which was left untouched in our fourth book itself, just as it has been entirely neglected by all philosophers before me. This is the inner significance and real nature of sexual love, which sometimes rises to the most intense passion, a subject the taking up of which in the ethical part of philosophy would not be paradoxical, if its importance had been recognized.

On Death and Its Relation to the Indestructibility of Our Inner Nature

Death is the real inspiring genius or Musagetes of philosophy, and for this reason Socrates defined philosophy as θανάτου μελέτη.[2] Indeed, without death there would hardly have been any philosophizing. It will therefore be quite in order for a special consideration of this subject to have its place here at the beginning of the last, most serious, and most important of our books.

The animal lives without any real knowledge of death; therefore the individual animal immediately enjoys the absolute imperishableness and immortality of the species, since it is conscious of itself only as endless. With man the terrifying certainty of death necessarily appeared along with the faculty of reason. But just as everywhere in nature a remedy, or at any rate a compensation, is given for every evil, so the same reflection that introduced the knowledge of death also assists us in obtaining *metaphysical* points of view. Such views console us concerning death, and the animal is neither in need of nor capable of them. All religions and philosophical systems are directed principally to this end, and are thus primarily the antidote to the certainty of death which reflecting reason produces from its own resources. The degree in which they attain this end is, however, very different, and *one* religion or philosophy will certainly enable man, far more than the others will, to look death calmly in the face. Brahmanism and Buddhism, which teach man to regard himself as Brahman, as the original being himself, to whom all arising and passing away are essentially foreign, will achieve much more in this respect than will those religions that represent man as being made out of nothing and as actually beginning at his birth the existence he has received from another. In keeping with this we find in India a confidence and a contempt for death of which we in Europe have no

---

[1] This chapter refers to § 54 of volume 1.
[2] "Preparation for death." [Tr.]

conception. It is indeed a ticklish business to force on man through early impression weak and untenable notions in this important respect, and thus to render him for ever incapable of adopting more correct and stable views. For example, to teach him that he came but recently from nothing, that consequently he has been nothing throughout an eternity, and yet for the future is to be imperishable and immortal, is just like teaching him that, although he is through and through the work of another, he shall nevertheless be responsible to all eternity for his commissions and omissions. Thus if with a mature mind and with the appearance of reflection the untenable nature of such doctrines forces itself on him, he has nothing better to put in their place; in fact, he is no longer capable of understanding anything better, and in this way is deprived of the consolation that nature had provided for him as compensation for the certainty of death. In consequence of such a development, we now (1844) see in England the Socialists among the demoralized and corrupted factory workers, and in Germany the young Hegelians among the demoralized and corrupted students, sink to the absolutely physical viewpoint. This leads to the result: *edite, bibite, post mortem nulla voluptas,*[3] and to this extent can be described as bestiality.

According, however, to all that has been taught about death, it cannot be denied that, at any rate in Europe, the opinion of men, often in fact even of the same individual, very frequently vacillates afresh between the conception of death as absolute annihilation and the assumption that we are, so to speak with skin and hair, immortal. Both are equally false, but we have not so much to find a correct mean as rather to gain the higher standpoint from which such views disappear of themselves.

With these considerations, I wish to start first of all from the entirely empirical viewpoint. Here we have primarily before us the undeniable fact that, according to natural consciousness, man not only fears death for his own person more than anything else, but also weeps violently over the death of his friends and relations. It is evident, indeed, that he does this not egoistically over his own loss, but out of sympathy for the great misfortune that has befallen them. He therefore censures as hard-hearted and unfeeling those who in such a case do not weep and show no grief. Parallel with this is the fact that, in its highest degrees, the thirst for revenge seeks the death of the adversary as the greatest evil that can be inflicted on him. Opinions change according to time and place, but the voice of nature remains always and everywhere the same, and is therefore to be heeded before everything else. Now here it seems clearly to assert that

---

[3] "Eat and drink, after death there is no more rejoicing." [Tr.]

death is a great evil. In the language of nature, *death* signifies annihilation; and that death is a serious matter could already be inferred
from the fact that, as everyone knows, life is no joke. Indeed we
must not deserve anything better than these two.

The fear of death is, in fact, independent of all knowledge, for the
animal has it, although it does not know death. Everything that is
born already brings this fear into the world. Such fear of death, however, is *a priori* only the reverse side of the will-to-live, which indeed
we all are. Therefore in every animal the fear of its own destruction,
like the care for its maintenance, is inborn. Thus it is this fear of
death, and not the mere avoidance of pain, that shows itself in the
anxious care and caution with which the animal seeks to protect
itself, and still more its brood, from everyone who might become
dangerous. Why does the animal flee, tremble, and try to conceal
itself? Because it is simply the will-to-live, but as such it is forfeit to
death and would like to gain time. By nature man is just the same.
The greatest of evils, the worst thing that can threaten anywhere, is
death; the greatest anxiety is the anxiety of death. Nothing excites
us so irresistibly to the most lively interest as does danger to the
lives of others; nothing is more dreadful than an execution. Now the
boundless attachment to life which appears here cannot have sprung
from knowledge and reflection. To these, on the contrary, it appears
foolish, for the objective value of life is very uncertain, and it remains at least doubtful whether existence is to be preferred to non-
existence; in fact, if experience and reflection have their say, non-
existence must certainly win. If we knocked on the graves and asked
the dead whether they would like to rise again, they would shake
their heads. In Plato's *Apology* this is also the opinion of Socrates,
and even the cheerful and amiable Voltaire cannot help saying: *On
aime la vie; mais le néant ne laisse pas d'avoir du bon:* and again:
*Je ne sais pas ce que c'est que la vie éternelle, mais celle-ci est une
mauvaise plaisanterie.*[4] Moreover, in any case life must end soon, so
that the few years which possibly we have still to exist vanish entirely
before the endless time when we shall be no more. Accordingly, to
reflection it appears even ludicrous for us to be so very anxious about
this span of time, to tremble so much when our own life or another's
is endangered, and to write tragedies whose terrible aspect has as its
main theme merely the fear of death. Consequently, this powerful
attachment to life is irrational and blind; it can be explained only
from the fact that our whole being-in-itself is the will-to-live, to which
life therefore must appear as the highest good, however embittered,

---

[4] "We like life, but all the same nothingness also has its good points. . . .
I do not know what eternal life is, but this present life is a bad joke." [Tr.]

short, and uncertain it may be; and that that will is originally and in itself without knowledge and blind. Knowledge, on the contrary, far from being the origin of that attachment to life, even opposes it, since it discloses life's worthlessness, and in this way combats the fear of death. When it is victorious, and man accordingly faces death courageously and calmly, this is honoured as great and noble. Therefore we then extol the triumph of knowledge over the blind will-to-live which is nevertheless the kernel of our own inner being. In the same way we despise him in whom knowledge is defeated in that conflict, who therefore clings unconditionally to life, struggles to the utmost against approaching death, and receives it with despair;[5] yet in him is expressed only the original inner being of our own self and of nature. Incidentally, it may here be asked how the boundless love of life and the endeavour to maintain it in every way as long as possible could be regarded as base and contemptible, and likewise considered by the followers of every religion as unworthy thereof, if life were the gift of the good gods to be acknowledged with thanks. How then could it appear great and noble to treat it with contempt? Meanwhile, these considerations confirm for us: (1) that the will-to-live is the innermost essence of man; (2) that in itself the will is without knowledge and blind; (3) that knowledge is an adventitious principle, originally foreign to the will; (4) that knowledge conflicts with the will, and our judgement applauds the triumph of knowledge over the will.

If what makes death seem so terrible to us were the thought of *non-existence,* we should necessarily think with equal horror of the time when as yet we did not exist. For it is irrefutably certain that non-existence after death cannot be different from non-existence before birth, and is therefore no more deplorable than that is. An entire infinity ran its course when we did *not yet* exist, but this in no way disturbs us. On the other hand, we find it hard, and even unendurable, that after the momentary intermezzo of an ephemeral existence, a second infinity should follow in which we shall exist *no longer.* Now could this thirst for existence possibly have arisen through our having tasted it and found it so very delightful? As was briefly set forth above, certainly not; the experience gained would far rather have been capable of causing an infinite longing for the lost paradise

---

[5] *In gladiatoriis pugnis timidos et supplices, et, ut vivere liceat, obsecrantes etiam odisse solemus; fortes et animosos, et se acriter ipsos morti offerentes servare cupimus.* Cicero, *Pro Milone,* c. 34.

["In gladiatorial conflicts we usually abhor and abominate the cowards who beg and implore us to let them live. On the other hand, we seek to preserve the lives of the brave, the courageous, and those who of their own free will impetuously face death." Tr.]

of non-existence. To the hope of immortality of the soul there is always added that of a "better world"; an indication that the present world is not worth much. Notwithstanding all this, the question of our state after death has certainly been discussed verbally and in books ten thousand times more often than that of our state before birth. Theoretically, however, the one is a problem just as near at hand and just as legitimate as the other; moreover, he who answered the one would likewise be fully enlightened about the other. We have fine declamations about how shocking it would be to think that the mind of man, which embraces the world and has so many excellent ideas, should sink with him into the grave; but we hear nothing about this mind having allowed a whole infinity of time to elapse before it arose with these its qualities, and how for just as long a time the world had to manage without it. Yet to knowledge uncorrupted by the will no question presents itself more naturally than this, namely: An infinite time has run its course before my birth; what was I throughout all that time? Metaphysically, the answer might perhaps be: "I was always I; that is, all who throughout that time said I, were just I." But let us turn away from this to our present entirely empirical point of view, and assume that I did not exist at all. But I can then console myself for the infinite time after my death when I shall not exist, with the infinite time when I did not as yet exist, as a quite customary and really very comfortable state. For the infinity *a parte post*[6] without me cannot be any more fearful than the infinity *a parte ante*[6] without me, since the two are not distinguished by anything except by the intervention of an ephemeral life-dream. All proofs of continued existence after death may also be applied just as well *in partem ante,* where they then demonstrate existence before life, in assuming which the Hindus and Buddhists therefore show themselves to be very consistent. Only Kant's ideality of time solves all these riddles; but we are not discussing this at the moment. But this much follows from what has been said, namely that to mourn for the time when we shall no longer exist is just as absurd as it would be to mourn for the time when we did not as yet exist; for it is all the same whether the time our existence does not fill is related to that which it does fill as future or as past.

But quite apart even from these considerations of time, it is in and by itself absurd to regard non-existence as an evil; for every evil, like every good, presupposes existence, indeed even consciousness. But this ceases with life, as well as in sleep and in a fainting fit; therefore the absence of consciousness is well known and familiar to us as a state containing no evil at all; in any case, its occurrence is a matter

---

[6] "After life"; "before life." [Tr.]

of a moment. Epicurus considered death from this point of view, and therefore said quite rightly: ὁ θάνατος μηδὲν πρὸς ἡμᾶς (Death does not concern us), with the explanation that when we are, death is not, and when death is, we are not (Diogenes Laërtius, x, 27). To have lost what cannot be missed is obviously no evil; therefore we ought to be just as little disturbed by the fact that we shall not exist as by the fact that we did not exist. Accordingly, from the standpoint of knowledge, there appears to be absolutely no ground for fearing death; but consciousness consists in knowing, and thus for consciousness death is no evil. Moreover, it is not really this *knowing* part of our *ego* that fears death, but *fuga mortis* comes simply and solely from the blind *will*, with which every living thing is filled. But, as already mentioned, this *fuga mortis* is essential to it, just because it is the will-to-live, whose whole inner nature consists in a craving for life and existence. Knowledge is not originally inherent in it, but appears only in consequence of the will's objectification in animal individuals. Now if by means of knowledge the will beholds death as the end of the phenomenon with which it has identified itself, and to which it therefore sees itself limited, its whole nature struggles against this with all its might. We shall investigate later on whether it really has anything to fear from death, and shall then remember the real source of the fear of death which is indicated here with a proper distinction between the willing and knowing part of our true nature.

According to this, what makes death so terrible for us is not so much the end of life—for this cannot seem to anyone specially worthy of regret—as the destruction of the organism, really because this organism is the will itself manifested as body. But actually, we feel this destruction only in the evils of illness or of old age; on the other hand, for the *subject,* death itself consists merely in the moment when consciousness vanishes, since the activity of the brain ceases. The extension of the stoppage to all the other parts of the organism which follows this is really already an event after death. Therefore, in a subjective respect, death concerns only consciousness. Now from going to sleep everyone can, to some extent, judge what the vanishing of consciousness may be; and whoever has had a real fainting fit knows it even better. The transition here is not so gradual, nor is it brought about by dreams; but first of all, while we are still fully conscious, the power of sight disappears, and then immediately supervenes the deepest unconsciousness. As far as the accompanying sensation goes, it is anything but unpleasant; and undoubtedly just as sleep is the brother of death, so is the fainting fit its twin-brother. Violent death also cannot be painful, for, as a rule, even severe wounds are not felt at all till some time afterwards, and are often noticed only from their external symptoms. If they are rapidly fatal, consciousness will vanish before this discovery; if they result in death later, it is the same as with other illnesses. All who have lost consciousness in water, through charcoal fumes, or through hanging, also state, as is well known, that it happened without pain. And finally, even death through natural causes proper, death through old age, euthanasia, is a gradual vanishing and passing out of existence in an imperceptible manner. In old age, passions and desires, together with the susceptibility to their objects, are gradually extinguished; the emotions no longer find any excitement, for the power to make representations or mental pictures becomes weaker and weaker, and its images feebler. The impressions no longer stick to us, but pass away without a trace; the days roll by faster and faster; events lose their significance; everything grows pale. The old man, stricken in years, totters about or rests in a corner, now only a shadow, a ghost, of his former self. What still remains there for death to destroy? One day a slumber is his last, and his dreams are ————. They are the dreams that Hamlet asks about in the famous monologue. I believe that we dream them just now.

I have still to observe that, although the maintenance of the life-process has a metaphysical basis, it does not take place without resistance, and hence without effort. It is this to which the organism yields every evening, for which reason it then suspends the brain-function, and diminishes certain secretions, respiration, pulse, and the development of heat. From this it may be concluded that the entire cessation of the life-process must be a wonderful relief for its driving force. Perhaps this is partly responsible for the expression of sweet contentment on the faces of most of the dead. In general, the moment of dying may be similar to that of waking from a heavy nightmare.

So far, the result for us is that death cannot really be an evil, however much it is feared, but that it often appears even as a good thing, as something desired, as a friend. All who have encountered insuperable obstacles to their existence or to their efforts, who suffer from incurable disease or from inconsolable grief, have the return into the womb of nature as the last resource that is often open to them as a matter of course. Like everything else, they emerged from this womb for a short time, enticed by the hope of more favourable conditions of existence than those that have fallen to their lot, and from this the same path always remains open to them. That return is the *cessio bonorum*[7] of the living. Yet even here it is entered into

---

[7] "Surrender of property." [Tr.]

only after a physical or moral conflict, so hard does everyone struggle against returning to the place from which he came forth so readily and willingly to an existence that has so many sorrows and so few joys to offer. To Yama, the god of death, the Hindus give two faces, one very fearful and terrible, one very cheerful and benevolent. This is already explained in part from the observations we have just made.

From the empirical standpoint, at which we are still placed, the following consideration is one which presents itself automatically, and therefore merits being defined accurately by elucidation, and thus kept within its limits. The sight of a corpse shows me that sensibility, irritability, blood circulation, reproduction, and so on in it have ceased. From this I conclude with certainty that that which previously actuated them, which was nevertheless something always unknown to me, now actuates them no longer, and so has departed from them. But if I now wished to add that this must have been just what I have known only as consciousness, and consequently as intelligence (soul), this would be a conclusion not merely unjustified, but obviously false. For consciousness has always shown itself to me not as the cause, but as a product and result of organic life, since it rose and sank in consequence thereof at the different periods of life, in health and sickness, in sleep, in a faint, in awaking, and so on. Thus it always appeared as the effect, never as a cause, of organic life, always showed itself as something arising and passing away and again arising, so long as the conditions for this still exist, but not apart from them. Indeed, I may also have seen that the complete derangement of consciousness, madness, far from dragging down with it and depressing the other forces, or even endangering life, greatly enhances these, especially irritability or muscular force, and lengthens rather than shortens life, if there are no other competing causes. Then I knew individuality as a quality or attribute of everything organic, and when this was a self-conscious organism, of consciousness also. But there exists no occasion for concluding now that individuality is inherent in that vanished principle which imparts life and is wholly unknown to me; the less so, as everywhere in nature I see each particular phenomenon to be the work of a universal force active in thousands of similar phenomena. But on the other hand there is just as little occasion for concluding that, because organized life has here ceased, the force that actuated it hitherto has also become nothing; just as little as there is to infer from the stopping of the spinning-wheel the death of the spinner. If, by finding its centre of gravity again, a pendulum finally comes to rest, and thus its individual apparent life has ceased, no one will suppose that gravitation is annihilated, but everyone sees that now as always it is active in innumerable phenomena. Of course, it might be objected to this comparison that even in the pendulum gravitation has not ceased to be active, but has merely given up manifesting its activity visibly. He who insists on this may think, instead, of an electrical body in which, after its discharge, electricity has really ceased to be active. I wished only to show by this that we directly attribute an eternity and ubiquity even to the lowest forces of nature; and the transitoriness of their fleeting phenomena does not for a moment confuse us with regard thereto. So much the less, therefore, should it occur to us to regard the cessation of life as the annihilation of the living principle, and thus death as the entire destruction of man. Because the strong arm that three thousand years ago bent the bow of Ulysses no longer exists, no reflective and well-regulated understanding will look upon the force that acted so energetically in it as entirely annihilated. Therefore, on further reflection, it will not be assumed that the force that bends the bow today, first began to exist with that arm. Much nearer to us is the idea that the force that formerly actuated a life now vanished is the same force that is active in the life now flourishing; indeed this thought is almost inevitable. However, we certainly know that, as was explained in the second book, only that is perishable which is involved in the causal chain; but merely the states and forms are so involved. Untouched, however, by the change of these, which is produced by causes, there remain matter on the one hand, and the natural forces on the other; for both are the presupposition of all those changes. But the principle that gives us life must first be conceived at any rate as a force of nature, until a profounder investigation may perhaps let us know what it is in itself. Thus, taken already as a force of nature, vital force remains entirely untouched by the change of forms and states, which the bond of cause and effect introduces and carries off again, and which alone are subject to arising and passing away, just as these processes lie before us in experience. To this extent, therefore, the imperishableness of our true inner nature could already be certainly demonstrated. But this, of course, will not satisfy the claims usually made on proofs of our continued existence after death, nor will it afford the consolation expected from such proofs. Yet it is always something, and whoever fears death as his absolute annihilation cannot afford to disdain the perfect certainty that the innermost principle of his life remains untouched by it. In fact, we might advance the paradox that that second thing which, like the forces of nature, remains untouched by the continuous change of states under the guidance of causality, i.e., matter, also assures us through its absolute permanence of an indestructibility; and by virtue of this, he who might be incapable of grasping any other could yet be confident of a certain imperishability. But it will be asked: "How is the permanence of mere dust, of crude matter, to be regarded as a continuance of our true inner nature?" Oh! do you know this dust then? Do you know what it is and what it can do? Learn to know it before you despise it. This matter, now lying there as dust and ashes, will soon form into crystals when dissolved in water; it will shine as metal; it will then emit electric sparks. By means of its galvanic tension it will manifest a force which, decomposing the strongest and firmest combinations, reduces earths to metals. It will, indeed of its own accord, form itself into plant and animal; and from its mysterious womb it will develop that life, about the loss of which you in your narrowness of mind are so nervous and anxious. Is it, then, so absolutely and entirely nothing to continue to exist as such matter? Indeed, I seriously assert that even this permanence of matter affords evidence of the indestructibility of our true inner being, although only as in an image and simile, or rather only as in a shadowy outline. To see this, we need only recall the discussion on matter given in chapter 24, the conclusion of which was that mere formless matter—this basis of the world of experience, never perceived by itself alone, but assumed as always permanent—is the immediate reflection, the visibility in general, of the thing-in-itself, that is, of the will. There-fore, what absolutely pertains to the will in itself holds good of matter under the conditions of experience, and it reproduces the true eternity of the will under the image of temporal imperish-ability. Because, as we have already said, nature does not lie, no view which has sprung from a purely objective comprehension of her, and has been logically thought out, can be absolutely and entirely false; in the worst case it is only very one-sided and imper-fect. But such a view is unquestionably consistent materialism, for instance that of Epicurus, just as is the absolute idealism opposed to it, like that of Berkeley, and generally every fundamental view of philosophy which has come from a correct *aperçu* and has been honestly worked out. Only they are all extremely one-sided interpre-tations, and therefore, in spite of their contrasts, are *simultaneously* true, each from a definite point of view. But as soon as we rise above this point, they appear to be true only relatively and conditionally. The highest standpoint alone, from which we survey them all and recognize them in their merely relative truth, and also beyond this in their falseness, can be that of absolute truth, in so far as such a truth is in general attainable. Accordingly, as was shown above, we see even in the really very crude, and therefore very old, fundamental view of materialism the indestructibility of our true inner being-in-itself still represented as by a mere shadow of it, namely through the imperishability of matter; just as in the already higher naturalism of an absolute physics we see it represented by the ubiquity and eternity of natural forces, among which vital force is at least to be reckoned. Hence even these crude fundamental views contain the assertion that the living being does not suffer any absolute annihilation through death, but continues to exist in and with the whole of nature.

The considerations which have brought us to this point, and with which the further discussions are connected, started from the remarkable fear of death which affects all living beings. But now we wish to alter the point of view, and to consider how, in contrast to individual beings, the *whole* of nature behaves with regard to death; yet here we still remain always on the ground and soil of the empirical.

We know, of course, of no higher gamble than that for life and death. We watch with the utmost attention, interest, and fear every decision concerning them; for in our view all in all is at stake. On the other hand, *nature,* which never lies, but is always frank and sincere, speaks quite differently on this theme, as Krishna does in the *Bhagavadgita.* Her statement is that the life or death of the individual is of absolutely no consequence. She expresses this by abandoning the life of every animal, and even of man, to the most insignificant accidents without coming to the rescue. Consider the insect on your path; a slight unconscious turning of your foot is decisive as to its life or death. Look at the wood-snail that has no means of flight, of defence, of practising deception, of concealment, a ready prey to all. Look at the fish carelessly playing in the still open net; at the frog prevented by its laziness from the flight that could save it; at the bird unaware of the falcon soaring above it; at the sheep eyed and examined from the thicket by the wolf. Endowed with little caution, all these go about guilelessly among the dangers which at every moment threaten their existence. Now, since nature abandons without reserve her organisms constructed with such inexpressible skill, not only to the predatory instinct of the stronger, but also to the blindest chance, the whim of every fool, and the mischievousness of every child, she expresses that the annihilation of these individuals is a matter of indifference to her, does her no harm, is of no significance at all, and that in these cases the effect is of no more consequence than is the cause. Nature states this very clearly, and she never lies; only she does not comment on her utterances, but rather expresses them in the laconic style of the oracle. Now if the universal mother carelessly sends forth her children without protection to a thousand threatening dangers, this can be only because she knows that, when they fall, they fall back into her womb, where they are safe and secure; therefore their fall is only a jest. With man she does not act otherwise than she does with the animals; hence her declaration extends also to him; the life or death of the individual is a matter of indifference to her. Consequently, they should be, in a certain sense, a matter of indifference to us; for in fact, we ourselves are nature. If only we saw deeply enough, we should certainly agree with nature, and regard life or death as indifferently as does she. Meanwhile, by means of reflection, we must attribute nature's careless and indifferent attitude concerning the life of individuals to the fact that the destruction of such a phenomenon does not in the least disturb its true and real inner being.

As we have just been considering, not only are life and death dependent on the most trifling accidents, but the existence of organic beings generally is also ephemeral; animal and plant arise today and tomorrow pass away; birth and death follow in quick succession, whereas to inorganic things, standing so very much lower, an incomparably longer duration is assured, but an infinitely long one only to absolutely formless matter, to which we attribute this even *a priori*. Now if we ponder over all this, I think the merely empirical, but objective and unprejudiced, comprehension of such an order of things must be followed as a matter of course by the thought that this order is only a superficial phenomenon, that such a constant arising and passing away cannot in any way touch the root of things, but can be only relative, indeed only apparent. The true inner being of everything, which, moreover, evades our glance everywhere and is thoroughly mysterious, is not affected by that arising and passing away, but rather continues to exist undisturbed thereby. Of course, we can neither perceive nor comprehend the way in which this happens, and must therefore think of it only generally as a kind of *tour de passe-passe*[8] that took place here. For whereas the most imperfect thing, the lowest, the inorganic, continues to exist unassailed, it is precisely the most perfect beings, namely living things with their infinitely complicated and inconceivably ingenious organizations, which were supposed always to arise afresh from the very bottom, and after a short span of time to become absolutely nothing, in order to make room once more for new ones like them coming into existence out of nothing. This is something so obviously absurd that it can never be the true order

---

[8] "Conjuring trick." [Tr.]

of things, but rather a mere veil concealing such an order, or more correctly a phenomenon conditioned by the constitution of our intellect. In fact, the entire existence and non-existence of these individual beings, in reference to which life and death are opposites, can be only relative. Hence the language of nature, in which it is given to us as something absolute, cannot be the true and ultimate expression of the quality and constitution of things and of the order of the world, but really only a *patois du pays*,[9] in other words, something merely relatively true, something self-styled, to be understood *cum grano salis,* or properly speaking, something conditioned by our intellect. I say that an immediate, intuitive conviction of the kind I have here tried to describe in words will force itself on everyone, of course only on everyone whose mind is not of the utterly common species. Such common minds are capable of knowing absolutely only the particular thing, simply and solely as such, and are strictly limited to knowledge of individuals, after the manner of the animal intellect. On the other hand, whoever, through an ability of an only somewhat higher power, even just begins to see in individual beings their universal, their Ideas, will also to a certain extent participate in that conviction, a conviction indeed that is immediate and therefore certain. Indeed, it is also only small, narrow minds that quite seriously fear death as their annihilation; those who are specially favoured with decided capacity are entirely remote from such terrors. Plato rightly founded the whole of philosophy on knowledge of the doctrine of Ideas, in other words, on the perception of the universal in the particular. But the conviction here described and arising directly out of the apprehension of nature must have been extremely lively in those sublime authors of the *Upanishads* of the *Vedas,* who can scarcely be conceived as mere human beings. For this conviction speaks to us so forcibly from an immense number of their utterances that we must ascribe this immediate illumination of their mind to the fact that, standing nearer to the origin of our race as regards time, these sages apprehended the inner essence of things more clearly and profoundly than the already enfeebled race, οἷοι νῦν βροτοί εἰσιν,[10] is capable of doing. But, of course, their comprehension was also assisted by the natural world of India, which is endowed with life in quite a different degree from that in which our northern world is. Thorough reflection, however, as carried through by Kant's great mind, also leads to just the same result by a different path; for it teaches us that our intellect, in which that rapidly changing phenomenal world exhibits itself,

---

[9] "Provincial dialect." [Tr.]

[10] "As mortals now are." [Tr.]

does not comprehend the true, ultimate essence of things, but merely its appearance or phenomenon; and indeed, as I add, because originally such an intellect is destined only to present motives to our will, in other words, to be serviceable to it in the pursuit of its paltry aims.

But let us continue still farther our objective and unprejudiced consideration of nature. If I kill an animal, be it a dog, a bird, a frog, or even only an insect, it is really inconceivable that this being, or rather the primary and original force by virtue of which such a marvellous phenomenon displayed itself only a moment before in its full energy and love of life, could through my wicked or thoughtless act have become nothing. Again, on the other hand, the millions of animals of every kind which come into existence at every moment in endless variety, full of force and drive, can never have been absolutely nothing before the act of their generation, and can never have arrived from nothing to an absolute beginning. If in this way I see one of these creatures withdraw from my sight without my ever knowing where it goes to, and another appear without my ever knowing where it comes from; moreover, if both still have the same form, the same inner nature, the same character, but not the same matter, which they nevertheless continue to throw off and renew during their existence; then of course the assumption that what vanishes and what appears in its place are one and the same thing, which has experienced only a slight change, a renewal of the form of its existence, and consequently that death is for the species what sleep is for the individual—this assumption, I say, is so close at hand, that it is impossible for it not to occur to us, unless our minds, perverted in early youth by the impression of false fundamental views, hurry it out of the way, even from afar, with superstitious fear. But the opposite assumption that an animal's birth is an arising out of nothing, and accordingly that its death is an absolute annihilation, and this with the further addition that man has also come into existence out of nothing, yet has an individual and endless future existence, and that indeed with consciousness, whereas the dog, the ape, and the elephant are annihilated by death—is really something against which the sound mind must revolt, and must declare to be absurd. If, as is often enough repeated, the comparison of a system's result with the utterances of common sense is supposed to be a touchstone of its truth, I wish that the adherents of that fundamental view, handed down by Descartes to the pre-Kantian eclectics, and indeed still prevalent even now among the great majority of cultured people in Europe, would once apply this touchstone here.

The genuine symbol of nature is universally and everywhere the circle, because it is the schema or form of recurrence; in fact, this is the most general form in nature. She carries it through in everything from the course of the constellations down to the death and birth of organic beings. In this way alone, in the restless stream of time and its content, a continued existence, i.e., a nature, becomes possible.

In autumn we observe the tiny world of insects, and see how one prepares its bed, in order to sleep the long, benumbing winter-sleep; another spins a cocoon, in order to hibernate as a chrysalis, and to awake in spring rejuvenated and perfected; finally, how most of them, intending to rest in the arms of death, carefully arrange a suitable place for depositing their eggs, in order one day to come forth from these renewed. This is nature's great doctrine of immortality, which tries to make it clear to us that there is no radical difference between sleep and death, but that the one endangers existence just as little as the other. The care with which the insect prepares a cell, or hole, or nest, deposits therein its egg, together with food for the larva that will emerge from it in the following spring, and then calmly dies, is just like the care with which a person in the evening lays out his clothes and his breakfast ready for the following morning, and then calmly goes to bed; and at bottom it could not take place at all, unless the insect that dies in autumn were in itself and according to its true essence just as identical with the insect hatched in spring as the person who lies down to sleep is with the one who gets up.

After these considerations, we now return to ourselves and our species; we then cast our glance forward far into the future, and try to picture to ourselves future generations with the millions of their individuals in the strange form of their customs and aspirations. But then we interpose with the question: Whence will all these come? Where are they now? Where is the abundant womb of that nothing which is pregnant with worlds, and which still conceals them, the coming generations? Would not the smiling and true answer to this be: Where else could they be but there where alone the real always was and will be, namely in the present and its content?—hence with you, the deluded questioner, who in this mistaking of his own true nature is like the leaf on the tree. Fading in the autumn and about to fall, this leaf grieves over its own extinction, and will not be consoled by looking forward to the fresh green which will clothe the tree in spring, but says as a lament: "I am not these! These are quite different leaves!" Oh, foolish leaf! Whither do you want to go? And whence are the others supposed to come? Where is the nothing, the abyss of which you fear? Know your own inner being, precisely that which is so filled with the thirst for existence; recognize it once more in the inner, mysterious, sprouting force of the tree. This force is always *one* and the same in all the generations of leaves, and it remains untouched by arising and passing away. And now

οἵη περ φύλλων γενεή, τοίη δὲ καὶ ἀνδρῶν
(*Qualis foliorum generatio, talis et hominum.*)[11]

Whether the fly now buzzing round me goes to sleep in the evening and buzzes again the following morning, or whether it dies in the evening and in spring another fly buzzes which has emerged from its egg, this in itself is the same thing. But then the knowledge that presents these as two fundamentally different things is not unconditioned, but relative, a knowledge of the phenomenon, not of the thing-in-itself. In the morning the fly exists again; it also exists again in the spring. For the fly what distinguishes the winter from the night? In Burdach's *Physiologie,* Vol. I, § 275, we read: "Up till ten o'clock in the morning no *Cercaria ephemera* (one of the infusoria) is yet to be seen (in the infusion), and at twelve the whole water swarms with them. In the evening they die, and the next morning new ones come into existence again. It was thus observed for six days in succession by Nitzsch."

Thus everything lingers only for a moment, and hurries on to death. The plant and the insect die at the end of the summer, the animal and man after a few years; death reaps unweariedly. But despite all this, in fact as if this were not the case at all, everything is always there and in its place, just as if everything were imperishable. The plant always flourishes and blooms, the insect hums, animal and man are there in evergreen youth, and every summer we again have before us the cherries that have already been a thousand times enjoyed. Nations also exist as immortal individuals, though sometimes they change their names. Even their actions, what they do and suffer, are always the same, though history always pretends to relate something different; for it is like the kaleidoscope, that shows us a new configuration at every turn, whereas really we always have the same thing before our eyes. Therefore, what forces itself on us more irresistibly than the thought that that arising and passing away do not concern the real essence of things, but that this remains untouched by them, hence is imperishable, consequently that each and every thing that *wills* to exist actually does exist continuously

---

[11] "As the leaves on the tree, so are the generations of human beings." [*Iliad,* vi, 146. Tr.]

and without end? Accordingly, at every given point of time all species of animals, from the gnat to the elephant, exist together complete. They have already renewed themselves many thousands of times, and withal have remained the same. They know nothing of others like them who have lived before them, or who will live after them; it is the species that always lives, and the individuals cheerfully exist in the consciousness of the imperishability of the species and their identity with it. The will-to-live manifests itself in an endless present, because this is the form of the life of the species, which therefore does not grow old, but remains always young. Death is for the species what sleep is for the individual, or winking for the eye; when the Indian gods appear in human form, they are recognized by their not winking. Just as at nightfall the world vanishes, yet does not for a moment cease to exist, so man and animal apparently pass away through death, yet their true inner being continues to exist just as undisturbed. Let us now picture to ourselves that alternation of birth and death in infinitely rapid vibrations, and we have before us the persistent and enduring objectification of the will, the permanent Ideas of beings, standing firm like the rainbow on the waterfall. This is temporal immortality. In consequence of this, in spite of thousands of years of death and decay, there is still nothing lost, no atom of matter, still less anything of the inner being exhibiting itself as nature. Accordingly we can at any moment cheerfully exclaim: "In spite of time, death, and decay, we are still all together!"

Perhaps an exception would have to be made of the man who should once have said from the bottom of his heart with regard to this game: "I no longer like it." But this is not yet the place to speak of that.

Attention, however, must indeed be drawn to the fact that the pangs of birth and the bitterness of death are the two constant conditions under which the will-to-live maintains itself in its objectification, in other words, our being-in-itself, untouched by the course of time and by the disappearance of generations, exists in an everlasting present, and enjoys the fruit of the affirmation of the will-to-live. This is analogous to our being able to remain awake during the day only on condition that we sleep every night; indeed, this is the commentary furnished by nature for an understanding of that difficult passage. For the suspension of the animal functions is sleep; that of the organic functions is death.

The substratum or filling out, the πλήρωμα or material of the *present,* is really the same through all time. The impossibility of directly recognizing this identity is just *time,* a form and limitation of our intellect. The fact that by virtue of it, for example, the future event does not as yet exist, rests on a delusion of which we become aware when the event has come to pass. The essential form of our intellect produces such a delusion, and this is explained and justified from the fact that the intellect has come forth from the hands of nature by no means for the purpose of comprehending the inner being of things, but merely for the purpose of comprehending motives, and hence to serve an individual and temporal phenomenon of will.*

If we comprehend the observations that concern us here, we shall also understand the true meaning of the paradoxical doctrine of the Eleatics, that there is no arising and passing away at all, but that the whole stands firm and immovable: Παρμενίδης καὶ Μέλισσος ἀνῄρουν γένεσιν καὶ φθοράν, διὰ τὸ νομίζειν τὸ πᾶν ἀκίνητον. (*Parmenides et Melissus ortum et interitum tollebant, quoniam nihil moveri putabant.* Stobaeus, *Eclogues,* I, 21.)[12] In the same way light is also thrown here on the fine passage of Empedocles, which Plutarch has preserved for us in the book *Adversus Coloten,* c. 12:

Νήπιοι· οὐ γάρ σφιν δολιχόφρονές εἰσι μέριμναι,
Οἳ δὴ γίνεσθαι πάρος οὐκ ἐὸν ἐλπίζουσι,
Ἤ τι καταθνῄσκειν καὶ ἐξόλλυσθαι ἁπάντη.
Οὐκ ἂν ἀνὴρ τοιαῦτα σοφὸς φρεσὶ μαντεύσαιτο,
Ὡς ὄφρα μέν τε βιῶσι (τὸ δὴ βίοτον καλέουσι),
Τόφρα μὲν οὖν εἰσίν, καὶ σφιν πάρα δεινὰ καὶ ἐσθλά,
Πρὶν δὲ πάγεν τε βροτοὶ, καὶ ἐπεὶ λύθεν, οὐδέν ἄρ' εἰσίν.
(*Stulta, et prolixas non admittentia curas*
Pectora: qui sperant, existere posse, quod ante
Non fuit, aut ullam rem pessum protinus ire;
Non animo prudens homo quod praesentiat ullus,
Dum vivunt [namque hoc vitaï nomine signant],

---

* There is only *one present,* and this always exists: for it is the sole form of actual existence. We must arrive at the insight that the *past* is not *in itself* different from the present, but is so only in our apprehension. This has *time* as its form, by virtue of which alone the present shows itself as different from the past. To make this insight easier, let us imagine all the events and scenes of human life, good and bad, fortunate and unfortunate, delightful and dreadful, which are presented to us successively in the course of time and variety of places, in the most motley multifariousness and succession, as existing *all at once and simultaneously* and for ever, in the *Nunc stans,* whereas only apparently now this now that exists; then we shall understand what the objectification of the will-to-live really means. Our pleasure in genre pictures is also due mainly to their fixing the fleeting scenes of life. The dogma of metempsychosis resulted from the feeling of the truth just expressed.

[12] Parmenides and Melissus denied arising and passing away, because they believed the universe to be immovable." [Tr.]

Sunt, et fortuna tum conflictantur utraque;
Ante ortum nihil est homo, nec post funera quidquam.)[13]

The very remarkable passage in Diderot's *Jacques le Fataliste,* which in its place is surprising, deserves just as much to be mentioned: *Un château immense, au frontispice duquel on lisait: "Je n'appartiens à personne, et j'appartiens à tout le monde: vous y étiez avant que d'y entrer, vous y serez encore, quand vous en sortirez."*[14]

Of course in *that* sense in which he arises out of nothing when he is begotten, man becomes nothing through death. But really to become so thoroughly acquainted with this nothing would be very interesting, for it requires only moderate discernment to see that this empirical nothing is by no means an absolute nothing, in other words, such as would be nothing in every sense. We are already led to this insight by the empirical observation that all the features and characteristics of the parents are found once again in their children, and have thus surmounted death. Of this, however, I shall speak in a special chapter.

There is no greater contrast than that between the ceaseless, irresistible flight of time carrying its whole content away with it, and the rigid immobility of what is actually existing, which is at all times one and the same; and if, from this point of view, we fix our really objective glance on the immediate events of life, the *Nunc stans* becomes clear and visible to us in the centre of the wheel of time. To the eye of a being who lived an incomparably longer life and took in at a single glance the human race in its whole duration, the constant alternation of birth and death would present itself merely as a continuous vibration. Accordingly, it would not occur to it at all to see in it a constantly new coming out of nothing and passing into nothing, but, just as to our glance the rapidly turning spark appears as a continuous circle, the rapidly vibrating spring as a permanent triangle, the vibrating cord as a spindle, so

---

[13] "Foolish and lacking far-sighted reflection are they
Who imagine there could arise what had not already been,
Or that it could pass away and become entirely nothing . . .
Never will such things occur to the sage,
That so long as we live—what is thus described as life—
Only for so long also are we subject to good and bad,
And that before birth and after death we are nothing." [Tr.]

[14] "An immense castle over the front entrance of which one read: 'I belong to no one, and I belong to all the world; you were in it before you entered it, and you will still be in it when you have gone out of it.'" [Tr.]

to its glance the species would appear as that which is and remains, birth and death as vibrations.

We shall have false notions about the indestructibility of our true nature through death, so long as we do not make up our minds to study it first of all in the animals, and claim for ourselves alone a class apart from them under the boastful name of immortality. But it is this presumption alone and the narrowness of view from which it proceeds, on account of which most people struggle so obstinately against recognizing the obvious truth that, essentially and in the main, we are the same as the animals; in fact that such people recoil at every hint of our relationship with these. Yet it is this denial of the truth which, more than anything else, bars to them the way to real knowledge of the indestructibility of our true nature. For if we seek anything on a wrong path, we have in so doing forsaken the right; and on the wrong path we shall never attain to anything in the end but belated disillusionment. Therefore, pursue truth straight away, not according to preconceived freaks and fancies, but guided by the hand of nature! First of all learn to recognize, when looking at every young animal, the never-ageing existence of the species, which, as a reflection of its own eternal youth, bestows on every new individual a temporal youth, and lets it step forth as new, as fresh, as if the world were of today. Ask yourself honestly whether the swallow of this year's spring is an entirely different one from the swallow of the first spring, and whether actually between the two the miracle of creation out of nothing has been renewed a million times, in order to work just as often into the hands of absolute annihilation. I know quite well that anyone would regard me as mad if I seriously assured him that the cat, playing just now in the yard, is still the same one that did the same jumps and tricks there three hundred years ago; but I also know that it is much more absurd to believe that the cat of today is through and through and fundamentally an entirely different one from that cat of three hundred years ago. We need only become sincerely and seriously engrossed in the contemplation of one of these higher vertebrates, in order to become distinctly conscious that this unfathomable inner being, taken as a whole as it exists, cannot possibly become nothing, and yet, on the other hand, we know its transitoriness. This rests on the fact that in this animal the eternity of its Idea (species) is distinctly marked in the finiteness of the individual. For in a certain sense it is of course true that in the individual we always have before us a different being, namely in the sense resting on the principle of sufficient reason, under which are also included time and space; these constitute the *principium individuationis*. But in another it is not true, namely in the sense in which reality belongs only to the permanent forms of things, to the Ideas, and which was so clearly evident to Plato that it became his fundamental thought, the centre of his philosophy; the comprehension of it became his criterion for the ability to philosophize generally.

Just as the spraying drops of the roaring waterfall change with lightning rapidity, while the rainbow, of which they are the supporter, remains immovably at rest, quite untouched by that restless change, so every Idea, i.e., every *species* of living beings remains entirely untouched by the constant change of its individuals. But it is the *Idea* or the species in which the will-to-live is really rooted and manifests itself; therefore the will is really concerned only in the continuance of the species. For example, the lions that are born and that die are like the drops of the waterfall; but *leonitas,* the Idea or form or shape of the lion, is like the unshaken and unmoved rainbow on the waterfall. Plato therefore attributed real and true being only to the *Ideas,* i.e., to the species; but to the individuals he attributed only a restless arising and passing away. From the deepest consciousness of his imperishable nature there also spring the confidence and serenity with which every animal and even every human individual move along light-heartedly amid a host of chances and hazards that may annihilate them at any moment, and moreover move straight on to death. Out of his eyes, however, there glances the peace of the species, which is unaffected and untouched by that destruction and extinction. Not even to man could this peace and calm be vouchsafed by uncertain and changing dogmas. As I have said, however, the sight of every animal teaches us that death is no obstacle to the kernel of life, the will in its manifestation. Yet what an unfathomable mystery lies in every animal! Look at the nearest one; look at your dog, and see how cheerfully and calmly he stands there! Many thousands of dogs have had to die before it was this dog's turn to live; but the death and extinction of those thousands have not affected the *Idea* of the dog. This Idea has not in the least been disturbed by all that dying. Therefore the dog stands there as fresh and endowed with original force as if this day were his first and none could be his last, and out of his eyes there shines the indestructible principle in him, the archaeus. Now what has died throughout those thousands of years? Not the dog; he stands there before us intact and unscratched; merely his shadow, his image or copy in our manner of knowing, which is bound to time. Yet how can we ever believe that that passes away which exists for ever and ever, and fills all time? The matter is, of course, explainable empirically, namely according as death destroyed the individuals, generation brought forth new ones. This empirical explanation, however, is only an apparent explanation; it puts one riddle in place of the other. Although a metaphysical understanding of the matter is not to be had so cheaply, it is nevertheless the only true and satisfactory one.

In his subjective method, Kant brought to light the great though negative truth that time cannot belong to the thing-in-itself, because it lies preformed in our apprehension. Now death is the temporal end of the temporal phenomenon; but as soon as we take away time, there is no longer any end at all, and the word has lost all meaning. But here, on the objective path, I am now trying to show the positive aspect of the matter, namely that the thing-in-itself remains untouched by time and by that which is possible only through time, that is, by arising and passing away, and that the phenomena in time could not have even that restless, fleeting existence that stands next to nothingness, unless there were in them a kernel of eternity. It is true that *eternity* is a concept having no perception as its basis; for this reason, it is also of merely negative content, and thus implies a timeless existence. *Time,* however, is a mere image of eternity, ὁ χρόνος εἰκὼν τοῦ αἰῶνος,[15] as Plotinus has it; and in just the same way, our temporal existence is the mere image of our true inner being. This must lie in eternity, just because time is only the form of our knowing; but by virtue of this form alone we know our own existence and that of all things as transitory, finite, and subject to annihilation.

In the second book I have explained that the adequate objectivity of the will as thing-in-itself is the (Platonic) *Idea* at each of its grades. Similarly in the third book I have shown that the Ideas of beings have as their correlative the pure subject of knowing, consequently that the knowledge of them appears only by way of exception and temporarily under specially favourable conditions. For individual knowledge, on the other hand, and hence in time, the *Idea* exhibits itself under the form of the *species,* and this is the Idea drawn apart by entering into time. The *species* is therefore the most immediate objectification of the thing-in-itself, i.e., of the will-to-live. Accordingly, the innermost being of every animal and of man also lies in the *species;* thus the will-to-live, which is so powerfully active, has its root in the species, not really in the individual. On the other hand, immediate consciousness is to be found only in the individual; therefore it imagines itself to be different from the species, and thus fears death. The will-to-live manifests itself in reference to the individual as hunger and fear of death; in reference to the species, as

---

[15] "Time is a copy or image of eternity." [Tr.]

sexual impulse and passionate care for the offspring. In agreement with this, we find nature, as being free from that delusion of the individual, just as careful for the maintenance of the species as she is indifferent to the destruction of the individuals; for her the latter are always only means, the former the end. Therefore, a glaring contrast appears between her niggardliness in the equipment of individuals and her lavishness when the species is at stake. From *one* individual often a hundred thousand seeds or more are obtained annually, for example, from trees, fish, crabs, termites, and many others. In the case of her niggardliness, on the other hand, only barely enough in the way of strength and organs is given to each to enable it with ceaseless exertion to maintain a bare living. If, therefore, an animal is crippled or weakened, it must, as a rule, die of starvation. And where an occasional economy was possible, through the circumstance that a part could be dispensed with in an emergency, it has been withheld, even out of order. Hence, for example, many caterpillars are without eyes; the poor animals grope about in the dark from leaf to leaf, and in the absence of antennae they do this by moving three quarters of their body to and fro in the air, till they come across an object. In this way they often miss their food that is to be found close at hand. But this happens in consequence of the *lex parsimoniae naturae,* to the expression of which, *natura nihil facit supervacaneum,* can still be added *et nihil largitur.*[16] The same tendency of nature shows itself also in the fact that the fitter an individual is for propagation by virtue of his age, the more powerfully does the *vis naturae medicatrix*[17] manifest itself in him. His wounds, therefore, heal easily, and he easily recovers from illnesses. This diminishes with the power of procreation, and sinks low after this power is extinguished; for in the eyes of nature the individual has now become worthless.

Now if we cast a glance at the scale of beings together with the gradation of consciousness that accompanies them, from the polyp to man, we see this wonderful pyramid kept in ceaseless oscillation certainly by the constant death of the individuals, yet enduring in the species throughout the endlessness of time by means of the bond of generation. Now, whereas, as was explained above, the *objective,* the species, manifests itself as indestructible, the *subjective,* consisting merely in the self-consciousness of these beings, seems to be of the shortest duration, and to be incessantly destroyed, in order just as often to come forth again out of nothing in an incompre-

---

[16] "Nature does nothing in vain and creates nothing superfluous; . . . and she gives away nothing." [Tr.]

[17] "The healing power of nature." [Tr.]

hensible way. But a man must really be very short-sighted to allow himself to be deceived by this appearance, and not to understand that, although the form of temporal permanence belongs only to the objective, the subjective—i.e., the *will,* living and appearing in everything, and with it the subject of *knowing* in which this exhibits itself—must be no less indestructible. For the permanence of the objective, or the external, can indeed be only the phenomenal appearance of the indestructibility of the subjective, or the internal, since the former cannot possess anything that it had not received in fee from the latter; it cannot be essentially and originally something objective, a phenomenon, and then secondarily and accidentally something subjective, a thing-in-itself, something conscious of itself. For obviously, the former as phenomenon or appearance presupposes something that appears, just as being-for-another presupposes being-for-self, and object presupposes subject; but not conversely, since everywhere the root of things must lie in that which they are by themselves, hence in the subjective, not in the objective, not in that which they are only for others, not in the consciousness of another. Accordingly we found in the first book that the correct starting-point for philosophy is essentially and necessarily the subjective, i.e., the idealistic, just as the opposite starting-point, proceeding from the objective, leads to materialism. Fundamentally, however, we are far more at one with the world than we usually think; its inner nature is our will, and its phenomenal appearance our representation. The difference between the continuance of the external world after his death and his own continuance after death would vanish for anyone who could bring this unity or identity of being to distinct consciousness; the two would present themselves to him as one and the same thing; in fact, he would laugh at the delusion that could separate them. For an understanding of the indestructibility of our true nature coincides with that of the identity of macrocosm and microcosm. Meanwhile we can elucidate what has here been said by a peculiar experiment that is to be carried out by means of the imagination, and might be called metaphysical. Let a person attempt to present vividly to his mind the time, not in any case very distant, when he will be dead. He then thinks himself away, and allows the world to go on existing; but soon, to his own astonishment, he will discover that nevertheless he still exists. For he imagined he made a mental representation of the world without himself; but the I or ego is in consciousness that which is immediate, by which the world is first brought about, and for which alone the world exists. This centre of all existence, this kernel of all reality, is to be abolished, and yet the world is to be allowed to go on existing; it is an idea that may, of course, be conceived in the abstract, but not realized. The endeavour to achieve this, the attempt to think the secondary without the primary, the conditioned without the condition, the supported without the supporter, fails every time, much in the same way as the attempt fails to conceive an equilateral right-angled triangle, or an arising and passing away of matter, and similar impossibilities. Instead of what was intended, the feeling here forces itself on us that the world is no less in us than we are in it, and that the source of all reality lies within ourselves. The result is really that the time when I shall not be will come objectively; but subjectively it can never come. Indeed, it might therefore be asked how far anyone in his heart actually believes in a thing that he cannot really conceive at all; or whether, since the deep consciousness of the indestructibility of our real inner nature is associated with that merely intellectual experiment that has, however, already been carried out more or less distinctly by everyone, whether, I say, our own death is not perhaps for us at bottom the most incredible thing in the world.

The deep conviction of the impossibility of our extermination by death, which, as the inevitable qualms of conscience at the approach of death also testify, everyone carries at the bottom of his heart, depends entirely on the consciousness of our original and eternal nature; therefore Spinoza expresses it thus: *sentimus experimurque nos AETERNOS esse.*[18] For a reasonable person can think of himself as imperishable only in so far as he thinks of himself as beginningless, as eternal, in fact as timeless. On the other hand, he who regards himself as having come out of nothing must also think that he becomes nothing again; for it is a monstrous idea that an infinity of time elapsed before he was, but that a second infinity has begun throughout which he will never cease to be. Actually the most solid ground for our imperishable nature is the old aphorism: *Ex nihilo nihil fit, et in nihilum nihil potest reverti.*[19] Therefore, Theophrastus Paracelsus (*Works,* Strasburg, 1603, Vol. II, p. 6) says very pertinently: "The soul in me has come from something, therefore it does not come to nothing; for it comes out of something." He states the true reason. But he who regards man's birth as his absolute beginning must regard death as his absolute end. For both are what they are in the same sense; consequently everyone can think of himself as *immortal* only in so far as he also thinks of himself as *unborn,* and in the same sense. What birth is, that also

---

[18] "We feel and experience that we are *eternal.*" [Tr.]

[19] "Nothing comes out of nothing, and nothing can again become nothing." [Tr.]

is death, according to its true nature and significance; it is the same line drawn in two directions. If the former is an actual arising out of nothing, the latter is also an actual annihilation. In truth, however, it is only by means of the *eternity* of our real inner nature that an imperishableness of it is conceivable; consequently such an imperishableness is not temporal. The assumption that man is created out of nothing necessarily leads to the assumption that death is his absolute end. In this respect, therefore, the Old Testament is quite consistent; for no doctrine of immortality is appropriate to a creation out of nothing. New Testament Christianity has such a doctrine, because it is Indian in spirit, and therefore, more than probably, Indian in origin, although only indirectly, through Egypt. Such a doctrine, however, is as little suited to the Jewish stem on which that Indian wisdom had to be grafted in the Holy Land as the freedom of the will is to the will's being created, or as

> *Humano capiti cerviçem pictor equinam*
> *Jungere si velit.*[20]

It is always bad if we are not allowed to be thoroughly original and to carve out of the whole wood. Brahmanism and Buddhism, on the other hand, quite consistently with a continued existence after death, have an existence before birth, and the purpose of this life is to atone for the guilt of that previous existence. The following passage from Colebrooke's *History of Indian Philosophy* in the *Transactions of the Asiatic London Society,* Vol. I, p. 577, shows also how clearly conscious they are of the necessary consistency in this: "Against the system of the Bhagavatas, which is but partially heretical, the objection upon which the chief stress is laid by Vyasa is, that the soul would not be eternal, if it were a production, and consequently had a beginning." Further, in Upham's *Doctrine of Buddhism,* p. 110, it is said: "The lot in hell of impious persons call'd Deitty is the most severe: these are they who, discrediting the evidence of Buddha, adhere to the heretical doctrine, that all living beings had their beginning in the mother's womb, and will have their end in death."

He who conceives his existence as merely accidental, must certainly be afraid of losing it through death. On the other hand he who sees, even only in a general way, that his existence rests on some original necessity, will not believe that this necessity, which has produced so wonderful a thing, is limited to such a brief span of time, but that it is active at all times. But whoever reflects that up till now, when he exists, an infinite time, and thus an infinity of changes, has

---

[20] "If a painter wanted to join a human head to the neck of a horse." [Horace, *Ars poetica*, 1.—Tr.]

run its course, but yet notwithstanding this he exists, will recognize his existence as a necessary one. Therefore the entire possibility of all states and conditions has exhausted itself already without being able to eliminate his existence. *If ever he could not be, he would already not be now.* For the infinity of the time that has already elapsed, with the exhausted possibility of its events in it, guarantees that what *exists necessarily exists.* Consequently, everyone has to conceive himself as a necessary being, in other words, as a being whose existence would follow from its true and exhaustive definition, if only we had this. Actually in this train of thought is to be found the only immanent proof of the imperishableness of our real inner nature, that is to say, the only proof that keeps within the sphere of empirical data. Existence must be inherent in this inner nature, since it shows itself to be independent of all states or conditions that can possibly be brought about through the causal chain; for these states have already done what they could, and yet our existence has remained just as unshaken thereby, as the ray of light is by the hurricane that it cuts through. If from its own resources time could bring us to a happy state, we should already have been there long ago; for an infinite time lies behind us. But likewise, if time could lead us to destruction, we should already long ago have ceased to exist. It follows from the fact that we now exist, if the matter is well considered, that we are bound to exist at all times. For we ourselves are the inner nature that time has taken up into itself, in order to fill up its void; therefore this inner nature fills the *whole* of time, present, past, and future, in the same way; and it is just as impossible for us to fall out of existence as it is for us to fall out of space. If we carefully consider this, it is inconceivable that what once exists in all the force of reality could ever become nothing, and then not exist throughout an infinite time. From this have arisen the Christian doctrine of the restoration of all things, the Hindu doctrine of the constantly renewed creation of the world by Brahma, together with similar dogmas of the Greek philosophers. The great mystery of our existence and non-existence, to explain which these and all kindred dogmas were devised, ultimately rests on the fact that the same thing that objectively constitutes an infinite course of time is subjectively a point, an indivisible, ever-present present-moment; but who comprehends it? It has been most clearly expounded by Kant in his immortal doctrine of the ideality of time and of the sole reality of the thing-in-itself. For it follows from this that what is really essential in things, in man, in the world, lies permanently and enduringly in the *Nunc stans,* firm and immovable; and that the change of phenomena and of events is a mere consequence of our apprehension of it by means of our perception-form of time. Accordingly, instead of saying to men: "Ye have arisen through birth, but are immortal," one should say: "Ye are not nothing," and teach them to understand this in the sense of the saying attributed to Hermes Trismegistus: Τὸ γὰρ ὂν ἀεὶ ἔσται. (*Quod enim est, erit semper.* Stobaeus, *Eclogues,* I, 43, 6.)[21] Yet if this does not succeed, but the anxious heart breaks out into its old lament: "I see all beings arise out of nothing through birth, and again after a brief term return to nothing; even my existence, now in the present, will soon lie in the remote past, and I shall be nothing!" then the right answer is: "Do you not exist? Do you not possess the precious present, to which you children of time all aspire so eagerly, actually at this moment? And do you understand how you have attained to it? Do you know the paths which have led you to it, that you could see them barred to you by death? An existence of yourself after the destruction of your body is not possibly conceivable to you; but can it be more inconceivable to you than are your present existence and the way you have attained to it? Why should you doubt that the secret paths that stood open to you up to this present, will not also stand open to you to every future present?"

Therefore, if considerations of this kind are certainly calculated to awaken the conviction that there is something in us that death cannot destroy, this nevertheless happens only by our being raised to a point of view from which birth is not the beginning of our existence. It follows from this, however, that what is proved to be indestructible through death is not really the individual. Moreover, having arisen through generation and carrying within himself the qualities of the father and mother, this individual exhibits himself as a mere difference of the species, and as such can be only finite. Accordingly, just as the individual has no recollection of his existence before his birth, so can he have no recollection of his present existence after death. Everyone, however, places his I or ego in *consciousness;* therefore this seems to him to be tied to individuality. Moreover, with individuality there disappears all that which is peculiar to him, as to this, and which distinguishes him from others. Therefore his continued existence without individuality becomes for him indistinguishable from the continuance of all other beings, and he sees his I or ego become submerged. Now he who thus links his existence to the identity of *consciousness,* and therefore desires for this an endless existence after death, should bear in mind that in any case he can attain to this only at the price of just as endless a past before birth. For as he has no recollection of an existence before birth, and so his consciousness begins with birth, he must look upon his birth as

---

[21] "For that which is must always be." [Tr.]

an arising of his existence out of nothing. But then he purchases the endless time of his existence after death for just as long a time before birth; in this way the account is balanced without any profit to him. On the other hand, if the existence left untouched by death is different from that of individual consciousness, then it must be independent of birth just as it is of death. Accordingly, with reference to it, it must be equally true to say "I shall always be" and "I have always been," which then gives us two infinities for one. However, the greatest equivocation really lies in the word "I," as will be seen at once by anyone who calls to mind the contents of our second book and the separation there carried out of the willing part of our true inner nature from the knowing part. According as I understand this word, I can say: "Death is my entire end"; or else: "This my personal phenomenal appearance is just as infinitely small a part of my true inner nature as I am of the world." But the I or ego is the dark point in consciousness, just as on the retina the precise point of entry of the optic nerve is blind, the brain itself is wholly insensible, the body of the sun is dark, and the eye sees everything except itself. Our faculty of knowledge is directed entirely *outwards* in accordance with the fact that it is the product of a brain-function that has arisen for the purpose of mere self-maintenance, and hence for the search for nourishment and the seizing of prey. Therefore everyone knows of himself only as of this individual, just as it exhibits itself in external perception. If, on the other hand, he could bring to consciousness what he is besides and beyond this, he would willingly give up his individuality, smile at the tenacity of his attachment thereto, and say: "What does the loss of this individuality matter to me? for I carry within myself the possibility of innumerable individualities." He would see that, although there is not in store for him a continued existence of his individuality, it is nevertheless just as good as if he had such an existence, since he carries within himself a complete compensation for it. Besides this, however, it might also be taken into consideration that the individuality of most people is so wretched and worthless that they actually lose nothing in it, and that what in them may still have some value is the universal human element; but to this we can promise imperishableness. In fact, even the rigid unalterability and essential limitation of every individuality as such would, in the case of its endless duration, inevitably and necessarily produce ultimately such great weariness by its monotony, that we should prefer to become nothing, merely in order to be relieved of it. To desire immortality for the individual is really the same as wanting to perpetuate an error for ever; for at bottom every individuality is really only a special error, a false step, something that it would be better should not be, in fact something from which it is the real purpose of life to bring us back. This also finds confirmation in the fact that most, indeed really all, people are so constituted that they could not be happy, no matter in what world they might be placed. Insofar as such a world would exclude want and hardship, they would become a prey to boredom, and insofar as this was prevented, they would fall into misery, vexation, and suffering. Thus, for a blissful condition of man, it would not be by any means sufficient for him to be transferred to a "better world"; on the contrary, it would also be necessary for a fundamental change to occur in man himself, and hence for him to be no longer what he is, but rather to become what he is not. For this, however, he must first of all cease to be what he is; as a preliminary, this requirement is fulfilled by death, and the moral necessity of this can from this point of view already be seen. To be transferred to another world and to change one's entire nature are at bottom one and the same thing. On this also ultimately rests that dependence of the objective on the subjective which is explained by the idealism of our first book; accordingly, here is to be found the point of contact between transcendental philosophy and ethics. If we bear this in mind, we shall find that the awakening from the dream of life is possible only through the disappearance along with it of its whole fundamental fabric as well; but this is its organ itself, the intellect together with its forms. With this the dream would go on spinning itself for ever, so firmly is it incorporated with that organ. That which really dreamt the dream is, however, still different from it, and alone remains over. On the other hand, the fear that with death everything might be over and finished may be compared to the case of a person who in a dream should think that there were mere dreams without a dreamer. But would it even be desirable for an individual consciousness to be kindled again, after it had once been ended by death, in order that it might continue for ever? For the most part, often in fact entirely, its content is nothing but a stream of paltry, earthly, poor ideas, and endless worries and anxieties; let these then be finally silenced! Therefore with true instinct the ancients put on their tombstones: *Securitati perpetuae;* or *Bonae quieti.*[22] But if even here, as has happened so often, we wanted continued existence of the individual consciousness, in order to connect with it a reward or punishment in the next world, then at bottom the aim would be merely the compatibility of virtue with egoism. But these two will never embrace; they are fundamentally opposed. On the other hand, the immediate conviction, which the sight of noble actions calls forth, is well founded, that the spirit of love enjoining one man to spare

---

[22] "To eternal security; . . . to good repose." [Tr.]

his enemies, and another, even at the risk of his life, to befriend a person never previously seen, can never pass away and become nothing.

The most complete answer to the question of the individual's continued existence after death is to be found in Kant's great doctrine of the *ideality of time*. Just here does this doctrine show itself to be specially fruitful and rich in important results, since it replaces dogmas, which lead to the absurd on the one path as on the other, by a wholly theoretical but well proved insight, and thus at once settles the most exciting of all metaphysical questions. To begin, to end, and to continue are concepts that derive their significance simply and solely from time; consequently they are valid only on the presupposition of time. But time has no absolute existence; it is not the mode and manner of the being-in-itself of things, but merely the form of our *knowledge* of the existence and inner being of ourselves and of all things; and for this reason such knowledge is very imperfect, and is limited to mere phenomena. Thus in reference to this knowledge alone do the concepts of ceasing and continuing find application, not in reference to that which manifests itself in them, namely the being-in-itself of things; applied to this, such concepts therefore no longer have any true meaning. For this is also seen in the fact that an answer to the question arising from those time-concepts becomes impossible, and every assertion of such an answer, whether on the one side or the other, is open to convincing objections. We might indeed assert that our being-in-itself continues after death, because it would be wrong to say that it was destroyed; but we might just as well assert that it is destroyed, because it would be wrong to say that it continues; at bottom, the one is just as true as the other. Accordingly, something like an antinomy could certainly be set up here, but it would rest on mere negations. In it one would deprive the subject of the judgement of two contradictorily opposite predicates, but only because the whole category of these predicates would not be applicable to that subject. But if one deprives it of those two predicates, not together but separately, it appears as if the contradictory opposite of the predicate, denied in each case, were thus proved of the subject of the judgement. This, however, is due to the fact that incommensurable quantities are here compared, inasmuch as the problem removes us to a scene that abolishes time, but yet asks about time-determinations. Consequently, it is equally false to attribute these to the subject and to deny them, which is equivalent to saying that the problem is transcendent. In this sense death remains a mystery.

On the other hand, adhering to that very distinction between phenomenon and thing-in-itself, we can make the assertion that man as phenomenon is certainly perishable, yet his true inner being is not affected by this. Hence this true inner being is indestructible, although, on account of the elimination of the time-concepts which is connected with this, we cannot attribute continuance to it. Accordingly, we should be led here to the concept of an indestructibility that was nevertheless not a continuance. Now this concept is one which, obtained on the path of abstraction, may possibly be thought in the abstract; yet it cannot be supported by any perception; consequently, it cannot really become distinct. On the other hand, we must here keep in mind that we have not, like Kant, absolutely given up the ability to know the thing-in-itself; on the contrary, we know that it is to be looked for in the will. It is true that we have never asserted an absolute and exhaustive knowledge of the thing-in-itself; indeed, we have seen quite well that it is impossible to know anything according to what it may be absolutely in and by itself. For as soon as I *know,* I have a representation, a mental picture; but just because this representation is mine, it cannot be identical with what is known; on the contrary, it reproduces in an entirely different form that which is known by making it a being-for-others out of a being-for-self; hence it is still always to be regarded as the *phenomenal appearance* of this. However, therefore, a *knowing* consciousness may be constituted, there can always be for it only phenomena. This is not entirely obviated even by the fact that my own inner being is that which is known; for, in so far as it falls within my *knowing* consciousness, it is already a reflex of my inner being, something different from this inner being itself, and so already in a certain degree phenomenon. Thus, in so far as I am that which knows, I have even in my own inner being really only a phenomenon; on the other hand, in so far as I am directly this inner being itself, I am not that which knows. For it is sufficiently proved in the second book that knowledge is only a secondary property of our inner being, and is brought about through the animal nature of this. Strictly speaking, therefore, we know even our own will always only as phenomenon, and not according to what it may be absolutely in and by itself. But in that second book, as well as in my work *On the Will in Nature,* it is fully discussed and demonstrated that if, in order to penetrate into the essence of things, we leave what is given only indirectly and from outside, and stick to the only phenomenon into whose inner nature an immediate insight is accessible to us from within, we quite definitely find in this the will as the ultimate thing and the kernel of reality. In the will, therefore, we recognize the thing-in-itself in so far as it no longer has space, but time for its form; consequently, we really know it only in its most immediate manifestation, and thus with the reservation that this knowledge of it is still not exhaustive and entirely adequate. In this sense, therefore, we here retain the concept of the will as that of the thing-in-itself.

The concept of ceasing to be is certainly applicable to man as phenomenon in time, and empirical knowledge plainly presents death as the end of this temporal existence. The end of the person is just as real as was its beginning, and in just that sense in which we did not exist before birth, shall we no longer exist after death. But no more can be abolished through death than was produced through birth; and so that cannot be abolished by which birth first of all became possible. In this sense *natus et denatus*[23] is a fine expression. Now the whole of empirical knowledge affords us mere phenomena; thus only phenomena are affected by the temporal processes of arising and passing away, not that which appears, namely the being-in-itself. For this inner being the contrast, conditioned by the brain, between arising and passing away, does not exist at all; on the contrary, it has lost meaning and significance. This inner being, therefore, remains unaffected by the temporal end of a temporal phenomenon, and always retains that existence to which the concepts of beginning, end, and continuance are not applicable. But in so far as we can follow up this inner being, it is in every phenomenal being its will; so too in man. Consciousness, on the other hand, consists in knowledge; but this, as has been sufficiently demonstrated, belongs, as activity of the brain, and consequently as function of the organism, to the mere phenomenon, and therefore ends therewith. The will alone, of which the work or rather the copy was the body, is what is indestructible. The sharp distinction between will and knowledge, together with the former's primacy, a distinction that constitutes the fundamental characteristic of my philosophy, is therefore the only key to the contradiction that shows itself in many different ways, and always arises afresh in every consciousness, even the crudest. This contradiction is that death is our end, and yet we must be eternal and indestructible; hence it is the *sentimus, experimurque nos aeternos esse* of Spinoza.[24] All philosophers have made the mistake of placing that which is metaphysical, indestructible, and eternal in man in the *intellect*. It lies exclusively in the *will,* which is entirely different from the intellect, and alone is original. As was most thoroughly explained in the second book, the intellect is a secondary phenomenon, and is conditioned by the brain, and therefore begins and ends with this. The will alone is that which conditions, the kernel of the

---

[23] "Born and unborn." [Tr.]
[24] "We feel and experience that we are eternal." [Tr.]

whole phenomenon; consequently, it is free from the forms of the phenomenon, one of which is time, and hence it is also indestructible. Accordingly, with death consciousness is certainly lost, but not what produced and maintained consciousness; life is extinguished, but with it not the principle of life which manifested itself in it. Therefore a sure and certain feeling says to everyone that there is in him something positively imperishable and indestructible. Even the freshness and vividness of recollections from earliest times, from early childhood, are evidence that something in us does not pass away with time, does not grow old, but endures unchanged. However, we were not able to see clearly what this imperishable element is. It is not consciousness any more than it is the body, on which consciousness obviously depends. On the contrary, it is that on which the body together with consciousness depends. It is, however, just that which, by entering into consciousness, exhibits itself as *will*. Of course, we cannot go beyond this most immediate phenomenal appearance of it, because we cannot go beyond consciousness. Therefore the question what that something may be in so far as it does *not* enter into consciousness, in other words, what it is absolutely in itself, remains unanswerable.

In the phenomenon, and by means of its forms time and space, as *principium individuationis,* it is thus evident that the human individual perishes, whereas the human race remains and continues to live. But in the being-in-itself of things which is free from these forms, the whole difference between the individual and the race is also abolished, and the two are immediately one. The entire will-to-live is in the individual, as it is in the race, and thus the continuance of the species is merely the image of the individual's indestructibility.

Now, since the infinitely important understanding of the indestructibility of our true nature by death rests entirely on the difference between phenomenon and thing-in-itself, I wish to put this very difference in the clearest light by elucidating it in the opposite of death, hence in the origin of animal beings, i.e., in *generation.* For this process, that is just as mysterious as death, places most directly before our eyes the fundamental contrast between phenomenon and the being-in-itself of things, i.e., between the world as representation and the world as will, and also shows us the entire heterogeneity of the laws of these two. The act of procreation thus presents itself to us in a twofold manner: firstly for self-consciousness, whose sole object is, as I have often shown, the will with all its affections; and secondly for the consciousness of other things, i.e., of the world of the representation, or the empirical reality of things. Now from the side of the will, and thus inwardly, subjectively, for self-consciousness, that act manifests itself as the most immediate and complete satisfaction of the will, i.e., as sensual pleasure. On the other hand, from the side of the representation, and thus outwardly, objectively, for the consciousness of other things, this act is just the woof of the most ingenious of all fabrics, the foundation of the inexpressibly complicated animal organism which then needs only development in order to become visible to our astonished eyes. This organism, whose infinite complication and perfection are known only to the student of anatomy, is not to be conceived and thought of, from the side of the representation, as other than a system, devised with the most carefully planned combination and carried out with the most consummate skill and precision, the most arduous work of the profoundest deliberation. Now from the side of the will, we know through self-consciousness that the production of the organism is the result of an act the very opposite of all reflection and deliberation, of an impetuous, blind craving, an exceedingly voluptuous sensation. This contrast is exactly akin to the infinite contrast, shown above, between the absolute facility with which nature produces her works, together with the correspondingly boundless carelessness with which she abandons such works to destruction—and the incalculably ingenious and well-thought-out construction of these very works. To judge from these, it must have been infinitely difficult to make them, and therefore to provide for their maintenance with every conceivable care, whereas we have the very opposite before our eyes. Now if, by this naturally very unusual consideration, we have brought together in the sharpest manner the two heterogeneous sides of the world, and so to speak grasped them with one hand, we must now hold them firmly, in order to convince ourselves of the entire invalidity of the laws of the phenomenon, or of the world as representation, for that of the will, or of things-in-themselves. It will then become clearer to us that whereas, on the side of the representation, i.e., in the phenomenal world, there is exhibited to us first an arising out of nothing, then a complete annihilation of what has arisen, from that other side, or in itself, there lies before us an essence or entity, and when the concepts of arising and passing away are applied to it, they have absolutely no meaning. For by going back to the root, where, by means of self-consciousness, the phenomenon and the being-in-itself meet, we have just palpably apprehended, as it were, that the two are absolutely incommensurable. The whole mode of being of the one, together with all the fundamental laws of this being, signifies nothing, and less than nothing, in the other. I believe that this last consideration will be rightly understood only by a few, and that it will be unpleasant and even offensive to all who do not understand it. However, I shall never on this account omit anything that can serve to illustrate my fundamental idea.

At the beginning of this chapter I explained that the great attachment to life, or rather the fear of death, by no means springs from *knowledge*, for in that case it would be the result of the known value of life, but that that fear of death has its root directly in the *will*; it proceeds from the will's original and essential nature, in which that will is entirely without knowledge, and is therefore the blind will-to-live. Just as we are allured into life by the wholly illusory inclination for sensual pleasure, so are we firmly retained in life by the fear of death, certainly just as illusory. Both spring directly from the will that is in itself without knowledge. On the other hand, if man were a merely *knowing* being, death would necessarily be not only a matter of indifference, but even welcome to him. Now the consideration we have reached here teaches us that what is affected by death is merely the *knowing* consciousness; that the *will*, on the other hand, in so far as it is the thing-in-itself that lies at the root of every individual phenomenon, is free from everything that depends on determinations of time, and so is imperishable. Its striving for existence and manifestation, from which the world results, is always satisfied, for it is accompanied by this world just as the body is by the shadow, since the world is merely the visibility of the true inner nature of the will. Nevertheless, the will in us fears death, and this is because knowledge presents to this will its true nature merely in the individual phenomenon. From this there arises for the will the illusion that it perishes with this phenomenon, just as when the mirror is smashed my image in it seems to be destroyed at the same time. Therefore this fills the will with horror, because it is contrary to its original nature, which is a blind craving for existence. It follows from this that that in us which alone is capable of fearing death, and also alone fears it, namely the *will*, is not affected by it; and that, on the other hand, what is affected by it and actually perishes is that which, by its nature, is not capable of any fear, and generally of any desire or emotion, and is therefore indifferent to existence and non-existence. I refer to the mere subject of knowledge, the intellect, the existence of which consists in its relation to the world of the representation, in other words the objective world; it is the correlative of this objective world, with whose existence its own existence is at bottom identical. Thus, although the individual consciousness does not survive death, that survives it which alone struggles against it, the will. From this is also explained the contradiction that, from the standpoint of knowledge, philosophers have at all times with cogent arguments shown death to be no evil; yet the fear of death remains impervious to them all, simply because it is rooted not in knowledge, but in the will alone. Just because the will alone, not the intellect, is the indestructible element, it follows that all religions and philosophies promise a reward in eternity only to the virtues of the will or heart, not to those of the intellect or head.

The following may also serve to illustrate this consideration. The will, which constitutes our being-in-itself, is of a simple nature; it merely wills and does not know. The subject of knowing, on the other hand, is a secondary phenomenon, arising out of the objectification of the will; it is the point of unity of the nervous system's sensibility, the focus, as it were, in which the rays of activity of all parts of the brain converge. Therefore with this brain the subject of knowing is bound to perish. In self-consciousness, as that which alone knows, the subject of knowing stands facing the will as a spectator, and although it has sprung from the will, it knows that will as something different from itself, something foreign to it, and thus only empirically, in time, piecemeal, in the successive agitations and acts of the will; only *a posteriori* and often very indirectly does it come to know the will's decisions. This is why our own inner being is a riddle to us, in other words, to our intellect, and why the individual regards himself as newly arisen and as perishable, although his inner being-in-itself is something timeless, and therefore eternal. Now just as the *will* does not *know,* so, conversely, the intellect, or the subject of knowledge, is simply and solely *knowing,* without ever willing. This can be proved even physically from the fact that, as already mentioned in the second book, the various emotions, according to Bichat, directly affect all parts of the organism and disturb their functions, with the exception of the brain as that which can be affected by them at most indirectly, in other words, in consequence of those very disturbances (*De la vie et de la mort,* art. 6, § 2). Yet it follows from this that the subject of knowing, by itself and as such, cannot take any part or interest in anything, but that the existence or non-existence of everything, in fact even of itself, is a matter of indifference to it. Now why should this indifferent being be immortal? It ends with the temporal phenomenon of the will, i.e., with the individual, just as it originated therewith. It is the lantern that after it has served its purpose is extinguished. The intellect, like the world of perception which exists in it alone, is mere phenomenon; but the finiteness of both does not affect that of which they are the phenomenal appearance. The intellect is the function of the cerebral nervous system; but this, like the rest of the body, is the objectivity of the *will.* The intellect, therefore, depends on the somatic life of the organism; but this organism itself depends on the will. Thus, in a certain sense, the organic body can be regarded as the link between the will and the intellect; although, properly speaking, the body is only the will itself spatially exhibiting itself in the perception of the intellect. Death and birth are the constant renewal and revival of the will's consciousness. In itself this will is endless and beginningless; it alone is, so to speak, the substance of existence (every such renewal, however, brings a new possibility of the denial of the will-to-live). Consciousness is the life of the subject of knowing, or of the brain, and death is its end. Therefore consciousness is finite, is always new, beginning each time at the beginning. The *will* alone is permanent; but permanence also concerns it alone, for it is the will-to-live. Nothing is of any consequence to the knowing subject by itself; yet the will and the knowing subject are united in the I or ego. In every animal being the will has achieved an intellect, and this is the light by which the will here pursues its ends. Incidentally, the fear of death may also be due partly to the fact that the individual will is so reluctant to separate itself from the intellect that has fallen to its lot through the course of nature, from its guide and guard, without which it knows that it is helpless and blind.

Finally, this explanation agrees also with that daily moral experience, teaching us that the will alone is real, while its objects, on the other hand, as conditioned by knowledge, are only phenomena, mere froth and vapour, like the wine provided by Mephistopheles in Auerbach's cellar; thus after every pleasure of the senses we say; "And yet it seemed as I were drinking wine." [25]

The terrors of death rest for the most part on the false illusion that then the I or ego vanishes, and the world remains. But rather is the opposite true, namely that the world vanishes; on the other hand, the innermost kernel of the ego endures, the bearer and producer of that subject in whose representation alone the world had its existence. With the brain the intellect perishes, and with the intellect the objective world, this intellect's mere representation. The fact that in other brains a similar world lives and moves, now as before, is a matter of indifference with reference to the intellect that is perishing. If, therefore, reality proper did not lie in the *will,* and if the *moral* existence were not that which extended beyond death, then, as the intellect and with it its world are extinguished, the true essence of things generally would be nothing more than an endless succession of short and troubled dreams without connexion among themselves; for the permanence of nature-without-knowledge consists merely in the time-representation of nature that knows. Therefore a world-

---

[25] Goethe's *Faust,* Bayard Taylor's translation. [Tr.]

spirit, dreaming without aim or purpose dreams that are often heavy and troubled, would then be all in all.

When an individual experiences the dread of death, we really have the strange, and even ludicrous, spectacle of the lord of the worlds, who fills everything with his true nature, and through whom alone everything that is has its existence, in despair and afraid of perishing, of sinking into the abyss of eternal nothingness; whereas, in truth, everything is full of him, and there is no place where he would not be, no being in whom he would not live, for existence does not support him, but he existence. Yet it is he who despairs in the individual who suffers the dread of death, since he is exposed to the illusion, produced by the *principium individuationis,* that his existence is limited to the being that is now dying. This illusion is part of the heavy dream into which he, as will-to-live, has fallen. However, we might say to the dying individual: "You are ceasing to be something which you would have done better never to become."

As long as no denial of that will has taken place, that of us which is left over by death is the seed and kernel of quite another existence, in which a new individual finds himself again so fresh and original, that he broods over himself in astonishment. Hence the enthusiastic, visionary, and dreamy disposition of noble youths at the time when this fresh consciousness has just been fully developed. What sleep is for the individual, death is for the will as thing-in-itself. It could not bear to continue throughout endless time the same actions and sufferings without true gain, if memory and individuality were left to it. It throws them off; this is Lethe; and through this sleep of death it reappears as a new being, refreshed and equipped with another intellect; "A new day beckons to a newer shore!" [26]

As the self-affirming will-to-live, man has the root of his existence in the species. Accordingly, death is the losing of one individuality and the receiving of another, and consequently a changing of the individuality under the exclusive guidance of his own will. For in this alone lies the eternal force which was able to produce his existence with his ego, yet, on account of the nature of this ego, is unable to maintain it in existence. For death is the *démenti* that the essence (*essentia*) of everyone receives in its claim to existence (*existentia*), the appearance of a contradiction lying in every individual existence:

> for all things, from the Void
> Called forth, deserve to be destroyed.[26]

Yet an infinite number of just such existences, each with its ego, stands within reach of the same force, that is, of the will, but these

---

[26] Goethe's *Faust,* Bayard Taylor's translation. [Tr.]

again will be just as perishable and transitory. Now as every ego has its separate consciousness, that infinite number of them, in respect of such an ego, is not different from a single one. From this point of view, it does not appear to me accidental that *aevum,* αἰών, signifies both the individual term of life and infinite time; thus it may be seen from this point, though indistinctly, that ultimately and in themselves both are the same. According to this it would really make no difference whether I existed only through my term of life or throughout an infinite time.

But of course we cannot obtain a notion of all that has been said above entirely without time-concepts; yet these should be excluded when we are dealing with the thing-in-itself. But it is one of the unalterable limitations of our intellect that it can never entirely cast off this first and most immediate form of all its representations, in order to operate without it. Therefore we naturally come here on a kind of metempsychosis, though with the important difference that this does not affect the whole ψυχή, and hence the *knowing* being, but the *will* alone, whereby so many absurdities that accompany the doctrine of metempsychosis disappear; and with the consciousness that the form of time here appears only as an unavoidable accommodation to the limitation of our intellect. If we now call in the assistance of the fact, to be discussed in chapter 43, that the character, i.e., the will, is inherited from the father, whereas the intellect comes from the mother, then this agrees very well with our view that the will of man, in itself individual, separates itself in death from the intellect that was obtained from the mother at procreation, and receives a new intellect in accordance with its now modified nature under the guidance of the absolutely necessary course of the world which harmonizes with this nature. With this new intellect, the will would become a new being that would have no recollection of a previous existence; for the intellect, alone having the faculty of recollection, is the mortal part or the form, whereas the will is the eternal part, the substance. Accordingly, the word palingenesis is more correct than metempsychosis for describing this doctrine. These constant rebirths then constitute the succession of the life-dreams of a will in itself indestructible, until, instructed and improved by so much and such varied and successive knowledge in a constantly new form, it would abolish itself.

The proper and, so to speak, esoteric doctrine of Buddhism, as we have come to know it through the most recent researches, also agrees with this view, since it teaches not metempsychosis, but a peculiar palingenesis resting on a moral basis, and it expounds and explains this with great depth of thought. This may be seen from the exposition of the subject, well worth reading and considering, given in Spence Hardy's *Manual of Buddhism,* pp. 394-96 (with which are to be compared pp. 429, 440, and 445 of the same book). Confirmations of it are to be found in Taylor's *Prabodha Chandro Daya,* London, 1812, p. 35; also in Sangermano's *Burmese Empire,* p. 6, as well as in the *Asiatic Researches,* Vol. VI, p. 179, and Vol. IX, p. 256. The very useful German compendium of Buddhism by Köppen is also right on this point. Yet for the great mass of Buddhists this doctrine is too subtle; and so plain metempsychosis is preached to them as a comprehensible substitute.

Moreover, it must not be overlooked that even empirical grounds support a palingenesis of this kind. As a matter of fact, there does exist a connexion between the birth of the newly appearing beings and the death of those who are decrepit and worn out. It shows itself in the great fertility of the human race, arising as the result of devastating epidemics. When, in the fourteenth century, the Black Death had for the most part depopulated the Old World, a quite abnormal fertility appeared among the human race, and twin births were very frequent. Most remarkable also was the circumstance that none of the children born at this time acquired all their teeth; thus nature, exerting herself to the utmost, was niggardly in details. This is stated by F. Schnurrer in the *Chronik der Seuchen* (1825). Casper, *Die wahrscheinliche Lebensdauer des Menschen* (1835), also confirms the principle that, in a given population, the number of procreations has the most decided influence on the duration of life and on mortality, as it always keeps pace with the mortality; so that, everywhere and at all times, the births and deaths increase and decrease in equal ratio. This he places beyond doubt by accumulated evidence from many countries and their different provinces. And yet there cannot possibly be a *physical* causal connexion between my previous death and the fertility of a couple who are strangers to me, or *vice versa.* Here, then, the metaphysical appears undeniably and in an astonishing way as the immediate ground of explanation of the physical. Every new-born being comes fresh and blithe into the new existence, and enjoys it as a gift; but nothing is or can be freely given. Its fresh existence is paid for by the old age and death of a worn-out and decrepit existence which has perished, but which contained the indestructible seed. Out of this seed the new existence arose; the two existences are *one* being. To show the bridge between the two would, of course, be the solution to a great riddle.

The great truth here expressed has never been entirely overlooked, although it could not be reduced to its precise and correct meaning. This becomes possible only through the doctrine of the primacy and metaphysical nature of the will and the secondary, merely organic, nature of the intellect. Thus we find the doctrine of metempsychosis, springing from the very earliest and noblest ages of the human race, always world-wide, as the belief of the great majority of mankind, in fact really as the doctrine of all religions, with the exception of Judaism and the two religions that have arisen from it. But, as already mentioned, we find this doctrine in its subtlest form, and coming nearest to the truth, in Buddhism. Accordingly, while Christians console themselves with the thought of meeting again in another world, in which they regain their complete personality and at once recognize one another, in those other religions the meeting is going on already, though incognito. Thus, in the round of births, and by virtue of metempsychosis or palingenesis, the persons who now stand in close connexion or contact with us will also be born simultaneously with us at the next birth, and will have the same, or analogous, relations and sentiments towards us as they now have, whether these are of a friendly or hostile nature. (See, for example, Spence Hardy's *Manual of Buddhism*, p. 162.) Of course, recognition is limited here to an obscure inkling, a reminiscence which is not to be brought to distinct consciousness, and which points to an infinite remoteness; with the exception, however, of the Buddha himself. He has the prerogative of distinctly knowing his own previous births and those of others; this is described in the *Jatakas*. But, in fact, if at favourable moments we look at the doings and dealings of men in real life in a purely objective way, the intuitive conviction is forced on us that they not only are and remain the same according to the (Platonic) Ideas, but also that the present generation, according to its real kernel, is precisely and substantially identical with every generation that previously existed. The question is only in what this kernel consists; the answer given to it by my teaching is well known. The above-mentioned intuitive conviction can be conceived as arising from the fact that the multiplying glasses, time and space, for a moment lose their effectiveness. With regard to the universal nature of the belief in metempsychosis, Obry rightly says in his excellent book *Du Nirvana indien*, p. 13: *Cette vieille croyance a fait le tour du monde, et était tellement répandue dans la haute antiquité, qu'un docte Anglican l'avait jugée sans père, sans mère, et sans généalogie*[27] (T. Burnet, in Beausobre, *Histoire du Manichéisme*, II, p. 391).

[27] "This old belief has journeyed round the world, and was so widespread in ancient times that a learned follower of the Anglican Church judged it to be without father, without mother, without genealogy." [Tr.]

Taught already in the *Vedas,* as in all the sacred books of India, metempsychosis is well known to be the kernel of Brahmanism and Buddhism. Accordingly it prevails even now in the whole of non-Mohammedan Asia, and thus among more than half of the human race, as the firmest of convictions, with an incredibly strong practical influence. It was also the belief of the Egyptians (Herodotus, ii, 123), from whom it was received with enthusiasm by Orpheus, Pythagoras, and Plato; the Pythagoreans in particular held firmly to it. That it was taught also in the mysteries of the Greeks follows undeniably from the ninth book of Plato's *Laws* (pp. 38 and 42, *ed. Bip.*). Nemesius even says (*De natura hominum,* c. 2): Κοινῇ μὲν οὖν πάντες Ἕλληνες, οἱ τὴν ψυχὴν ἀθάνατον ἀποφηνάμενοι, τὴν μετενσωμάτωσιν δογματίζουσι. (*Communiter igitur omnes Graeci, qui animam immortalem statuerunt, eam de uno corpore in aliud transferri censuerunt.*)[28] The *Edda,* particularly in the *Völuspá,* also teaches metempsychosis. No less was it the foundation of the religion of the Druids (Caesar, *De Bello Gallico,* vi. A. Pictet, *Le Mystère des Bardes de l'île de Bretagne,* 1856). Even a Mohammedan sect in India, the Bohrahs, of whom Colebrooke gives a detailed account in the *Asiatic Researches,* Vol. VII, pp. 336 *seqq.,* believe in metempsychosis, and accordingly abstain from all animal food. Among American Indians and Negro tribes, indeed even among the natives of Australia, traces of this belief are found, as appears from an exact description, given in *The Times* of 29 January 1841, of the execution of two Australian savages for arson and murder. It says: "The younger of the 2 prisoners met his end with a dogged and determinate spirit, as it appear'd of revenge; the only intelligible expression he made use of conveyed an impression that he would rise up 'a white fellow,' which, it was considered, strengthened his resolution." In a book by Ungewitter, *Der Welttheil Australien* (1853), it is related also that the Papuans of New Holland regarded the whites as their own relations who had returned to the world. As the result of all this, belief in metempsychosis presents itself as the natural conviction of man whenever he reflects at all in an unprejudiced way. Accordingly, it would actually be that which Kant falsely asserts of his three pretended Ideas of reason, namely a philosopheme natural to human reason, and resulting from the forms of that faculty; and where this belief is not found, it would only be supplanted by positive religious doctrines coming from a different source. I have also noticed that it is at once obvious to everyone who hears of it for the first time. Just see how seriously even Lessing defends it in the last seven

---

[28] "Belief in a wandering from one body to another is common to all the Greeks, who declared that the soul was immortal." [Tr.]

paragraphs of his *Erziehung des Menschengeschlechts*. Lichtenberg
also says in his *Selbstcharakteristik:* "I cannot get rid of the idea that
I had died before I was born." Even the exceedingly empirical Hume
says in his sceptical essay on immortality, p. 23: "The metempsychosis is therefore the only system of this kind that philosophy can
hearken to." [29] What opposes this belief, which is spread over the
whole human race and is evident to the wise as well as to the vulgar,
is Judaism, together with the two religions that have sprung from it,
inasmuch as they teach man's creation out of nothing. He then has
the hard task of connecting this with the belief in an endless future
existence *a parte post*. Of course, they have succeeded, with fire and
sword, in driving that consoling, primitive belief of mankind out of
Europe and of a part of Asia; for how long is still uncertain. The
oldest Church history is evidence of precisely how difficult this was.
Most of the heretics were attached to that primitive belief; for example, the Simonians, Basilidians, Valentinians, Marcionites, Gnostics, and Manichaeans. The Jews themselves have come to it to some
extent, as is reported by Tertullian and Justin (in his dialogues).
In the *Talmud* it is related that Abel's soul passed into the body of
Seth, and then into that of Moses. Even the biblical passage, Matthew xvi, 13-15, takes on a rational meaning only when we understand it as spoken on the assumption of the dogma of metempsychosis. Luke, of course, who also has the passage (ix, 18-20), adds
the words ὅτι προφήτης τις τῶν ἀρχαίων ἀνέστη;[30] he thus attributes
to the Jews the assumption that an ancient prophet can thus rise
again with skin and hair; but, as they know that he has already been
in the grave for six or seven hundred years, and consequently has
long since turned to dust, such rising again would be a palpable
absurdity. However, in Christianity the doctrine of original sin, in
other words of atonement for the sin of another individual, has taken
the place of the transmigration of souls and of the expiation by
means thereof of all the sins committed in a previous life. Thus both
identify, and indeed with a moral tendency, the existing person with

---

[29] This posthumous essay is found in the *Essays on Suicide and the Immortality of the Soul* by the late David Hume (Basel, 1799), sold by James
Decker. Through this Basel reprint, those two works of one of England's
greatest thinkers and authors have been saved from destruction, after they had
been suppressed in their own country, in consequence of the stupid and
utterly contemptible bigotry there prevailing, through the influence of a
powerful and insolent clergy, to England's lasting discredit. They are entirely
dispassionate, coldly rational investigations of the two subjects mentioned
above.

[30] "That one of the old prophets is risen again." [Tr.]

one who has existed previously; transmigration of souls does this directly, original sin indirectly.

Death is the great reprimand that the will-to-live, and more particularly the egoism essential thereto, receive through the course of nature; and it can be conceived as a punishment for our existence.* Death is the painful untying of the knot that generation with sensual pleasure had tied; it is the violent destruction, bursting in from outside, of the fundamental error of our true nature, the great disillusionment. At bottom, we are something that ought not to be; therefore we cease to be. Egoism really consists in man's restricting all reality to his own person, in that he imagines he lives in this alone, and not in others. Death teaches him something better, since it abolishes this person, so that man's true nature, that is his will, will henceforth live only in other individuals. His intellect, however, which itself belonged only to the phenomenon, i.e., to the world as representation, and was merely the form of the external world, also continues to exist in the condition of being representation, in other words, in the *objective* being, *as such,* of things, hence also only in the existence of what was hitherto the external world. Therefore, from this time forward, his whole ego lives only in what he had hitherto regarded as non-ego; for the difference between external and internal ceases. Here we recall that the better person is the one who makes the least difference between himself and others, and does not regard them as absolutely non-ego; whereas to the bad person this difference is great, in fact absolute. I have discussed this at length in the essay *On the Basis of Morality.* The conclusion from the above remarks is that the degree in which death can be regarded as man's annihilation is in proportion to this difference. But if we start from the fact that the difference between outside me and inside me, as a spatial difference, is founded only in the phenomenon, not in the thing-in-itself, and so is not an absolutely real difference, then in the losing of our own individuality we shall see only the loss of a phenomenon, and thus only an apparent loss. However much reality that difference has in empirical consciousness, yet from the metaphysical standpoint the sentences "I perish, but the world endures," and "The world perishes, but I endure," are not really different at bottom.

But beyond all this, death is the great opportunity no longer to be I; to him, of course, who embraces it. During life, man's will is without freedom; on the basis of his unalterable character, his

---

* Death says: You are the product of an act that ought not to have taken place; therefore, to wipe it out, you must die.

conduct takes place with necessity in the chain of motives. Now everyone carries in his memory very many things which he has done, about which he is not satisfied with himself. If he were to go on living, he would go on acting in the same way by virtue of the unalterability of his character. Accordingly, he must cease to be what he is, in order to be able to arise out of the germ of his true nature as a new and different being. Death, therefore, loosens those bonds; the will again becomes free, for freedom lies in the *esse,* not in the *operari. Finditur nodus cordis, dissolvuntur omnes dubitationes, ejusque opera evanescunt,*[31] is a very famous saying of the *Veda* often repeated by all Vedantists.[32] Dying is the moment of that liberation from the one-sidedness of an individuality which does not constitute the innermost kernel of our true being, but is rather to be thought of as a kind of aberration thereof. The true original freedom again enters at this moment which in the sense stated can be regarded as a *restitutio in integrum.*[33] The peace and composure on the countenance of most dead people seem to have their origin in this. As a rule, the death of every good person is peaceful and gentle; but to die willingly, to die gladly, to die cheerfully, is the prerogative of the resigned, of him who gives up and denies the will-to-live. For he alone wishes to die *actually* and not merely *apparently,* and consequently needs and desires no continuance of his person. He willingly gives up the existence that we know; what comes to him instead of it is in our eyes *nothing,* because our existence in reference to that one is *nothing.* The Buddhist faith calls that existence *Nirvana,* that is to say, extinction.[34]

---

[31] "[Whoever beholds the highest and profoundest], has his heart's knot cut, all his doubts are resolved, and his works come to nought." [Tr.]

[32] *Sankara, seu de theologumenis Vedanticorum,* ed. F. H. H. Windischmann, p. 37; *Oupnekhat,* Vol. I, pp. 387 and 78; Colebrooke's *Miscellaneous Essays,* Vol. I, p. 363.

[33] "Restoration to the former state." [Tr.]

[34] The etymology of the word *Nirvana* is given in various ways. According to Colebrooke (*Transactions of the Royal Asiatic Society,* Vol. I, p. 566), it comes from *va,* "to blow" like the wind, with the prefixed negative *nir;* hence it signifies a lull or calm, but as adjective "extinguished." Obry, *Du Nirvana indien,* p. 3, says: *Nirvanam en sanscrit signifie à la lettre extinction, telle que celle d'un feu.* ("Nirvanam in Sanskrit literally means extinction, e.g., as of a fire." Tr.) According to the *Asiatic Journal,* Vol. XXIV, p. 735, it is really *Neravana,* from *nera,* "without," and *vana,* "life," and the meaning would be *annihilatio.* In Spence Hardy's *Eastern Monachism,* p. 295, *Nirvana* is derived from *vana,* "sinful desires," with the negative *nir.* I. J. Schmidt, in his translation of the *History of the Eastern Mongolians,* p. 307, says that the Sanskrit *Nirvana* is translated into Mongolian by a phrase meaning "departed from misery," "escaped from misery." According to the same scholar's lectures at the St. Petersburg Academy, *Nirvana* is the opposite of

Samsara, which is the world of constant rebirths, of craving and desire, of the illusion of the senses, of changing and transient forms, of being born, growing old, becoming sick, and dying. In *Burmese* the word *Nirvana,* on the analogy of other Sanskrit words, is transformed into *Nieban,* and is translated by "complete vanishing." See Sangermano's *Description of the Burmese Empire,* transl. by Tandy, Rome 1833, § 27. In the first edition of 1819, I also wrote *Nieban,* because at that time we knew Buddhism only from inadequate accounts of the Burmese.

CHAPTER XLII

Life of the Species

In the preceding chapter we called to mind that the (Platonic) *Ideas* of the different grades of beings, which are the adequate objectification of the will-to-live, present themselves in the individual's knowledge, bound to the form of *time,* as the *species,* in other words, as the successive and homogeneous individuals connected by the bond of generation, and that the species is therefore the *Idea* (εἶδος, *species*) drawn out in time. Consequently, the true being-in-itself of every living thing lies primarily in its species; yet this species again has its existence only in the individuals. Although the will attains to self-consciousness only in the individual, and thus knows itself directly only as the individual, yet the deep-seated consciousness that it is really the species in which its true being objectifies itself appears in the fact that the affairs of the species as such, i.e., the relations of the sexes, the generation and nourishment of the offspring, are to the individual of incomparably greater importance and consequence than everything else. Hence heat or rut among the animals (an excellent description of the vehemence of which is found in Burdach's *Physiologie,* Vol. I, §§ 247, 257), and, in the case of man, the careful and capricious selection of the other individual for the satisfaction of the sexual impulse, which can rise to the height of passionate love, to whose fuller investigation I shall devote a special chapter; hence, finally, the excessive love of parents for their offspring.

In the supplements to the second book, the will was compared to the root of the tree, the intellect to its crown; and so inwardly or psychologically it is. But outwardly or physiologically, the genitals are the root, and the head is the crown. The nourishing part, it is true, is not the genitals, but the villi of the intestines; yet not the latter, but the former are the root, for through them the individual is connected with the species in which it is rooted. For physically the individual is a production of the species, metaphysically a more or less imperfect picture of the *Idea* that, in the form of time, exhibits itself as species. In agreement with the relation here expressed, the maximum vitality, and also the decrepitude, of the brain and of the genitals, are simultaneous and closely connected. The sexual impulse is to be regarded as the inner impulse of the tree (the species) on which the life of the individual thrives, just like a leaf which is nourished by the tree, and assists in nourishing it. That impulse is therefore very strong, and springs from the depths of our nature. To castrate an individual is to cut him off from the tree of the species on which he thrives, and to let him, thus severed, wither away; hence the degradation of his powers of mind and body. The service of the species, fertilization or impregnation, is followed in the case of every animal individual by momentary exhaustion and debility of all its powers, and in the case of most insects even by speedy death; for this reason Celsus said: *Seminis emissio est partis animae jactura.*[1] In the case of man, the extinction of the procreative power shows that the individual is approaching death; at every age excessive use of that power shortens life, whereas moderation enhances all the powers, especially muscular strength. For this reason abstemiousness and moderation were part of the training of Greek athletes. The same moderation lengthens the insect's life even to the following spring. All this indicates that the life of the individual is at bottom only something borrowed from the species, and that all vital force is, so to speak, force of the species checked by damming up. But this is to be explained from the fact that the metaphysical substratum of life reveals itself directly in the species, and only by means of this in the individual. Accordingly, in India the lingam with the yoni, as the symbol of the species and of its immortality, is revered, and, as the counterpoise of death, it is ascribed as an attribute to Shiva, the very divinity presiding over death.

However, without myth and symbol, the vehemence of the sexual impulse, the keen ardour and profound seriousness with which every animal, and man also, pursues the business of that impulse, are evidence that, through the function that serves it, the animal belongs to that in which its true inner being really and mainly lies, namely the *species;* whereas all the other functions and organs serve directly only the individual, whose existence is at bottom only secondary. In the vehemence of that impulse which is the concentration of the whole animal inner nature is further expressed the consciousness that the individual does not endure, and that everything therefore has to be staked on the maintenance of the *species,* as that in which the individual's true existence lies.

To illustrate what has been said, let us picture to ourselves an animal on heat and in the act of procreation. We see in it a

---

[1] "The ejaculation of sperm is the casting away of part of the soul." [Tr.]

seriousness and ardour never known at any other time. Now what occurs in it? Does it know that it must die, and that through its present business a new individual, though one wholly similar to it, will arise, in order to take its place? It knows nothing of all this, for it does not think; but it is as keenly concerned about the continuance of its species in time as if it did know it all. For it is conscious that it desires to live and exist, and it expresses the highest degree of this willing through the act of procreation; this is all that takes place in its consciousness. This is also quite sufficient for the continued existence of beings, just because the will is the radical, and knowledge the adventitious. For this reason, the will does not need to be guided throughout by knowledge; but as soon as it has made a decision in its primitive originality, this willing will automatically objectify itself in the world of the representation. Now if in such a way it is that definite animal form we have pictured to ourselves that wills life and existence, then it wills life and existence not in general, but in precisely this form. Therefore it is the sight of its form in the female of its species that stimulates the animal's will to procreation. Looked at from outside and under the form of time, this willing of the animal presents itself as such an animal form maintained throughout an infinite time by the ever-repeated replacement of one individual by another, and hence by the alternation of death and generation. Thus considered, death and generation appear to be the pulsation of that form (ἰδέα, εἶδος, *species*) enduring through all time. We can compare them to the forces of attraction and repulsion, through whose antagonism matter continues to exist. What is here demonstrated in the animal applies also to man; for although with him the act of procreation is accompanied by complete knowledge of its final cause, it is nevertheless not guided by this knowledge, but proceeds immediately from the will-to-live as its concentration. Accordingly, it is to be reckoned as one of the instinctive actions; for in procreation the animal is guided by knowledge of the end in view just as little as it is in mechanical instincts. In these also the will manifests itself, in the main, without the mediation of knowledge which, here as there, is concerned only with details. To a certain extent, generation is the most marvellous of the instincts, and its work the most astonishing.

From these considerations, it is clear why sexual desire bears a character very different from that of any other; it is not only the strongest of desires, but is even specifically of a more powerful kind than all the others are. It is everywhere tacitly assumed as necessary and inevitable, and is not, like other desires, a matter of taste and caprice. For it is the desire that constitutes even the very nature of man. In conflict with it, no motive is so strong as to be certain of victory. It is so very much the chief thing, that no other pleasures make up for the deprivation of its satisfaction; for its sake, moreover, animal and man undertake every peril and conflict. A very naïve expression of this natural sentiment is the well-known inscription on the door of the *fornix* at Pompeii, adorned with the phallus: *Heic habitat felicitas.*[2] For those going in this was naïve, for those coming out ironical, and in itself it was humorous. On the other hand, the excessive power of the procreative impulse is seriously and worthily expressed in the inscription that (according to Theon of Smyrna, *De Musica,* c. 47) Osiris had placed on the column erected by him to the eternal gods: "To Eros, the spirit, the heaven, the sun, the moon, the earth, the night, the day, and the father of all that is and is to be"; likewise in the beautiful apostrophe with which Lucretius opens his work:

> *Aeneadum genetrix, hominum divômque voluptas,*
> *Alma Venus etc.*[3]

In keeping with all this is the important role played by the sex-relation in the world of mankind, where it is really the invisible central point of all action and conduct, and peeps up everywhere, in spite of all the veils thrown over it. It is the cause of war and the aim and object of peace, the basis of the serious and the aim of the joke, the inexhaustible source of wit, the key to all hints and allusions, and the meaning of all secret signs and suggestions, all unexpressed proposals, and all stolen glances; it is the daily thought and desire of the young and often of the old as well, the hourly thought of the unchaste, and the constantly recurring reverie of the chaste even against their will, the ever ready material for a joke, only because the profoundest seriousness lies at its root. This, however, is the piquant element and the jest of the world, that the principal concern of all men is pursued secretly and ostensibly ignored as much as possible. Indeed, we see it take its seat at every moment as the real and hereditary lord of the world, out of the fulness of its own strength, on the ancestral throne, look down thence with scornful glances, and laugh at the arrangements made to subdue it, to imprison it, or at any rate to restrict it, and if possible to keep it concealed, or indeed so to master it that it appears only as an entirely subordinate and secondary concern of life. But all this agrees with the fact that the sexual impulse is the kernel of the will-

---

[2] "Here dwells happiness." [Tr.]
[3] "Mother of Aeneas' race, delight and desire of gods and men, lovely and enchanting Venus." [Tr.]

to-live, and consequently the concentration of all willing; in the text, therefore, I have called the genitals the focus of the will. Indeed, it may be said that man is concrete sexual impulse, for his origin is an act of copulation, and the desire of his desires is an act of copulation, and this impulse alone perpetuates and holds together the whole of his phenomenal appearance. It is true that the will-to-live manifests itself primarily as an effort to maintain the individual; yet this is only a stage towards the effort to maintain the species. This latter effort must be more intense in proportion as the life of the species surpasses that of the individual in duration, extension, and value. The sexual impulse is therefore the most complete manifestation of the will-to-live, its most distinctly expressed type. The origin of individuals from this impulse, as well as its primacy over all other desires of the natural person, are both in complete agreement with this.

Yet another physiological observation is relevant here; it throws light on my fundamental doctrine expounded in the second book. The sexual impulse is the most vehement of cravings, the desire of desires, the concentration of all our willing. Accordingly, its satisfaction, corresponding exactly to the individual desire of anyone, thus to a desire directed to a definite individual, is the summit and crown of his happiness, the ultimate goal of his natural endeavours, with whose attainment everything seems to him to be attained, and with the missing of which everything seems to have been missed. In just the same way we find, as the physiological correlative of all this, in the objectified will, and thus in the human organism, the sperm or semen as the secretion of secretions, the quintessence of all humours, the final result of all organic functions, and in this we have one more proof of the fact that the body is only objectivity of the will, in other words the will itself under the form of the representation.

Connected with procreation is the maintenance of the offspring, and with the sexual impulse parental love; thus in these the life of the species is carried on. Accordingly, the animal's love for its offspring has, like the sexual impulse, a strength far surpassing that of the efforts which are directed merely towards itself as an individual. This shows itself in the fact that even the mildest animals are ready to undertake on behalf of their offspring the most unequal fight to the death; and with almost all species of animals, the mother encounters every danger for the protection of her young, in fact in many cases she even faces certain death. In the case of man, this instinctive parental love is guided and directed by the faculty of reason, in other words, by reflection; but sometimes it is also checked, and in the case of bad characters this can amount to its complete renunciation. We can therefore observe its effects most clearly in the case of the animals. In itself, however, this parental love is no less strong in man; here too in particular cases we see it entirely overcome self-love, and even go so far as a man's sacrificing his own life. Thus, for example, newspapers from France have just reported that at Cahors in the department of Lot, a father took his own life, in order that his son, whose name had been drawn for military service, should be the eldest son of a widow, and as such exempt from service (*Galignani's Messenger*, 22 June 1843). Since, however, animals are incapable of any reflection, the instinctive maternal affection in their case (the male is generally not conscious of his paternity) shows itself directly and genuinely, and hence with perfect distinctness and in all its strength. At bottom, it is the expression of the consciousness in the animal that its true inner being lies more immediately in the species than in the individual. Therefore, in case of necessity, the animal sacrifices its own life, so that the species may be maintained in the young. Here therefore, as well as in the sexual impulse, the will-to-live becomes to a certain extent transcendent, since its consciousness extends beyond the individual, in which it is inherent, to the species. To avoid expressing this second manifestation of the life of the species in a merely abstract way, and to bring it home to the reader in its magnitude and reality, I will mention a few examples of the extraordinary power of instinctive maternal love.

The sea-otter, when pursued, seizes her young one and dives with it; when she comes to the surface again to breathe, she covers it with her body and receives the hunter's harpoon, while it makes good its escape. A young whale is killed merely to decoy the mother, who hurries to it, and seldom forsakes it so long as it still lives, although she is hit by several harpoons. (Scoresby's *Tagebuch einer Reise auf den Walfischfang,* from the English by Kries, p. 196.) On Three Kings Island near New Zealand there are colossal seals called sea-elephants (*Phoca proboscidea*). Swimming round the island in a regular herd, they feed on fish, yet under the water they have certain terrible enemies, unknown to us, by which they are often severely wounded; hence their swimming together requires special tactics. The females bring forth their young on the shore; while they are suckling them, a business lasting from seven to eight weeks, all the males form a circle round them to prevent them, driven by hunger, from entering the sea; and when this is attempted, they prevent it by biting. Thus they all fast together for seven or eight weeks, and become thin, merely in order that the young may not enter the sea before they are able to swim well, and to observe the proper tactics that are then taught them by blows and bites (Freycinet, *Voyage aux terres australes,* 1826). Here we also see how parental love, like every strong exertion of the will (see chap. xix, 6) enhances the intelligence. Wild duck, whitethroats, and many other birds fly in front of the hunter's feet with loud cries, and flap about when he approaches their nest, as though their wings were injured, in order to distract his attention from their young to themselves. The lark tries to entice the dog away from her nest by exposing herself. In just the same way, hinds and does induce the hunter to pursue them, so that their young may not be attacked. Swallows have flown into burning houses in order to save their young or to perish with them. At Delft in a great fire, a stork allowed itself to be burnt in its nest rather than forsake its frail and delicate young that were still unable to fly. (Hadr. Junius, *Descriptio Hollandiae.*) Mountain-cocks and woodcocks allow themselves to be caught when brooding on the nest. *Muscicapa tyrannus* defends her nest with particular courage, and offers resistance even to eagles. An ant has been cut in two, and the front half has been seen to bring its pupae into safety. A bitch, whose litter had been surgically removed from her womb, crept up to them dying, caressed them, and began to whine furiously only when they were taken from her. (Burdach, *Physiologie als Erfahrungswissenschaft,* Vols. II and III.)

CHAPTER XLIII

The Hereditary Nature of Qualities

The most ordinary everyday experience teaches that, with procreation, the combined seed of the parents transmits not only the characteristics of the species, but those of the individuals also, as regards the bodily (objective, external) qualities; and this has at all times been recognized:

Naturae sequitur semina quisque suae.[1]

Whether this holds good of mental (subjective, internal) qualities also, so that these too are transmitted from parents to children, is a question that has often been raised, and almost always answered in the affirmative. More difficult, however, is the problem whether it is possible to distinguish what belongs to the father and what to the mother, what is the mental and spiritual inheritance coming to us from each of our parents. If we throw light on this problem by means of our fundamental knowledge that the *will* is the true inner being, the kernel, the radical element in man, while the *intellect* is the secondary, the adventitious, the accident of that substance, then before questioning experience we shall assume it as at least probable that at procreation the father, as *sexus potior* and the procreative principle, imparts the basis, the radical element, of the new life, that is, the *will,* but the mother, as *sexus sequior* and the merely conceiving principle, the secondary element, the *intellect.* We shall therefore assume that man inherits his moral nature, his character, his inclinations, his heart, from the father, but the degree, quality, and tendency of his intelligence from the mother. This assumption finds its actual confirmation in experience, though this cannot be decided by a physical experiment on the table, but follows partly from careful and keen observation over many years, and partly from history.

Our own experience has the advantage of complete certainty

---

[1] "Each is guided by the talents with which nature has endowed him." Propertius IV, 8, 20 (not Catullus as cited by Schopenhauer). [Tr.]

and the greatest speciality, and this outweighs the disadvantage that attaches to it, arising from the fact that its sphere is limited, and its examples not generally known. I therefore refer everyone in the first instance to his own experience. Let him first of all consider himself, admit to himself his own inclinations and passions, his characteristic errors and weaknesses, his vices, as well as his good points and virtues, if he has any; then let him recall his father to mind, and he will not fail to notice all these characteristic traits in him also. On the other hand he will often find his mother of an entirely different character, and a moral agreement with her, will occur extremely rarely, and only through the exceptional accident of a similarity of character between the two parents. Let him make this examination, for example, with regard to quick temper or patience, avarice or extravagance, tendency to sensuality, intemperance, or gambling, callousness or kindness, honesty or duplicity, pride or affability, courage or cowardice, peaceableness or quarrelsomeness, conciliatory attitude or resentment, and so on. Then let him make the same investigation in all those whose character and parents have come to be accurately known to him. If he proceeds with attention, correct judgement, and sincerity, confirmation of our principle will not be wanting. Thus, for example, he will find the special tendency to tell lies, peculiar to many people, equally present in two brothers, because they have inherited it from the father; for this reason, the comedy *The Liar and his Son* is psychologically correct. But two inevitable limitations are here to be borne in mind, which only downright injustice could interpret as evasions. Firstly, *pater semper incertus.*[2] Only a decided bodily resemblance to the father removes this limitation; a superficial resemblance is not enough to do so; for there is an after-effect from earlier impregnation, by virtue of which the children of a second marriage sometimes still have a slight resemblance to the first husband, and those begotten in adultery a resemblance to the legitimate father. Such an after-effect has been observed even more distinctly in the case of animals. The second limitation is that the father's moral character does indeed appear in the son, yet with the modification it has received through another and often very different *intellect* (the inheritance from the mother), whence a correction of the observation becomes necessary. In proportion to that difference, this modification may be important or unimportant, yet never so great that the fundamental traits of the father's character would not still always appear sufficiently easy to recognize even under such modification, somewhat like a person who had tried to disguise himself by an entirely strange kind of dress,

---

[2] "The father is always uncertain." [Tr.]

wig, and beard. For example, if, by virtue of his inheritance from the mother, a person is preeminently endowed with the faculty of reason, and thus with the capacity for reflection and deliberation, then his passions, inherited from his father, will be partly restrained and partly concealed thereby; and accordingly they will attain only to methodical and systematic or secret manifestation. From this, then, will result a phenomenon very different from that of the father, who may possibly have had quite a limited intelligence. In just the same way the opposite can occur. On the other hand, the mother's inclinations and passions do not reappear in the children at all; indeed, we often see the very opposite of them.

The examples of history have the advantage over those of private life of being universally known; on the other hand they are, of course, impaired by the uncertainty and frequent falsification of all tradition, and also by the fact that, as a rule, they contain only the public, not the private life, and accordingly only the political actions, not the finer manifestations of the character. But I wish to support the truth put forward here by some examples from history. Those who have made a special study of history will no doubt be able to add a far greater number of cases just as striking.

It is well known that P. Decius Mus sacrificed his life for his country with heroic magnanimity, for, solemnly dedicating himself and the enemy to the infernal gods, he plunged with covered face into the army of the Latins. About forty years later, his son of the same name did exactly the same thing in the war against the Gauls. (Livy, viii, 6; x, 28.) Hence a positive proof of Horace's *fortes creantur fortibus et bonis;*[3] the converse of this is supplied by Shakespeare;

> Cowards father cowards, and base things sire base.
> *Cymbeline*, IV, 2.

Early Roman history presents us with whole families, whose members distinguished themselves in a long succession by self-sacrificing patriotism and bravery; such were the gens Fabia and the gens Fabricia. Alexander the Great, again, was, like his father Philip, fond of power and conquest. The pedigree of Nero, which Suetonius (c. 4 and 5) gives with a moral purpose at the beginning of his description of this monster, is well worth considering. The gens Claudia, which he is describing, flourished in Rome through six centuries and produced men of action who were nevertheless arrogant and cruel. From it sprang Tiberius, Caligula, and finally Nero. In his grandfather, and even more strongly in his father, all those atrocious

---

[3] "From the brave and the good are the brave descended." Horace, *Odes,* iv, 4, 29. [Tr.]

qualities already show themselves which were able to obtain their full development only in Nero, partly because his high rank allowed them freer scope, and partly because he had in addition as his mother the irrational Bacchante, Agrippina, who was unable to endow him with any intellect for curbing his passions. Suetonius, therefore, relates wholly in our sense that at his birth *praesagio fuit etiam Domitii, patris, vox, inter gratulationes amicorum, negantis, quidquam ex se et Agrippina, nisi detestabile et malo publico nasci potuisse.*[4] On the other hand, Cimon was the son of Miltiades, Hannibal the son of Hamilcar, and the Scipios produced a whole family of heroes and noble defenders of their country. The son of Pope Alexander VI, however, was his hideous image Caesar Borgia. The son of the notorious Duke of Alba was just as cruel and wicked as his father. The malicious and unjust Philip IV of France, known specially for his cruel torture and execution of the Templars, had as his daughter Isabella, wife of Edward II of England. This woman rose against her husband, took him prisoner, and, after he had signed his abdication, since the attempt to kill him by ill-treatment proved unsuccessful, had him put to death in prison in a manner too horrible for me to mention here. Henry VIII of England, the bloodthirsty tyrant and *defensor fidei,* had by his first marriage a daughter, Queen Mary, distinguished equally for bigotry and cruelty, who from her numerous burnings of heretics won for herself the title of Bloody Mary. His daughter by his second marriage, namely Elizabeth, inherited an excellent understanding from her mother, Anne Boleyn, which ruled out bigotry, and curbed, yet did not eliminate, her father's character in her, so that this still shone through on occasion, and distinctly appeared in her cruel treatment of Mary of Scotland. Van Geuns,[5] after Marcus Donatus, speaks of a Scottish girl whose father had been burnt as a highwayman and cannibal when she was only a year old. Although she grew up among quite different people, there developed in her, with increasing age, the same craving for human flesh, and, caught in the act of satisfying this craving, she was buried alive. In the *Freimütige* of 13 July 1821 we read that in the department of Aube the police hunted for a girl, because she had murdered two children, whom she was to take to the foundling hospital, in order to keep the little money allowed for them. The police finally found the girl on the road to Paris, drowned near

---

[4] "A prophecy was also the utterance of his father Domitius who assured the friends on their congratulating him that from him and Agrippina only something detestable and tending to the general ruin could be born." [Tr.]

[5] *Disputatio de corporum habitudine, animae, hujusque virium indice.* Harderov., 1789, § 9.

Romilly; and her own father gave himself up as her murderer. Finally, let me mention here a couple of cases from recent times, which accordingly have only the newspapers to vouch for them. In October 1836 a Count Belecznai was condemned to death in Hungary, because he had murdered an official, and severely wounded his own relations. His elder brother had previously been executed for parricide; and his father had likewise been a murderer. (*Frankfurter Postzeitung,* 26 October 1836.) A year later, the youngest brother of this count fired a pistol at, but missed, the steward of his estates in the very street in which the official had been murdered. (*Frankfurter Journal,* 16 September 1837.) In the *Frankfurter Postzeitung* of 19 November 1857, a despatch from Paris announces the condemnation to death of a very dangerous highway robber, Lemaire, and his companions, and adds: "The criminal tendency appears to be hereditary in his family and in those of his confederates, since several of their stock have died on the scaffold." It follows from a passage in the *Laws* of Plato that similar cases were known to the Greeks. (Stobaeus, *Florilegium,* Vol. II, p. 213.) The annals of crime will certainly have many similar pedigrees to show. The tendency to suicide is specially hereditary.

On the other hand, when we see the admirable Marcus Aurelius have the wicked Commodus for a son, this does not lead us astray, for we know that Diva Faustina was an *uxor infamis.* On the contrary, we remember this case in order to presume in analogous cases an analogous reason; for example, that Domitian was the full brother of Titus I can never believe, but rather that Vespasian also was a deceived husband.

Now as regards the second part of the principle set up, namely the inheritance of the intellect from the mother, this enjoys a far more general acceptance than does the first, which in itself is opposed by the *liberum arbitrium indifferentiae,*[6] but the separate conception of which is opposed by the simple and indivisible nature of the soul. The old and popular expression "mother wit" in itself testifies to the early recognition of this second truth that is based on the experience gained with both small and great intellectual endowments, namely that they are the ability and capacity of those whose mothers relatively distinguished themselves by their intelligence. On the other hand, that the father's intellectual qualities are not transmitted to the son is proved both by the fathers and by the sons of men who were distinguished by the most eminent abilities, since, as a rule, they were men of quite ordinary intelligence and without a trace of the father's mental gifts. But if for once an

---

[6] "The will's free determination not influenced in any direction." [Tr.]

isolated exception to this frequently confirmed experience appears, such, for example, as that presented by Pitt and his father Lord Chatham, we are entitled, indeed obliged, to ascribe it to an accident, although, on account of the extreme rarity of great talents, such an accident is certainly one of the most extraordinary. But here the rule holds good that it is improbable that the improbable *never* happens. Moreover, great statesmen (as mentioned already in chapter 22) are such just as much through qualities of their character, and hence through the paternal inheritance, as through the superior qualities of their mind. On the other hand, among artists, poets, and philosophers, whose achievements alone are ascribed to *genius* proper, I know of no case analogous to this. It is true that Raphael's father was a painter, but not a great one; Mozart's father and also his son were musicians, but not great ones. However, we cannot help admiring how fate, which had allotted to those two men, each the greatest in his sphere, only a very short life, saw to it, by way of compensation so to speak, that they were already born in their workshop. In this way, without suffering the loss of time in youth which often occurs in the case of other men of genius, they received from childhood, through paternal example and instruction, the necessary introduction into the art to which they were exclusively destined. This secret and mysterious power, appearing to guide the life of the individual, has been the subject of special investigations on my part which I have recorded in the essay "On the apparent deliberateness in the fate of the individual" (*Parerga,* Vol. I). It is also to be noted here that there are certain scientific occupations which presuppose, of course, good, innate abilities, yet not really rare and extraordinary ones; the main requirements, on the contrary, are zealous effort, diligence, patience, early and good instruction, sustained study, and much practice. From this, and not from inheritance of the father's intellect, is to be explained the fact that, as the son always willingly follows the path prepared by his father, and almost all businesses are hereditary in certain families, individual families can show a succession of men of merit even in some branches of knowledge which require above all diligence and perseverance; such are the Scaligers, the Bernouillis, the Cassinis, the Herschels.

The number of proofs of the real inheritance of the intellect from the mother would be very much greater than it is, were it not that the character and disposition of the female sex are such that women rarely give public proof of their mental faculties; therefore these do not become historical, and thus do not come to the knowledge of posterity. Moreover, on account of the generally weaker nature of the female sex, these faculties themselves never reach in the woman the degree to which in favourable circumstances they subsequently rise in the son; but as for woman herself, we have to estimate her achievements more highly in this very connexion. Accordingly, for the present, only the following examples appear to me to be proofs of our truth. Joseph II was the son of Maria Thercsa. Cardanus says in the third chapter of *De vita propria; Mater mea fuit memoria et ingenio pollens.*[7] In the first book of the *Confessions,* J. J. Rousseau says: *La beauté de ma mère, son esprit, ses talents,— elle en avait de trop brillans pour son état,*[8] and so on, and he then quotes a most delightful couplet by her. D'Alembert was the illegitimate son of Claudine de Tencin, a woman of superior intellect and the author of several works of fiction and similar writings which met with great approval in their day, and are said to be still readable. (See her biography in the *Blätter für literarische Unterhaltung,* March 1845, Nos. 71-73). That Buffon's mother was a distinguished woman is seen from the following passage in the *Voyage à Montbar,* by Hérault de Séchelles, quoted by Flourens in his *Histoire des travaux de Buffon,* p. 288: *Buffon avait ce principe qu'en général les enfants tenaient de leur mère leurs qualités intellectuelles et morales: et lorsqu'il l'avait développé dans la conversation, il en faisait sur-le-champ l'application à lui-même, en faisant un éloge pompeux de sa mère, qui avait en effet, beaucoup d'esprit, des connaissances étendues, et une tête très bien organisée.*[9] That he mentions the moral qualities also is either an error made by the reporter, or is due to the fact that his mother accidentally had the same character that he and his father had. The contrary of this is presented by innumerable cases in which mother and son have opposite characters. Hence in *Orestes* and *Hamlet* the greatest dramatists could present mother and son in hostile conflict, in which the son appears as the moral representative and avenger of the father. On the other hand, the converse case, namely of the son appearing as the moral representative and avenger of the mother against the father, would be revolting, and at the same time almost ludicrous. This is due to the fact that between father and son there exists actual identity of being, which is the will, but between mother and son there exists mere identity of the intellect, and even this subject to certain conditions.

---

[7] "My mother was distinguished for her memory and for her intellect." [Tr.]

[8] "The beauty of my mother, her mind, and her gifts,—they were all too brilliant for her social position." [Tr.]

[9] "Buffon upheld this principle that children generally inherit their intellectual and moral qualities from their mother. And when he had developed this theme in conversation, he at once applied it to himself and indulged in fulsome praise of his mother who, in fact, had great intellect, extensive knowledge, and a very well organized mind." [Tr.]

Between mother and son there can exist the greatest moral contrast, between father and son only an intellectual. From this point of view the necessity of the Salic law should also be recognized, that woman cannot carry on the line. In his short autobiography Hume says: "Our mother was a woman of singular merit." Of Kant's mother it says in the most recent biography by F. W. Schubert that "according to her son's own judgement, she was a woman of great natural understanding. For those days, when there was so little opportunity for the education of girls, she was exceptionally well informed, and later continued by herself to look after her further education. . . . When out walking, she drew her son's attention to all kinds of natural phenomena, and tried to explain them through the power of God." What an intelligent, clever, and superior woman Goethe's mother was is now generally known. How much she has been spoken of in literature, though his father has not been mentioned at all! Goethe himself describes him as a man of inferior abilities. Schiller's mother was susceptible to poetry; she herself made verses, a fragment of which is to be found in his biography by Schwab. Bürger, that genuine poetic genius, to whom is due perhaps the first place among German poets after Goethe, for, compared with his ballads, those of Schiller seem cold and artificial, has furnished an account of his parents which is significant for us, and which his friend and physician Althof repeats in these words in his biography, published in 1798: "It is true that Bürger's father had various kinds of knowledge, after the manner of study prevalent at the time, and that he was also a good and honest man. Nevertheless, he liked his quiet comfort and his pipe of tobacco so much that, as my friend used to say, he always first had to pull himself together, if he were to apply himself for a brief quarter of an hour to the instruction of his son. His wife was a woman of the most extraordinary mental gifts, which, however, were so little cultivated that she scarcely learnt to write legibly. Bürger was of the opinion that, with proper culture, his mother would have become the most famous of her sex, although several times he expressed a marked dislike of different traits of her moral character. Yet he believed he had inherited some intellectual gifts from his mother, but from his father an agreement with his moral character." Sir Walter Scott's mother was a poetess, and was in touch with the fine intellects of her time, as we learn from the obituary notice of Sir Walter in the *Globe* of 24 September, 1832. That poems by her appeared in print in 1789 I find from an article entitled "Mother-wit," published by Brockhaus in the *Blätter für literarische Unterhaltung* of 4 October 1841. This gives a long list of clever mothers of famous men, from which I will take only two.

"Bacon's mother was a distinguished linguist, wrote and translated several works, and showed in each of them erudition, discernment, and taste. Boerhaave's mother distinguished herself by medical knowledge." On the other hand, Haller has preserved for us a strong proof of the inheritance of feeble-mindedness from mothers, for he states: *E duabus patriciis sororibus, ob divitias maritos nactis, quum tamen fatuis essent proximae, novimus in nobilissimas gentes nunc a seculo retro ejus morbi manasse seminia, ut etiam in quarta generatione, quintave, omnium posterorum aliqui fatui supersint.* (*Elementa physiologiae, lib.* XXIX, § 8.)[10] According to Esquirol, madness also is inherited more frequently from the mother than from the father. But if it is inherited from the father, I attribute this to the disposition of feeling, the effect of which gives rise to it.

From our principle, it seems to follow that sons of the same mother have equal mental powers, and that if one were highly gifted, the other would of necessity be so also. Occasionally this is the case; for example, we have the Carracci, Joseph and Michael Haydn, Bernard and Andreas Romberg, George and Frederick Cuvier. I would also add the brothers Schlegel, were it not that the younger, namely Friedrich, had made himself unworthy of the honour of being mentioned along with his admirable, blameless, and highly distinguished brother, August Wilhelm, by the disgraceful obscurantism displayed by him in the last quarter of his life conjointly with Adam Müller. For obscurantism is a sin, perhaps not against the Holy Spirit, but certainly against the human. Therefore we ought never to forgive it, but always and everywhere implacably hold it against the person who has made himself guilty of it, and take every opportunity of showing our contempt for him, as long as he lives, and even after he is dead. Just as often, however, the above conclusion does not follow; for example, Kant's brother was quite an ordinary person. To explain this, I recall what was said in chapter 31 on the physiological conditions of genius. Not only an extraordinarily developed brain formed absolutely for the purpose (the mother's share) is required, but also a very energetic heart action to animate it, that is to say, subjectively a passionate will, a lively temperament; this is the inheritance from the father. But this very quality is at its height only during the father's most vigorous years, and the mother ages even more rapidly. Accordingly, the highly gifted sons will, as

---

[10] "From two aristocratic sisters, who on account of their wealth had obtained husbands, although they were almost imbeciles, the seeds of this malady have, as we know, penetrated for a century into the most distinguished families, so that even in the fourth or fifth generation some of their descendants are imbeciles." [Tr.]

a rule, be the eldest, begotten in the full vigour of both parents; thus Kant's brother was eleven years younger than he. Even in the case of two distinguished brothers, the elder will as a rule be the superior. Yet not only the age, but every temporary ebb of the vital forces, or other disturbance of health in the parents at the time of procreation is capable of curtailing the share of one or the other parent, and of preventing the appearance of an eminent man of talent, a phenomenon that is for this very reason so exceedingly rare. Incidentally, in the case of twins, the absence of all the differences just mentioned is the cause of the quasi-identity of their nature.

If isolated cases should be found where a highly gifted son had had no mentally distinguished mother, this might be explained from the fact that this mother herself had had a phlegmatic father. For this reason, her unusually developed brain had not been properly excited by the corresponding energy of the blood circulation, a requirement I have already discussed in chapter 31. Nevertheless, her extremely perfect nervous and cerebral system had been transmitted to the son. But in his case there had been in addition a lively and passionate father with energetic heart action, whereby the other somatic condition of great mental power first appeared in him. Perhaps this was Byron's case, as we do not find the good mental qualities of his mother mentioned anywhere. The same explanation may also be applied to the case where the mother of a son of genius, herself distinguished for mental gifts, had not had a clever mother, since the latter's father had been a man of phlegmatic nature.

The discordant, changeable, and uncertain element in the character of most people may possibly be traceable to the fact that the individual has not a simple origin, but obtains the will from the father and the intellect from the mother. The more heterogeneous and unsuited to each other the parents, the greater will that disharmony, that inner variance be. While some excel through their heart and others through their head, there are still others whose superiority is to be found merely in a certain harmony and unity of the whole inner nature. This results from the fact that with them heart and head are so thoroughly suited to each other that they mutually support and bring one another into prominence. This leads us to suppose that their parents were specially suited to, and in harmony with, each other.

As regards the physiological aspect of the theory expounded, I wish only to mention that Burdach, who erroneously assumes that the same psychic quality can be inherited now from the father, now from the mother, nevertheless adds (*Physiologie als Erfahrungs-*

wissenschaft, Vol. I, § 306): "On the whole, the male element has more influence in determining the irritable life, but the female element more influence on sensibility." What Linnaeus says in the *Systema naturae,* Vol. I, p. 8, is also to the point: *Mater prolifera promit, ante generationem, vivum compendium MEDULLARE novi animalis, suique simillimi, carinam Malpighianam dictum, tanquam plumulam vegetabilium: hoc ex genitura COR adsociat ramificandum in corpus. Punctum enim saliens ovi incubantis avis ostendit primum cor micans, cerebrumque cum medulla: corculum hoc, cessans a frigore, excitatur calido halitu, premitque bulla aërea, sensim dilatata, liquores, secundum canales fluxiles. Punctum vitalitatis itaque in viventibus est tanquam a prima creatione continuata medullaris vitae ramificatio, cum ovum sit GEMMA MEDULLARIS MATRIS a primordio viva, licet non sua ante proprium COR PATERNUM.*[11]

We now connect the conviction, thus gained, of the inheritance of the character from the father and of the intellect from the mother with our previous consideration of the wide gulf placed by nature between one person and another in a moral as well as an intellectual regard. We also connect this conviction with our knowledge of the complete unalterability both of character and of mental faculties, and we are then led to the view that a real and thorough improvement of the human race might be reached not so much from outside as from within, not so much by theory and instruction as rather by the path of generation. Plato had something of the kind in mind when, in the fifth book of his *Republic,* he explained his strange plan for increasing and improving his warrior caste. If we could castrate all scoundrels and stick all stupid geese in a convent, and give men of noble character a whole harem, and procure men, and indeed thorough men, for all girls of intellect and understanding, then a generation would soon arise which would produce a better age than that of Pericles. However, without entering into such Utopian plans, it might be taken into consideration that if, as, unless I am mistaken,

---

[11] "A fertile mother before procreation brings forth from the *medulla* a living compendium of the new animal which is absolutely like her, and is called *carina Malpighiana,* similar to the *plumula* (plumule) of plants. After generation the *heart* attaches itself to this, in order to spread it out into the body. For the salient point in the egg which the bird hatches, shows at the beginning a palpitating heart, and the brain together with the medulla. This small heart stops under the influence of cold, is stimulated to movement by warm breath, and presses the fluids along the ducts by means of a vesicle that gradually expands. The point of vitality in living beings is, so to speak, a marrowy ramification of life continued from the first generation; for the egg is a *marrowy gemma in the mother,* which from the very first lives, although it has no life of its own before a *heart of its own originating from the father.*" [Tr.]

was actually the case with some ancient races, castration were the severest punishment after death, the world would be relieved of whole pedigrees of scoundrels, all the more certainly since it is well known that most crimes are committed between the ages of twenty and thirty.* In the same way it might be considered whether, as regards results, it would not be more advantageous to provide dowries to the public to be distributed on certain occasions not, as is now the custom, to girls ostensibly the most virtuous, but to the cleverest and most intelligent, especially as it is very difficult to judge of virtue, for only God, as they say, sees the heart. The opportunities for displaying a noble character are rare and a matter of chance; moreover, the virtue of many a girl is powerfully supported by her ugliness. But those who are themselves gifted with understanding can judge of it with great certainty after some investigation. The following is another practical application. In many countries, even in South Germany, the bad practice prevails of women carrying loads, often very considerable ones, on their heads. This must have a detrimental effect on the brain, whereby in the female sex of the nation this organ gradually deteriorates; and as from the female sex the male receives his brain, the whole nation becomes more and more stupid; in many cases this is not necessary at all. Accordingly, by abolishing this practice, the nation's quantum of intelligence as a whole would be increased, and this would positively be the greatest increase of the national wealth.

But if we now leave such practical applications to others, and return to our own special standpoint, the ethico-metaphysical, then, by connecting the contents of chapter 41 with those of the present chapter, the following result will present itself, which, in spite of all its transcendence, has an immediate empirical support. It is the same character, the same individually determined will, that lives in all the descendants of a stock from the remote ancestor down to the present descendant. But in each of these a different intellect is given to it, and thus a different grade and a different kind of knowledge. In this way life is now presented to it, in each of these, from a different aspect and in a different light; it obtains a new fundamental view of life, a new instruction. As the intellect is extinguished

---

* In his *Vermischte Schriften* (Göttingen, 1801, Vol. II, p. 477) Lichtenberg says: "In England it has been proposed to castrate thieves. The proposal is not bad; the punishment is very severe; it makes men contemptible, and yet leaves them still fit for trades; and if stealing is hereditary, it is then not transmitted by birth. Courage also ceases, and as the sexual impulse so frequently leads to theft, this cause also disappears. The remark that women would all the more eagerly prevent their husbands from stealing is merely mischievous, for as things are at present, they risk losing them altogether."

with the individual, it is true that that will cannot directly supplement the insight of the one course of life by that of the other. But in consequence of each new fundamental view of life, such as only a renewed personality can impart to the will, its willing itself receives a different tendency, and so in this way experiences a modification; and, what is the main point, the will in this new modification has either to affirm life anew, or to deny it. In such a way the arrangement of nature, which springs from the necessity of two sexes for procreation, that is, the arrangement of the ever-changing connexion of a will with an intellect, becomes the basis of a method of salvation. For by virtue of this arrangement, life constantly presents new aspects to the will (of which life is the copy and mirror), turns round without intermission, so to speak, before its glance, allows different and ever different modes of perception to try their effect on it, in order that on each of these it may decide for affirmation or for denial, both of which are constantly open to it; only that, when once denial is resorted to, the entire phenomenon ceases for it with death. Now according to this, it is just the constant renewal and complete change of the intellect which, as imparting a new world-view, holds open to the same will the path of salvation; but it is the intellect that comes from the mother. Therefore, here may be the real reason why all nations (with very few and doubtful exceptions) abhor and forbid the marriage of brother and sister, and even why sexual love does not arise at all between brother and sister, unless in extremely rare exceptions due to an unnatural perversity of the instincts and impulses, if not to the illegitimacy of one of them. For from a marriage of brother and sister nothing could result but always the same will with the same intellect, just as the two exist already united in both parents; thus the result would be the hopeless repetition of the already existing phenomenon.

Now if in the particular case, and close at hand, we contemplate the incredibly great, and so obvious, difference of characters; if we find one so good and benevolent, another so wicked and indeed merciless, and again behold one who is just, honest, and sincere, and another who is completely false as a sneak, a swindler, a traitor, or an incorrigible scoundrel, then there is opened before us an abysmal depth in our contemplation, since we ponder in vain when reflecting on the origin of such a difference. Hindus and Buddhists solve the problem by saying that "it is the consequence of the deeds of the preceding course of life." This solution is indeed the oldest as well as the most comprehensible, and has come from the wisest of mankind; yet it merely pushes the question farther back; nevertheless a more satisfactory solution will hardly be found. From the standpoint of my whole teaching, it remains for me to say that here, where we are speaking of the will as thing-in-itself, the principle of sufficient reason, as the mere form of the phenomenon, no longer finds any application, but with this principle all why and whence vanish. Absolute freedom consists simply in there being something not at all subject to the principle of sufficient reason as the principle of all necessity; such a freedom, therefore, belongs only to the thing-in-itself; but this is precisely the will. Accordingly, in its phenomenon, and consequently in the *operari*,[12] the will is subject to necessity; but in the *esse*,[12] where it has determined itself as thing-in-itself, it is *free*. Therefore, as soon as we come to this, as happens here, all explanation by means of reasons and consequents ceases, and there is nothing left for us but to say that the true freedom of the will here manifests itself. This freedom belongs to the will in so far as it is thing-in-itself, which, however, precisely as such, is groundless, in other words knows no why. But on this account all understanding here ceases, because all our understanding rests on the principle of sufficient reason, since it consists in the mere application of this principle.

---

[12] "Acting," "being." The will is free to be this or that phenomenon, but once it has assumed phenomenal form, its acting is necessitated. [Tr.]

CHAPTER XLIV

The Metaphysics of Sexual Love

> Ye wise men, highly and deeply learned,
> Who think it out and know,
> How, when, and where do all things pair?
> Why do they love and kiss?
> Ye lofty sages, tell me why!
> What happened to me then?
> Find out and tell me where, how, when,
> And why this happened to me.
>
> Bürger

This chapter is the last of four, and their varied and mutual references to one another, by virtue of which they form to a certain extent a subordinate whole, will be recognized by the attentive reader without its being necessary for me to interrupt my discussion by recalling and referring to them.

We are accustomed to see the poets mainly concerned with describing sexual love. As a rule, this is the principal theme of all dramatic works, tragedies as well as comedies, romantic as well as classical, Indian as well as European. It is no less the material of by far the greater part of lyric, and likewise of epic poetry, especially if we are ready to class with the latter the enormous piles of romances that have been produced every year for centuries in all the civilized countries of Europe, as regularly as the fruits of the earth. As regards the main contents of all these works, they are nothing but many-sided, brief, or lengthy descriptions of the passion we are discussing. The most successful descriptive accounts of this passion, such, for example, as *Romeo and Juliet, La Nouvelle Héloïse,* and *Werther,* have gained immortal fame. Yet when La Rochefoucauld imagines it is the same with passionate love as with ghosts, of which all speak, but no one has seen; and when Lichtenberg disputes and denies the reality and naturalness of that passion in his essay *Über die Macht der Liebe,* they are greatly mistaken. For it is impossible that anything foreign to, and inconsistent with, human nature, and thus a merely imaginary caricature, could at all times be untiringly

[531]

described and presented by poetic genius, and accepted by mankind with unaltered interest; since nothing artistically beautiful can be without truth:

> *Rien n'est beau que le vrai; le vrai seul est aimable.*[1]
> Boileau [*Epîtres*, ix, 23]

But it is certainly confirmed by experience, though not by everyday experience, that that which occurs, as a rule, only as a lively yet still controllable inclination, can, in certain circumstances, grow to be a passion exceeding every other in intensity. It then sets aside all considerations, and overcomes all obstacles with incredible force and persistence, so that for its satisfaction life is risked without hesitation; indeed, when that satisfaction is denied, life is given as the price. Werthers and Jacopo Ortis exist not merely in works of fiction, but every year can show us at least half a dozen of them in Europe: *sed ignotis perierunt mortibus illi:*[2] for their sorrows find no other chroniclers than writers of official records and newspaper reporters. Yet readers of the police court reports in English and French daily papers will testify to the correctness of my statement. But even greater is the number of those brought to the madhouse by the same passion. Finally, every year provides us with one or two cases of the common suicide of two lovers thwarted by external circumstances. But it is inexplicable to me why those who are certain of mutual love and expect to find supreme bliss in its enjoyment, do not withdraw from every connexion by the most extreme steps, and endure every discomfort, rather than give up with their lives a happiness that for them is greater than any other they can conceive. However, as regards the lower degrees and slight attacks of that passion, everyone has them daily before his eyes, and, so long as he is not old, often in his heart also.

Therefore, after what has here been recalled, we cannot doubt either the reality or the importance of the matter, and so, instead of wondering why a philosopher for once makes this constant theme of all the poets his own, we should be surprised that a matter that generally plays so important a part in the life of man has hitherto been almost entirely disregarded by philosophers, and lies before us as a raw and untreated material. It is Plato who has been most concerned with it, especially in the *Banquet* and the *Phaedrus;* yet what he says about it is confined to the sphere of myths, fables, and jokes, and for the most part concerns only the Greek love of boys. The little

---

[1] "Nothing is beautiful but truth; truth alone is agreeable." [Tr.]

[2] "Yet there was no knowledge of the death which they died." [Horace, *Sat.* i, 3, 108. Tr.]

that Rousseau says about our theme in the *Discours sur l'inégalité* (p. 96, *ed. Bip.*) is false and inadequate. Kant's discussion of the subject in the third section of the essay *On the Feeling of the Beautiful and the Sublime* (pp. 435 *seq.* of Rosenkranz's edition) is very superficial and without special knowledge; thus it also is partly incorrect. Finally, Platner's treatment of the subject in his *Anthropologie,* §§ 1347 *seq.,* will be found dull and shallow by everyone. Spinoza's definition, on the other hand, deserves to be mentioned for the sake of amusement, on account of its excessive naïvety: *Amor est titillatio, concomitante idea causae externae* (*Ethics,* IV, *Prop.* 44, *dem.*).[3] Accordingly, I have no predecessors either to make use of or to refute; the subject has forced itself on me objectively, and has become connected of its own accord with my consideration of the world. Moreover, least of all can I hope for approval from those who are themselves ruled by this same passion, and who accordingly try to express the excess of their feelings in the most sublime and ethereal figures of speech. To them my view will appear too physical, too material, however metaphysical, indeed transcendent, it may be at bottom. Meanwhile they may reflect that, if the object which today inspires them to write madrigals and sonnets had been born eighteen years earlier, it would have won scarcely a glance from them.

For all amorousness is rooted in the sexual impulse alone, is in fact absolutely only a more closely determined, specialized, and indeed, in the strictest sense, individualized sexual impulse, however ethereally it may deport itself. Now, keeping this in mind, we consider the important role played by sexual love in all its degrees and nuances, not merely in theatrical performances and works of fiction, but also in the world of reality. Next to the love of life, it shows itself here as the strongest and most active of all motives, and incessantly lays claim to half the powers and thoughts of the younger portion of mankind. It is the ultimate goal of almost all human effort; it has an unfavourable influence on the most important affairs, interrupts every hour the most serious occupations, and sometimes perplexes for a while even the greatest minds. It does not hesitate to intrude with its trash, and to interfere with the negotiations of statesmen and the investigations of the learned. It knows how to slip its love-notes and ringlets even into ministerial portfolios and philosophical manuscripts. Every day it brews and hatches the worst and most perplexing quarrels and disputes, destroys the most valuable relationships, and breaks the strongest bonds. It demands the sac-

---

[3] "Love is a titillation accompanied by the notion of an external cause." [Tr.]

rifice sometimes of life or health, sometimes of wealth, position, and happiness. Indeed, it robs of all conscience those who were previously honourable and upright, and makes traitors of those who have hitherto been loyal and faithful. Accordingly, it appears on the whole as a malevolent demon, striving to pervert, to confuse, and to overthrow everything. If we consider all this, we are induced to exclaim: Why all this noise and fuss? Why all the urgency, uproar, anguish, and exertion? It is merely a question of every Jack finding his Jill.[4] Why should such a trifle play so important a role, and constantly introduce disturbance and confusion into the well-regulated life of man? To the earnest investigator, however, the spirit of truth gradually reveals the answer. It is no trifle that is here in question; on the contrary, the importance of the matter is perfectly in keeping with the earnestness and ardour of the effort. The ultimate aim of all love-affairs, whether played in sock or in buskin, is actually more important than all other aims in man's life; and therefore it is quite worthy of the profound seriousness with which everyone pursues it. What is decided by it is nothing less than the *composition of the next generation*. The *dramatis personae* who will appear when we have retired from the scene are determined, according to their existence and their disposition, by these very frivolous love-affairs. Just as the being, the *existentia,* of these future persons is absolutely conditioned by our sexual impulse in general, so is their true nature, their *essentia,* by the individual selection in the satisfaction of this impulse, i.e., by sexual love; and by this it is in every respect irrevocably fixed. This is the key to the problem; we shall become more accurately acquainted with it in its application when we go through the degrees of amorousness from the most casual inclination up to the most intense passion. Then we shall recognize that the variety of these degrees springs from the degree of individualization of the choice.

The collected *love-affairs* of the present generation, taken together, are accordingly the human race's serious *meditatio compositionis generationis futurae, e qua iterum pendent innumerae generationes.*[5] This high importance of the matter is not a question of *individual* weal and woe, as in all other matters, but of the existence and special constitution of the human race in times to come; therefore the will of the individual appears at an enhanced power as the will of the species. It is this high importance on which the pathetic and sublime elements of love-affairs, the transcendent element of their ecstasies

---

[4] I have not dared to express myself precisely here; the patient and gracious reader must therefore translate the phrase into Aristophanic language.

[5] "Meditation on the composition of the future generation on which in their turn innumerable generations depend." [Tr.]

and pains, rest. For thousands of years poets have never wearied of presenting these in innumerable examples, for no theme can equal this in interest. As it concerns the weal and woe of the species, it is related to all the rest, which concern only the weal of the individual, as a solid body is to a surface. This is the reason why it is so hard to impart interest to a drama without love-affairs; on the other hand, this theme is never worn out even by daily use.

That which makes itself known to the individual consciousness as sexual impulse in general, and without direction to a definite individual of the other sex, is in itself, and apart from the phenomenon, simply the will-to-live. But what appears in consciousness as sexual impulse, directed to a definite individual, is in itself the will-to-live as a precisely determined individual. Now in this case the sexual impulse, though in itself a subjective need, knows how to assume very skilfully the mask of an objective admiration, and thus to deceive consciousness; for nature requires this stratagem in order to attain her ends. But in every case of being in love, however objective and touched with the sublime that admiration may appear to be, what alone is aimed at is the generation of an individual of a definite disposition. This is confirmed first of all by the fact that the essential thing is not perhaps mutual affection, but possession, in other words, physical enjoyment. The certainty of the former, therefore, cannot in any way console us for the want of the latter; on the contrary, in such a situation many a man has shot himself. On the other hand, when those who are deeply in love cannot obtain mutual affection, they are easily satisfied with possession, i.e., with physical enjoyment. This is proved by all forced marriages, and likewise by a woman's favour, so often purchased, in spite of her dislike, with large presents or other sacrifices, and also by cases of rape. The true end of the whole love-story, though the parties concerned are unaware of it, is that this particular child may be begotten; the method and manner by which this end is attained is of secondary importance. However loudly those persons of a lofty and sentimental soul, especially those in love, may raise an outcry over the gross realism of my view, they are nevertheless mistaken. For is not the precise determination of the individualities of the next generation a much higher and worthier aim than those exuberant feelings and immaterial soap-bubbles of theirs? Indeed, of earthly aims can there be one that is more important and greater? It alone corresponds to the depth with which we feel passionate love, to the seriousness with which it appears, and to the importance attached by it even to the trifling details of its sphere and occasion. Only in so far as *this* end is assumed to be the true one do the intricacies and difficulties, the endless exertions and annoyances, encountered for the attainment of the beloved object, appear appropriate to the matter. For it is the future generation in the whole of its individual definiteness which is pressing into existence by means of these efforts and exertions. In fact, it is itself already astir in that far-sighted, definite, and capricious selection for the satisfaction of the sexual impulse which is called love. The growing attachment of two lovers is in itself in reality the will-to-live of the new individual, an individual they can and want to produce. Its new life, indeed, is already kindled in the meeting of their longing glances, and it announces itself as a future individuality, harmonious and well constituted. They feel the longing for an actual union and fusion into a single being, in order then to go on living only as this being; and this longing receives its fulfilment in the child they produce. In the child the qualities transmitted by both parents continue to live, fused and united into one being. Conversely, the mutual, decided, and persistent dislike between a man and a girl is the announcement that what they might produce would only be a badly organized, unhappy being, wanting in harmony in itself. Therefore a deeper meaning lies in the fact that, although Calderón calls the atrocious Semiramis the daughter of the air, yet he introduces her as the daughter of a rape followed by the murder of the husband.

But what ultimately draws two individuals of different sex exclusively to each other with such power is the will-to-live which manifests itself in the whole species, and here anticipates, in the individual that these two can produce, an objectification of its true nature corresponding to its aims. Hence this individual will have the will or character from the father, the intellect from the mother, and the corporization from both. But the form will depend more on the father, the size more on the mother, in accordance with the law which comes to light in the breeding of hybrids among animals, and rests mainly on the fact that the size of the foetus must conform to that of the uterus. The quite special and individual passion of two lovers is just as inexplicable as is the quite special individuality of any person, which is exclusively peculiar to him; indeed at bottom the two are one and the same; the latter is *explicite* what the former was *implicite*. The moment when the parents begin to love each other—*to fancy each other,* as a very apposite English expression has it—is actually to be regarded as the very first formation of a new individual, and the true *punctum saliens* of its life; and, as I have said, in the meeting and fixation of their longing glances there arises the first germ of the new being, which of course, like all germs, is often crushed out. To a certain extent this new individual is a new (Platonic) Idea; and, just as all the Ideas strive to enter into the phenomenon with the greatest vehemence, avidly seizing for this purpose the matter which the law of causality divides among them all, so does this particular Idea of a human individuality strive with the greatest eagerness and vehemence for its realization in the phenomenon. This eagerness and vehemence is precisely the two future parents' passion for each other. It has innumerable degrees, the two extremes of which at any rate may be described as 'Αφροδίτη πάνδημος and οὐρανία;[6] but essentially it is everywhere the same. On the other hand, it will be the more powerful in degree the more *individualized* it is, in other words, the more the beloved individual is exclusively suited, by virtue of all his or her parts and qualities, to satisfy the desire of the lover and the need established through his or her own individuality. The point here in question will become clear to us in the further course of our discussion. Primarily and essentially, the amorous inclination is directed to health, strength, and beauty, and consequently to youth as well, since the will strives first of all to exhibit the specific character of the human species as the basis of all individuality; ordinary flirtation ('Αφροδίτη πάνδημος) does not go much farther. Connected with these, then, are the more special demands which we shall investigate in detail later, and with which the passion rises, where they see satisfaction before them. The highest degrees of this passion, however, spring from that suitability of the two individualities to each other. By virtue of this, the will, i.e., the character, of the father and the intellect of the mother bring about in their union precisely that individual for which the will-to-live in general, exhibiting itself in the whole species, feels a longing. This longing is in keeping with the magnitude of the will, and therefore exceeds the measure of a mortal heart; in just the same way, its motives lie beyond the sphere of the individual intellect. This, therefore, is the soul of a true and great passion. Now the more perfect the mutual suitability to each other of two individuals in each of the many different respects to be considered later, the stronger will their mutual passion prove to be. As there are no two individuals exactly alike, one particular woman must correspond most perfectly to each particular man—always with regard to what is to be produced. Really passionate love is as rare as is the accident of these two meeting. Since, however, the possibility of such a love is present in everyone, the descriptions of it in the works of the poets are intelligible to us. Just because the passion of being in love really turns on what is to be produced and on its qualities, and because the kernel of this passion lies in this, a friendship without any admixture of sexual love can exist between two young and comely persons of different sex by

---

[6] "Vulgar and celestial love." [Tr.]

virtue of the harmony of their disposition, their character, and their mental tendency; in fact, as regards sexual love, there may even exist between them a certain aversion. The reason for this is to be found in the fact that a child produced by them would have unharmonious bodily or mental qualities; in short, the child's existence and nature would not be in keeping with the aims of the will-to-live as it exhibits itself in the species. In the opposite case, in spite of difference of disposition, character, and mental tendency, and of the dislike and even hostility resulting therefrom, sexual love can nevertheless arise and exist; if it then blinds us to all that, and leads to marriage, such a marriage will be very unhappy.

Now to the more thorough investigation of the matter. Egoism is so deep-rooted a quality of all individuality in general that, in order to rouse the activity of an individual being, egotistical ends are the only ones on which we can count with certainty. It is true that the species has a prior, closer, and greater claim to the individual than has the perishable individuality itself. Yet when the individual is to be active, and even to make sacrifices for the sake of the continuance and constitution of the species, the importance of the matter cannot be made so comprehensible to his intellect, calculated as this is merely for individual ends, that its effect would be in accordance with the matter. Therefore in such a case, nature can attain her end only by implanting in the individual a certain *delusion,* and by virtue of this, that which in truth is merely a good thing for the species seems to him to be a good thing for himself, so that he serves the species, whereas he is under the delusion that he is serving himself. In this process a mere chimera, which vanishes immediately afterwards, floats before him, and, as motive, takes the place of a reality. This *delusion* is *instinct.* In the great majority of cases, instinct is to be regarded as the sense of the *species* which presents to the will what is useful to *it.* Since, however, the will has here become individual, it must be deceived in such a way that it perceives through the sense of the *individual* what the sense of the *species* presents to it. Thus it imagines it is pursuing individual ends, whereas in truth it is pursuing merely general ends (taking this word in the most literal sense). We observe the external phenomenon of instinct best in animals, where its role is most important; but only in ourselves can we become acquainted with the internal process, as with everything internal. Now it is supposed of course that man has hardly any instinct at all, at any rate only the instinct by which the new-born baby seeks and seizes its mother's breast. But we have in fact a very definite, distinct, and indeed complicated instinct, namely that to select the other individual for sexual satisfaction, a selection that is so fine, so serious, and so capricious. The beauty or ugliness of the other individual has absolutely nothing to do with this satisfaction in itself, that is to say, in so far as this satisfaction is a sensual pleasure resting on the individual's pressing need. Therefore the regard for this beauty or ugliness which is nevertheless pursued with such ardour, together with the careful selection that springs therefrom, evidently refers not to the chooser himself, although he imagines it does so, but to the true end and purpose, namely that which is to be produced; for this is to receive the type of the species as purely and correctly as possible. Thus through a thousand physical accidents and moral misfortunes there arises a very great variety of deteriorations of the human form; yet its true type in all its parts is always re-established. This takes place under the guidance of that sense of beauty which generally directs the sexual impulse, and without which this impulse sinks to the level of a disgusting need. Accordingly, in the first place, everyone will decidedly prefer and ardently desire the most beautiful individuals; in other words, those in whom the character of the species is most purely and strongly marked. But in the second place he will specially desire in the other individual *those* perfections that he himself lacks; in fact, he will even find beautiful those imperfections that are the opposite of his own. Hence, for example, short men look for tall women, persons with fair hair like those with dark, and so on. The delusive ecstasy that seizes a man at the sight of a woman whose beauty is suited to him, and pictures to him a union with her as the highest good, is just the *sense of the species*. Recognizing the distinctly expressed stamp of the species, this sense would like to perpetuate the species with this man. The maintenance of the type of the species rests on this decided inclination to beauty; hence it acts with such great power. Later on, we shall specially examine the considerations that it follows. Therefore, what here guides man is really an instinct directed to what is best for the species, whereas man himself imagines he is seeking merely a heightening of his own pleasure. In fact, we have in this an instructive explanation of the inner nature of *all* instinct, which, as here, almost always sets the individual in motion for the good of the species. For obviously the care with which an insect hunts for a particular flower, or fruit, or dung, or meat, or, like the ichneumon, for the larva of another insect, in order to lay its eggs only *there,* and to attain this does not shrink from trouble or danger, is very analogous to the care with which a man specially selects for sexual satisfaction a woman with qualities that appeal to him individually. He strives after her so eagerly that, to attain this end, he often, in defiance of all reason, sacrifices his own happiness in life by a foolish marriage, by love-affairs that cost him his fortune, his honour, and his life, even by crimes, such as adultery or rape; all merely in order to serve the species in the most appropriate way, in accordance with the will of nature that is everywhere supreme, although at the expense of the individual. Thus instinct is everywhere an action as if in accordance with the conception of an end or purpose, and yet entirely without such a conception. Nature implants it, wherever the acting individual would be incapable of understanding the end, or unwilling to pursue it. Therefore, as a rule, instinct is given only to the animals, especially indeed to the lowest of them, as having the least understanding; but almost only in the case here considered is it given also to·man, who, it is true, might understand the end, but would not pursue it with the necessary ardour, that is to say, even at the cost of his individual welfare. Here then, as in the case of all instinct, truth assumes the form of delusion, in order to act on the will. It is a voluptuous delusion which leads a man to believe that he will find a greater pleasure in the arms of a woman whose beauty appeals to him than in those of any other, or which, exclusively directed to a *particular* individual, firmly convinces him that her possession will afford him boundless happiness. Accordingly, he imagines he is making efforts and sacrifices for his own enjoyment, whereas he is doing so merely for the maintenance of the regular and correct type of the species; or there is to attain to existence a quite special and definite individuality that can come only from these parents. The character of instinct is here so completely present, namely an action as though in accordance with the conception of an end and yet entirely without such a conception, that whoever is urged by that delusion often abhors and would like to prevent the end, procreation, which alone guides it; this is the case with almost all illicit love-affairs. According to the character of the matter expounded, everyone who is in love will experience an extraordinary disillusionment after the pleasure he finally attains; and he will be astonished that what was desired with such longing achieves nothing more than what every other sexual satisfaction achieves, so that he does not see himself very much benefited by it. That desire was related to all his other desires as the species is to the individual, hence as the infinite to something finite. On the other hand, the satisfaction is really for the benefit only of the species, and so does not enter into the consciousness of the individual, who, inspired by the will of the species, here served with every kind of sacrifice a purpose that was not his own at all. Therefore, after the consummation of the great work, everyone who is in love finds himself duped; for the delusion by means of which the individual was the dupe of the species has disappeared. Accordingly,

Plato says very pertinently: ἡδονὴ ἀπάντων ἀλαζονέστατον (*Voluptas omnium maxime vaniloqua*), *Philebus* [65 c] 319.[7]

All this throws light once more on the instincts and mechanical tendencies of animals. These are also undoubtedly involved in a kind of delusion that deceives them with the prospect of their own pleasure, whereas they work so laboriously and with self-denial for the species. Thus the bird builds its nest; the insect looks for the only suitable place for its eggs, or even hunts for prey which, unsuitable for its own consumption, must be laid beside the eggs as food for the future larvae; the bee, the wasp, the ant attend to the work of their ingenious structures, and their highly complicated economy. They are all undoubtedly guided by a delusion that conceals the service of the species under the mask of an egotistical end. This is probably the only way to obtain a clear idea of the *inner* or subjective process lying at the root of the manifestations of instinct. But outwardly or objectively, we find in the case of those animals that are largely governed by instinct, especially of insects, a preponderance of the ganglionic system, i.e., the *subjective* nervous system, over the *objective* or cerebral system. From this it is to be concluded that they are urged not so much by an objective, correct apprehension, as by subjective representations which stimulate the desire, and result from the influence of the ganglionic system on the brain, and that accordingly they are urged by a certain *delusion;* and this will be the *physiological* process in the case of all instinct. By way of illustration, I mention as another example of instinct in man, though a weaker one, the capricious appetite of pregnant women. This seems to spring from the fact that the nourishment of the embryo sometimes requires a special or definite modification of the blood flowing to it; whereupon the food that produces such a modification at once presents itself to the pregnant woman as an object of ardent longing; thus a *delusion* arises. Accordingly, woman has one more instinct than has man; and in her the ganglionic system is much more developed. In the case of man, the great preponderance of the brain explains why he has fewer instincts than have animals, and why even these few can easily be led astray. Thus the sense of beauty, which instinctively guides selection for sexual satisfaction, is led astray when it degenerates into a tendency to pederasty. This is analogous to the bluebottle (*Musca vomitoria*) which, instead of laying its eggs, in accordance with its instinct, in tainted meat, lays them in the blossom of the *Arum dracunculus,* being led astray by the corpse-like smell of that plant.

---

[7] "For nothing is so boastful as cupidity." [Tr.]

That an instinct, directed absolutely to what is to be produced, underlies all sexual love, will obtain complete certainty from more detailed analysis; we cannot therefore omit this. First of all, it is not out of place to mention here that by nature man is inclined to inconstancy in love, woman to constancy. The man's love diminishes perceptibly from the moment it has obtained satisfaction; almost every other woman charms him more than the one he already possesses; he longs for variety. On the other hand, the woman's love increases from that very moment. This is a consequence of nature's aim, which is directed to the maintenance, and thus the greatest possible increase, of the species. The man can easily beget over a hundred children in a year, if there are that number of women available; on the other hand, no matter with how many men, the woman could bring into the world only one child in a year (apart from twin births). The man, therefore, always looks around for other women; the woman, on the contrary, cleaves firmly to the one man; for nature urges her, instinctively and without reflection, to retain the nourisher and supporter of the future offspring. Accordingly, conjugal fidelity for the man is artificial, for the woman natural; and so adultery on the part of the woman is much less pardonable than on the part of the man, both objectively on account of the consequences, and subjectively on account of its being unnatural.

However, to be thorough and to gain full conviction that pleasure in the other sex, however objective it may seem, is yet merely disguised instinct, i.e., sense of the species, striving to maintain its type, we must investigate more fully the very considerations that guide us in this pleasure. We must enter into their details, strange as such details to be mentioned here may appear to be in a philosophical work. These considerations are divided into those directly concerning the type of the species, i.e., beauty, those directed to psychic qualities, and finally the merely relative ones, which arise from the requisite correction or neutralization by each other of the one-sided qualities and abnormalities of the two individuals. We will go over them one by one.

Age is the primary consideration that guides our choice and inclination. On the whole, we accept it as the age from the years when menstruation begins to those when it ceases; but we give a decided preference to the period between the ages of eighteen and twenty-eight. Outside those years no woman can attract us; an old woman, that is to say a woman who no longer menstruates, excites our aversion. Youth without beauty always has attraction; beauty without youth has none. Here the purpose that unconsciously guides us is clearly the possibility of procreation in general. Therefore every individual loses attraction for the opposite sex to the extent that he or she is removed from the fittest period for procreation or conception. The second consideration is *health;* acute diseases disturb us only temporarily, chronic diseases, or even cachexia, repel us, because they are transmitted to the child. The third consideration is the *skeleton* or bony structure, because it is the foundation of the type of the species. Next to age and disease, nothing repels us so much as a deformed figure; even the most beautiful face cannot make up for it; whereas even the ugliest face, when accompanied by a straight stature, is preferred without question. Further, we feel most strongly every want of proportion in the *skeleton;* for example, a stunted, dumpy, short-legged figure, and many such; also a limping gait, where this is not the result of an external accident. On the other hand, a strikingly fine stature can make up for every defect; it enchants us. Here also we see the great value that all attach to smallness of the feet; this rests on their being an essential characteristic of the species, since no animal has so small a tarsus and metatarsus taken together as man has; and this is associated with his walking upright; he is a plantigrade. Accordingly, Jesus ben Sirach also says (Ecclus. xxvi, 23, according to the revised translation by Kraus): "Golden columns on a silver base, and beautiful feet on well-set heels." [8] The teeth are also important to us, because they are essential to nourishment, and are above all hereditary. The fourth consideration is a certain *fulness of flesh,* a predominance of the vegetative function, of plasticity, since this promises abundant nourishment for the foetus; hence great leanness repels us strongly. A full female bosom exerts an exceptional charm on the male, because, being directly connected with the woman's functions of propagation, it promises the new-born child abundant nourishment. On the other hand, *excessively* fat women excite our repugnance, because this condition points to atrophy of the uterus, and thus to barrenness; this is known not by the head, but by instinct. The last consideration is *beauty of the face.* Here the parts of the bones are considered first; hence we look principally for a beautiful nose, and a short, turned-up nose mars everything. A slight downward or upward curvature of the nose has decided the happiness in life of innumerable girls, and rightly, for the type of the species is at stake. A mouth small because of small maxillae is very essential as a specific characteristic of the human countenance, in contrast to the muzzles of animals. A receding chin, cut away as it were, is particularly repugnant, because *mentum*

---

[8] The above is taken from Deussen's translation. A translation of the quotation as given by Schopenhauer is: "A woman with straight figure and beautiful feet is like golden columns on silver chairs." [Tr.]

prominulum[9] is an exclusive characteristic of our species. Finally, there is the regard for beautiful eyes and forehead; this is associated with psychic qualities, especially those of the intellect which are inherited from the mother.

The unconscious considerations observed, on the other hand, by the inclination and tendency of women, we naturally cannot state so precisely. On the whole, the following may be asserted. They prefer the ages from thirty to thirty-five, and regard these as superior to the age of youths, who really offer the height of human beauty. The reason is that they are guided not by taste but by instinct, which recognizes in the age aforesaid the acme of procreative power. In general they are less concerned with beauty, especially of the face; it is as if they alone took it upon themselves to give this to the child. They are won mainly by a man's strength, and the courage connected with it; for these promise the production of strong children, and at the same time a courageous protector for them. Every bodily defect in the man, every variation from the type, can be eliminated, as regards the child, by the woman in reproduction through the fact that she herself is faultless in these respects, or even exceeds in the opposite direction. Only *those* qualities of the man are excluded from them which are peculiar to his sex, and which the mother, therefore, cannot give to the child. Such are the male structure of the skeleton, broad shoulders, narrow hips, straight legs, muscular strength, courage, beard, and so on. The result is that women often love ugly men, but never an unmanly man, because they cannot neutralize his defects.

The second kind of considerations underlying sexual love are those that concern psychic qualities. Here we shall find that the woman is generally attracted by the man's qualities of heart or character, as being those which are inherited from the father. The woman is won especially by firmness of will, resoluteness, and courage, perhaps also by honesty and kindness of heart. Intellectual merits, on the other hand, do not exercise any direct and instinctive power over her, just because they are *not* inherited from the father. With women want of understanding does not matter; in fact, extraordinary mental power, or even genius, as something abnormal, might have an unfavourable effect. Hence we often see an ugly, stupid, and coarse fellow get the better of a cultured, clever, and amiable man when dealing with women. Marriages from love are occasionally contracted between natures widely different intellectually; for example, the *man* is rough, powerful, and narrow-minded, the *woman* tenderly sensitive, deli-

---

[9] "Prominent chin." [Tr.]

cately thoughtful, cultured, aesthetic, and so on; or *he* is even a
genius and learned, whereas *she* is a silly goose:

> Sic visum Veneri; cui placet impares
> Formas atque animos sub juga aënea
> Saevo mittere cum joco.[10]

The reason is that quite different considerations from those of the
intellect predominate here, namely those of instinct. What is looked
for in marriage is not intellectual entertainment, but the procreation
of children; it is an alliance of hearts, not of heads. It is a vain and
ridiculous pretence when women assert that they have fallen in love
with a man's mind, or it is the overstraining of a degenerate nature.
On the other hand, in their instinctive love, men are not determined
by the woman's *qualities of character;* hence so many Socrateses
have found their Xanthippes, for example Shakespeare, Albrecht
Dürer, Byron, and others. But the qualities of *intellect* do have an
influence here, because they are inherited from the mother; yet their
influence is easily outweighed by that of physical beauty, which, as
something that concerns more essential points, has a more direct
effect. Nevertheless, from the feeling or experience of that influence,
it happens that mothers have their daughters taught the fine arts,
languages, and so forth, to make them attractive to men. In this they
try to assist the intellect by artificial means, just as they do the hips
and bust, should the occasion arise. It should be noted that here we
always speak only of the wholly immediate, instinctive attraction,
from which alone springs the condition of *being in love* proper. That
a woman of understanding and culture values understanding and
intellect in a man, that from rational reflection a man tests and takes
his bride's character into account, has nothing to do with the matter
with which we are dealing. Such things are the basis of a rational
choice in marriage, but not of the passionate love that is our theme.

So far, I have taken into account only the *absolute* considerations,
that is to say, those that apply to everyone. I now come to the
relative considerations, which are individual, because what is intended with them is a rectification of the type of the species already
defectively presented, a correction of the divergences from the type
which are already borne in the chooser's own person, and hence a
return to the pure presentation of the type. Therefore, everyone loves
what he himself lacks. Starting from the individual constitution, and
directed thereto, the choice resting on such *relative* considerations

---

[10] "And thus has Venus willed it; with cruel jest she often loves to send
uncongenial forms and spirits under the brazen yoke." [Horace, *Odes,* i, 33,
10. Tr.]

is much more definite, decided, and exclusive than is that which proceeds merely from absolute considerations. Therefore, as a rule, the origin of really passionate love is to be found in these relative considerations, and only that of the ordinary and slighter inclination in absolute considerations. Accordingly, it is not usual for precisely regular and perfect beauties to kindle great passions. For such a truly passionate inclination to arise, something is required that can be expressed only by a chemical metaphor; thus two persons must neutralize each other, just as an acid and an alkali do to make a neutral salt. The conditions required for this are in essence the following. In the first place, all sexuality is partiality. This partiality or one-sidedness is more decidedly expressed and present in a higher degree in one individual than in another. Therefore in every individual it can be better supplemented and neutralized by one individual of the opposite sex than by another, since every individual requires a one-sidedness, individually the opposite of his or her own, to supplement the type of mankind in the new individual to be produced, to whose constitution everything always tends. Physiologists know that manliness and womanliness admit of innumerable degrees. Through these the former sinks down to the repulsive gynander and hypospadaeus, and the latter rises to the graceful androgyne. Complete hermaphroditism can be reached from both sides, and at this point there are individuals who, holding the exact mean between the two sexes, cannot be attributed to either, and are consequently unfit for propagation. Accordingly, the neutralization, here under discussion, of the two individualities by each other requires that the particular degree of *his* manliness shall correspond exactly to the particular degree of *her* womanliness, so that the one-sidedness of each exactly cancels that of the other. Accordingly, the most manly man will look for the most womanly woman, and *vice versa;* and in just the same way will every individual look for the one corresponding to him or her in degree of sexuality. How far the required relation occurs between two individuals is instinctively felt by them, and, together with the other *relative* considerations, lies at the root of the higher degrees of being in love. Therefore, while the lovers speak pathetically of the harmony of their souls, the core of the matter is often the agreement, here pointed out, with regard to the being that is to be produced and to its perfection. Moreover, such agreement is obviously of much more importance than is the harmony of their souls; not long after the wedding this harmony often resolves itself into a howling discord. Here come in the further relative considerations, resting on the fact that everyone endeavours to eliminate through the other individual his own weaknesses, defects, and deviations from the type, lest they be perpetuated or even grow into complete abnormalities in the child to be produced. The weaker a man is in regard to muscular strength, the more will he look for robust women; and the woman on her part will do just the same. Now, as a lesser degree of muscular strength in the woman is natural and regular, woman will, as a rule, give the preference to stronger men. Further, size is an important consideration. Short men have a decided inclination for tall women, and *vice versa;* indeed in a short man the preference for tall women will be the more passionate, according as he himself was begotten by a tall father, and has remained short only through the influence of his mother, because he has inherited from the father the vascular system and its energy that is able to supply a large body with blood. On the other hand, if his father and grandfather were short, that inclination will be less decided. At the root of a tall woman's aversion to tall men is nature's intention to avoid too tall a race, lest with the strength to be imparted by *this* woman, the race should prove to be too weak to live long. But if such a woman chooses a tall husband, perhaps for the sake of being more presentable in society, then, as a rule, the offspring will atone for the folly. Further, the consideration as regards complexion is very definite. Blondes prefer absolutely dark persons or brunettes, but only rarely do the latter prefer the former. The reason for this is that fair hair and blue eyes constitute a variation, almost an abnormality, analogous to white mice, or at least to white horses. In no other quarter of the globe, not even in the vicinity of the poles, are they indigenous, but only in Europe; and they have obviously come from Scandinavia. Incidentally, I here express my opinion that a white colour in the skin is not natural to man, but that by nature he has a black or brown skin, just as had our forefathers the Hindus; consequently, a white human being has never sprung originally from the womb of nature, and therefore there is no white race, however much this is talked about, but every white human being is bleached. Driven into the north, which is strange and foreign to him, and in which he exists only like exotic plants, and like these requires a hothouse in winter, man became white in the course of thousands of years. The gypsies, an Indian race that immigrated about four centuries ago, show the transition from the complexion of the Hindus to our own.[11] Therefore in sexual love, nature strives to return to dark hair and brown eyes as the archetype; but the white colour of the skin has become a second nature, though not so that the brown of the Hindus would repel us. Finally, each individual also seeks in the particular parts of the body the corrective

---

[11] The fuller discussion of this is found in *Parerga,* Vol. II, § 92 of the first edition.

of his own defects and deviations, and does this the more decidedly, the more important is the part. Therefore pug-nosed individuals have an inexpressible liking for hawk-like noses, for parrot-faces; it is just the same as regards all the other parts. Persons with excessively slim, long bodies and limbs can find beauty even in a stumpy and exceedingly short body. Considerations of temperament rule in an analogous manner; each will prefer the opposite of his own, yet only to the extent that his is a decided one. He who is himself very perfect in some respect does not, of course, seek out and love the imperfection in that very respect, but he is more easily reconciled to it than are others, because he himself ensures the children against great imperfection in this particular instance. For example, one who is himself very white will not be repelled by a yellowish complexion; but one who has this colour will find a dazzling white divinely beautiful. The rare case in which a man falls in love with a decidedly ugly woman occurs when, besides the above-discussed exact harmony of the degree of sexuality, the whole of her abnormalities are precisely the opposite to, and thus the corrective of, his own. It is then usual for the infatuation to reach a high degree.

The profound seriousness with which we scrutinize and consider each part of the woman's body, and with which she on her part does the same, the critical scrupulousness with which we examine a woman who begins to please us, the capricious nature of our choice, the close attention with which the bridegroom observes the bride, the care he takes not to be deceived in any part, and the great value he attaches to every excess or deficiency in the essential parts; all this is quite in keeping with the importance of the end. For the new being to be produced will have to bear a similar part throughout its whole life. For example, if the woman is but slightly crooked or uneven, this can easily impart a hump to her son; and so with everything else. Of course, consciousness of all this does not exist; on the contrary, everyone imagines he makes that difficult selection only in the interest of his own sensual pleasure (which at bottom cannot be interested in this at all). But he makes it exactly as conforms, under the presupposition of his own corporization, to the interest of the species, and the secret task is to maintain the type of the species as purely as possible. Without knowing it, the individual here acts by order of something higher, the species; hence the importance he attaches to things that might, indeed would of necessity, be to him as such a matter of indifference. There is something quite peculiar to be found in the deep, unconscious seriousness with which two young people of opposite sex regard each other when they meet for the first time, the searching and penetrating glance they cast at each other, the careful inspection all the features and parts of their respective persons have to undergo. This scrutiny and examination is the *meditation of the genius of the species* concerning the individual possible through these two, and the combination of its qualities. The degree of their mutual pleasure in and longing for each other proves to be in accordance with the result of this meditation. After this longing has reached a significant degree, it can be suddenly extinguished again by the discovery of something that had previously remained unobserved. In all who are capable of procreation, therefore, the genius of the species meditates thus concerning the race to come. The constitution of this race is the great work with which Cupid is occupied, incessantly active, speculating, and pondering. Compared with the importance of his great business concerning the species and all the generations to come, the affairs of individuals in all their ephemeral totality are very insignificant; hence he is always ready to sacrifice these arbitrarily. For he is related to them as an immortal is to mortals, and his interests are related to theirs as the infinite to the finite. Therefore, conscious of managing affairs of a higher order than all those that concern only individual weal and woe, he pursues them with sublime and undisturbed calm amid the tumult of war, in the turmoil of business life, or during the raging of a plague; and follows them even into the seclusion of the cloister.

In the foregoing discussion, we have seen that the intensity of the state of being in love increases with its individualization, since we showed how the physical constitution of two individuals can be such that, for the purpose of restoring the type of the species as far as possible, the one individual is quite specially and completely the complement of the other, who therefore desires it exclusively. Even in this case there comes about a considerable passion; and this at once gains a nobler and more sublime appearance from the very fact that it is directed to an individual object and to this alone, and thus appears, so to speak, at the *special* order of the species. For the opposite reason, mere sexual impulse is base and ignoble, because it is directed to all without individualization, and strives to maintain the species merely as regards quantity, with little consideration for quality. But individualization and with it the intensity of being in love can reach so high a degree that without their satisfaction all the good things of the world and even life itself lose their value. It is then a desire that exceeds in intensity every other; hence it makes a person ready for any sacrifice, and, if its fulfilment remains for ever denied, can lead to madness or suicide. Besides the considerations we have previously set forth, there must at the root of such excessive passion be also other unconscious considerations that we do not have before our eyes. We must therefore assume that not only the corporization, but also the *will* of the man and the *intellect* of the woman are specially suited to each other. In consequence of this, one particular individual can be produced by them alone, and its existence is intended by the genius of the species for reasons inaccessible to us, since they lie in the inner nature of the thing-in-itself. Or, to speak more precisely, the will-to-live desires to objectify itself here in a quite particular individual that can be produced only by this father together with this mother. This metaphysical desire of the will-in-itself has primarily no other sphere of action in the series of beings than the hearts of the future parents. These, accordingly, are seized with this intense desire, and then imagine they are desiring on their own account what has merely for the moment a purely metaphysical end, in other words, an end that lies outside the series of actually existing things. Therefore it is the intense desire of the future individual to enter into existence, an individual that has here first become possible. This longing proceeds from the primary source of all beings, and exhibits itself in the phenomenon as the exalted passion of the future parents for each other, which pays little regard to everything outside itself. Indeed it exhibits itself as a delusion which is unique, by virtue of which such a man in love would give up all the good things of the world for cohabitation with this woman; and yet this does not actually achieve for him more than does any other cohabitation. That it is, however, this cohabitation alone that is kept in view, is seen from the fact that even this exalted passion, like every other, is extinguished in the enjoyment—to the great astonishment of those involved in it. The passion is extinguished also when, through the woman's eventual barrenness (which, according to Hufeland, may arise from nineteen accidental constitutional defects), the real metaphysical purpose is frustrated, just as happens daily in millions of seeds trampled under foot. Yet in these seeds the same metaphysical life-principle strives for existence, and there is no other consolation for this than the fact that an infinity of space, time, and matter, and consequently an inexhaustible opportunity for return, stand open to the will-to-live.

The view here expounded must have been present in the mind of Theophrastus Paracelsus, though only in a fleeting form. He did not deal with this theme, and my whole train of thought was foreign to him; but in quite a different context, and in his desultory manner, he wrote the following remarkable words: *Hi sunt, quos Deus copulavit, ut eam quae fuit Uriae et David; quamvis ex diametro (sic enim sibi humana mens persuadebat) cum justo et legitimo matrimonio pugnaret hoc. . . . sed propter Salomonem, QUI ALIUNDE NASCI*

NON POTUIT nisi ex Bathseba, conjuncto David semine, quamvis meretrice, conjunxit eos Deus (De Vita Longa, I, 5).[12]

The longing of love, the ἵμερος, that the poets of all ages are for ever concerned to express in innumerable forms, a subject which they do not exhaust, in fact to which they cannot do justice; this longing that closely associates the notion of an endless bliss with the possession of a definite woman, and an unutterable pain with the thought that this possession is not attainable; this longing and this pain of love cannot draw their material from the needs of an ephemeral individual. On the contrary, they are the sighs of the spirit of the species, which sees here, to be won or lost, an irreplaceable means to its ends, and therefore groans deeply. The species alone has infinite life, and is therefore capable of infinite desire, infinite satisfaction, and infinite sufferings. But these are here imprisoned in the narrow breast of a mortal; no wonder, therefore, when such a breast seems ready to burst, and can find no expression for the intimation of infinite rapture or infinite pain with which it is filled. This, then, affords the material for all erotic poetry of the sublime kind, which accordingly rises into transcendent metaphors that soar above all that is earthly. This is the theme of Petrarch, the material for the Saint-Preuxs, Werthers, and Jacopo Ortis, who apart from this could not be understood or explained. For that infinite appreciation of the beloved cannot rest on some spiritual excellences, or in general on her objective, actual qualities, because for this purpose she is often not well enough known to the lover; this was the case with Petrarch. The spirit of the species alone is able to see at a glance what value she has for *it,* for its ends. As a rule, great passions arise at the first glance:

> Who ever lov'd, that lov'd not at first sight?
> Shakespeare, *As You Like It,* III, 5.

A passage in the romance *Guzman de Alfarache,* by Mateo Alemán, which has been famous for two hundred and fifty years, is noteworthy in this respect: *No es necesario, para que uno ame, que pase distancia de tiempo, que siga discurso, ni haga eleccion, sino que con aquella primera y sola vista, concurran juntamente cierta correspondencia ó consonancia, ó lo que acá solemos vulgarmente decir, una CONFRONTACION DE SANGRE, á que por particular influxo*

---

[12] "It is those whom God has joined together, as, for example, David and the wife of Uriah; although this relationship (so at least the mind of man persuaded itself) is diametrically opposed to a just and legitimate marriage. But for Solomon's sake, *who could not be born* from parents *other than* Bathseba and the seed of David, although in adultery, God joined these two together." [Tr.]

suelen mover las estrellas. (In order that one may love, it is not necessary that much time should pass, that he should set to work with deliberation and make a choice, but merely that, at that first and only glance, a certain correspondence and consonance should be encountered on both sides, or what we are accustomed to call in ordinary life a *sympathy of the blood,* and a special influence of the stars usually prompts one to this.) (Part II, Bk. iii, c. 5.) Accordingly, the loss of the beloved through a rival or by death is also for the passionate lover a pain exceeding all others, just because it is of a transcendent nature, in that it not merely affects him as an individual, but attacks him in his *essentia aeterna,* in the life of the species, into whose special will and service he was summoned. Therefore jealousy is so tormenting and terrible, and the giving up of the beloved is the greatest of all sacrifices. A hero is ashamed of all lamentations except those of love, because in these it is not he but the species that wails. In Calderón's *Zenobia the Great,* there is in the second act a scene between Zenobia and Decius in which the latter says:

> *Cielos; ¿luego tu me quieres?*
> *Perdiera cien mil victorias,*
> *Volviérame, etc.*[13]

Here honour, which hitherto outweighed every interest, is driven from the field, as soon as sexual love, i.e., the interest of the species, comes into play, and sees a decided advantage before it. For this is infinitely superior to any interest of mere individuals, however important it be. Therefore honour, duty, and loyalty yield to this alone, after they have withstood every other temptation, even the threat of death. In just the same way we find in private life that in no point is conscientiousness so rare as in this. It is sometimes set aside here even by persons who are otherwise honest and just, and adultery is committed recklessly when passionate love, in other words the interest of the species, has taken possession of them. It seems as if they believed themselves to be conscious of a higher right than can ever be conferred by the interests of individuals, just because they act in the interest of the species. In this connexion Chamfort's remarks are noteworthy: *Quand un homme et une femme ont l'un pour l'autre une passion violente, il me semble toujours que, quelques soient les obstacles qui les séparent, un mari, des parens etc., les deux amans sont l'un à l'autre, DE PAR LA NATURE, qu'ils s'appartiennent de DROIT DIVIN, malgré les lois et les conventions*

---

[13] "Heaven! then you love me? For this I would give up a hundred thousand victories, I would turn back," etc.

humaines.[14] Whoever is inclined to be incensed at this should be referred to the remarkable indulgence shown in the Gospel by the Saviour to the woman taken in adultery, since he assumes at the same time the same guilt in all those present. From this point of view, the greatest part of the *Decameron* appears as mere mocking and jeering on the part of the genius of the species at the rights and interests of individuals which are trampled under foot by it. When differences of rank and similar circumstances oppose the union of passionate lovers, they are set aside with the same ease, and are treated as nothing by the genius of the species. Pursuing its ends that belong to generations without number, this genius blows away such human laws and scruples like chaff. For the same deep-lying reason, every danger is willingly encountered, and even the otherwise faint-hearted become courageous, when the ends of passionate love are at stake. In plays and novels, we see with ready sympathy young persons, asserting their love-affairs, i.e., the interest of the species, gain the victory over their elders, who are mindful only of the welfare of individuals. For the efforts of the lovers appear to us to be so much more important, sublime, and therefore right than anything that could be opposed to them, just as the species is more important than the individual. Thus the fundamental theme of almost all comedies is the appearance of the genius of the species with its aims. These run counter to the personal interests of the individuals who are presented in the comedy, and threaten to undermine their happiness. As a rule, the genius of the species achieves its object; and, as this is in accordance with poetic justice, it satisfies the spectator, because he feels that the aims of the species take precedence of all those of individuals. Therefore at the conclusion he quite confidently leaves the lovers crowned with victory, since he shares with them the delusion that they have established their own happiness, whereas they have rather sacrificed it to the welfare of the species, in opposition to the will and foresight of their elders. In isolated, abnormal comedies, the attempt has been made to reverse the matter, and to bring about the happiness of the individuals at the expense of the aims of the species; but the spectator feels the pain suffered by the genius of the species, and is not consoled by the advantage thereby assured to the individuals. A couple of very well known little pieces occur to me as examples of this kind, namely *La Reine de seize ans* and *Le Mariage de raison*. Since the aims of the species are frustrated in

---

[14] "When a man and a woman have a very strong passion for each other, it always seems to me that, whatever obstacles there may be that separate them, such as husband or parents, the two lovers belong to each other *by nature* and *by divine right*, in spite of laws and human conventions." [Tr.]

tragedies with love-affairs, the lovers, who were the tools of the species, generally perish at the same time, as for example, in *Romeo and Juliet, Tancred, Don Carlos, Wallenstein, The Bride of Messina,* and many others.

A person's being in love often furnishes comic, and sometimes even tragic, phenomena, both because, taken possession of by the spirit of the species, he is now ruled by it, and no longer belongs to himself; in this way his conduct becomes inappropriate to the individual. In the higher degrees of being in love, his thoughts are given such a poetical and sublime touch, even a transcendent and hyperphysical tendency, by virtue of which he appears wholly to lose sight of his real, very physical aim. What gives this to his thoughts is ultimately the fact that he is now inspired by the spirit of the species, whose affairs are infinitely more important than all those that concern mere individuals, in order to establish under the special directions of this spirit the entire existence of an indefinitely long posterity with *this* individually and precisely determined nature, a nature that it can obtain simply and solely from *him* as father and from his beloved as mother. Otherwise this posterity, *as such,* never comes to existence, whereas the objectification of the will-to-live expressly demands this existence. It is the feeling of acting in affairs of such transcendent importance that raises the lover so far above everything earthly, indeed even above himself, and gives to his very physical desires such a hyperphysical clothing that love becomes a poetical episode even in the life of the most prosaic person; in this latter case, the matter sometimes assumes a comic aspect. That mandate of the will, objectifying itself in the species, exhibits itself in the lover's consciousness under the mask of the anticipation of an infinite bliss which he is to find in the union with this female individual. In the highest degree of being in love this chimera becomes so radiant that, if it cannot be attained, life itself loses all charm, and appears so cheerless, flat, and unpalatable, that disgust at it overcomes even the dread of death, so that it is sometimes voluntarily cut short. The will of such a person has been caught up in the whirlpool of the will of the species, or that will of the species has obtained so great an ascendancy over the individual will that if such a person cannot be effective in the first capacity, he disdains to be so in the last. Here the individual is too weak a vessel to be capable of enduring the infinite longing of the will of the species which is concentrated on a definite object. Therefore in this case the issue is suicide, sometimes the double suicide of the two lovers, unless, to save life, nature should allow madness to intervene, which then envelops with its veil the consciousness of that hopeless state. No year passes without proving by several cases of all these kinds the reality of what has been set forth.

Not only, however, does the unsatisfied passion of being in love sometimes have a tragic issue, but even the satisfied passion leads more often to unhappiness than to happiness. For its demands often clash so much with the personal welfare of the man or woman concerned as to undermine it, since they are incompatible with his or her other circumstances, and upset the plan of life built on these. In fact, love is often in contradiction not only with external circumstances, but even with the lover's own individuality, since it casts itself on persons who, apart from the sexual relation, would be hateful, contemptible, and even abhorrent to the lover. But the will of the species is so much more powerful than that of the individual, that the lover shuts his eyes to all the qualities repugnant to him, overlooks everything, misjudges everything, and binds himself for ever to the object of his passion. He is so completely infatuated by that delusion, which vanishes as soon as the will of the species is satisfied, and leaves behind a detested partner for life. Only from this is it possible to explain why we often see very rational, and even eminent, men tied to termagants and matrimonial fiends, and cannot conceive how they could have made such a choice. For this reason the ancients represented love as blind. In fact, a man in love may even clearly recognize and bitterly feel in his bride the intolerable faults of temperament and character which promise him a life of misery, and yet not be frightened away:

> I ask not, I care not,
> If guilt's in thy heart;
> I know that I love thee,
> Whatever thou art.[15]

For ultimately he seeks not *his* interest, but that of a third person who has yet to come into existence, although he is involved in the delusion that what he seeks is his own interest. But it is precisely this not seeking *one's own* interest, everywhere the stamp of greatness, which gives even to passionate love a touch of the sublime, and makes it a worthy subject of poetry. Finally, sexual love is compatible even with the most extreme hatred towards its object; hence Plato compared it to the love of the wolf for the sheep. Therefore, the case appears when a passionate lover is unable to meet with a favourable response under any condition, in spite of all his efforts and entreaties:

---

[15] Thomas Moore, *Irish Melodies.* [Tr.]

I love and hate her.
Shakespeare, *Cymbeline,* III, 5.

The hatred that is then kindled towards the beloved sometimes goes
so far that the lover murders her and then commits suicide. A
few instances of this kind usually happen every year; they will be
found in the English and French newspapers. Goethe's verse is therefore quite correct:

By all love ever rejected! By hell-fire hot and unsparing!
I wish I knew something worse, that I might use it for swearing! [16]

It is really no hyperbole when a lover describes as *cruelty* the
coldness of the beloved, and the delight of her vanity in gloating over
his sufferings. For he is under the influence of an impulse akin to
the instinct of insects, which compels him to pursue his purpose unconditionally, in spite of all the arguments of his faculty of reason,
and to set aside everything else; he cannot give it up. Not one but
many a Petrarch has there been, who has had to drag through life
the unsatisfied ardour of love, like a fetter, like an iron weight tied
to his foot, and has breathed out his sighs in solitary woods; but
only in the one Petrarch did there dwell at the same time the gift of
poetry, so that Goethe's fine verse holds good of him.

And when in his torment man was dumb,
A god gave me the power to say how I suffer.

In fact, the genius of the species generally wages war with the
guardian geniuses of individuals; it is their pursuer and enemy,
always ready ruthlessly to destroy personal happiness in order to
carry out its ends; indeed, the welfare of whole nations has sometimes been sacrificed to its whims. Shakespeare gives us an example
of this in *Henry VI, Part III,* act III, scenes 2 and 3. All this rests
on the fact that the species, as that in which the root of our true
nature lies, has a closer and prior right to us than has the individual;
hence its affairs take precedence. From a feeling of this, the ancients
personified the genius of the species in Cupid, a malevolent, cruel, and
therefore ill-reputed god, in spite of his childish appearance, a
capricious, despotic demon, yet lord of gods and men:

σὺ δ'ὦ θεῶν τύραννε κ'ἀνθρώπων, Ἔρως!
(*Tu, deorum hominumque tyranne, Amor!*)[17]

A deadly dart, blindness, and wings are his attributes. These last

---

[16] Goethe's *Faust,* Bayard Taylor's translation. [Tr.]
[17] "Eros, tyrant of gods and men!" [Euripides, *Andromeda,* fragm. Tr.]

signify changeableness; this appears, as a rule, only with the disillusionment that is the consequence of satisfaction.

Thus, because the passion rested on a delusion that presented as valuable for the individual what is of value only for the species, the deception is bound to vanish after the end of the species has been attained. The spirit of the species, which had taken possession of the individual, sets him free again. Forsaken by this spirit, the individual falls back into his original narrowness and neediness, and sees with surprise that, after so high, heroic, and infinite an effort, nothing has resulted for his pleasure but what is afforded by any sexual satisfaction. Contrary to expectation, he finds himself no happier than before; he notices that he has been the dupe of the will of the species. As a rule, therefore, a Theseus made happy will forsake his Ariadne. If Petrarch's passion had been satisfied, his song would have been silenced from that moment, just as is that of the bird, as soon as the eggs are laid.

Incidentally, it may here be remarked that, however much my metaphysics of love may displease the very persons who are ensnared in this passion, yet if rational considerations in general could avail anything against it, the fundamental truth I reveal would, more than anything else, necessarily enable one to overcome it. But the saying of the old comedian will, no doubt, remain true: *Quae res in se neque consilium, neque modum habet ullum, eam consilio regere non potes.*[18]

Marriages from love are contracted in the interest of the species, not of individuals. It is true that the persons concerned imagine they are advancing their own happiness; but their actual aim is one that is foreign to themselves, since it lies in the production of an individual that is possible only through them. Brought together by this aim, they ought then to get on with each other as well as possible. However, the two persons, brought together by that instinctive delusion that is the essence of passionate love, will in other respects be very often of quite different natures. This comes to light when the delusion vanishes, as it necessarily must. Accordingly, marriages contracted from love prove as a rule unhappy, for through them the coming generation is provided for at the expense of the present. *Quien se casa por amores, ha de vivir con dolores* (He who marries for love has to live in sorrow) says the Spanish proverb. The opposite is the case with marriages contracted from convenience, often in accordance with the parents' choice. Here the governing considerations, be they of whatever kind they may, are at any rate real, and cannot vanish

---

[18] "What is not endowed either with reason or moderation cannot possibly be ruled by reason." [Terence, *Eunuchus*, 57-8. Tr.]

of themselves. Through them the happiness of the present generation is provided for, but of course to the detriment of the coming generation, yet the former happiness remains problematical. The man, having his eye on money instead of on the satisfaction of his inclination in the case of his marriage, lives more in the individual than in the species. This is directly opposed to the truth; hence it appears contrary to nature, and excites a certain contempt. A girl who rejects the proposal of a wealthy and not old man, against her parents' advice, in order to choose, setting aside all considerations of convenience, according to her instinctive inclination, sacrifices her individual welfare to that of the species. But on this very account, we cannot withhold a certain approbation; for she has preferred what is more important, and has acted in the spirit of nature (more precisely of the species), whereas the parents advised her in the spirit of individual egoism. In consequence of all this, it seems as if, in making a marriage, either the individual or the interest of the species must come off badly. Often this must be the case, for that convenience and passionate love should go hand in hand is the rarest stroke of good fortune. The wretched physical, moral, or intellectual state of most people may have its cause partly in the fact that marriages are usually contracted not from pure choice and inclination, but from all kinds of external considerations and according to accidental circumstances. But if inclination is, to a certain extent, taken into consideration along with convenience, this is, so to speak, a compromise with the genius of the species. It is well known that happy marriages are rare, just because it is of the essence of marriage that the principal aim is not the present, but the coming generation. However, let it be added for the consolation of tender and loving natures that passionate sexual love is sometimes associated with a feeling of an entirely different origin, namely real friendship based on harmony of disposition, which nevertheless often appears only when sexual love proper is extinguished in its satisfaction. That friendship will then often spring from the fact that the supplementary and corresponding physical, moral, and intellectual qualities of the two individuals, from which arose the sexual love with regard to the child to be produced, are also related to one another with reference to the individuals themselves, in a supplementary manner as opposite qualities of temperament and mental gifts, and thereby form the basis of a harmony of dispositions.

The whole metaphysics of love here discussed is closely connected with my metaphysics in general, and the light which it reflects on this may be summarized as follows.

We have seen that, in the satisfaction of the sexual impulse, the careful selection that rises through innumerable degrees up to passionate love rests on the extremely serious interest taken by man in the personal constitution of the coming generation. Now this exceedingly remarkable interest confirms two truths set forth in the preceding chapters: (1) The indestructibility of man's true being-in-itself, which continues to live in that coming generation. For that interest, so lively and eager, and not springing from reflection and intention, but from the innermost impulse and urge of our true nature, could not be present so indelibly, and exercise so great a power over man, if he were absolutely perishable, and were merely followed in time by a race actually and entirely different from him. (2) That his true being-in-itself lies rather in the species than in the individual. For that interest in the special constitution of the species, which forms the root of all love-affairs from the passing inclination up to the most serious passion, is for everyone really the most important matter, whose success or failure touches him most acutely; hence it is called preeminently the *affair of the heart.* Moreover, when this interest has expressed itself strongly and decidedly, every interest that concerns merely one's own person is thought less of, and is necessarily sacrificed to it. In this way, therefore, man shows that the species is nearer to him than the individual, and that he lives more immediately in the former than in the latter. Why, then, does the man in love hang with complete abandon on the eyes of his chosen one, and is ready to make every sacrifice for her? Because it is his *immortal part* that longs for her; it is always the mortal part alone that longs for everything else. That eager or even ardent longing, directed to a particular woman, is therefore an immediate pledge of the indestructibility of the kernel of our true nature, and of its continued existence in the species. But to regard this continued existence as something trifling and insufficient is a mistake, which arises from the fact that, by the continued life of the species, we understand nothing more than the future existence of beings similar to, but in no respect identical with, ourselves; and this again because, starting from knowledge directed outwards, we take into consideration only the external form of the species, as we apprehend this in perception, and not its inner nature. But it is precisely this inner nature that is the basis of our own consciousness as its kernel, and so is even more immediate than this itself is, and, as thing-in-itself, free from the *principium individuationis,* is really the same identical thing in all individuals, whether they exist side by side or one after another. Now this is the will-to-live, and hence precisely that which has so pressing and urgent a desire for life and continuance. Accordingly, this remains immune from, and unaffected by, death. But there is also the fact that it cannot attain to a better state or condition than its present one; consequently, with life, the constant suffering and dying of individuals are certain to it. To free it from this is reserved for the *denial* of the will-to-live; through this denial, the individual will tears itself away from the stem of the species, and gives up that existence in it. We lack concepts for what the will now is; indeed, we lack all data for such concepts. We can only describe it as that which is free to be or not to be the will-to-live. For the latter case, Buddhism describes it by the word *Nirvana,* whose etymology was given in a note at the end of chapter 41. It is the point that remains for ever inaccessible to all human knowledge precisely as such.

If, from the standpoint of this last consideration, we now contemplate the bustle and turmoil of life, we see everyone concerned with its cares and troubles, exerting all his strength to satisfy infinite needs and to ward off suffering in many forms, yet without daring to hope for anything else in place of it except just the preservation of this tormented existence for a short span of time. In between, however, we see in the midst of the tumult the glances of two lovers meet longingly: yet why so secretly, nervously, and furtively? Because these lovers are the traitors who secretly strive to perpetuate the whole trouble and toil that would otherwise rapidly come to an end. Such an end they try to frustrate, as others like them have frustrated it previously. But this consideration already encroaches on the following chapter.

APPENDIX TO THE PRECEDING CHAPTER

> Οὕτως ἀναιδῶς ἐξεκίνησας τόδε
> τὸ ῥῆμα· καὶ ποῦ τοῦτο φεύξεσθαι δοκεῖς;
> Πέφευγα· τ'ἀληθὲς γὰρ ἰσχυρὸν τρέφω.
> (Sophocles, *Oedipus Rex,* 354)[19]

On page 541 I casually mentioned pederasty, describing it as a misguided instinct. This seemed to me sufficient when I was working on the second edition. Further reflection on this aberration has since enabled me to discover a remarkable problem, and its solution also. This presupposes the preceding chapter, but also throws light on it, and therefore helps to supplement and support the fundamental view there expounded.

---

[19] "Do you make bold so shamelessly to utter such a word, and think to escape punishment? 'I have escaped, for truth bears me witness.' " [Tr.]

Considered in itself, pederasty appears to be a monstrosity, not merely contrary to nature, but in the highest degree repulsive and abominable; it seems an act to which only a thoroughly perverse, distorted, and degenerate nature could at any time descend, and which would be repeated in quite isolated cases at most. But if we turn to experience, we find the opposite; we see this vice fully in vogue and frequently practised at all times and in all countries of the world, in spite of its detestable nature. We all know that it was generally widespread among the Greeks and Romans, and was publicly admitted and practised unabashed. All the authors of antiquity give more than abundant proof of this. In particular, the poets one and all are full of this topic; not even the respectable Virgil is an exception (*Eclogue* 2). It is ascribed even to the poets of remote antiquity, to Orpheus (who was torn to pieces for it by the Maenads), to Thamyris, and even to the gods themselves. The philosophers also speak much more of this love than of the love of women; in particular, Plato seems to know of hardly any other, and likewise the Stoics, who mention it as worthy of the sage. (Stobaeus, *Eclog. eth.,* bk. II, c. 7.) In the *Symposium,* Plato even mentions to the credit of Socrates, as an unexampled act of heroism, that he scorned Alcibiades who offered himself to him for the purpose. In Xenophon's *Memorabilia,* Socrates speaks of pederasty as a thing blameless and even praiseworthy. (Stobaeus, *Florilegium,* Vol. I, p. 57.) Likewise in the *Memorabilia* (Bk. I, *cap.* 3, § 8), where Socrates warns of the dangers of love, he speaks so exclusively of love of boys that one would imagine there were no women at all. Even Aristotle (*Politics,* ii, 9) speaks of pederasty as of a usual thing, without censuring it. He mentions that it was held in public esteem by the Celts, that the Cretans and their laws countenanced it as a means against overpopulation, and he recounts (c. 10) the male love-affair of Philolaus the legislator, and so on. Even Cicero says: *Apud Graecos opprobrio fuit adolescentibus, si amatores non haberent.*[20] Here in general there is no need of proofs for well-informed readers; they can recall them by the hundred, for with the ancients everything is full of it. But even among less cultured peoples, particularly the Gauls, the vice was very much in vogue. If we turn to Asia, we see all the countries of that continent permeated with the vice from the earliest times down to the present day, and likewise with no special attempt to conceal it; Hindus and Chinese, no less than the peoples of Islam, whose poets also we find much more concerned with love of boys than with love of women; for

---

[20] "Among the Greeks it was regarded as disgraceful for youths not to have lovers." [Tr.]

example in Sadi's *Gulistan* the book "On Love" speaks exclusively of the former. Even to the Hebrews this vice was not unknown, for the Old and New Testaments mention it as punishable. Finally, in Christian Europe religion, legislation, and public opinion have had to oppose it with all their force. In the Middle Ages it was everywhere a capital offence; in France it was punishable even in the sixteenth century by burning at the stake, and in England, even up to about 1830, the death penalty for it was rigorously carried out; the punishment now is deportation for life. Such strong measures therefore were needed to put a stop to the vice; indeed, they were remarkably successful, yet they did not by any means succeed in exterminating it. On the contrary, it slinks around at all times and in all places, in all countries and among all classes, under the veil of the deepest secrecy; and it often comes to light where least expected. Even in earlier centuries it was no different, in spite of all the death penalties. The mentions of and allusions to it in the works of all those times are evidence of this. If we realize all this, and think it over carefully, we see pederasty appearing at all times and in all countries in a way very far removed from that which we had at first presupposed, when we considered it merely in itself, and hence *a priori*. Thus the universal nature and persistent ineradicability of the thing show that it arises in some way from human nature itself; since for this reason alone could it inevitably appear always and everywhere, as a proof of the saying:

Naturam expelles furca, tamen usque recurret.[21]

Therefore we cannot possibly escape this conclusion if we intend to proceed openly and honestly. To overlook these facts and to rest content with reviling and rebuking the vice would of course be easy; this, however, is not my way of settling problems, but, faithful even here to my innate disposition to investigate truth everywhere and to get to the bottom of things, I first of all acknowledge the phenomenon that presents itself for explanation, together with the inevitable conclusion to be drawn from it. Now that something so thoroughly contrary to nature, indeed going against nature in a matter of the greatest importance and concern to her, should arise from nature herself is such an unheard-of paradox, that its explanation confronts us as a difficult problem. However, I shall now solve it by discovering the secret of nature which lies at its root.

As a starting-point, let me make use of a passage in Aristotle's *Politics,* vii, 16. Here he first of all explains that people who are too

---

[21] "Expel nature with a pitchfork, she still comes back." [Horace, *Epist.* i, 10, 24. Tr.]

young produce inferior, feeble, defective, and undersized children; and further that the same thing applies to the offspring of those who are too old. Τὰ γὰρ τῶν πρεσβυτέρων ἔκγονα, καθάπερ τὰ τῶν νεωτέρων, ἀτελῆ γίγνεται, και τοῖς σώμασι, καὶ ταῖς διανοίαις, τὰ δὲ τῶν γεγηρακότων ἀσθενῆ (*Nam, ut juniorum, ita et grandiorum natu foetus inchoatis atque imperfectis corporibus mentibusque nascuntur: eorum vero qui senio confecti sunt, suboles infirma et imbecilla est*).[22] Now what Aristotle states as the rule for the individual is laid down by Stobaeus as a law for the community at the end of his exposition of the Peripatetic philosophy (Stobaeus, *Ecl. eth.*, bk. ii, c. 7 *in fine*): πρὸς τὴν ῥώμην τῶν σωμάτων και τελειότητα δεῖν μήτε νεωτέρων ἄγαν, μήτε πρεσβυτέρων τοὺς γάμους ποιεῖσθαι, ἀτελῆ γὰρ γίγνεσθαι, κατ' ἀμφοτέρας τὰς ἡλικίας, καὶ τελείως ἀσθενῆ τὰ ἔκγονα (*oportet, corporum roboris et perfectionis causa, nec juniores justo, nec seniores matrimonio jungi, quia circa utramque aetatem proles fieret imbecillis et imperfecta*).[23] Aristotle, therefore, lays down that a man who is fifty-four years of age should not have any more children, though he may still continue cohabitation for the sake of his health or for any other reason. He does not say how this is to be carried into effect, but he is obviously of the opinion that children conceived when their parents are of such an age should be disposed of by abortion, for he had recommended this a few lines previously. Now nature on her part cannot dispute the fact that forms the basis of Aristotle's precept, nor can she eliminate it. For, in consequence of her principle that *natura non facit saltus,* she could not suddenly stop a man's secretion of semen, but here, as in every case of mortification and decay, a gradual deterioration had to precede it. But procreation during this deterioration would bring into the world human beings who would be weak, dull, sickly, wretched, and short-lived. In fact, only too often this does happen; children conceived by elderly parents frequently die off at an early age; in any case, they never reach a great age. They are more or less frail, sickly, feeble, and their offspring are similarly constituted. What is said here about procreation during the years of decline applies just as much to procreation at an immature age. But there is nothing so dear to the heart of nature as the maintenance and preservation of the species

---

[22] "For children of people too old as well as too young leave much to be desired in both a physical and mental regard, and children of those in advanced years are weaklings." [Tr.]

[23] "But to obtain strong and perfect bodies, marriages should not be contracted either by those too young or by those too old, for the offspring of people of these ages leave much to be desired, and in the end only weaklings are born." [Tr.]

and of its genuine type. The means to this end are strong and vigorous individuals of sound constitution; nature desires these alone. In fact, at bottom she regards and treats individuals only as means, and the species alone as the end (as was shown in chapter 41). Accordingly, in consequence of nature's own laws and aims, we here see her in a critical situation and actually in great straits. As a result of her essential condition, she could not possibly count on a high-handed expedient, depending on the arbitrary will of some person, such as that suggested by Aristotle; and just as little could she rely on men's being taught by experience to recognize the disadvantages of too early or too late procreation, and accordingly curbing their desires as a result of cold and rational deliberation. Therefore, in so important a matter, nature could not risk either of these expedients. There was then nothing left for her but to choose the lesser of two evils. But for this purpose she had to make use here in her own interests of her favourite instrument, instinct. As was shown in the preceding chapter, this everywhere guides and directs so important a business as procreation, and creates such strange illusions. But this could happen here only by her misdirecting the instinct (*lui donna le change*). Thus nature knows only the physical, not the moral; in fact, there is even a decided antagonism between her and morality. Her sole aim is the preservation of the individual, and especially of the species, in the greatest possible perfection. Now it is true that pederasty is detrimental to those youths who have been seduced into practising it, yet not so much so that it would not be the lesser of two evils. Nature accordingly chooses this, in order to avoid by a wide margin the far greater evil, depravation of the species, and so to avert a lasting and growing misfortune.

As a result of this prudence on nature's part, a tendency to pederasty gradually and almost imperceptibly appears at about the age stated by Aristotle. This tendency becomes more and more definite and decided in proportion as the ability to beget strong and healthy children grows less and less; this is how nature arranges things. It should be noted, however, that it is still a very long way from the first appearance of this tendency to the vice itself. It is true that if, as in ancient Greece and Rome, or in Asia at all times, this tendency is not checked, it can easily lead to the vice through encouragement by example; the result then is that it becomes very widespread. In Europe, on the other hand, it is opposed by such powerful motives of religion, morality, law, and honour, that almost everyone shrinks at the mere thought of it, and we may assume accordingly that out of some three hundred who feel the tendency, hardly more than one will be so feeble and crazy as to give way to it. This is all the more certain, as this tendency appears only at that age when the blood has cooled down and the sexual impulse in general has declined. On the other hand, the tendency finds such strong opponents in mature reason, in the caution and discretion gained through experience, and in steadiness and firmness exercised in many different ways, that only a thoroughly depraved nature will succumb to it.

Meanwhile, nature's object here is attained by the fact that this tendency entails an indifference towards women; and this increases more and more, turns into aversion, and finally grows into loathing and disgust. Nature here achieves her real purpose with the greater certainty, the more the procreative power decreases in the man, the more decided its unnatural tendency becomes. In keeping with this, we find that pederasty is usually a vice of old men. Only those who have brought matters to a public scandal are caught in the act. To the really manly age it is something foreign, strange, and even incomprehensible. If there happens to be an exception to this, I think that it can only be the result of an accidental and premature depravation of the procreative power, which could produce only inferior offspring; and to prevent this, nature diverts this power. Therefore, the young pederasts who unfortunately are not uncommon in large cities always direct their hints and proposals to elderly gentlemen, never to those of a vigorous and robust age, or to young men. Even among the Greeks, where custom and example may at times have involved an exception to this rule, we usually find the lover expressly represented by authors as elderly, especially by philosophers, in particular by Plato and Aristotle. In this connexion a passage from Plutarch's *Liber Amatorius,* c. 5, is specially worth noting: Ὁ παιδικὸς ἔρως, ὀψὲ γεγονώς, καὶ παρ' ὥραν τῷ βίῳ, νόθος καὶ σκότιος, ἐξελαύνει τὸν γνήσιον ἔρωτα καὶ πρεσβύτερον. (*Puerorum amor, qui, quum tarde in vita et intempestive, quasi spurius et occultus, exstitisset, germanum et natu majorem amorem expellit.*)[24] Even among the gods we find only the elderly, like Zeus and Hercules, attended by male paramours, not Mars, Apollo, Bacchus or Mercury. Moreover in the East, shortage of women resulting from polygamy may at times give rise to forced exceptions to this rule. This can also happen in colonies still new and therefore without women, such as California and others. In keeping with this is also the fact that both immature sperm and that depraved through age can produce only

---

[24] "The love for boys appears late in life and untimely as a spurious and sombre affection, and then expels the genuine and original love." [Tr.]

feeble, inferior, and unhappy offspring; and, as in old age, so too in youth an erotic tendency of such a kind often exists between youths. But it is only extremely rarely that this leads to the actual vice, since it is opposed not only by the motives above-mentioned, but also by innocence, chastity, purity, scruples of conscience, and the bashfulness of youth.

The result of this discussion is that, whereas the vice we are considering appears to work directly against the aims and ends of nature, and that in a matter that is all-important and of the greatest concern to her, it must in fact serve these very aims, although only indirectly, as a means for preventing greater evils. Thus it is a phenomenon of the dying, and again of the immature, procreative force, both of which threaten the species with danger; and although they should both cease on moral grounds, yet these could not be relied on; for in her activities, nature generally does not take the truly moral into account. Accordingly, in consequence of her own laws, nature was hard pressed, and resorted to a makeshift, a stratagem, by a perversion of the instinct. In fact, it might be said that she built herself an asses' bridge, in order, as explained above, to escape from the greater of two evils. Thus she has in view the important object of preventing miserable and wretched offspring which might gradually deprave the whole species; and, as we have seen, she has no scruples in the choice of means. The spirit in which she goes to work here is the same as that in which she urges wasps to sting their young to death, as mentioned above in chapter 27. For in both cases she resorts to what is bad in order to avoid what is worse; thus she leads the sexual impulse astray, in order to frustrate its most pernicious consequences.

In this discussion, my intention has primarily been to solve the striking problem stated at the beginning, and then to confirm my theory discussed at length in the preceding chapter. This theory states that, in all sexual love, instinct holds the reins, and creates illusions, since for nature the interest of the species takes precedence over all others. This holds good even in the case of the disgusting depravity of the sexual impulse which we are considering; for even here, as the ultimate reason, the aims and ends of the species are the result, although in this case they are of a merely negative kind, since nature follows a prophylactic course. Therefore this discussion throws light on the whole of my metaphysics of sexual love; but a truth hitherto concealed has through it been brought to light. In spite of its strangeness, it still sheds new light on the inner essence, the spirit, and the workings of nature. Accordingly, there was here no question of moral admonition against the vice, but of a proper understanding of the essential nature of the matter. For the rest, the true, ultimate, and profoundly metaphysical reason for the objectionable nature of pederasty is that, whereas in it the will-to-live affirms itself, the effect of that affirmation, which holds open the path to salvation, and hence the resumption of life, is completely cut off. Finally, by expounding these paradoxical ideas, I wanted to grant to the professors of philosophy a small favour, for they are very disconcerted by the ever-increasing publicization of my philosophy which they so carefully concealed. I have done so by giving them the opportunity of slandering me by saying that I defend and commend pederasty.

On the Affirmation of the Will-to-Live

If the will-to-live exhibited itself merely as an impulse to self-preservation, that would be only an affirmation of the individual phenomenon for the span of time of its natural duration. The cares and troubles of such a life would not be great, and consequently existence would prove easy and cheerful. Since, on the contrary, the will wills life absolutely and for all time, it exhibits itself at the same time as sexual impulse which has an endless series of generations in view. This impulse does away with that unconcern, cheerfulness, and innocence that would accompany a merely individual existence, since it brings into consciousness unrest, uneasiness, and melancholy, and into the course of life misfortunes, cares and misery. On the other hand, if it is voluntarily suppressed, as we see in rare exceptions, then this is the turning of the will, which changes its course. It is then absorbed in, and does not go beyond, the individual; but this can happen only through his doing a painful violence to himself. If this has taken place, that unconcern and cheerfulness of the merely individual existence are restored to consciousness, and indeed raised to a higher power. On the other hand, tied up with the satisfaction of that strongest of all impulses and desires is the origin of a new existence, and hence the carrying out of life afresh with all its burdens, cares, wants, and pains, in *another* individual, it is true; yet if the two, who are different in the phenomenon, were such absolutely and in themselves, where then would eternal justice be found? Life presents itself as a problem, a task to be worked out, and in general therefore as a constant struggle against want and affliction. Accordingly everyone tries to get through with it and come off as well as he can; he disposes of life as he does of a compulsory service that he is in duty bound to carry out. But who has contracted this debt? His begetter, in the enjoyment of sensual pleasure. Therefore, because the one has enjoyed this pleasure, the other must live, suffer, and die. However, we know and look back to the fact that the differ-

---

[1] This chapter refers to § 60 of volume 1.

ence of the homogeneous is conditioned by space and time, which I have called in this sense the *principium individuationis;* otherwise eternal justice would be irretrievably lost. Paternal love, by virtue of which the father is ready to do, to suffer, and to take a risk more for his child than for himself, and at the same time recognizes this as his obligation, is due to the very fact that the begetter recognizes himself once more in the begotten.

The life of a man, with its endless care, want, and suffering, is to be regarded as the explanation and paraphrase of the act of pro-creation, of the decided affirmation of the will-to-live. Further, it is also due to this that he owes nature the debt of death, and thinks of this debt with uneasiness. Is not this evidence of the fact that our existence involves guilt? But we certainly always exist on periodical payment of the toll, birth and death, and we enjoy successively all the sorrows and joys of life, so that none can escape us. This is just the fruit of the affirmation of the will-to-live. Thus the fear of death, which holds us firmly to life in spite of all its miseries, is really illu-sory; but just as illusory is the impulse that has enticed us into it. This enticement itself can be objectively perceived in the reciprocal longing glances of two lovers; they are the purest expression of the will-to-live in its affirmation. How gentle and tender it is here! It wills well-being, and quiet enjoyment, and mild pleasures for itself, for others, for all. This is the theme of Anacreon. Thus by allure-ment and flattery it works its way into life; but when it is in life, then misery introduces crime, and crime misery; horror and desolation fill the scene. This is the theme of Aeschylus.

But the act by which the will affirms itself and man comes into existence is one of which all in their heart of hearts are ashamed, and which therefore they carefully conceal; in fact, if they are caught in the act, they are as alarmed as if they had been detected in a crime. It is an action of which, on cool reflection, we think often with repugnance, and in an exalted mood with disgust. Considerations going more closely into the matter in this sense are afforded by Montaigne in the fifth chapter of his third book under the marginal heading *Ce que c'est que l'amour.* A peculiar sadness and remorse follows close on it; yet these are felt most after the consummation of the act for the first time, and generally they are the more distinct, the nobler the character. Hence even the pagan Pliny says: *Homini tan-tum primi coitus poenitentia; augurium scilicet vitae, a poenitenda origine (Historia Naturalis,* X, 83).[2] On the other hand, in Goethe's *Faust* what do devil and witches practise and sing on their Sabbath?

---

[2] "Only man feels remorse after the first copulation; a course characteristic of life, that we feel remorse for our origin." [Tr.]

Lewdness and obscene jokes. In the very same work (in the admirable Paralipomena to *Faust*) what does Satan incarnate preach before the assembled multitude? Lewdness and obscene talk, nothing more. But the human race continues to exist simply and solely by means of the constant practice of such an act as this. Now if optimism were right, if our existence were to be gratefully acknowledged as the gift of the highest goodness guided by wisdom, and accordingly if it were in itself praiseworthy, commendable, and delightful, then certainly the act that perpetuates it would necessarily bear quite a different complexion. If, on the other hand, this existence is a kind of false step or wrong path, if it is the work of an originally blind will, the luckiest development of which is that it comes to itself in order to abolish itself, then the act perpetuating that existence must appear precisely as in fact it does.

With regard to the first fundamental truth of my teaching, the remark merits a place here that the above-mentioned shame over the business of procreation extends even to the parts that serve it, although, like all the other parts, they are given us by nature. Once again, this is a striking proof of the fact that not merely man's actions, but even his body, are to be regarded as the phenomenon, the objectification, of his *will,* and as its work. For he could not be ashamed of a thing that existed without his will.

The act of procreation is further related to the world as the solution is to the riddle. Thus the world is wide in space and old in time, and has an inexhaustible multiplicity of forms. Yet all this is only the phenomenon of the will-to-live; and the concentration, the focus of this will is the act of generation. Hence in this act the inner nature of the world most distinctly expresses itself. In this respect it is even worth noting that the act itself is also positively called "the will" in the very significant German phrase: *Er verlangte von ihr, sie sollte ihm zu Willen sein.*[3] Therefore that act, as the most distinct expression of the will, is the kernel, the compendium, the quintessence of the world. Hence we obtain through it a light as to the true nature and tendency of the world; it is the solution to the riddle. Accordingly, it is understood by the "tree of knowledge"; for, after acquaintance with it, everyone begins to see life in its true light, as Byron also says:

> The tree of knowledge has been pluck'd—all's known.
> *Don Juan,* I, 128.

No less in keeping with this quality is the fact that it is the great

---

[3] "He expected her to be willing to serve him." [Tr.]

ἄρρητον,[4] the public secret which must never be distinctly mentioned anywhere, but is always and everywhere understood to be the main thing as a matter of course, and is therefore always present in the minds of all. For this reason, even the slightest allusion to it is instantly understood. The principal role played in the world by this act and by what is connected with it, because everywhere love-intrigues are pursued on the one hand, and assumed on the other, is quite in keeping with the importance of this *punctum saliens* of the world-egg. What is amusing is to be found only in the constant concealment of the main thing.

But see now how the young, innocent human intellect is startled at the enormity, when that great secret of the world first becomes known to it! The reason for this is that, on the long path that the will, originally without knowledge, had to traverse before it rose to intellect, especially to human, rational intellect, it became such a stranger to itself; and so it no longer knows its origin, that *poenitenda origo,* and from the standpoint of pure, hence innocent, knowledge is horrified thereat.

Now, as the focus of the will, that is to say, its concentration and highest expression, are the sexual impulse and its satisfaction, it is expressed very significantly and naively in the symbolical language of nature by the fact that individualized will, hence man and the animal, makes its entry into the world through the portal of the sexual organs.

The *affirmation of the will-to-live,* which accordingly has its centre in the act of generation, is inevitable and bound to happen in the case of the animal. For the will that is the *natura naturans* first of all arrives at *reflection* in man. To arrive at reflection means not merely to know for the momentary need and necessity of the individual will, for its service in the urgent present moment—as is the case with the animal according to its completeness and its needs which go hand in hand—but to have reached a greater breadth of knowledge, by virtue of a distinct recollection of the past, of an approximate anticipation of the future, and, in this way, of a comprehensive survey of the individual life, of one's own, of another, indeed of existence generally. Actually, the life of every animal species throughout the thousands of years of its existence is to a certain extent like a single moment; for it is mere consciousness of the *present* without that of the past and of the future, and consequently without that of death. In this sense it is to be regarded as a steady and enduring moment, a *nunc stans.* Incidentally, we here see most distinctly that in general the form of life, or of the phenomenon of

---

[4] "Unspeakable." [Tr.]

the will with consciousness, is primarily and immediately only the *present*. Past and future are added only in the case of man, and indeed only in the concept; they are known *in abstracto,* and are possibly illustrated by pictures of the imagination. Hence, after the will-to-live, i.e., the inner being of nature, has run through the whole series of animals in restless striving towards complete objectification and complete enjoyment—and this often happens at various intervals of successive animal series arising anew on the same planet—it ultimately arrives at *reflection* in the being endowed with the faculty of reason, namely man. Here the matter now begins to be grave ·and critical for him; the question forces itself on him whence is all this and for what purpose, and principally whether the trouble and misery of his life and effort are really repaid by the profit. *Le jeu vaut-il bien la chandelle?* [5] Accordingly, here is the point where, in the light of distinct knowledge, he decides for the affirmation or denial of the will-to-live, although he can as a rule bring the latter to consciousness only in a mythical cloak. Consequently, we have no ground for assuming that an even more highly developed objectification of the will is reached anywhere, for it has already reached its turning-point here.

---

[5] "Is the game worth the candle?" [Tr.]

CHAPTER XLVI[1]

On the Vanity and Suffering of Life

Awakened to life out of the night of unconsciousness, the will finds itself as an individual in an endless and boundless world, among innumerable individuals, all striving, suffering, and erring; and, as if through a troubled dream, it hurries back to the old unconsciousness. Yet till then its desires are unlimited, its claims inexhaustible, and every satisfied desire gives birth to a new one. No possible satisfaction in the world could suffice to still its craving, set a final goal to its demands, and fill the bottomless pit of its heart. In this connexion, let us now consider what as a rule comes to man in satisfactions of any kind; it is often nothing more than the bare maintenance of this very existence, extorted daily with unremitting effort and constant care in conflict with misery and want, and with death in prospect. Everything in life proclaims that earthly happiness is destined to be frustrated, or recognized as an illusion. The grounds for this lie deep in the very nature of things. Accordingly, the lives of most people prove troubled and short. The comparatively happy are often only apparently so, or else, like those of long life, they are rare exceptions; the possibility of these still had to be left, as decoy-birds. Life presents itself as a continual deception, in small matters as well as in great. If it has promised, it does not keep its word, unless to show how little desirable the desired object was; hence we are deluded now by hope, now by what was hoped for. If it has given, it did so in order to take. The enchantment of distance shows us paradises that vanish like optical illusions, when we have allowed ourselves to be fooled by them. Accordingly, happiness lies always in the future, or else in the past, and the present may be compared to a small dark cloud driven by the wind over the sunny plain; in front of and behind the cloud everything is bright, only it itself always casts a shadow. Consequently, the present is always inadequate, but the future is uncertain, and the past irrecoverable. With its misfortunes, small, greater, and great, occurring hourly, daily, weekly, and

---

[1] This chapter refers to §§ 56-59 of volume 1. Compare with it also chapters 11 and 12 of volume 2 of the *Parerga and Paralipomena*.

yearly; with its deluded hopes and accidents bringing all calculations to nought, life bears so clearly the stamp of something which ought to disgust us, that it is difficult to conceive how anyone could fail to recognize this, and be persuaded that life is here to be thankfully enjoyed, and that man exists in order to be happy. On the contrary, that continual deception and disillusionment, as well as the general nature of life, present themselves as intended and calculated to awaken the conviction that nothing whatever is worth our exertions, our efforts, and our struggles, that all good things are empty and fleeting, that the world on all sides is bankrupt, and that life is a business that does not cover the costs; so that our will may turn away from it.

The way in which this *vanity* of all objects of the will makes itself known and comprehensible to the intellect that is rooted in the individual, is primarily *time*. It is the form by whose means that vanity of things appears as their transitoriness, since by virtue of this all our pleasures and enjoyments come to nought in our hands, and afterwards we ask in astonishment where they have remained. Hence that vanity itself is the only *objective* element of time, in other words, that which corresponds to it in the inner nature of things, and so that of which it is the expression. For this reason, time is the *a priori* necessary form of all our perceptions; everything must present itself in time, even we ourselves. Consequently, our life is primarily like a payment made to us in nothing but copper coins, for which we must then give a receipt; the coins are the days, and the receipt is death. For in the end time proclaims the judgement of nature on the worth of all beings that appear in it, since it destroys them:

> And justly so: for all things, from the Void
> Called forth, deserve to be destroyed:
> 'Twere better, then, were naught created.[2]

Thus old age and death, to which every life necessarily hurries, are a sentence of condemnation on the will-to-live which comes from the hands of nature herself. It states that this will is a striving that is bound to frustrate itself. "What you have willed," it says, "ends thus: will something better." Therefore the instruction afforded to everyone by his life consists on the whole in the fact that the objects of his desires constantly delude, totter, and fall; that in consequence they bring more misery than joy, until at last even the whole foundation on which they all stand collapses, since his life itself is destroyed. Thus he obtains the final confirmation that all his striving and willing was a perversity, a path of error:

---

[2] From Bayard Taylor's translation of Goethe's *Faust*. [Tr.]

> Then old age and experience, hand in hand,
> Lead him to death, and make him understand,
> After a search so painful and so long,
> That all his life he has been in the wrong.

But I wish to go into the matter in more detail, for it is these views in which I have met with most contradiction. First of all, I have to confirm by the following remarks the proof given in the text of the negative nature of all satisfaction, and hence of all pleasure and happiness, in opposition to the positive nature of pain.

We feel pain, but not painlessness; care, but not freedom from care; fear, but not safety and security. We feel the desire as we feel hunger and thirst; but as soon as it has been satisfied, it is like the mouthful of food which has been taken, and which ceases to exist for our feelings the moment it is swallowed. We painfully feel the loss of pleasures and enjoyments, as soon as they fail to appear; but when pains cease even after being present for a long time, their absence is not directly felt, but at most they are thought of intentionally by means of reflection. For only pain and want can be felt positively; and therefore they proclaim themselves; well-being, on the contrary, is merely negative. Therefore, we do not become conscious of the three greatest blessings of life as such, namely health, youth, and freedom, as long as we possess them, but only after we have lost them; for they too are negations. We notice that certain days of our life were happy only after they have made room for unhappy ones. In proportion as enjoyments and pleasures increase, susceptibility to them decreases; that to which we are accustomed is no longer felt as a pleasure. But in precisely this way is the susceptibility to suffering increased; for the cessation of that to which we are accustomed is felt painfully. Thus the measure of what is necessary increases through possession, and thereby the capacity to feel pain. The hours pass the more quickly the more pleasantly they are spent, and the more slowly the more painfully they are spent, since pain, not pleasure, is the positive thing, whose presence makes itself felt. In just the same way we become conscious of time when we are bored, not when we are amused. Both cases prove that our existence is happiest when we perceive it least; from this it follows that it would be better not to have it. Great and animated delight can be positively conceived only as the consequence of great misery that has preceded it; for nothing can be added to a state of permanent contentment except some amusement or even the satisfaction of vanity. Therefore, all poets are obliged to bring their heroes into anxious and painful situations, in order to be able to liberate them therefrom again. Accordingly dramas and epics generally describe only fighting, suffering, tormented men and women, and every work of fiction is a peep-show in which we observe the spasms and convulsions of the agonized human heart. Sir Walter Scott has naively set forth this aesthetic necessity in the "Conclusion" to his novel *Old Mortality*. Voltaire, so highly favoured by nature and good fortune, also says, entirely in agreement with the truth I have demonstrated: *Le bonheur n'est qu'un rêve, et la douleur est réelle;* and he adds: *il y a quatre-vingts ans que je l'éprouve. Je n'y sais autre chose que me résigner, et me dire que les mouches sont nées pour être mangées par les araignées, et les hommes pour être dévorés par les chagrins.*[3]

Before we state so confidently that life is desirable or merits our gratitude, let us for once calmly compare the sum of the pleasures which are in any way possible, and which a man can enjoy in his life, with the sum of the sufferings which are in any way possible, and can come to him in his life. I do not think it will be difficult to strike the balance. In the long run, however, it is quite superfluous to dispute whether there is more good or evil in the world; for the mere existence of evil decides the matter, since evil can never be wiped off, and consequently can never be balanced, by the good that exists along with or after it.

> *Mille piacer' non vagliono un tormento.*[4]

For that thousands had lived in happiness and joy would never do away with the anguish and death-agony of one individual; and just as little does my present well-being undo my previous sufferings. Therefore, were the evil in the world even a hundred times less than it is, its mere existence would still be sufficient to establish a truth that may be expressed in various ways, although always only somewhat indirectly, namely that we have not to be pleased but rather sorry about the existence of the world; that its non-existence would be preferable to its existence; that it is something which at bottom ought not to be, and so on. Byron's expression of the matter is exceedingly fine [*Childe Harold,* iv, 126]:

> Our life is a false nature,—'tis not in
> The harmony of things, this hard decree,
> This uneradicable taint of sin,
> This boundless Upas, this all-blasting tree

---

[3] "Happiness is only a dream, and pain is real. . . . I have experienced this for eighty years. I know of nothing better than to resign myself to this and to say that flies are born to be eaten by spiders, and men to be devoured by trouble and affliction." [Tr.]

[4] "A thousand pleasures do not compensate for one pain." [Tr.]
                                                          Petrarch.

Whose root is earth, whose leaves and branches be
The skies, which rain their plagues on men like dew—
Disease, death, bondage—all the woes we see—
And worse, the woes we see not—which throb through
The immedicable soul, with heart-aches ever new.

If the world and life were an end in themselves, and accordingly were to require theoretically no justification, and practically no compensation or amends, but existed, perhaps as represented by Spinoza and present-day Spinozists, as the single manifestation of a God who, *animi causa,* or even to mirror himself, undertook such an evolution of himself, and consequently its existence needed neither to be justified by reasons nor redeemed by results—then the sufferings and troubles of life would not indeed have to be fully compensated by the pleasures and well-being in it. For, as I have said, this is impossible, because my present pain is never abolished by future pleasures, since the latter fill up their time just as the former fills its own. On the contrary, there would have to be no sufferings at all, and of necessity there would also not be death, or else it would have no terrors for us. Only thus would life pay for itself.

Now since our state or condition is rather something that it were better should not be, everything that surrounds us bears the traces of this—just as in hell everything smells of sulphur—since everything is always imperfect and deceptive, everything agreeable is mixed with something disagreeable, every enjoyment is always only half an enjoyment, every gratification introduces its own disturbance, every relief new worries and troubles, every expedient for our daily and hourly needs leaves us in the lurch at every moment, and denies its service. The step on to which we tread so often gives way under us; in fact, misfortunes and accidents great and small are the element of our life, and in a word, we are like Phineus, all of whose food was contaminated and rendered unfit to eat by the Harpies. All that we lay hold on resists us, because it has a will of its own which must be overcome. Two remedies for this are tried; firstly εὐλάβεια, i.e., prudence, foresight, cunning; it does not teach us fully, is not sufficient, and comes to nought. Secondly, stoical equanimity, seeking to disarm every misfortune by preparedness for all and contempt for everything; in practice, this becomes cynical renunciation which prefers to reject once for all every means of help and every alleviation. It makes us dogs, like Diogenes in his tub. The truth is that we ought to be wretched, and are so. The chief source of the most serious evils affecting man is man himself; *homo homini lupus.*[5] He who

---

[5] "Man is a wolf for man." [Tr.]

keeps this last fact clearly in view beholds the world as a hell, surpassing that of Dante by the fact that one man must be the devil of another. For this purpose, of course, one is more fitted than another, indeed an archfiend is more fitted than all the rest, and appears in the form of a conqueror, he sets several hundred thousand men, facing one another, and exclaims to them: "To suffer and die is your destiny; now shoot one another with musket and cannon!" and they do so. In general, however, the conduct of men towards one another is characterized as a rule by injustice, extreme unfairness, hardness, and even cruelty; an opposite course of conduct appears only by way of exception. The necessity for the State and for legislation rests on this fact, and not on your shifts and evasions. But in all cases not lying within the reach of the law, we see at once a lack of consideration for his like which is peculiar to man, and springs from his boundless egoism, and sometimes even from wickedness. How man deals with man is seen, for example, in Negro slavery, the ultimate object of which is sugar and coffee. However, we need not go so far; to enter at the age of five a cotton-spinning or other factory, and from then on to sit there every day first ten, then twelve, and finally fourteen hours, and perform the same mechanical work, is to purchase dearly the pleasure of drawing breath. But this is the fate of millions, and many more millions have an analogous fate.

We others, however, can be made perfectly miserable by trifling incidents, but perfectly happy by nothing in the world. Whatever we may say, the happiest moment of the happy man is that of his falling asleep, just as the unhappiest moment of the unhappy man is that of his awaking. An indirect but certain proof of the fact that people feel unhappy, and consequently are so, is also abundantly afforded by the terrible envy that dwells in all. In all the circumstances of life, on the occasion of every superiority or advantage, of whatever kind it be, this envy is roused and cannot contain its poison. Because people feel unhappy, they cannot bear the sight of one who is supposed to be happy. Whoever feels happy for the moment would at once like to make all around him happy, and says:

Que tout le monde ici soit heureux de ma joie.[6]

If life in itself were a precious blessing, and decidedly preferable to non-existence, the exit from it would not need to be guarded by such fearful watchmen as death and its terrors. But who would go on living life as it is, if death were less terrible? And who could bear even the mere thought of death, if life were a pleasure? But the former still always has the good point of being the end of life, and

---

[6] "May everyone here be happy in my joy." [Tr.]

we console ourselves with death in regard to the sufferings of life, and with the sufferings of life in regard to death. The truth is that the two belong to each other inseparably, since they constitute a deviation from the right path, and a return to this is as difficult as it is desirable.

If the world were not something that, *practically* expressed, ought not to be, it would also not be *theoretically* a problem. On the contrary, its existence would either require no explanation at all, since it would be so entirely self-evident that astonishment at it and enquiry about it could not arise in any mind; or its purpose would present itself unmistakably. But instead of this it is indeed an insoluble problem, since even the most perfect philosophy will always contain an unexplained element, like an insoluble precipitate or the remainder that is always left behind by the irrational proportion of two quantities. Therefore, if anyone ventures to raise the question why there is not nothing at all rather than this world, then the world cannot be justified from itself; no ground, no final cause of its existence can be found in itself; it cannot be demonstrated that it exists for its own sake, in other words, for its own advantage. In pursuance of my teaching, this can, of course, be explained from the fact that the principle of the world's existence is expressly a groundless one, namely a blind will-to-live, which, as *thing-in-itself,* cannot be subject to the principle of sufficient reason or ground; for this principle is merely the form of phenomena, and through it alone every why is justified. But this is also in keeping with the nature and constitution of the world, for only a blind, not a seeing, will could put itself in the position in which we find ourselves. On the contrary, a seeing will would soon have made the calculation that the business does not cover the costs, since such a mighty effort and struggle with the exertion of all one's strength, under constant care, anxiety, and want, and with the inevitable destruction of every individual life, finds no compensation in the ephemeral existence itself, which is obtained by such effort, and comes to nothing in our hands. Therefore, the explanation of the world from the νοῦς of Anaxagoras, in other words, from a will guided by *knowledge,* necessarily demands for its extenuation optimism, which is then set up and maintained in spite of the loudly crying evidence of a whole world full of misery. Life is then given out as a gift, whereas it is evident that anyone would have declined it with thanks, had he looked at it and tested it beforehand; just as Lessing admired the understanding of his son. Because this son had absolutely declined to come into the world, he had to be dragged forcibly into life by means of forceps; but hardly was he in it, when he again hurried away from it. On the other hand, it is well said that life should be, from one end to the other, only a lesson, to which, however, anyone could reply: "For this reason, I wish I had been left in the peace of the all-sufficient nothing, where I should have had no need either of lessons or of anything else." But if it were added that one day he was to give an account of every hour of his life, he would rather be justified in first himself asking for an account as to why he was taken away from that peace and quiet and put into a position so precarious, obscure, anxious, and painful. To this, then, false fundamental views lead. Far from bearing the character of a *gift,* human existence has entirely the character of a contracted *debt.* The calling in of this debt appears in the shape of the urgent needs, tormenting desires, and endless misery brought about through that existence. As a rule, the whole lifetime is used for paying off this debt, yet in this way only the interest is cleared off. Repayment of the capital takes place through death. And when was this debt contracted? At the begetting.

Accordingly, if man is regarded as a being whose existence is a punishment and an atonement, then he is already seen in a more correct light. The myth of the Fall of man (although probably, like the whole of Judaism, borrowed from the *Zend Avesta: Bundahish,* 15), is the only thing in the Old Testament to which I can concede a metaphysical, although only allegorical, truth; indeed it is this alone that reconciles me to the Old Testament. Thus our existence resembles nothing but the consequence of a false step and a guilty desire. New Testament Christianity, the ethical spirit of which is that of Brahmanism and Buddhism, and which is therefore very foreign to the otherwise optimistic spirit of the Old Testament, has also, extremely wisely, started from that very myth; in fact, without this, it would not have found one single point of connexion with Judaism. If we wish to measure the degree of guilt with which our existence itself is burdened, let us look at the suffering connected with it. Every great pain, whether bodily or mental, states what we deserve; for it could not come to us if we did not deserve it. That Christianity also looks at our existence in this light is proved by a passage from Luther's *Commentary on Galatians,* ch. 3, which I have before me only in Latin: *Sumus autem nos omnes corporibus et rebus subjecti Diabolo, et hospites sumus in mundo, cujus ipse princeps et Deus est. Ideo panis quem edimus, potus quem bibimus, vestes quibus utimur, imo aër et totum quo vivimus in carne, sub ipsius imperio est.*[7] An outcry has been raised about the melancholy and cheerless

---

[7] "In our bodies and circumstances, however, we are all subject to the devil and are strangers in this world, of which he is prince and lord. Hence everything is under his rule, the bread we eat, the beverage we drink, the clothes we use, even the air and everything by which we live in the flesh." [Tr.]

nature of my philosophy; but this is to be found merely in the fact that, instead of inventing a future hell as the equivalent of sins, I have shown that where guilt is to be found, there is already in the world something akin to hell; but he who is inclined to deny this can easily experience it.

This world is the battle-ground of tormented and agonized beings who continue to exist only by each devouring the other. Therefore, every beast of prey in it is the living grave of thousands of others, and its self-maintenance is a chain of torturing deaths. Then in this world the capacity to feel pain increases with knowledge, and therefore reaches its highest degree in man, a degree that is the higher, the more intelligent the man. To this world the attempt has been made to adapt the system of *optimism,* and to demonstrate to us that it is the best of all possible worlds. The absurdity is glaring. However, an optimist tells me to open my eyes and look at the world and see how beautiful it is in the sunshine, with its mountains, valleys, rivers, plants, animals, and so on. But is the world, then, a peep-show? These things are certainly beautiful to *behold,* but to *be* them is something quite different. A teleologist then comes along and speaks to me in glowing terms about the wise arrangement by virtue of which care is taken that the planets do not run their heads against one another; that land and sea are not mixed up into pulp, but are held apart in a delightful way; also that everything is neither rigid in continual frost nor roasted with heat; likewise that, in consequence of the obliquity of the ecliptic, there is not an eternal spring in which nothing could reach maturity, and so forth. But this and everything like it are indeed mere *conditiones sine quibus non.* If there is to be a world at all, if its planets are to exist at least as long as is needed for the ray of light from a remote fixed star to reach them, and are not, like Lessing's son, to depart again immediately after birth, then of course it could not be constructed so unskilfully that its very framework would threaten to collapse. But if we proceed to the *results* of the applauded work, if we consider the *players* who act on the stage so durably constructed, and then see how with sensibility pain makes its appearance, and increases in proportion as that sensibility develops into intelligence, and then how, keeping pace with this, desire and suffering come out ever more strongly, and increase, till at last human life affords no other material than that for tragedies and comedies, then whoever is not a hypocrite will hardly be disposed to break out into hallelujahs. The real but disguised origin of these latter has moreover been exposed, mercilessly but with triumphant truth, by David Hume in his *Natural History of Religion,* Secs. 6, 7, 8, and 13. He also explains without reserve in the tenth and eleventh books of his *Dialogues on Natural Religion,* with arguments very convincing yet quite different from mine, the miserable nature of this world and the untenableness of all optimism; here at the same time he attacks optimism at its source. Both these works of Hume are as well worth reading as they are at the present time unknown in Germany, where, on the other hand, incredible pleasure is found patriotically in the most repulsive drivel of native, boastful mediocrities, who are lauded to the skies as great men. Nevertheless, Hamann translated those dialogues; Kant looked through the translation, and late in life wished to induce Hamann's son to publish them, because the translation by Platner did not satisfy him (see Kant's biography by F. W. Schubert, pp. 81 and 165). There is more to be learnt from each page of David Hume than from the collected philosophical works of Hegel, Herbart, and Schleiermacher taken together.

Again, the founder of systematic *optimism* is Leibniz, whose services to philosophy I have no wish to deny, although I could never succeed in really thinking myself into the monadology, pre-established harmony, and *identitas indiscernibilium.*[8] His *Nouveaux essais sur l'entendement* are, however, merely an excerpt with a detailed yet weak criticism, with a view to correction, of Locke's work that is justly world-famous. He here opposes Locke with just as little success as he opposes Newton in his *Tentamen de Motuum Coelestium Causis* directed against the system of gravitation. The *Critique of Pure Reason* is very specially directed against this Leibniz-Wolffian philosophy and has a polemical, indeed a destructive, relation to it, just as to Locke and Hume it has a relation of continuation and of further development. That the professors of philosophy are everywhere engaged at the present time in setting Leibniz on his feet again with his humbug, in fact in glorifying him, and, on the other hand, in disparaging and setting aside Kant as much as possible, has its good reason in the *primum vivere.*[9] The *Critique of Pure Reason* does not permit of one's giving out Jewish mythology as philosophy, or speaking summarily of the "soul" as a given reality, as a well known and well accredited person, without giving some account of how one has arrived at this concept, and what justification one has for using it scientifically. But *primum vivere, deinde philosophari!* [9] Down with Kant, *vivat* our Leibniz! Therefore, to return to Leibniz, I cannot assign to the *Théodicée,* that methodical and broad development of optimism, in such a capacity, any other merit than that it later gave rise to the immortal *Candide* of the great Voltaire. In this

---

[8] The principle of Leibniz, according to which two indistinguishable things are identical. [Tr.]

[9] "First live, then philosophize!" [Tr.]

way, of course, Leibniz's oft-repeated and lame excuse for the evil of the world, namely that the bad sometimes produces the good, obtained proof that for him was unexpected. Even by the name of his hero, Voltaire indicated that it needed only sincerity to recognize the opposite of optimism. Actually optimism cuts so strange a figure on this scene of sin, suffering, and death, that we should be forced to regard it as irony if we did not have an adequate explanation of its origin in its secret source (namely hypocritical flattery with an offensive confidence in its success), a source so delightfully disclosed by Hume, as previously mentioned.

But against the palpably sophistical proofs of Leibniz that this is the best of all possible worlds, we may even oppose seriously and honestly the proof that it is the *worst* of all possible worlds. For possible means not what we may picture in our imagination, but what can actually exist and last. Now this world is arranged as it had to be if it were to be capable of continuing with great difficulty to exist; if it were a little worse, it would be no longer capable of continuing to exist. Consequently, since a worse world could not continue to exist, it is absolutely impossible; and so this world itself is the worst of all possible worlds. For not only if the planets ran their heads against one another, but also if any one of the actually occurring perturbations of their course continued to increase, instead of being gradually balanced again by the others, the world would soon come to an end. Astronomers know on what accidental circumstances—in most cases on the irrational relation to one another of the periods of revolution—all this depends. They have carefully calculated that it will always go on well, and consequently that the world can also last and go on. Although Newton was of the opposite opinion, we will hope that the astronomers have not miscalculated, and consequently that the mechanical perpetual motion realized in such a planetary system will also not, like the rest, ultimately come to a standstill. Again, powerful forces of nature dwell under the firm crust of the planet. As soon as some accident affords these free play, they must necessarily destroy that crust with everything living on it. This has occurred at least three times on our planet, and will probably occur even more frequently. The earthquake of Lisbon, of Haiti, the destruction of Pompeii are only small, playful hints at the possibility. An insignificant alteration of the atmosphere, not even chemically demonstrable, causes cholera, yellow fever, black death, and so on, which carry off millions of people; a somewhat greater alteration would extinguish all life. A very moderate increase of heat would dry up all rivers and springs. The animals have received barely enough in the way of organs and strength to enable them with the greatest exertion to procure sustenance for their own lives and food for their offspring. Therefore, if an animal loses a limb, or even only the complete use of it, it is in most cases bound to perish. Powerful as are the weapons of understanding and reason possessed by the human race, nine-tenths of mankind live in constant conflict with want, always balancing themselves with difficulty and effort on the brink of destruction. Thus throughout, for the continuance of the whole as well as for that of every individual being, the conditions are sparingly and scantily given, and nothing beyond these. Therefore the individual life is a ceaseless struggle for existence itself, while at every step it is threatened with destruction. Just because this threat is so often carried out, provision had to be made, by the incredibly great surplus of seed, that the destruction of individuals should not bring about that of the races, since about these alone is nature seriously concerned. Consequently, the world is as bad as it can possibly be, if it is to exist at all. *Q.E.D.* The fossils of entirely different kinds of animal species which formerly inhabited the planet afford us, as proof of our calculation, records of worlds whose continuance was no longer possible, and which were in consequence somewhat worse than the worst of possible worlds.

At bottom, optimism is the unwarranted self-praise of the real author of the world, namely of the will-to-live which complacently mirrors itself in its work. Accordingly optimism is not only a false but also a pernicious doctrine, for it presents life as a desirable state and man's happiness as its aim and object. Starting from this, everyone then believes he has the most legitimate claim to happiness and enjoyment. If, as usually happens, these do not fall to his lot, he believes that he suffers an injustice, in fact that he misses the whole point of his existence; whereas it is far more correct to regard work, privation, misery, and suffering, crowned by death, as the aim and object of our life (as is done by Brahmanism and Buddhism, and also by genuine Christianity), since it is these that lead to the denial of the will-to-live. In the New Testament, the world is presented as a vale of tears, life as a process of purification, and the symbol of Christianity is an instrument of torture. Therefore, when Leibniz, Shaftesbury, Bolingbroke, and Pope appeared with *optimism,* the general offence caused by it was due mainly to the fact that optimism is irreconcilable with Christianity. This is stated and explained by Voltaire in the preface to his excellent poem *Le Désastre de Lisbonne,* which also is expressly directed against optimism. This great man, whom I so gladly commend in the face of the slanders of mercenary German ink-slingers, is placed decidedly higher than Rousseau by the insight to which he attained in three respects, and which testifies to the greater depth of his thinking: (1) insight into the preponderating magnitude of the evil and misery of existence with which he is deeply penetrated; (2) insight into the strict necessitation of the acts of will; (3) insight into the truth of Locke's principle that what thinks may possibly be also material. Rousseau, on the other hand, disputes all this by declamations in his *Profession de foi du vicaire Savoyard,* the superficial philosophy of a Protestant pastor. In this very spirit he also attacks, in the interests of optimism, Voltaire's fine poem just mentioned. This he does with distorted, shallow, and logically false reasoning in his long letter to Voltaire of 18 August 1756, which was devoted simply to this purpose. Indeed, the fundamental characteristic and πρῶτον ψεῦδος[10] of Rousseau's whole philosophy is that he puts in the place of the Christian doctrine of original sin and of the original depravity of the human race an original goodness and unlimited perfectibility thereof, which had been led astray merely by civilization and its consequences; and on this he then establishes his optimism and humanism.

Just as in *Candide* Voltaire in his facetious manner wages war on optimism, so has Byron done the same, in his serious and tragic way, in his immortal masterpiece *Cain,* and for this reason he too has been glorified by the invectives of the obscurantist Friedrich Schlegel. If in conclusion, to confirm my view, I wished to record the sayings of great minds of all ages in this sense, which is opposed to optimism, there would be no end to the citations: for almost every one of them has expressed in strong terms his knowledge of the world's misery. Hence at the end of this chapter a few statements of this kind may find a place, not to confirm, but merely to embellish it.

First of all, let me mention here that, remote as the Greeks were from the Christian and lofty Asiatic world-view, and although they were decidedly at the standpoint of the affirmation of the will, they were nevertheless deeply affected by the wretchedness of existence. The invention of tragedy, which belongs to them, is already evidence of this. Another proof of it is given by the custom of the Thracians, first mentioned by Herodotus (v, 4), and often referred to later, of welcoming the new-born child with lamentation, and recounting all the evils that face it, and, on the other hand, of burying the dead with mirth and merriment, because they have escaped from so many great sufferings. This runs as follows in a fine verse preserved for us by Plutarch (*De audiend. poët., in fine*):

> Τὸν φύντα θρηνεῖν, εἰς ὅσ'ἔρχεται κακά·
> Τὸν δ'αὖ θανόντα καὶ πόνων πεπαυμένον

---

[10] "First false step." [Tr.]

Χαίροντας εὐφημοῦντας ἐκπέμπειν δόμων.
(*Lugere genitum, tanta qui intrarit mala:
At morte si quis finiisset miserias,
Hunc laude amicos atque laetitia exsequi.*)[11]

It is to be attributed not to historical relationship, but to the moral identity of the matter, that the Mexicans welcomed the new-born child with the words: "My child, you are born to endure; therefore endure, suffer, and keep silence." And in pursuance of the same feeling, Swift (as Sir Walter Scott relates in his *Life of Swift*) early adopted the custom of celebrating his birthday, not as a time of joy, but of sadness, and of reading on that day the passage from the Bible where Job laments and curses the day on which it was said in the house of his father that a man-child is born.

Well known and too long to copy out is the passage in the *Apology of Socrates,* where Plato represents this wisest of mortals as saying that, even if death deprived us of consciousness for ever, it would be a wonderful gain, for a deep, dreamless sleep is to be preferred to any day, even of the happiest life.

A saying of Heraclitus ran:

Τῷ οὖν βίῳ ὄνομα μὲν βίος, ἔργον δὲ θάνατος.
(*Vitae nomen quidem est vita, opus autem mors. Etymologicum magnum*, s.v. βίος; also Eustathius *ad Iliad.*, i, p. 31.)[12]

The fine lines of Theognis are well known:

Ἀρχὴν μὲν μὴ φῦναι ἐπιχθονίοισιν ἄριστον,
Μηδ' εἰσιδεῖν αὐγὰς ὀξέος ἠελίου·
Φύντα δ'ὅπως ὤκιστα πύλας Ἀΐδαο περῆσαι,
Καὶ κεῖσθαι πολλὴν γῆν ἐπαμησάμενον.
(*Optima sors homini natum non esse, nec unquam
Adspexisse diem, flammiferumque jubar.
Altera jam genitum demitti protinus Orco,
Et pressum multa mergere corpus humo.*[13]

In *Oedipus Colonus* (1225) Sophocles has the following abbreviation of this:

---

[11] "Pity him who is born, because he faces so many evils; but the dead are to be accompanied with mirth and blessings, because they have escaped from so many sufferings." [Tr.]

[12] "Life has the name of life, but in reality it is death." [Tr.]

[13] "Not to be born at all would be the best thing for man, never to behold the sun's scorching rays; but if one is born, then one is to press as quickly as possible to the portals of Hades, and rest there under the earth." [Tr.]

> Μὴ φῦναι τὸν ἄπαντα νι-
> κᾷ λόγον · τὸ δ'ἐπεὶ φανῇ,
> βῆναι κεῖθεν, ὅθεν περ ἥκει,
> πολὺ δεύτερον, ὡς τάχιστα.

(*Natum non esse sortes vincit alias omnes: proxima autem est, ubi quis in lucem editus fuerit, eodem redire, unde venit, quam ocissime.*) [14]

Euripides says:

> Πᾶς δ'ὀδυνηρὸς βίος ἀνθρώπων,
> Κ'οὐκ ἔστι πόνων ἀνάπαυσις.
> (*Omnis hominum vita est plena dolore,*
> *Nec datur laborum remissio. Hippolytus,* 189.) [15]

And Homer already said:

> Οὐ μὲν γὰρ τί πού ἐστιν ὀϊζυρώτερον ἀνδρὸς
> Πάντων, ὅσσα δε γαῖαν ἔπι πνείει τε καὶ ἔρπει.
> (*Nom enim quidquam alicubi est calamitosius homine omnium,*
> *quotquot super terram spirantque et moventur. Iliad,* xvii, 446.) [16]

Even Pliny says:

Quapropter hoc primum quisque in remediis animi sui habeat, ex omnibus bonis, quae homini natura tribuit, nullum melius esse tempestiva morte. (*Hist. Nat.* 28, 2.) [17]

Shakespeare puts into the mouth of the old King Henry IV the words:

> O heaven! that one might read the book of fate,
> And see the revolution of the times
> . . . how chances mock,
> And changes fill the cup of alteration
> With divers liquors! O, if this were seen,
> The happiest youth,—viewing his progress through
> What perils past, what crosses to ensue,—
> Would shut the book and sit him down and die.

---

[14] "Never to be born is far best; yet if a man lives, the next best thing is for him to return as quickly as possible to the place from which he came." [Tr.]

[15] "All the life of man is full of misery, and there is no end to affliction and despair." [Tr.]

[16] "Of all that breathes and creeps on earth there is no more wretched being than man." [Tr.]

[17] "Therefore may everyone acknowledge first of all, as a means for saving his soul, the view that, of all the good things meted out to man by nature, none is more valuable than a timely death." [Tr.]

Finally, Byron [*Euthanasia*]:

> Count o'er the joys thine hours have seen,
>   Count o'er thy days from anguish free,
> And know, whatever thou hast been,
>   'Tis something better not to be.

Balthasar Gracián also brings before our eyes the misery of our existence in the darkest colours in the *Criticón, Parte* 1, *Crisi* 5, at the beginning, and *Crisi* 7 at the end, where he presents life in detail as a tragic farce.

But no one has treated this subject so thoroughly and exhaustively as Leopardi in our own day. He is entirely imbued and penetrated with it; everywhere his theme is the mockery and wretchedness of this existence. He presents it on every page of his works, yet in such a multiplicity of forms and applications, with such a wealth of imagery, that he never wearies us, but, on the contrary, has a diverting and stimulating effect.

On Ethics

Here is the great gap which results in these supplements from the fact that I have already dealt with morality in the narrower sense in the two essays published under the title *Die Grundprobleme der Ethik*. As I have said, I assume an acquaintance with these, in order to avoid needless repetitions. Hence there remains for me only a small gleaning of isolated reflections that could not be discussed in those essays where the contents were, in the main, prescribed by the Academies, and least of all those that require a higher point of view than the one common to all, at which I was compelled to stop in those essays. Accordingly, it will not surprise the reader to find these reflections here in a very fragmentary collection. This has been continued again in chapters 8 and 9 of the second volume of the *Parerga*.

Moral investigations are incomparably more important than physical, and in general than all others; this follows from the fact that they almost immediately concern the thing-in-itself, namely that phenomenon of it in which, directly discovered by the light of knowledge, it reveals its true nature as *will*. Physical truths, on the other hand, remain entirely within the sphere of the representation, i.e., of the phenomenon, and show merely how the lowest phenomena of the will manifest themselves in the representation in conformity to law. Moreover, consideration of the world from the *physical* angle, however far and successfully it may be pursued, remains in its results without consolation for us; only on the *moral* side is consolation to be found, since here the depths of our own inner nature are disclosed for consideration.

My philosophy, however, is the only one that grants to morality its complete and entire rights; for only if the true nature of man is his own *will*, consequently only if he is, in the strictest sense, his own work, are his deeds actually entirely his and attributable to him. On the other hand, as soon as he has another origin, or is the work

---

[1] This chapter refers to §§ 55, 62, 67 of volume 1.

of a being different from himself, all his guilt falls back on to this origin or originator. For *operari sequitur esse.*[2]

Since Socrates, the problem of philosophy has been to connect the force which produces the phenomenon of the world and in consequence determines its nature, with the morality of the disposition or character, and thus to demonstrate a *moral* world-order as the basis of the *physical. Theism* achieved this in a childlike manner which was unable to satisfy mature mankind. Therefore *pantheism* opposed itself to theism, as soon as it ventured to do so, and demonstrated that nature carries within herself the power by virtue of which she appears. With this, however, *ethics* was bound to be lost. It is true that here and there Spinoza attempts to save it by sophisms, but he often gives it up altogether, and with an audacity that excites astonishment and indignation he declares the difference between right and wrong, and in general between good and evil, to be merely conventional, and therefore in itself hollow and empty (e.g., *Ethics,* IV, prop. 37, schol. 2). After Spinoza had met with unmerited neglect for more than a hundred years, he has been again overrated in this century through the reaction caused by the swing of the pendulum of opinion. All pantheism must ultimately be shipwrecked on the inescapable demands of ethics, and then on the evil and suffering of the world. If the world is a theophany, then everything done by man, and even by the animal, is equally divine and excellent; nothing can be more censurable and nothing more praiseworthy than anything else; hence there is no ethics. Therefore, in consequence of the renewed Spinozism of our day, and thus of pantheism, the treatment of ethics has sunk so low and has become so shallow, that there has been made from it a mere set of instructions for a proper public and family life, in which the ultimate aim of human existence was supposed to consist, that is, in methodical, perfect, smug, and comfortable Philistinism. Pantheism, of course, has led to such shallow absurdities only by the fact that (by a shameful misuse of the *e quovis ligno fit Mercurius*)[3] Hegel, a man with a common mind, has been falsely stamped by the well-known means as a great philosopher, and a herd of his disciples, at first suborned but afterwards merely stupid, got the big words. Such outrages on the human mind do not remain unpunished; the seed has sprung up. In the same spirit, it was then asserted that ethics ought to have for its material not the conduct of individuals, but that of masses of people, and that this alone was a theme worthy of it. Nothing can be more preposterous than this view, which rests on the shallowest realism. For in every

---

[2] "What we do follows from what we are." [Tr.]
[3] "Out of any piece of wood a god may be carved." [Tr.]

individual the whole undivided will-to-live, the being-in-itself, appears, and the microcosm is like the macrocosm. The masses have no more substance than has any individual. In ethics the question is not one of action and result, but of *willing,* and willing itself occurs only in the individual. What is decided *morally* is not the fate of nations, which exists only in the phenomenon, but that of the individual. Nations are in reality mere abstractions; only individuals actually exist. Hence in this way is pantheism related to ethics. The evils and misery of the world, however, are not in accord even with *theism;* and so it tried to help itself by all kinds of shifts, evasions, and theodicies which nevertheless succumbed irretrievably to the arguments of Hume and Voltaire. But *pantheism* is wholly untenable in face of that evil side of the world. Thus, only when we consider the world entirely *from without* and solely from the *physical* side, and keep in view nothing but the order of things which always renews itself, and thereby the comparative imperishableness of the whole, is it perhaps feasible to declare the world to be a God, yet always only symbolically. But if we enter within, and therefore take in addition the *subjective* and the *moral* side, with its preponderance of want, suffering, and misery, of dissension, wickedness, infamy, and absurdity, we soon become aware with horror that we have before us anything but a theophany. But I have shown, and have proved especially in my work *On the Will in Nature,* that the force working and operating in nature is identical with the *will* in ourselves. In this way, the *moral* world-order actually enters into direct connexion with the force that produces the phenomenon of the world. For the *phenomenal appearance of the will* must correspond exactly to its mode of existence. On this rests the explanation of *eternal justice,* which is given in §§ 63, 64 of volume 1; and, although it continues to exist by its own power, the world receives throughout a *moral* tendency. Consequently, the problem raised since the time of Socrates is now actually solved for the first time, and the demand of our thinking reason, that is directed to what is moral, is satisfied. But I have never professed to propound a philosophy that would leave no questions unanswered. In this sense, philosophy is actually impossible; it would be the science of omniscience. But *est quadam prodire tenus, si non datur ultra;*[4] there is a limit up to which reflection can penetrate, and *so far* illuminate the night of our existence, although the horizon always remains dark. This limit is reached by my doctrine in the will-to-live that affirms or denies itself in its own phenomenon. To want to go beyond this is, in my view,

---

[4] "There is a limit up to which one can go, even if one cannot go beyond it." [Tr.]

like wanting to fly beyond the atmosphere. We must stop here, although new problems arise from those that are solved. Moreover, we must refer to the fact that the validity of the principle of sufficient reason or ground is limited to the phenomenon; this was the theme of my first essay on that principle, published as early as 1813.

I now go on to supplement particular observations, and will begin by supporting with a couple of passages from classical poetry my explanation of *weeping,* given in § 67 of volume 1, namely that it springs from sympathy, the object of which is one's own self. At the end of the eighth book of the *Odyssey,* Ulysses, who is never represented as weeping in spite of his many sufferings, bursts into tears, when, still unknown, he hears his previous heroic life and deeds chanted by the bard Demodocus at the court of the Phaeacian king, since the remembrance of the brilliant period of his life contrasts with his present wretchedness. Hence not this wretchedness itself directly, but the objective consideration of it, the picture of his present plight brought into prominence by the past, provokes his tears; he feels sympathy for himself. Euripides makes Hippolytus, innocently condemned and bemoaning his own fate, express the same feeling:

Φεῦ· εἴθ' ἦν ἐμαυτὸν προσβλέπειν ἐναντίον
στάνθ', ὡς ἐδάκρυσ' οἷα πάσχομεν κακά. (1084)
(*Heu, si liceret mihi, me ipsum extrinsecus spectare, quantopere deflerem mala, quae patior*).[5]

Finally, as proof of my explanation, there may be cited here an anecdote that I take from the English paper *The Herald* of 16 July, 1836. A client, after listening to the presentation of his case in court by his counsel, burst into tears, and exclaimed: "I never thought I had suffered half so much till I listened to it here today!"

I have of course shown in § 55 of the first volume how, in spite of the unalterability of character, in other words of the real, fundamental willing of man, an actual moral *repentance* is yet possible. However, I will add the following explanation, which I must preface with one or two definitions. *Inclination* is any strong susceptibility of the will to motives of a certain kind. *Passion* is an inclination so strong, that the motives that excite it exercise a power over the will which is stronger than that of any possible motive acting against them. Its mastery over the will thus becomes absolute; consequently, the attitude of the will towards it is *passive,* an attitude of *suffering.* Here, however, it is to be observed that passions seldom reach the

---

[5] "Ah, if it were granted to me to see myself as I stand there and weep over my distress." [Tr.]

degree in which they correspond to the definition completely; on the contrary, they bear their name as mere approximations to this degree; and so there are then counter-motives that are able at least to restrict their effect, if only they distinctly enter consciousness. The *emotion* is a stirring of the will, just as irresistible yet only temporary, by a motive that does not obtain its power through a deeprooted inclination. On the contrary, such a motive gets its power merely by suddenly appearing and excluding for the moment the counter-effect of all other motives, since it consists in a representation which wholly obscures the others by its excessive vividness, or entirely conceals them, as it were, by its too close proximity, so that they cannot enter consciousness and act on the will. Hence in this way, the capacity for reflection, and with it *intellectual freedom,*[6] are to a certain extent abolished. Accordingly, the emotion is related to the passion as the fancy of an overwrought brain is to madness.

A moral *repentance* is now conditioned by the fact that, before the deed, the inclination thereto did not leave the intellect free scope, since it did not allow it to contemplate clearly and completely the motives opposing the deed, but rather directed it again and again to motives urging the deed. But now, when the deed is done, these motives are neutralized by this deed itself, and have consequently become ineffective. Now reality brings the opposing motives before the intellect as consequences of the deed which have already taken place, and the intellect then knows that they would have been the stronger, if only it had properly contemplated and carefully weighed them. The man, therefore, becomes aware of having done what was not really in accordance with his will; this knowledge is repentance. For he has not acted with full intellectual freedom, since not all the motives attained to effectiveness. What excluded the motives opposed to the deed was, in the case of the hasty deed, the emotion, and in the case of the deliberate deed, the passion. Often it is also due to the fact that the man's faculty of reason presented the countermotives to him in the abstract, it is true, but was not supported by an imagination strong enough to present to him their whole content and true significance in pictures or images. Examples of what has been said are the cases in which thirst for revenge, jealousy, and avarice lead to murder. After the murder is committed, these are extinguished, and then justice, sympathy, the remembrance of former friendship raise their voice, and say all that they would have said earlier had they been allowed to have their say. Then bitter repentance appears and says: "If it had not happened already, it would never happen." A unique presentation of this is afforded by the

---

[6] This is discussed in the appendix to my essay *On the Freedom of the Will.*

famous old Scottish ballad *Edward, Edward!,* which has been translated by Herder. In an analogous way, the neglect of one's own well-
being can bring about an egotistical repentance. For example, when
an otherwise inadvisable marriage is contracted in consequence of a
passionate love that by such marriage is then extinguished, whereupon the counter-motives of personal interest, lost independence, and
so on only then enter consciousness, and speak as they would have
spoken previously had they been allowed to have their say. Accordingly, all such actions spring ultimately from a relative weakness
of the intellect, in so far as this intellect allows itself to be mastered
by the will, when it should have inexorably fulfilled its function of
presenting motives, without allowing itself to be disturbed by the
will. Here the vehemence of the will is only *indirectly* the cause, in so
far as it interferes with the intellect, and thereby prepares repentance
for itself. The *reasonableness* of the character, σωφροσύνη, which is
opposed to passionateness, really consists in the will's never over-
powering the intellect to such an extent as to prevent it from
correctly exercising its function of presenting motives distinctly,
completely, and clearly, in the abstract for our faculty of reason, and
in the concrete for our imagination. This can rest just as well on the
moderation and mildness of the will as on the strength of the
intellect. All that is required is that the intellect be *relatively* strong
enough for the existing will, hence that the two stand in a suitable
relation to each other.

The following explanations have still to be added to the characteristics of *jurisprudence,* discussed in § 62 of volume 1, as well
as in § 17 of the essay *On the Basis of Morality.*

Those who deny with Spinoza that there is a *right* apart from the
State, confuse the means of enforcing the right with the right itself.
The right, of course, is assured *protection* only in the State, but it
itself exists independently of the State. For by force it can be
merely suppressed, never abolished. Accordingly, the *State* is nothing
more than an *institution of protection,* rendered necessary by the
manifold attacks to which man is exposed, and which he is not able
to ward off as an individual, but only in alliance with others. Accordingly, the aims of the State are:

(1) First of all protection directed outwards, which may become
necessary against inanimate forces of nature or wild beasts as well
as against man, and consequently against other nations; although this
case is the most frequent and important, for man's worst enemy is
man: *homo homini lupus.*[7] Since, in consequence of this aim, nations

---

[7] "Man is a wolf to man." [Tr.]

lay down the principle in words, though not in deeds, of always wishing to maintain only a defensive, never an aggressive, attitude to one another, they recognize *international law.* At bottom, this is nothing but natural right in the only sphere of practical efficacy left to it, namely between nation and nation, where it alone must reign, because its stronger son, positive law, cannot assert itself, since that requires a judge and executive. Accordingly, international law consists in a certain degree of morality in the dealings of nations with one another, the maintenance of which is a matter of honour for mankind. Public opinion is the tribunal of cases based on this law.

(2) Protection directed inwards, that is, protection of the members of a State against one another, and consequently the safeguarding of *private right,* by means of the maintenance of an *honest and fair state of things.* This consists in the protection of each individual by the concentrated forces of all, from which there results a phenomenon as though all were honest, that is to say, just, as if no one wanted to injure anyone else.

But, as is usual in things human, the removal of one evil generally opens the way to a fresh one; thus the granting of this twofold protection brings about the need for a third, namely:

(3) Protection against the protector, in other words, against him, or those, to whom society has handed over the management of the protection; and thus guarantee of *public right.* This seems most completely attainable by dividing and separating from one another the threefold unity of the protective power, the legislature, the judicature, and the executive, so that each is managed by others, and independently of the rest. The great value, in fact the fundamental idea, of monarchy seems to me to lie in the fact that, because men remain men, one must be placed so high, and be given so much power, wealth, security, and absolute inviolability, that *for himself* there is nothing left to desire, to hope, or to fear. In this way, the egoism that dwells in him, as in everyone, is annihilated, as it were, by neutralization; and, just as if he were not a human being, he is now enabled to practise justice, and to have in view no longer his own welfare, but only that of the public. This is the origin of the seemingly superhuman character which everywhere accompanies the dignity of royalty, and distinguishes it so entirely from mere presidency. Therefore it must also be hereditary, not subject to election, so that no one may be able to see in the king his own equal, and also so that the king can provide for his descendants only by caring for the welfare of the State, as such welfare is absolutely identical with that of his own family.

If other aims besides that of protection, here discussed, are ascribed to the State, this can easily endanger its true aim.

According to my explanation, the *right of property* arises only through the *manufacture or working up* of things. This truth has often been stated already; and it finds a noteworthy confirmation in that it is maintained even in a practical regard, in a statement of the American ex-president, Quincy Adams, which is to be found in the *Quarterly Review* for 1840, No. 130, and also in French in the *Bibliothèque universelle de Genève,* July 1840, No. 55. I repeat it here: "There are moralists who have questioned the right of the Europeans to intrude upon the possessions of the aboriginals in any case, and under any limitations whatsoever; but have they maturely considered the whole subject? The Indian right of possession itself stands, with regard to the greatest part of the country, upon a *questionable* foundation. Their cultivated fields, their constructed habitations, a space of ample sufficiency for their subsistence, and whatever they had annexed of themselves by personal labour, was undoubtedly by the laws of nature theirs. But what is the right of a huntsman to the forest of a thousand miles over which he has accidentally ranged in quest of prey?" and so on. In just the same way, those who in our own day saw themselves impelled to combat communism with arguments (for example, the Archbishop of Paris in a pastoral letter of June 1851), have always advanced the argument that property is the fruit of one's own labour, is only, so to speak, embodied work. This shows once more that the right of property is to be established only by work applied to things, since only in this respect does it meet with free recognition, and assert itself morally.

A proof of an entirely different kind in support of the same truth is afforded by the moral fact that, while the law punishes poaching just as severely as, and in many countries even more severely than, it punishes theft, civil honour, which through theft is irretrievably lost, is yet not really forfeited by poaching, but in so far as the poacher has not made himself guilty of anything else, he is of course burdened with a stigma, yet not regarded as dishonest and shunned by all, as is the thief. For the principles of a citizen's honour rest on moral and not on merely positive right; game, however, is not an object of treatment or elaboration, and so is not an object of morally valid possession. The right to it is therefore entirely positive, and is not morally recognized.

According to my view, the basis of *criminal* law should be the principle that it is not the *person,* but only the *deed* that is punished, so that it may not recur. The criminal is merely the subject *in which* the deed is punished, so that the power to deter may be retained by the law in consequence of which the punishment takes place. This is the meaning of the expression "he is forfeit to the law." According to Kant's explanation, amounting to a *jus talionis,* it is not the deed but the person who is punished. The penitentiary system also tries to punish not so much the deed as the person, so that he may change for the better. In this way it sets aside the real aim of punishment, determent from the deed, in order to achieve the very problematical aim of improvement. But it is always a doubtful thing to try to secure two different ends by *one* means; how much more so when the two ends are in any sense opposite. Education is a benefit, punishment is supposed to be an evil; the penitentiary prison is supposed to achieve both. Moreover, however large may be the share that brutality and ignorance, in conjunction with external distress, have in many crimes, we must not regard them as the principal cause of these, since innumerable persons living under the same hard conditions and in entirely similar circumstances do not commit any crimes. The principal matter, therefore, reverts to the personal, moral character, but, as I have explained in the essay *On the Freedom of the Will,* this character is absolutely unalterable. Therefore, real moral reform is not at all possible, but only determent from the deed. Moreover, correction of knowledge and the awakening of a desire to work may of course be attained; it will be seen how far this can be effective. Besides this, it is clear from the aim of punishment, which I advance in the text, that, where possible, the apparent suffering of the punishment should exceed the actual; but solitary confinement achieves the reverse. Its great severity has no witnesses, and is by no means anticipated by anyone who has not yet experienced it; hence it does not deter. It threatens the person, tempted to crime by want and misery, with the opposite pole of human wretchedness, boredom; but as Goethe rightly observes:

> If real affliction is our lot,
> Then do we wish for boredom.

Therefore the prospect of it will deter him as little as will the sight of the palatial prisons that are built by honest persons for rogues. If it is desired, however, to regard these penitentiary prisons as educational institutions, it is to be regretted that admission to them is obtained only by crimes, instead of which the prisons should have preceded these.

That punishment should bear a correct proportion to the crime, as Beccaria taught, does not rest on its being an expiation thereof, but on the fact that the pledge must be appropriate to the value of that for which it answers. Therefore everyone is justified in demanding as a pledge the life of another, as a guarantee for the security of his own, but not for the security of his property, for which the freedom and so forth of another is sufficient pledge. For safeguarding the lives of the citizens, capital punishment is therefore absolutely necessary. Those who would like to abolish it should be given the answer: "First remove murder from the world, and then capital punishment ought to follow." It should be inflicted even for the definite attempt at murder, just as for murder itself; for the law's desire is to punish the deed, not to avenge the result. In general, the injury to be prevented provides the correct measure for the punishment to be threatened, but this is not given by the moral worthlessness of the forbidden action. Therefore the law can rightly impose penal servitude for letting a flower-pot fall from a window, or hard labour for smoking in a wood during summer, and yet permit this in winter. But to inflict the punishment of death for shooting an aurochs, as is done in Poland, is too much, for the preservation of the species of the aurochs must not be purchased with human life. In determining the measure of the punishment along with the magnitude of the injury to be prevented, we take into consideration the strength of the motives prompting us to the forbidden action. Quite a different standard would apply to punishment, if expiation, retaliation, *jus talionis,* were its true purpose. But the criminal code should be nothing but a register of counter-motives to possible criminal actions. Each of these counter-motives must therefore decidedly outweigh the motives that lead to these actions, and indeed the more so, the greater the injury that would spring from the action to be guarded against, the stronger the temptation to it, and the more difficult the conviction of the evil-doer; always on the correct assumption that the will is not free, but determinable by motives, otherwise it could not be got at at all. So much for jurisprudence.

In my essay *On the Freedom of the Will* (pp. 50 *seqq.;* second ed., pp. 48 *seqq.*), I have demonstrated the original and unalterable nature of the innate character, from which the moral content of the course of life proceeds. It is well established as a fact; but, in order to grasp problems in their full extent, it is sometimes necessary to contrast opposites sharply. Therefore let us picture in these how incredibly great is the innate difference between one person and another in a moral and intellectual respect. Here magnanimity and wisdom; there wickedness and stupidity. In one goodness of heart shines from his eyes, or the stamp of genius is enthroned on his countenance. The base and mean physiognomy of another is the stamp of moral turpitude and intellectual dulness, unmistakably and indelibly impressed by the hand of nature herself; he looks as though he ought to be ashamed of his existence. And the inner being actually corresponds to this outer appearance. We cannot possibly assume that such differences, which transform the man's whole being, which are not to be abolished by anything, and which further determine his course of life in conflict with the circumstances, could exist without guilt or merit on the part of those affected by them, and that they were the mere work of chance. It is at once evident from this that man must be in a certain sense his own work. But on the other hand we can show empirically the origin of those differences in the character and disposition of the parents; moreover, the coming together and connexion of these parents were obviously the work of the most accidental circumstances. By such considerations we are then forcibly referred to the difference between the phenomenon and the being-in-itself of things, a difference that alone can contain the solution to this problem. The thing-in-itself is revealed only by means of the forms of the phenomenon; therefore, what proceeds from the thing-in-itself must nevertheless appear in those forms, and so also in the bond of causality. Accordingly it will present itself to us here as a mysterious guidance of things incomprehensible to us, the mere tool of which would be the external empirical connexion. But all that happens in this empirical connexion is produced by causes, and so is determined necessarily and from outside, whereas its true ground lies in the inner nature of the real essence that thus appears. Here, of course, we can see the solution to the problem only from a distance, and, by reflecting on it, we fall into an abyss of thought, as Hamlet rightly says, "Thoughts beyond the reaches of our souls." In the essay "On the Apparent Deliberateness in the Fate of the Individual" in the first volume of the *Parerga,* I have expounded my ideas on this mysterious guidance of things, a guidance indeed which is to be conceived only figuratively.

In § 14 of my essay *On the Basis of Morality* is to be found a discussion on *egoism* according to its nature; and the following attempt to discover its root is to be regarded as supplementary to that discussion. Nature flatly contradicts herself, according as she speaks from the particular or the universal, from inside or outside, from the centre or the periphery. Thus nature has her centre in every individual, for each one is the entire will-to-live. Therefore, even if this individual is only an insect or a worm, nature herself speaks out of it as follows: "I alone am all in all; in my maintenance is everything involved; the rest may perish, it is really nothing." Thus nature speaks from the *particular* standpoint, from that of self-consciousness, and to this is due the *egoism* of every living thing. On the other hand, from the *universal* standpoint, from that of the *consciousness of other things,* and thus from that of objective knowledge, for the moment looking away from the individual to whom knowledge adheres,—hence from outside, from the periphery, nature speaks thus: "The individual is nothing and less than nothing. I destroy millions of individuals every day for sport and pastime; I abandon their fate to chance, to the most capricious and wanton of my children, who harasses them at his pleasure. Every day I produce millions of new individuals without any diminution of my productive power; just as little as the power of a mirror is exhausted by the number of the sun's images that it casts one after another on the wall. The individual is nothing." Only he who really knows how to reconcile and eliminate this obvious contradiction of nature has a true answer to the question concerning the perishableness or imperishableness of his own self. I believe I have given an adequate introduction to such knowledge in the first four chapters of this fourth book of supplements. The above remarks may be further illustrated in the following manner. By looking inwards, every individual recognizes in his inner being, which is his will, the thing-in-itself, and hence that which alone is everywhere real. Accordingly, he conceives himself as the kernel and centre of the world, and considers himself infinitely important. On the other hand, if he looks outwards, he is then in the province of the representation, of the mere phenomenon, where he sees himself as an individual among an infinite number of other individuals, and consequently as something extremely insignificant, in fact quite infinitesimal. Accordingly every individual, even the most insignificant, every I, seen from within, is all in all; seen from without, on the other hand, he is nothing, or at any rate as good as nothing. To this, therefore, is due the great difference between what each one necessarily is in his own eyes, and what he is in the eyes of others, consequently *egoism,* with which everyone reproaches everyone else.

In consequence of this egoism, the most fundamental of all our errors is that, with reference to one another, we are not-I. On the other hand, to be just, noble, and benevolent is nothing but to translate my metaphysics into actions. To say that time and space are mere forms of our knowledge, not determinations of things-in-themselves, is the same as saying that the teaching of metempsychosis, namely that "One day you will be born again as the man whom you now injure, and will suffer the same injury," is identical with the frequently mentioned formula of the Brahmans, *Tat tvam asi,* "This thou art." All genuine virtue proceeds from the immediate and *intuitive* knowledge of the metaphysical identity of all beings, as I have often shown, especially in § 22 of the essay *On the Basis of Morality*. But it is not on this account the result of a special preeminence of intellect; on the contrary, even the feeblest intellect is sufficient to see through the *principium individuationis,* which is the main point here. Accordingly, the most excellent character can be found even with a weak understanding; moreover, the excitement of our sympathy is not accompanied by any exertion of our intellect. On the contrary, it seems that the required penetration of the *principium individuationis* would be present in everyone, if his *will* were not opposed to it. By virtue of the will's immediate, mysterious, and despotic influence over the intellect, it prevents this penetration from arising, so that ultimately all guilt falls back on to the *will,* as is also in conformity with the fact.

The doctrine of metempsychosis, previously touched on, deviates from the truth merely by transferring to the future what is already now. Thus it represents my true inner being-in-itself as existing in others only after my death, whereas the truth is that it already lives in them now, and death abolishes merely the illusion by reason of which I am not aware of this; just as the innumerable hosts of stars always shine above our heads, but become visible only when the one sun near the earth has set. From this point of view, however much my individual existence, like that sun, outshines everything for me, at bottom it appears only as an obstacle which stands between me and the knowledge of the true extent of my being. And because in his knowledge every individual succumbs to this obstacle, it is simply individuation that keeps the will-to-live in error as to its own true nature; it is the *Maya* of Brahmanism. Death is a refutation of this error and abolishes it. I believe that, at the moment of dying, we become aware that a mere illusion has limited our existence to our person. Even empirical traces of this may be seen in many states or conditions akin to death through abolition of the concentration of consciousness in the brain, and of these states magnetic sleep is the most conspicuous. When this sleep reaches the higher degrees, our existence shows itself in it through various symptoms, beyond our persons and in other beings, most strikingly by direct participation in the thoughts of another individual, and ultimately even by the ability to know the absent, the distant, and also the future, that is, by a kind of omnipresence.

On this metaphysical identity of the will as thing-in-itself rest in general three phenomena, in spite of the infinite multiplicity of its appearances, and these three can be brought under the common concept of *sympathy:* (1) *sympathy or compassion,* which is, as I have shown, the basis of justice and philanthropy, *caritas;* (2) *sexual love,* with capricious selection, *amor,* which is the life of the species, asserting its precedence over that of individuals; (3) *magic,* to which also belong animal magnetism and sympathetic cures. Accordingly, *sympathy* is to be defined as the empirical appearance of the will's metaphysical identity, through the physical multiplicity of its phenomena. In this way a connexion shows itself; and this is entirely different from that which is brought about by the forms of the phenomenon, and which we comprehend under the principle of sufficient reason.

CHAPTER XLVIII[1]

On the Doctrine of the Denial of the Will-to-Live

Man has his existence and being either *with* his will, in other words, with his consent, or *without* it; in the latter case such an existence, embittered by inevitable sufferings of many kinds, would be a flagrant injustice. The ancients, particularly the Stoics, and also the Peripatetics and Academics, laboured in vain to prove that virtue is enough to make life happy; experience loudly cried out against this. Although they were not clearly aware of it, what was really at the root of the attempt of those philosophers was the assumed *justice* of the case; he who was *without guilt* ought to be free from suffering, and hence happy. But the serious and profound solution of the problem is to be found in the Christian doctrine that works do not justify. Accordingly, although a man has practised all justice and philanthropy, consequently the ἀγαθόν, *honestum,* he is still not *culpa omni carens*[2] as Cicero imagines (*Tusc.,* V, 1); but *el delito mayor del hombre es haber nacido* (Man's greatest offence is that he was born) as the poet Calderón, inspired by Christianity, has expressed it from a knowledge far profounder than was possessed by those wise men. Accordingly, that man comes into the world already involved in guilt can appear absurd only to the person who regards him as just having come from nothing, and as the work of another. Hence in consequence of *this* guilt, which must therefore have come from his will, man rightly remains abandoned to physical and mental sufferings, even when he has practised all those virtues, and so he is *not* happy. This follows from the *eternal justice* of which I spoke in § 63 of volume 1. However, as St. Paul (Rom. iii, 21 *seqq.*), Augustine, and Luther teach, works cannot justify, since we all are and remain essentially sinners. This is due in the last resort to the fact that, since *operari sequitur*

---

[1] This chapter refers to § 68 of volume 1. Compare it also with chapter 14 of volume 2 of the *Parerga.*

[2] "Free from all guilt." [Tr.]

esse,[3] if we acted as we ought to act, we should also necessarily be what we ought to be. But then we should not need any *salvation* from our present condition, and such salvation is represented as the highest goal not only by Christianity, but also by Brahmanism and Buddhism (under the name expressed in English by *final emancipation*); in other words, we should not need to become something quite different from, indeed the very opposite of, what we are. However, since we are what we ought *not* to be, we also necessarily do what we ought *not* to do. We therefore need a complete transformation of our nature and disposition, i.e., the new spiritual birth, regeneration, as the result of which salvation appears. Although the guilt lies in conduct, in the *operari,* yet the root of the guilt lies in our *essentia et existentia,* for the *operari* necessarily proceeds from these, as I have explained in the essay *On the Freedom of the Will.* Accordingly, original sin is really our only true sin. Now it is true that the Christian myth makes original sin arise only after man already existed, and for this purpose ascribes to him, *per impossibile,* a free will; it does this, however, simply as a myth. The innermost kernel and spirit of Christianity is identical with that of Brahmanism and Buddhism; they all teach a heavy guilt of the human race through its existence itself, only Christianity does not proceed in this respect directly and openly, like those more ancient religions. It represents the guilt not as being established simply by existence itself, but as arising through the act of the first human couple. This was possible only under the fiction of a *liberum arbitrium indifferentiae,*[4] and was necessary only on account of the Jewish fundamental dogma, into which that doctrine was here to be implanted. According to the truth, the very origin of man himself is the act of his free will, and is accordingly identical with the Fall, and therefore the original sin, of which all others are the result, appeared already with man's *essentia* and *existentia;* but the fundamental dogma of Judaism did not admit of such an explanation. Therefore Augustine taught in his books *De Libero Arbitrio* that only as Adam before the Fall was man guiltless and had a free will, whereas for ever after he is involved in the necessity of sin. The law, ὁ νόμος, in the biblical sense, always demands that we should change our conduct, while our essential nature would remain unchanged. But since this is impossible, Paul says that no one is justified before the law; we can be transferred from the state of sinfulness into that of freedom and salvation only by the new birth or regeneration in Jesus Christ, in

---

[3] "What we do follows from what we are." [Tr.]

[4] "The free decision of the will not influenced in any direction." [Tr.]

consequence of the effect of grace, by virtue of which a new man arises, and the old man is abolished (in other words, a fundamental change of disposition). This is the Christian myth with regard to ethics. But of course Jewish theism, on to which the myth was grafted, must have received marvellous additions in order to attach itself to that myth. Here the fable of the Fall presented the only place for the graft of the old Indian stem. It is to be ascribed just to this forcibly surmounted difficulty that the Christian mysteries have obtained an appearance so strange and opposed to common sense. Such an appearance makes proselytizing more difficult; on this account and from an inability to grasp their profound meaning, Pelagianism, or present-day rationalism, rises up against them, and tries to explain them away by exegesis, but in this way it reduces Christianity to Judaism.

However, to speak without myth; as long as our will is the same, our world cannot be other than it is. It is true that all men wish to be delivered from the state of suffering and death; they would like, as we say, to attain to eternal bliss, to enter the kingdom of heaven, but not on their own feet; they would like to be carried there by the course of nature. But this is impossible; for nature is only the copy, the shadow, of our will. Therefore, of course, she will never let us fall and become nothing; but she cannot bring us anywhere except always into nature again. Yet everyone experiences in his own life and death how precarious it is to exist as a part of nature. Accordingly, existence is certainly to be regarded as an error or mistake, to return from which is salvation; it bears this character throughout. Therefore it is conceived in this sense by the ancient Samana religions, and also by real and original Christianity, although in a roundabout way. Even Judaism itself contains the germ of such a view, at any rate in the Fall of man; this is its redeeming feature. Only Greek paganism and Islam are wholly optimistic; therefore in the former the opposite tendency had to find expression at least in tragedy. In Islam, however, the most modern as well as the worst of all religions, this opposite tendency appeared as *Sufism,* that very fine phenomenon which is entirely Indian in spirit and origin, and has now continued to exist for over a thousand years. In fact, nothing else can be stated as the aim of our existence except the knowledge that it would be better for us not to exist. This, however, is the most important of all truths, and must therefore be stated, however much it stands in contrast with the present-day mode of European thought. On the other hand, it is nevertheless the most universally recognized fundamental truth in the whole of non-Mohammedan Asia, today as much as three thousand years ago.

Now if we consider the will-to-live as a whole and objectively, we have to think of it, according to what has been said, as involved in a *delusion*. To return from this, and hence to deny its whole present endeavour, is what religions describe as self-denial or self-renunciation, *abnegatio sui ipsius;*[5] for the real self is the will-to-live. The moral virtues, hence justice and philanthropy, if pure, spring, as I have shown, from the fact that the will-to-live, seeing through the *principium individuationis,* recognizes itself again in all its phenomena; accordingly they are primarily a sign, a symptom, that the appearing will is no longer firmly held in that delusion, but that disillusionment already occurs. Thus it might be said figuratively that the will already flaps its wings, in order to fly away from it. Conversely, injustice, wickedness, cruelty are signs of the opposite, that is, of deep entanglement in that delusion. But in the second place, these moral virtues are a means of advancing self-renunciation, and accordingly of denying the will-to-live. For true righteousness, inviolable justice, that first and most important cardinal virtue, is so heavy a task, that whoever professes it unconditionally and from the bottom of his heart has to make sacrifices which soon deprive life of the sweetness required to make it enjoyable, and thereby turn the will from it, and thus lead to resignation. Yet the very thing that makes righteousness venerable is the sacrifices it costs; in trifles it is not admired. Its true nature really consists in the righteous man's not throwing on others, by craft or force, the burdens and sorrows incidental to life, as is done by the unrighteous, but in his bearing what has fallen to his lot. In this way he has to endure undiminished the full burden of the evil imposed on human life. Justice thereby becomes a means for advancing the denial of the will-to-live, since want and suffering, those actual conditions of human life, are its consequence; but these lead to resignation. *Caritas,* the virtue of philanthropy which goes farther, certainly leads even more quickly to the same result. For on the strength of it, a person takes over also the sufferings that originally fall to the lot of others; he therefore appropriates to himself a greater share of these than would come to him as an individual in the ordinary course of things. He who is inspired by this virtue has again recognized in everyone else his own inner nature. In this way he now identifies his own lot with that of mankind in general; but this is a hard lot, namely that of striving, suffering, and dying. Therefore, whoever, by renouncing every accidental advantage, desires for himself no other lot than that of mankind in general, can no longer desire even this for any length

---

[5] "Denial of one's own self." [Tr.]

of time. Clinging to life and its pleasures must now soon yield, and make way for a universal renunciation; consequently, there will come about the denial of the will. Now since, according to this, poverty, privations, and special sufferings of many kinds are produced by the most complete exercise of moral virtues, *asceticism* in the narrowest sense, the giving up of all property, the deliberate search for the unpleasant and repulsive, self-torture, fasting, the hairy garment, mortification of the flesh; all these are rejected by many as super-fluous, and perhaps rightly so. Justice itself is the hairy garment that causes its owner constant hardship, and philanthropy that gives away what is necessary provides us with constant fasting.[6] For this reason, *Buddhism* is free from that strict and excessive asceticism that plays a large part in Brahmanism, and thus from deliberate self-mortification. It rests content with the celibacy, voluntary poverty, humility, and obedience of the monks, with abstinence from animal food, as well as from all worldliness. Further, since the goal to which the moral virtues lead is the one here indicated, the Vedanta philosophy[7] rightly says that, after the entrance of true knowledge with complete resignation in its train, and so after the arrival of the new birth, the morality or immorality of previous conduct becomes a matter of indifference; and it uses here the saying so often quoted by the Brahmans: *Finditur nodus cordis, dissolvuntur omnes dubita-tiones, ejusque opera evanescunt, viso supremo illo* (Sankara, *sloka* 32).[8] Now, however objectionable this view may be to many, to whom a reward in heaven or a punishment in hell is a much more satisfactory explanation of the ethical significance of human action, just as even the good Windischmann rejects that teaching with horror while expounding it; yet he who is able to get to the bottom of things will find that, in the end, this teaching agrees with the Christian doctrine that is urged especially by Luther. This doctrine teaches that it is not works that save us, but only faith appearing through the effect of grace, and that therefore we can never be

---

[6] On the other hand, in so far as asceticism is admitted, the statement of the ultimate motives of human conduct given in my essay *On the Basis of Morality*, namely (1) one's own weal, (2) another's woe, and (3) another's weal, is to be supplemented by a fourth, namely one's own woe. I mention this here incidentally merely in the interest of systematic consistency. In that essay, this fourth motive had to be passed over in silence, since the prize-question was stated in the spirit of the philosophical ethics prevailing in Protestant Europe.

[7] See F. H. H. Windischmann's *Sancara, sive de theologumenis Vedanti-corum,* pp. 116, 117 and 121-23: also *Oupnekhat,* Vol. I, pp. 340, 356, 360.

[8] "He who beholds the highest and profoundest, has his heart's knot cut, all his doubts are resolved, and his works come to nought." [Tr.]

justified by our actions, but obtain forgiveness for our sins only by virtue of the merits of the Mediator. In fact, it is easy to see that, without such assumptions, Christianity would have to teach endless punishments for all, and Brahmanism endless rebirths, and hence that no salvation would be attained by either. Sinful works and their consequence must be annulled and annihilated at some time either by the pardon of another, or by the appearance of our own better knowledge, otherwise the world cannot hope for any salvation; afterwards, however, these become a matter of indifference. This is also the μετάνοια καὶ ἄφεσις ἁμαρτιῶν,[9] the announcement of which is finally imposed by the already risen Christ on his Apostles as the sum of their mission (Luke, xxiv, 47). The moral virtues are not really the ultimate end, but only a step towards it. In the Christian myth, this step is expressed by the eating of the tree of knowledge of good and evil, and with this moral responsibility appears simultaneously with original sin. This original sin itself is in fact the affirmation of the will-to-live; on the other hand, the denial of this will, in consequence of the dawning of better knowledge, is salvation. Therefore, what is moral is to be found between these two; it accompanies man as a light on his path from the affirmation to the denial of the will, or, mythically, from the entrance of original sin to salvation through faith in the mediation of the incarnate God (Avatar): or, according to the teaching of the *Veda*, through all the rebirths that are the consequence of the works in each case, until right knowledge appears, and with it salvation (final emancipation), *Moksha,* i.e., reunion with *Brahma.* But the Buddhists with complete frankness describe the matter only negatively as *Nirvana,* which is the negation of this world or of *Samsara.* If *Nirvana* is defined as nothing, this means only that *Samsara* contains no single element that could serve to define or construct *Nirvana.* For this reason the *Jains,* who differ from the Buddhists only in name, call the Brahmans who believe in the *Vedas,* Sabdapramans, a nickname supposed to signify that they believe on hearsay what cannot be known or proved (*Asiatic Researches,* Vol. VI, p. 474).

When certain ancient philosophers, such as Orpheus, the Pythagoreans, Plato (e.g., in the *Phaedo,* pp. 151, 183 *seq., ed. Bip.,* and see Clement of Alexandria, *Stromata,* iii, p. 400 *seq.*), deplore the soul's connexion with the body, as the Apostle Paul does, and wish to be liberated from this connexion, we understand the real and true meaning of this complaint, in so far as we recognize in the

---

[9] "Repentance and remission of sins." [Tr.]

second book that the body is the will itself, objectively perceived as spatial phenomenon.

In the hour of death, the decision is made whether man falls back into the womb of nature, or else no longer belongs to her, but ——: we lack image, concept, and word for this opposite, just because all these are taken from the objectification of the will, and therefore belong to that objectification; consequently, they cannot in any way express its absolute opposite; accordingly, this remains for us a mere negation. However, the death of the individual is in each case the unweariedly repeated question of nature to the will-to-live: "Have you had enough? Do you wish to escape from me?" The individual life is short, so that the question may be put often enough. The ceremonies, prayers, and exhortations of the Brahmans at the time of death are conceived in this sense, as we find them preserved in several passages of the *Upanishad*. In just the same way, the Christian concern is for the proper employment of the hour of death by means of exhortation, confession, communion, and extreme unction; hence the Christian prayers for preservation from a sudden end. That many desire just such an end at the present day simply shows that they no longer stand at the Christian point of view, which is that of the denial of the will-to-live, but at that of its affirmation, which is the heathen.

However, he will be least afraid of becoming nothing in death who has recognized that he is already nothing now, and who consequently no longer takes any interest in his individual phenomenon, since in him knowledge has, so to speak, burnt up and consumed the will, so that there is no longer any will, any keen desire for individual existence, left in him.

Individuality, of course, is inherent above all in the intellect; reflecting the phenomenon, the intellect is related thereto, and the phenomenon has the *principium individuationis* as its form. But individuality is also inherent in the will, in so far as the character is individual; yet this character itself is abolished in the denial of the will. Thus individuality is inherent in the will only in its affirmation, not in its denial. The holiness attaching to every purely moral action rests on the fact that ultimately such action springs from the immediate knowledge of the numerical identity of the inner nature of all living things.[10] But this identity is really present only in the state of the denial of the will (Nirvana), as the affirmation of the will (Samsara) has for its form the phenomenal appearance of this

---

[10] Compare *Die beiden Grundprobleme der Ethik*, p. 274 (2nd edn., p. 271).

in plurality and multiplicity. Affirmation of the will-to-live, the phenomenal world, diversity of all beings, individuality, egoism, hatred, wickedness, all spring from *one* root. In just the same way, on the other hand, the world as thing-in-itself, the identity of all beings, justice, righteousness, philanthropy, denial of the will-to-live, spring from *one* root. Now, as I have sufficiently shown, moral virtues spring from an awareness of that identity of all beings; this, however, lies not in the phenomenon, but in the thing-in-itself, in the root of all beings. If this is the case, then the virtuous action is a momentary passing through the point, the permanent return to which is the denial of the will-to-live.

It is a deduction from what has been said that we have no ground for assuming that there are even more perfect intelligences than those of human beings. For we see that this intelligence is already sufficient for imparting to the will that knowledge in consequence of which the will denies and abolishes itself. With this knowledge, individuality, and therefore intelligence, as being merely a tool of individual nature, of animal nature, cease. To us this will appear less objectionable when we consider that we cannot conceive even the most perfect possible intelligences, which we may tentatively assume for this purpose, as indeed continuing to exist throughout an endless time, a time that would prove to be much too poor to afford them constantly new objects worthy of them. Thus, because the inner essence of all things is at bottom identical, all knowledge of it is necessarily tautological. If this inner essence is once grasped, as it soon would be by those most perfect intelligences, what would be left for them but mere repetition and its tedium throughout endless time? Thus, even from this point of view, we are referred to the fact that the aim of all intelligence can only be reaction to a will; but since all willing is error, the last work of intelligence is to abolish willing, whose aims and ends it had hitherto served. Accordingly, even the most perfect intelligence possible can be only a transition stage to that which no knowledge can ever reach; in fact, such an intelligence, in the nature of things, can take only the place of the moment of attained, perfect insight.

In agreement with all these considerations, and with what was shown in the second book to be the origin of knowledge from the will, since knowledge is serviceable to the aims of the will, and in this way reflects the will in its affirmation, whereas true salvation lies in the denial of the will, we see all religions at their highest point end in mysticism and mysteries, that is to say, in darkness and veiled obscurity. These really indicate merely a blank spot for knowledge, the point where all knowledge necessarily ceases. Hence for thought this can be expressed only by negations, but for sense-perception it is indicated by symbolical signs, in temples by dim light and silence, in Brahmanism even by the required suspension of all thought and perception for the purpose of entering into the deepest communion with one's own self, by mentally uttering the mysterious *Om*.* In the widest sense, mysticism is every guidance to the immediate awareness of that which is not reached either by perception or conception, or generally by any knowledge. The mystic is opposed to the philosopher by the fact that he begins from within, whereas the philosopher begins from without. The mystic starts from his inner, positive, individual experience, in which he finds himself as the eternal and only being, and so on. But nothing of this is communicable except the assertions that we have to accept on his word; consequently he is unable to convince. The philosopher, on the other hand, starts from what is common to all, the objective phenomenon lying before us all, and from the facts of self-consciousness as they are to be found in everyone. Therefore reflection on all this, and the combination of the data given in it, are his method; for this reason he is able to convince. He should therefore beware of falling into the way of the mystics, and, for instance, by assertion of intellectual intuitions, or of pretended immediate apprehensions of the faculty of reason, of trying to give in bright colours a positive knowledge of what is for ever inaccessible to all knowledge, or at most can be expressed only by a negation. Philosophy has its value and virtue in its rejection of all assumptions that cannot be substantiated, and in its acceptance as its data only of that which can be proved with certainty in the external world given by perception, in the forms constituting our intellect for the apprehension of the world, and in the consciousness of one's own self common to all. For this reason it must remain

---

* If we keep in view this essential *immanence of our knowledge and of all knowledge,* which springs from its being something secondary, something that has arisen for the aims of the will—it becomes easy to explain that all the mystics of all religions ultimately arrive at a kind of *ecstasy.* In this each and every kind of *knowledge* together with its fundamental form, *object and subject,* entirely ceases. Only in this sphere, lying beyond all knowledge, do they claim to have attained their highest goal, since they have reached the point where there are no longer any subject and object, consequently no kind of knowledge, just because there is no longer any will, to serve which is the sole destiny of knowledge.

Whoever has grasped this will no longer regard it as excessively extravagant for fakirs to sit down, contemplate the tip of their noses, and attempt to banish all ideas and representations, or that in many a passage of the *Upanishad* guidance is given to sink oneself, silently and inwardly uttering the mysterious *Om,* into the depths of one's own being, where subject and object and all knowledge vanish.

cosmology, and cannot become theology. Its theme must restrict itself to the world; to express from every aspect *what* this world *is,* what it *may be* in its innermost nature, is all that it can honestly achieve. Now it is in keeping with this that, when my teaching reaches its highest point, it assumes a *negative* character, and so ends with a negation. Thus it can speak here only of what is denied or given up; but what is gained in place of this, what is laid hold of, it is forced (at the conclusion of the fourth book) to describe as nothing; and it can add only the consolation that it may be merely a relative, not an absolute, nothing. For, if something is no one of all the things that we know, then certainly it is for us in general nothing. Yet it still does not follow from this that it is nothing absolutely, namely that it must be nothing from every possible point of view and in every possible sense, but only that we are restricted to a wholly negative knowledge of it; and this may very well lie in the limitation of our point of view. Now it is precisely here that the mystic proceeds positively, and therefore, from this point, nothing is left but mysticism. Anyone, however, who desires this kind of supplement to the negative knowledge to which alone philosophy can guide him, will find it in its most beautiful and richest form in the *Oupnekhat,* in the *Enneads* of Plotinus, in Scotus Erigena, in passages of Jacob Böhme, and especially in the wonderful work of Madame de Guyon, *Les Torrens,* and in Angelus Silesius, and finally also in the poems of the Sufis, of which Tholuck has given us one collection in Latin and another translation into German, and in many other works. The Sufis are the Gnostics of Islam; hence also Sadi describes them by an expression that is translated by "full of insight." Theism, calculated with reference to the capacity of the crowd, places the primary source of existence outside us, as an object. All mysticism, and so Sufism also, at the various stages of its initiation, draw this source gradually back into ourselves as the subject, and the adept at last recognizes with wonder and delight that he himself is it. We find this course of events expressed by Meister Eckhart, the father of German mysticism, not only in the form of a precept for the perfect ascetic "that he seek not God outside himself" (*Eckhart's Works,* edited by Pfeiffer, Vol. I, p. 626), but also exhibited extremely naïvely by the fact that, after Eckhart's spiritual daughter had experienced that conversion in herself, she sought him out, in order to cry out to him jubilantly: "Sir, rejoice with me, I have become God!" (*loc. cit.,* p. 465). The mysticism of the Sufis also expresses itself generally in this same spirit, principally as a revelling in the consciousness that we ourselves are the kernel of the world and the source of all existence, to which everything returns. It is true that there also frequently occurs the call to give up all willing as the only way in which deliverance from individual existence and its sufferings is possible; yet it is subordinated and is required as something easy. In the mysticism of the Hindus, on the other hand, the latter side comes out much more strongly, and in Christian mysticism it is quite predominant, so that the pantheistic consciousness, essential to all mysticism, here appears only in a secondary way, in consequence of the giving up of all willing, as union with God. In keeping with this difference of conception Mohammedan mysticism has a very cheerful, Christian mysticism a melancholy and painful character, while that of the Hindus, standing above both, holds the mean in this respect.

Quietism, i.e., the giving up of all willing, asceticism, i.e., intentional mortification of one's own will, and mysticism, i.e., consciousness of the identity of one's own inner being with that of all things, or with the kernel of the world, stand in the closest connexion, so that whoever professes one of them is gradually led to the acceptance of the others, even against his intention. Nothing can be more surprising than the agreement among the writers who express those teachings, in spite of the greatest difference of their age, country, and religion, accompanied as it is by the absolute certainty and fervent assurance with which they state the permanence and consistency of their inner experience. They do not form some *sect* that adheres to, defends, and propagates a dogma theoretically popular and once adopted; on the contrary, they generally do not know of one another; in fact, the Indian, Christian, and Mohammedan mystics, quietists, and ascetics are different in every respect except in the inner meaning and spirit of their teachings. A most striking example of this is afforded by the comparison of Madame de Guyon's *Torrens* with the teaching of the *Vedas,* especially with the passage in the *Oupnekhat,* Vol. I, p. 63. This contains the substance of that French work in the briefest form, but accurately and even with the same figures of speech, and yet it could not possibly have been known to Madame de Guyon in 1680. In the *German Theology* (the only unmutilated edition, Stuttgart, 1851), it is said in Chapters 2 and 3 that the fall of the devil as well as that of Adam consisted in the fact that the one, like the other, had ascribed to himself I and me, mine and to me. On page 89 it says: "In true love there remains neither I nor me, mine, to me, thou, thine, and the like." In keeping with this, it says in the *Kural,* translated from the Tamil by Graul, p. 8: "The passion of the mind directed outwards and that of the I directed inwards cease" (cf. verse 346). And in the *Manual of Buddhism* by Spence Hardy, p. 258, the Buddha says: "My disciples, reject the idea that I am this or this is mine." If we turn from the forms, produced by external circumstances, and go to the root of things, we shall find generally that Sakya Muni and Meister Eckhart teach the same thing; only that the former dared to express his ideas plainly and positively, whereas the latter is obliged to clothe them in the garment of the Christian myth, and to adapt his expressions thereto. This goes to such lengths that with him the Christian myth is little more than a metaphorical language, in much the same way as the Hellenic myth is to the Neo-Platonists; he takes it throughout allegorically. In the same respect, it is noteworthy that the turning of St. Francis from prosperity to a beggar's life is entirely similar to the even greater step of the Buddha Sakya Muni from prince to beggar, and that accordingly the life of St. Francis, as well as the order founded by him, was only a kind of Sannyasi existence. In fact, it is worth mentioning that his relationship with the Indian spirit also appears in his great love for animals, and his frequent association with them, when he always calls them his sisters and brothers; and his beautiful *Cantico* is evidence of his inborn Indian spirit through the praise of the sun, moon, stars, wind, water, fire and earth.[11]

Even the Christian quietists must often have had little or no knowledge of one another, for example, Molinos and Madame de Guyon of Tauler and the *German Theology,* or Gichtel of the former. Likewise, the great difference of their culture, in that some of them, like Molinos, were learned, others, like Gichtel and many more, were illiterate, has no essential influence on their teachings. Their great inner agreement, together with the firmness and certainty of their utterances, proves all the more that they speak from actual inner experience, from an experience which is, of course, not accessible to everyone, but comes only to a favoured few. This experience has therefore been called the effect of grace, whose reality, however, is indubitable for the above reasons. But to understand all this we must read the mystics themselves, and not be content with second-hand reports; for everyone must himself be comprehended before we judge of him. Therefore I specially recommend for an acquaintance with quietism Meister Eckhart, the *German Theology,* Tauler, Madame de Guyon, Antoinette Bourignon, Bun-

---

[11] S. Bonaventure, *Vita S. Francisci,* c. 8; K. Hase, *Franz von Assisi,* ch. 10; *I cantici di S. Francesco,* edited by Schlosser and Steinle, Frankfurt a.M., 1842.

yan, Molinos,[12] and Gichtel. As practical proofs of the deep seriousness of asceticism, Pascal's life edited by Reuchlin together with his history of Port Royal, and also the *Histoire de Sainte Elisabeth* by the Comte de Montalembert and *La vie de Rancé* by Chateaubriand are also well worth reading; yet these by no means exhaust all that is important in this class. Whoever has read such works, and has compared their spirit with that of asceticism and quietism, as it runs through all the works of Brahmanism and Buddhism and speaks from every page, will admit that every philosophy, which, to be consistent, must reject that whole mode of thought, in that it declares the representatives of it to be impostors or madmen, must on this account necessarily be false. But all European systems, my own excepted, find themselves in this position. It must truly be a strange madness which, in circumstances and among persons of the widest possible difference, expressed itself with such agreement, and was, moreover, exalted to a principal teaching of their religion by the oldest and most numerous races on earth, by some three-quarters of all the inhabitants of Asia. But no philosophy can leave undecided the theme of quietism and asceticism, if the question is put to it, since this theme is in substance identical with that of all metaphysics and ethics. Here, then, is a point on which I expect and desire every philosophy with its optimism to express itself. And if, in the judgement of contemporaries, the paradoxical and unexampled agreement of my philosophy with quietism and asceticism appears as an obvious stumbling-block, yet I, on the other hand, see in this very agreement a proof of its sole accuracy and truth, and also a ground for explaining why it has been discreetly ignored and kept secret by *Protestant* universities.

For not only the religions of the East, but also true Christianity has throughout this fundamental ascetic character that my philosophy explains as denial of the will-to-live, although Protestantism, especially in its present-day form, tries to keep this dark. Yet even the open enemies of Christianity who have appeared in most recent times have attributed to it the teaching of renunciation, self-denial, perfect chastity, and generally mortification of the will, which they quite rightly describe by the name of *"anticosmic tendency"*; and they have thoroughly demonstrated that such doctrines are essentially peculiar to original and genuine Christianity. In this respect they are undeniably right; but they set up this very thing as an

---

[12] *Michaelis de Molinos manuductio spiritualis: hispanice 1675, italice 1680, latine 1687, gallice in libro non adeo raro, cui titulus: Recueil de diverses pièces concernant le quiétisme, ou Molinos et ses disciples.* Amsterdam, 1688.

obvious and patent reproach to Christianity, whereas just in this are its deepest truth, its high value, and its sublime character to be found. Such an attitude is evidence of a mental obscurity to be explained only from the fact that the minds of those men, unfortunately like thousands of others at the present time in Germany, are completely ruined and for ever confused by that miserable Hegelism, that school of dulness, that centre of stupidity and ignorance, that mind-destroying, spurious wisdom that people are at last beginning to recognize as such. Admiration of this school will soon be left to the Danish Academy alone; in their eyes, indeed, that coarse and clumsy charlatan is a *summus philosophus,* for whom it takes the field:

> *Car ils suivront la créance et estude,*
> *De l'ignorante et sotte multitude,*
> *Dont le plus lourd sera reçu pour juge.*[13]
> Rabelais

The ascetic tendency is certainly unmistakable in genuine and original Christianity, as it was developed in the writings of the Church Fathers from the kernel of the New Testament; this tendency is the highest point to which everything strives upwards. We find, as its principal teaching, the recommendation of genuine and pure celibacy (that first and most important step in the denial of the will-to-live) already expressed in the New Testament.[14] In his *Life of Jesus* (Vol. I, p. 618), Strauss also says with regard to the recommendation of celibacy given in Matthew xix, 11 *seq.* "That in order not to represent Jesus as saying anything running counter to present-day ideas, men hasten to *introduce surreptitiously* the idea that Jesus commends celibacy only with regard to the circumstances of the time, and in order to leave unfettered the activity of the Apostles; but in the context there is even less indication of this than there is in the kindred passage, I Cor. vii, 25 *seq.* On the contrary, we have here again one of the places where *ascetic principles* such as were widespread among the Essenes, and probably even more so among the Jews, appear in the teaching of Jesus also." This ascetic tendency later appears more decided than at the beginning, when, still looking for adherents, Christianity did not dare to pitch its demands too high; and by the beginning of the third century it is emphatically urged. In Christianity proper, marriage is regarded

---

[13] "For they will follow the belief and choice of the ignorant and stupid crowd whose dullest member will be welcomed as judge." [Tr.]

[14] Matth. xix, 11 *seq.;* Luke, xx, 35-37; I Cor. vii, 1-11 and 25-40; I Thess. iv, 3; I John iii, 3; Rev., xiv, 4.

merely as a compromise with man's sinful nature, as a concession, as something allowed to those who lack the strength to aspire to the highest, and as an expedient for preventing greater perdition. In this sense, it receives the sanction of the Church so that the bond may be indissoluble. But celibacy and virginity are set up as the higher inspiration of Christianity, by which one enters into the ranks of the elect. Through these alone does one attain the victor's crown, which is indicated even at the present time by a wreath on the coffin of the unmarried, as also by the wreath laid aside by the bride on the day of her marriage.

A piece of evidence on this point, coming certainly from the earliest days of Christianity, is the pregnant answer of the Lord quoted by Clement of Alexandria (*Stromata*, iii, 6 and 9) from the Gospel of the Egyptians: Τῇ Σαλώμῃ ὁ κύριος πυνθανομένῃ, μέχρι πότε θάνατος ἰσχύσει; μέχρις ἄν, εἶπεν, ὑμεῖς, αἱ γυναῖκες, τίκτητε (*Salomae interroganti "Quousque vigebit mors?" Dominus "Quoadusque," inquit, "vos, mulieres, paritis"*). τουτ' ἔστι, μέχρις ἄν αἱ ἐπιθυμίαι ἐνεργῶσι (*hoc est, quamdiu operabuntur cupiditates*)[15] Clement adds (c. 9) with which he connects at once the famous passage, Rom. v, 12. Further, in c. 13, he quotes the words of Cassianus: Πυνθανομένης τῆς Σαλώμης, πότε γνωσθήσεται τὰ περὶ ὧν ἤρετο, ἔφη ὁ κύριος, "Ὅταν τὸ τῆς αἰσχύνης ἔνδυμα πατήσητε, καὶ ὅταν γένηται τὰ δύο ἕν, καὶ τὸ ἄρρεν μετὰ τῆς θηλείας οὔτε ἄρρεν, οὔτε θῆλυ (*Cum interrogaret Salome, quando cognoscentur ea, de quibus interrogabat, ait Dominus: 'Quando pudoris indumentum conculcaveritis, et quando duo facta fuerint unum, et masculum cum femina nec masculum nec femineum.'*),[16] in other words, when she no longer needs the veil of modesty, since all distinction of sex will have disappeared.

On this point the heretics have certainly gone farthest, thus the Tatianites or Encratites, the Gnostics, the Marcionites, the Montanists, Valentinians, and Cassians in the second century, yet only by their paying honour to truth with reckless consistency, and therefore teaching, according to the spirit of Christianity, complete abstinence, ἐγκράτεια, whereas the Church prudently declared heresy all that ran counter to her far-seeing policy. Of the Tatianites Augustine says: *Nuptias damnant, atque omnino pares eas fornicationibus aliisque corruptionibus faciunt: nec recipiunt in suum numerum conjugio*

---

[15] "When Salome asked the Lord how long death would reign, he replied 'As long as you women continue to be born'; in other words, as long as desires show their strength." [Tr.]

[16] "When Salome asked at what time that which she enquired about would be known, the Lord answered: 'When you trample on the veil of modesty and when the two sexes become one, and when male as well as female are neither male nor female.'" [Tr.]

utentem, sive marem, sive feminam. Non vescuntur carnibus, easque abominantur. (De haeresibus ad Quodvultdeum, haer. 25).[17] But even the orthodox fathers consider marriage in the light indicated above, and zealously preach complete abstinence, ἀγνεία. Athanasius states as the cause of marriage: ὅτι ὑποπίπτουνιές, ἐσμεν τῇ τοῦ προπάτορος καταδίκη· . . . ἐπειδὴ ὁ προηγούμενος σκοπὸς τοῦ Θεοῦ ἦν, τὸ μὴ διὰ γάμου γενέσθαι ἡμᾶς καὶ φθορᾶς· ἡ δὲ παράβασις τῆς ἐντολῆς τὸν γάμον εἰσήγαγεν διὰ τὸ ἀνομῆσαι τὸν Ἀδάμ. (*Quia subjacemus condemnationi propatoris nostri; . . . nam finis, a Deo praelatus, erat, nos non per nuptias et corruptionem fieri: sed transgressio mandati nuptias introduxit, propter legis violationem Adae. Exposit. in psalm.* 50).[18] Tertullian calls marriage *genus mali inferioris, ex indulgentia ortum (De Pudicitia,* c. 16) and says: *Matrimonium et stuprum est commixtio carnis; scilicet cujus concupiscentiam Dominus stupro adaequavit. Ergo, inquis, jam et primas, id est unas nuptias destruis? Nec immerito: quoniam et ipsae ex eo constant, quod est stuprum (De Exhortatione Castitatis,* c. 9).[19] In fact, Augustine himself acknowledges entirely this teaching and all its results, since he says: *Novi quosdam, qui murmurent: Quid si, inquiunt, omnes velint ab omni concubitu abstinere, unde subsistet genus humanum? Utinam omnes hoc vellent! dumtaxat in caritate, de corde puro, et conscientia bona, et fide non ficta: multo citius Dei civitas compleretur, et acceleraretur terminus mundi (De bono conjugali,* c. 10). And again: *Non vos ab hoc studio, quo multos ad imitandum vos excitatis, frangat querela vanorum, qui dicunt: Quomodo subsistet genus humanum, si omnes fuerint continentes? Quasi propter aliud retardetur hoc seculum, nisi ut impleatur praedestinatus numerus ille sanctorum, quo citius impleto, profecto nec terminus seculi differetur (De bono viduitatis,* c. 23).[20] At the same time, we see that he identifies salvation with

---

[17] "They reject marriage and put it on a level with fornication and other vices; also they do not receive any married people into their ranks, either men or women. They do not eat meat and detest it." [Tr.]

[18] "That the damnation of our progenitor has fallen to our lot; . . . since the aim intended by God was that we should not be born through marriage and corruption; but the transgressing of the commandment gave rise to marriage, because Adam had been disobedient." [Tr.]

[19] "A kind of inferior evil resting on indulgence,"—"Marriage, like adultery, is a carnal intercourse; for the Lord has put strong desire for it on a level with adultery. Therefore can one object that you condemn also the first of all marriages, and at the time the only one? Certainly, and rightly so, for it too consists in what is called adultery." [Tr.]

[20] "I know some who grumble and say: If all were to abstain from procreation, how would the human race continue to exist? Would that all wanted to abstain! provided it were done in love, from a pure heart, with a good conscience, and sincere belief, then the kingdom of God would be

the end of the world. The remaining passages bearing on this point from the works of Augustine are found collected in the *Confessio Augustiniana e D. Augustini operibus compilata a Hieronymo Torrense*, 1610, under the headings *De Matrimonio, De Coelibatu*, and so on. From these anyone can convince himself that in old, genuine Christianity marriage was a mere concession; moreover that it was supposed to have only the begetting of children as its object; and that, on the other hand, total abstinence was the true virtue much to be preferred to marriage. To remove all doubts about the tendency of the Christianity we are discussing, I recommend for those who do not wish to go back to the sources, two works: Carové, *Ueber das Cölibatgesetz* (1832), and Lind, *De Coelibatu Christianorum per tria priora secula* (*Havniae* [Copenhagen], 1839). But it is by no means the views of these writers themselves to which I refer, as these are opposed to mine, but simply the accounts and quotations carefully collected by them, which merit complete trust and confidence as being quite undesigning, just because these two authors are opponents of celibacy, the former a rationalistic Catholic, and the latter a Protestant theological student who speaks exactly like one. In the first-named work we find (Vol. I, p. 166), the following result expressed in that regard: "By virtue of the Church view, as it may be read in the canonical Church Fathers, in Synodal and Papal instructions, and in innumerable writings of orthodox Catholics, perpetual chastity is called a divine, heavenly, angelic virtue, and the obtaining of the assistance of divine grace for this purpose is made dependent on the earnest entreaty therefor. We have already shown that this Augustinian teaching is found expressed by Canisius and by the Council of Trent as the invariable belief of the Church. But that it has been retained till the present day as a dogma may be sufficiently established by the June 1831 number of the periodical *Der Katholik*. On p. 263 it says: 'In Catholicism the observance of a *perpetual chastity*, for God's sake, appears *in itself* as the *highest* merit of man. The view that the observance of perpetual chastity as an *end in itself sanctifies* and exalts man, is, as every instructed Catholic is convinced, deep-rooted in Christianity according to its spirit and its express precept. The Council of Trent has removed all possible doubt about this.' It must certainly be admitted by every unbiassed person

---

realized far more quickly, since the end of the world would be hastened."

"Might not the futile complaint of those who ask how the human race could continue to exist if all were to practise abstinence, perplex you in this endeavour by which you inspire many to emulate you? As though a reprieve would be given to this world for yet another reason than that the predestined number of saints was complete. But the more quickly this becomes complete, the less need is there for the end of the world to be postponed." [Tr.]

not only that the teaching expressed by *Der Katholik* is really Catholic, but also that the arguments adduced may be absolutely irrefutable for a Catholic's faculty of reason, as they are drawn directly from the fundamental ecclesiastical view of the Church on life and its destiny." Further, it is said on p. 270 of the same work: "Although Paul describes the prohibition to marry as a false teaching, and the even more Judaistic author of the Epistle to the Hebrews enjoins that 'Marriage shall be honourable in all, and the marriage bed undefiled' (Hebr. xiii, 4), yet the main tendency of these two sacred writers must not on this account be misunderstood. To both virginity was perfection, marriage only a makeshift for the weaker, and only as such was it to be held inviolate. The highest endeavour, on the other hand, was directed to complete, material casting off of self. The self should turn away and refrain from everything that contributes only to *its* pleasure and to this *only temporarily*." Finally on p. 288: "We agree with the Abbé Zaccaria, who asserts that celibacy (not the law of celibacy) is derived above all from the teaching of Christ and of the Apostle Paul."

What is opposed to this really Christian fundamental view is everywhere and always only the Old Testament, with its πάντα καλὰ λίαν.[21] This appears with particular distinctness from that important third book of the *Stromata* of Clement. Arguing against the above-mentioned Encratite heretics, he there always confronts them merely with Judaism and its optimistic history of creation, with which the world-denying tendency of the New Testament is most certainly in contradiction. But the connexion of the New Testament with the Old is at bottom only an external, accidental, and in fact forced one; and, as I have said, this offered a sole point of contact for the Christian teaching only in the story of the Fall, which, moreover, in the Old Testament is isolated, and is not further utilized. Yet according to the Gospel account, it is just the orthodox followers of the Old Testament who bring about the crucifixion of the Founder, because they consider his teachings to be in contradiction with their own. In the above-mentioned third book of the *Stromata* of Clement the antagonism between optimism together with theism on the one hand, and pessimism together with asceticism on the other, comes out with surprising distinctness. This book is directed against the Gnostics, who taught precisely pessimism and asceticism, particularly ἐγκράτεια (abstinence of every kind, but especially from all sexual satisfaction); for this reason, Clement vigorously censures them. But at the same time it becomes apparent that the spirit of the Old Testament stands in this antagonism with that of the New. For, apart from the

---

[21] "[And God saw] all [that he had made, and behold it] was very good." [Tr.]

Fall which appears in the Old Testament like an *hors d'œuvre,* the spirit of the Old Testament is diametrically opposed to that of the New; the former is optimistic, and the latter pessimistic. This contradiction is brought out by Clement himself at the end of the eleventh chapter (προσαποτεινόμενον τὸν Παῦλον τῷ Κτίστη κ.τ.λ.),[22] although he will not admit it, but declares it to be apparent, like the good Jew that he is. In general, it is interesting to see how for Clement the New and Old Testaments always get mixed up, and how he strives to reconcile them, yet often drives out the New Testament with the Old. At the very beginning of the third chapter he objects to the Marcionites for having found fault with the creation, after the manner of Plato and Pythagoras, since Marcion teaches that nature is bad and made of bad material (φύσις κακή, ἐκ τὲ ὕλης κακής); hence this world should not be populated, but man should abstain from marriage (μὴ βουλόμενοι τὸν κόσμον συμπλήρουν, ἀπέχεσθαι γάμου). Now Clement, to whom the Old Testament is generally much more congenial and convincing than the New, takes this very much amiss. He sees in this their flagrant ingratitude, enmity, and resentment towards him who made the world, towards the just demiurge, whose work they themselves are. In godless rebellion "forsaking the natural disposition," they nevertheless disdained to make use of his creatures (ἀντιτασσόμενοι τῷ ποιητῇ τῷ σφων, . . . ἐγκρατεῖς τῇ πρὸς τὸν πεποιηκότα ἔχθρᾳ, μὴ βουλόμενοι χρῆσθαι τοῖς ὑπ' αὐτοῦ κτισθεῖσιν, . . . ἀσεβεῖ θεομαχίᾳ τῶν κατὰ φύσιν ἐκστάντες λογισμῶν).[23] Here in his holy ardour he will not allow the Marcionites even the honour of originality, but, armed with his well-known erudition, he reproaches them and supports his case with the finest quotations, that the ancient philosophers, that Heraclitus and Empedocles, Pythagoras and Plato, Orpheus and Pindar, Herodotus and Euripides, and in addition the Sibyls, already deeply deplored the wretched nature of the world, and thus taught pessimism. Now he does not notice in this scholarly enthusiasm that precisely in this way he is providing grist to the mill of the Marcionites, for he shows indeed that "All the wisest of all the ages" have taught and sung the same thing as they. On the contrary, he confidently and boldly quotes the most decided and emphatic utterances of the ancients in that sense. Of course, he is not put out by them; sages may lament the melancholy

---

[22] "That Paul (by words like Rom. vii, 18) puts himself in opposition to the Creator." [Tr.]

[23] "Since they resist him who has created them, . . . persisting in their hostility to their creator, in that they do not wish to make any use of his creatures, . . . and in wanton and wicked conflict with God, they forsake the natural disposition." [Tr.]

nature of existence, poets may pour out the most affecting lamentations about it, nature and experience may cry out ever so loudly against optimism; all this does not disturb our Church Father; he still holds his Jewish revelation in his hand, and remains confident. The demiurge has made the world; from this it is *a priori* certain that it is excellent, no matter what it looks like. It is then just the same with the second point, with the ἐγκράτεια, by which, according to his view, the Marcionites reveal their ingratitude to the demiurge (ἀχαριστεῖν τῷ δημιουργῷ), and the stubbornness with which they reject his gifts (δι' ἀντίταξιν πρὸς τὸν δημιουργόν, τὴν χρῆσιν τῶν κοσμικῶν παραίτουμενοι). The tragic poets had already paved the way for the Encratites (to the detriment of their originality), and had said the same thing. Thus they lamented the infinite misery of existence, and added that it is better to bring no children into such a world. Again he supports this with the finest passages, and at the same time accuses the Pythagoreans of having renounced sexual pleasure for this reason. All this, however, does not worry him at all; he sticks to his principle that through their abstinence all these sin against the demiurge, since they teach that one should not marry, should not beget children, should not bring into the world new miserable beings, should not produce fresh fodder for death (δι' ἐγκρατείας ἀσεβοῦσιν εἴς τε τὴν κτίσιν καὶ τὸν ἅγιον δημιουργόν, τὸν παντοκράτορα μόνον θεόν, καὶ διδάσκουσι, μὴ δεῖν παραδέχεσθαι γάμον καὶ παιδοποιίαν, μηδὲ ἀντεισάγειν τῷ κόσμῳ δυστυχήσοντας ἑτέρους, μηδὲ ἐπιχορηγεῖν θανάτῳ τροφήν. c. 6).[24] Since the learned Church Father thus denounces ἐγκράτεια, he does not appear to have foreseen that, just after his time, the celibacy of the Christian priesthood would be introduced more and more, and finally in the eleventh century would be passed into law, because it is in keeping with the spirit of the New Testament. It is precisely this spirit that the Gnostics grasped more profoundly and understood better than did our Church Father, who was more of a Jew than a Christian. The point of view of the Gnostics stands out very clearly at the beginning of the ninth chapter, where the following is quoted from the Gospel of the Egyptians: αὐτὸς εἶπεν ὁ Σωτήρ, "ἦλθον καταλῦσαι τὰ ἔργα τῆς θηλείας"· θηλείας μὲν τῆς ἐπιθυμίας ἔργα δέ, γένεσιν καὶ φθοράν (*Aiunt enim dixisse Servatorem: "Veni ad dissolvendum opera feminae": feminae quidem, cupiditatis; opera autem, generationem et interitum*);[25] but partic-

---

[24] "For through their abstinence they sin against creation and the holy Creator, against the sole, almighty God; and they teach that one should not enter into matrimony and beget children, should not bring further unhappy beings into the world, and produce fresh fodder for death." [Tr.]

[25] "For they say that the Saviour himself said: 'I have come that I may bring to nought the works of woman'; of woman, in other words of desire; but the works are generation and destruction." [Tr.]

ularly at the end of the thirteenth chapter and at the beginning of the
fourteenth. The Church, of course, had to consider how to set
on its feet a religion that could also walk and stand in the world
as it is, and among men; she therefore declared these men to be
heretics. At the conclusion of the seventh chapter, our Church
Father sets up Indian asceticism as bad in opposition to the Christian-
Jewish; here is clearly brought out the fundamental difference in
the spirit of the two religions. In Judaism and Christianity, everything runs back to obedience or disobedience to God's command,
ὑπακοὴ καὶ παρακοή, as befits us creatures, ἡμῖν, τοῖς πεπλασμένοις
ὑπὸ τῆς τοῦ Παντοκράτορος βουλήσεως (*nobis qui ab Omnipotentis
voluntate effecti sumus*)[26] c. 14. Then comes, as a second duty,
λατρεύειν θεῷ ζῶντι, to serve the Lord, to praise his works, and to
overflow with thankfulness. In Brahmanism and Buddhism, of course,
the matter has quite a different aspect, since in the latter all improvement, conversion, and salvation to be hoped for from this
world of suffering, from this Samsara, proceed from knowledge of the
four fundamental truths: (1) *dolor*, (2) *doloris ortus*, (3) *doloris
interitus*, (4) *octopartita via ad doloris sedationem*.[27] *Dhammapada*,
ed. Fausböll, pp. 35 and 347. The explanation of these four truths is
found in Burnouf, *Introduction à l'histoire du Buddhisme*, p. 629,
and in all descriptions of Buddhism.

In truth it is not Judaism with its πάντα καλὰ λίαν,[28] but Brahmanism and Buddhism that in spirit and ethical tendency are akin to
Christianity. The spirit and ethical tendency, however, are the
essentials of a religion, not the myths in which it clothes them. Therefore I do not abandon the belief that the teachings of Christianity are
to be derived in some way from those first and original religions. I
have already pointed out some traces of this in the second volume of
the *Parerga*, § 179. In addition to these is the statement of Epipha-
nius (*Haereses*, xviii) that the first Jewish Christians of Jerusalem,
who called themselves Nazarenes, abstained from all animal food. By
virtue of this origin (or at any rate of this agreement), Christianity
belongs to the ancient, true, and sublime faith of mankind. This
faith stands in contrast to the false, shallow, and pernicious *optimism*
that manifests itself in Greek paganism, Judaism, and Islam. To a
certain extent the Zend religion holds the mean, since it opposes to
Ormuzd a pessimistic counterpoise in Ahriman. The Jewish religion
resulted from this Zend religion, as J. G. Rhode has thoroughly
demonstrated in his book *Die heilige Sage des Zendvolks;* Jehovah
came from Ormuzd, and Satan from Ahriman. The latter, however,

---

[26] "Us, who have been created by the will of the Almighty." [Tr.]
[27] The Four Noble Truths of Buddhism. [Tr.]
[28] "All was very good." [Tr.]

plays only a very subordinate role in Judaism, in fact almost entirely disappears. In this way optimism gains the upper hand, and there is left only the myth of the Fall as a pessimistic element, which (as the fable of Meshian and Meshiane) is also taken from the Zend-Avesta, but nevertheless falls into oblivion until it, as well as Satan, is again taken up by Christianity. But Ormuzd himself is derived from Brahmanism, although from a lower region thereof; he is no other than *Indra,* that subordinate god of the firmament and the atmosphere, who is frequently in competition with men. This has been very clearly shown by the eminent scholar I. J. Schmidt in his work *Ueber die Verwandtschaft der gnostisch-theosophischen Lehren mit den Religionssystemen des Orients, vorzüglich dem Buddhismus.* This Indra-Ormuzd-Jehovah afterwards had to pass into Christianity, as that religion arose in Judaea. But in consequence of the cosmopolitan character of Christianity, he laid aside his proper name, in order to be described in the language of each converted nation by the appellative of the superhuman individuals he supplanted, as θεός, *Deus,* which comes from the Sanskrit *Deva* (from which also devil, *Teufel* is derived), or among the Gothic-Germanic nations by the word God, *Gott,* which comes from *Odin,* or *Wodan, Guodan, Godan.* In just the same way he assumed in Islam, which also springs from Judaism, the name of Allah, which existed previously in Arabia. Analogously to this, when the gods of the Greek Olympus were transplanted to Italy in prehistoric times, they assumed the names of the gods who reigned there previously; hence among the Romans Zeus is called Jupiter, Hera Juno, Hermes Mercury, and so on. In China the first embarrassment of the missionaries arose from the fact that the Chinese language has absolutely no appellative of the kind, and also no word for creating;[29] for the three religions of China know of no gods either in the plural or in the singular.

However it may be in other respects, that πάντα καλὰ λίαν[30] of the Old Testament is really foreign to Christianity proper; for in the New Testament the world is generally spoken of as something to which we do not belong, which we do not love, the ruler of which, in fact, is the devil.[31] This agrees with the ascetic spirit of the denial

---

[29] Cf. *On the Will in Nature,* second edition, p. 124.

[30] "All was very good." [Tr.]

[31] For example, John xii, 25 and 31; xiv, 30; xv, 18, 19; xvi, 33; Coloss. ii, 20; Eph. ii, 1-3; I John ii, 15-17, and iv, 4, 5. Here is an opportunity to see how, in their efforts to misinterpret the text of the New Testament in conformity with their rationalistic, optimistic, and unutterably shallow worldview, certain Protestant theologians go to the length of positively falsifying this text in their translations. Thus, in his new Latin version, added to the Griesbach text of 1805, H. A. Schott translates the word κόσμος, John xv,

of one's self and the overcoming of the world. Like boundless love of one's neighbour, even of one's enemy, this spirit is the fundamental characteristic which Christianity has in common with Brahmanism and Buddhism, and which is evidence of their relationship. There is nothing in which we have to distinguish the kernel from the shell so much as in Christianity. Just because I value this kernel highly, I sometimes treat the shell with little ceremony; yet it is thicker than is often supposed.

By eliminating asceticism and its central point, the meritorious nature of celibacy, Protestantism has already given up the innermost kernel of Christianity, and to this extent is to be regarded as a breaking away from it. In our day, this has shown itself in the gradual transition of Protestantism into shallow rationalism, that modern Pelagianism. In the end, this results in a doctrine of a loving father who made the world, in order that things might go on very pleasantly in it (and in this, of course, he was bound to fail), and who, if only we conform to his will in certain respects, will afterwards provide an even much pleasanter world (in which case it is only to be regretted that it has so fatal an entrance). This may be a good religion for comfortable, married, and civilized Protestant parsons, but it is not Christianity. Christianity is the doctrine of the deep guilt of the human race by reason of its very existence, and of the heart's intense longing for salvation therefrom. That salvation, however, can be attained only by the heaviest sacrifices and by the denial of one's own self, hence by a complete reform of man's nature. From a practical point of view, Luther may have been perfectly right, that is to say, with reference to the Church scandal of his time which he wished to stop, but not so from a theoretical point of view. The more sublime a teaching is, the more open is it to abuse at the hands of human nature, which is, on the whole, of a mean and evil disposition; for this reason, the abuses in Catholicism are much more numerous and much greater than those in Protestantism. Thus, for example, monasticism, that methodical denial of the will, practised in common for the purpose of mutual encouragement, is an institution of a sublime nature. For this reason, however, it often becomes untrue to its spirit. The revolting abuses of the Church provoked in Luther's honest mind a lofty indignation. In consequence of this, however, he was led to a desire to reduce the claims of Christianity itself as much as possible. For this purpose, he first of all restricted it to the words of the Bible; for he went too far in his well-meant zeal, for he

---

18, 19 by *Judaei,* I John iv, 4 by *profani homines,* and Coloss. ii, 20 στοιχεῖα τοῦ κοσμοῦ by *elementa Judaica;* whereas Luther everywhere renders the word honestly and correctly by "world."

attacked the heart of Christianity in the ascetic principle. For, after the withdrawal of this, the optimistic principle of necessity soon stepped into its place. But in religions, as well as in philosophy, optimism is a fundamental error that bars the way to all truth. From all this, it seems to me that Catholicism is a disgracefully abused, and Protestantism a degenerate, Christianity. Christianity in general thus appears to have suffered the fate that falls to the lot of everything that is noble, sublime, and great, as soon as it has to exist among mankind.

However, even in the very midst of Protestantism, the essentially ascetic and Encratite spirit of Christianity has again asserted itself, and the result of this is a phenomenon that perhaps has never previously existed in such magnitude and definiteness, namely the extremely remarkable sect of the *Shakers* in North America, founded in 1774 by an Englishwoman, Ann Lee. The followers of this sect have already increased to six thousand; they are divided into fifteen communities, and inhabit several villages in the states of New York and Kentucky, especially in the district of New Lebanon near Nassau village. The fundamental characteristic of their religious rule of life is celibacy and complete abstinence from all sexual satisfaction. It is unanimously admitted even by English and American visitors, who in every other respect laugh and jeer at them, that this rule is observed strictly and with perfect honesty, although brothers and sisters sometimes even occupy the same house, eat at the same table, in fact *dance* together in church during divine service. For whoever has made that heaviest of all sacrifices, may *dance* before the Lord; he is the victor, he has overcome. Their hymns in church are generally cheerful; in fact, some of them are merry songs. That church dance which follows the sermon is also accompanied by the singing of the rest; it is executed rhythmically and briskly, and ends with a galopade that is carried on till all are exhausted. After each dance, one of their teachers cries aloud: "Remember that ye rejoice before the Lord for having mortified your flesh! For this is the only use that we can here make of our refractory limbs." Most of the other conditions are automatically tied up with celibacy. There is no family, and hence no private property, but community of ownership. All are dressed alike, similarly to Quakers and very neatly. They are industrious and diligent; idleness is by no means tolerated. They also have the enviable rule of avoiding all unnecessary noise, such as shouting, door-slamming, whip-cracking, loud knocking, and so on. One of them has thus expressed their rule of life: "Lead a life of innocence and purity, love your neighbours as yourself, live in peace with all men, and refrain from war, bloodshed, and all acts of violence towards others, as well as from all striving after worldly honour and distinction. Give to each what is his, and observe *holiness,* without which no man can see the Lord. Do good to all in so far as there is opportunity and as long as your strength lasts." They do not persuade anyone to join them, but test those who present themselves for admission by a novitiate of several years. Everyone is free to leave them; very rarely is anyone expelled for misconduct. Children by a former husband or wife are carefully educated, and only when they have grown up do they take the vow voluntarily. It is said that during the controversies of their ministers with Anglican clergy the latter often come off the worse, for the arguments consist of passages from the New Testament. More detailed accounts of them are found especially in Maxwell's *Run through the United States,* 1841; also in Benedict's *History of All Religions,* 1830; likewise in *The Times* of 4 November 1837, and also in the May 1831 number of the German periodical *Columbus.* A German sect in America, very similar to them, is the Rappists, who also live in strict celibacy and abstinence. An account of them is given in F. Löher's *Geschichte und Zustände der Deutschen in Amerika,* 1853. In Russia the Raskolniki are said to be a similar sect. The Gichtelians likewise live in strict chastity. We find also among the ancient Jews a prototype of all these sects, namely the Essenes, of whom even Pliny gives an account (*Historia Naturalis,* V, 15), and who were very similar to the Shakers, not only in celibacy, but also in other respects, even in the dance during divine service.[32] This leads to the supposition that the woman who founded the Shakers took the Essenes as a pattern. In the face of such facts, how does Luther's assertion appear: *Ubi natura, quemadmodum a Deo nobis insita est, fertur ac rapitur, FIERI NULLO MODO POTEST, ut extra matrimonium caste vivatur. (Catech. maj.)*?[33]

Although, in essential respects, Christianity taught only what the whole of Asia knew already long before and even better, for Europe it was nevertheless a new and great revelation. In consequence of this, the spiritual tendency of European nations was entirely transformed. For it disclosed to them the metaphysical significance of existence, and accordingly taught them to look beyond the narrow, paltry, and ephemeral life on earth, and no longer to regard that as an end in itself, but as a state or condition of suffering, guilt, trial, struggle and purification, from which we can soar upwards

---

[32] Bellermann, *Geschichtliche Nachrichten über Essäer und Therapeuten,* 1821, p. 106.

[33] "Where nature, as implanted in us by God, is carried away, then *it is in no way possible* for a chaste life to be lived outside matrimony." [Tr.]

to a better existence, inconceivable to us, by means of moral effort, severe renunciation, and the denial of our own self. Thus it taught the great truth of the affirmation and denial of the will-to-live in the garment of allegory by saying that, through the Fall of Adam, the curse had come upon all men, sin had come into the world, and guilt was inherited by all; but that through the sacrificial death of Jesus, on the other hand, all were purged of sin, the world was saved, guilt abolished, and justice appeased. But in order to understand the truth itself contained in this myth, we must regard human beings not merely in time as entities independent of one another, but must comprehend the (Platonic) Idea of man. This is related to the series of human beings as eternity in itself is to eternity drawn out in time. Hence the eternal Idea *man,* extended in time to the series of human beings, appears once more in time as a whole through the bond of generation that unites them. Now if we keep in view the Idea of man, we see that the Fall of Adam represents man's finite, animal, sinful nature, in respect of which he is just a being abandoned to limitation, sin, suffering, and death. On the other hand, the conduct, teaching, and death of Jesus Christ represent the eternal, supernatural side, the freedom, the salvation of man. Now, as such and *potentiâ,* every person is Adam as well as Jesus, according as he comprehends himself, and his will thereupon determines him. In consequence of this, he is then damned and abandoned to death, or else saved and attains to eternal life. Now these truths were completely new, both in the allegorical and in the real sense, as regards the Greeks and Romans, who were still entirely absorbed in life, and did not seriously look beyond this. Whoever doubts this last statement should see how even Cicero (*Pro Cluentio,* c. 61) and Sallust (*Catilina,* c. 47) speak of the state after death. Although the ancients were far advanced in almost everything else, they had remained children in the principal matter; and in this they were surpassed even by the Druids, who indeed taught metempsychosis. The fact that one or two philosophers, like Pythagoras and Plato, thought otherwise, alters nothing as regards the whole.

Therefore that great fundamental truth contained in Christianity as well as in Brahmanism and Buddhism, the need for salvation from an existence given up to suffering and death, and its attainability through the denial of the will, hence by a decided opposition to nature, is beyond all comparison the most important truth there can be. But it is at the same time entirely opposed to the natural tendency of mankind, and is difficult to grasp as regards its true grounds and motives; for, in fact, all that can be thought only generally and in the abstract is quite inaccessible to the great majority of people.

Therefore, in order to bring that great truth into the sphere of practical application, a *mythical vehicle* for it was needed everywhere for this great majority, a receptacle, so to speak, without which it would be lost and dissipated. The truth had therefore everywhere to borrow the garb of fable, and, in addition, had to try always to connect itself in each case with what is historically given, and is already known and revered. That which *sensu proprio* was and remained inaccessible to the great masses of all times and countries with their low mentality, their intellectual stupidity, and their general brutality, had to be brought home to them *sensu allegorico* for practical purposes, in order to be their guiding star. Thus the above-mentioned religions are to be regarded as sacred vessels in which the great truth, recognized and expressed for thousands of years, possibly indeed since the beginning of the human race, and yet remaining in itself an esoteric doctrine as regards the great mass of mankind, is made accessible to them according to their powers, and preserved and passed on through the centuries. Yet because everything that does not consist throughout of the indestructible material of pure truth is subject to destruction, whenever this fate befalls such a vessel through contact with a heterogeneous age, the sacred contents must be saved in some way by another vessel, and preserved for mankind. But philosophy has the task of presenting those contents, since they are identical with pure truth, pure and unalloyed, hence merely in abstract concepts, and consequently without that vehicle, for those who are capable of thinking, the number of whom is at all times extremely small. Philosophy is related to religions as a straight line is to several curves running near it; for it expresses *sensu proprio,* and consequently reaches directly, that which religions show under disguises, and reach in roundabout ways.

Now if, in order to illustrate by an example what has just been said, and at the same time to follow a philosophical fashion of my time, I wish perhaps to try to resolve the deepest mystery of Christianity, namely that of the Trinity, into the fundamental conceptions of my philosophy, this might be done in the following manner with the licence granted in the case of such interpretations. The Holy Ghost is the decided denial of the will-to-live; the person in whom this exhibits itself *in concreto* is the Son. He is identical with the will that affirms life, and thereby produces the phenomenon of this world of perception, i.e., with the Father, in so far as affirmation and denial are opposite acts of the same will. The ability of the will to affirm or deny is the only true freedom. This, however, is to be regarded as a mere *lusus ingenii.*[34]

---

[34] "Playful fancy." [Tr.]

Before ending this chapter I will quote a few proofs in support of what I denoted in § 68 of the first volume by the expression Δεύτερος πλοῦς,[35] namely the bringing about of the denial of the will by one's own deeply felt suffering, thus not merely by the appropriation of others' suffering and by the knowledge, introduced thereby, of the vanity and wretchedness of our existence. We can understand what goes on in a man's heart in the case of an exaltation of this kind, and of the process of purification introduced by it, if we consider what every sensitive person experiences when looking on at a tragedy, as it is of a similar nature to this. Thus possibly in the third and fourth acts such a person is painfully affected and filled with anxiety by the sight of the ever more clouded and threatened happiness of the hero. On the other hand, when in the fifth act this happiness is entirely wrecked and shattered, he feels a certain elevation of mind. This affords him a pleasure of an infinitely higher order than any which could ever have been derived from the sight of the hero's happiness, however great this might have been. Now in the weak water-colours of fellow-feeling, such as can be stirred by a well-known illusion, this is the same as that which occurs with the force of reality in the feeling of our own fate, when it is grave misfortune that finally drives man into the haven of complete resignation. All those conversions that completely transform man, such as I have described in the text, are due to this occurrence. The story of the conversion of the Abbé Rancé may be given here in a few words, as one that is strikingly similar to that of Raymond Lull given in the text; moreover, it is notable on account of its result. His youth was devoted to pleasure and enjoyment; finally, he lived in a passionate relationship with a Madame de Montbazon. When he visited her one evening, he found her room empty, dark, and in disorder. He struck something with his foot; it was her head, which had been severed from the trunk because, after her sudden death, her corpse could not otherwise have been put into the leaden coffin that was standing beside it. After recovering from a terrible grief, Rancé became in 1663 the reformer of the order of the Trappists, which at that time had departed entirely from the strictness of its rules. He at once entered this order, and through him it was brought back to that terrible degree of renunciation in which it continues to exist at La Trappe even at the present time. As the denial of the will, methodically carried out and supported by the severest renunciations, and by an incredibly hard and painful way of life, this order fills the visitor with sacred awe after he has been touched at his reception by the humility of these genuine monks. Emaciated by fasting, shivering, night-

---

[35] "The next best course." [Tr.]

watches, praying, and working, these monks kneel before him, the worldling and sinner, to ask for his blessing. In France, of all the monastic orders this one alone has maintained itself completely after all the revolutionary changes. This is to be ascribed to the deep seriousness which is unmistakable in it, and which excludes all secondary purposes. It has remained untouched, even by the decline of religion, because its root is to be found deeper in human nature than is any positive doctrine of belief.

I have mentioned in the text that the great and rapid revolutionary change in man's innermost nature, which has here been considered, and has hitherto been entirely neglected by philosophers, occurs most frequently when, fully conscious, he goes out to a violent and certain death, as in the case of executions. But to bring this process much more closely before our eyes, I do not regard it as in any way unbecoming to the dignity of philosophy to record the statements of a few criminals before execution, although I might in this way incur the sneer that I encourage gallows-sermons. On the contrary, I certainly believe that the gallows is a place of quite peculiar revelations, and a watch-tower from which the person who still retains his senses often obtains a much wider view and a clearer insight into eternity than most philosophers have over the paragraphs of their rational psychology and theology. The following gallows-sermon was given at Gloucester on 15 April 1837, by a certain Bartlett who had murdered his mother-in-law: "Englishmen and fellow-countrymen! I have a few words to say, and very few they shall be. Yet let me entreat you, one and all, that these few words may strike deep into your hearts. Bear them in your minds, not only while you are witnessing this sad scene, but take them to your homes, take them and repeat them to your children and friends; I implore you as a dying man, one for whom the instrument of death is even now prepared. And these words are, that you may loose yourselves from the love of this dying world and its vain pleasures. Think less of it and more of your God. Do this: repent, repent! For be assured, that without deep and true repentance, without turning to your heavenly Father, you will never attain, nor can hold the slightest hope of ever reaching those bowers of bliss and that land of peace, to which I trust I am now fast advancing, etc." (From *The Times* 18, April, 1837.) Even more remarkable is a last statement of the well-known murderer Greenacre, who was executed in London on 1 May, 1837. The English newspaper *The Post* gives the following account of it, which is also reprinted in *Galignani's Messenger* of 6 May, 1837. "On the morning of his execution a gentleman recommended him to put his trust in God and pray to be forgiven through the intercession of Jesus Christ.

Greenacre made answer that praying through the intercession of Christ was a matter of opinion: as for himself, he believed that a Mahommetan in the eyes of the supreme being was equal to a Christian and had as great a claim to salvation. He remarked that since his confinement he had turned his attention to theological matters, and had come to the conclusion: that the gallows was a pass-port to Heaven." The indifference here displayed towards positive religions is just what gives this statement greater weight, since it shows that the basis of such a statement is no fanatical delusion, but the man's own immediate knowledge. The following extract, taken from the *Limerick Chronicle* and given in *Galignani's Messenger* of 15 August, 1837, may also be mentioned: "Mary Cooney, for the revolting murder of Mrs. Anne Anderson, was executed at Gallowsgreen on Monday last. So deeply sensible of her crime was the wretched woman, that she kissed the rope which encircled her neck, and humbly implored God for mercy." Finally also this: *The Times* of 29 April 1845 gives several letters, written on the day before his execution by Hocker, who was condemned for the murder of Delarue. In one of them he says: "I am persuaded that unless the natural heart be broken, and renewed by divine mercy, however noble and amiable it may be deemed by the world, it can never think of eternity without inwardly shuddering." These are the outlooks into eternity mentioned above, which are disclosed from that watch-tower, and I have the less hesitation in giving them here, since Shakespeare also says:

> out of these convertites
> There is much matter to be heard and learn'd.
> (*As You Like It*, last scene.)

In his *Life of Jesus* (Vol. I, Sec. 2, chap. 6, §§ 72 and 74), Strauss has shown that Christianity also attributes to suffering as such the purifying and sanctifying power here described, and, on the other hand, ascribes to great prosperity an opposite effect. Thus he says that the beatitudes in the Sermon on the Mount have a different meaning in Luke (vi, 21) from that which they have in Matthew (v, 3), for only the latter adds τῷ πνεύματι to μακάριοι οἱ πτωχοί and τὴν δικαιοσύνην to πεινῶντες.[36] Thus only with him are the ingenuous, the innocent, the humble, and so on meant; with Luke, on the other hand, the really poor are meant, so that here the contrast is that between present suffering and future well-being. With the Ebionites it was a cardinal principle that whoever takes his share at the *present*

---

[36] "In spirit" to "blessed are the poor"; "after righteousness" to "those who hunger." [Tr.]

time, gets nothing in the future, and *vice versa*. Accordingly, in Luke the blessings are followed by as many οὐαί, woes, which are addressed to the rich, πλούσιοι, to the satisfied, ἐμπεπλησμένοι, and to those who laugh, γελῶντες, in the Ebionite sense. On p. 604 Strauss says that the parable of the rich man and Lazarus (Luke xvi, 19) is given in the same sense. This parable does not mention at all any transgression of the former or any merit of the latter, and takes as the standard of future requital not the good done or the wickedness practised in this life, but the evil suffered and the good enjoyed here, in the Ebionite sense. Strauss goes on to say that "a similar appreciation of outward poverty is also ascribed to Jesus by the other synoptists (Matth. xix, 16; Mark x, 17; Luke xviii, 18) in the story of the rich young man, and in the maxim about the camel and the eye of a needle."

If we go to the bottom of things, we shall recognize that even the most famous passages of the Sermon on the Mount contain an indirect injunction to voluntary poverty, and thus to the denial of the will-to-live. For the precept (Matth. v, 40 *seq.*), to comply unconditionally with all demands made on us, to give also our cloak to him who will take away our coat, and so on; likewise (Matth. vi, 25-34) the precept to banish all cares for the future, even for the morrow, and so to live for the day, are rules of life whose observance inevitably leads to complete poverty. Accordingly, they state in an indirect manner just what the *Buddha* directly commands his followers to do, and confirmed by his own example, namely to cast away everything and become *bhikkhus,* that is to say, mendicants. This appears even more decidedly in the passage Matthew x, 9-15, where the Apostles are not allowed to have any possessions, not even shoes and staff, and are directed to go and beg. These precepts afterwards became the foundation of the mendicant order of St. Francis (Bonaventure, *Vita S. Francisci,* c. 3). I say therefore that the spirit of Christian morality is identical with that of Brahmanism and Buddhism. In accordance with the whole view discussed here, Meister Eckhart also says (*Works,* Vol. I, p. 492): "Suffering is the fleetest animal that bears you to perfection."

CHAPTER XLIX

The Road to Salvation

There is only one inborn error, and that is the notion that we exist in order to be happy. It is inborn in us, because it coincides with our existence itself, and our whole being is only its paraphrase, indeed our body is its monogram. We are nothing more than the will-to-live, and the successive satisfaction of all our willing is what we think of through the concept of happiness.

So long as we persist in this inborn error, and indeed even become confirmed in it through optimistic dogmas, the world seems to us full of contradictions. For at every step, in great things as in small, we are bound to experience that the world and life are certainly not arranged for the purpose of containing a happy existence. Now, while the thoughtless person feels himself vexed and annoyed hereby merely in real life, in the case of the person who thinks, there is added to the pain in reality the theoretical perplexity as to why a world and a life that exist so that he may be happy in them, answer their purpose so badly. At first it finds expression in pious ejaculations such as, "Ah! why are the tears beneath the moon so many?" and many others; but in their train come disquieting doubts about the assumptions of those preconceived optimistic dogmas. We may still try to put the blame for our individual unhappiness now on the circumstances, now on other people, now on our own bad luck or even lack of skill, and we may know quite well how all these have worked together to bring it about, but this in no way alters the result, that we have missed the real purpose of life, which in fact consists in being happy. The consideration of this then often proves to be very depressing, especially when life is already drawing to an end; hence the countenances of almost all elderly persons wear the expression of what is called *disappointment*. In addition to this, however, every day of our life up to now has taught us that, even when joys and pleasures are attained, they are in themselves deceptive, do not perform what they promise, do not satisfy the heart, and finally that their possession is at least embittered by the vexations and unpleasantnesses that accompany or spring from them. Pains and sorrows, on the other hand, prove very real, and often exceed all expectation. Thus everything in life is certainly calculated to bring us back from that original error, and to convince us that the purpose of our existence is not to be happy. Indeed, if life is considered more closely and impartially, it presents itself rather as specially intended to show us that we are *not* to feel happy in it, since by its whole nature it bears the character of something for which we have lost the taste, which must disgust us, and from which we have to come back, as from an error, so that our heart may be cured of the passion for enjoying and indeed for living, and may be turned away from the world. In this sense, it would accordingly be more correct to put the purpose of life in our woe than in our welfare. For the considerations at the end of the previous chapter have shown that the more one suffers, the sooner is the true end of life attained, and that the more happily one lives, the more is that end postponed. Even the conclusion of Seneca's last letter is in keeping with this: *bonum tunc habebis tuum, quum intelliges infelicissimos esse felices,*[1] which certainly seems to indicate an influence of Christianity. The peculiar effect of the tragedy rests ultimately on the fact that it shakes that inborn error, since it furnishes a vivid illustration of the frustration of human effort and of the vanity of this whole existence in a great and striking example, and thereby reveals life's deepest meaning; for this reason, tragedy is recognized as the sublimest form of poetry. Now whoever has returned by one path or the other from that error which is *a priori* inherent in us, from that πρῶτον ψεῦδος[2] of our existence, will soon see everything in a different light, and will find that the world is in harmony with his insight, though not with his wishes. Misfortunes of every sort and size will no longer surprise him, although they cause him pain; for he has seen that pain and trouble are the very things that work towards the true end of life, namely the turning away of the will from it. In all that may happen, this will in fact give him a wonderful coolness and composure, similar to that with which a patient undergoing a long and painful cure bears the pain of it as a sign of its efficacy. Suffering expresses itself clearly enough to the whole of human existence as its true destiny. Life is deeply steeped in suffering, and cannot escape from it; our entrance into it takes place amid tears, at bottom its course is always

---

[1] "Then will you have for yourself your own good, when you see that the lucky ones are the unhappiest of all." [Tr.]
[2] "First false step." [Tr.]

tragic, and its end is even more so. In this there is an unmistakable touch of deliberation. As a rule, fate passes in a radical way through the mind of man at the very summit of his desires and aspirations, and in this way his life then receives a tragic tendency, by virtue of which it is calculated to free him from the passionate desire of which every individual existence is a manifestation, and to bring him to the point where he parts with life without retaining any desire for it and its pleasures. In fact, suffering is the process of purification by which alone man is in most cases sanctified, in other words, led back from the path of error of the will-to-live. Accordingly, the salutary nature of the cross and of suffering is so often discussed in Christian devotional books, and in general the cross, an instrument of suffering not of doing, is very appropriately the symbol of the Christian religion. In fact, even the Preacher, Jewish indeed but very philosophical, rightly says: "Sorrow is better than laughter: for by the sadness of the countenance the heart is made better" (Eccles. vii, 3). Under the expression δεύτερος πλοῦς[3] I have presented suffering to a certain extent as a substitute for virtue and holiness; but here I must state boldly that, having carefully considered everything, we have to hope for our salvation and deliverance rather from what we suffer than from what we do. Precisely in this sense Lamartine very finely says in his *Hymne à la douleur,* apostrophizing pain:

> *Tu me traites sans doute en favori des cieux,*
> *Car tu n'épargnes pas les larmes à mes yeux.*
> *Eh bien! je les reçois comme tu les envoies,*
> *Tes maux seront mes biens, et tes soupirs mes joies.*
> *Je sens qu'il est en toi, sans avoir combattu,*
> *UNE VERTU DIVINE AU LIEU DE MA VERTU,*
> *Que tu n'es pas la mort de l'âme, mais sa vie,*
> *Que ton bras, en frappant, guérit et vivifie.*[4]

Therefore, if suffering has such a sanctifying force, this will belong in an even higher degree to death, which is more feared than any suffering. Accordingly, in the presence of every person who has died, we feel something akin to the awe that is forced from us by great suffering; in fact, every case of death presents itself to a certain extent as a kind of apotheosis or canonization. Therefore we do not contemplate the corpse of even the most insignificant person without

---

[3] "The next best course." [Tr.]

[4] "Doubtless you treat me as heaven's favourite, for you do not spare my eyes their tears. Well, these I receive as sent by you. Your woes will be my weal, your sighs my joys. Without a fight, I feel in you *virtue divine instead of mine.* You are not the death, but the life of the soul, and the blows of your arm revive and heal." [Tr.]

awe, and indeed, strange as the remark may sound in this place, the guard gets under arms in the presence of every corpse. Dying is certainly to be regarded as the real aim of life; at the moment of dying, everything is decided which through the whole course of life was only prepared and introduced. Death is the result, the *résumé,* of life, or the total sum expressing at one stroke all the instruction given by life in detail and piecemeal, namely that the whole striving, the phenomenon of which is life, was a vain, fruitless, and self-contradictory effort, to have returned from which is a deliverance. Just as the whole slow vegetation of the plant is related to the fruit that at one stroke achieves a hundredfold what the plant achieved gradually and piecemeal, so is life with its obstacles, deluded hopes, frustrated plans, and constant suffering related to death, which at one stroke destroys all, all that the person has willed, and thus crowns the instruction given him by life. The completed course of life, on which the dying person looks back, has an effect on the whole will that objectifies itself in this perishing individuality, and such an effect is analogous to that exercised by a motive on man's conduct. The completed course gives his conduct a new direction that is accordingly the moral and essential result of the life. Just because a *sudden* death makes this retrospect impossible, the Church regards such a death as a misfortune, and prayers are offered to avert it. Because this retrospect, like the distinct foreknowledge of death, is conditioned by the faculty of reason, and is possible in man alone, not in the animal, and therefore he alone actually drains the cup of death, humanity is the only stage at which the will can deny itself, and completely turn away from life. To the will that does not deny itself, every birth imparts a new and different intellect; until it has recognized the true nature of life, and, in consequence, no longer wills it.

In the natural course, the decay of the body coincides in old age with that of the will. The passion for pleasures easily disappears with the capacity to enjoy them. The occasion of the most vehement willing, the focus of the will, the sexual impulse, is the first to be extinguished, whereby the man is placed in a position similar to the state of innocence which existed before the genital system developed. The illusions that set up chimeras as exceedingly desirable benefits vanish, and in their place comes the knowledge of the vanity of all earthly blessings. Selfishness is supplanted by love for children, and in this way the man begins to live in the ego of others rather than in his own, which soon will be no more. This course is at any rate the most desirable; it is the euthanasia of the will. In the hope of this, the Brahmin, after passing the best years of his life, is ordered to forsake property and family, and to lead the life of a recluse (*Manu,*

VI, 2). But if, on the contrary, the desire outlives the capacity to
enjoy, and we then regret particular pleasures missed in life, instead
of seeing the emptiness and vanity of it all; and if money, the abstract representative of all the objects of desire, for which the sense
is dead, then takes their place, and excites the same vehement passions that were formerly awakened more excusably by the objects
of actual pleasure, and thus, with deadened senses, an inanimate but
indestructible object is desired with equally indestructible eagerness;
or even if, in the same way, existence in the opinion of others is to
take the place of the existence and action in the real world, and now
kindles the same passions; then the will has been sublimated and
etherealized in avarice and ambition. In this way, however, it has
cast itself into the last stronghold, in which it is still besieged only
by death. The purpose of existence is missed.

All these considerations furnish a fuller explanation of the purification, the turning of the will, and salvation, which were denoted in
the previous chapter by the expression δεύτερος πλοῦς,[5] and which
are brought about by the sufferings of life, and are undoubtedly the
most frequent; for they are the way of sinners, as we all are. The
other way, leading to just the same goal by means of mere knowledge
and accordingly the appropriation of the sufferings of a whole world,
is the narrow path of the elect, of the saints, and consequently is to
be regarded as a rare exception. Therefore, without that first path,
it would be impossible for the majority to hope for any salvation.
But we struggle against entering on this path, and strive rather with
all our might to prepare for ourselves a secure and pleasant existence, whereby we chain our will ever more firmly to life. The conduct of ascetics is the opposite of this, for they deliberately make
their life as poor, hard, and cheerless as possible, because they have
their true and ultimate welfare in view. Fate and the course of things,
however, take care of us better than we ourselves do, since they
frustrate on all sides our arrangements for a Utopian existence,
whose folly is apparent enough from its shortness, uncertainty, emptiness, and termination in bitter death. Thorns upon thorns are strewn
on our path, and everywhere we are met by salutary suffering, the
panacea of our misery. What gives our life its strange and ambiguous
character is that in it two fundamental purposes, diametrically opposed, are constantly crossing each other. One purpose is that of the
individual will, directed to chimerical happiness in an ephemeral,
dreamlike, and deceptive existence, where, as regards the past, happiness and unhappiness are a matter of indifference, but at every moment the present is becoming the past. The other purpose is that of

---

[5] "The next best course." [Tr.]

fate, directed obviously enough to the destruction of our happiness, and thus to the mortification of our will, and to the elimination of the delusion that holds us chained to the bonds of this world.

The current and peculiarly Protestant view that the purpose of life lies solely and immediately in moral virtues, and hence in the practice of justice and philanthropy, betrays its inadequacy by the fact that so deplorably little real and pure morality is to be found among men. I do not wish to speak of lofty virtue, noble-mindedness, generosity, and self-sacrifice, which are hardly ever met with except in plays and novels, but only of those virtues that are everyone's duty. He who is old should think back to all those with whom he has had any dealings, and ask himself how many people whom he has come across were really and truly *honest*. Were not by far the greater number of them, to speak plainly, the very opposite, in spite of their shameless indignation at the slightest suspicion of dishonesty, or even of untruthfulness? Were not mean selfishness, boundless avarice, well-concealed knavery, poisonous envy, and devilish delight at the misfortunes of others, so universally prevalent, that the slightest exception was received with admiration? And philanthropy, how extremely rarely does it extend beyond a gift of something so superfluous that it can never be missed! Was the whole purpose of existence supposed to lie in such exceedingly rare and feeble traces of morality? If, on the other hand, we put this purpose in the complete reversal of this nature of ours (which bears the evil fruits just mentioned), a reversal brought about by suffering, the matter assumes a different aspect, and is brought into agreement with what actually lies before us. Life then presents itself as a process of purification, the purifying lye of which is pain. If the process is carried out, it leaves the previous immorality and wickedness behind as dross, and there appears what the *Veda* says; *Finditur nodus cordis, dissolvuntur omnes dubitationes, ejusque opera evanescunt.*[6] In agreement with this view, the fifteenth sermon of Meister Eckhart will be found well worth reading.

---

[6] "Whoever beholds the highest and profoundest, has his heart's knot cut, all his doubts are resolved, and his works come to nought." [Tr.]

CHAPTER L

Epiphilosophy

At the conclusion of my discussion, a few remarks on my philosophy itself may find place. As I have already said, this philosophy does not presume to explain the existence of the world from its ultimate grounds. On the contrary, it sticks to the actual facts of outward and inward experience as they are accessible to everyone, and shows their true and deepest connexion, yet without really going beyond them to any extramundane things, and the relations of these to the world. Accordingly, it arrives at no conclusions as to what exists beyond all possible experience, but furnishes merely an explanation and interpretation of what is given in the external world and in self-consciousness. It is therefore content to comprehend the true nature of the world according to its inner connexion with itself. Consequently, it is *immanent* in the Kantian sense of the word. But for this reason it still leaves many questions untouched, for instance, why what is proved as a fact is as it is and not otherwise, and others. But all such questions, or rather the answers to them, are really transcendent, that is to say, they cannot be thought by means of the forms and functions of our intellect; they do not enter into these. Our intellect is therefore related to them as our sensibility is to the possible properties of bodies for which we have no senses. After all my explanations, it can still be asked, for example, from what this will has sprung, which is free to affirm itself, the phenomenal appearance of this being the world, or to deny itself, the phenomenal appearance of which we do not know. What is the fatality lying beyond all experience which has put it in the extremely precarious dilemma of appearing as a world in which suffering and death reign, or else of denying its own inner being? Or what may have prevailed upon it to forsake the infinitely preferable peace of blessed nothingness? An individual will, it may be added, can direct itself to its own destruction only through error in the choice, hence through the fault of knowledge; but how could the will-in-itself, prior to all phenomenon, and consequently still without knowledge, go astray, and fall into the ruin of its present condition? In general, whence comes the great discord which permeates this world? Further, it may be asked how deeply in the being-in-itself of the world do the roots of individuality go. In any case, the answer to this might be that they go as deeply as the affirmation of the will-to-live; where the denial of the will occurs, they cease, for with the affirmation they sprang into existence. We might even put the question: "What would I be, if I were not the will-to-live?" and more of the same kind. To all such questions the reply would have to be, first, that the expression of the most universal and general form of our intellect is the *principle of sufficient ground or reason (Grund)*, but that, on this very account, this principle finds application only to the phenomenon, not to the being-in-itself of things; but all whence and why rest on this principle alone. In consequence of the Kantian philosophy, it is no longer an *aeterna veritas,* but merely the form, i.e., the function, of our intellect. This intellect is essentially cerebral, and originally a mere instrument in the service of our will; and this will, together with all its objectifications, is therefore presupposed by it. But our whole knowing and conceiving are bound to the forms of the intellect; accordingly, we must conceive everything in time, consequently as a before and an after, then as cause and effect, and also as above, below, as whole and parts, and so on. We cannot possibly escape from this sphere, in which all possibility of our knowledge is to be found. But these forms are quite inappropriate to the problems here raised, and even supposing their solution were given, it would not be such as to be capable of being grasped. With our intellect, with this mere instrument of the will, we therefore come up against insoluble problems everywhere, as against the walls of our prison. But besides this it may be assumed, at any rate as probable, that not only *for us* is knowledge of all that has been asked about impossible, but that such knowledge is not possible in general, hence not ever or anywhere possible; that those relations are not only relatively but absolutely inscrutable; that not only does no one know them, but that they are in themselves unknowable, since they do not enter into the form of knowledge in general. (This is in keeping with what Scotus Erigena says *de mirabili divina ignorantia, qua Deus non intelligit quid ipse sit.* Bk. II.)[1] For knowableness in general, with its most essential, and therefore constantly necessary, form of subject and object, belongs merely to the *phenomenon,* not to the being-in-itself of things. Where there is knowledge, and consequently representation, there is also only phenomenon, and there we already stand in

---

[1] "About the wonderful, divine ignorance, by virtue of which God does not know what he himself is." [Tr.]

the province of the phenomenon. In fact, knowledge in general is known to us only as a brain-phenomenon, and we are not only not justified in conceiving it otherwise, but even incapable of doing so. What the world is as world may be understood; it is phenomenon, and we can know what appears in this world directly from ourselves, by virtue of a thorough analysis of self-consciousness. But by means of this key to the inner nature of the world, the whole phenomenon can be deciphered according to its continuity and connexion, and I believe I have succeeded in doing this. But if we leave the world, in order to answer the questions indicated above, then we have left the whole ground on which not only connexion according to reason or ground and consequent, but even knowledge in general is possible; everything is then *instabilis tellus, innabilis unda.*² The essence of things before or beyond the world, and consequently beyond the will, is not open to any investigation, because knowledge in general is itself only phenomenon, and therefore it takes place only *in* the world, just as the world comes to pass only in it. The inner being-in-itself of things is not something that knows, is not an intellect, but something without knowledge. Knowledge is added only as an accident, as an expedient for the phenomenal appearance of that inner being; it can therefore take up that inner being itself only in accordance with its own nature which is calculated for quite different ends (namely those of an individual will), and consequently very imperfectly. This is why a perfect understanding of the existence, inner nature, and origin of the world, extending to the ultimate ground and meeting every requirement, is impossible. So much as regards the limits of my philosophy and of all philosophy.

The ἓν καὶ πᾶν,³ in other words, that the inner essence in all things is absolutely one and the same, has by my time already been grasped and understood, after the Eleatics, Scotus Erigena, Giordano Bruno, and Spinoza had taught it in detail, and Schelling had revived this doctrine. But *what* this one is, and how it manages to exhibit itself as the many, is a problem whose solution is first found in my philosophy. From the most ancient times, man has been called the microcosm. I have reversed the proposition, and have shown the world as the macranthropos, in so far as will and representation exhaust the true nature of the world as well as that of man. But obviously it is more correct to learn to understand the world from man than man from the world, for we have to explain what is indirectly

---

² "Land on which one cannot stand, water in which one cannot swim." [Tr.]

³ "One and all." [Tr.]

given, and thus external perception, from what is directly given, self-consciousness, not *vice versa*.

Now it is true that I have that ἓν καὶ πᾶν in common with the *Pantheists*, but not the πᾶν θεός,[4] because I do not go beyond experience (taken in the widest sense), and still less do I put myself in contradiction with the data lying before me. Quite consistently in the sense of pantheism, Scotus Erigena declares every phenomenon to be a theophany; but then this concept must be applied also to terrible and ghastly phenomena: fine theophanies! What further distinguishes me from the Pantheists is principally the following: (1) That their θεός is an *x*, an unknown quantity; the *will,* on the other hand, is, of all possible things, the one most intimately known to us, the only thing immediately given, and therefore exclusively fitted for explaining everything else. For what is unknown must everywhere be explained from what is better known, not *vice versa.* (2) That their θεός manifests himself *animi causa,* in order to display his glory and majesty, or even to let himself be admired. Apart from the vanity here attributed to him, they are thus put in the position of having to sophisticate away the colossal evils in the world. The world, however, remains in glaring and terrible contradiction with that fancied eminence. With me, on the other hand, the *will* arrives at self-knowledge through its objectification, however this may come about, whereby its abolition, conversion, and salvation become possible. Accordingly, with me alone ethics has a sure foundation, and is completely worked out in agreement with the sublime and profound religions Brahmanism, Buddhism, and Christianity, not merely with Judaism and Islam. The metaphysics of the beautiful is also first fully cleared up as a result of my fundamental truths, and no longer needs to take refuge behind empty words. Only with me are the evils of the world honestly admitted in all their magnitude; this is possible, because the answer to the question of their origin coincides with the answer to the question of the origin of the world. On the other hand, since all other systems are optimistic, the question of the origin of evil is the incurable disease ever breaking out in them anew. Affected with this complaint, they struggle along with palliatives and quack remedies. (3) That I start from experience and the natural self-consciousness given to everyone, and lead to the will as what alone is metaphysical; thus I take the ascending, analytic course. The Pantheists, on the other hand, go the opposite way, and take the descending, synthetic course. They start from their θεός, which they get by entreaty or defiance, although occasionally under

---

[4] "All is God." [Tr.]

the name of *substantia* or absolute; and then this wholly unknown thing is supposed to explain everything better known. (4) That with me the world does not fill the entire possibility of all being, but that in this world there is still left much room for what we describe only negatively as the denial of the will-to-live. Pantheism, on the other hand, is essentially optimism; but if the world is what is best, then we must leave the matter at that. (5) That the world of perception, the world as representation, is to the Pantheists just an intentional manifestation of God dwelling within it. This contains no proper explanation of the world's appearance, but rather itself requires explanation. With me, on the other hand, the world as representation appears merely *per accidens,* since the intellect with its external perception is primarily only the medium of motives for the more perfect phenomena of will, and this medium is gradually enhanced to that objectivity of perceptibility in which the world exists. In this sense, a real account of its origin is given as of an object of perception, and certainly not, as with the Pantheists, by means of untenable fictions.

In consequence of Kant's criticism of all speculative theology, almost all the philosophizers in Germany cast themselves back on to Spinoza, so that the whole series of unsuccessful attempts known by the name of post-Kantian philosophy is simply Spinozism tastelessly got up, veiled in all kinds of unintelligible language, and otherwise twisted and distorted. Therefore I wish to indicate the relation in which my teaching stands to Spinozism in particular, after I have explained its relation to Pantheism in general. It is related to Spinozism as the New Testament is to the Old; that is to say, what the Old Testament has in common with the New is the same God-Creator. Analogously to this, the world exists, with me as with Spinoza, by its own inner power and through itself. But with Spinoza his *substantia aeterna,* the inner nature of the world, which he himself calls *Deus,* is also, as regards its moral character and worth, Jehovah, the God-Creator, who applauds his creation, and finds that everything has turned out excellently, πάντα καλὰ λίαν.[5] Spinoza has deprived him of nothing more than personality. Hence for him the world with everything in it is wholly excellent and as it ought to be; therefore man has nothing further to do than *vivere, agere, suum Esse conservare, ex fundamento proprium utile quaerendi (Ethics* iv, prop. 67):[6] he should just enjoy his life as long as it lasts, wholly in accordance with Ecclesiastes ix, 7-10. In short, it is optimism;

[5] "All was very good." [Tr.]

[6] "Man should live, act, maintain his existence, since ultimately he seeks his own advantage." [Tr.]

hence its ethical side is weak, as in the Old Testament, in fact it is even false, and in part revolting.[7] With me, on the other hand, the will, or the inner nature of the world, is by no means Jehovah; on the contrary, it is, so to speak, the crucified Saviour, or else the crucified thief, according as it is decided. Consequently, my ethical teaching agrees with the Christian completely and in its highest tendencies, and no less with that of Brahmanism and Buddhism. Spinoza, on the other hand, could not get rid of the Jews: *quo semel est imbuta recens servabit odorem.*[8] His contempt for animals, who, as mere things for our use, are declared by him to be without rights, is thoroughly Jewish, and, in conjunction with Pantheism, is at the same time absurd and abominable (*Ethics* IV, appendix, c. 27). In spite of all this, Spinoza remains a very great man; but to form a correct estimate of his worth, we must keep in view his relation to Descartes. This philosopher had divided nature sharply into mind and matter, i.e., into thinking and extended substance, and had also set up God and the world in complete contrast to each other. As long as Spinoza was a Cartesian, he taught all this in his *Cogitata Metaphysica*, c. 12, in the year 1665. Only in his last years did he see the fundamental mistake of that twofold dualism; consequently, his own philosophy consists mainly in the indirect abolition of these two antitheses. Yet, partly to avoid hurting his teacher, partly to be less offensive, he gave it a positive appearance by means of a strictly dogmatic form, although the contents are mainly negative. Even his identification of the world with God has only this negative significance. For to call the world God is not to explain it; it remains a riddle under the one name as under the other. But these two negative truths were of value for their time, as for all times in which there are still conscious or unconscious Cartesians. In common with all philosophers before Locke, he makes the great mistake of starting from concepts without having previously investigated their origin, such, for example, as substance, cause, and so on. In such a method of procedure, these concepts then receive a much too extensive validity. Those who in most recent times were unwilling to acknowledge the Neo-Spinozism that had arisen, were scared of doing so,

---

[7] *Unusquisque tantum juris habet, quantum potentiâ valet. Tractatus Politicus,* c. 2, § 8. *Fides alicui data tamdiu rata manet, quamdiu ejus, qui fidem dedit, non mutatur voluntas. Ibid.* § 12. *Uniuscujusque jus potentiâ ejus definitur. Ethics* iv, prop. 37, schol. 1—("Each is right in proportion to his might."—"A given promise remains valid as long as the will of the person who gave it does not change."—"Each man's right is determined by the might which he has." [Tr.]). In particular chap. 16 of the *Tractatus Theologico-politicus* is the true compendium of the immorality of Spinoza's philosophy.

[8] "(A smelling bottle) long retains the smell of that which filled it." [Tr.]

like Jacobi for example, principally by the bugbear of *fatalism.* By this is to be understood every doctrine that refers the existence of the world, together with the human race's critical position in it, to some absolute necessity, in other words, to a necessity incapable of further explanation. On the other hand, those afraid of fatalism believed it to be all-important to deduce the world from the free act of will of a being existing outside it; as though it were certain beforehand which of the two would be more correct, or even better merely in reference to us. But in particular, *non datur tertium*[9] is here assumed, and accordingly, every philosophy hitherto has represented the one or the other. I am the first to depart from this, since I actually set up the *Tertium,* namely that the act of will, from which the world springs, is our own. It is free; for the principle of sufficient reason or ground, from which alone all necessity has its meaning, is merely the form of the will's phenomenal appearance. Just on this account, this phenomenal appearance is absolutely necessary in its course, when once it exists. In consequence of this alone can we recognize from the phenomenon the nature of the act of will, and accordingly *eventualiter* will otherwise.

---

[9] "There is no third possibility." [Tr.]

INDEX

A

A posteriori, I, 11, 64, 98, 100, 113, 213, 222, 289, 290, 302, 323, 418, 427, 448, 464f., 480f., 485, 503; II, 10, 42, 97, 127, 182, 195f., 209, 240, 289, 370f., 499.

A priori, I, 3f., 11, 13, 23, 25, 42, 50, 52, 64f., 66-7, 71f., 74f., 98, 100, 104, 121, 123, 128, 154, 172, 174, 222, 245, 247, 262, 289, 296, 302, 316, 323f., 342, 418, 421, 427, 430-1, 436f., 453, 457, 462f., 472f., 480f., 493f., 495, 497, 502f., 522f., 528f.; II, 11, 21f., 32f., 65, 82, 85, 89, 97, 111, 121, 127, 130, 176, 179f., 194f., 204, 240, 277, 285, 289f., 301, 305f., 314f., 320, 348, 413-14, 420, 427, 465, 474, 562, 574, 622, 635.

A propos, II, 133.

Abortion, II, 563.

Absent, I, 192.

Absolute, I, 26, 273, 483-4, 521; II, 43, 82, 185, 351, 644.

Abstract, I, 6, 35f., 39f., 45, 51f., 62, 82, 84f., 95, 100, 102, 109, 111, 116, 151, 178, 186f., 190, 193, 213, 234-5, 237f., 240, 242, 261f., 271-2, 275, 281, 285, 297f., 333, 335, 354, 365, 367f., 383-4, 404, 431, 437, 439, 441, 448f., 466f., 473f., 485, 519, 530, 532; II, 5, 20, 23, 44, 59f., 63f., 71f., 85, 88, 91f., 103f., 186, 192, 205, 208, 276f., 366, 369, 406, 409, 450, 494, 572, 629.

Abstracta, I, 41, 263; II, 41, 73, 82-3, 85, 105, 120, 180, 193, 305, 379, 442, 494, 591.

Absurd, I, x, xxvii, 324f., 437, 465, 474, 483, 485, 509, 526; II, 4, 9, 69, 87, 92, 96-7, 121, 124, 130, 162, 166, 181, 192, 230, 265, 267, 302-3, 321, 344, 378, 423, 426, 431,

467, 474, 476, 482, 493, 502, 506, 581, 590f., 645.

Abyss, II, 323, 325, 599.

Abyssinia, II, 69, 226.

Academics, II, 603.

Academies, I, 513; II, 268.

Accident (see Chance).

Accounts, II, 218.

Achilles, I, 238; II, 172, 449.

Acids, II, 546.

Acoustic Figures (in Sand), II, 109, 301.

Actio in distans, II, 326.

Actors, I, 225, 228, 266; II, 262, 400, 456.

Actu and Potentia, I, 500; II, 47, 54, 66, 140.

Acuteness, I, 22; II, 77-8, 89.

Adagio, I, 261.

Adam, I, 328-9, 405, 604, 613, 628.

Adams, J. Q., II, 596.

Adelung, J. C., II, 378.

Adultery, II, 518, 540, 542, 552-3.

Advantage, II, 217, 241.

Advice, II, 218-9.

Aelian, C., II, 216.

Aenesidemus (see Schulze).

Aeschylus, II, 434, 569.

Aesthetics, I, 45, 195-6, 199f., 239, 256, 271, 327, 363, 368, 390, 515, 527, 530; II, 122, 244, 291, 368f., 374f.

Aevum, II, 502.

Affectation, I, 236.

Affirmation (of the Will), I, 285, 308, 326, 328f., 340f., 354, 362, 366, 370f., 379f., 392, 398, 401, 405; II, 419, 437, 462, 479, 529, 568ff., 585, 608f., 641.

Africa, I, 159.

African Deys, I, 364.

Agamemnon, I, 152; II, 449.

'Αγάπη, I, 374-5.

'Αγαθόν, I, 603.

122, 126, 130, 136, 141-2, 145, 148, 149, 243, 251, 416, 534; II, 47, 110, 127, 173, 182, 209, 265, 297, 546.

Cherries, II, 226, 478.

Cherubs (winged), I, 99; II, 394.

Chess, I, 231, 390, 516.

Chevreul, M. E., II, 315.

Chicanery, II, 86, 92, 226.

Children, I, 251, 272, 293, 299, 306, 327, 377, 400, 405, 411; II, 60-1, 79f., 95, 98, 162, 165f., 186-7, 208, 211f., 216, 233f., 238, 242, 280, 347, 393f., 416, 473, 481, 496, 503, 517f., 535f., 544f., 563-4, 569, 619, 622, 637.

Chiliasts, II, 69.

Chimeras, I, 488, 520; II, 69, 84, 234, 315, 538, 554, 637.

Chimpanzees, II, 312.

China and Chinese, I, 27, 144, 239, 265, 486; II, 75, 119, 404, 429, 561, 624.

Chivalry, II, 124.

Chladni, E., I, 266.

Chlorine, II, 108.

Chord, I, 65, 72.

Christianity, I, xxvi, 86, 91, 213, 232, 233, 239, 242, 293, 326, 328, 355, 358, 383-4, 386f., 486, 512, 515, 522, 524f.; II, 150, 159, 167f., 176, 187, 199, 287, 418, 431, 434f., 444, 488f., 504, 506, 580, 584f., 603f., 607f., 613f., 619f., 623f., 632-3, 635f., 643, 645.

Christina of Sweden, I, 340.

Chronos, I, 31.

Chrysippus, I, 88, 89, 302, 467; II, 151.

Church, I, 368, 387, 395, 403-4-5, 408, 504; II, 617, 623, 625, 637.

Chyle, II, 251.

Chyme, II, 252.

Cicero, M. T., I, 88, 89, 191, 302, 345, 467, 517-8, 520-1; II, 91, 92, 150f., 158f., 226, 383, 466, 561, 603, 628.

Ciphers, II, 184, 445.

Circles, I, 42, 72, 77, 247, 407; II, 92, 110, 477, 481.

Circulation (of Blood), I, 115; II, 216, 240, 253, 255, 262, 280, 333, 368, 393, 470, 526.

Circulus vitiosus, I, 459.

Civilization, I, 37, 312; II, 164, 585.

Clairvoyance, I, 151; II, 186, 255.

Clarke, S., I, 407, 509.

Claudius, Gens Claudia, II, 519.

Claudius, Emperor, II, 237.

Claudius, M., I, 394-5, 398, 403.

Clay, II, 173.

Cleanthes, I, 89, 510.

Clement of Alexandria, I, 329, 487, 520; II, 32, 608, 617, 620f.

Climate, I, 132, 156, 159, 216-7, 322, 364; II, 404, 416, 420.

Clocks (Clockwork), I, 322; II, 35, 171, 213, 319, 358, 402.

Clothing, I, 229, 306, 477f.; II, 280.

Cloud Cuckoo-land, I, 273.

Clouds, I, 142, 182-3, 185, 461; II, 72, 236, 375, 442-3, 573.

Clowns, I, 60; II, 95, 101.

Codrus, I, 375.

Coexistence, I, 10, 120, 441, 462, 472; II, 185.

Cohesion, I, 80, 122, 125, 126, 142, 214f., 533; II, 298, 304, 314, 414.

Coins, I, 77, 306, 425; II, 8, 76, 78, 125.

Colebrooke, H. T., I, 381-2, 488, 505, 508.

Colour (Theory of Colour), I, 21, 123, 189, 199, 226, 239, 531; II, 26, 28, 89, 143, 218, 315, 375, 423, 433.

Colour Organ, II, 31.

Columns, I, 214; II, 411f.

Comedy, I, 249, 322, 331, 333, 358; II, 96, 437, 442, 531, 553, 581.

Comets, II, 390.

Commodus, L. A. A., II, 521.

Common, I, 187, 385; II, 73, 101, 124, 138, 380, 382.

Common Sense, I, 406; II, 7.

Commonwealth, I, 337.

Communism, II, 596.

Company (Society), I, 198; II, 231.

Compass, I, 85.

Compassion, I, 295, 324, 374, 526; II, 435, 592f., 601-2.

Compendiums (Fabricator of), II, 461.

Composers, I, 57, 260, 263; II, 449, 455.

Mice, II, 547.
Microcosm and Macrocosm, I, 162, 332; II, 281, 385, 443, 486, 591, 642.
Microscope, II, 389.
Midas, I, 189.
Midday, I, 280-1.
Middle Ages, I, 48, 488, 507; II, 124, 418, 428, 446, 562.
Migratory Birds, II, 61, 343.
Milan, II, 386.
Miltiades, II, 520.
Milton, J., II, 410.
Mimicry, II, 379.
Mimosa pudica, I, 116.
Mind, I, 129, 178-9, 185, 192-3, 197, 223, 225, 229, 234-5, 237-8, 245, 250, 252, 273-4, 281, 300, 302-3, 306, 311, 317-18, 376, 379, 394, 428, 446, 452, 463, 509; II, 20, 28f., 34, 78f., 89, 122, 131f., 139, 144f., 159, 165, 227, 231f., 283, 335, 369, 426, 456, 467, 511, 522, 645.
Mine, II, 316.
Mineralogy, I, 96; II, 122, 127.
Minerva (see Athene).
Ministers (Statesmen), I, 231; II, 283.
Miracles, I, 102, 251, 512; II, 36, 164-5-6, 203, 248f., 313, 482.
Mirror, I, 152, 165, 178, 186, 245, 249, 252, 266, 274-5, 278, 288, 300, 302, 320, 325, 331, 351, 365, 369, 382, 385, 390, 410, 518; II, 140, 202, 206, 216, 226, 256, 277-8, 282, 311, 324, 367, 373-4, 380, 436, 498, 529, 584, 600.
Misers, I, 152; II, 222.
Misery, I, 323f., 351f., 366, 373, 378-9, 380, 397, 400f., 516; II, 161, 164, 184, 359, 449, 492, 555, 568f., 573, 575, 579f., 584f., 591, 622, 638.
Missionaries, II, 624.
Missouri, I, 147.
Mist, I, 317, 484; II, 407.
Mithra, I, 242.
Mnemonics, II, 133f.
Mob, I, 234-5; II, 146, 148, 268, 426.
Mock existence, II, 358.
Modality, I, 44, 463f., 471, 473, 479, 493; II, 110.
Models, II, 414.

Modesty, I, 234; II, 426, 617.
Mohammed, I, 295, 302, 346; II, 113, 425, 444, 505, 561, 605, 613, 623f., 643.
Moksha, II, 608.
Molecules, II, 302.
Moles, I, 304; II, 330, 353-4.
Molinos, M. de, II, 614.
Moloch, II, 69.
Monads, II, 582.
Monarchy, I, 343; II, 595.
Money, II, 638.
Money-lender, II, 236.
Monkeys, I, 23; II, 97, 280, 312f., 396, 476.
Monogram, I, 450.
Monologue, II, 102.
Monstrum per defectum, II, 377.
Monstrum per excessum, II, 89, 377.
Mont Blanc, I, 25; II, 383.
Montaigne, M. E. de, I, 358; II, 126, 243, 569.
Montalembert, C. R., II, 615.
Montanists, II, 617.
Montbazon, Mme., II, 630.
Monuments, II, 445-6.
Mood, I, 146, 316; II, 63, 100, 138, 140, 207, 374, 389, 404, 456.
Moon, I, 24, 35, 216, 292; II, 9, 79, 215, 299f., 374-5, 614.
Moore, T., II, 555.
Morality, I, 45, 60, 84, 86, 90, 265, 271, 284, 293, 307, 333, 341f., 358f., 367, 385f., 399, 408, 422, 424f., 494, 523f.; II, 85, 128, 150f., 159, 162, 175, 187, 215, 230, 232f., 384, 443, 461, 492, 500, 564, 589ff., 615, 639, 643.
Moravian Community, I, 356; II, 30.
Morphology, I, 96-7, 141, 184.
Mortal (Man), I, 186; II, 503.
Mosaic, I, 57, 59; II, 335.
Moses, I, 231, 487.
Most, G. F., II, 265.
Mote in Sunbeam, I, 124; II, 319.
Mother, II, 70, 107, 160, 265, 351, 392-3, 410, 474, 490, 502, 514, 517f., 525f., 536f., 544f., 550, 554.
Motion, I, 67, 97, 122-3, 148, 150, 163, 223, 224-5, 419; II, 20, 54, 65, 133, 192, 298, 303, 316.
Motives (Motivation), I, 28, 37, 86, 100, 102, 103, 105f., 111, 113f.,

Parents, I, 328, 400; II, 107, 481, 510, 514f., 526, 536f., 550, 557-8, 563, 599.
Pariah, I, 356.
Paris, Apple of, I, 239.
Parmenides, I, 71, 109, 330; II, 32, 480.
Parnassus, II, 75.
Parody, II, 95.
Paroxysm, II, 229.
Parricide, II, 43, 521.
Parrot-faces, II, 548.
Parsimony (Law of), II, 279f., 283, 485.
Parsons, I, 486; II, 338, 506, 625, 627.
Partes orationis, I, 477.
Particles, I, 477; II, 104, 126.
Particular, I, 62f., 68, 78, 88, 129, 177f., 180, 184f., 209, 230, 231f., 262, 283, 343, 379, 390, 396, 433, 443, 455, 469, 485, 508; II, 64f., 74, 76, 88, 105, 115, 121f., 141, 309, 343, 379, 389, 427, 439f., 449, 475, 599.
Pascal, B., I, 371; II, 615.
Passions, I, 38, 49, 107, 132, 183, 190, 197, 225, 250, 259, 296, 299, 321, 328, 385, 394, 398, 519; II, 118, 141, 203, 205f., 216, 224, 231, 235, 237f., 246, 261, 266, 276, 280, 368, 373, 394, 419, 437, 441, 448f., 462, 469, 510, 518f., 532, 534, 536f., 546, 549f., 559, 592f., 638.
Past, I, 31, 36, 84, 192-3, 198, 278f., 284, 311, 348, 364, 366-7, 453, 494; II, 59f., 98, 149, 402, 441, 445, 467, 480, 571f., 638.
Pastime, I, 313, 323.
Patent of Nobility, II, 388.
Pathology, II, 127, 260.
Patois du pays, II, 475.
Patriotism, II, 519.
Paul (Saint), I, 294, 329; II, 603f., 620.
Paws (of Man), II, 404.
Peace, I, 196, 202, 203f., 322, 390, 391f.; II, 28, 326, 357, 513.
Peace of Mind, I, 86, 89, 205, 212, 219, 250, 261, 303, 319, 335, 398, 411, 519; II, 233, 370.
Pearls (String of), II, 251, 432.
Peasants, II, 231.

Pedantry, I, 60f., 84; II, 77.
Pederasty, II, 541, 560f.
Peep-show, II, 576, 581.
Pelagianism, I, 406; II, 167-8, 605, 625.
Pendant, I, 431, 449, 514; II, 34.
Pendulum, I, 312, 461; II, 470-1, 590.
Penelope, II, 129, 178.
Penitentiary System, I, 313; II, 597.
Perception (intuitive), I, 11f., 24, 35, 38, 52f., 55, 57f., 62, 65, 67f., 73f., 75f., 79, 84-5, 95, 99f., 107, 112, 119, 121, 151f., 165, 175, 178, 181-2, 185-6, 190, 192, 197f., 199, 200, 213, 216, 231, 237, 239, 242f., 247, 250-1, 256, 263-4, 266, 296-7, 298-9, 417f., 434f., 450f., 474f., 490, 508, 520, 530f.; II, 5, 11, 15, 19f., 26, 33, 37, 40f., 60, 64f., 71f., 77, 88, 91, 98f., 120f., 130, 137, 141, 148, 179, 185f., 192f., 205, 221, 243, 247, 273f., 284, 295, 305, 308f., 317, 325, 354, 366f., 372, 374f., 406f., 445, 499, 611, 643f.
Perfection, I, 424-5; II, 129, 184, 232, 321f., 443, 633.
Perfidy, I, 338.
Pericles, II, 527.
Perihelion (and Aphelion), II, 300.
Peripatetics, I, 89, 517, 524; II, 563, 603.
Perpetuum mobile, I, 462; II, 316, 319, 583.
Persephone (Proserpina), I, 241, 329.
Persians, I, 48; II, 101.
Personality (Person), I, 131, 185-6, 194, 195, 198, 221, 229, 248, 288, 353, 373, 379, 387, 407; II, 6, 222-3, 225, 238, 495, 504, 507.
Perspective, I, 252; II, 403.
Persuasion, I, 49.
Perversity, I, 70, 253, 324, 373; II, 69, 214.
Pessimism, I, 323f.; II, 170, 356, 620f.
Pestalozzi, J. H., II, 35.
Petitio principii, I, 27, 427, 465, 496, 498; II, 121, 180, 314, 317, 350.
Petit-Thouars, Admiral, II, 310.
Petrarch, F., I, xxvi, xxviii, 377, 396; II, 126, 432, 551, 556-7, 576.
Petronius, G., I, 512.
Petulance, II, 393.
Pfeiffer, F., I, 381, 387; II, 612.

A CATALOG OF SELECTED DOVER
BOOKS IN ALL FIELDS OF INTEREST

CONCERNING THE SPIRITUAL IN ART, Wassily Kandinsky. Pioneering work by father of abstract art. Thoughts on color theory, nature of art. Analysis of earlier masters. 12 illustrations. 80pp. of text. 5⅜ x 8½. 23411-8 Pa. $4.95

ANIMALS: 1,419 Copyright-Free Illustrations of Mammals, Birds, Fish, Insects, etc., Jim Harter (ed.). Clear wood engravings present, in extremely lifelike poses, over 1,000 species of animals. One of the most extensive pictorial sourcebooks of its kind. Captions. Index. 284pp. 9 x 12. 23766-4 Pa. $14.95

CELTIC ART: The Methods of Construction, George Bain. Simple geometric techniques for making Celtic interlacements, spirals, Kells-type initials, animals, humans, etc. Over 500 illustrations. 160pp. 9 x 12. (USO) 22923-8 Pa. $9.95

AN ATLAS OF ANATOMY FOR ARTISTS, Fritz Schider. Most thorough reference work on art anatomy in the world. Hundreds of illustrations, including selections from works by Vesalius, Leonardo, Goya, Ingres, Michelangelo, others. 593 illustrations. 192pp. 7⅛ x 10¼. 20241-0 Pa. $9.95

CELTIC HAND STROKE-BY-STROKE (Irish Half-Uncial from "The Book of Kells"): An Arthur Baker Calligraphy Manual, Arthur Baker. Complete guide to creating each letter of the alphabet in distinctive Celtic manner. Covers hand position, strokes, pens, inks, paper, more. Illustrated. 48pp. 8¼ x 11. 24336-2 Pa. $3.95

EASY ORIGAMI, John Montroll. Charming collection of 32 projects (hat, cup, pelican, piano, swan, many more) specially designed for the novice origami hobbyist. Clearly illustrated easy-to-follow instructions insure that even beginning papercrafters will achieve successful results. 48pp. 8¼ x 11. 27298-2 Pa. $3.50

THE COMPLETE BOOK OF BIRDHOUSE CONSTRUCTION FOR WOOD-WORKERS, Scott D. Campbell. Detailed instructions, illustrations, tables. Also data on bird habitat and instinct patterns. Bibliography. 3 tables. 63 illustrations in 15 figures. 48pp. 5¼ x 8½. 24407-5 Pa. $2.50

BLOOMINGDALE'S ILLUSTRATED 1886 CATALOG: Fashions, Dry Goods and Housewares, Bloomingdale Brothers. Famed merchants' extremely rare catalog depicting about 1,700 products: clothing, housewares, firearms, dry goods, jewelry, more. Invaluable for dating, identifying vintage items. Also, copyright-free graphics for artists, designers. Co-published with Henry Ford Museum & Greenfield Village. 160pp. 8¼ x 11. 25780-0 Pa. $10.95

HISTORIC COSTUME IN PICTURES, Braun & Schneider. Over 1,450 costumed figures in clearly detailed engravings–from dawn of civilization to end of 19th century. Captions. Many folk costumes. 256pp. 8⅜ x 11¾. 23150-X Pa. $12.95

STICKLEY CRAFTSMAN FURNITURE CATALOGS, Gustav Stickley and L. & J. G. Stickley. Beautiful, functional furniture in two authentic catalogs from 1910. 594 illustrations, including 277 photos, show settles, rockers, armchairs, reclining chairs, bookcases, desks, tables. 183pp. 6½ x 9¼. 23838-5 Pa. $11.95

AMERICAN LOCOMOTIVES IN HISTORIC PHOTOGRAPHS: 1858 to 1949, Ron Ziel (ed.). A rare collection of 126 meticulously detailed official photographs, called "builder portraits," of American locomotives that majestically chronicle the rise of steam locomotive power in America. Introduction. Detailed captions. xi + 129pp. 9 x 12. 27393-8 Pa. $13.95

AMERICA'S LIGHTHOUSES: An Illustrated History, Francis Ross Holland, Jr. Delightfully written, profusely illustrated fact-filled survey of over 200 American lighthouses since 1716. History, anecdotes, technological advances, more. 240pp. 8 x 10¾. 25576-X Pa. $12.95

TOWARDS A NEW ARCHITECTURE, Le Corbusier. Pioneering manifesto by founder of "International School." Technical and aesthetic theories, views of industry, economics, relation of form to function, "mass-production split" and much more. Profusely illustrated. 320pp. 6⅛ x 9¼. (USO) 25023-7 Pa. $9.95

HOW THE OTHER HALF LIVES, Jacob Riis. Famous journalistic record, exposing poverty and degradation of New York slums around 1900, by major social reformer. 100 striking and influential photographs. 233pp. 10 x 7⅞. 22012-5 Pa. $11.95

FRUIT KEY AND TWIG KEY TO TREES AND SHRUBS, William M. Harlow. One of the handiest and most widely used identification aids. Fruit key covers 120 deciduous and evergreen species; twig key 160 deciduous species. Easily used. Over 300 photographs. 126pp. 5⅜ x 8½. 20511-8 Pa. $3.95

COMMON BIRD SONGS, Dr. Donald J. Borror. Songs of 60 most common U.S. birds: robins, sparrows, cardinals, bluejays, finches, more–arranged in order of increasing complexity. Up to 9 variations of songs of each species. Cassette and manual 99911-4 $8.95

ORCHIDS AS HOUSE PLANTS, Rebecca Tyson Northen. Grow cattleyas and many other kinds of orchids–in a window, in a case, or under artificial light. 63 illustrations. 148pp. 5⅜ x 8½. 23261-1 Pa. $5.95

MONSTER MAZES, Dave Phillips. Masterful mazes at four levels of difficulty. Avoid deadly perils and evil creatures to find magical treasures. Solutions for all 32 exciting illustrated puzzles. 48pp. 8¼ x 11. 26005-4 Pa. $2.95

MOZART'S DON GIOVANNI (DOVER OPERA LIBRETTO SERIES), Wolfgang Amadeus Mozart. Introduced and translated by Ellen H. Bleiler. Standard Italian libretto, with complete English translation. Convenient and thoroughly portable–an ideal companion for reading along with a recording or the performance itself. Introduction. List of characters. Plot summary. 121pp. 5¼ x 8½. 24944-1 Pa. $3.95

TECHNICAL MANUAL AND DICTIONARY OF CLASSICAL BALLET, Gail Grant. Defines, explains, comments on steps, movements, poses and concepts. 15-page pictorial section. Basic book for student, viewer. 127pp. 5⅜ x 8½. 21843-0 Pa. $4.95

THE CLARINET AND CLARINET PLAYING, David Pino. Lively, comprehensive work features suggestions about technique, musicianship, and musical interpretation, as well as guidelines for teaching, making your own reeds, and preparing for public performance. Includes an intriguing look at clarinet history. "A godsend," The Clarinet, Journal of the International Clarinet Society. Appendixes. 7 illus. 320pp. 5⅜ x 8½. 40270-3 Pa. $9.95

HOLLYWOOD GLAMOR PORTRAITS, John Kobal (ed.). 145 photos from 1926-49. Harlow, Gable, Bogart, Bacall; 94 stars in all. Full background on photographers, technical aspects. 160pp. 8⅜ x 11¼. 23352-9 Pa. $12.95

THE ANNOTATED CASEY AT THE BAT: A Collection of Ballads about the Mighty Casey/Third, Revised Edition, Martin Gardner (ed.). Amusing sequels and parodies of one of America's best-loved poems: Casey's Revenge, Why Casey Whiffed, Casey's Sister at the Bat, others. 256pp. 5⅜ x 8½. 28598-7 Pa. $8.95

THE RAVEN AND OTHER FAVORITE POEMS, Edgar Allan Poe. Over 40 of the author's most memorable poems: "The Bells," "Ulalume," "Israfel," "To Helen," "The Conqueror Worm," "Eldorado," "Annabel Lee," many more. Alphabetic lists of titles and first lines. 64pp. 5 3/16 x 8¼. 26685-0 Pa. $1.00

PERSONAL MEMOIRS OF U. S. GRANT, Ulysses Simpson Grant. Intelligent, deeply moving firsthand account of Civil War campaigns, considered by many the finest military memoirs ever written. Includes letters, historic photographs, maps and more. 528pp. 6⅛ x 9¼. 28587-1 Pa. $12.95

ANCIENT EGYPTIAN MATERIALS AND INDUSTRIES, A. Lucas and J. Harris. Fascinating, comprehensive, thoroughly documented text describes this ancient civilization's vast resources and the processes that incorporated them in daily life, including the use of animal products, building materials, cosmetics, perfumes and incense, fibers, glazed ware, glass and its manufacture, materials used in the mummification process, and much more. 544pp. 6⅛ x 9¼. (USO) 40446-3 Pa. $16.95

RUSSIAN STORIES/PYCCKNE PACCKA3bl: A Dual-Language Book, edited by Gleb Struve. Twelve tales by such masters as Chekhov, Tolstoy, Dostoevsky, Pushkin, others. Excellent word-for-word English translations on facing pages, plus teaching and study aids, Russian/English vocabulary, biographical/critical introductions, more. 416pp. 5⅜ x 8½. 26244-8 Pa. $9.95

PHILADELPHIA THEN AND NOW: 60 Sites Photographed in the Past and Present, Kenneth Finkel and Susan Oyama. Rare photographs of City Hall, Logan Square, Independence Hall, Betsy Ross House, other landmarks juxtaposed with contemporary views. Captures changing face of historic city. Introduction. Captions. 128pp. 8¼ x 11. 25790-8 Pa. $9.95

AIA ARCHITECTURAL GUIDE TO NASSAU AND SUFFOLK COUNTIES, LONG ISLAND, The American Institute of Architects, Long Island Chapter, and the Society for the Preservation of Long Island Antiquities. Comprehensive, well-researched and generously illustrated volume brings to life over three centuries of Long Island's great architectural heritage. More than 240 photographs with authoritative, extensively detailed captions. 176pp. 8¼ x 11. 26946-9 Pa. $14.95

NORTH AMERICAN INDIAN LIFE: Customs and Traditions of 23 Tribes, Elsie Clews Parsons (ed.). 27 fictionalized essays by noted anthropologists examine religion, customs, government, additional facets of life among the Winnebago, Crow, Zuni, Eskimo, other tribes. 480pp. 6⅛ x 9¼. 27377-6 Pa. $10.95

FRANK LLOYD WRIGHT'S DANA HOUSE, Donald Hoffmann. Pictorial essay of residential masterpiece with over 160 interior and exterior photos, plans, elevations, sketches and studies. 128pp. 9¼ x 10¾. 29120-0 Pa. $12.95

THE MALE AND FEMALE FIGURE IN MOTION: 60 Classic Photographic Sequences, Eadweard Muybridge. 60 true-action photographs of men and women walking, running, climbing, bending, turning, etc., reproduced from rare 19th-century masterpiece. vi + 121pp. 9 x 12. 24745-7 Pa. $10.95

1001 QUESTIONS ANSWERED ABOUT THE SEASHORE, N. J. Berrill and Jacquelyn Berrill. Queries answered about dolphins, sea snails, sponges, starfish, fishes, shore birds, many others. Covers appearance, breeding, growth, feeding, much more. 305pp. 5¼ x 8¼. 23366-9 Pa. $9.95

ATTRACTING BIRDS TO YOUR YARD, William J. Weber. Easy-to-follow guide offers advice on how to attract the greatest diversity of birds: birdhouses, feeders, water and waterers, much more. 96pp. 5³⁄₁₆ x 8¼. 28927-3 Pa. $2.50

MEDICINAL AND OTHER USES OF NORTH AMERICAN PLANTS: A Historical Survey with Special Reference to the Eastern Indian Tribes, Charlotte Erichsen-Brown. Chronological historical citations document 500 years of usage of plants, trees, shrubs native to eastern Canada, northeastern U.S. Also complete identifying information. 343 illustrations. 544pp. 6½ x 9¼. 25951-X Pa. $12.95

STORYBOOK MAZES, Dave Phillips. 23 stories and mazes on two-page spreads: Wizard of Oz, Treasure Island, Robin Hood, etc. Solutions. 64pp. 8¼ x 11. 23628-5 Pa. $2.95

AMERICAN NEGRO SONGS: 230 Folk Songs and Spirituals, Religious and Secular, John W. Work. This authoritative study traces the African influences of songs sung and played by black Americans at work, in church, and as entertainment. The author discusses the lyric significance of such songs as "Swing Low, Sweet Chariot," "John Henry," and others and offers the words and music for 230 songs. Bibliography. Index of Song Titles. 272pp. 6½ x 9¼. 40271-1 Pa. $9.95

MOVIE-STAR PORTRAITS OF THE FORTIES, John Kobal (ed.). 163 glamor, studio photos of 106 stars of the 1940s: Rita Hayworth, Ava Gardner, Marlon Brando, Clark Gable, many more. 176pp. 8⅜ x 11¼. 23546-7 Pa. $14.95

BENCHLEY LOST AND FOUND, Robert Benchley. Finest humor from early 30s, about pet peeves, child psychologists, post office and others. Mostly unavailable elsewhere. 73 illustrations by Peter Arno and others. 183pp. 5⅜ x 8½. 22410-4 Pa. $6.95

YEKL and THE IMPORTED BRIDEGROOM AND OTHER STORIES OF YIDDISH NEW YORK, Abraham Cahan. Film Hester Street based on Yekl (1896). Novel, other stories among first about Jewish immigrants on N.Y.'s East Side. 240pp. 5⅜ x 8½. 22427-9 Pa. $6.95

SELECTED POEMS, Walt Whitman. Generous sampling from *Leaves of Grass*. Twenty-four poems include "I Hear America Singing," "Song of the Open Road," "I Sing the Body Electric," "When Lilacs Last in the Dooryard Bloom'd," "O Captain! My Captain!"–all reprinted from an authoritative edition. Lists of titles and first lines. 128pp. 5³⁄₁₆ x 8¼. 26878-0 Pa. $1.00

CATALOG OF DOVER BOOKS

THE BEST TALES OF HOFFMANN, E. T. A. Hoffmann. 10 of Hoffmann's most important stories: "Nutcracker and the King of Mice," "The Golden Flowerpot," etc. 458pp. 5⅜ x 8½. 21793-0 Pa. $9.95

FROM FETISH TO GOD IN ANCIENT EGYPT, E. A. Wallis Budge. Rich detailed survey of Egyptian conception of "God" and gods, magic, cult of animals, Osiris, more. Also, superb English translations of hymns and legends. 240 illustrations. 545pp. 5⅜ x 8½. 25803-3 Pa. $13.95

FRENCH STORIES/CONTES FRANÇAIS: A Dual-Language Book, Wallace Fowlie. Ten stories by French masters, Voltaire to Camus: "Micromegas" by Voltaire; "The Atheist's Mass" by Balzac; "Minuet" by de Maupassant; "The Guest" by Camus, six more. Excellent English translations on facing pages. Also French-English vocabulary list, exercises, more. 352pp. 5⅜ x 8½. 26443-2 Pa. $9.95

CHICAGO AT THE TURN OF THE CENTURY IN PHOTOGRAPHS: 122 Historic Views from the Collections of the Chicago Historical Society, Larry A. Viskochil. Rare large-format prints offer detailed views of City Hall, State Street, the Loop, Hull House, Union Station, many other landmarks, circa 1904-1913. Introduction. Captions. Maps. 144pp. 9⅜ x 12¼. 24656-6 Pa. $12.95

OLD BROOKLYN IN EARLY PHOTOGRAPHS, 1865-1929, William Lee Younger. Luna Park, Gravesend race track, construction of Grand Army Plaza, moving of Hotel Brighton, etc. 157 previously unpublished photographs. 165pp. 8⅞ x 11¾. 23587-4 Pa. $13.95

THE MYTHS OF THE NORTH AMERICAN INDIANS, Lewis Spence. Rich anthology of the myths and legends of the Algonquins, Iroquois, Pawnees and Sioux, prefaced by an extensive historical and ethnological commentary. 36 illustrations. 480pp. 5⅜ x 8½. 25967-6 Pa. $10.95

AN ENCYCLOPEDIA OF BATTLES: Accounts of Over 1,560 Battles from 1479 B.C. to the Present, David Eggenberger. Essential details of every major battle in recorded history from the first battle of Megiddo in 1479 B.C. to Grenada in 1984. List of Battle Maps. New Appendix covering the years 1967-1984. Index. 99 illustrations. 544pp. 6½ x 9¼. 24913-1 Pa. $16.95

SAILING ALONE AROUND THE WORLD, Captain Joshua Slocum. First man to sail around the world, alone, in small boat. One of great feats of seamanship told in delightful manner. 67 illustrations. 294pp. 5⅜ x 8½. 20326-3 Pa. $6.95

ANARCHISM AND OTHER ESSAYS, Emma Goldman. Powerful, penetrating, prophetic essays on direct action, role of minorities, prison reform, puritan hypocrisy, violence, etc. 271pp. 5⅜ x 8½. 22484-8 Pa. $7.95

MYTHS OF THE HINDUS AND BUDDHISTS, Ananda K. Coomaraswamy and Sister Nivedita. Great stories of the epics; deeds of Krishna, Shiva, taken from puranas, Vedas, folk tales; etc. 32 illustrations. 400pp. 5⅜ x 8½. 21759-0 Pa. $12.95

THE TRAUMA OF BIRTH, Otto Rank. Rank's controversial thesis that anxiety neurosis is caused by profound psychological trauma which occurs at birth. 256pp. 5⅜ x 8½. 27974-X Pa. $7.95

A THEOLOGICO-POLITICAL TREATISE, Benedict Spinoza. Also contains unfinished Political Treatise. Great classic on religious liberty, theory of government on common consent. R. Elwes translation. Total of 421pp. 5⅜ x 8½. 20249-6 Pa. $9.95

CATALOG OF DOVER BOOKS

MY BONDAGE AND MY FREEDOM, Frederick Douglass. Born a slave, Douglass became outspoken force in antislavery movement. The best of Douglass' autobiographies. Graphic description of slave life. 464pp. 5⅜ x 8½. 22457-0 Pa. $8.95

FOLLOWING THE EQUATOR: A Journey Around the World, Mark Twain. Fascinating humorous account of 1897 voyage to Hawaii, Australia, India, New Zealand, etc. Ironic, bemused reports on peoples, customs, climate, flora and fauna, politics, much more. 197 illustrations. 720pp. 5⅜ x 8½. 26113-1 Pa. $15.95

THE PEOPLE CALLED SHAKERS, Edward D. Andrews. Definitive study of Shakers: origins, beliefs, practices, dances, social organization, furniture and crafts, etc. 33 illustrations. 351pp. 5⅜ x 8½. 21081-2 Pa. $8.95

THE MYTHS OF GREECE AND ROME, H. A. Guerber. A classic of mythology, generously illustrated, long prized for its simple, graphic, accurate retelling of the principal myths of Greece and Rome, and for its commentary on their origins and significance. With 64 illustrations by Michelangelo, Raphael, Titian, Rubens, Canova, Bernini and others. 480pp. 5⅜ x 8½. 27584-1 Pa. $9.95

PSYCHOLOGY OF MUSIC, Carl E. Seashore. Classic work discusses music as a medium from psychological viewpoint. Clear treatment of physical acoustics, auditory apparatus, sound perception, development of musical skills, nature of musical feeling, host of other topics. 88 figures. 408pp. 5⅜ x 8½. 21851-1 Pa. $11.95

THE PHILOSOPHY OF HISTORY, Georg W. Hegel. Great classic of Western thought develops concept that history is not chance but rational process, the evolution of freedom. 457pp. 5⅜ x 8½. 20112-0 Pa. $9.95

THE BOOK OF TEA, Kakuzo Okakura. Minor classic of the Orient: entertaining, charming explanation, interpretation of traditional Japanese culture in terms of tea ceremony. 94pp. 5⅜ x 8½. 20070-1 Pa. $3.95

LIFE IN ANCIENT EGYPT, Adolf Erman. Fullest, most thorough, detailed older account with much not in more recent books, domestic life, religion, magic, medicine, commerce, much more. Many illustrations reproduce tomb paintings, carvings, hieroglyphs, etc. 597pp. 5⅜ x 8½. 22632-8 Pa. $12.95

SUNDIALS, Their Theory and Construction, Albert Waugh. Far and away the best, most thorough coverage of ideas, mathematics concerned, types, construction, adjusting anywhere. Simple, nontechnical treatment allows even children to build several of these dials. Over 100 illustrations. 230pp. 5⅜ x 8½. 22947-5 Pa. $8.95

THEORETICAL HYDRODYNAMICS, L. M. Milne-Thomson. Classic exposition of the mathematical theory of fluid motion, applicable to both hydrodynamics and aerodynamics. Over 600 exercises. 768pp. 6⅛ x 9¼. 68970-0 Pa. $20.95

SONGS OF EXPERIENCE: Facsimile Reproduction with 26 Plates in Full Color, William Blake. 26 full-color plates from a rare 1826 edition. Includes "TheTyger," "London," "Holy Thursday," and other poems. Printed text of poems. 48pp. 5¼ x 7. 24636-1 Pa. $4.95

OLD-TIME VIGNETTES IN FULL COLOR, Carol Belanger Grafton (ed.). Over 390 charming, often sentimental illustrations, selected from archives of Victorian graphics—pretty women posing, children playing, food, flowers, kittens and puppies, smiling cherubs, birds and butterflies, much more. All copyright-free. 48pp. 9¼ x 12¼. 27269-9 Pa. $7.95

PERSPECTIVE FOR ARTISTS, Rex Vicat Cole. Depth, perspective of sky and sea, shadows, much more, not usually covered. 391 diagrams, 81 reproductions of drawings and paintings. 279pp. 5⅜ x 8½. 22487-2 Pa. $7.95

DRAWING THE LIVING FIGURE, Joseph Sheppard. Innovative approach to artistic anatomy focuses on specifics of surface anatomy, rather than muscles and bones. Over 170 drawings of live models in front, back and side views, and in widely varying poses. Accompanying diagrams. 177 illustrations. Introduction. Index. 144pp. 8⅜ x11¼. 26723-7 Pa. $8.95

GOTHIC AND OLD ENGLISH ALPHABETS: 100 Complete Fonts, Dan X. Solo. Add power, elegance to posters, signs, other graphics with 100 stunning copyright-free alphabets: Blackstone, Dolbey, Germania, 97 more–including many lower-case, numerals, punctuation marks. 104pp. 8⅛ x 11. 24695-7 Pa. $8.95

HOW TO DO BEADWORK, Mary White. Fundamental book on craft from simple projects to five-bead chains and woven works. 106 illustrations. 142pp. 5⅜ x 8. 20697-1 Pa. $5.95

THE BOOK OF WOOD CARVING, Charles Marshall Sayers. Finest book for beginners discusses fundamentals and offers 34 designs. "Absolutely first rate . . . well thought out and well executed."–E. J. Tangerman. 118pp. 7¾ x 10⅝. 23654-4 Pa. $7.95

ILLUSTRATED CATALOG OF CIVIL WAR MILITARY GOODS: Union Army Weapons, Insignia, Uniform Accessories, and Other Equipment, Schuyler, Hartley, and Graham. Rare, profusely illustrated 1846 catalog includes Union Army uniform and dress regulations, arms and ammunition, coats, insignia, flags, swords, rifles, etc. 226 illustrations. 160pp. 9 x 12. 24939-5 Pa. $10.95

WOMEN'S FASHIONS OF THE EARLY 1900s: An Unabridged Republication of "New York Fashions, 1909," National Cloak & Suit Co. Rare catalog of mail-order fashions documents women's and children's clothing styles shortly after the turn of the century. Captions offer full descriptions, prices. Invaluable resource for fashion, costume historians. Approximately 725 illustrations. 128pp. 8⅜ x 11¼. 27276-1 Pa. $11.95

THE 1912 AND 1915 GUSTAV STICKLEY FURNITURE CATALOGS, Gustav Stickley. With over 200 detailed illustrations and descriptions, these two catalogs are essential reading and reference materials and identification guides for Stickley furniture. Captions cite materials, dimensions and prices. 112pp. 6½ x 9¼. 26676-1 Pa. $9.95

EARLY AMERICAN LOCOMOTIVES, John H. White, Jr. Finest locomotive engravings from early 19th century: historical (1804–74), main-line (after 1870), special, foreign, etc. 147 plates. 142pp. 11⅜ x 8¼. 22772-3 Pa. $10.95

THE TALL SHIPS OF TODAY IN PHOTOGRAPHS, Frank O. Braynard. Lavishly illustrated tribute to nearly 100 majestic contemporary sailing vessels: Amerigo Vespucci, Clearwater, Constitution, Eagle, Mayflower, Sea Cloud, Victory, many more. Authoritative captions provide statistics, background on each ship. 190 black-and-white photographs and illustrations. Introduction. 128pp. 8⅞ x 11¾. 27163-3 Pa. $14.95

LITTLE BOOK OF EARLY AMERICAN CRAFTS AND TRADES, Peter Stockham (ed.). 1807 children's book explains crafts and trades: baker, hatter, cooper, potter, and many others. 23 copperplate illustrations. 140pp. 4⅝ x 6.
23336-7 Pa. $4.95

VICTORIAN FASHIONS AND COSTUMES FROM HARPER'S BAZAR, 1867–1898, Stella Blum (ed.). Day costumes, evening wear, sports clothes, shoes, hats, other accessories in over 1,000 detailed engravings. 320pp. 9⅜ x 12¼.
22990-4 Pa. $15.95

GUSTAV STICKLEY, THE CRAFTSMAN, Mary Ann Smith. Superb study surveys broad scope of Stickley's achievement, especially in architecture. Design philosophy, rise and fall of the Craftsman empire, descriptions and floor plans for many Craftsman houses, more. 86 black-and-white halftones. 31 line illustrations. Introduction 208pp. 6½ x 9¼. 27210-9 Pa. $9.95

THE LONG ISLAND RAIL ROAD IN EARLY PHOTOGRAPHS, Ron Ziel. Over 220 rare photos, informative text document origin (1844) and development of rail service on Long Island. Vintage views of early trains, locomotives, stations, passengers, crews, much more. Captions. 8⅞ x 11¾. 26301-0 Pa. $13.95

VOYAGE OF THE LIBERDADE, Joshua Slocum. Great 19th-century mariner's thrilling, first-hand account of the wreck of his ship off South America, the 35-foot boat he built from the wreckage, and its remarkable voyage home. 128pp. 5⅜ x 8½.
40022-0 Pa. $4.95

TEN BOOKS ON ARCHITECTURE, Vitruvius. The most important book ever written on architecture. Early Roman aesthetics, technology, classical orders, site selection, all other aspects. Morgan translation. 331pp. 5⅜ x 8½. 20645-9 Pa. $8.95

THE HUMAN FIGURE IN MOTION, Eadweard Muybridge. More than 4,500 stopped-action photos, in action series, showing undraped men, women, children jumping, lying down, throwing, sitting, wrestling, carrying, etc. 390pp. 7⅞ x 10⅝.
20204-6 Clothbd. $27.95

TREES OF THE EASTERN AND CENTRAL UNITED STATES AND CANADA, William M. Harlow. Best one-volume guide to 140 trees. Full descriptions, woodlore, range, etc. Over 600 illustrations. Handy size. 288pp. 4½ x 6⅜.
20395-6 Pa. $6.95

SONGS OF WESTERN BIRDS, Dr. Donald J. Borror. Complete song and call repertoire of 60 western species, including flycatchers, juncoes, cactus wrens, many more–includes fully illustrated booklet. Cassette and manual 99913-0 $8.95

GROWING AND USING HERBS AND SPICES, Milo Miloradovich. Versatile handbook provides all the information needed for cultivation and use of all the herbs and spices available in North America. 4 illustrations. Index. Glossary. 236pp. 5⅜ x 8½.
25058-X Pa. $7.95

BIG BOOK OF MAZES AND LABYRINTHS, Walter Shepherd. 50 mazes and labyrinths in all–classical, solid, ripple, and more–in one great volume. Perfect inexpensive puzzler for clever youngsters. Full solutions. 112pp. 8⅛ x 11.
22951-3 Pa. $5.95

PIANO TUNING, J. Cree Fischer. Clearest, best book for beginner, amateur. Simple repairs, raising dropped notes, tuning by easy method of flattened fifths. No previous skills needed. 4 illustrations. 201pp. 5⅜ x 8½. 23267-0 Pa. $6.95

HINTS TO SINGERS, Lillian Nordica. Selecting the right teacher, developing confidence, overcoming stage fright, and many other important skills receive thoughtful discussion in this indispensible guide, written by a world-famous diva of four decades' experience. 96pp. 5³/₈ x 8½. 40094-8 Pa. $4.95

THE COMPLETE NONSENSE OF EDWARD LEAR, Edward Lear. All nonsense limericks, zany alphabets, Owl and Pussycat, songs, nonsense botany, etc., illustrated by Lear. Total of 320pp. 5⅜ x 8½. (USO) 20167-8 Pa. $7.95

VICTORIAN PARLOUR POETRY: An Annotated Anthology, Michael R. Turner. 117 gems by Longfellow, Tennyson, Browning, many lesser-known poets. "The Village Blacksmith," "Curfew Must Not Ring Tonight," "Only a Baby Small," dozens more, often difficult to find elsewhere. Index of poets, titles, first lines. xxiii + 325pp. 5⅜ x 8¼. 27044-0 Pa. $8.95

DUBLINERS, James Joyce. Fifteen stories offer vivid, tightly focused observations of the lives of Dublin's poorer classes. At least one, "The Dead," is considered a masterpiece. Reprinted complete and unabridged from standard edition. 160pp. 5³/₁₆ x 8¼. 26870-5 Pa. $1.00

GREAT WEIRD TALES: 14 Stories by Lovecraft, Blackwood, Machen and Others, S. T. Joshi (ed.). 14 spellbinding tales, including "The Sin Eater," by Fiona McLeod, "The Eye Above the Mantel," by Frank Belknap Long, as well as renowned works by R. H. Barlow, Lord Dunsany, Arthur Machen, W. C. Morrow and eight other masters of the genre. 256pp. 5⅜ x 8½. (USO) 40436-6 Pa. $8.95

THE BOOK OF THE SACRED MAGIC OF ABRAMELIN THE MAGE, translated by S. MacGregor Mathers. Medieval manuscript of ceremonial magic. Basic document in Aleister Crowley, Golden Dawn groups. 268pp. 5⅜ x 8½. 23211-5 Pa. $9.95

NEW RUSSIAN-ENGLISH AND ENGLISH-RUSSIAN DICTIONARY, M. A. O'Brien. This is a remarkably handy Russian dictionary, containing a surprising amount of information, including over 70,000 entries. 366pp. 4½ x 6⅛. 20208-9 Pa. $10.95

HISTORIC HOMES OF THE AMERICAN PRESIDENTS, Second, Revised Edition, Irvin Haas. A traveler's guide to American Presidential homes, most open to the public, depicting and describing homes occupied by every American President from George Washington to George Bush. With visiting hours, admission charges, travel routes. 175 photographs. Index. 160pp. 8¼ x 11. 26751-2 Pa. $11.95

NEW YORK IN THE FORTIES, Andreas Feininger. 162 brilliant photographs by the well-known photographer, formerly with *Life* magazine. Commuters, shoppers, Times Square at night, much else from city at its peak. Captions by John von Hartz. 181pp. 9¼ x 10¾. 23585-8 Pa. $13.95

INDIAN SIGN LANGUAGE, William Tomkins. Over 525 signs developed by Sioux and other tribes. Written instructions and diagrams. Also 290 pictographs. 111pp. 6⅛ x 9¼. 22029-X Pa. $3.95

CATALOG OF DOVER BOOKS

ANATOMY: A Complete Guide for Artists, Joseph Sheppard. A master of figure drawing shows artists how to render human anatomy convincingly. Over 460 illustrations. 224pp. 8⅜ x 11¼. 27279-6 Pa. $11.95

MEDIEVAL CALLIGRAPHY: Its History and Technique, Marc Drogin. Spirited history, comprehensive instruction manual covers 13 styles (ca. 4th century thru 15th). Excellent photographs; directions for duplicating medieval techniques with modern tools. 224pp. 8⅜ x 11¼. 26142-5 Pa. $12.95

DRIED FLOWERS: How to Prepare Them, Sarah Whitlock and Martha Rankin. Complete instructions on how to use silica gel, meal and borax, perlite aggregate, sand and borax, glycerine and water to create attractive permanent flower arrangements. 12 illustrations. 32pp. 5⅜ x 8½. 21802-3 Pa. $1.00

EASY-TO-MAKE BIRD FEEDERS FOR WOODWORKERS, Scott D. Campbell. Detailed, simple-to-use guide for designing, constructing, caring for and using feeders. Text, illustrations for 12 classic and contemporary designs. 96pp. 5⅜ x 8½. 25847-5 Pa. $3.95

SCOTTISH WONDER TALES FROM MYTH AND LEGEND, Donald A. Mackenzie. 16 lively tales tell of giants rumbling down mountainsides, of a magic wand that turns stone pillars into warriors, of gods and goddesses, evil hags, powerful forces and more. 240pp. 5⅜ x 8½. 29677-6 Pa. $6.95

THE HISTORY OF UNDERCLOTHES, C. Willett Cunnington and Phyllis Cunnington. Fascinating, well-documented survey covering six centuries of English undergarments, enhanced with over 100 illustrations: 12th-century laced-up bodice, footed long drawers (1795), 19th-century bustles, 19th-century corsets for men, Victorian "bust improvers," much more. 272pp. 5⅝ x 8¼. 27124-2 Pa. $9.95

ARTS AND CRAFTS FURNITURE: The Complete Brooks Catalog of 1912, Brooks Manufacturing Co. Photos and detailed descriptions of more than 150 now very collectible furniture designs from the Arts and Crafts movement depict davenports, settees, buffets, desks, tables, chairs, bedsteads, dressers and more, all built of solid, quarter-sawed oak. Invaluable for students and enthusiasts of antiques, Americana and the decorative arts. 80pp. 6½ x 9¼. 27471-3 Pa. $8.95

WILBUR AND ORVILLE: A Biography of the Wright Brothers, Fred Howard. Definitive, crisply written study tells the full story of the brothers' lives and work. A vividly written biography, unparalleled in scope and color, that also captures the spirit of an extraordinary era. 560pp. 6⅛ x 9¼. 40297-5 Pa. $17.95

THE ARTS OF THE SAILOR: Knotting, Splicing and Ropework, Hervey Garrett Smith. Indispensable shipboard reference covers tools, basic knots and useful hitches; handsewing and canvas work, more. Over 100 illustrations. Delightful reading for sea lovers. 256pp. 5⅜ x 8½. 26440-8 Pa. $8.95

FRANK LLOYD WRIGHT'S FALLINGWATER: The House and Its History, Second, Revised Edition, Donald Hoffmann. A total revision–both in text and illustrations–of the standard document on Fallingwater, the boldest, most personal architectural statement of Wright's mature years, updated with valuable new material from the recently opened Frank Lloyd Wright Archives. "Fascinating"–*The New York Times*. 116 illustrations. 128pp. 9¼ x 10¾. 27430-6 Pa. $12.95

PHOTOGRAPHIC SKETCHBOOK OF THE CIVIL WAR, Alexander Gardner. 100 photos taken on field during the Civil War. Famous shots of Manassas Harper's Ferry, Lincoln, Richmond, slave pens, etc. 244pp. 10⅝ x 8¼. 22731-6 Pa. $10.95

FIVE ACRES AND INDEPENDENCE, Maurice G. Kains. Great back-to-the-land classic explains basics of self-sufficient farming. The one book to get. 95 illustrations. 397pp. 5⅜ x 8½. 20974-1 Pa. $7.95

SONGS OF EASTERN BIRDS, Dr. Donald J. Borror. Songs and calls of 60 species most common to eastern U.S.: warblers, woodpeckers, flycatchers, thrushes, larks, many more in high-quality recording. Cassette and manual 99912-2 $9.95

A MODERN HERBAL, Margaret Grieve. Much the fullest, most exact, most useful compilation of herbal material. Gigantic alphabetical encyclopedia, from aconite to zedoary, gives botanical information, medical properties, folklore, economic uses, much else. Indispensable to serious reader. 161 illustrations. 888pp. 6½ x 9¼. 2-vol. set. (USO) Vol. I: 22798-7 Pa. $9.95 Vol. II: 22799-5 Pa. $9.95

HIDDEN TREASURE MAZE BOOK, Dave Phillips. Solve 34 challenging mazes accompanied by heroic tales of adventure. Evil dragons, people-eating plants, blood-thirsty giants, many more dangerous adversaries lurk at every twist and turn. 34 mazes, stories, solutions. 48pp. 8¼ x 11. 24566-7 Pa. $2.95

LETTERS OF W. A. MOZART, Wolfgang A. Mozart. Remarkable letters show bawdy wit, humor, imagination, musical insights, contemporary musical world; includes some letters from Leopold Mozart. 276pp. 5⅜ x 8½. 22859-2 Pa. $7.95

BASIC PRINCIPLES OF CLASSICAL BALLET, Agrippina Vaganova. Great Russian theoretician, teacher explains methods for teaching classical ballet. 118 illustrations. 175pp. 5⅜ x 8½. 22036-2 Pa. $5.95

THE JUMPING FROG, Mark Twain. Revenge edition. The original story of The Celebrated Jumping Frog of Calaveras County, a hapless French translation, and Twain's hilarious "retranslation" from the French. 12 illustrations. 66pp. 5⅜ x 8½. 22686-7 Pa. $3.95

BEST REMEMBERED POEMS, Martin Gardner (ed.). The 126 poems in this superb collection of 19th- and 20th-century British and American verse range from Shelley's "To a Skylark" to the impassioned "Renascence" of Edna St. Vincent Millay and to Edward Lear's whimsical "The Owl and the Pussycat." 224pp. 5⅜ x 8½. 27165-X Pa. $5.95

COMPLETE SONNETS, William Shakespeare. Over 150 exquisite poems deal with love, friendship, the tyranny of time, beauty's evanescence, death and other themes in language of remarkable power, precision and beauty. Glossary of archaic terms. 80pp. 5³⁄₁₆ x 8¼. 26686-9 Pa. $1.00

BODIES IN A BOOKSHOP, R. T. Campbell. Challenging mystery of blackmail and murder with ingenious plot and superbly drawn characters. In the best tradition of British suspense fiction. 192pp. 5⅜ x 8½. 24720-1 Pa. $6.95

THE WIT AND HUMOR OF OSCAR WILDE, Alvin Redman (ed.). More than 1,000 ripostes, paradoxes, wisecracks: Work is the curse of the drinking classes; I can resist everything except temptation; etc. 258pp. 5⅜ x 8½.   20602-5 Pa. $6.95

SHAKESPEARE LEXICON AND QUOTATION DICTIONARY, Alexander Schmidt. Full definitions, locations, shades of meaning in every word in plays and poems. More than 50,000 exact quotations. 1,485pp. 6½ x 9¼. 2-vol. set.
Vol. 1: 22726-X Pa. $17.95
Vol. 2: 22727-8 Pa. $17.95

SELECTED POEMS, Emily Dickinson. Over 100 best-known, best-loved poems by one of America's foremost poets, reprinted from authoritative early editions. No comparable edition at this price. Index of first lines. 64pp. 5³⁄₁₆ x 8¼.
26466-1 Pa. $1.00

THE INSIDIOUS DR. FU-MANCHU, Sax Rohmer. The first of the popular mystery series introduces a pair of English detectives to their archnemesis, the diabolical Dr. Fu-Manchu. Flavorful atmosphere, fast-paced action, and colorful characters enliven this classic of the genre. 208pp. 5³⁄₁₆ x 8¼.   29898-1 Pa. $2.00

THE MALLEUS MALEFICARUM OF KRAMER AND SPRENGER, translated by Montague Summers. Full text of most important witchhunter's "bible," used by both Catholics and Protestants. 278pp. 6⅝ x 10.   22802-9 Pa. $12.95

SPANISH STORIES/CUENTOS ESPAÑOLES: A Dual-Language Book, Angel Flores (ed.). Unique format offers 13 great stories in Spanish by Cervantes, Borges, others. Faithful English translations on facing pages. 352pp. 5⅜ x 8½.
25399-6 Pa. $8.95

GARDEN CITY, LONG ISLAND, IN EARLY PHOTOGRAPHS, 1869–1919, Mildred H. Smith. Handsome treasury of 118 vintage pictures, accompanied by carefully researched captions, document the Garden City Hotel fire (1899), the Vanderbilt Cup Race (1908), the first airmail flight departing from the Nassau Boulevard Aerodrome (1911), and much more. 96pp. 8⅞ x 11³⁄₄.   40669-5 Pa. $12.95

OLD QUEENS, N.Y., IN EARLY PHOTOGRAPHS, Vincent F. Seyfried and William Asadorian. Over 160 rare photographs of Maspeth, Jamaica, Jackson Heights, and other areas. Vintage views of DeWitt Clinton mansion, 1939 World's Fair and more. Captions. 192pp. 8⅞ x 11.   26358-4 Pa. $12.95

CAPTURED BY THE INDIANS: 15 Firsthand Accounts, 1750-1870, Frederick Drimmer. Astounding true historical accounts of grisly torture, bloody conflicts, relentless pursuits, miraculous escapes and more, by people who lived to tell the tale. 384pp. 5⅜ x 8½.   24901-8 Pa. $8.95

THE WORLD'S GREAT SPEECHES (Fourth Enlarged Edition), Lewis Copeland, Lawrence W. Lamm, and Stephen J. McKenna. Nearly 300 speeches provide public speakers with a wealth of updated quotes and inspiration–from Pericles' funeral oration and William Jennings Bryan's "Cross of Gold Speech" to Malcolm X's powerful words on the Black Revolution and Earl of Spenser's tribute to his sister, Diana, Princess of Wales. 944pp. 5⅜ x 8⅜.   40903-1 Pa. $15.95

THE BOOK OF THE SWORD, Sir Richard F. Burton. Great Victorian scholar/adventurer's eloquent, erudite history of the "queen of weapons"–from prehistory to early Roman Empire. Evolution and development of early swords, variations (sabre, broadsword, cutlass, scimitar, etc.), much more. 336pp. 6⅛ x 9¼.
25434-8 Pa. $9.95

AUTOBIOGRAPHY: The Story of My Experiments with Truth, Mohandas K. Gandhi. Boyhood, legal studies, purification, the growth of the Satyagraha (nonviolent protest) movement. Critical, inspiring work of the man responsible for the freedom of India. 480pp. 5⅜ x 8½. (USO) 24593-4 Pa. $8.95

CELTIC MYTHS AND LEGENDS, T. W. Rolleston. Masterful retelling of Irish and Welsh stories and tales. Cuchulain, King Arthur, Deirdre, the Grail, many more. First paperback edition. 58 full-page illustrations. 512pp. 5⅜ x 8½. 26507-2 Pa. $9.95

THE PRINCIPLES OF PSYCHOLOGY, William James. Famous long course complete, unabridged. Stream of thought, time perception, memory, experimental methods; great work decades ahead of its time. 94 figures. 1,391pp. 5⅜ x 8½. 2-vol. set.
Vol. I: 20381-6 Pa. $13.95
Vol. II: 20382-4 Pa. $14.95

THE WORLD AS WILL AND REPRESENTATION, Arthur Schopenhauer. Definitive English translation of Schopenhauer's life work, correcting more than 1,000 errors, omissions in earlier translations. Translated by E. F. J. Payne. Total of 1,269pp. 5⅜ x 8½. 2-vol. set. Vol. 1: 21761-2 Pa. $12.95
Vol. 2: 21762-0 Pa. $12.95

MAGIC AND MYSTERY IN TIBET, Madame Alexandra David-Neel. Experiences among lamas, magicians, sages, sorcerers, Bonpa wizards. A true psychic discovery. 32 illustrations. 321pp. 5⅜ x 8½. (USO) 22682-4 Pa. $9.95

THE EGYPTIAN BOOK OF THE DEAD, E. A. Wallis Budge. Complete reproduction of Ani's papyrus, finest ever found. Full hieroglyphic text, interlinear transliteration, word-for-word translation, smooth translation. 533pp. 6½ x 9¼.
21866-X Pa. $11.95

MATHEMATICS FOR THE NONMATHEMATICIAN, Morris Kline. Detailed, college-level treatment of mathematics in cultural and historical context, with numerous exercises. Recommended Reading Lists. Tables. Numerous figures. 641pp. 5⅜ x 8½.
24823-2 Pa. $11.95

PROBABILISTIC METHODS IN THE THEORY OF STRUCTURES, Isaac Elishakoff. Well-written introduction covers the elements of the theory of probability from two or more random variables, the reliability of such multivariable structures, the theory of random function, Monte Carlo methods of treating problems incapable of exact solution, and more. Examples. 502pp. 5³/₈ x 8¹/₂. 40691-1 Pa. $16.95

THE RIME OF THE ANCIENT MARINER, Gustave Doré, S. T. Coleridge. Doré's finest work; 34 plates capture moods, subtleties of poem. Flawless full-size reproductions printed on facing pages with authoritative text of poem. "Beautiful. Simply beautiful."–*Publisher's Weekly*. 77pp. 9¼ x 12. 22305-1 Pa. $7.95

NORTH AMERICAN INDIAN DESIGNS FOR ARTISTS AND CRAFTSPEOPLE, Eva Wilson. Over 360 authentic copyright-free designs adapted from Navajo blankets, Hopi pottery, Sioux buffalo hides, more. Geometrics, symbolic figures, plant and animal motifs, etc. 128pp. 8⅜ x 11. (EUK) 25341-4 Pa. $8.95

SCULPTURE: Principles and Practice, Louis Slobodkin. Step-by-step approach to clay, plaster, metals, stone; classical and modern. 253 drawings, photos. 255pp. 8⅛ x 11.
22960-2 Pa. $11.95

THE INFLUENCE OF SEA POWER UPON HISTORY, 1660–1783, A. T. Mahan. Influential classic of naval history and tactics still used as text in war colleges. First paperback edition. 4 maps. 24 battle plans. 640pp. 5⅜ x 8½. 25509-3 Pa. $14.95

THE STORY OF THE TITANIC AS TOLD BY ITS SURVIVORS, Jack Winocour (ed.). What it was really like. Panic, despair, shocking inefficiency, and a little heroism. More thrilling than any fictional account. 26 illustrations. 320pp. 5⅜ x 8½. 20610-6 Pa. $8.95

FAIRY AND FOLK TALES OF THE IRISH PEASANTRY, William Butler Yeats (ed.). Treasury of 64 tales from the twilight world of Celtic myth and legend: "The Soul Cages," "The Kildare Pooka," "King O'Toole and his Goose," many more. Introduction and Notes by W. B. Yeats. 352pp. 5⅜ x 8½. 26941-8 Pa. $8.95

BUDDHIST MAHAYANA TEXTS, E. B. Cowell and Others (eds.). Superb, accurate translations of basic documents in Mahayana Buddhism, highly important in history of religions. The Buddha-karita of Asvaghosha, Larger Sukhavativyuha, more. 448pp. 5⅜ x 8½. 25552-2 Pa. $12.95

ONE TWO THREE . . . INFINITY: Facts and Speculations of Science, George Gamow. Great physicist's fascinating, readable overview of contemporary science: number theory, relativity, fourth dimension, entropy, genes, atomic structure, much more. 128 illustrations. Index. 352pp. 5⅜ x 8½. 25664-2 Pa. $8.95

EXPERIMENTATION AND MEASUREMENT, W. J. Youden. Introductory manual explains laws of measurement in simple terms and offers tips for achieving accuracy and minimizing errors. Mathematics of measurement, use of instruments, experimenting with machines. 1994 edition. Foreword. Preface. Introduction. Epilogue. Selected Readings. Glossary. Index. Tables and figures. 128pp. 5³/₈ x 8¹/₂. 40451-X Pa. $6.95

DALÍ ON MODERN ART: The Cuckolds of Antiquated Modern Art, Salvador Dalí. Influential painter skewers modern art and its practitioners. Outrageous evaluations of Picasso, Cézanne, Turner, more. 15 renderings of paintings discussed. 44 calligraphic decorations by Dalí. 96pp. 5⅜ x 8½. (USO) 29220-7 Pa. $5.95

ANTIQUE PLAYING CARDS: A Pictorial History, Henry René D'Allemagne. Over 900 elaborate, decorative images from rare playing cards (14th–20th centuries): Bacchus, death, dancing dogs, hunting scenes, royal coats of arms, players cheating, much more. 96pp. 9¼ x 12¼. 29265-7 Pa. $12.95

MAKING FURNITURE MASTERPIECES: 30 Projects with Measured Drawings, Franklin H. Gottshall. Step-by-step instructions, illustrations for constructing handsome, useful pieces, among them a Sheraton desk, Chippendale chair, Spanish desk, Queen Anne table and a William and Mary dressing mirror. 224pp. 8⅛ x 11¼. 29338-6 Pa. $13.95

THE FOSSIL BOOK: A Record of Prehistoric Life, Patricia V. Rich et al. Profusely illustrated definitive guide covers everything from single-celled organisms and dinosaurs to birds and mammals and the interplay between climate and man. Over 1,500 illustrations. 760pp. 7½ x 10⅛. 29371-8 Pa. $29.95

Prices subject to change without notice.

Available at your book dealer or write for free catalog to Dept. GI, Dover Publications, Inc., 31 East 2nd St., Mineola, N.Y. 11501. Dover publishes more than 500 books each year on science, elementary and advanced mathematics, biology, music, art, literary history, social sciences and other areas.